HPP Architects
Approaches

HPP Architects
Approaches

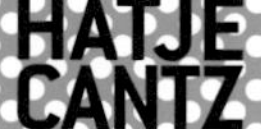

The Balance between Sustainability and Innovation

Remarks on HPP's Oeuvre

Frank R. Werner

Architectural firms are highly complex structures that are comparable in many ways to living organisms. Architectural associations, as a rule, arise more casually, and are often architecturally active for decades, until, along with the death of their founders, they quietly take their leave. From the standpoint of architectural history, only a few architectural firms have been able, or are still able, to outlive the lifetime of their founding fathers. In the Baroque period, generation-spanning dynasties of master builders—for instance, the Dientzenhofers of Upper Bavaria—were not exceptional. There are only a few today, though, one of them being a prominent family from Cologne that has produced third and fourth generations of architects. There is another dynamic involved in the influential partnerships of convenience that began to appear in the nineteenth century. One can truly count on one's fingers the names of the great firms that have made architectural history for decades, if not for almost a whole century.

Which firms that were prominent at the end of the nineteenth and beginning of the twentieth centuries immediately come to mind? Ones such as Adler & Sullivan, Burnham & Root, and McKim, Mead, and White, not to mention the great firm of Skidmore, Owings & Merrill, known around the world as SOM, which was founded in 1936 and is still extremely active today. There is only one institution in Germany that is comparable: three years before SOM was established, Helmut Hentrich founded an architectural firm bearing his name in 1933 in Düsseldorf. The management and employees of this firm, today called Hentrich Petschnigg & Partner GmbH + Co. KG and known by the acronym HPP, have erected more than a thousand buildings worldwide since 1933. But by their nature, numbers say little about architectural quality. Of necessity, the question therefore arises of how it is that one of the largest architectural firms in the world, in spite of changes in personnel and the turnover of generations, has managed to maintain such a high level of quality, and even increase it, since its founding? Without a doubt, given the fundamentally different conditions of the global building experience of today, HPP's oeuvre can be considered a true work of art.

If one reviews the seventy-five years of buildings that HPP has produced, one gets the impression that although there has been a basic ethical and aesthetic consistency in the firm's architectural approach, there has been no demonstratively binding canon of design or simple, space-and-time-transcending guidelines restricting its architectural expression. Although at first glance this may seem to be a flaw, it actually proves upon closer inspection to be a great asset: each generation of HPP's architects has had to develop their own design repertoire in a highly impressive way—their own generation-specific architectural language and repertoire of building typologies. This has happened with extraordinarily precise outlines and a clearly defined profile, and though it has been backed up by the corresponding architectural theory, it is always expressive of the discrete, invisible charm of the internal corporate identity of a firm that has been thoroughly successful for seventy-five years. One can only concur with Henry-Russell Hitchcock, who recognized as early as 1973 that multifacetedness and a wide spectrum of variation are the factors that characterize both the high, international level of HPP's work and the greatest achievements of postwar architecture.

If one could, so to speak, let HPP's buildings parade by in slow motion, then the projects of the firm's early phase, which were mostly residential buildings from the nineteen-thirties and -forties, radiate craftsmanlike solidity, elegance, and a consciousness of history. After

World War II, HPP turned increasingly to public buildings, that is, to administrative buildings and other prominent projects of this kind. In the process, HPP created buildings which have long since taken their places in the architectural history of the twentieth century. Among these remarkable projects are the Drahthaus (1952), the Aluminium Haus (1953), and the Dreischeibenhaus (1960), all of which were built in Düsseldorf.

The Dreischeibenhaus represented a groundbreaking investigation of the building typology of the skyscraper in Europe. Also known as the Thyssenhaus, this high-rise was mentioned in the same breath as Mies van der Rohe's Seagram Building (1958) in New York very early on in terms of its elegance and spatial qualities. But HPP continued to develop its own high-rise typologies. With the Europa Center (1964) in Berlin, the Unilever High-Rise (1964) in Hamburg, the Standard Bank Centre (1971) and the Highpoint Hillbrow in Johannesburg (1971), and the De Beers diamond sorting facility (1974) in Kimberly, South Africa, HPP produced high-rises that took on a prominent role in their respective cityscapes and offered innovative solutions for tower construction of both the towers themselves and the connecting zones between them and their urban surroundings. With the Ruhr University in Bochum (1970), which HPP recently partially overhauled in an impressive fashion, a complete university city surrounded by green spaces was created. In addition, there are very quiet, contemplative buildings, such as the sculptural Dietrich Bonhoeffer church (1965) in Düsseldorf-Garath, or the extraordinarily empathetic alterations made to the Expressionistic Rheinhalle, a multifunctional facility and planetarium building constructed by Wilhelm Kreis in 1926 that HPP converted into the Düsseldorf Concert Hall (1978).

The buildings of the nineteen-eighties and -nineties are characterized by a change in paradigm. According to what Tilmann Buddensieg, HPP's projects in this period were increasingly focused on the concept of the city, and even mutated into small "cities within cities." The Olivandenhof (1988), without a doubt one of the most extraordinary architectural structures from this period, reclaimed public and semi-public spaces in the heart of Cologne between old and new. The main administration building of the Cologne Stadtsparkasse (1992) strengthened the urban fabric vis-à-vis the medieval Hahnentor by interconnecting the preexisting buildings with new ones and by accentuating the newly created district from both inside and outside with an impressive rotunda. A similarly effective rotunda also dominates the main headquarters of the Hannoversche Leben insurance company in Hannover. Large-scale administration complexes in more peripheral locations, such as the TÜV Akademie in Cologne (1994) and the expansion and new construction of the LVM insurance company building in Münster (1994), were based on broadly laid out, clearly delineated, basic geometric forms from this point on.

Even the completely newly laid out residential areas, such as the residential Beethovenpark in Cologne, which was realized in collaboration with Büro dt 8, underscore HPP's desire to rehabilitate the dense, but nonetheless lovable and livable, atmosphere of downtown life. The same attitude is evident in one of the most remarkable HPP buildings of the 1990s, the retirement residence in Wesel (1996). Seeming more urban from the outside, in the sense of its strict peripheral configuration, this complex presents a riotous, intimate, almost villagelike residential landscape on the inside. Glassed-in verandas function as orientational lookout points over the complex's almost improvised-looking housing units grouped around green courtyards. But in addition, HPP's significantly more numerous multistory office buildings, such as the main administration building of the Provinzial insurance company in Düsseldorf (1995), the Anthropolis complex in Berlin (1997), and Neven DuMont's publishing center in Cologne (1998), break the customary, large-scale forms of the nineteen-sixties and -seventies down into smaller clusters with livable inner courtyards connected by lattice-enclosed atria and passages.

Projects dedicated to retrofitting landmark-protected buildings for modern use were not underrepresented in the eighties and nineties either, thereby maintaining Helmut Hentrich's passion for the scrupulous maintenance of historical structures. This was expressed programmatically in Pyrmont Castle in the Eifel region. Hubert Petschnigg had purchased the castle in a ruinous state, and from 1963 to 1970 HPP reworked and expanded the structure as a conference center and relaxation retreat. The scrupulous high-tech conversion of the Expressionistic Düsseldorf Rheinhalle completed in 1995, the revitalization and conversion of the historic Yenidze tobacco factory in Dresden (1996), originally built in the Moorish style, and the spectacular renovation and refurbishing of the main Leipzig train station (1997) with the addition of multistory commercial passageways are like contemporary references to HPP's founding father.

And what about the high-rise? This building type, of course, also had to undergo a new interpretation in the eighties and nineties. Whether the high-rises were integrated as urban development accents into vast complexes, as in the cases of the building of the Cologne publisher DuMont and the Düsseldorf main administration building of the Victoria insurance company (1998), or left freestanding, as in the case of the office tower erected at the end of the nineties in the Berlin Spittelmarkt, they are always clad in delicate, relieflike steel-and-glass structures and knit into their respective surroundings at their bases by means of spatially commanding settings.

In December 2007, HPP published a thoughtful book. It was thoughtful, because it was neither the typical architect's book nor a conventional monograph. Instead, it was small, thin, rather modestly designed, and sparsely illustrated, with only a few textual explanations of the projects addressed. What distinguished this little volume from the general masses of printed material on architecture was the fact that despite HPP's extensive oeuvre, only a few representative works were selected and presented by means of appropriate keywords and without lengthy accompanying texts. The keywords included terms such as flexibility, significance, poetry, identity, sustainability, and time. With the use of keywords as a means of cross-referencing and interconnecting the design paradigms underlying the building projects, this little book escaped the dilemma of more ponderous publications. Instead, it evolved into a sort of diary that illuminates the buildings and their concepts, so that they explain themselves without requiring wordy descriptions.

In order to assign keywords to HPP's most recent projects, let us return to the categories of content in this earlier book. We see that the new construction of the Breidenbacher Hof hotel in Düsseldorf (2008) belongs to the group of buildings grouped under the title "Context" in the book. HPP provides a straightforward explanation of the importance of context for the Breidenbacher Hof: "In our design, we bring together a building whose origins lie in the classical hotel architecture of the nineteenth century with the highest demands of a modern, five-star-plus hotel. . . . The new Breidenbacher Hof represents a certain challenge for modern architecture. Therefore, we looked at pictures of the old Grand Hotels of European metropolises, and with our new design we were able to add an additional fresh layer of meaning to the charm of these buildings." In fact, the new, externally targeted, "un-modern" conception of the Breidenbacher Hof provides a worthy element of closure to the urban ensemble of the Wilhelm Marx Haus, the Carschhaus, and the Kaufhof an der Kö.

The model project of the buildings grouped under the keyword "Construction" is, as one would expect, the AufSchalke Arena in Gelsenkirchen, which was completed in 2001. Entire construction and building segments were designed modularly and organized with the mandate that the resulting structure be multifunctional and capable of facilitating rapid changes of use. This made the arena the first soccer stadium in the world to be able to be converted within just a few hours into a monumental hall with a closed roof for rock concerts or other large-scale events. Even the grass playing field can be rolled in or out on short notice. The external effect of the "plain" construction was developed solely on the basis of the technical and atmospheric demands of the inside of the stadium.

The building category labeled "Shell" is best represented by one of the supposedly most unpretentious of HPP's buildings, namely, the parking garage of the Leipzig Zoo (2004). The façade and roof of the gently swaying "Bamboo Parkhaus," as it is called in Leipzig, consist of an alignment of ten thousand identical bamboo stalks, which because of their natural growth diverge only a very little from each other. The enclosure of the prosaic parking garage with an exotic building material makes it easier for visitors to connect the structure to the world of experience awaiting them at the zoo.

Whoever has seen the glamorous resurrection of the main Leipzig train station (1997) will not have any difficulty understanding that one of the largest landmark-protected "cathedrals" of the era of the railroad was virtually predestined to be the flagship of the HPP building projects grouped under the keyword "Function." It was only with a substantial functional upgrading of the large, seventeen-meter-high, 8,600-square-meter transverse platform hall, where more than 600,000 passengers arrive every day, that the historic ensemble could be both preserved and prepared for modern use. Therefore, beneath the floor of the hall, which had been completely cleared of all installations, subterranean shopping areas were installed on two levels and connected with the historic hall by means of broad openings and atria. Shoppers can thus roam around a total area of 35,000 square meters underneath the hall without distraction. This has made the main Leipzig train station the much discussed pilot project of a whole series of subsequent conversions of historic train stations.

The keyword "Flexibility" is represented in HPP's oeuvre by the Santander Consumer Bank building in Mönchengladbach, which was completed in 2006. HPP notes that fostering communication within the division structures of the bank required especially open and flexible, but no less comfortably appointed, offices: "Unterritorial work environments allow spaces to become workstations rather than personal encampments." This loss of individual workplace identity is compensated for especially by the highly attractive communication locations. Light-flooded atria and floor-to-ceiling glass walls free up the interior of the meandering building structure and help to merge it with its surroundings.

Under the heading of "Materiality" is the project that is one of the most ambitious of the selected works being presented: the Expo Village that HPP is erecting for the world's fair that will take place in Shanghai in 2010. The project has been designed with very consciously European urban characteristics and is currently rising within the "boomtown" of Shanghai on forty-four hectares with a gross floor area of almost 700,000 square meters. This Expo Village on the bank of the Huangpu River must address particularly complex demands on its materiality and sustainability. Sixteen hectares of parking area are planned to facilitate the networking of the grounds with both the urbanistic surroundings and the adjoining landscape spaces. A displaced but rigorous north-south orientation of the building is intended to minimize the heat input without blocking the views of the city, countryside, and river. Ideas about the project's potential uses after the end of the world's fair were already being discussed in the planning stages. HPP points out that the building structure is set up in such a way that after the world's fair it can be turned over to the private real estate sector and adapted to reuse with relatively little effort. Farsighted access plans, flexible construction systems, and an adaptive expansion grid will provide the basis for the project's sustainability by allowing its conversion into a residential district for thousands of people. According to HPP, the successful development of this district will "not be due to its architectural quality alone. Above all, it is the project's inner values, disposition, and use structure, as well as its technical and physical building parameters that contribute to its sustainability." This is particularly true of the materials employed, because they transport this sustainability both visually and tangibly to a country whose architectural tradition does not lack a delicate use of materials.

In the much less spectacular river setting, HPP constructed a new Justice Center for the city of Wuppertal in connection with the preexisting court building on a little island in the Wupper River in 2005. With this structure wrapped around a central atrium, static conventions, at least visually, have been turned upside down. An almost monolithic building structure clad in natural stone appears to be floating weightlessly on top of a high, glass-enclosed base. Its double-layered glass skin is printed on both sides with what seems to be a delicate filigree pattern. Seen from up close, however, this pattern reveals itself to be an endlessly repeated sentence: "All human beings are equal before the law." With this discreet but nevertheless powerful detail, the Justice Center in Wuppertal presents an example of the building category of "Detail."

The Europe Tower in Sofia, which is scheduled to be completed in 2011, is on an entirely different scale. It represents the category of "Significance" just as naturally as it does emphatically. With this new, crystalline, manifoldly tapered "urban crown" set within the Bulgarian capital, HPP has not only fulfilled the imposing real estate expectations of the building's sponsors. By actually reflecting the mountain landscape of the surrounding Vitosha Mountains, an innovative urban building block that will contribute to the city's development of a unique visual identity has also been inserted. In addition, the designers of this striking skyscraper have made a powerful and self-conscious reference to HPP's long tradition of designing remarkable high-rises. Once again, HPP has left behind a meaningful and optimistic metropolitan "footprint."

There is no greater contrast between two construction tasks than the one between the buildings representing the keyword "Destination" and those representing that of "Continuity." While the elongated Loop 5 shopping center (2009) situated on the edge of a multilane highway in Weiterstadt provides a new "destination" in a peripheral urban no-man's-land thanks to the cascades of color and culminating band of advertising on its vertically laminated façades, HPP's renewed involvement with Düsseldorf's concert hall transpired under very different auspices. In Weiterstadt, in analogy to Paul Virilio's thesis of the constriction of dromological perception, the determination of location and purpose had to be developed and accentuated by taking into account the fleeting perspective of the movement of passengers driving by in automobiles. In contrast, in the case of the Düsseldorf Concert Hall, the Expressionistic building by Wilhelm Kreis that HPP had already been involved with from 1975 to 1978, the architects' first concern was restoring the fitness of a building that was getting on in years, as well as the verification of internal office continuity. More than thirty years after the first renovation campaign carried out by Helmut Hentrich, it seemed time to bring the concert hall up to date in terms of the demands of modern building engineering and fire prevention. In the course of doing so, the ticket offices, dressing rooms, foyer, entryways, and roof terrace were redesigned. But above all, the acoustics of the dome's construction had to be brought up to international standards. As a result, the cupola was completely redesigned and its acoustics optimized. In addition, the carefully staged deployment of light ensured that the cupola could be transformed as needed into a transparent, starry sky.

As a result of an international competition, HPP received the commission to build a more than 100,000-square-meter office environment for Allianz Versicherung's 2,400 employees in Frankfurt am Main. Named the Allianz Kai and completed in 2002, the building had to be two things above all: light and transparent. This might seem an impossible task, bearing in mind the structure's almost 300-meter length and forty-five-meter width, but the project succeeded with the help of an internal access structure connecting the individual buildings that is more than 150 meters long and seven stories high. With its bridges, elevators, and staircases, all enclosed by glass, this access structure creates the effect of transforming the entire complex into a glassed-in "city within a city" with a radiant force of which Paul Scheerbart and the architects of the "Glass Chain" in the 1920s could only dream. It is no wonder that the Allianz Kai heads the buildings associated with the keyword "Poetry."

The inclusion of the Grand Hotel in Heiligendamm (2003) in the group of buildings within the category of "Identity" is just as appropriate. Since the Baltic Sea spa was founded in Heiligendamm in 1793 by the Grand Duke Friedrich Franz I of Mecklenburg, it was long considered one of the most elegant seaside resorts in Germany. After the fall of the Berlin Wall, a rather rundown ensemble of five historical buildings comprised of the Orangerie, Hohenzollern Castle, the Kurhaus, Mecklenburg House, and the Grand Hotel was in a position to be brought up to the standards of a modern hotel and wellness and recreational facility in the luxury resort category. With its renovation, Heiligendamm has been resurrected again as the "white city" on the Baltic Sea—the city of the beautiful, rich, and powerful that it has always truly been. The identity-generating effect of the building ensemble is in large part due to the fact that HPP's work on this project was distinguished with the MIPIM Award at the 2004 MIPIM international real estate fair in Cannes in the category of "Hotel & Tourism Resorts."

HPP has also produced a whole series of large construction projects that can be categorized under the keyword "Ecology," the best example of which are the various building segments of the main headquarters of Victoria in Düsseldorf, which are still under construction. A multitude of innovative façade concepts, photovoltaic systems, co-generation units, and lighting and sun protection were incorporated in this project. The energy optimization achieved here as well as in other HPP projects through a combination of passive energy-saving systems and innovative regenerative energies underscores the significance of the individual building segments.

A similar principle applies, if under different conditions, to the Media Library in Krefeld (2008), which one can interpret as both a successful example of the renovation of a public square and an innovative impulse embodying the keyword "Economy." Ultimately, the Media Library accomplishes the trick of generating highly effective external as well as internal spatial and design qualities without an excessive cost. The core idea here is an unusual organizational typology: a system of ramps wrapped around the foyer and the central exhibition area that continuously and fluidly connects the terraced, climbing levels on which books are issued with one another. Visitors stroll through the building as if they were on a boardwalk, continuously enjoying new spatial impressions as they move. Both natural and mechanical ventilation and exhaust systems eliminate the need for additional cooling and air-conditioning. The building's energy-efficient operation and economical construction costs demonstrate once again that HPP can also realize unconventional and demanding spatial concepts in economical and innovative ways.

An administrative complex of an entirely different nature offers the best reflection of the keyword "Sustainability" within HPP's oeuvre, the Henkel Asia-Pacific and China Headquarters, which were finished in 2007 in Pudong, Shanghai's flourishing economic center on the east bank of the Huangpu River. In addition to incorporating the most modern Western building standards, the planning precepts of this imposing facility for leading high-tech firms placed particular emphasis on environmental compatibility and sustainability. The Chinese influence, however, is not to be understated. As the official symbol of the city of Shanghai, the magnolia flower became the starting point for the project's planning. In addition, a feng shui consultant was brought in and played a significant role in the configuration of all aspects of the building. The result is a gently swung, glassed-in reinforced concrete skeleton construction devoid of right angles. By deploying heat-insulating glass, thermally decoupled façade profiles, and a type of external sun protection typical to the area, the building's energy consumption could be lowered by forty percent in comparison with the regional average.

At the same time, the building's convex/concave glass skin, as well as its organic, swinging forms, and the surfaces, floor coverings, and materials in the entryway atrium and the restaurant, as well as in the inner courtyard, all underscore the new structure's roots in Chinese tradition. Far Eastern traditions and Western building standards have thus been harmonically united here in a symbiotic sustainability.

The last group of recent buildings to be addressed is indebted to a factor that actually subsumes all the projects, especially since HPP can look back on seventy-five years of activity. The factor is that of "Time." One of the best examples of how HPP manages the factor of time is the Cologne Rheinhallen project, which is scheduled for completion in 2009. After the Cologne Fair left its ancestral Expressionistic brick halls in Cologne-Deutz, the extensive grounds became available. After substantially gutting the old halls according to the guidelines of the landmark preservation principles applying to brick façades, new administration and editorial offices as well as television studios for the broadcaster RTL and its approximately 2,000 employees were installed from the ground up with a gross floor area of about 160,000 square meters. The result was a broad, light-flooded office and studio landscape with courtyards and roofed halls, with the old and new merging at the edges. The old is updated in the new here, thus opening a new chapter in architectural design.

This closes the circle of observation which began with Helmut Hentrich's masterful residential houses of the 1930s, in order for the time being to end with the space permeating cities-in-the-city, those great office landscapes and intruders in the clouds of the early twenty-first century. Context, construction, shell, function, flexibility, materiality, detail, significance, destination, continuity, poetry, identity, ecology, economy, sustainability and time—these are the memorable keywords which we have applied to HPP's buildings as they slid by us like the individual, iridescent pearls on a necklace. Of course, one term is missing from this list, one which would have addressed the notion of sensuousness. In spite of the sheer magnitude of many of these projects, one thing is always palpable: HPP's sure sense of poetry and sensuousness. Both of these qualities will bestow inestimable value upon building projects with even the most prosaic of uses.

The day-to-day business of urbanistic and architectural design and its realization is in reality much more than a "jeu magnifique," or magnificent game, as Le Corbusier once provocatively said. Much more than this, architectural thought and action embody the difficult daily confrontation of the conventions of banality. In a period of seventy-five years, the founding fathers of HPP and their successors have extended their impressive cosmos of intellectual edifices generation by generation—edifices which seem to abrogate the banal. The countless ideas—which, like it or not, were left behind, and had to be left behind—will, however, leave their traces between the covers of a book. It is apparently only due to a pronounced ethical sense of responsibility that continuity and congruence are so astoundingly articulated in HPP's oeuvre, down through the twenty-first century. The architecture presented in this volume can truly bear scrutiny, not because it relies on gimmickry, but because project after project, in the best sense of this word, it leaves behind evidence of curiosity and openness—curiosity and openness for people living and working more humanly in dynamic equilibrium with new sustainable constructions and building technologies. And is it a step too far in the realm of speculation if one seems to discover increased evidence of sensuousness in the last decades of HPP's work? Be that as it may, as one of the grand old architectural firms in Europe, HPP produces architecture that is not only lively, but also conscious of its responsibilities. That would seem, therefore, to make it equipped as well as possible for the future, and the hundredth anniversary of the firm's founding is only twenty-five years away!

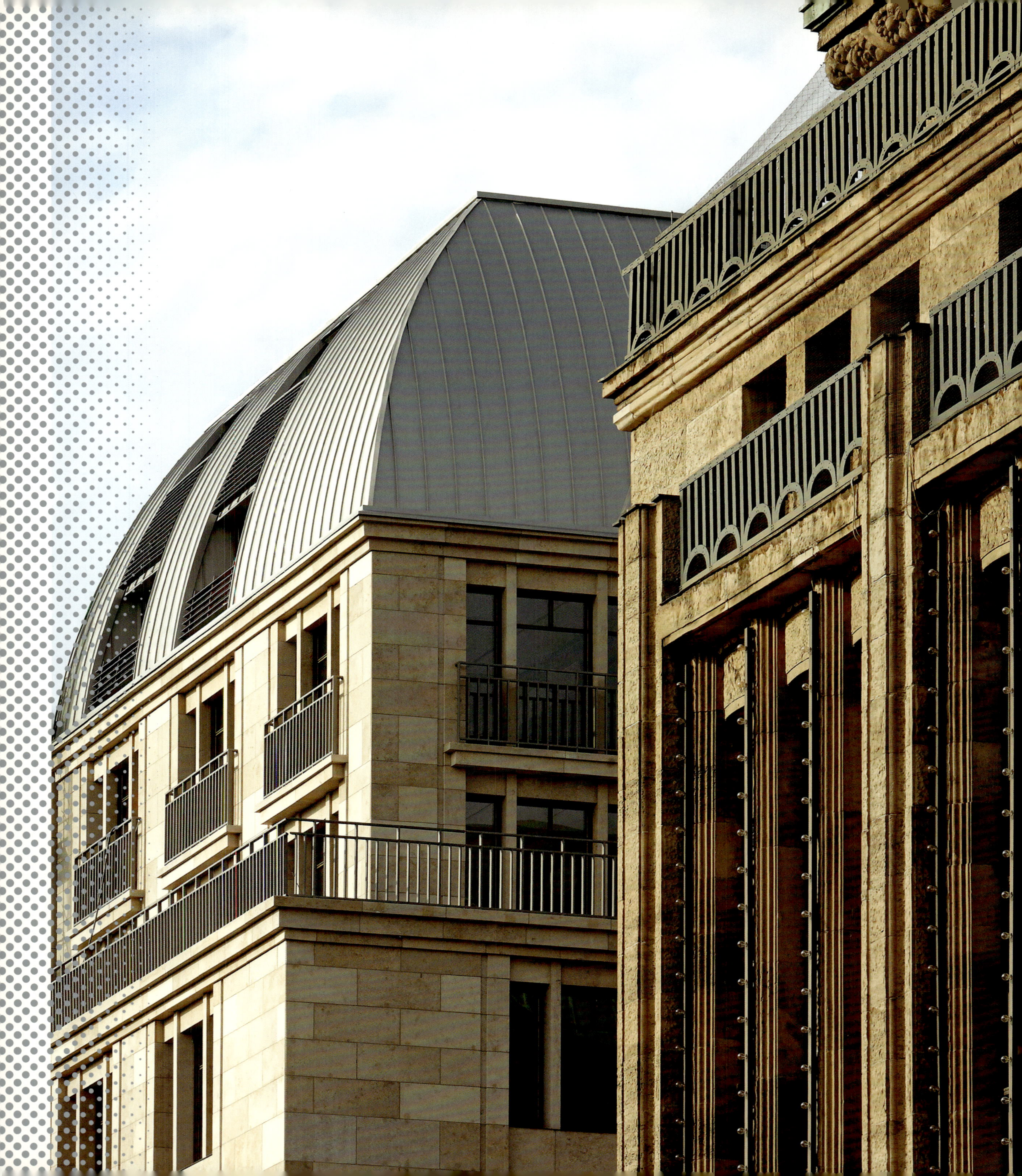

The Königsallee in the heart of Düsseldorf is the scene of the history of two extraordinary buildings whose contours have helped characterized the face of the city for decades. It is indeed one of the best known and most impressive promenades in all of Germany. And where but here, between Heinrich-Heine-Allee and Königsallee, the transition from the "Kö" to the historic district, could we locate Düsseldorf's urban center of gravity? In 1909, an architectural ensemble was created in this urbanistically prominent location that was dominated by the Tietz department store, which is the Kaufhof an der Kö today, and the Breidenbacher Hof. Over the years, these two structures have engaged in an architectural conversation with one another in the heart of Düsseldorf.

The boulevard where these buildings are located has had a turbulent history. At the beginning of the nineteenth century, after the withdrawal of the French troops and the dismantling of their fortifications, the Königsallee emerged to the east of the historic district. The magnificent boulevard is marked by the central city moat, luxurious trees, and the green embankments bordering the water and patrolled by swans and ducks.

Separated by the water of the moat but also connected by several bridges, the east and west sides of Königsallee have developed differently. On the west side the great private banks are strongly represented, while on the east side exclusive retail sets the tone. The sophisticated avenue has left its mark on the city for more than 200 years, and the Breidenbacher Hof hotel, which opened in 1812, long offered Düsseldorf's finest lodgings.

From very early on, the hotel became an interface between the new train station on the Königsallee and the auxiliary post offices in the historic district. As a result, travelers who were heading to or returning from the train station passed by the luxury hotel. The guest book from the hotel's early years reads like a German, as well as international, who's who. After the building's destruction during World War II and subsequent reconstruction, the Breidenbacher Hof remained the preferred choice of the upper classes. When the luxury hotel was later closed and demolished in 1999, the penultimate chapter of the long dialogue between the Breidenbacher Hof and the Kaufhof began.

Just like the city itself, the Kaufhof, a department store exemplifying Jugendstil design, waited patiently for the completion of the Breidenbacher Hof. Now it looks as if the latter had been there all along—which was the precise aim of HPP's design for the new reconstruction. The new building's façade was designed with a thorough respect for the tradition of the historic structure that had preceded it, but the building's interior is completely fresh and tailored to the needs and demands of the shoppers of today. Classic, timeless, and comparable to the kinds of historic buildings found in large European cities, the hotel exudes the solid and discreet elegance that only ones with stone façades can. It makes do without the slightest reference to contemporary design fads, reprising the appearance of the centuries-old structure almost as a matter of course. With the new structure's reference to the Breidenbacher Hof's historic design, it is at the same time a point of orientation, architectural trademark, and urban development constant for Düsseldorf.

Let us end with the words of Heinrich Heine: "Düsseldorf is very beautiful. … And if one has no fixed address, then one prefers to stop at the Breidenbacher Hof, [for] this trademark signif[ies] exquisite hospitality in the heart of the region's capital on the Rhine."

Context Breidenbacher Hof

Client: **Pearl of Kuwait Real Estate Co.** | Hotel operator: **Capella Hotels & Resorts**
Location: **Düsseldorf** | GFA Hotel: **17,520 m²** | GFA Residences: **4,875 m²**
GFA Retail: **4,125 m²** | GFA Office: **3,995 m²** | Hotel rooms: **79 guest rooms and 16 suites**
Completion date: **2008**

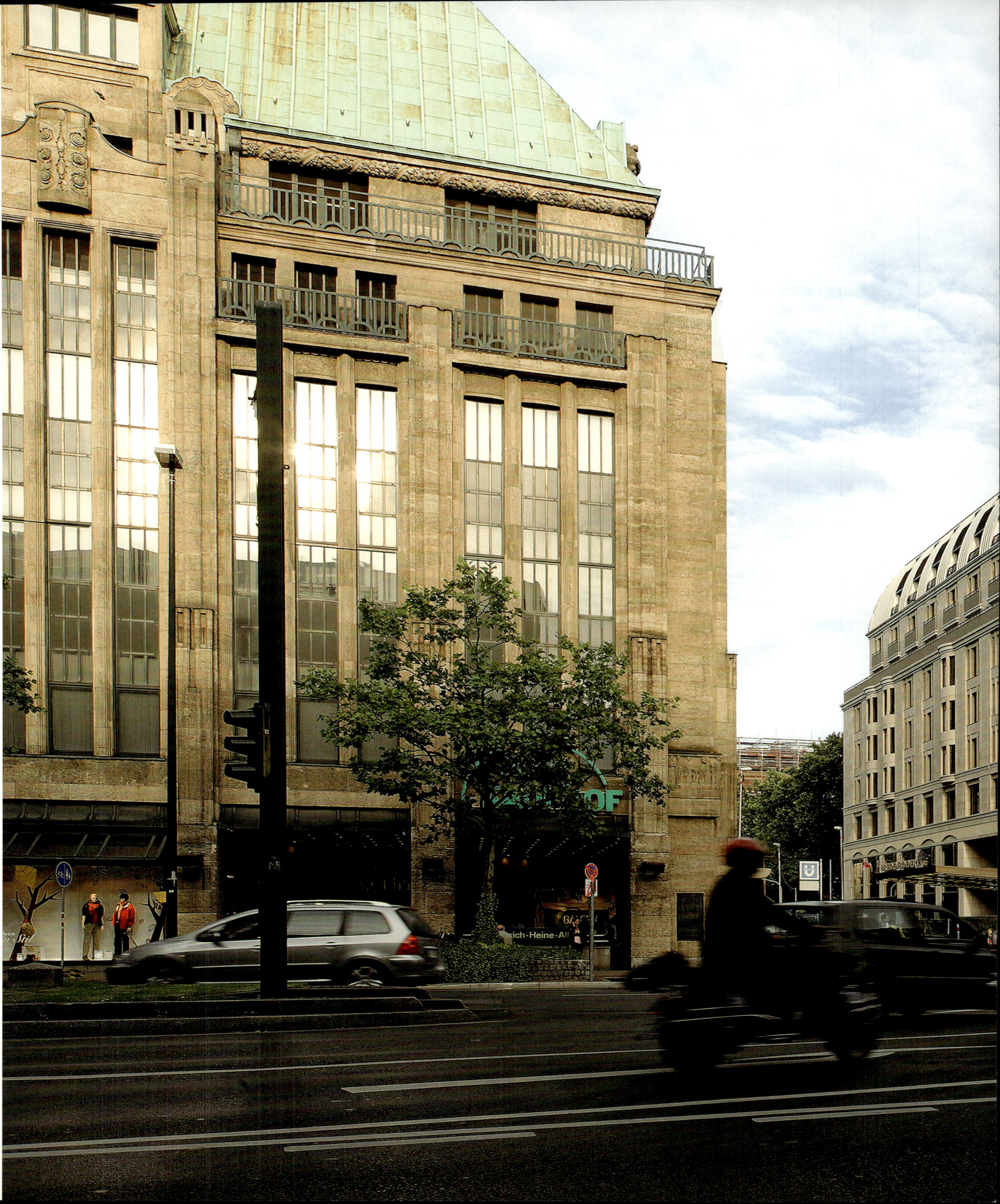

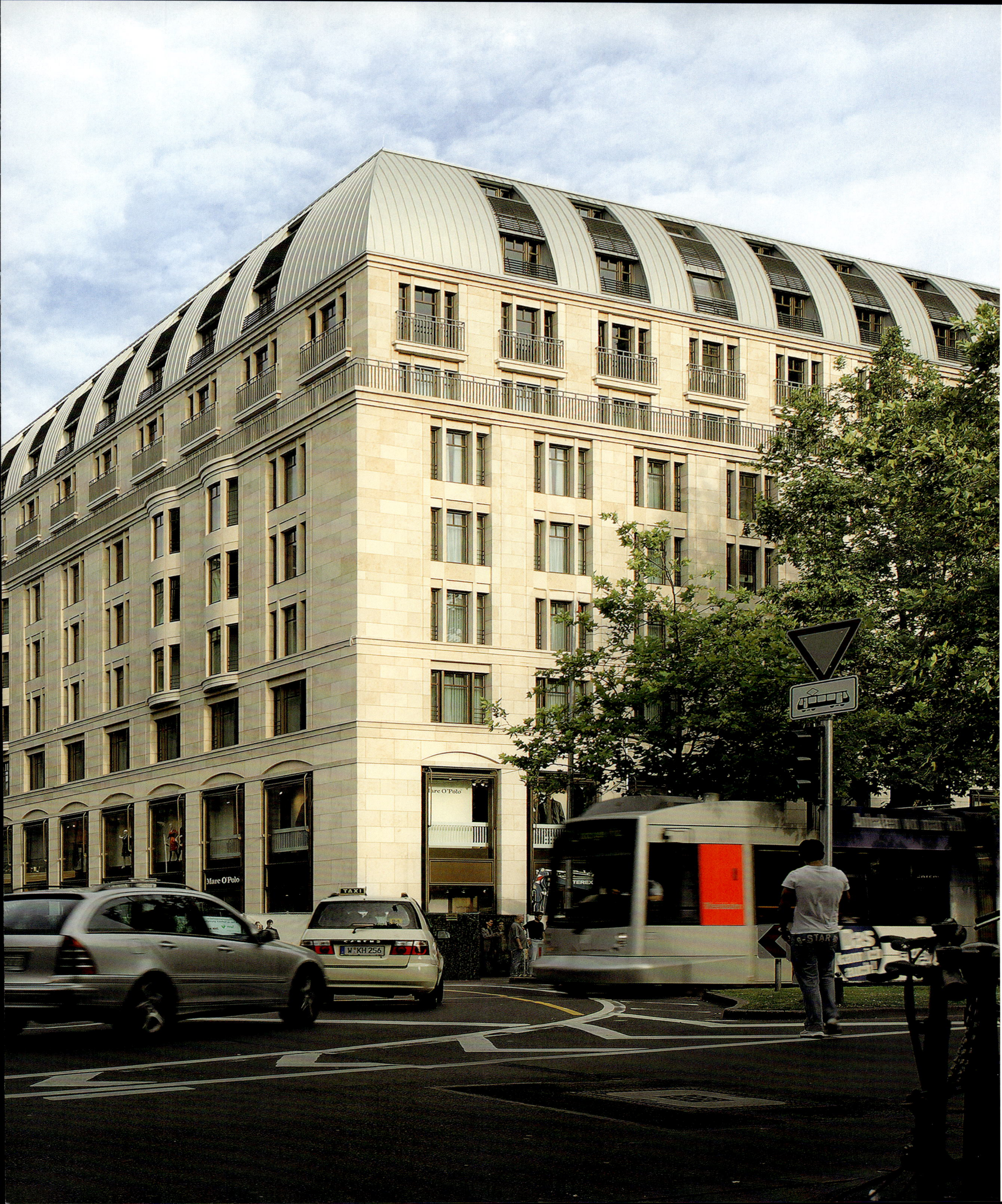

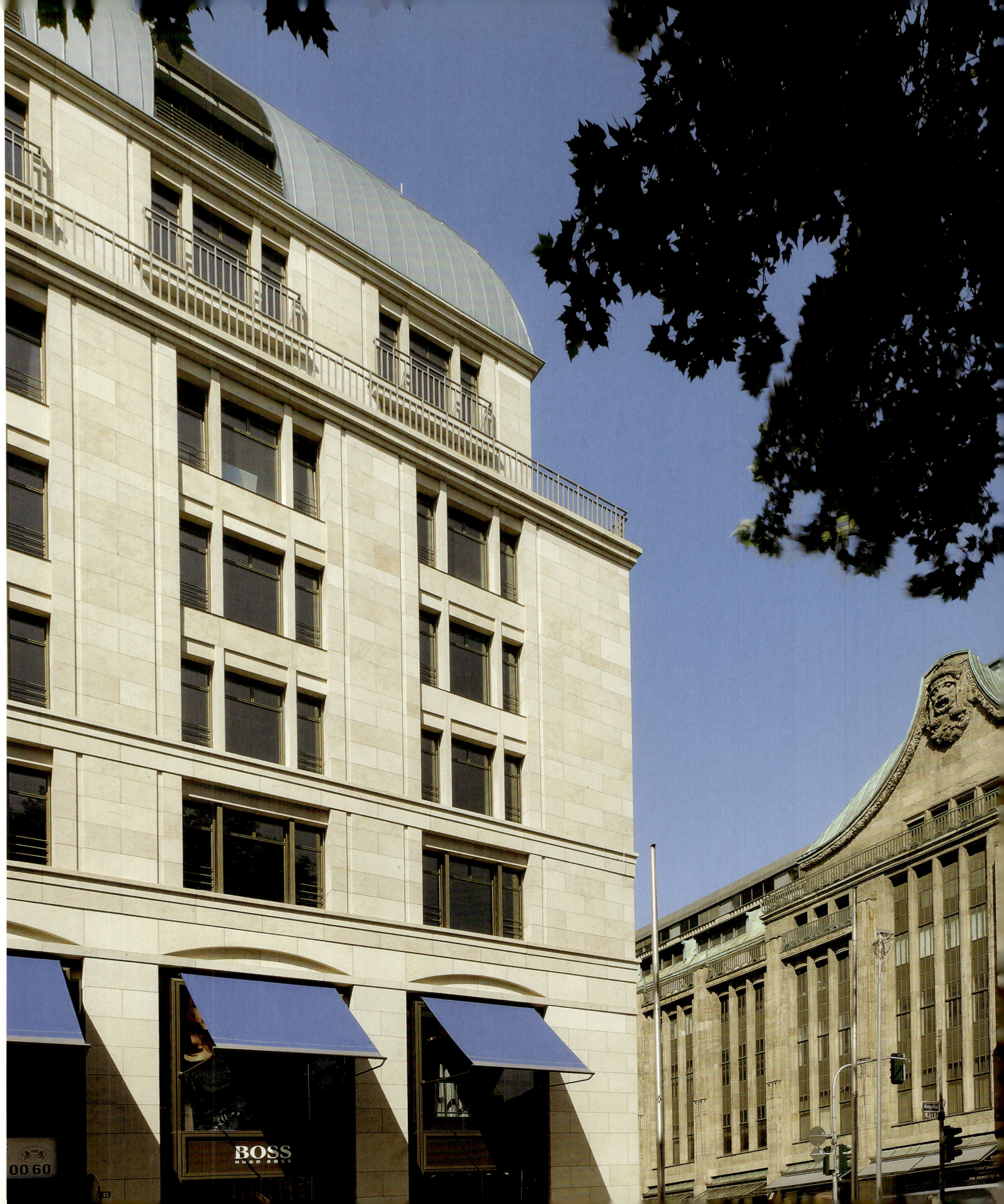

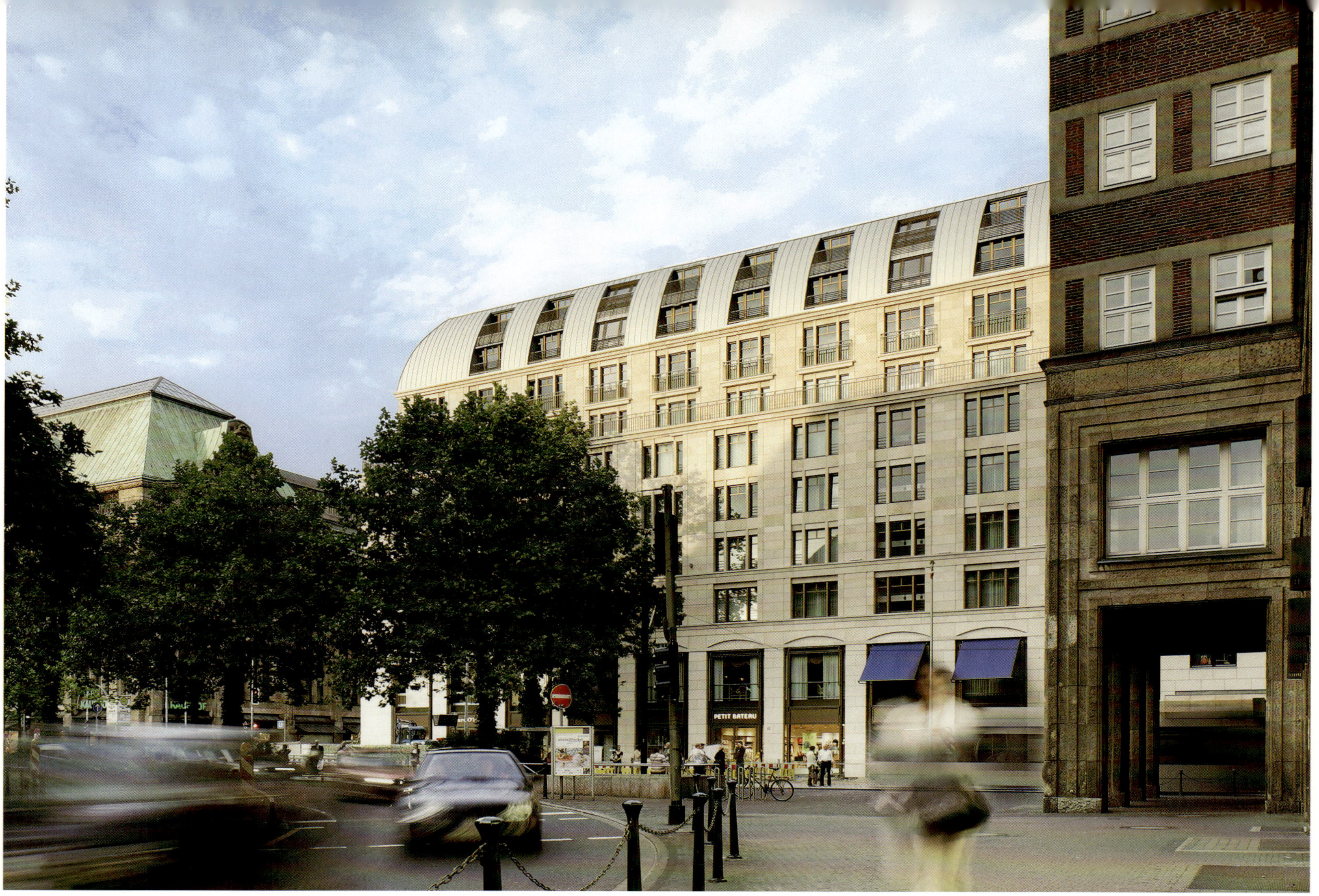

The building ensemble of Heinrich-Heine-Platz

← Königsallee view
↞ The Breidenbacher Hof in dialogue with the Kaufhof, Heinrich-Heine-Allee view

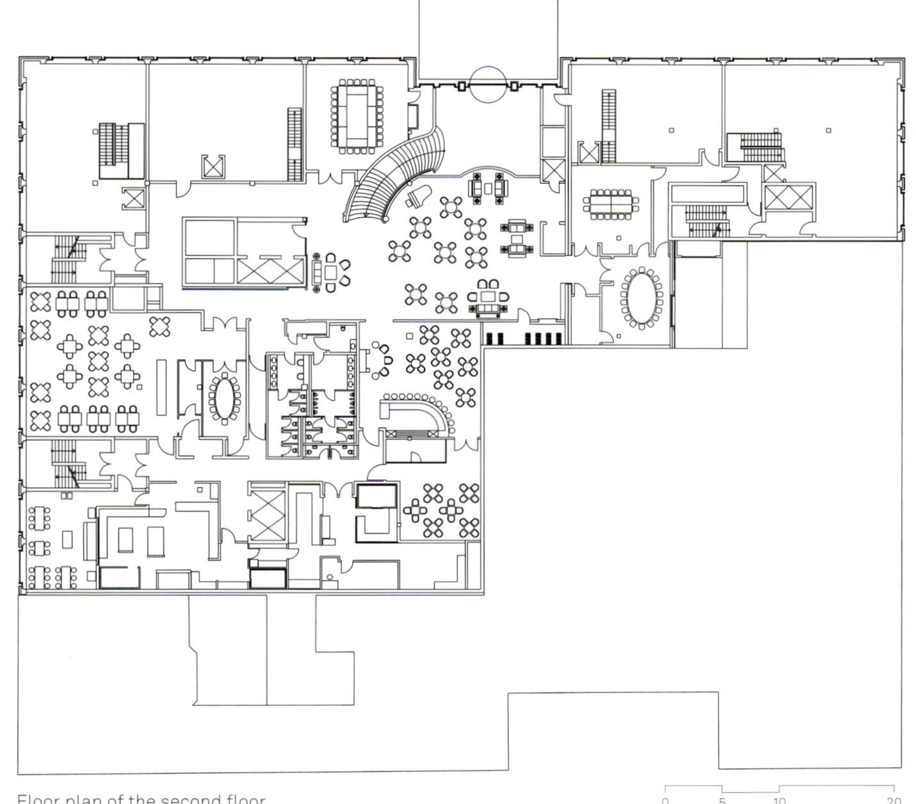

Floor plan of the second floor

The Breidenbacher Hof For 175 years the Breidenbacher Hof's name was synonymous with the highest level of hotel comfort. However, the building was eventually shut down and then demolished in 1999 due to its decrepit state. The new Breidenbacher Hof now stands on the very same location that its historical predecessor once did, on the west side of the Königsallee in Düsseldorf in the context of the urbanistically important ensemble of the Wilhelm-Marx-Haus, the Carschhaus, and the Kaufhof an der Kö.

Today the new building, which was completed in 2008, is once again one of the best hotels in Düsseldorf. In addition, the nine-story structure also has space for upscale retail stores and well-appointed offices, as well as a total of eighteen luxury apartments, whose sizes range from 110 to 330 square meters, on the upper three stories.

In honor of the location and the history of the hotel, which goes back to 1806, the new Breidenbacher Hof displays a traditional mode of organization: the first five stories comprise the base of the structure, the sixth and seventh stories are recessed, and the final two stories are nestled under a vaulted Mansard roof. The building's consciously classicizing architectural vocabulary is underscored by the profiling and articulation of the façade with large natural stone slabs. While the horizontal lines of the building's shell are defined by cornices on each floor, distinct, vertical joints and three-light windows set deeply within their reveals s gnal the inner division of the building. Design elements such as basket-handle arches, bays, and awnings in the pedestrian area also lend the "urban stone" of the façade a marked plasticity as well as a haptic quality.

Access to the hotel is provided via the main entrance on Theodor-Körner-Strasse, which is visible at quite a distance through the covered drive with its carefully orchestrating lighting. The reception area with an adjoining club lounge is located on the ground floor of the two-story hotel lobby. The guests ascend a broad, curved marble stairway to the second floor, where the restaurant, bar, cigar lounge, and conference and event rooms are located.

The hotel has space for 79 guest rooms and 16 suites. The rooms, which range from 41 to 83 square meters, have a width of approximately 4.5 meters and a height of 2.7 meters. From the attractive building's corners, the 96- to 222-square-meter suites have a view of the Heinrich-Heine-Platz and the old downtown district. The central positioning of the elevator units ensures that the distance to the rooms is short for guests and service personnel.

Flexibly dividable space for exclusive retail shops is located on the first two floors and the first basement level along the adjoining streets of Königsallee, Theodor-Körner-Strasse, and Heinrich-Heine-Allee. The office spaces, which can also be divided flexibly, are located on the third to seventh floors and are reached via a separate entrance on Königsallee. This multiple-use capability of the building contributes substantially to the activation of the urban space and provides an answer to the future needs of the city's downtown: a highly attractive combination of first-class residences, services, and recreation opportunities.

The timeless, classic appearance of the new Breidenbacher Hof consciously calls to mind the grand hotels of nineteenth-century Europe. Through the language of its design and scale, the building engages in a dialogue with the surrounding architectural landmarks and constitutes a striking new element in the architectural ensemble of Heinrich-Heine-Platz. A new urbanity has emerged.

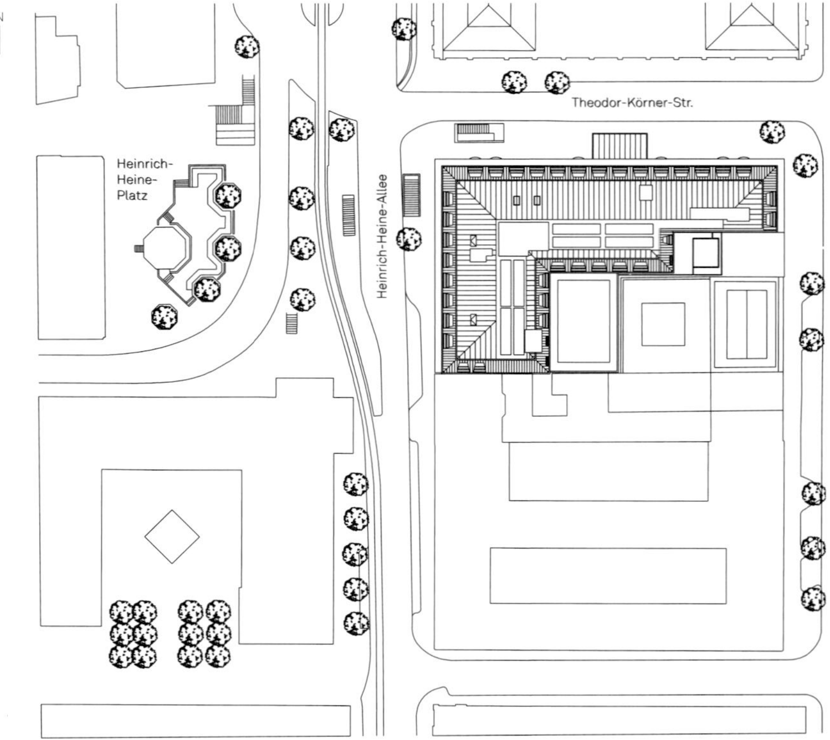

→ View of Theodor-Körner-Strasse

Site plan

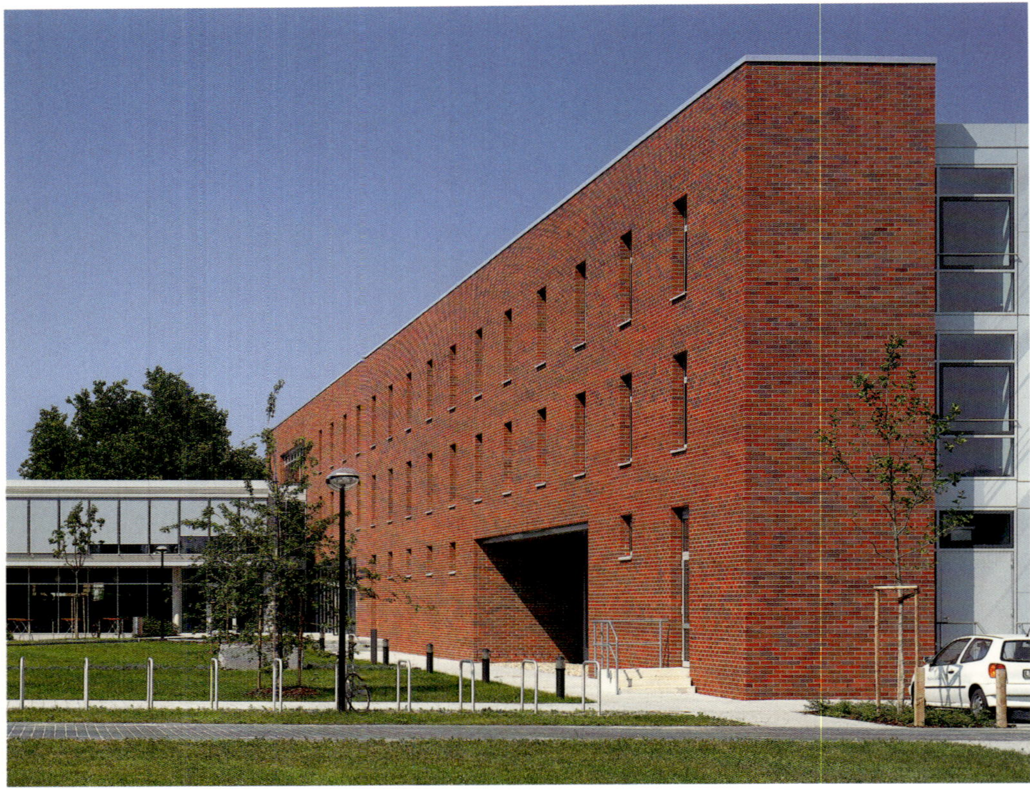

Leipzig Public Utility Facility

The new building complex is oriented towards the volumes of the historic landmark of the decommissioned gas tank and the smokestack of the South Heating Plant. In its materiality and colorfulness it reflects the character of the other buildings in the vicinity.

Client: Stadtwerke Leipzig
Location: Leipzig
GFA: 7,908 m²
Work stations: 300
Completion date: 2000
Competition: 1st Prize, 1998
Award: Architecture Prize of the City of Leipzig, 2001

Context

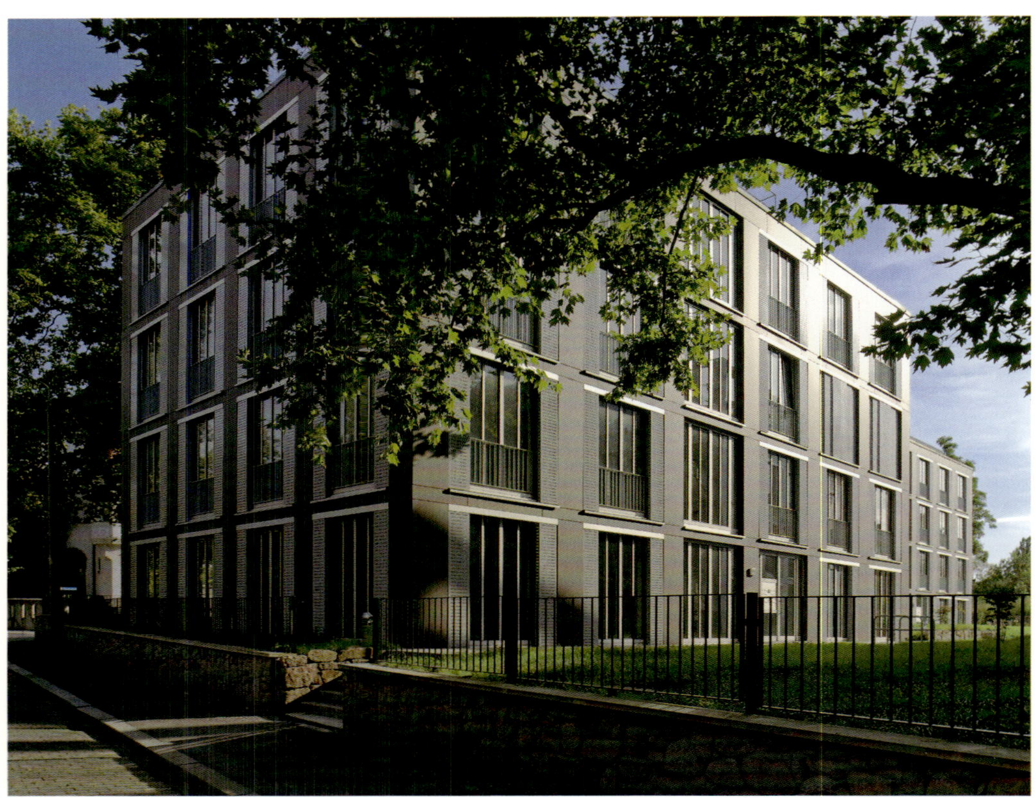

Park Mansions, Kickerlingsberg

The urban surroundings of the Park Mansions in the Kickerlingsberg district are characterized by Jugendstil buildings and extended green areas. This context, as well as a unique stock of trees, lends the lot on which the seven new buildings are located its own special character. Thanks to the extensive surface area of the building's windows, the broad grounds that open up within the loose arrangement of the Park Mansions may also be enjoyed from the living areas inside the mansions themselves.

Client: City Projektbau Leipzig GmbH
Location: Leipzig-Gohlis
GFA: 9,498 m²
Residential units: 71
Completion date: 1st phase of construction in 2007

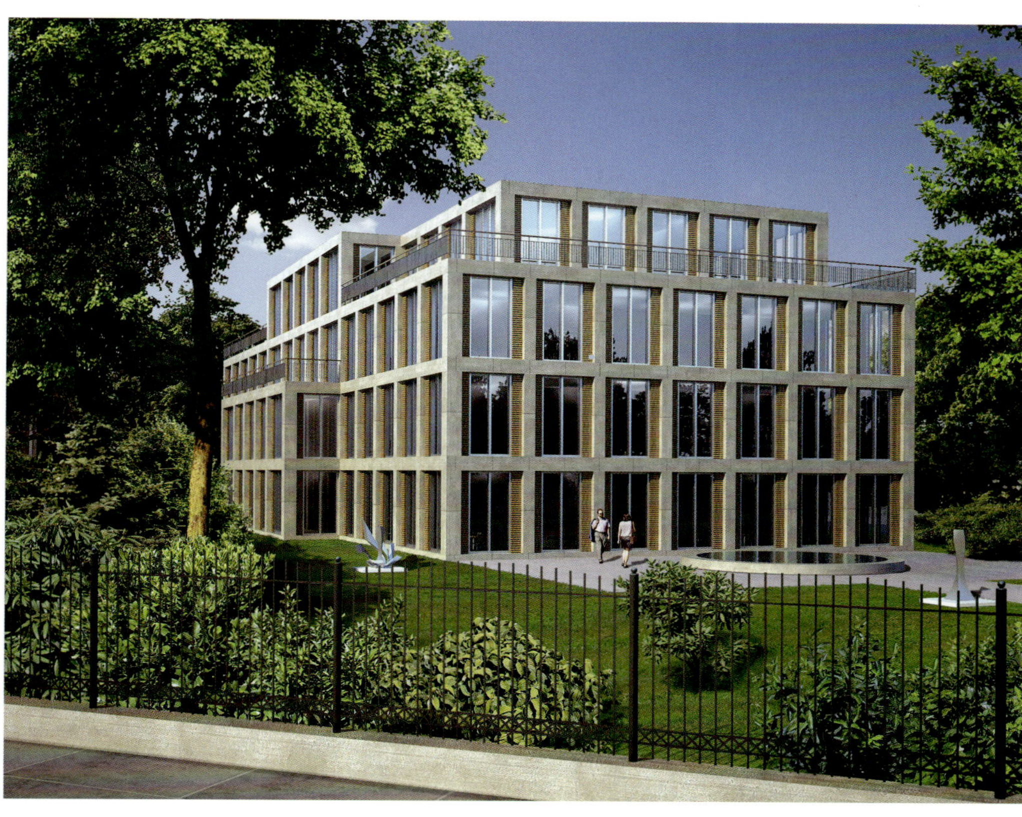

Cecilien-Palais

This imposing new office building is located on Cecilienallee and has an unencumbered view of the riverside park across the way. The building, which is constructed on a rectangular ground plan, has three full stories, an open penthouse, and a basement. The generously segmented natural stone façades underscore the prestigious character of the new building while its scale integrates it into the physical context of its urban surroundings.

Client: BEMA Unternehmensgruppe
Location: Düsseldorf
GFA: 5,340 m²
Completion date: 2009

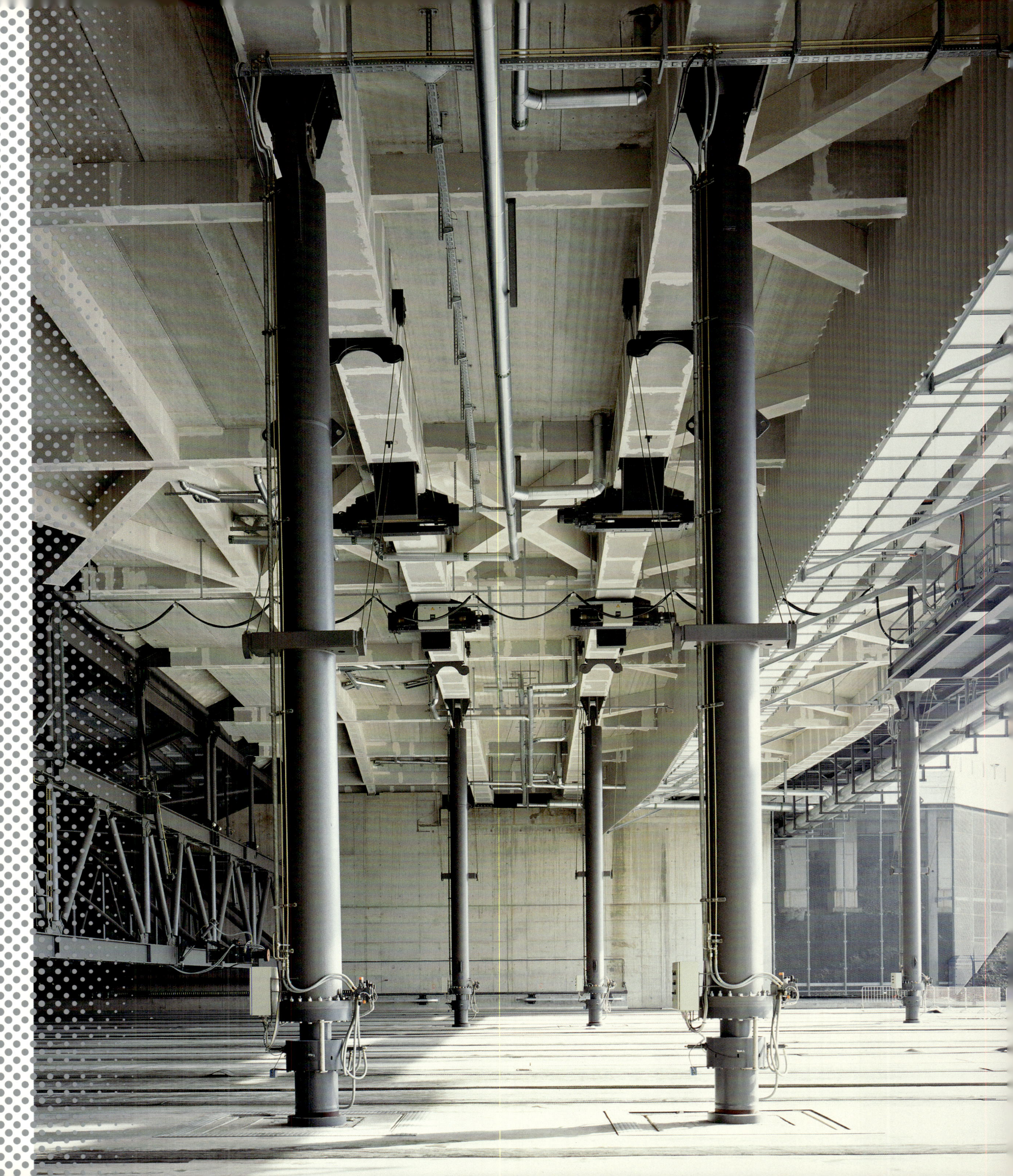

Construction AufSchalke Arena

Client: **FC Schalke 04 Stadion-Beteiligungs-GmbH & Co. Immobilienverwaltungs-KG**
Location: **Gelsenkirchen** | GFA: **40,816 m²** | Seats: **max. 61,482**
Completion date: **2001** | Award: **IOC / IAKS AWARD, Special Distinction, 2005**

Buildings have left a deep mark on the development of humanity, and extraordinary building is a source of inspiration. The great Gothic cathedrals, breathtaking bridges, and the skyscrapers of modern megacities imbue thought and imagination with a new dimension. For many, the discovery of building often begins in childhood by playing with wooden blocks. Space is playfully occupied, a feeling for materials is developed, and the capability of combining smaller, individual parts into larger, more complex objects emerges. That is how master builders have realized their constructions over the centuries: through trial and error, and through the dissemination of the knowledge of materials and their characteristics and stability.

At the beginning of a building project, the design represents the plan for the spatial realization of an idea in the form of a building. This is what characterizes the architect and his activity. There is no recipe for such work, no precise set of guidelines. Each building must be thought through afresh and calculated down to the level of the most minor details. Visible construction—principles such as making the load transfer and the clear formal inclusion in the building's configuration visible—is the high art of design. Principle, calculation, and procedure are the essential steps which explain the appearance of architecture.

There is hardly another type of building that makes a more striking visual impression than a stadium, in which everything revolves around the game played within it. Building was also one of the central subjects in the planning and realization of the AufSchalke Arena, which consists of two massively elaborated stands prefabricated in units. These fit snugly around the grassy playing field, which every second weekend becomes the most important location in the region. At exactly 3:30 PM, over and over again, the bowl seems to spill over and a wave seems to roll through the stadium every time the Schalke Miners score a goal. What is created is an incomparable atmosphere that spreads throughout the stadium.

The arena, at 220 meters in length, is spanned by an unsupported construction of steel girders and has outer surfaces covered with sheets of Teflon. It is especially exciting when in good weather the roof automatically opens up over the playing field like the top of a convertible, providing an unencumbered view of the sky and letting the sun's rays heat up the mood in the stadium even further. In order for the grass to stay green on the playing field, it is carted out of the arena during the week on sleeve bearings. The lower bleachers on the south side of the stadium can be raised, and, as if by magic, the playing field glides out from under them to its storage position out-side the stadium.

Building, then, is a process that challenges the architect every day anew. Even today—despite computerized processes—playful thought, experiments, a knowledge of materials, and a large measure of technical expertise provide the basic foundations of architectural design. The development process, a process by which something emerges from the mind of the architect, makes possible the realization of everything from a building's broader spatial concept to its more precise details. No technical aids will ever be able to replace this creative process.

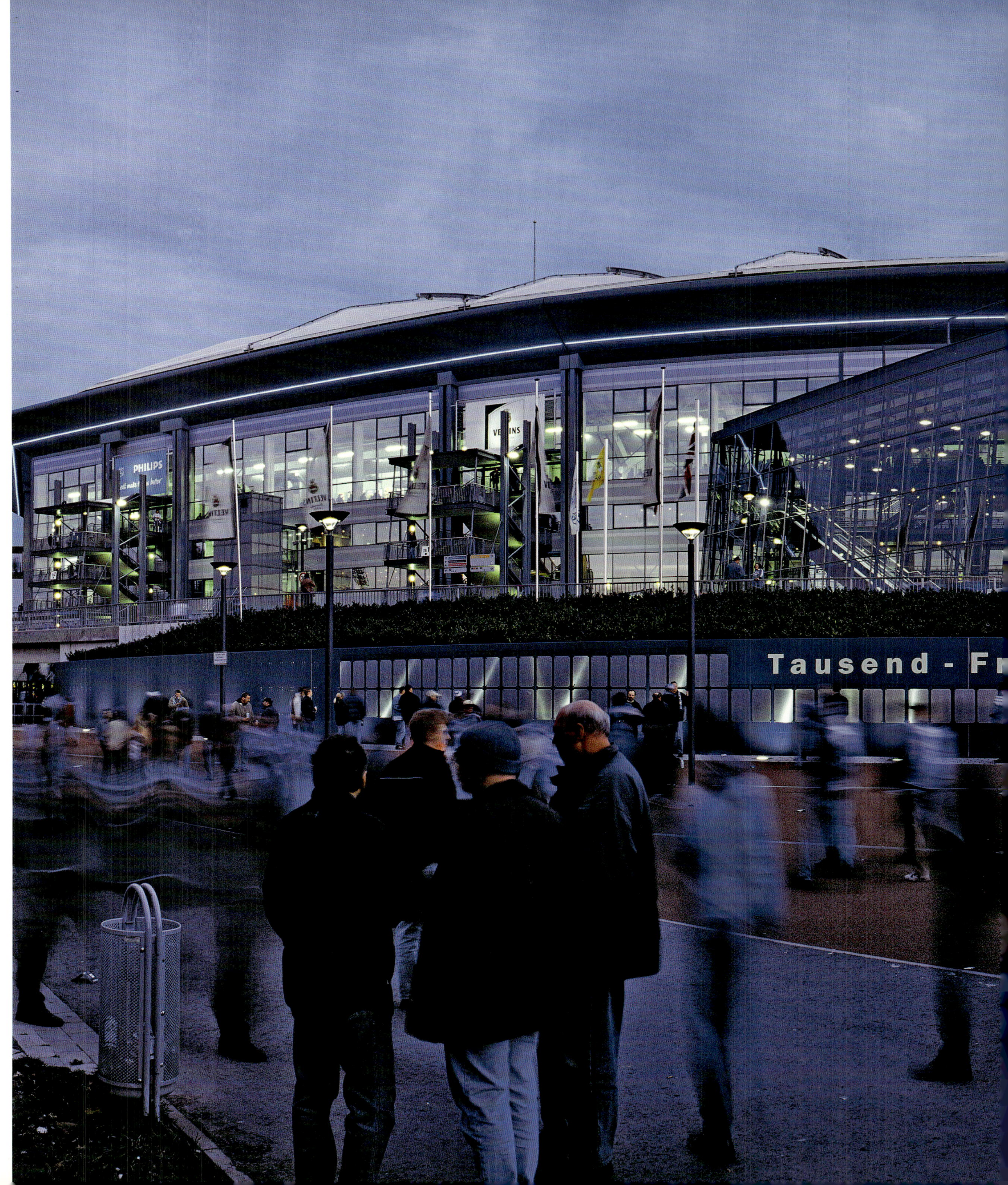
PHILIPS
VELTINS
Tausend - Fr

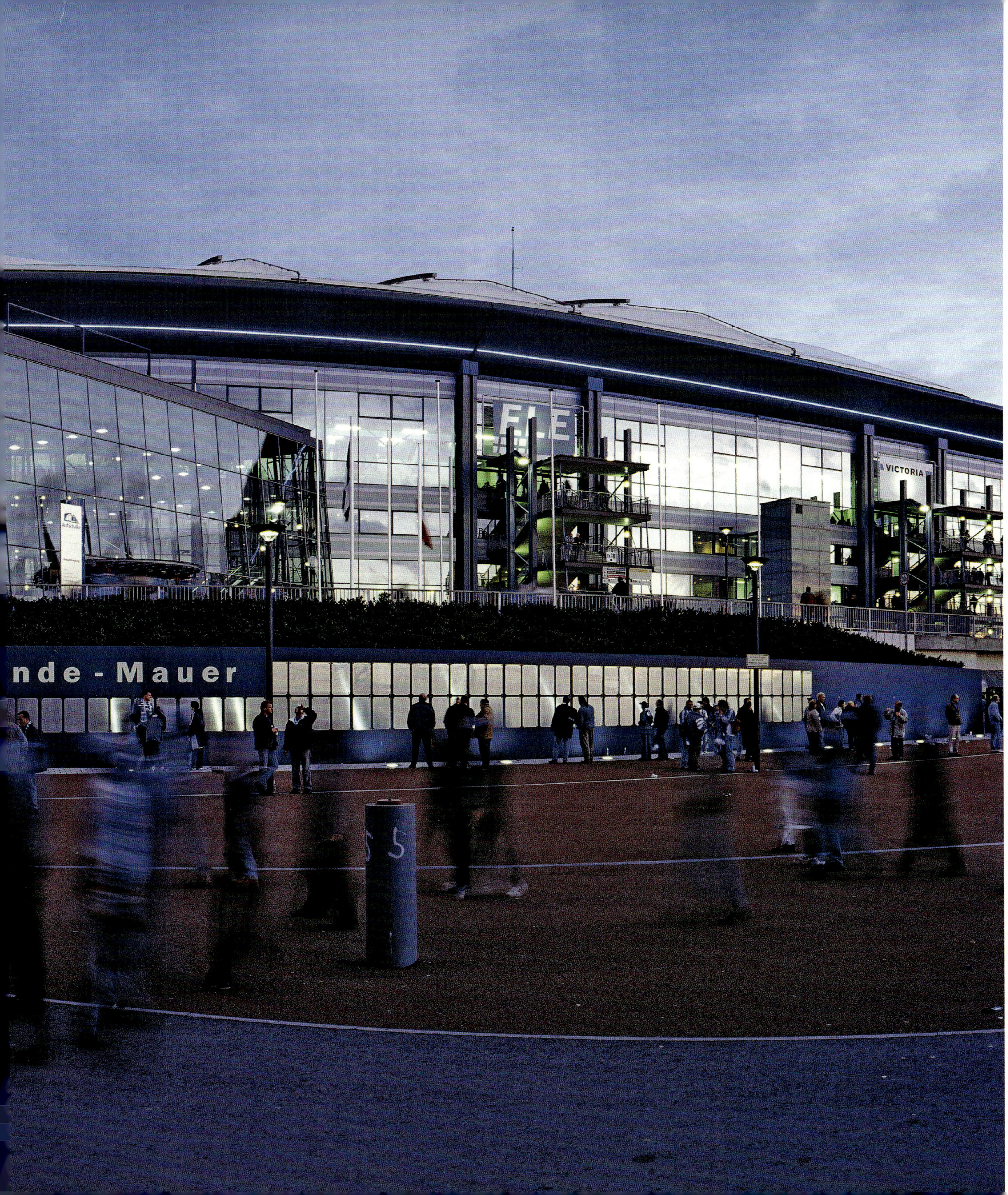

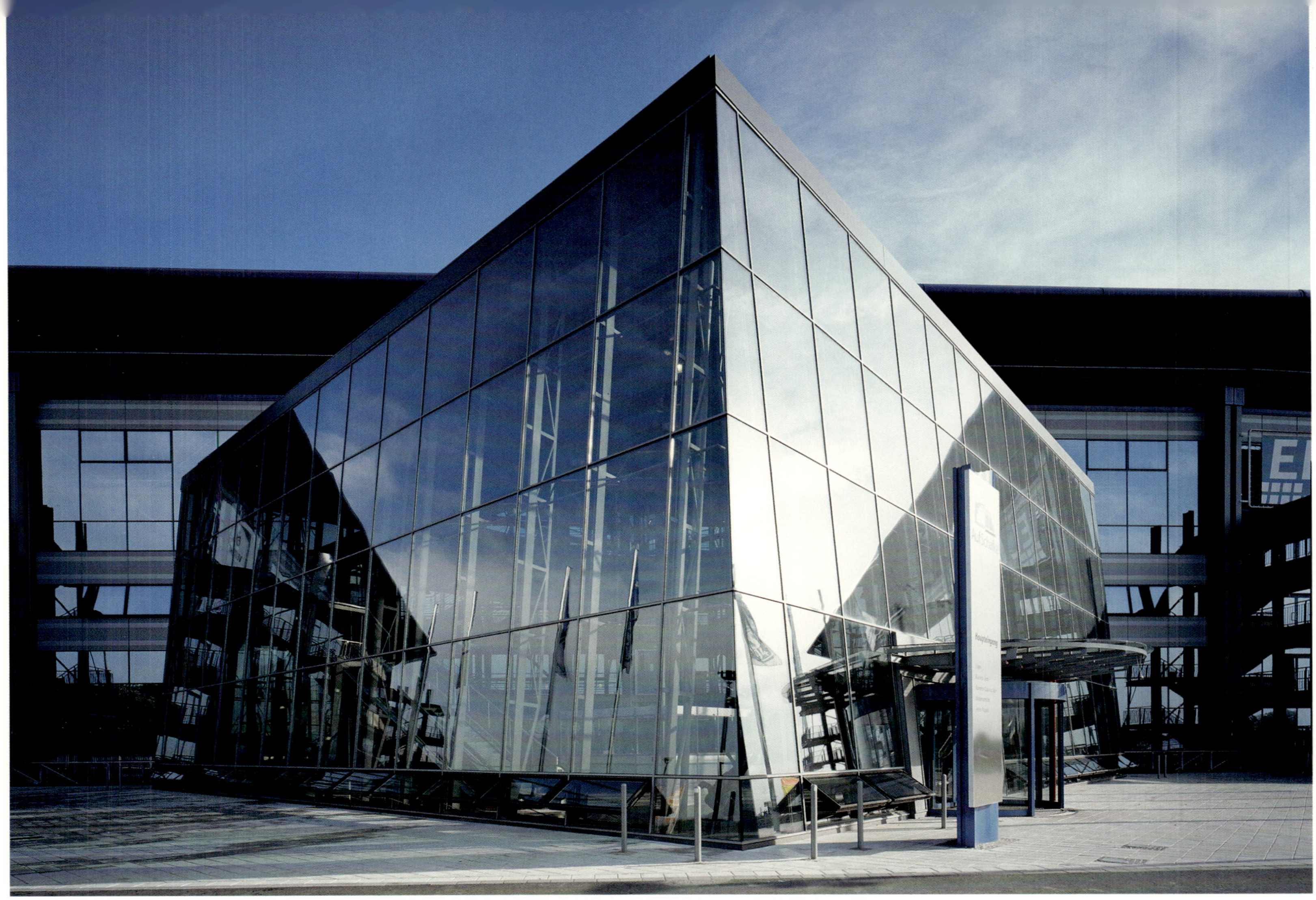

Glass-enclosed entry building

← Main entrance, west side
→ Steel-encased elevator shaft

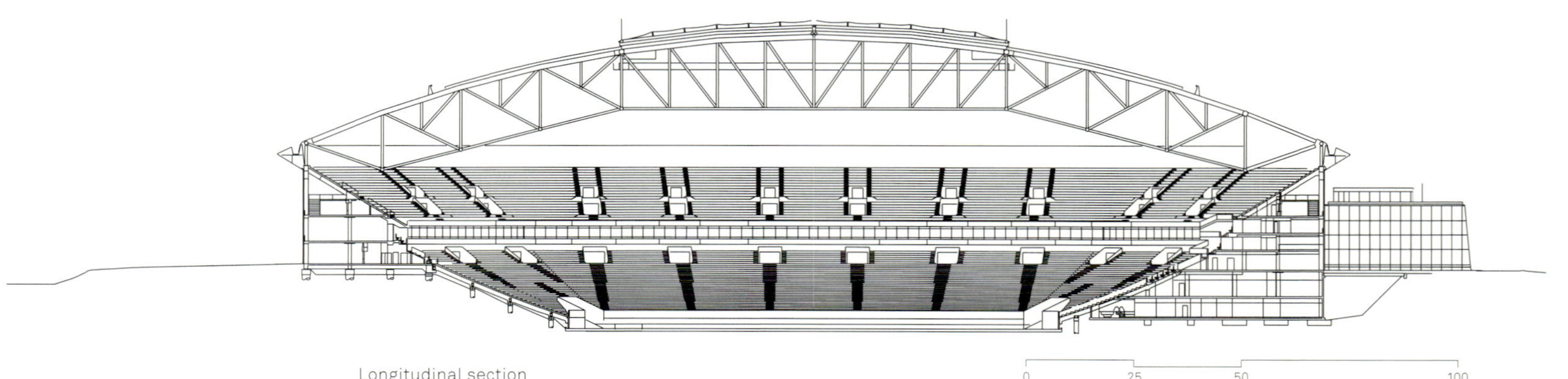

Longitudinal section

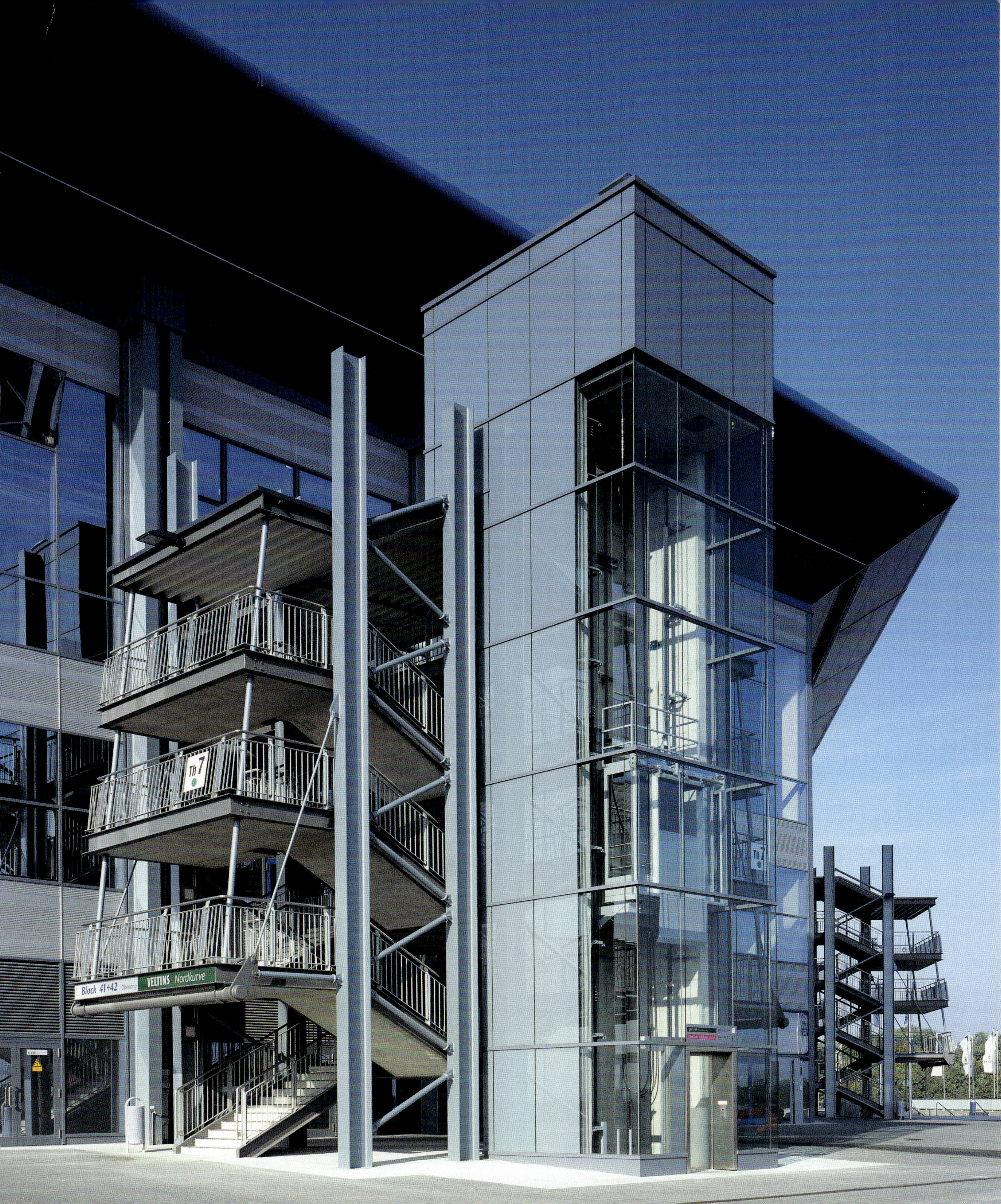
Th 7
Block 41+42
VELTINS Nordkurve

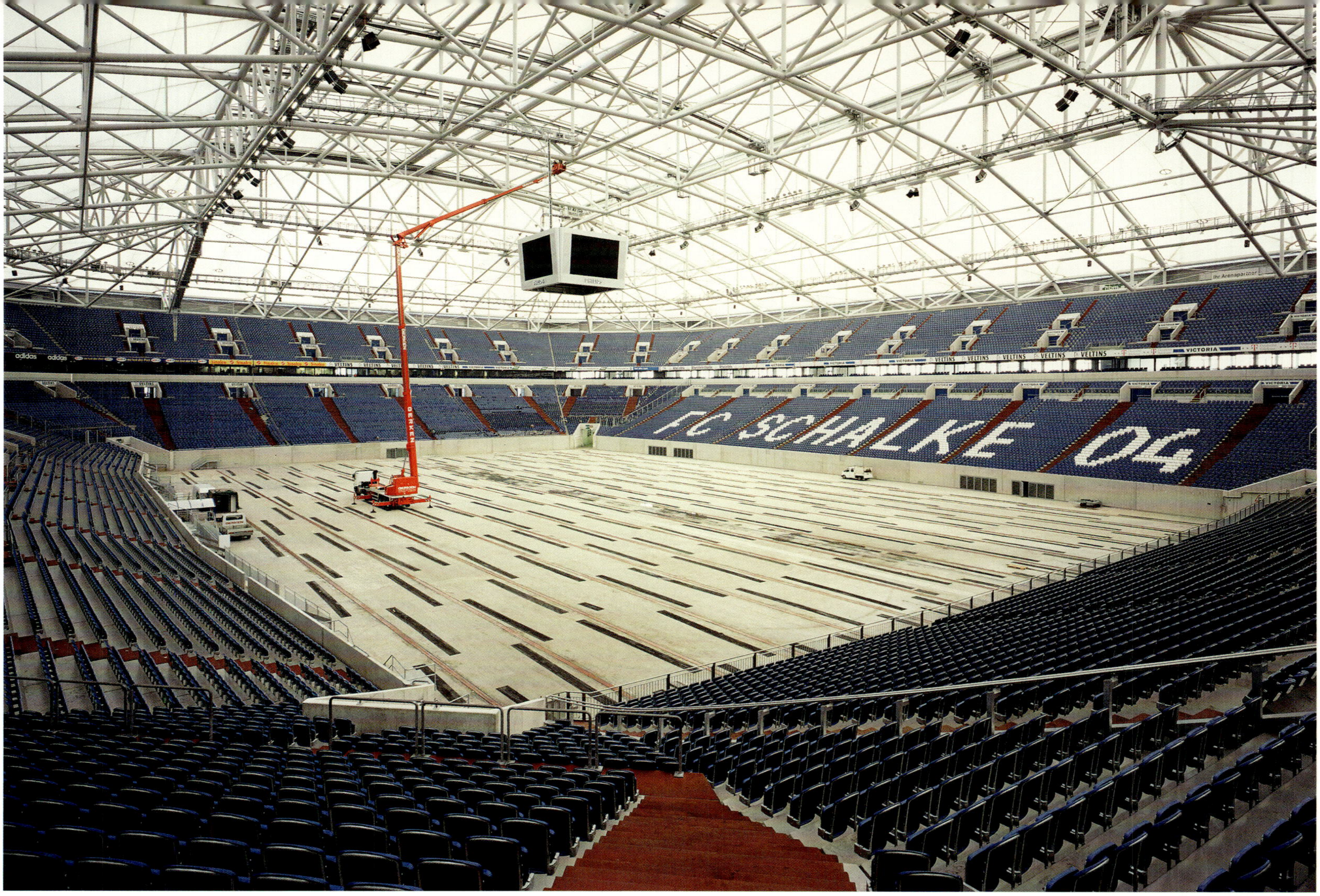

Secondary floor of reinforced concrete

→ Retractable playing field mechanism

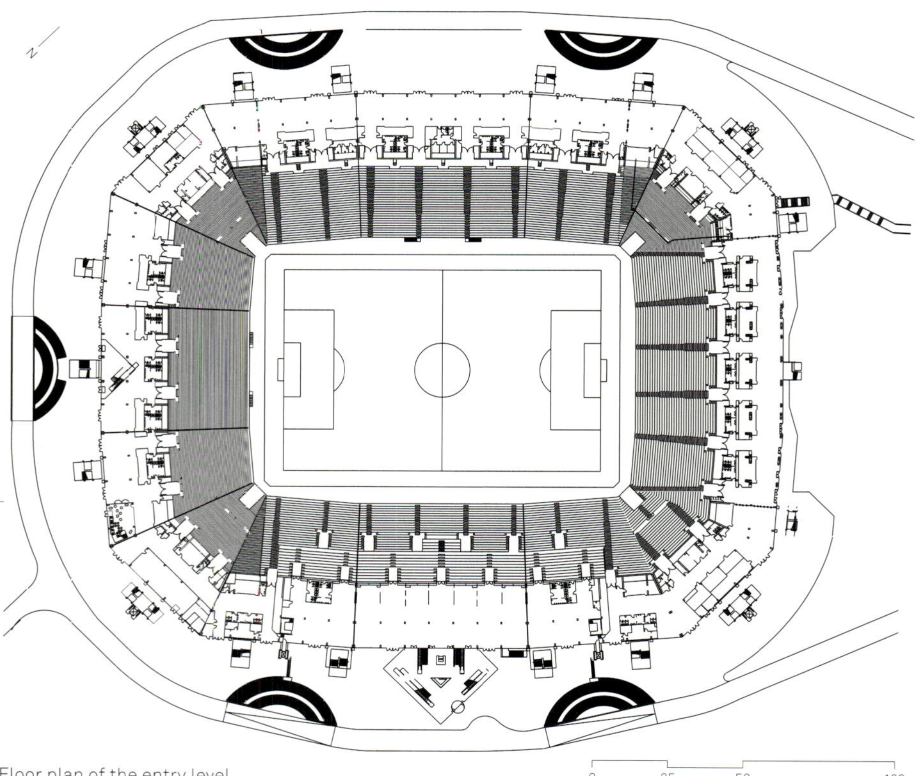

Floor plan of the entry level

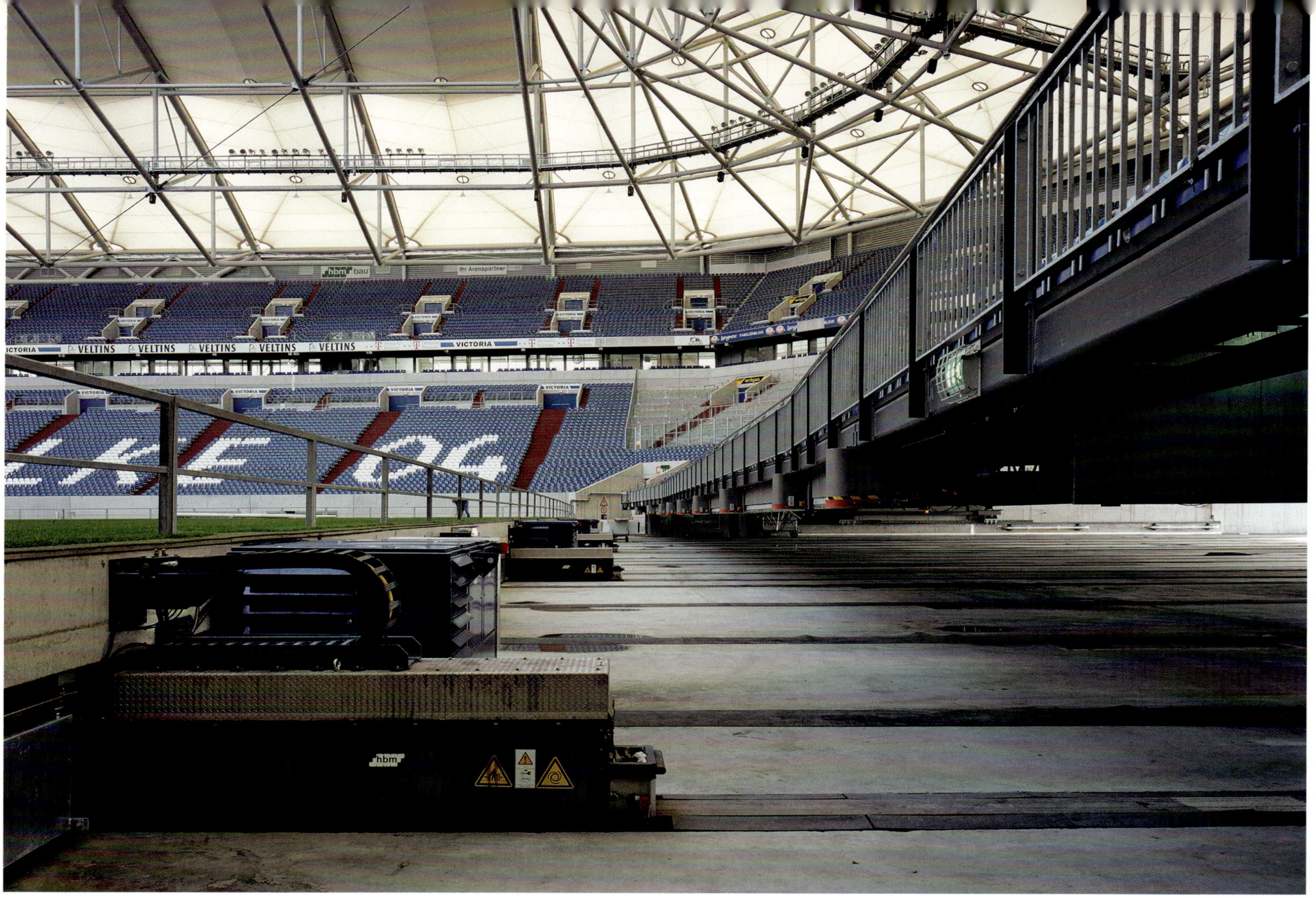

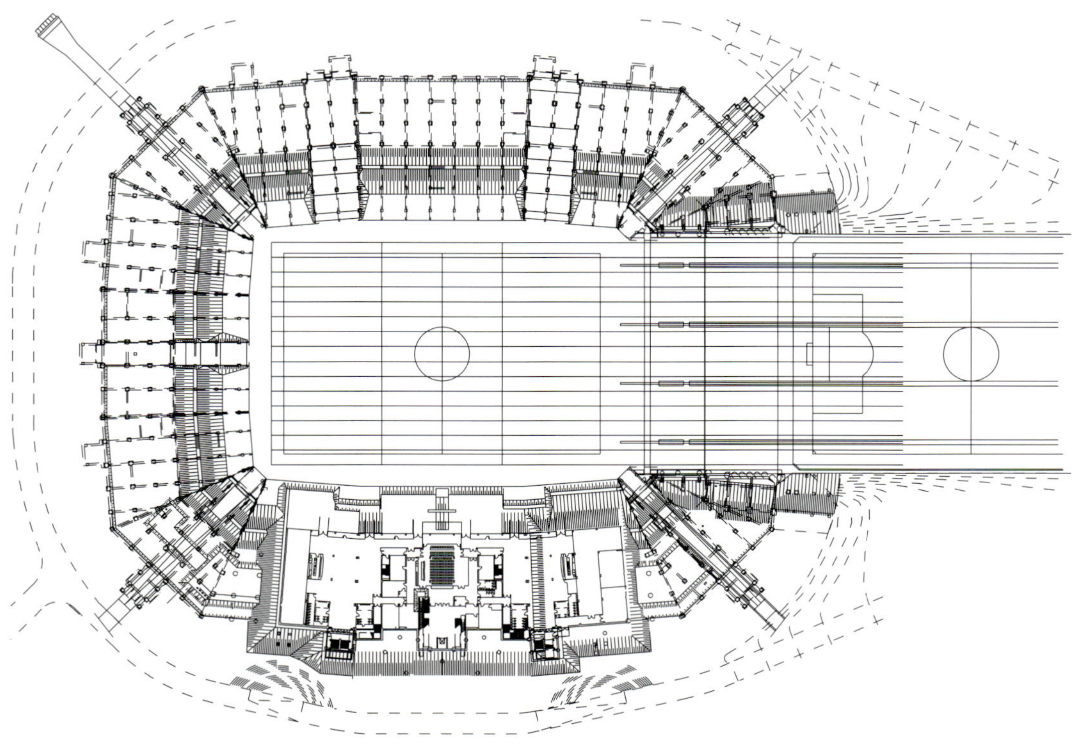

Floor plan of the playing field level

30 **The AufSchalke Arena** The AufSchalke Arena is located in Berger Field, the geographical middle of Gelsenkirchen, in the direct line of sight of the old Park Stadium. This new arena was constructed to replace Park Stadium during the 2001–02 National League soccer season due to problems of mining subsidence.

The design for the 225-meter-long, 187-meter-wide, 53.5-meter-tall structure was the result of the requirement that the stadium be multifunctional. Because the structure's use is not dependent upon good weather, in addition to its main function as a soccer stadium with seating for 60,000 fans, AufSchalke Arena can also be used to host fairs, exhibitions, concerts, and other large-scale events. With its basic form of a rounded-off rectangle, it is the first soccer stadium in the world of its size that can be transformed in just thirty minutes into a giant hall with a closed roof. In order to do this, the moveable part of the two-part roof construction slides laterally over a framework of steel pipes. In order to protect the grass during non-sporting events, the entire playing field (118 by 79 meters) can be driven out of the stadium in six hours by simply pressing a button. Like a drawer, the turf slides out of the stadium on Teflon tracks through an opening underneath the south bleachers. After the playing field has been rolled out, a secondary floor surface of reinforced concrete can be used for other events. Once the sliding procedure has been completed, the lower level of the south bleachers can be hydraulically moved approximately sixteen meters underneath the upper one, thus allowing the resulting free surface area to be used to set up a stage. In cases such as this one, the stadium's spectator capacity is only slightly reduced.

The supporting structure of the bleachers is made of reinforced concrete, with the exception of the south bleachers. The latter are supported by an eighty-meter-long, overarching steel bridge construction, in order to make it possible to drive on and off of the playing field. The bleachers are placed snugly along all four sides of the field and are each divided into two galleries. This balances out the stadium's interior space and creates the infamous "witch's cauldron" effect when the stadium is full, an effect previously encountered only in stadiums built exclusively for soccer.

In the arena's west building there is the VIP area divided into five levels with loges, the Business Club, and team and media rooms. These are all accessed through the forward-positioned, pyramidal, crystalline entry building. In the other areas of the stadium, visitors gain access via eighteen open outdoor stairways. On the ground floor as well as in the upper gallery, thirty-two concession stands attend to the food and beverage needs of the stadium's guests in the promenades running under the bleachers.

The building's exterior consists of a fully glassed-in, unitized, aluminum curtain wall that is united with protruding steel pillars as well as exterior staircases. Because of the initial design requirement that the stadium be multifunctional, all construction groups—roofs, bleachers, loges, and access points—are designed as modular elements, just as if they were parts of a set of building blocks. Using these, the building was developed from the inside outwards, but the important membrane-covered steel framework can nonetheless be seen from outside the building in the roof area to good effect.

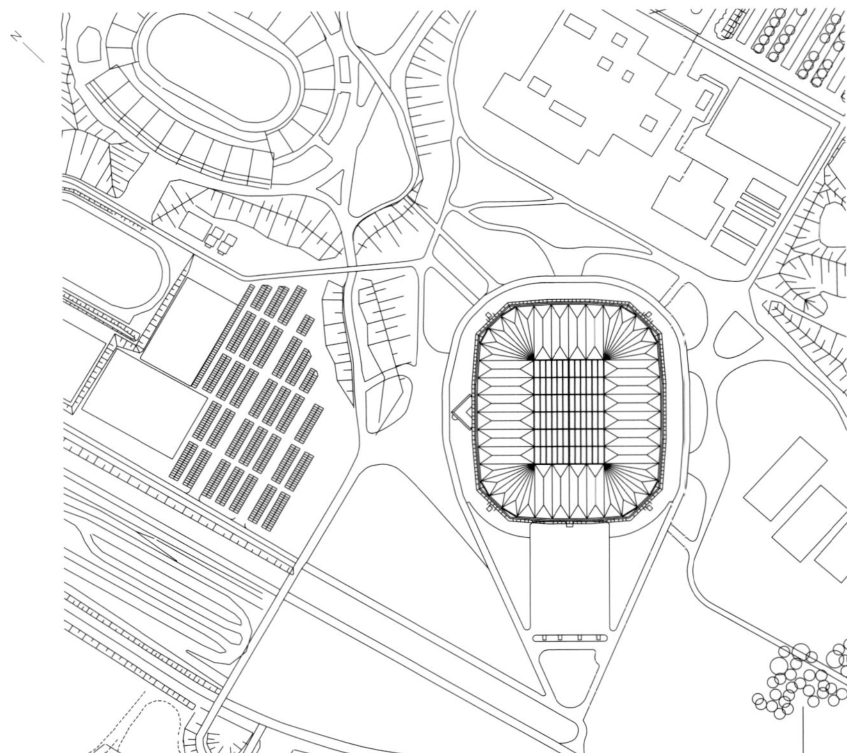

Site plan

→ Access foyer for VIP areas
→→ The AufSchalke "witch's cauldron"

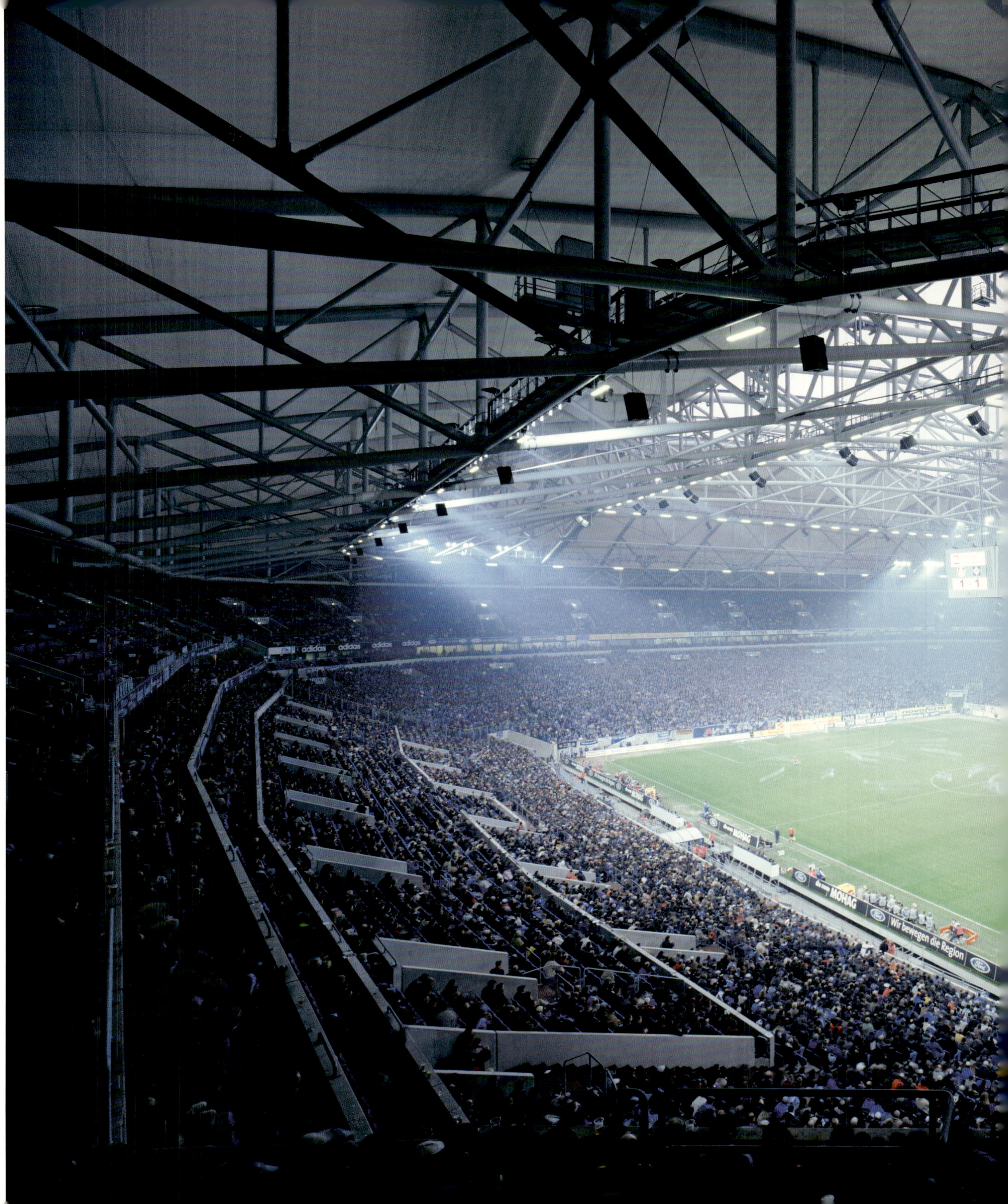
adidas
Wir bewegen die Region
MOHAG

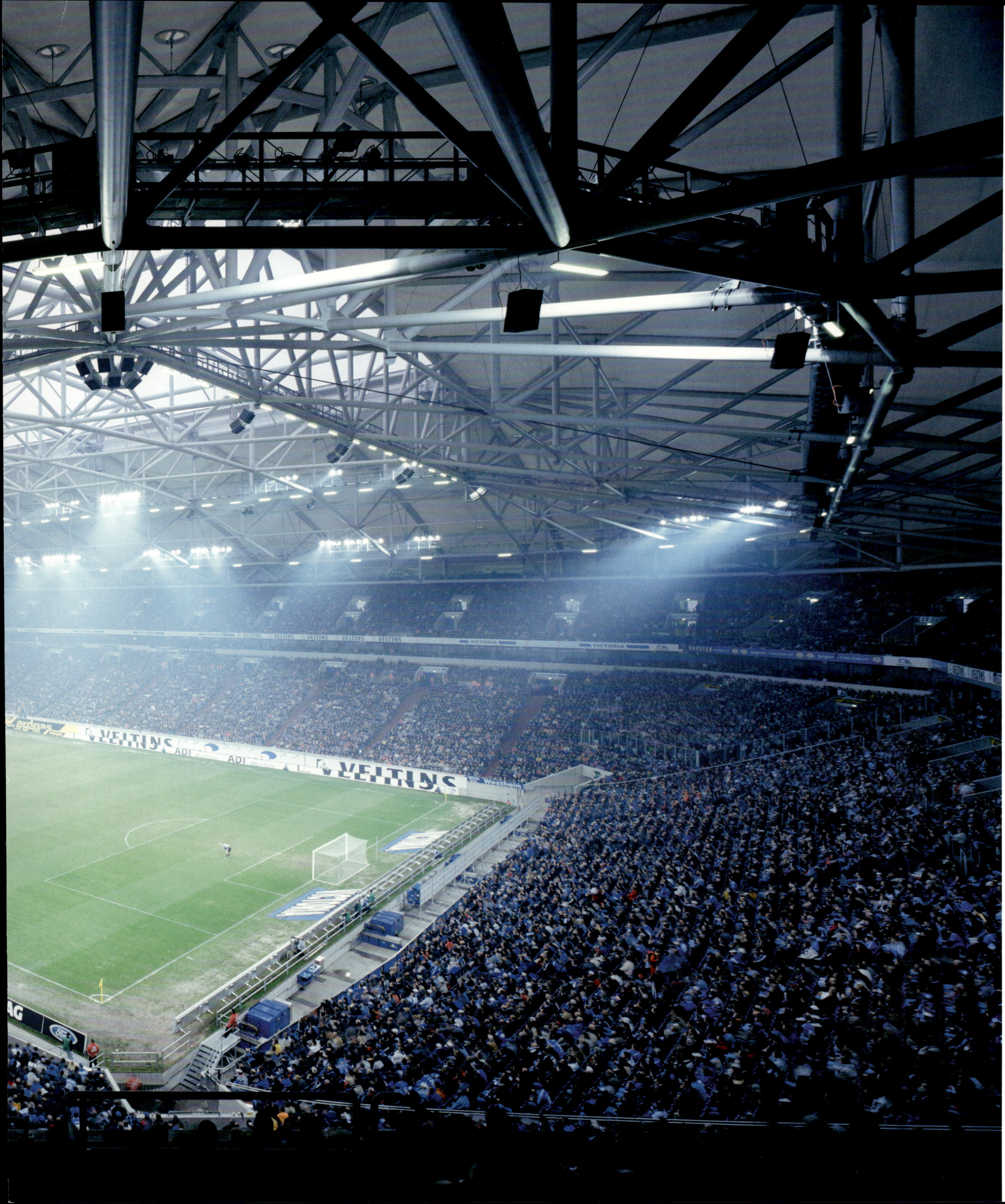

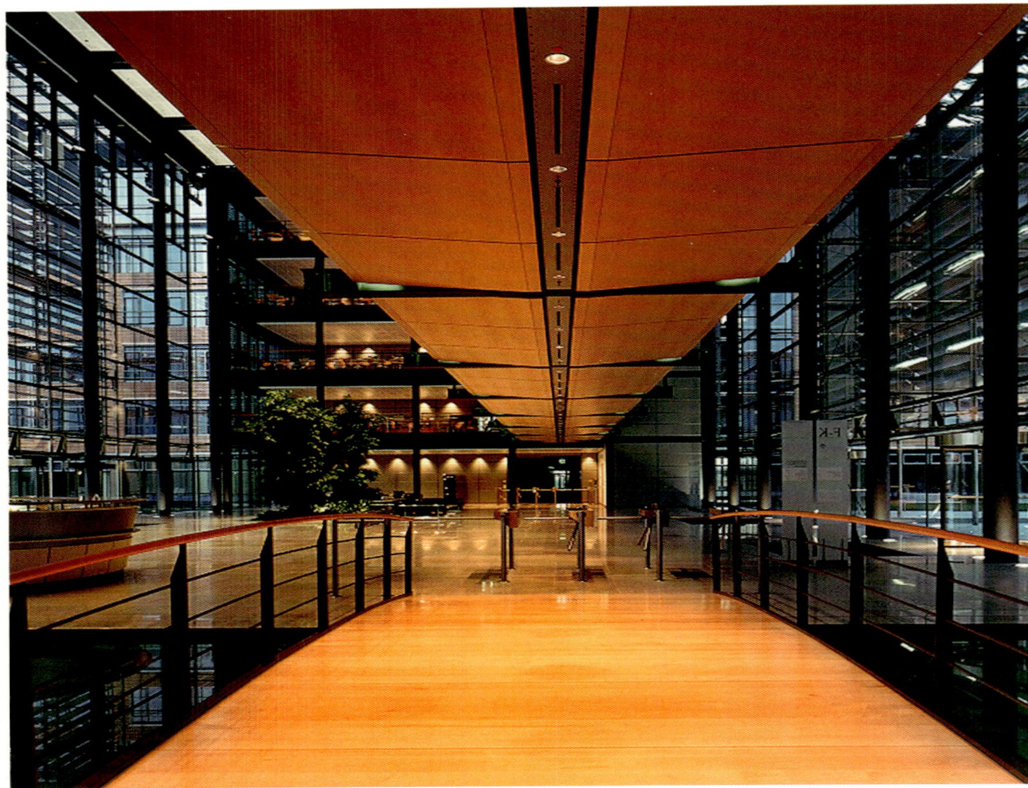

HUK-COBURG

This administration building is divided in an eastern section comprised of three building units and a western one of five units. The entrance hall, a completely glassed-in, open steel construction, is connected with the two construction sections via suspended bridges. By means of height-adjustable ceiling panels, the volume of the room can be adapted in response to changing acoustic requirements.

Client: HUK-COBURG Immobiliengesellschaft Bertelsdorfer Höhe GbR
Location: Coburg
GFA: 108,580 m²
Work stations: 1,840
Completion date: 1998
Competition: 1st Prize, 1993

Construction

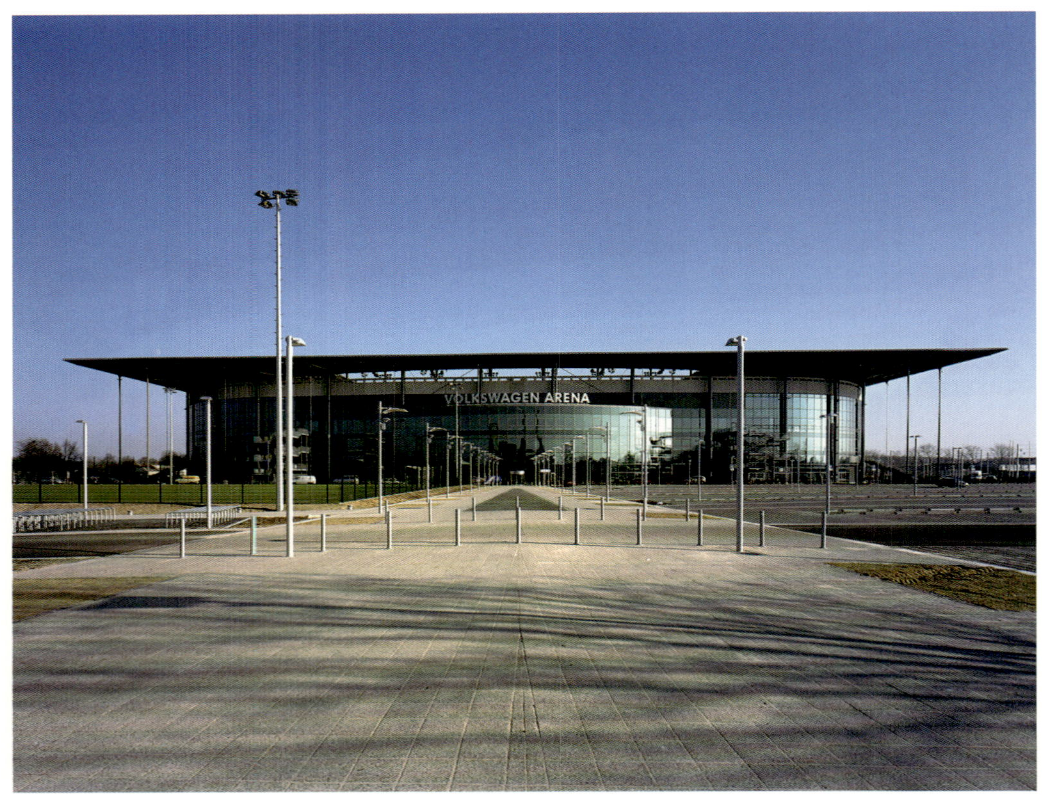

Volkswagen Arena

The individual functional building blocks of the arena, such as the roof elements, bleachers, loges, and access points, were designed as modular elements in order to meet the requirement that the facility be multifunctional. From the outside, the rectangular, metallic roof slices the Wolfsburg cityscape, while a translucent membrane roof reveals the constructive finesse of the interior.

Client: Wolfsburg AG
Location: Wolfsburg
GFA: 25,300 m²
Seats: 30,000
Completion date: 2002

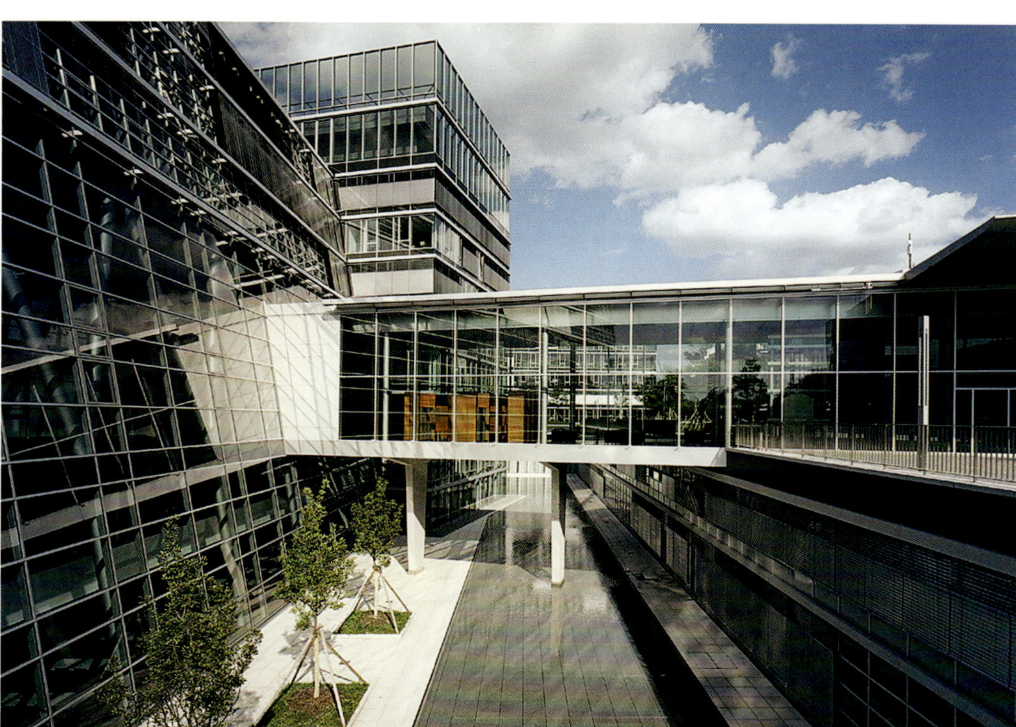

Allianz Headquarters, Unterföhring

This new six-story building complements Allianz's other two existing administration buildings. In its linearity, it also defines the backbone of the entire facility. The shared entryway is accentuated by a slightly rotated, two-story-tall pavilion borne by a transparent bridge construction.

Client: **Allianz Immobilien GmbH**
Location: **Munich-Unterföhring**
GFA: **100,000 m²**
Work stations: **2,000**
Completion date: **2004**
Competition: **1st Prize, 2000**

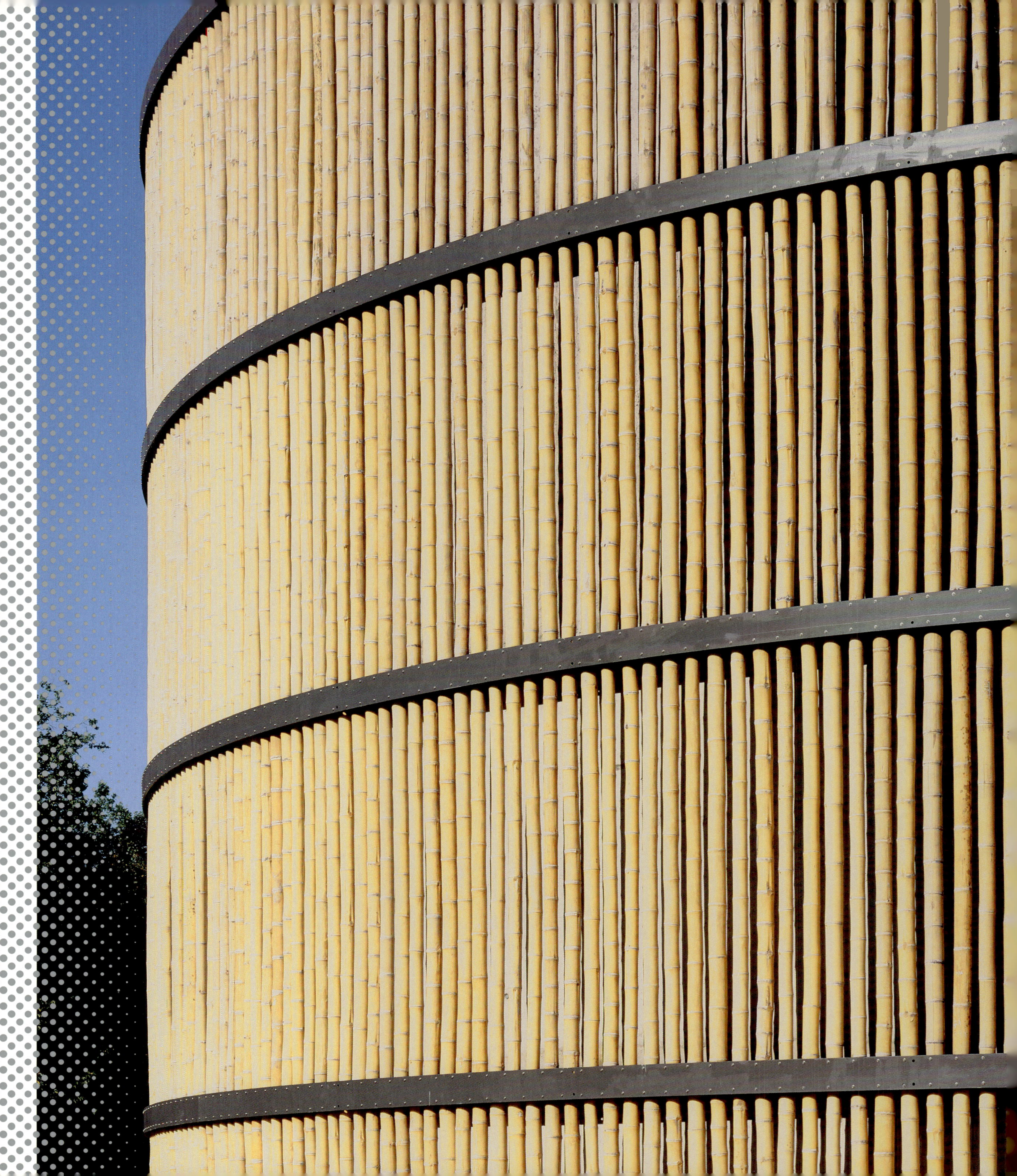

"The clothes make the man." In the past, this was a phrase by which some people measured themselves, and time and again less prominent personalities intentionally, or perhaps only unconsciously, try to enhance their own position by "polishing" their appearance. This happens in Gottfried Keller's short story of 1874, in which the tailor Wenzel Strapinski is taken for a count because of his cultivated appearance in the town of Seldwyla. He falls in love with the daughter of an upper class family, and she remains true to him even when the class difference is exposed.

The façade makes the building—but this is not another title of a short story by Keller. And it is also not a well-known saying. But perhaps it is a good description of the shells that lend external expression to buildings, giving them unmistakable visages and protecting the activities performed inside them.

Today architecture is increasingly thought of as a duality of space and shell. In this sense, the light shell covers the load-bearing construction and mass of the underlying structure. However, a building's shell is not just an element of design, protection, or thermal insulation. It also serves as a connecting element that interconnects a building's interior and the outside world. A still new approach to architecture is to perceive the shell of a building as a means of communicating company messages through the creation of a trademark appearance within the urban space. As a consequence, this means that the façade is raised to the status of the external, visible element of "brand-name architecture."

This is the perspective from which the parking lot of the Leipzig Zoo is designed. In the first approximation, the building task of a parking garage must be seen purely functionally, because it is mainly there to create the greatest amount of space for parking cars. As a result, the majority of parking garages are purely utilitarian buildings, dark horizontal blocks from whose interiors the caravans of parked cars project a disordered image to the outside. Starting with the task of designing a parking garage for the zoo, the opportunity arose to create something unusual, to offer the observer "something more."

This "more" displays aspects of nature and the world of the jungle, and is understood as an abstracted prologue to what visitors will experience in the zoo after parking their vehicles. A sort of dialogue thus arises between the parking garage and the zoo. The use of natural stalks of bamboo for the creation of the structure's shell builds a design bridge to the zoo, making the garage a visible trademark with the increased architectural value of immediate recognizability. Furthermore, the bamboo has a more refreshing effect than the usual anonymous design of parking garage façades. The stalks are also arranged horizontally at intervals in order to ensure sufficient ventilation and natural lighting on the parking levels.

In this way, an image and a trademark can be communicated through a structure. The project has an added value because it underscores creativity and a capacity for innovation in architecture. In the final analysis, the bamboo stalks are precisely the right "clothes" for this building. Thus, the form of an unusual love, as Keller describes the love of the tailor and the councilor's daughter in spite of adverse circumstances, can also be seen in Leipzig, though naturally on another level and in a different context: the affection of the city of Leipzig for its zoo parking garage.

Shell
Parking Garage of the Leipzig Zoo

Client: **Zoo Leipzig GmbH** | Location: **Leipzig** | GFA: **16,500 m²** | Parking spaces: **527**
Completion date: **2004** | Competition: **1st Prize, 2002** | Award: **BDA Prize of Saxony, recognition, 2004**

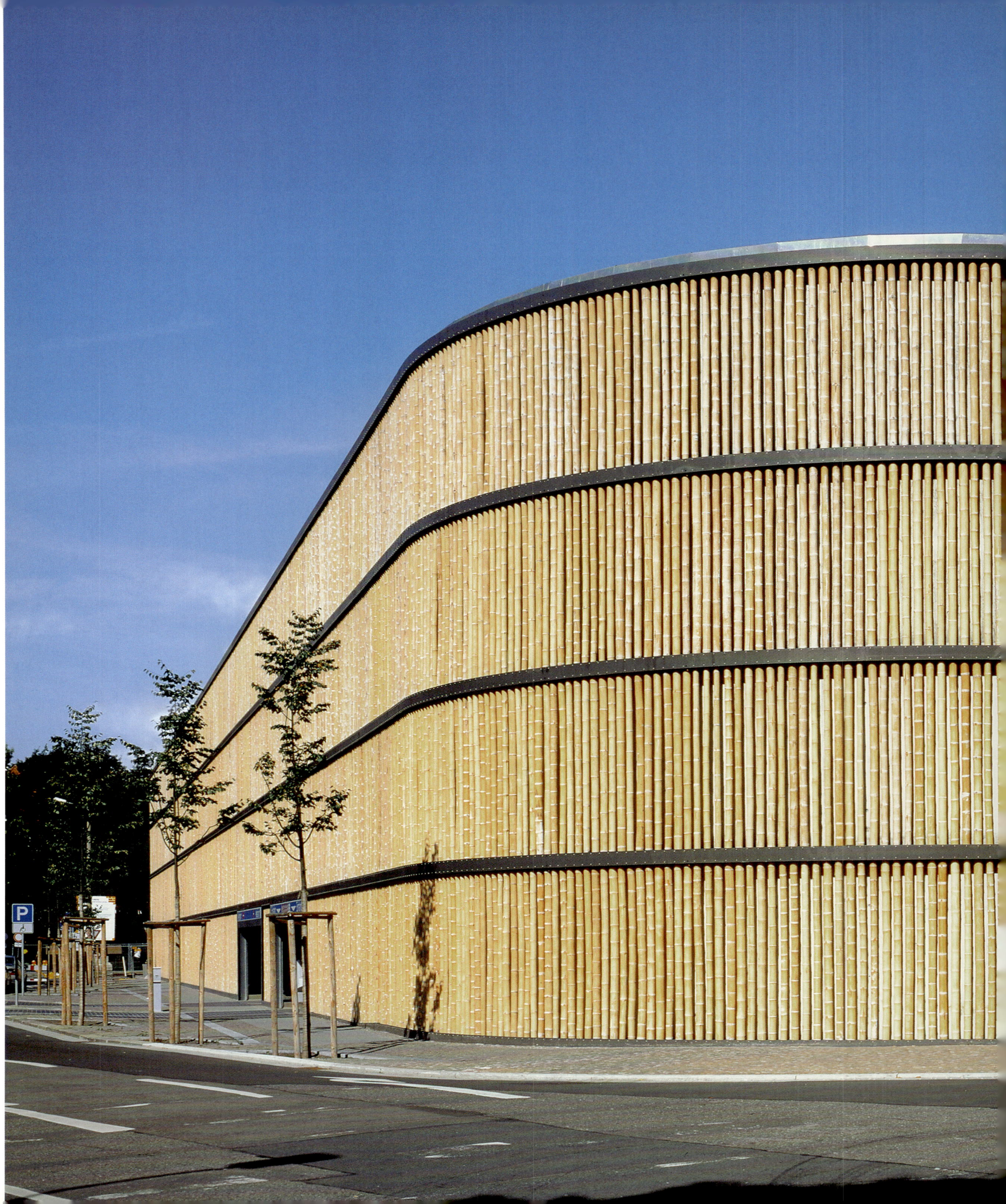

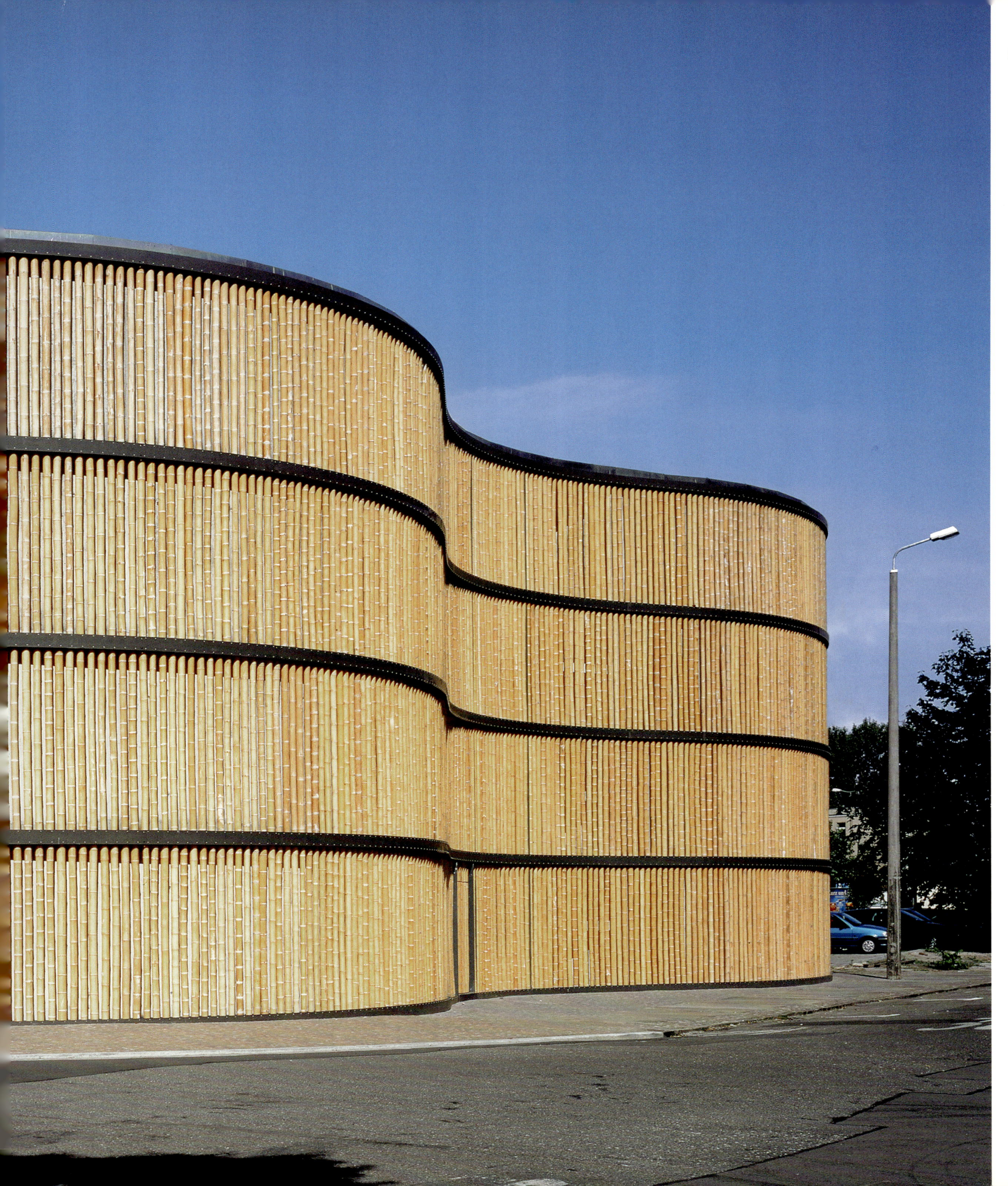

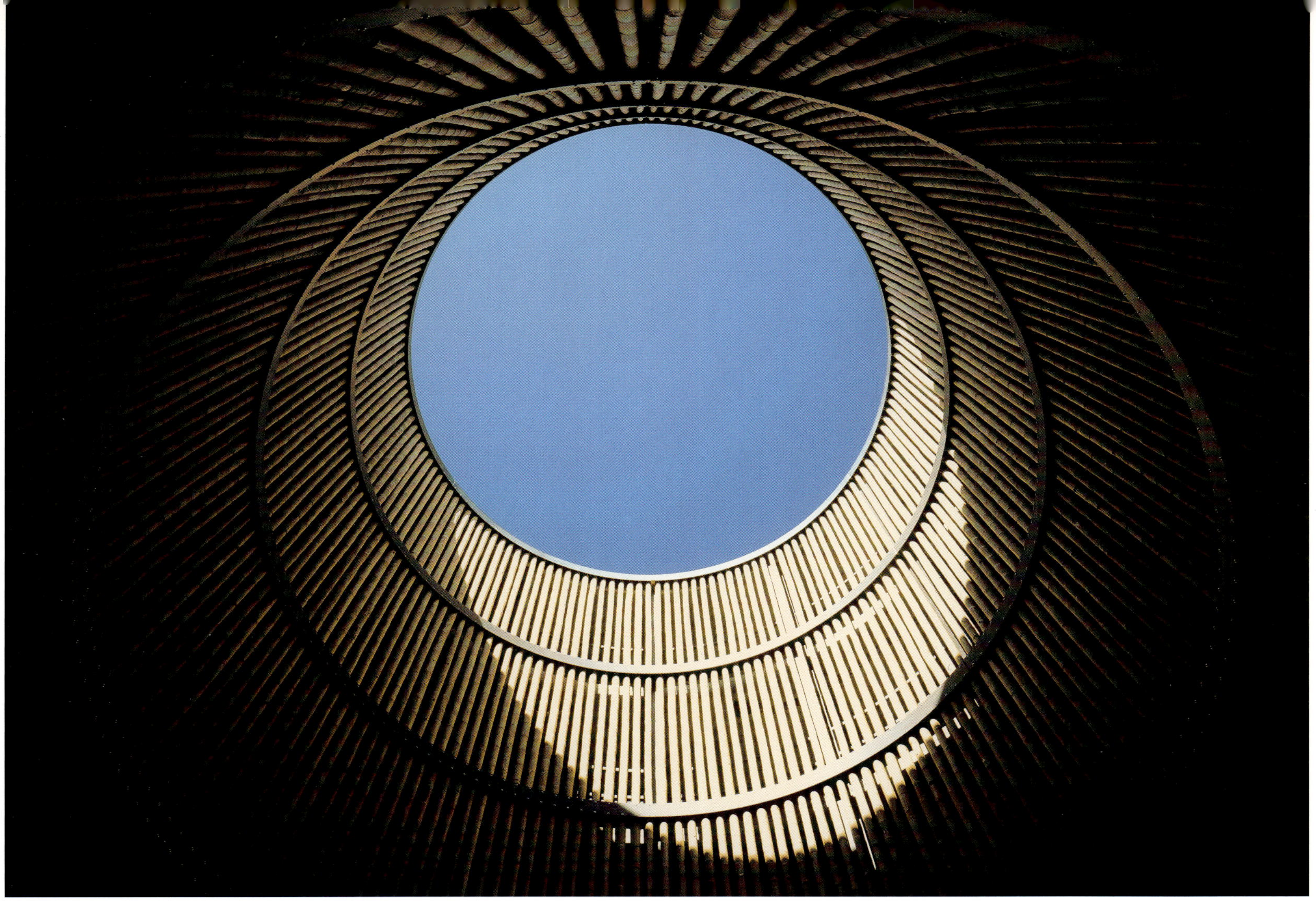

Air space in ascent and descent shaft

← Thematic shell made of 10,000 bamboo stalks
↞ Shell as a central design idea

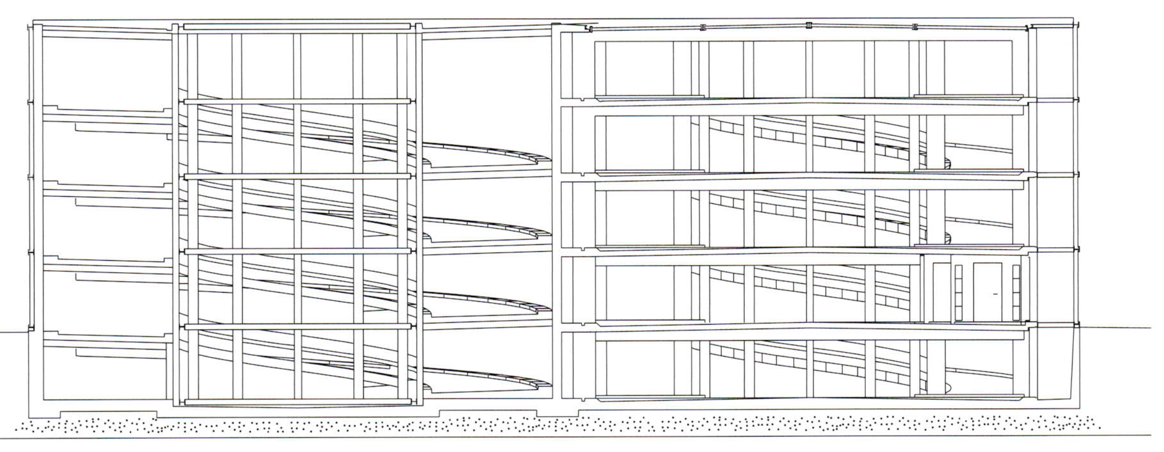

Cross section of ascent and descent shaft

The Parking Garage of the Leipzig Zoo With around 1.3 million visitors per year, the Leipzig Zoo is one of the favorite animal parks in Germany. In order to provide the zoo's visitors with enough parking, a competition was held in 2002 for the design of a parking garage with an attractive as well as economical design concept.

In a three-day workshop, the notion of a "shell" was chosen as a central concept. The parking garage was supposed to express a unity with the adjacent zoo grounds. As a result, the designers sought a façade material that would both make reference to the exotic world of the zoo and lend the structure a soft and haptic impression.

The parking garage is located across from the zoo's main entrance, and is thereby in the immediate vicinity of downtown Leipzig. The unusual façade made of bamboo stalks already sets the tone for a visit to the zoo. The building has a rectangular floor plan with dimensions of approximately 100 by 40 meters and is given an organic shaped on its eastern façade through the incorporation of two recessed spiral ramps. The concrete and steel construction was conceived as an open, large-scale garage with five parking levels that provide a total of 527 parking spaces. The width of the parking spaces is 2.5 meters, with parking for the handicapped on every floor in the vicinity of the spacious elevator building on the west side of the façade. In addition, the parking garage has two emergency stairways facing each other, as well as an open stairwell and a landing with access to the main entrance.

The filling and emptying of the parking garage occurs via two separate entrance and exit gates on Parthenstrasse. In order to unscramble the traffic flow inside, only one-way traffic is possible in the garage. The separate parking decks are connected to one another with spiral ramps set at an angle of nine degrees. For safety reasons, the intersections in front of the descent and ascent departure points are open. In order to prevent the sound of the garage's traffic from being propagated in the direction of the housing, the spiral ramps are surrounded by concrete walls.

The elongated building structure was completely wrapped with 10,000 Guadua bamboo stalks at intervals of 7.5 centimeters, with the exception of the stairway and elevator buildings, where the parking garage opens its story-high glass entrance façade to the zoo entrance. In addition to its thematic relevance, the bamboo mantle acts as a safety restraint and allows for the necessary ventilation. However, in a first approximation the unusual façade material lends the building a unique character that in turn thematically bridges the functional requirements of a parking garage and the exotic world of the zoo.

→ Side access passages on façade

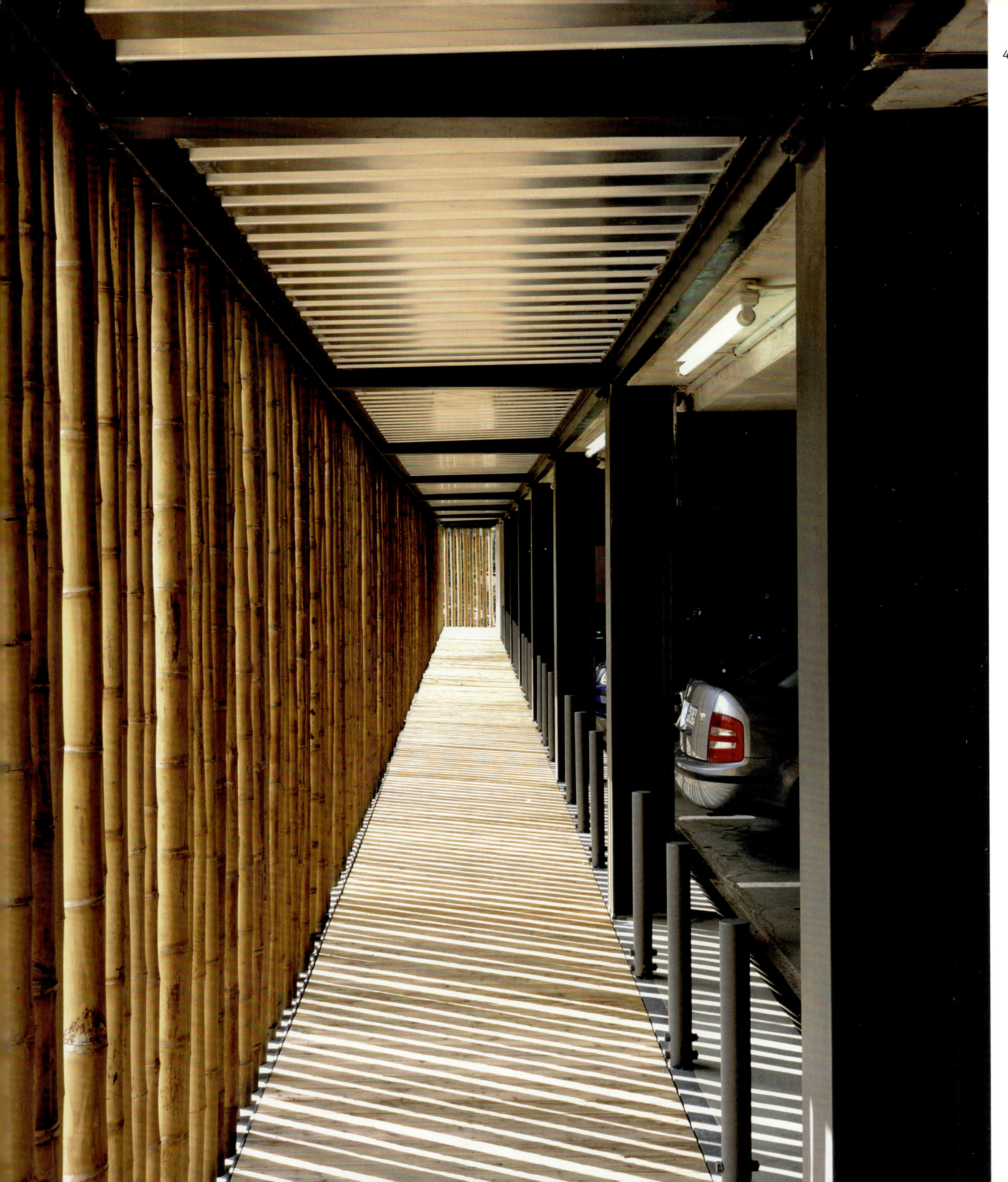

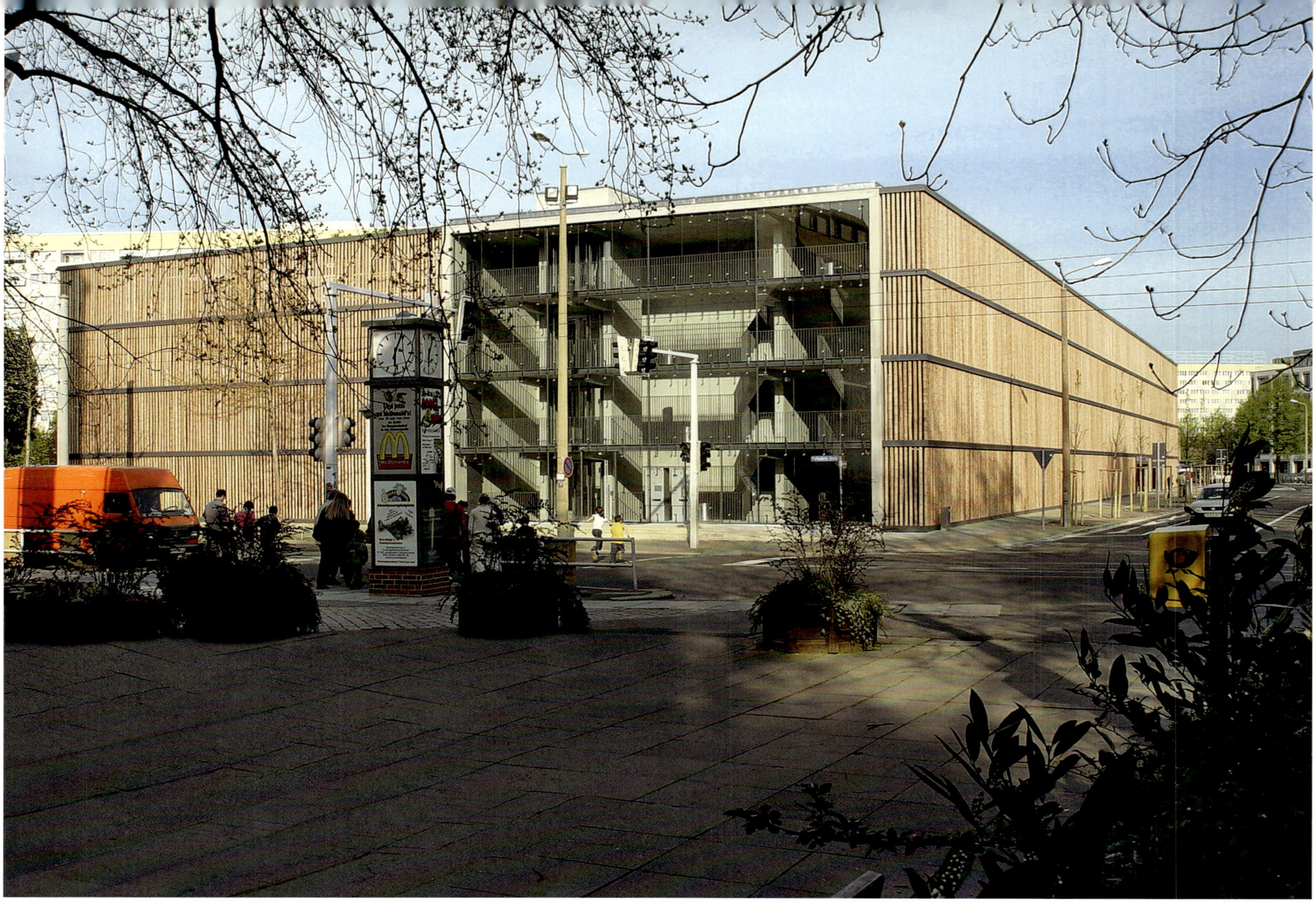

Completely glass-encased stairway and elevator building

→ Parking garage with tower of the Congress Hall

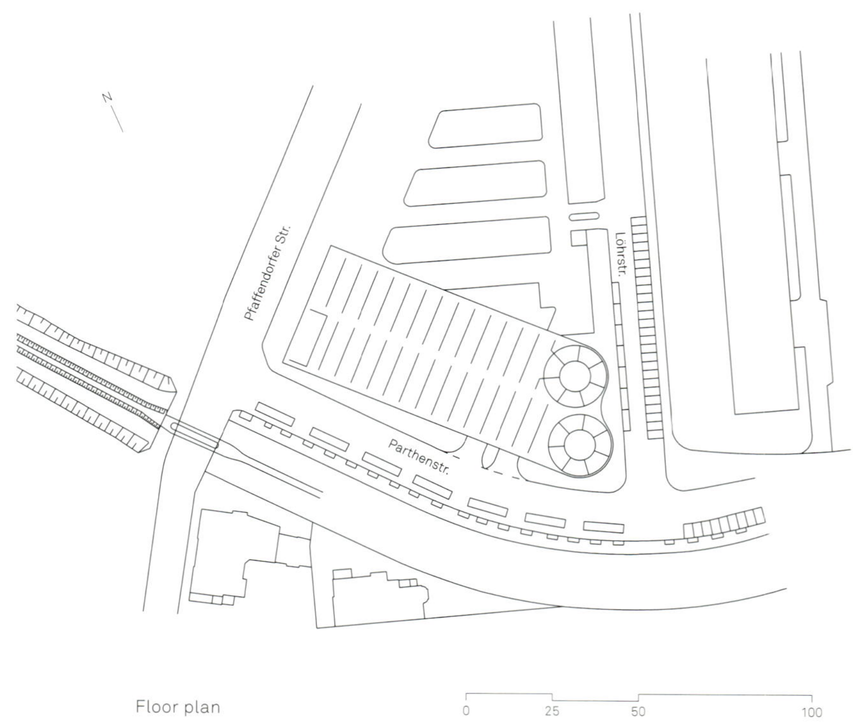

Floor plan

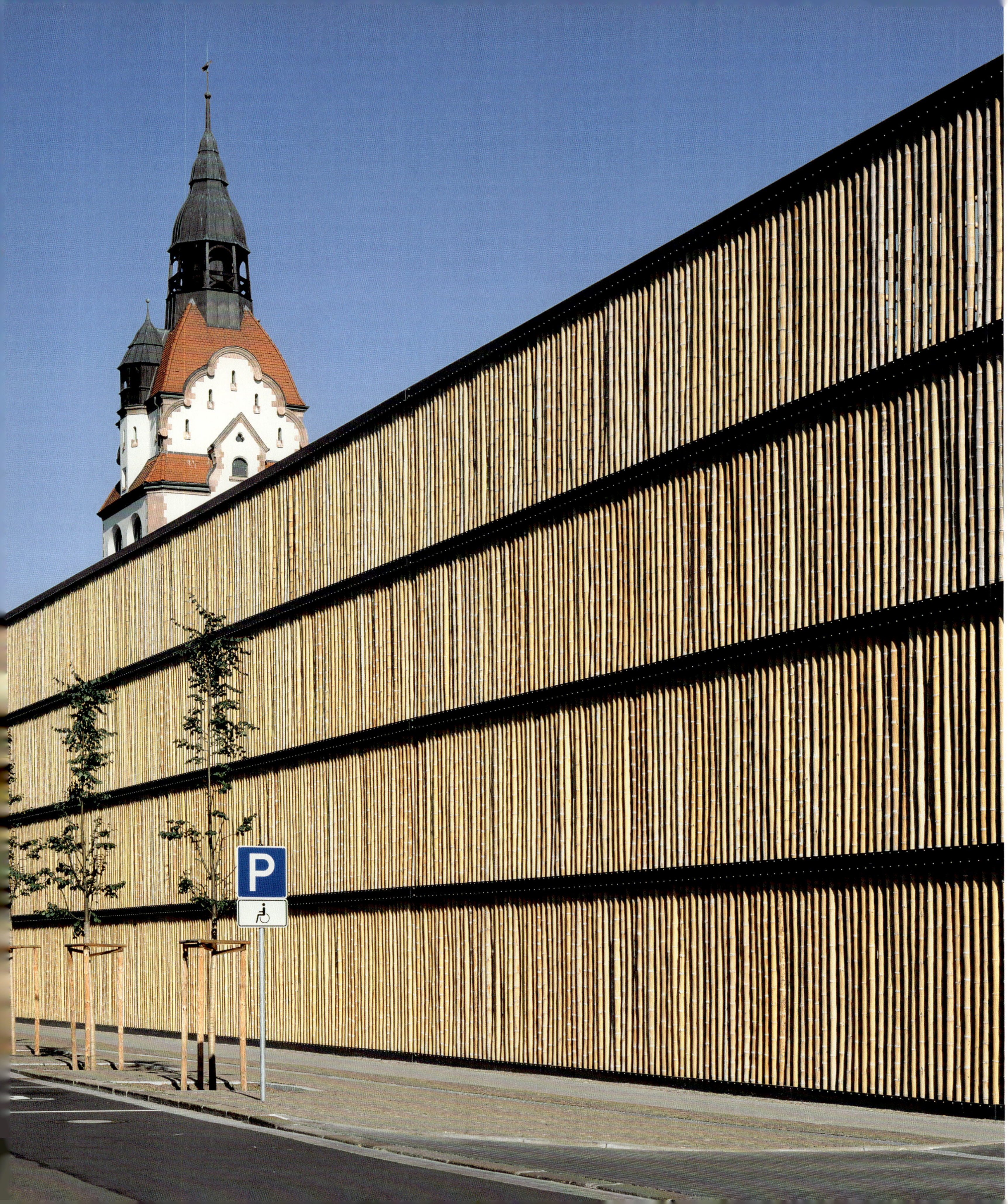

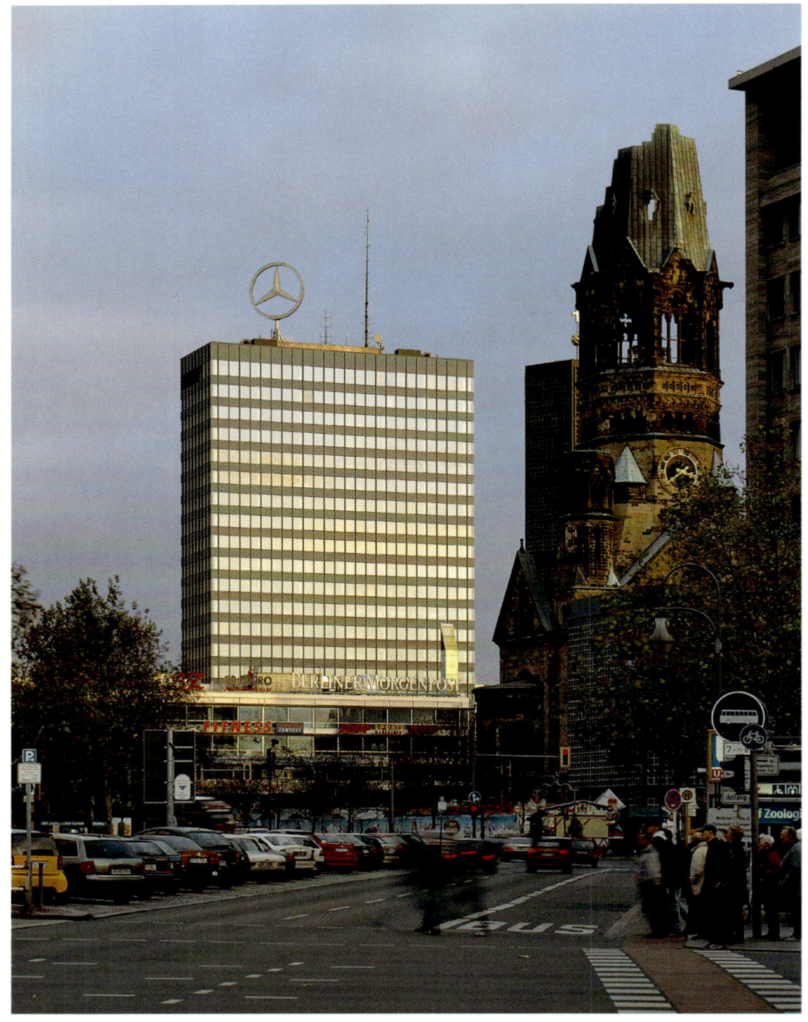

Shell

Europa Center

Within the framework of this revitalization project, the façade of the building, which is protected as a historic landmark, was redone. The device of a double façade makes possible the introduction of both exterior sun protection and windows that can be opened. By using the original aluminum profile system for the outer, single-paned façade layer, the overall impression of the building is retained, thereby meeting landmark protection requirements.

Client: **Europa-Center Europahaus Grundstücksgesellschaft mbH & Co. KG**
Location: **Berlin**
GFA: **14,500 m²**
Height: **89.1 m**
Completion date: **1964**
Restoration and revitalization according to landmark protection criteria: **2001**
Competition: **1st Prize, 1960**

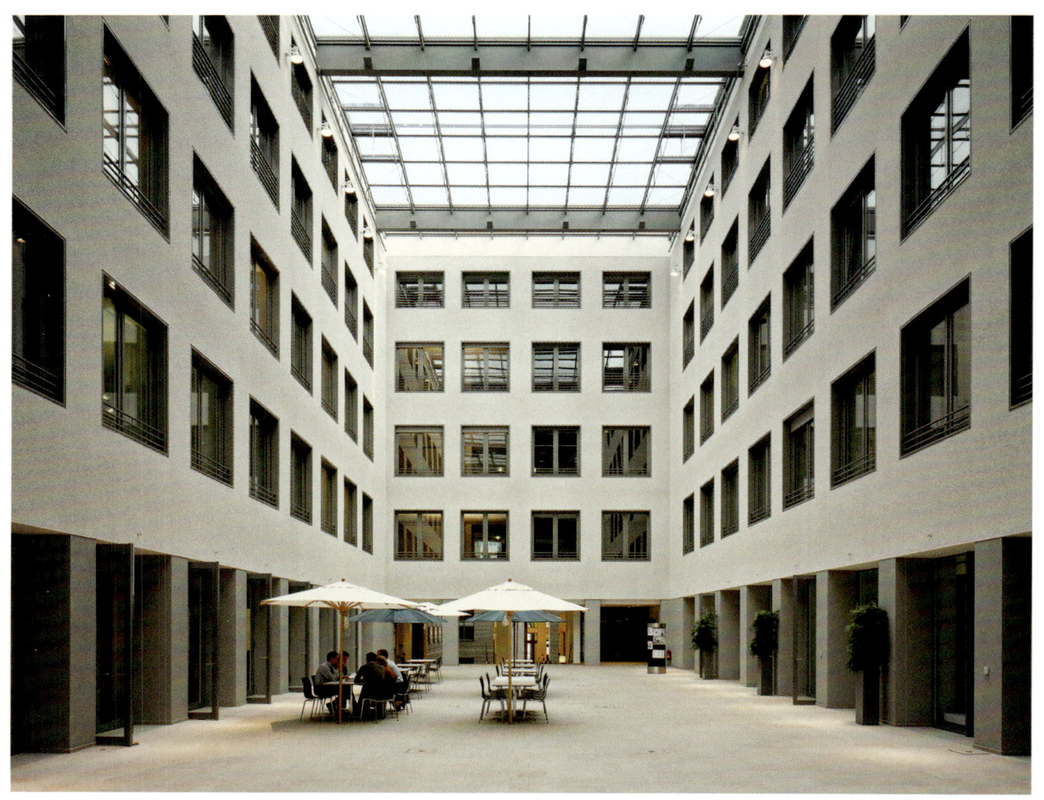

Allianz Munich, Ludwigstrasse

This building in the Maxvorstadt, one of Munich's most popular districts, was gutted after the previous user moved out. While the landmark-protected, classicizing façade was retained, the interior was modernized from the ground up with a glass-roofed inner courtyard, a new roof construction, state-of-the-art engineering, and flexibly laid out, communication-facilitating office areas.

Client: **Allianz Versicherungs AG**
Main user: **The Boston Consulting Group**
Location: **Munich**
GFA: **30,000 m²**
Work stations: **750**
Completion date: **2002**
Architecture: **HPP in collaboration with K + P Architekten**
Interior design: **Wiegmann und Trübenbach**
Award: **Façade Prize of the Capital City of Munich, 2004**

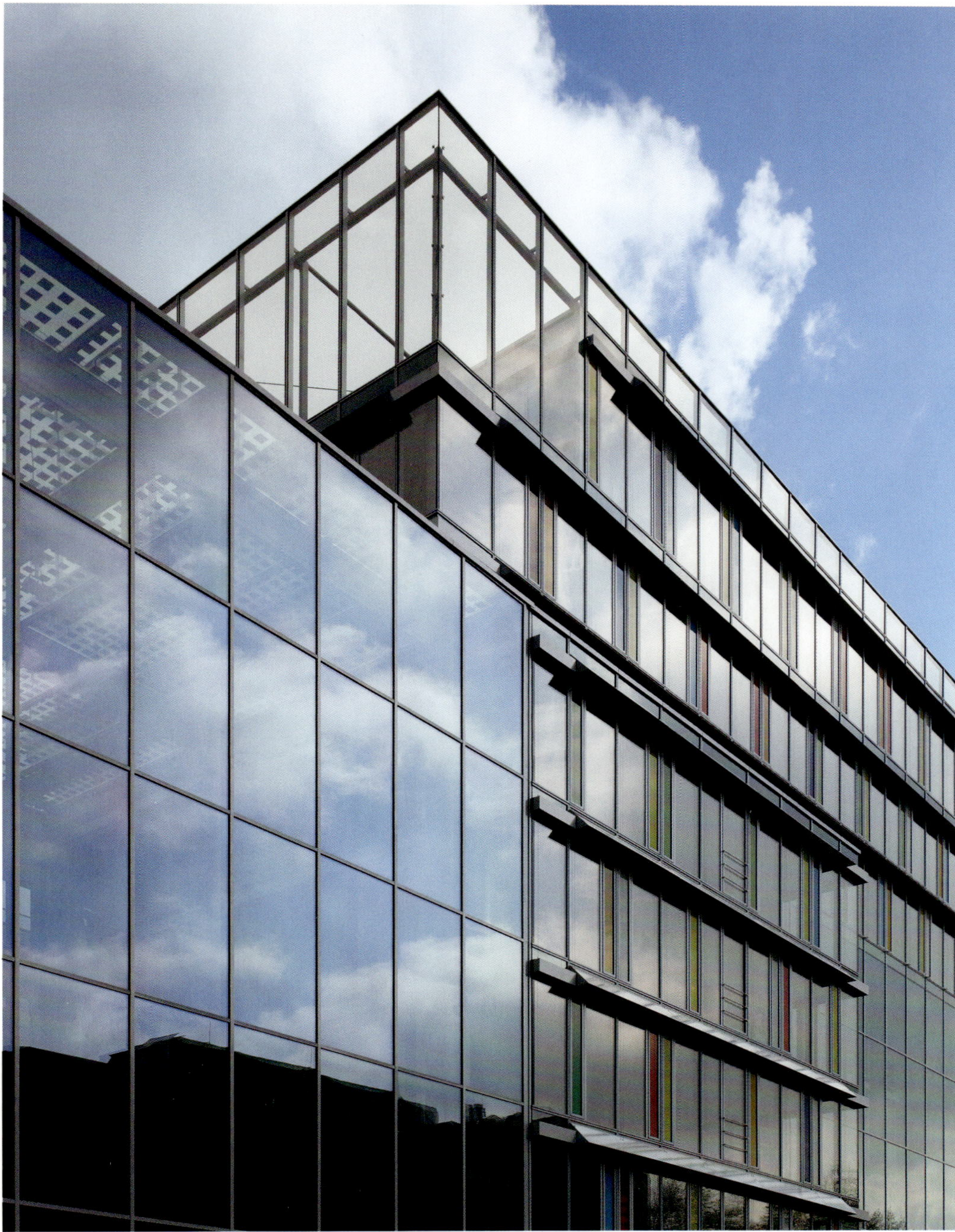

LVM 7

In the immediate vicinity of its headquarters, LVM has erected this structure as its seventh expansion building. Delicate glass cubes were placed in an alternating comb system by connecting them via a main glass thoroughfare. In addition to its striking, colorfully designed exterior, the three- to eight-story building is distinguished by its innovative energy-use concept, which, along with windows that can be opened, features geothermal energy probes and a photovoltaic unit.

Client: LVM Landwirtschaftlicher Versicherungsverein Münster a.G.
Location: Münster
GFA: 23,400 m^2
Work stations: 460
Completion date: 2008
Competition: 1st Prize, 2004
(Design: Prof. Duk-Kyu Ryang, MA Architecture)

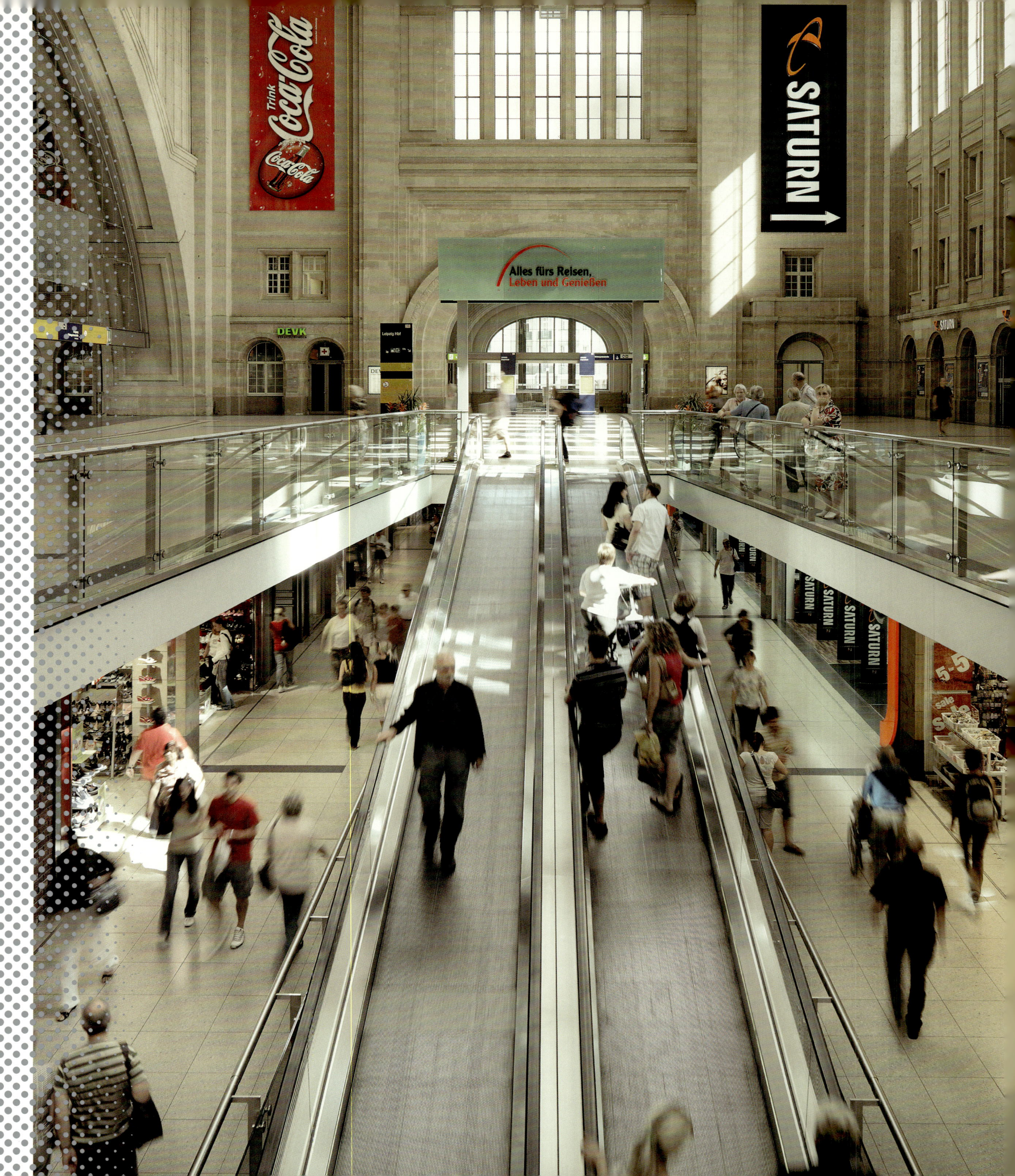

Trink
Coca-Cola
Coca-Cola
SATURN
Alles fürs Reisen,
Leben und Genießen
DEVK
SATURN
SATURN
SATURN

Function Leipzig Central Train Station

Client: **ECE Projektmanagement representing the DB Immobilienfonds 7 Wieland KG** | Location: **Leipzig**
Retail surface: **30,000 m²** | Year of completion: **1915** | Conversion and restoration according to landmark protection criteria: **1997** | International competition: **1st Prize, 1994** | Award: **Saxon State Prize for Architecture, 1999**

The word "function" describes the task which a building has to fulfill. In connection with the evolution of a structure's construction and design, functionality develops out of a laborious searching process.

This is how things worked in the development of the revitalization concept for the main train station in Leipzig. Until late in the twentieth century, the great train terminals were places of desire. Even the travelers of today can confirm the continued presence of that kind of romanticism in these spaces.

The train stations were one of the great construction tasks of the nineteenth century. They had rapidly advanced from purely utilitarian structures to prominent and engaging buildings. This is how Leipzig's main train station, a 300-meter-long terminal station inaugurated in 1915, developed. Almost as fast as the development of the steam locomotive revolutionized transportation and communication, the increasing mobility of individuals in the nineteen-sixties represented a turning point for train stations. The latter went into decline, and the once vital works of architecture called train stations were degraded to visual amusement parks and gathering places for prostitutes and the homeless. It was no longer a pleasure or a positive experience to arrive in or depart from a train station.

Then another technical innovation came along, one which helped train stations regain some of their old glamour: the high-speed ICE, or InterCity Express train. The great changes that the new technology introduced brought many of the functions that had been assigned to the passenger reception buildings over the years into question. Contemporary use concepts have to be developed for the train stations in order to rescue these urban trademarks of our cities. What could be more natural than to combine the needs of the traveler with shopping opportunities, services, and an enjoyable layover?

In the main train station in Leipzig, this new world appears as a three-story-tall, lens-shaped passageway, which for the most part occupies preexisting building volume and thereby sustainably increases the use efficiency of the passenger reception area. Retail spaces dominate the levels below the concourse, because in Leipzig the trains travel at one story above street level. This opened the world of commerce to the street with rows of businesses, retail shops, and cafés. The grand concourse is confirmed in its new function by the spatial effect of the horizontal addition of the stores. Thanks to these newly introduced uses, the station gallery fills the Leipzig train station with people and generates a new sense of life within its spaces.

Naturally there were also many practical planning aspects to consider. Railroad service counters and information distribution facilities, for example, had to be discreetly tucked away in the new hybrid organism. Today the railroad-related functions are located where the baggage check once was, with a central connection to the station forecourt, the concourse, and the gallery.

This is how the new picture of the Leipzig train station has been put together. As an urban orientation point, the station not only facilitates the arrival and departure of travelers, but also represents an opportunity for strolling and whiling away the time. In 2010, HPP will write another chapter in the history of the Leipzig train station. With the opening of the Leipzig City Tunnel, the terminal will graduate to a through station, if only an underground one.

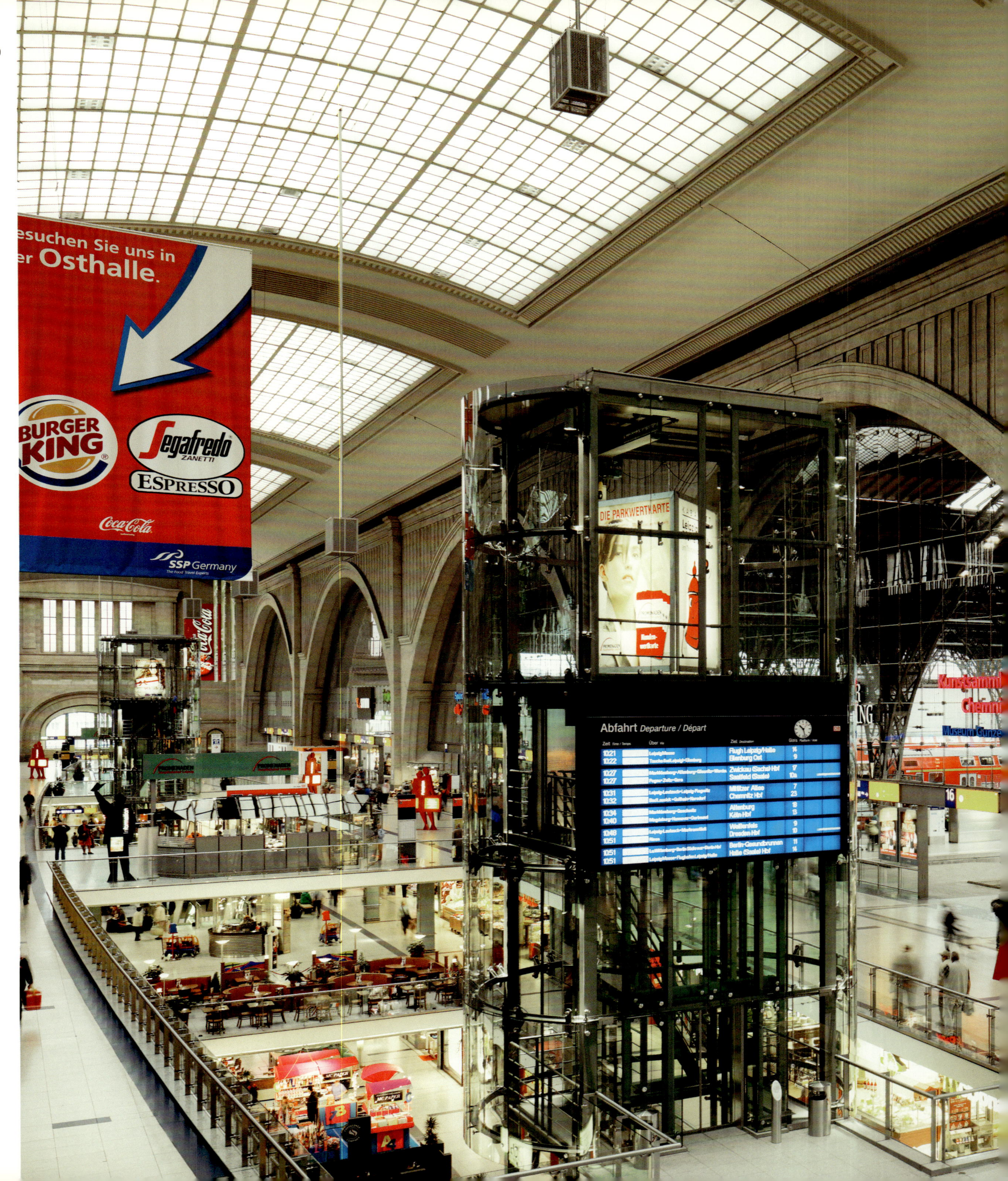
esuchen Sie uns in
er Osthalle.
BURGER KING
Segafredo ZANETTI
ESPRESSO
Coca-Cola
SSP Germany
DIE PARKWERTKARTE
Abfahrt Departure / Départ

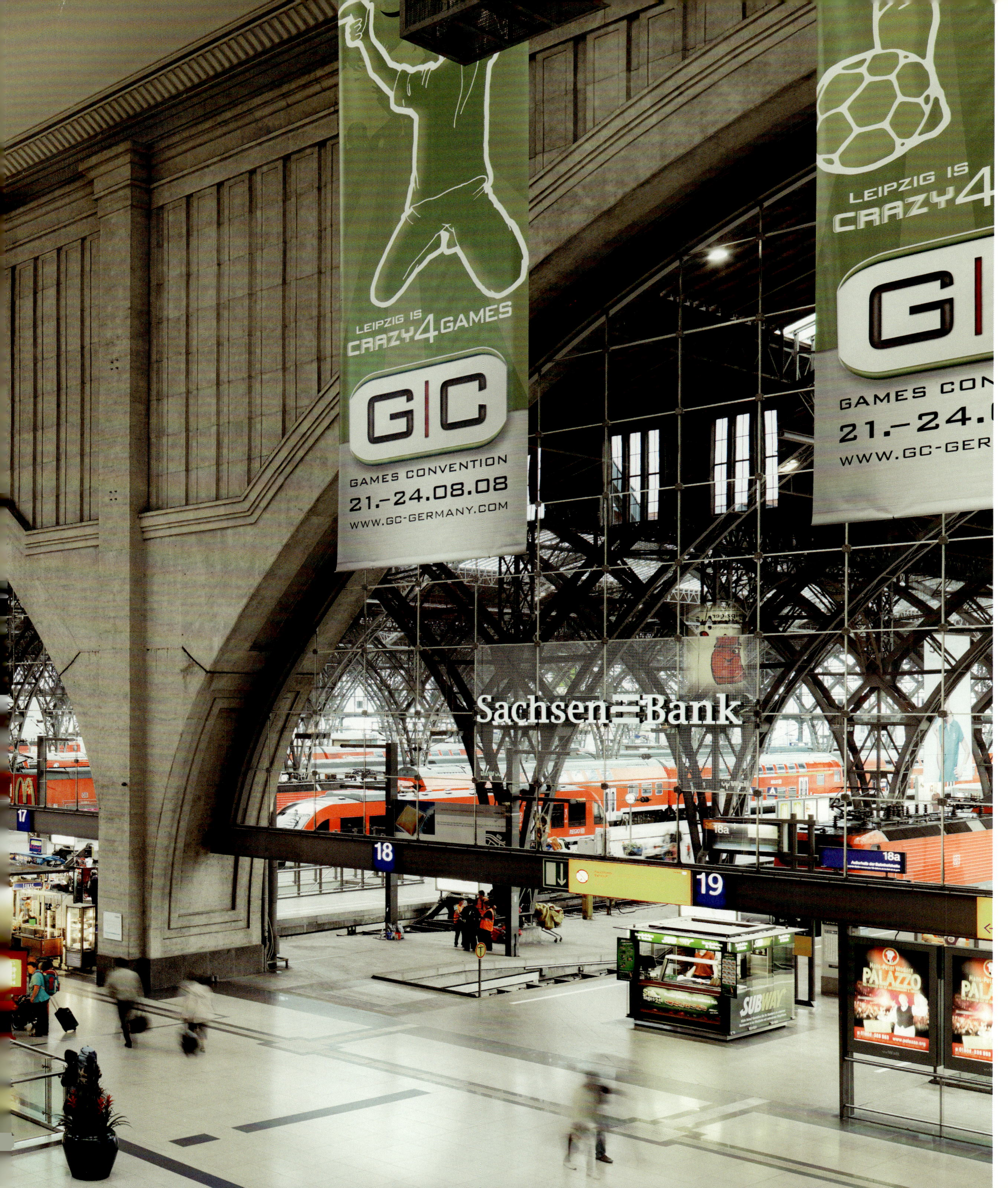
LEIPZIG IS
CRAZY4GAMES
GC
GAMES CONVENTION
21.-24.08.08
WWW.GC-GERMANY.COM
Sachsen Bank
17
18
19
18a
SUBWAY
PALAZZO

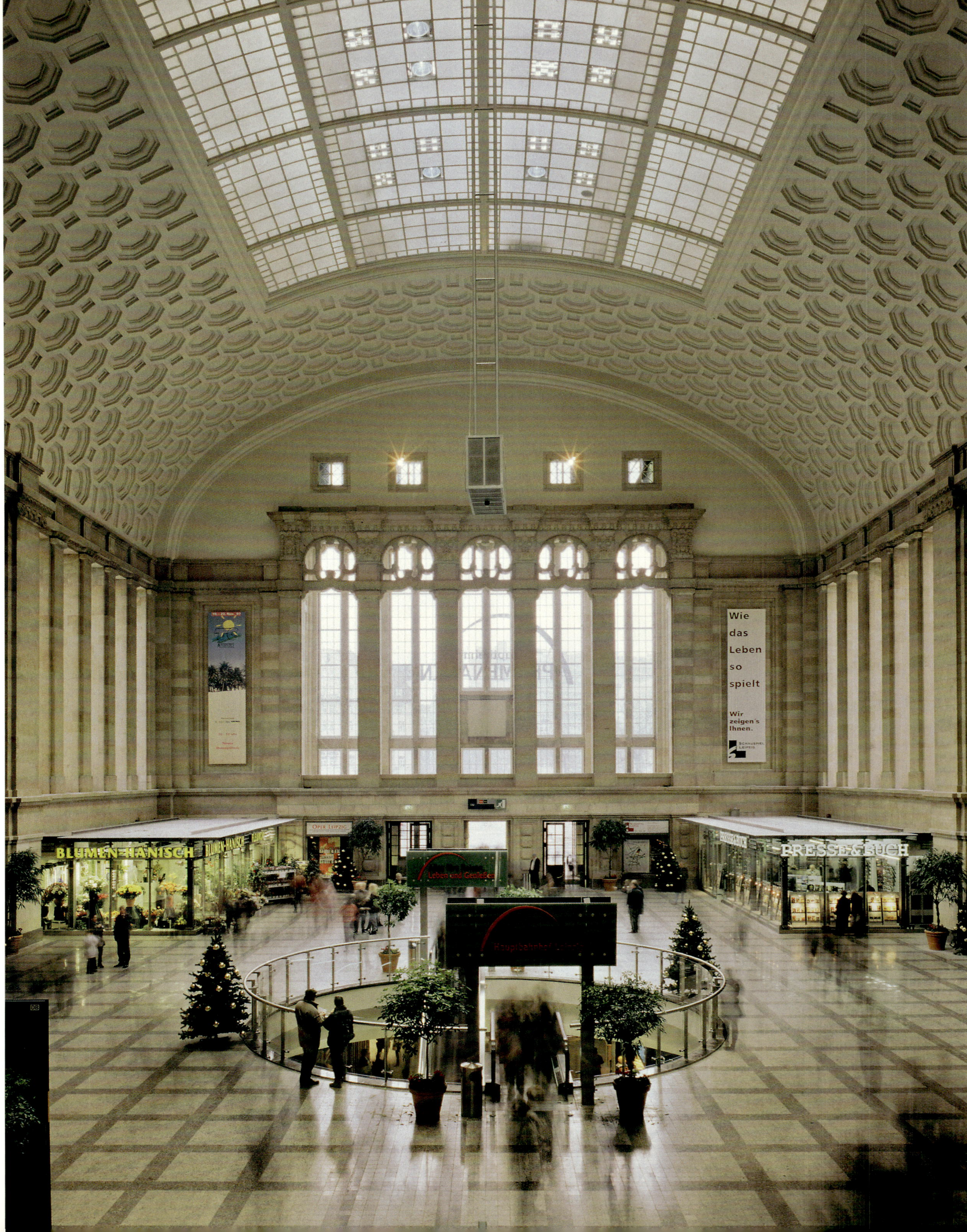
Wie
das
Leben
so
spielt
Wir
zeigen's
Ihnen.
BLUMEN-HANISCH
OPER LEIPZIG
PRESSE&BUCH

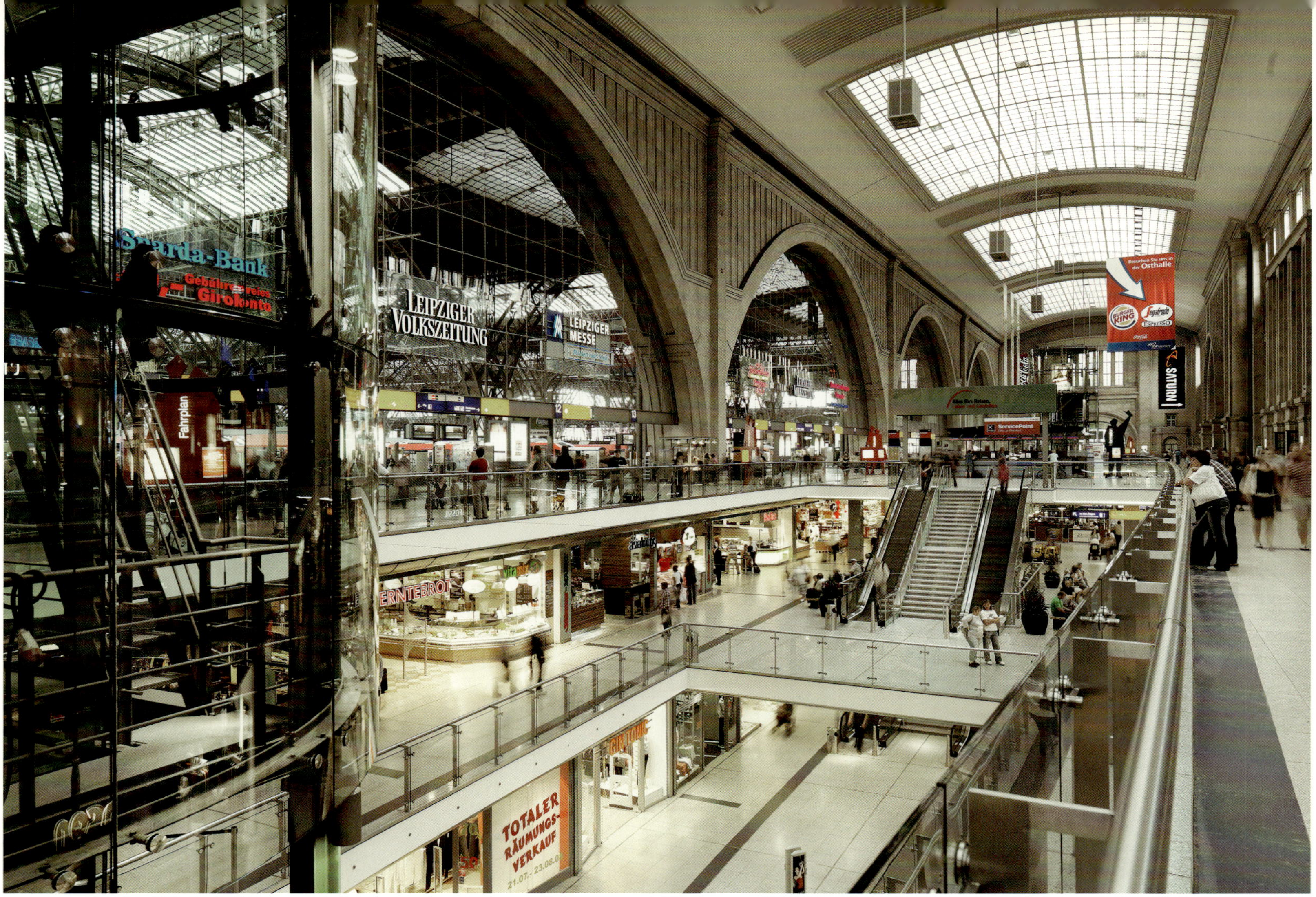

Concourse hall with new shopping levels

← Entrance hall viewed from the west
↞ Concourse hall with new shopping levels

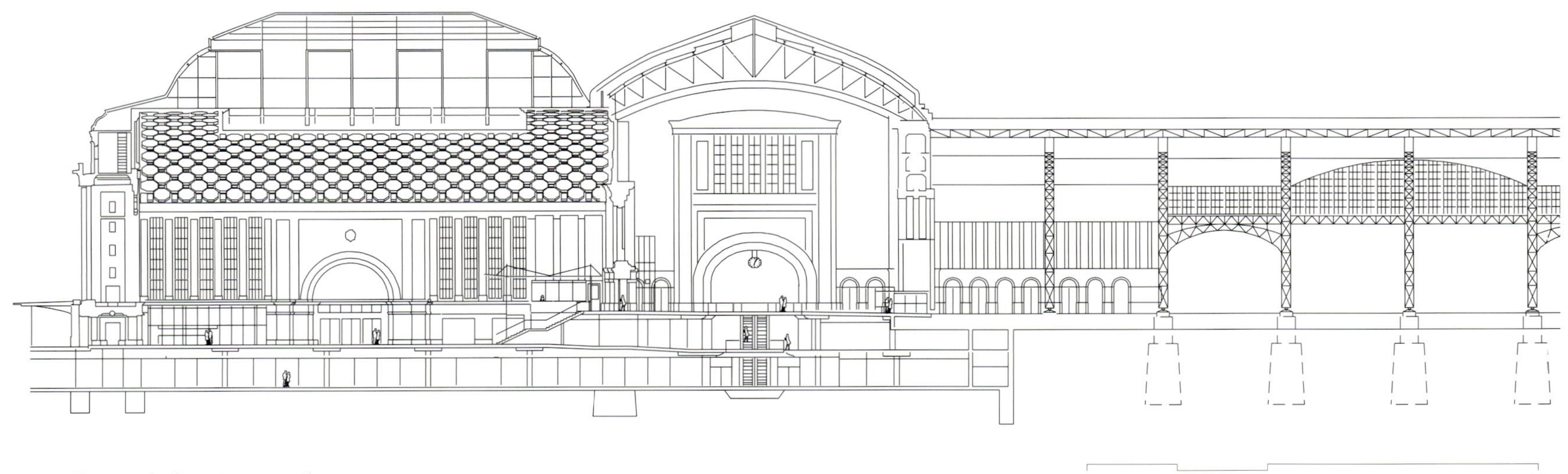

Entrance hall, west cross section

The Leipzig Central Train Station The plans for the historical Leipzig main railroad station by the architects of the firm of Lossow und Kühne were submitted in the 1906 competition for a "Passenger Railway Station with Terminal." At the time of its inauguration in 1915, it was the largest terminal in Europe. Beyond its function as a transportation hub, it rapidly developed into an architectural showcase. After being destroyed in World War II it was rebuilt in 1965, but it lost some of its significance as a result of the increase in automobile travel.

The uses of the railroad as well as the requirements of railway stations have changed over the years. In addition to providing functionality, flexibility, comfort, and design, today's railway station architecture must measure up to the standards of upscale urban pedestrian areas. This was the idea behind reestablishing the main Leipzig railroad station as the focus of urban life in the city. HPP received the first prize in the architectural competition for the station's reconfiguration in 1994 and was contracted immediately thereafter to follow through with the realization of its proposal.

As a result, the conversion of the largest railway terminal in Europe became a pilot project with the mission of incorporating a retail and services center in the reception building. In doing so, HPP had to guarantee that while the structure of the landmark-protected station building would not be altered, the new design would meet the project's functional, constructive, and economic needs while maintaining the fascinating impact of the 270-meter-long concourse hall. In its conversion of the station the design allowed for one major alteration to the existing structure: the addition of a lens-shaped opening in the concourse hall which respected the historical nature of the structure while creating a formal and functional element of spatial connection. The lens-shaped opening and the space it creates make the forum the central hub of the multipurpose center. The access level of the station is given a new orientation with the allocation of retail and service outlets. Complementing the traditional uses of the railway station, this aspect is also evident on the second story of the track level and the third story in a direct spatial interaction with the station. The railroad company's offices and other office spaces occupy the upper part of the structure on the fourth and fifth floors.

A total of about 140 businesses, cafés, and restaurants occupying approximately 17,500 square meters of floor space are distributed over the three retail levels beneath the concourse hall on what are called promenade decks, all of which are interconnected by spacious stairways, elevators, moving walkways, and travelators. The concourse thereby takes on the character of a gallery that offers travelers a new concept of the railway station: the railway station as a "travel respite." In addition to the conversion of the concourse, the historical areas of the old waiting rooms assume new functions and are imbued with new content by being transformed into spaces for cultural events and conferences.

The completely revitalized building was assigned its new identity and renamed the "Promenaden Hauptbahnhof Leipzig" on November 12, 1997.

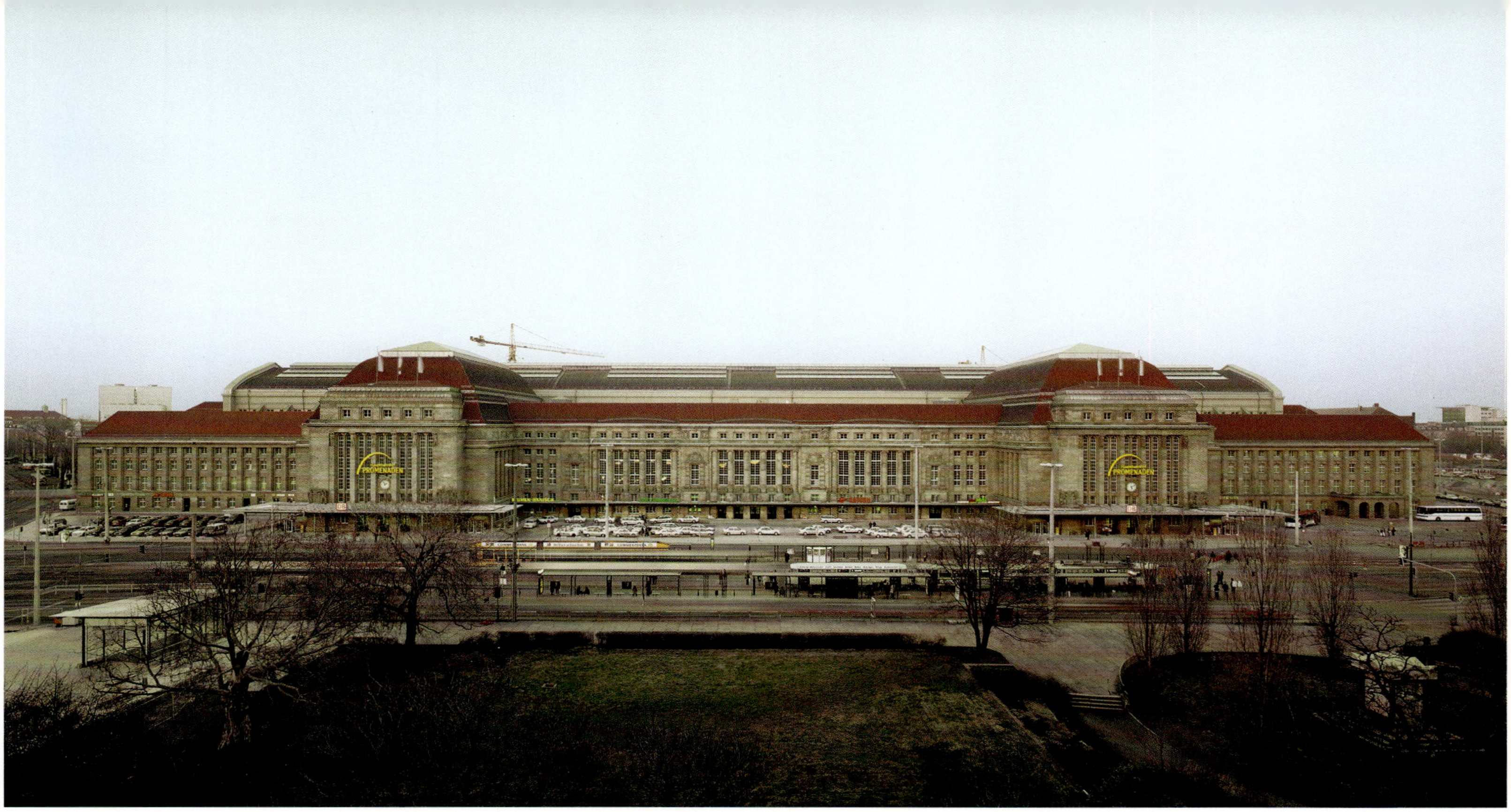

Downtown view of reception building
→ Lens-shaped cutout in concourse hall

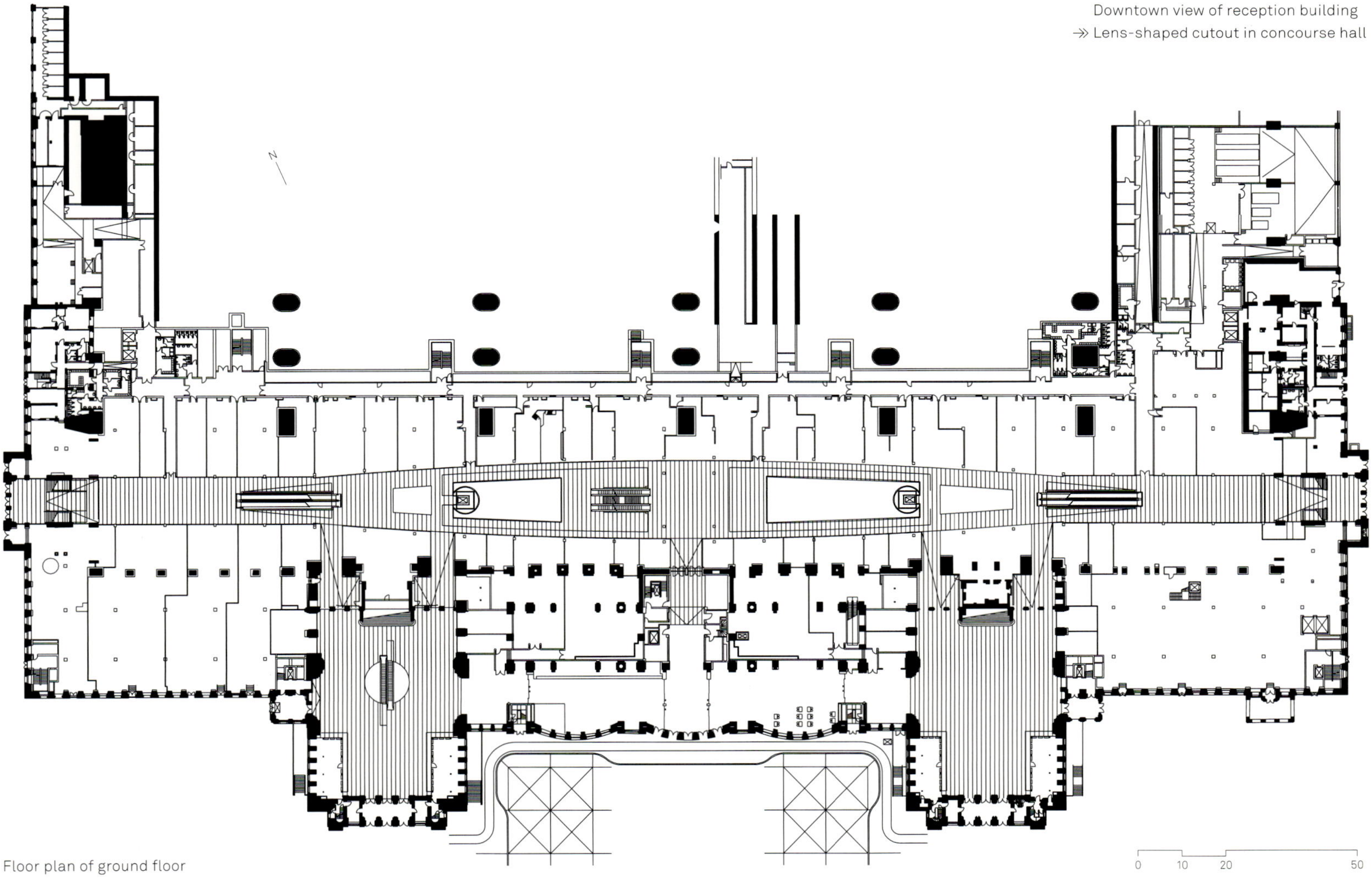

Floor plan of ground floor

0 10 20 50

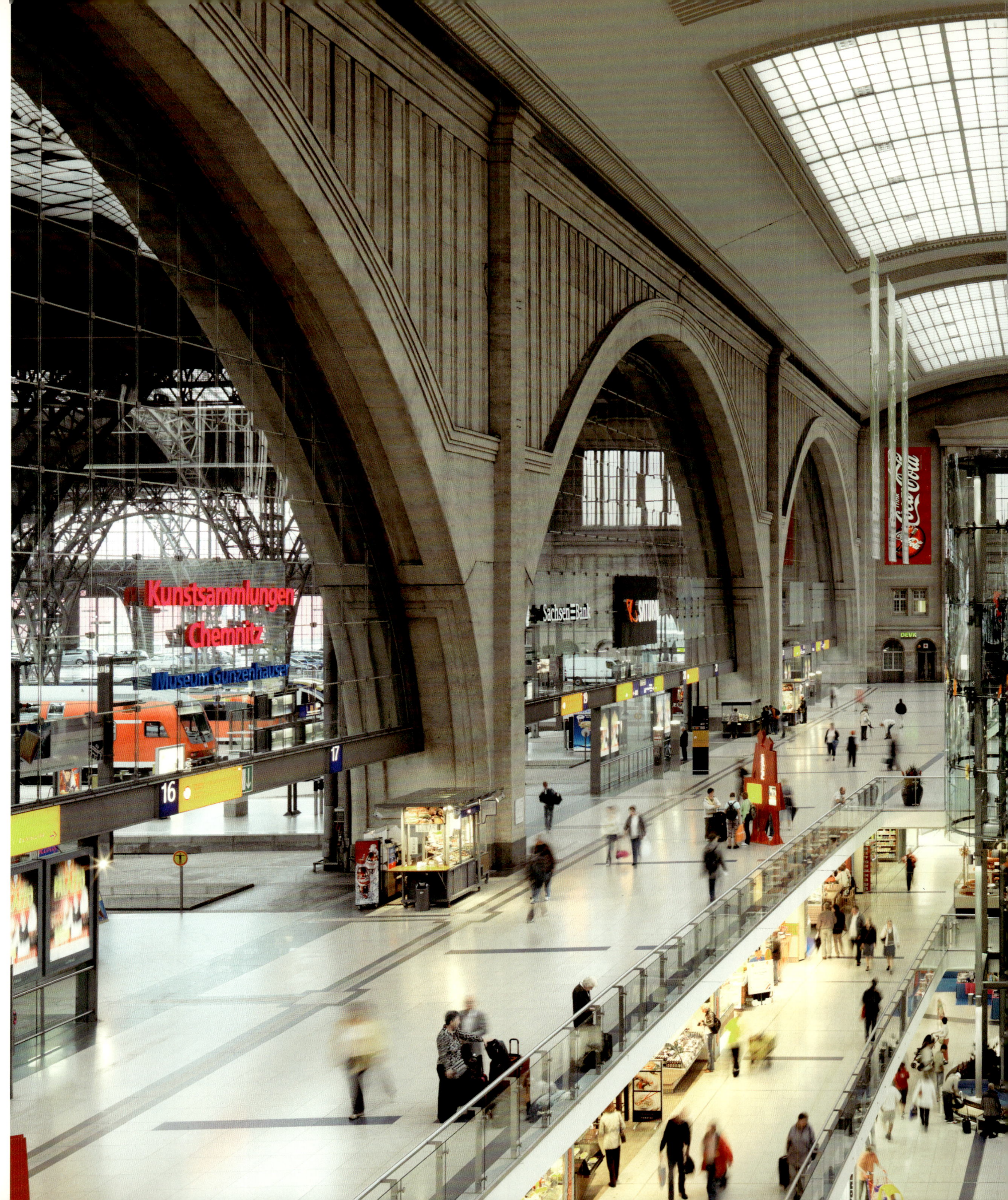
Kunstsammlungen
Chemnitz
Museum Gunzenhauser
Sachsen Bank
SATURN
DEVK
16
17

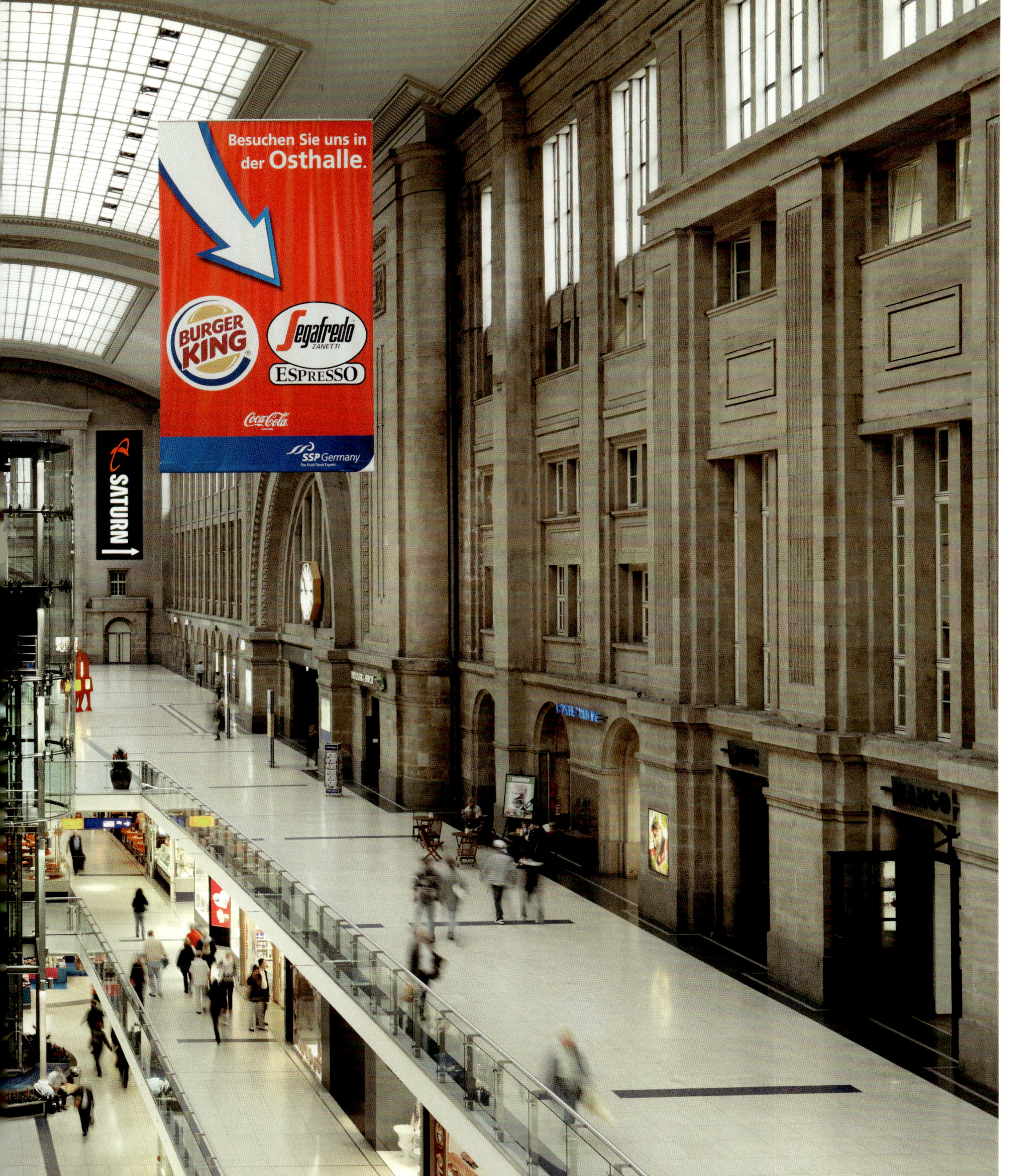
Besuchen Sie uns in der Osthalle.
BURGER KING
Segafredo ZANETTI
ESPRESSO
Coca-Cola
SSP Germany
SATURN

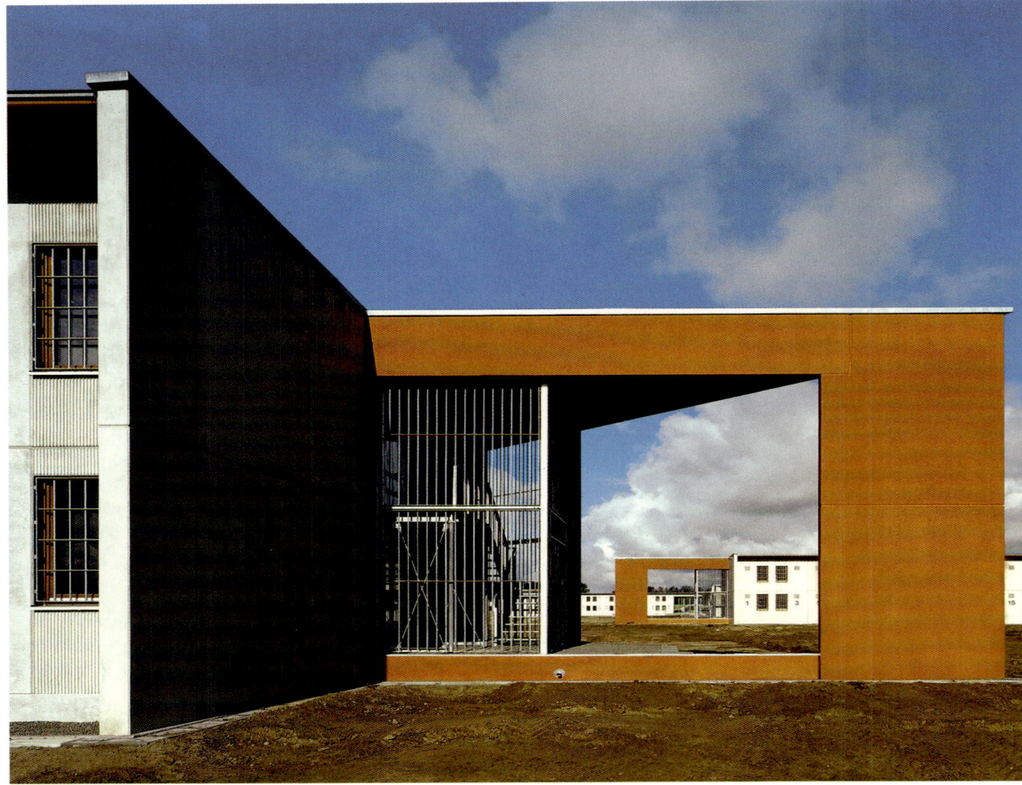

JVA (Reformatory), Billwerder

The design of this building is that of a differentiated campus facility with an orthogonal building structure and a moderate building height situated in the Billwerder-Allermöhe landscape. An exterior "building trail" consisting of the reception building, the kitchen, the canteen, the sports hall, and owner-operated businesses defines the area. Inside, a total of seven incarceration units comprise the variously defined building complex.

Client: City of Hamburg
Location: Hamburg
GFA: 53,918 m²
Completion date: 2005
Competition: 1st Prize, 1993

Function

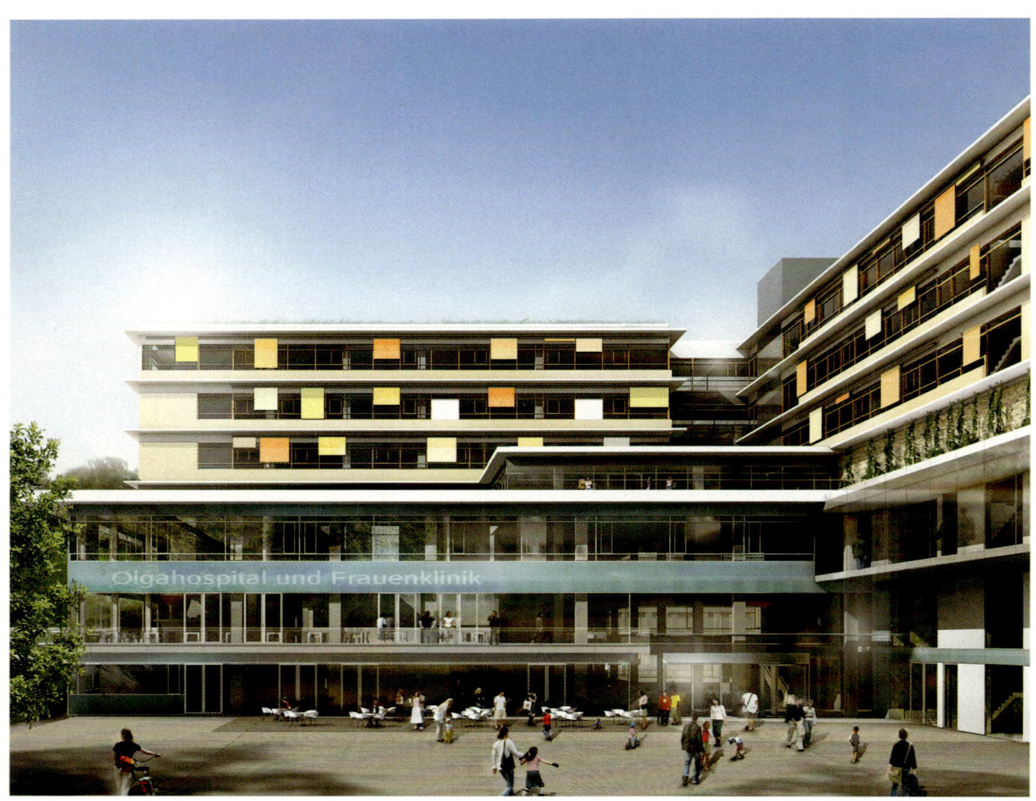

Olga Hospital and Women's Clinic

The task of the competition consisted in the accommodation of the children's and women's clinic in its own building areas on a sloped, spatially cramped piece of property. By filling out the dormitories as square pavilions, it was possible to efficiently place bright, light-suffused stations on top of the multistoried treatment and diagnostic areas.

Client: Capital City of Stuttgart
Location: Stuttgart
GFA: 94,000 m²
Beds: 405
Completion date: 2012
Competition: 1st Prize, 2006
Architecture: HPP in collaboration with Sorg und Frosch

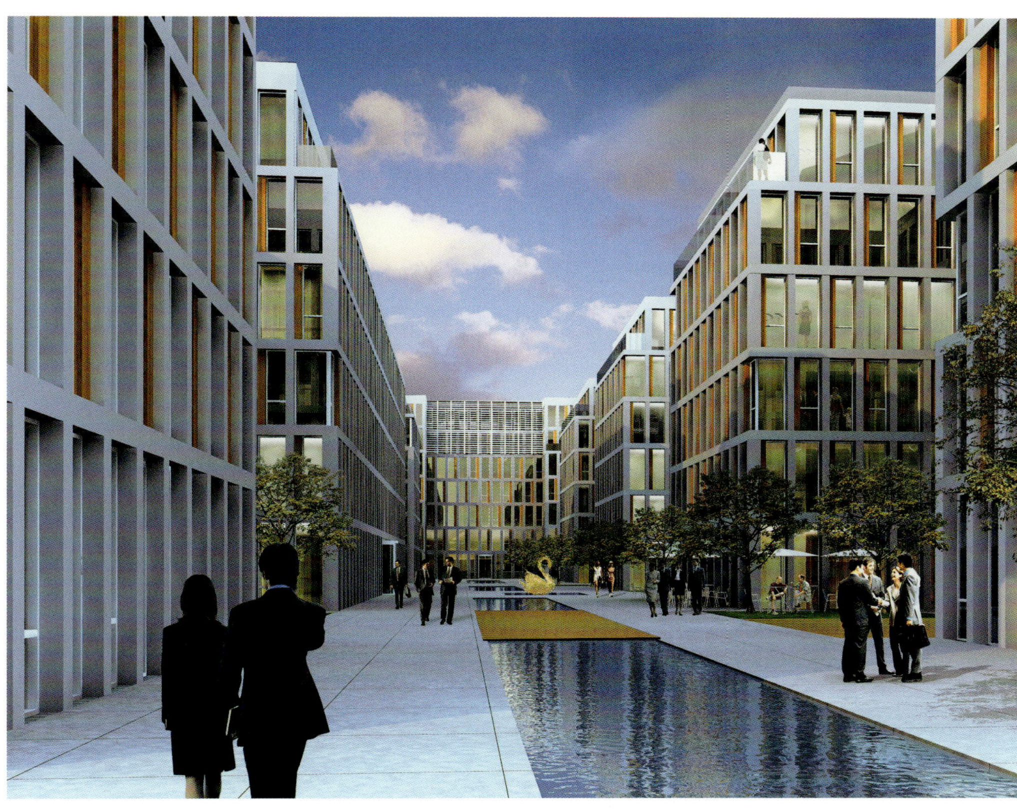

Swan Office Park

Between the international airport and downtown Bucharest, this classic office park is being built within the framework of a broad area of urban development. The complex includes five modules offering a total of 55,000 square meters of gross floor area of office and service areas and 900 parking places, which are for the most part located in underground garages. All of the building structures are spatially as well as functionally accessed by a central axis.

Client: **Swan Property S.R.L.**
Location: **Bucharest**
GFA: **95,000 m²**
Completion date: **2009**

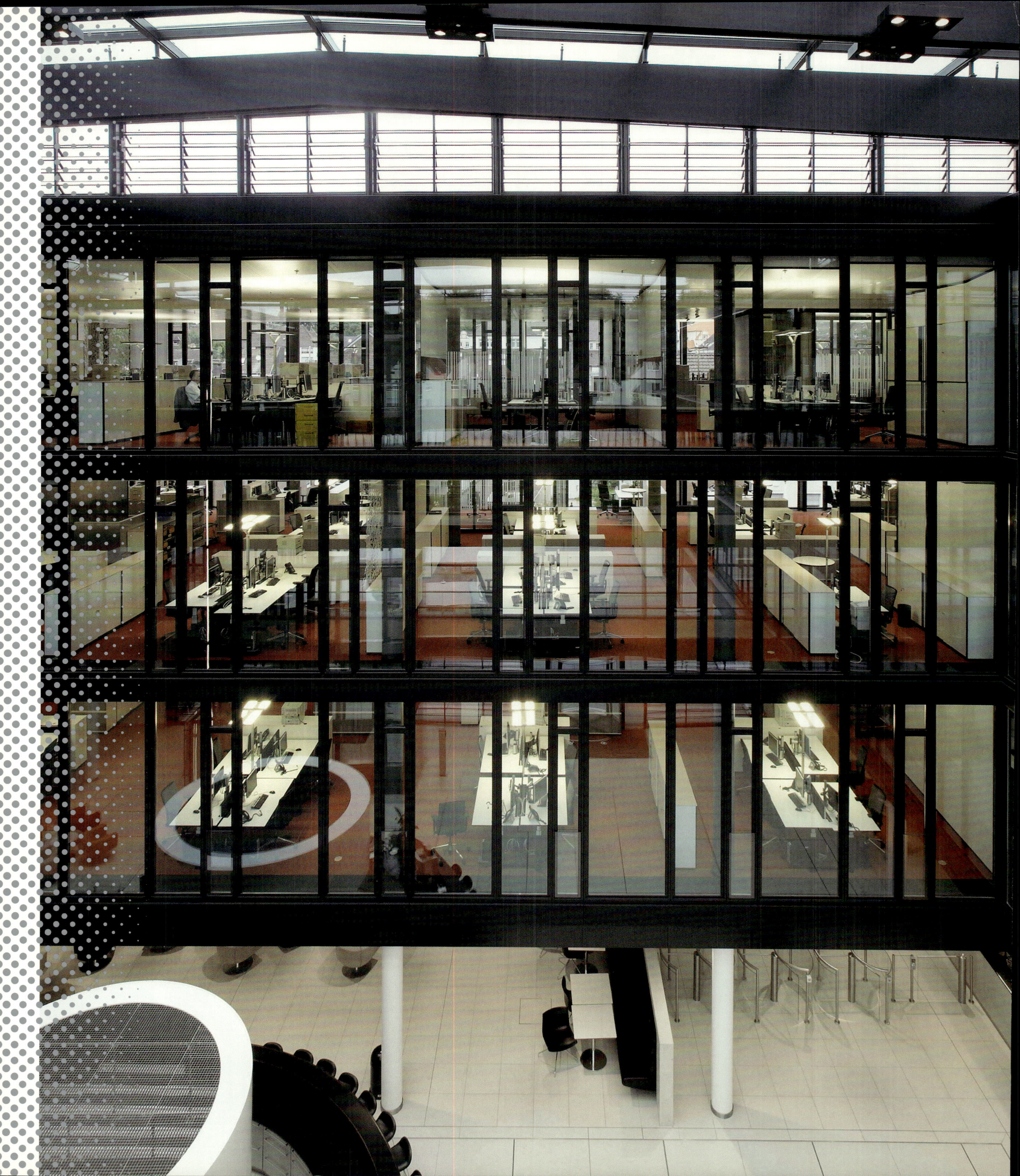

How often do we overuse the term "flexibility" as a synonym for malleability or adaptability? Originally, flexibility meant "to bend or deflect," being derived from the Latin *flectere*. A blade of grass that bends in the wind and does not snap as a brittle branch would provides an effective image drawn from nature of successful adaptation to changing circumstances. Most of the time, being flexible is rewarded with success.

Everyone's life is characteristically shaped by incisive changes. We are forced to accept that we are subject to transformations, and that we must constantly begin all over again—and thus react flexibly—in order to adjust to previously unforeseen situations. To a great extent, flexibility consists of a positive attitude toward change. Globalization, the individualization of society, and demographic change are generating new circumstances and require adaptation at all levels of society.

This concept of flexibility as a life-sustaining factor can be applied under certain conditions to architecture, too. Just like people, buildings and structures must also be able to respond to different uses. For the design of a building in concrete terms, this means that spatial structures, construction, and expansion grids or supply systems should not be planned with reference to just one possible use. On the contrary, they should be flexibly designed and allow latitude for subsequent adaptation to new demands and uses.

This spatial latitude runs like a recurring theme through the opportunities for different use configurations and communication structures in the administration building of the Santander Consumer Bank in Mönchengladbach. The building's unconventional access structure sets the tone of the project right away. It runs in a straight line through the meandering building structure and creates space for different scenarios of use within the daily operation of the bank. The structure is not built to provide just an efficient means of access to the building's various areas or the best possible spatial orientation; it also makes space for communication, exhibition, and company representation.

In a similar way, flexibility is continued as a spatial concept on the building's upper stories. Here, however, the flexibility supports the efficiency of the internal work flow of the building's users. Spaces can be changed at a moment's notice with just a few adjustments. Room arrangements that are created in this way can be spatially understood as a reaction to changes in the modes of work of the bank's administration.

The building's internal dynamic and the vital work domain and its flexible use structure are mirrored in the seemingly transparent external appearance of the Santander Consumer Bank Building. Its uniqueness is achieved by the subtle, asymmetric arrangement of the opening wing as well as the colorfulness of the profile. Black, unmistakable, and unusual in their sharp-edged wing shape, the sun blinds lend a note of distinction to the building and constitute an easily recognizable architectural detail. As a consequence, the content and appearance of the bank are woven together in a dense architectural construct. The fact that this architectural fabric is always experienced differently depending upon the changing demands of the building's users calls to mind the blade of grass bending in the wind.

Flexibility
Santander Consumer Bank Building

Client: VR-Leasing ONYX GmbH & Co. Immobilien KG | Location: Mönchengladbach | GFA: 31,600 m²
Work stations: 1,200 | Completion date: 2006 | Competition: 1st Prize, 2003

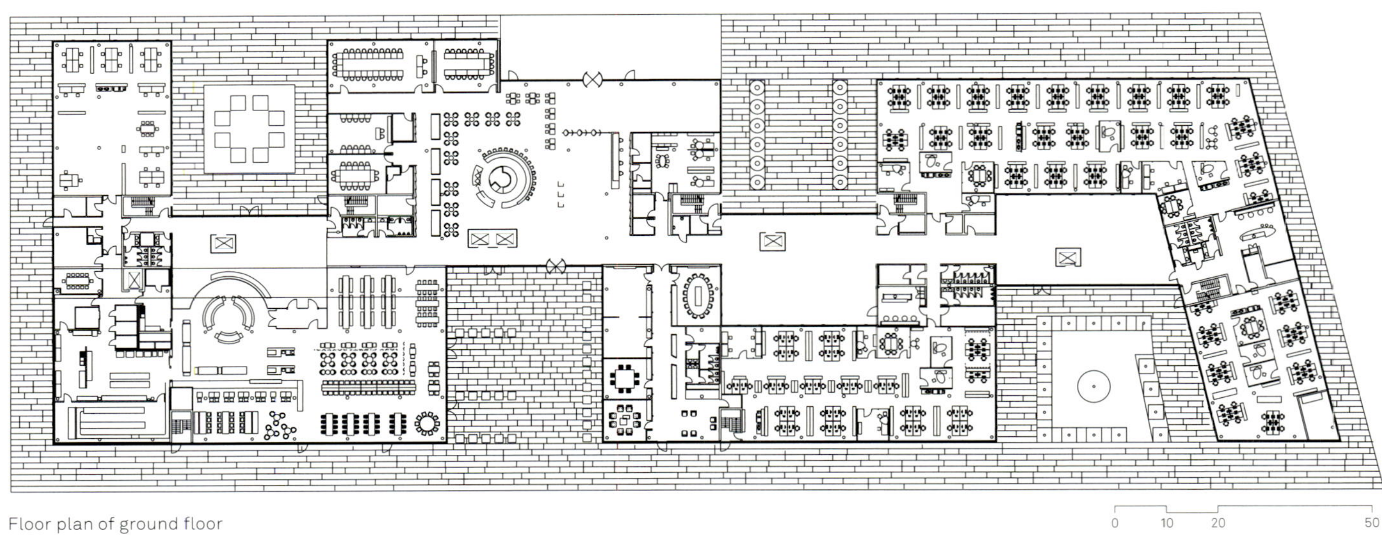

Floor plan of ground floor

→ Connection bridge on third floor
Entrance atrium reception area

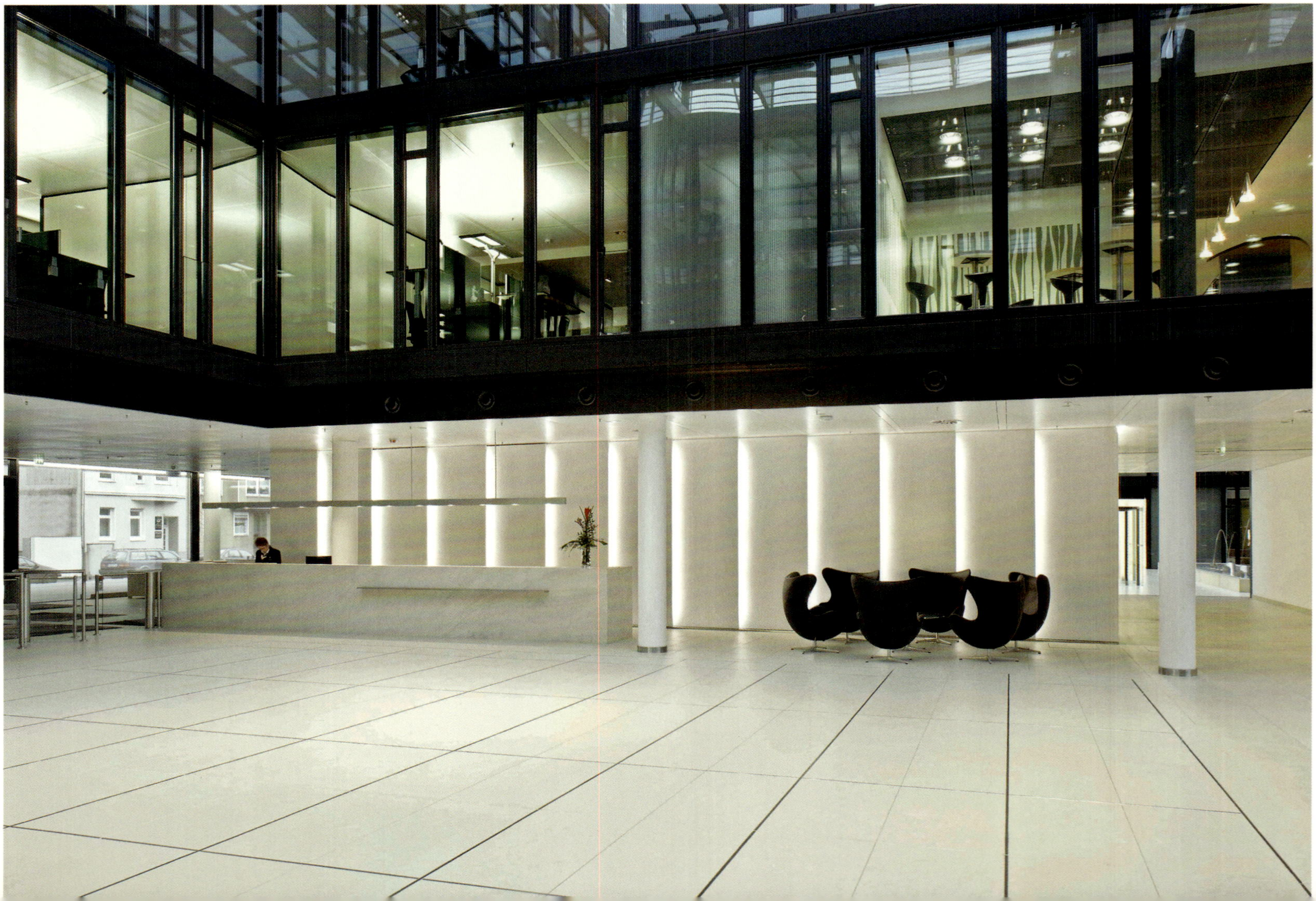

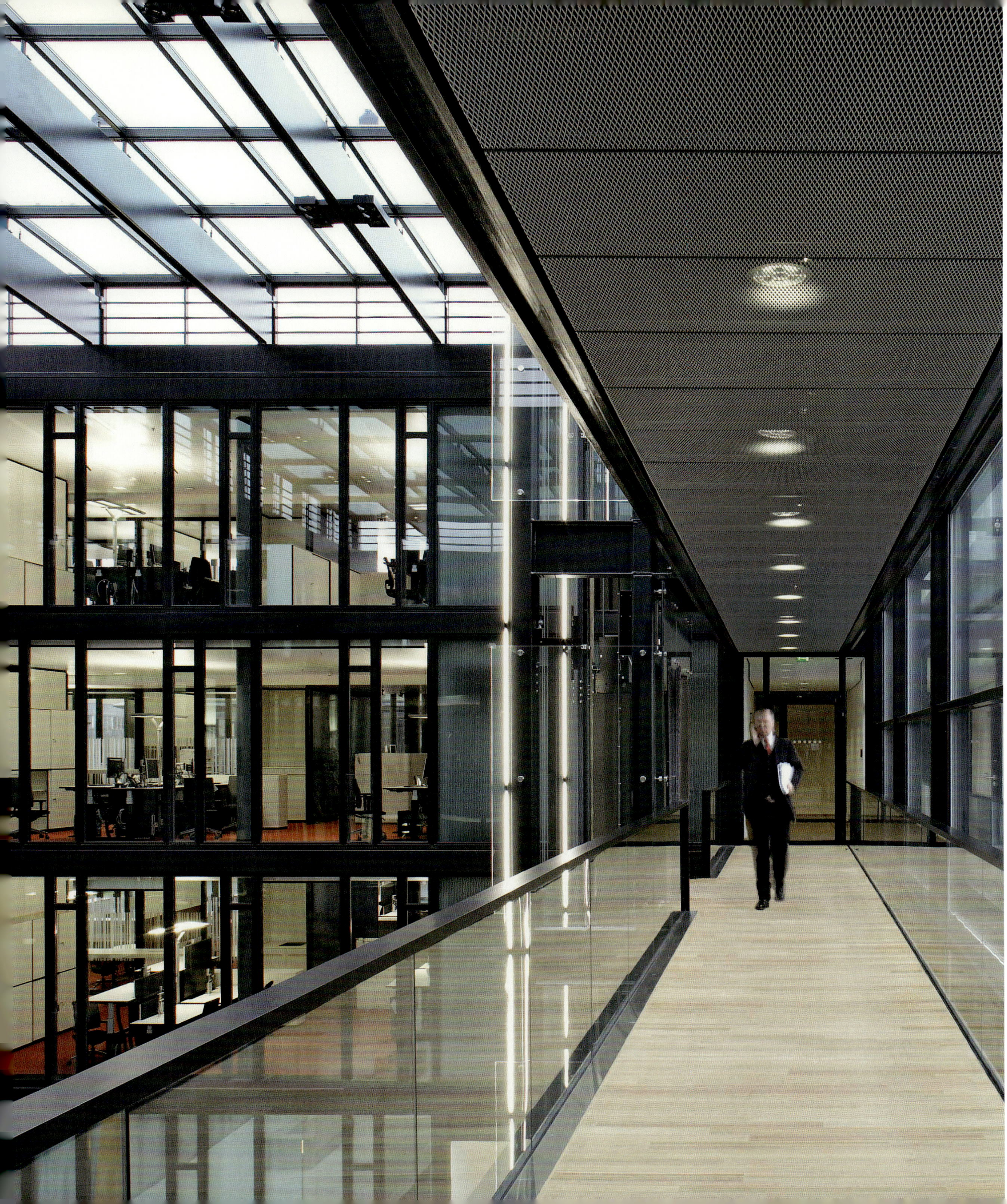

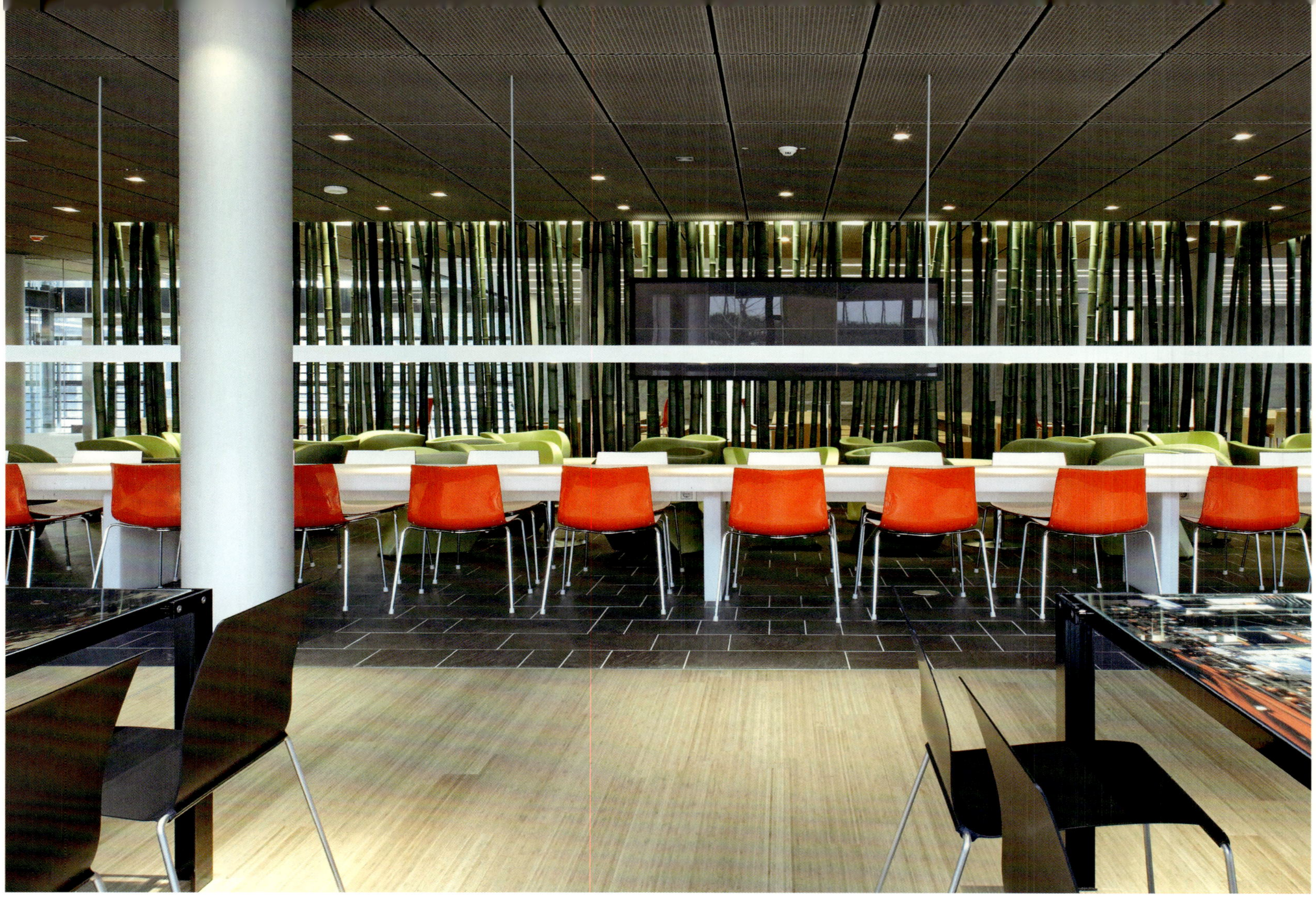

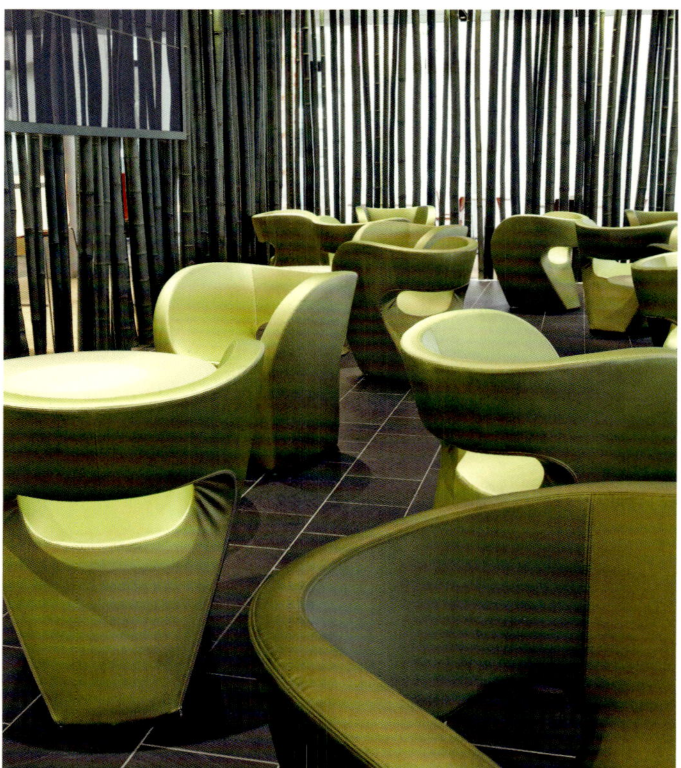

"Urban Eating" cafeteria
"Bamboo Lounge" cafeteria

→ Nonterritorial work areas in the flexible office layout

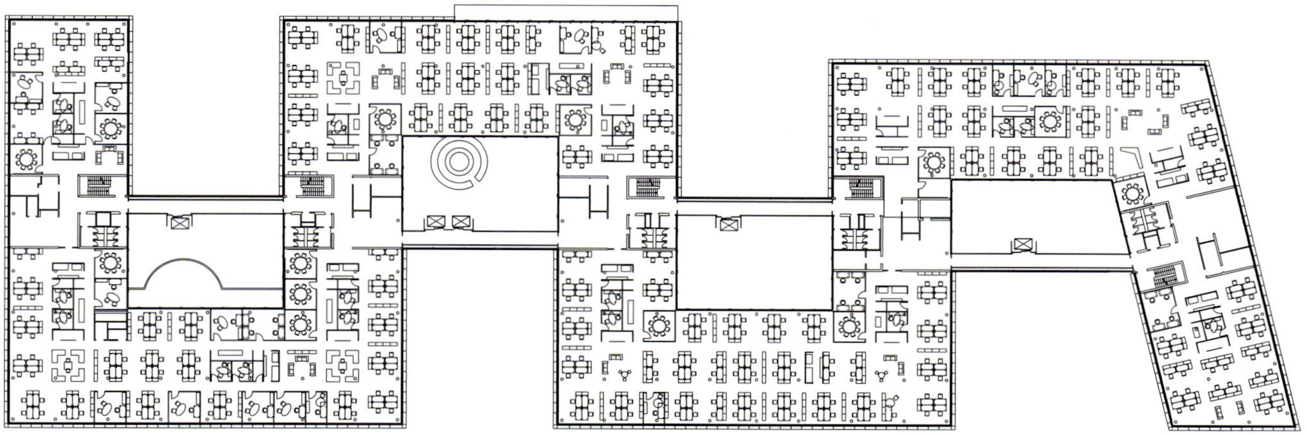

Floor plan of second floor

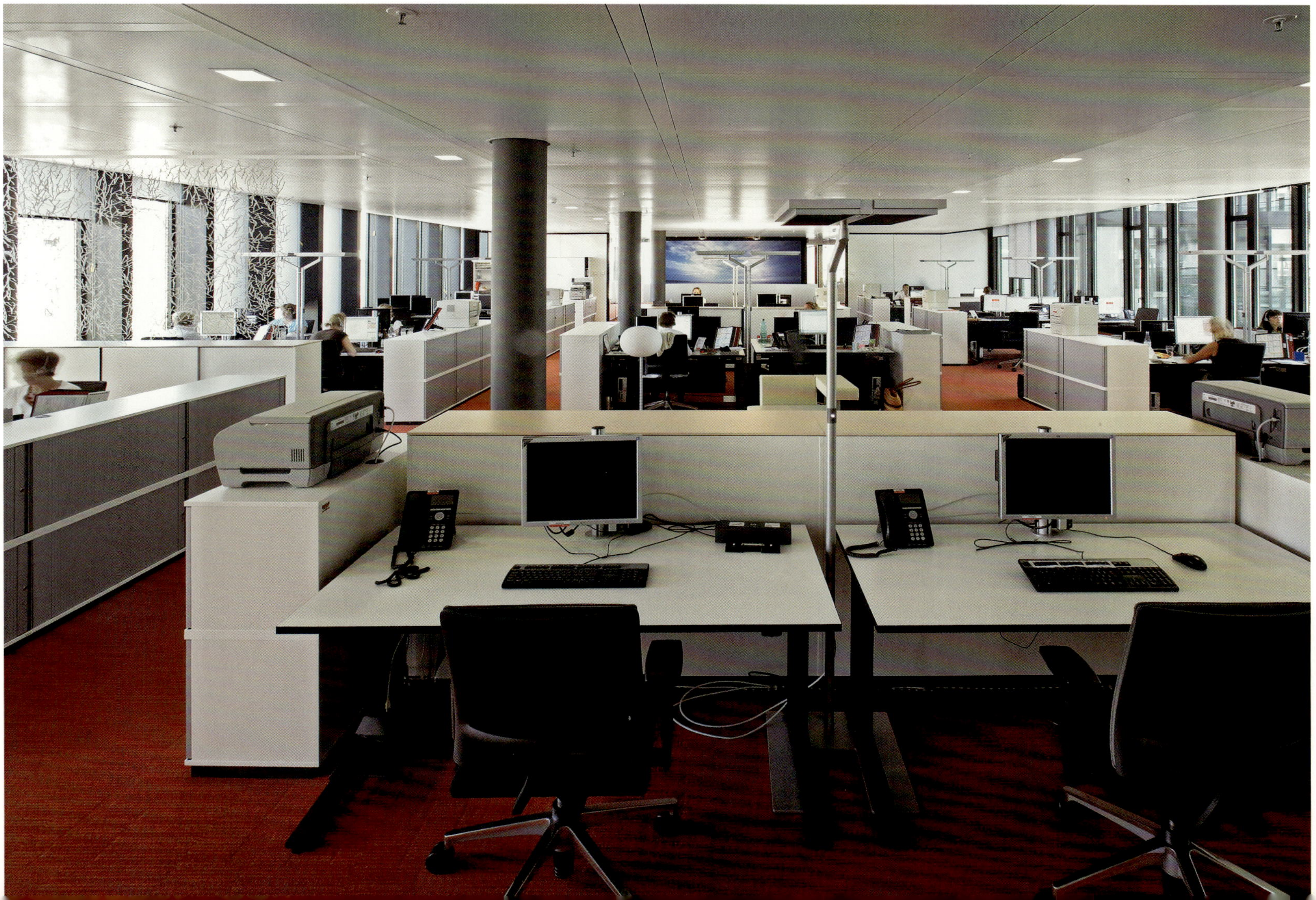

The Santander Consumer Bank Building In a downtown, mixed-use area at the foot of the Abteiberg in the city of Mönchengladbach stands a transparent corporate administration building with unusual work and leisure qualities. This is where the Banco Santander, Spain's largest bank, has erected its German headquarters on a former industrial area. Since the spring of 2007, the facility has provided office space for the 1,200 employees who were consolidated in Mönchengladbach from different locations.

From the very start, the well-being of the employees was the central concern informing the architectural design. With the new building, the bank wanted to create the appropriate conditions for realizing the process of change it calls the "New Work" project, a work concept based on the results of the "Office 21" study conducted by the Fraunhofer Institute. "Office 21" asserts that in an increasingly automated and networked professional world, creativity becomes the new raw material of society. The motivation of Santander's employees to find new solutions to the challenges they face in their work and to share these with others thus becomes the basis for the bank's continued and future success.

Given this conceptual backdrop, the goal of the architectural competition for the building's design was to find and develop innovation-promoting modes of work, as well as economical and flexible spatial concepts, that would support the internal flow of information. As a result, the final design idea was focused on the internal organization of a team-oriented, communication-based work environment. The building site's geographical proximity to the Rhine River influenced the basic concept of designing a building that "flowed into" the city landscape. In addition, openness, transparency, and flexibility were to be designed to facilitate the work processes of the building's users as much as possible and to promote the exchange of information.

The ultimate result of these basic ideas is a meandering glass building divided into sections along its length by four glass atria. From an urban development standpoint, the new building consolidates the formerly commercial use of the grounds and, with its varying height, mediates between the different heights of the surrounding structures and the grounds themselves. The open, green-surfaced courtyards and the setbacks from the building line generate a stimulating street layout, which breaks up and expands the road space.

The new Santander Consumer Bank Building is a three- to four-story structure whose upper story is recessed. The lively horizontal division is thereby also extended vertically. Spatially and organizationally, the administration building is unified by a main thoroughfare that runs along its length. On the upper levels, this access principle is echoed through the use of connecting bridges crossing the glass atria. All of the important sections of the building, such as the office spaces, the conference and training areas, the reception area, and the cafeteria, can thus always be quickly and efficiently reached.

→ Main entrance with courtyard

The building is accessed via the central forecourt and the entryway atrium. In addition to the coffee bar, a branch of the bank for employees, training rooms, and a conference room are also located here. The employee restaurant, with a generous "free flow" zone, is located on the ground floor, which can be converted to a meeting room for 750 people when necessary by using the adjoining atria. The conference areas next to the atria can be extended just as easily. The atria were variously designed with natural, elemental themes—such as water, air, stone, or wood—in mind, in order to assist with visitor orientation in the interior and provide space for communication and brainstorming.

The layouts of the sixteen-meter-deep office zones are continuously integrated into the meandering ground plan on all floors and are easy to combine with one another. Working groups or organizational units can be fluidly arranged in a constant planning grid of 1.4 meters, thus guaranteeing optimal flexibility and facilitating information exchange. In consideration of varying workplace demands, a mix of open office spaces and glass-partitioned thinking cubicles and project rooms was created. Chill-out zones serving as retreat areas were incorporated at the junctures of these areas.

The new flexible conception of the office workspace requires the sophisticated integration of architectural design and building engineering. A combination of natural window ventilation and mechanical ventilation, which includes air inlets hidden within the ceiling panels, provides comfortable and draft-free air circulation in all work areas with a minimum expenditure of energy. Absorption surfaces in the ceilings, as well as furniture designed especially for the building, provide noise-free acoustic conditions in the open office layout. The façades are equipped with light-diverting, outdoor sun protection lamellae, which are daylight controlled and connected to the interior lighting. With three-meter room clearances, there are also excellent lighting conditions in the middle zones of the office spaces.

The transparency of the building in the interior was consciously set off by different spatial qualities. With its orangey-red flooring, the color concept of the office spaces corresponds to Santander's corporate identity. Similarly, the high-quality interior details and furnishings were also selected to make reference to the bank's corporate image, as well as to convey a sense of confidence and to coordinate with the exterior appearance of the black framing of the glass façade. Materials such as wood, leather, and natural stone were also incorporated to generate a sense of warmth and comfort.

The innovative approaches demanded by Santander's "New Work" concept are what made it possible to realize such a trailblazing administrative building. Because of the requirement that the building be adaptable in response to the ever-changing organizational demands of the bank's operation, the structure was intentionally designed to have greater flexibility in its use, something which will ultimately optimize the duration of the building's life.

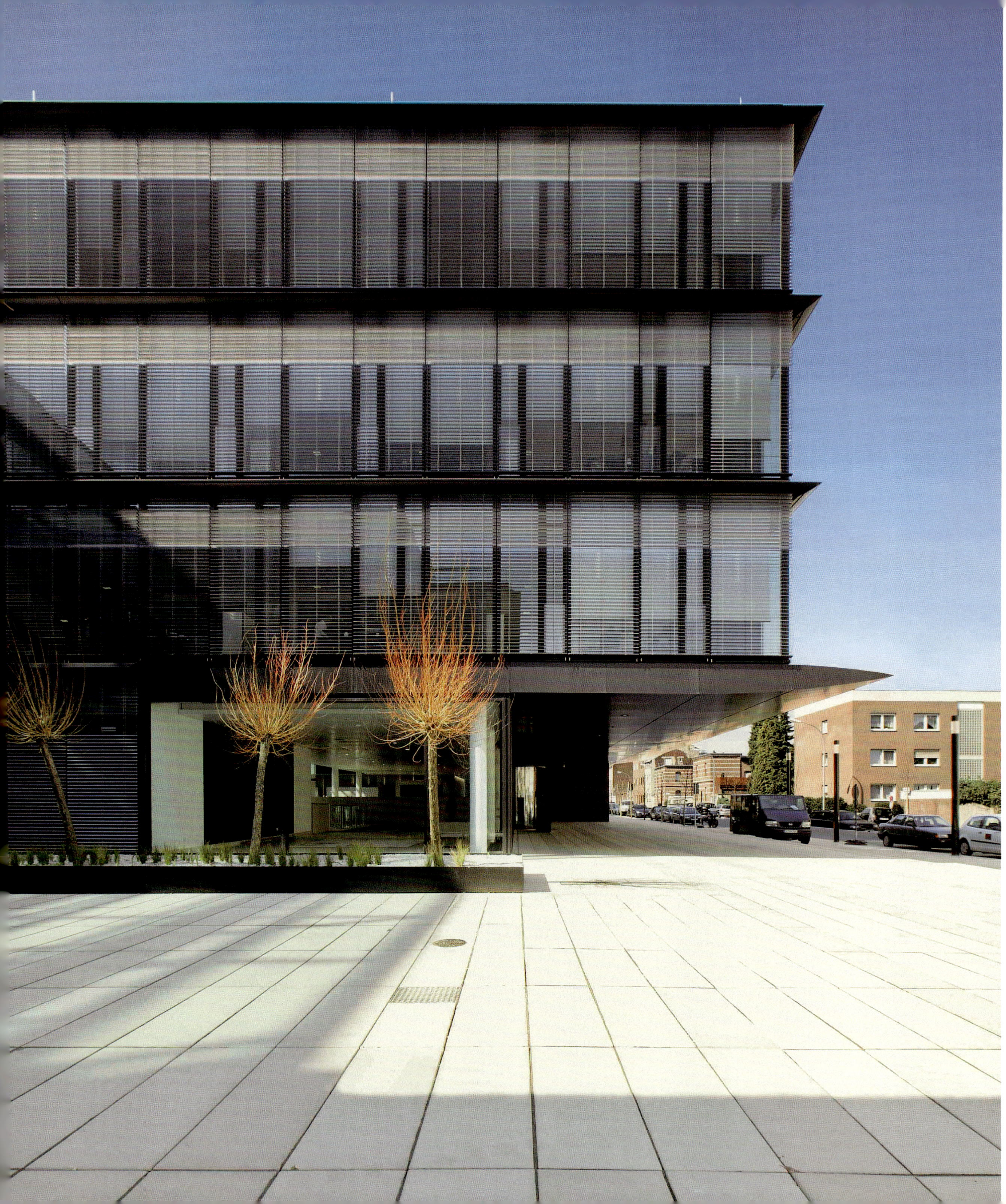

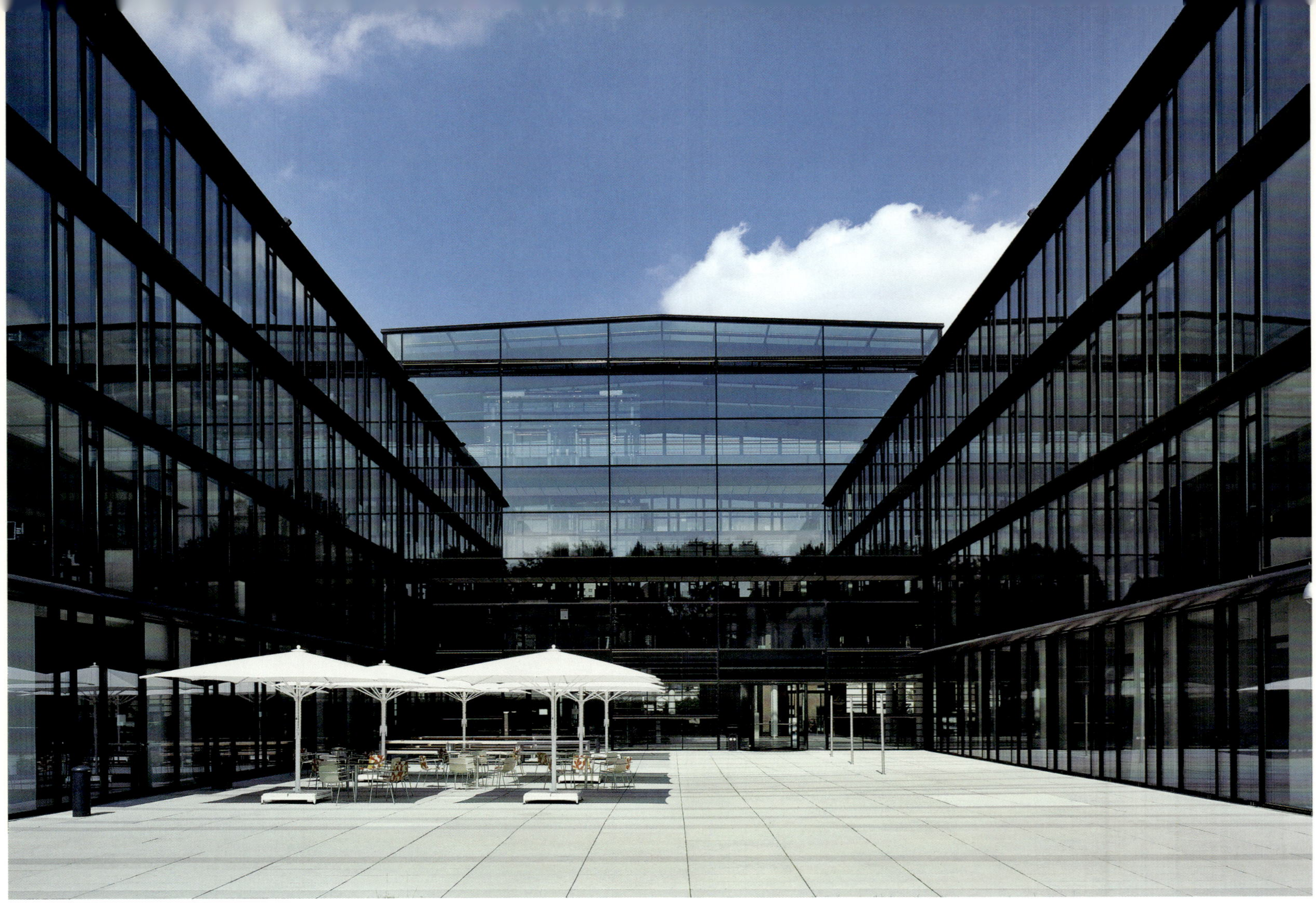

Employee restaurant terrace, south side
→ Main entrance, north side

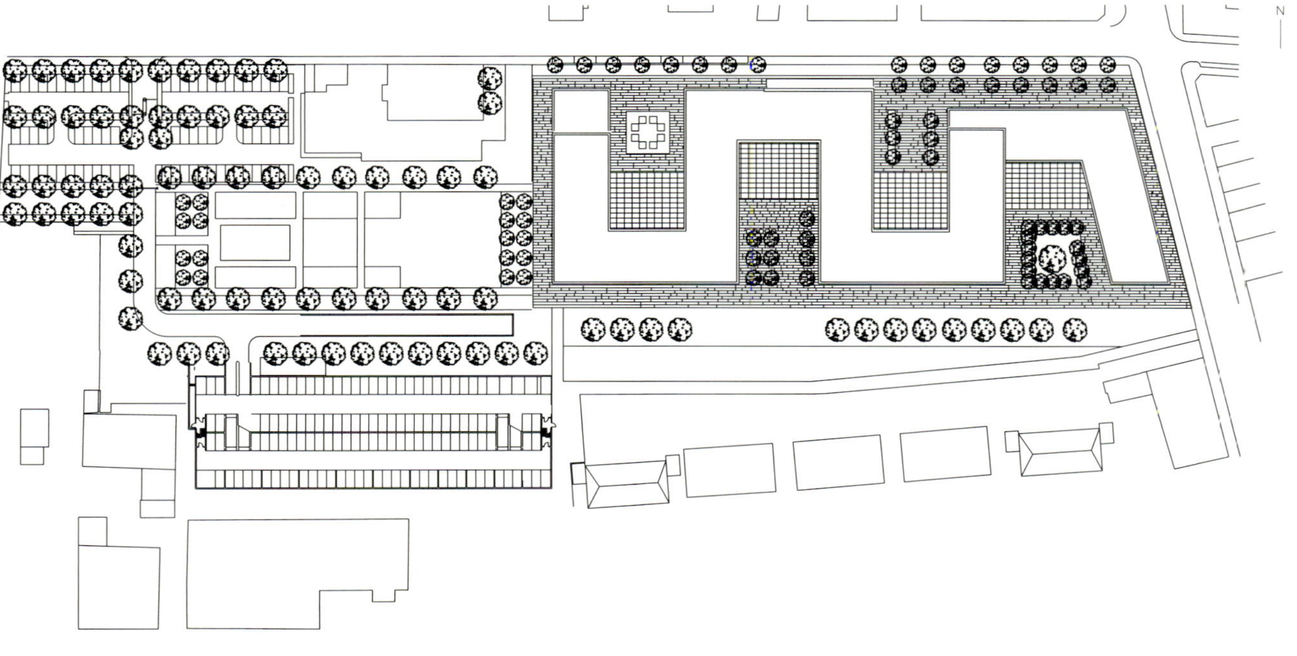

Site plan

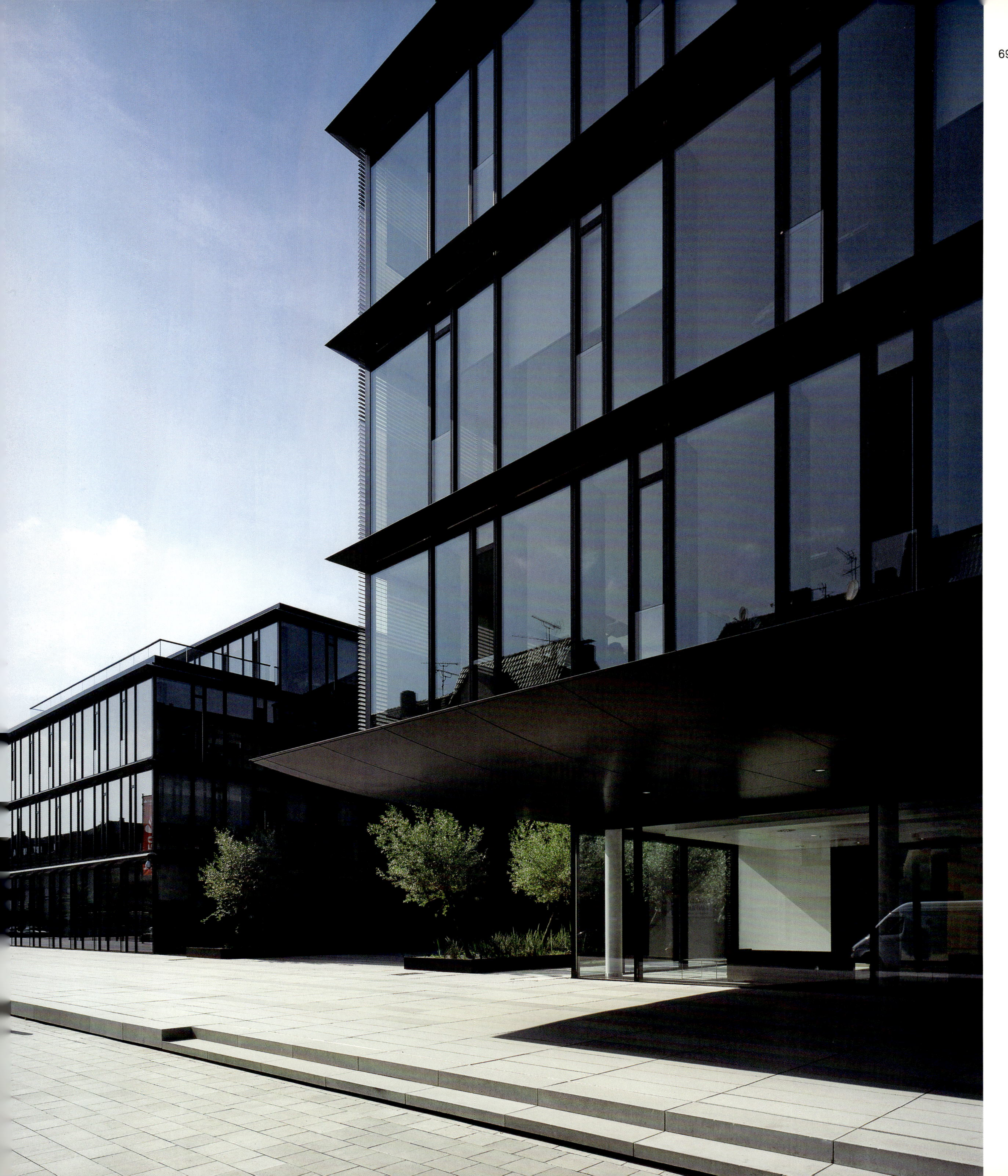

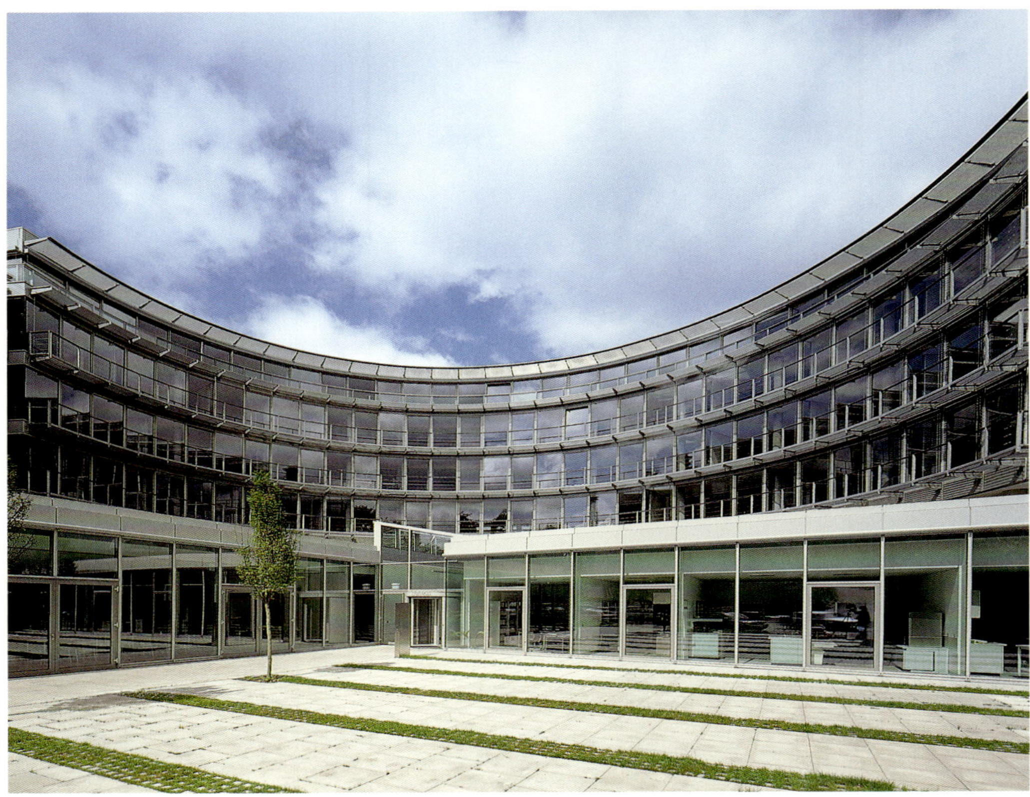

Lüdenscheid Public Utility Facility

With a building depth of fourteen meters, this five-story public utility administration building in Lüdenscheid makes possible the variable organization of its office spaces for the use of individuals or teams, thereby creating a surface use that is very flexible and economical from the standpoint of possible future changes in the function and use of the existing structure.

Client: Stadtwerke Lüdenscheid GmbH
Location: Lüdenscheid
GFA: 6,000 m²
Work stations: 145
Completion date: 1999
Competition: 1st Prize, 1997

Flexibility

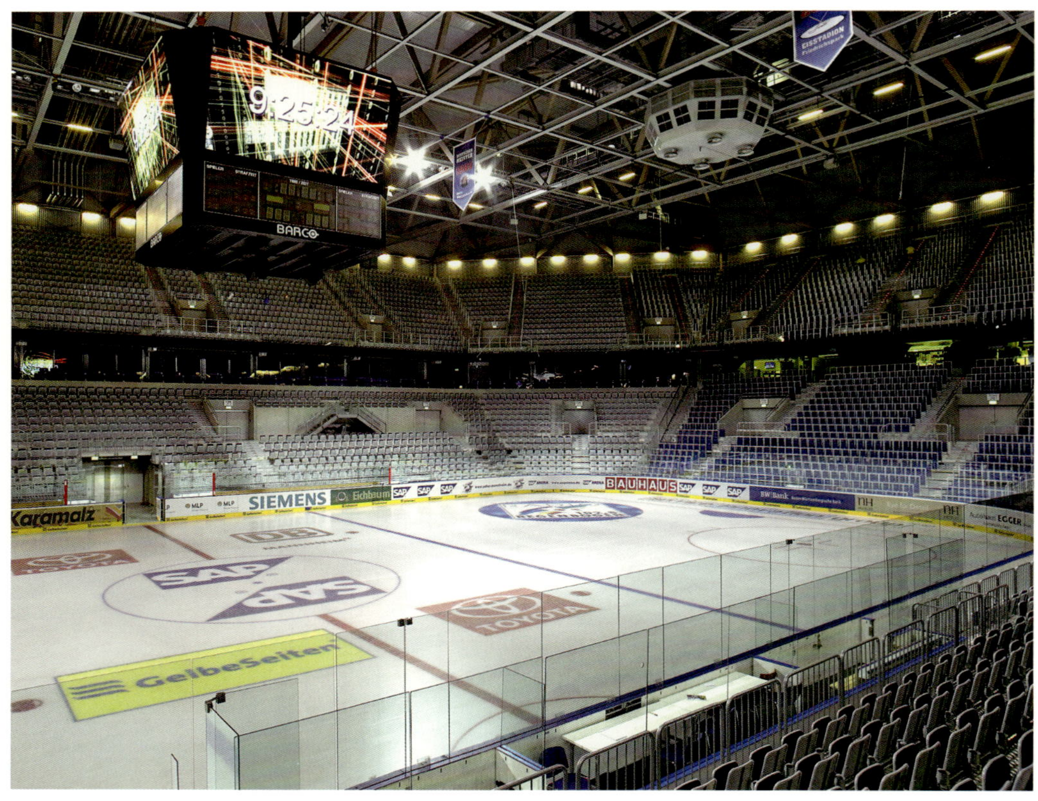

SAP ARENA

The SAP ARENA was planned as a multipurpose arena and can be used for sporting events as well as other large events. In order to increase, or, as the case may be, decrease, the surface being used, the bleachers can be telescopically slid into and out of one another.

Client: Arena Mannheim Besitzgesellschaft mbH & Co. KG
Location: Mannheim
GFA: 36,200 m²
Seats: max. 14,000
Completion date: 2005

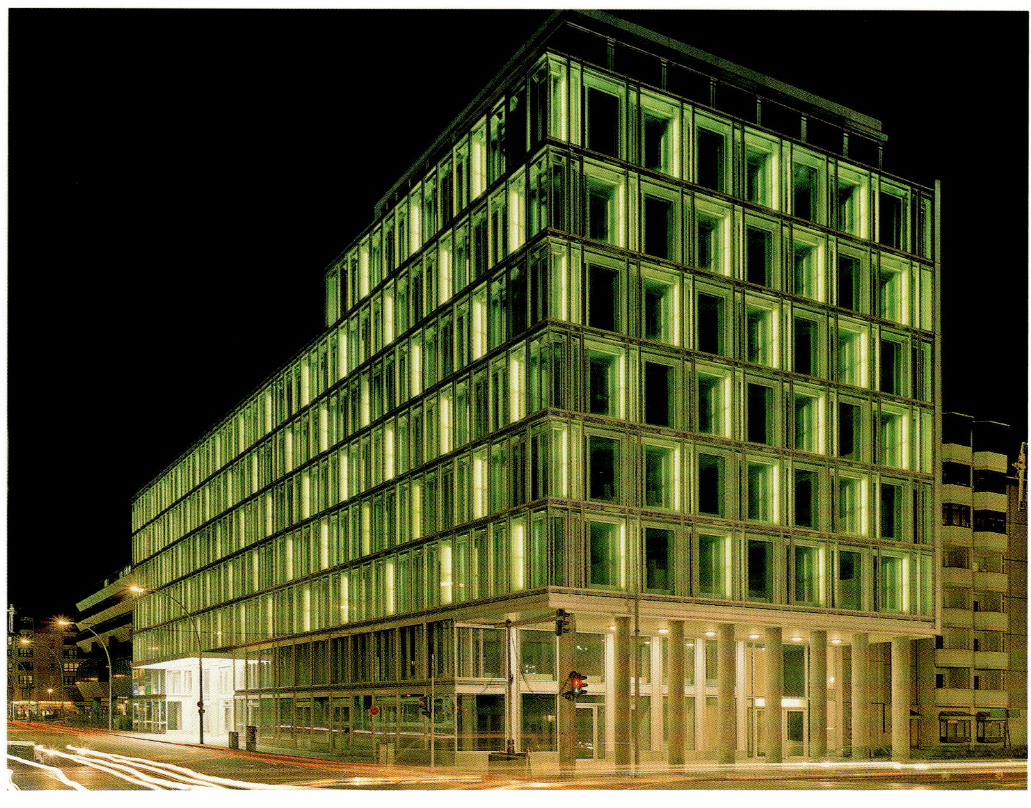

Residential and Commercial Building, Wilhelmstrasse

This seven-story building within Berlin's parliamentary and governmental district is divided into a comb-like structure and a building in behind with two stepped floors. Providing access to the building via a landscaped courtyard allows for a flexible division of the structure into multiple rental areas measuring up to 150 square meters. The story-high glass winter windows make open window ventilation on the side of the building that is exposed to high noise levels possible. This in turn allows for the flexible arrangement of office functions throughout the building.

Client: **ABG Allgemeine Bauträger- und Gewerbeimmobiliengesellschaft mbH Objekt Wilhelmstrasse KG**
Location: **Berlin**
GFA: **38,100 m²**
Completion date: **2002**

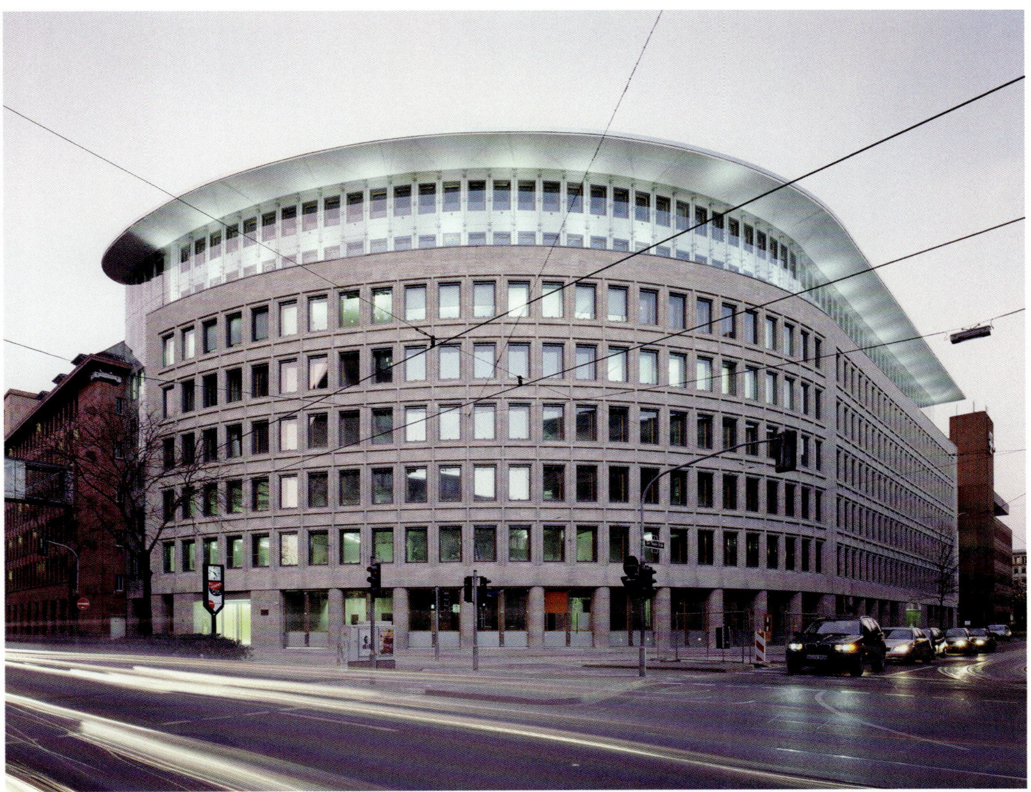

Galileo House

Within the confines of this project's tight budget, it was possible to renovate this building, which has great significance within its urban context, in an innovative way. Since the existing office structure and its vertical access did not facilitate the new user requirement of flexibility, a centrally located stairway was expanded in coordination with the existing stairways on each floor in order to create new usable units measuring up to 400 square meters. This kind of organizational floor plan now permits the free and flexible division of the area units for purposes ranging from cellular office plans to combined office structures and open-plan offices.

Client: **Euro-Invest KTS Ltd.**
Location: **Düsseldorf**
GFA: **13,500 m²**
Rental units: **24 possible**
Year of completion: **1955**
Restoration: **2002**

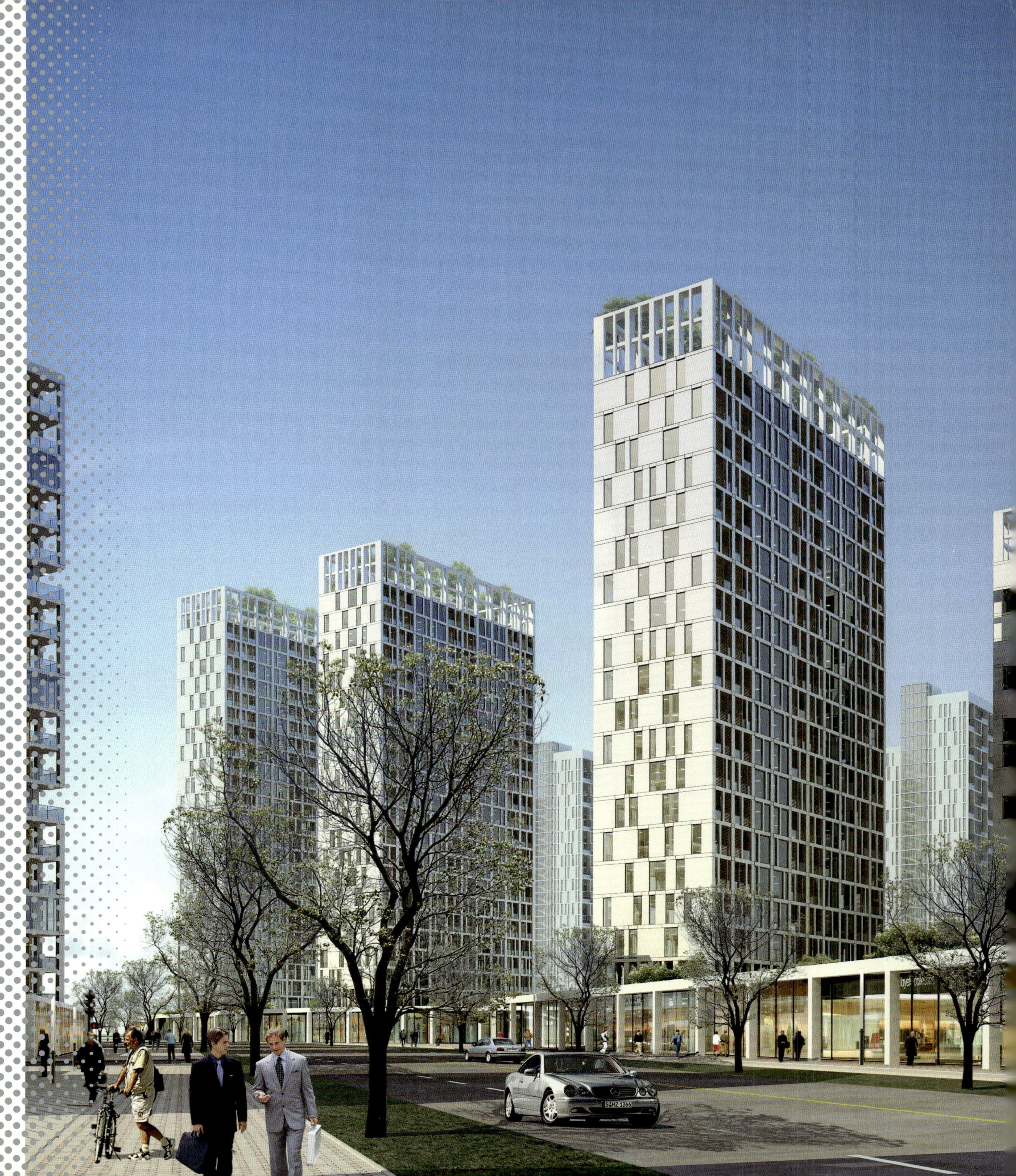

Materiality World Expo Village

Client: **EXPO Land** | Location: **Shanghai** | GFA: **700,000 m²**
Completion date: **2010** | International Competition: **1st Prize, 2006**

What are old objects like? To give just one example, one can think of the heavy, large wooden doors with brass latches that one finds in historic school buildings. The materials of these objects—brass and high-quality wood—are what characterize the image of many old classrooms down to this day. In today's school buildings, however, due to tight budget restraints, resort is often made to cheaper options, such as economical plywood doors. They look contemporary and modern, but they put up next to no resistance and have no soul, and are therefore easily replaced.

Things can be experienced via a multitude of qualities. They can have design, mass, surface texture, elasticity, color, odor, and taste. Materials provide sensuous enjoyment; in our interaction with them, the materiality of things determines the specific nature of their handling and perception.

Materials make a difference. In the case of architecture, their textures, characteristics, and surface effects influence the design and execution of a building. The sure and considered handling of materials and their deployment is a basic building block of architectural design. For centuries certain materials have left their mark on the appearance, and hence the character, of our cities. They are mainly stone, plaster, and brick, and to a certain extent wood. Glass, steel, and concrete were introduced in this order much later and revolutionized architecture at approximately the same time as the advent of industrialization. Natural stone, however, occupies the place of pride, for it is the preferred building material of choice and influenced the visual character of all noteworthy architectural styles until the nineteenth century.

When Walter Benjamin said that "the city wears gray," he was alluding first and foremost to the prominence of natural stone, which characterized the streets as well as the city districts in the metropolises of the nineteenth and twentieth centuries. This strong presence of stone still remains today in large European cities; the grey materiality of their appearance is familiar to us. It gives us the feeling of intimacy—it has come to signify our cultural homeland. Any given building culture is recognized by its formal expression, particularly with regard to its materiality.

Materiality was also one of the guiding design ideas in the development of the concept for the World Expo Village in Shanghai. In addition to the urban planning involved in the project and the Village's requirements in terms of function and content, the desire to develop a special character or charisma for this "village" was of particular significance. The guiding principle of giving the Village the atmosphere of a European city was quickly established, as was the decision to employ the buildings materials in a homogeneous manner. The heart of the 2010 world's fair will thus be European in character and made of stone. This will set it apart from the randomness of the fast paced, anonymous developments that characterize the megacity of Shanghai and will make it a unique point of reference.

The Expo Village will not just employ natural stone, nor incorporate just one building type. Rather, each of the seven basic types will be distinguished by its own natural stone. An architectural design family will thus emerge, one whose character is clearly derived from European building culture. We are hoping for a bit of intimacy—spatial and formal intimacy.

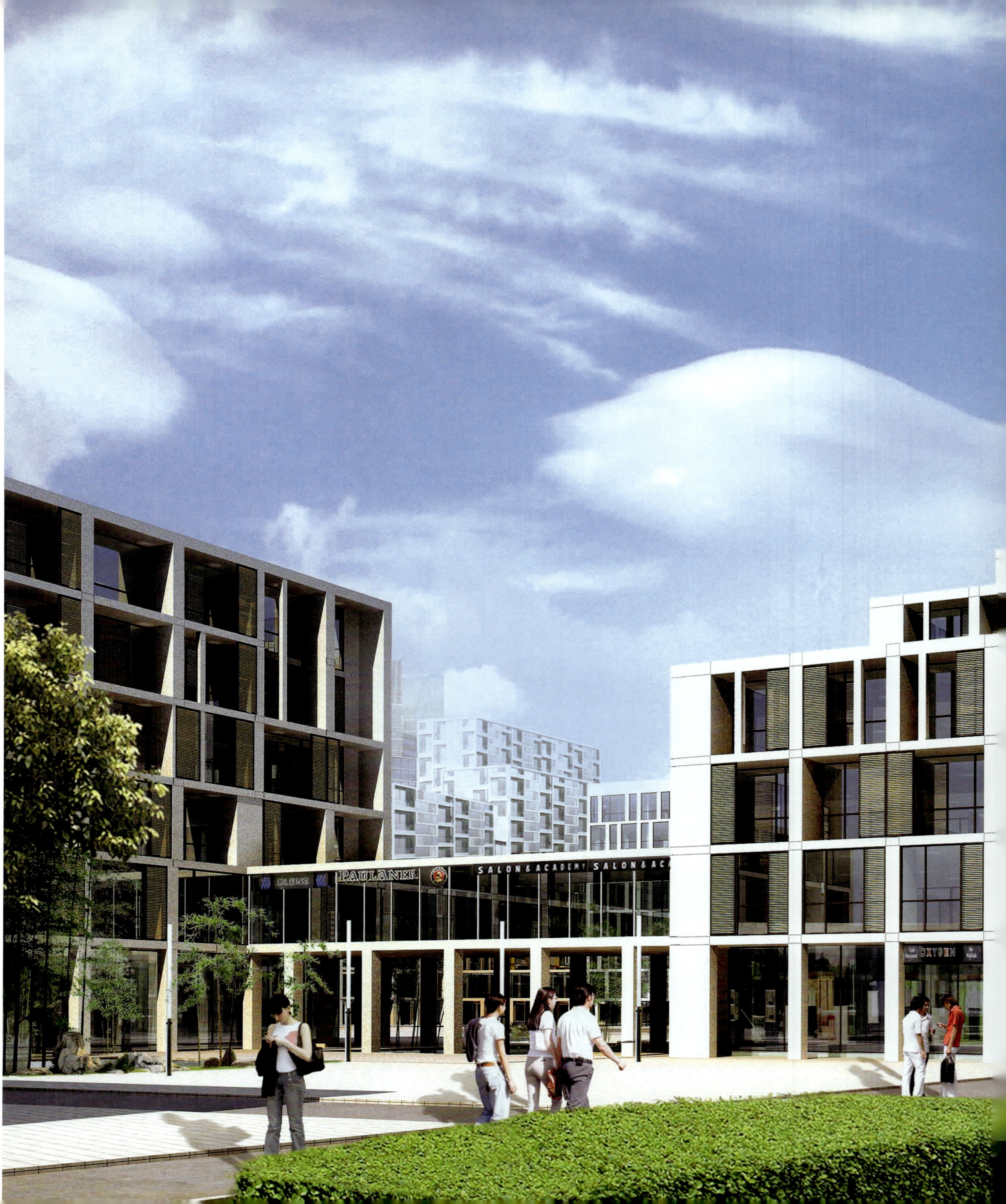
PAULANER
SALON&ACADEMY SALON&AC
OXYGEN

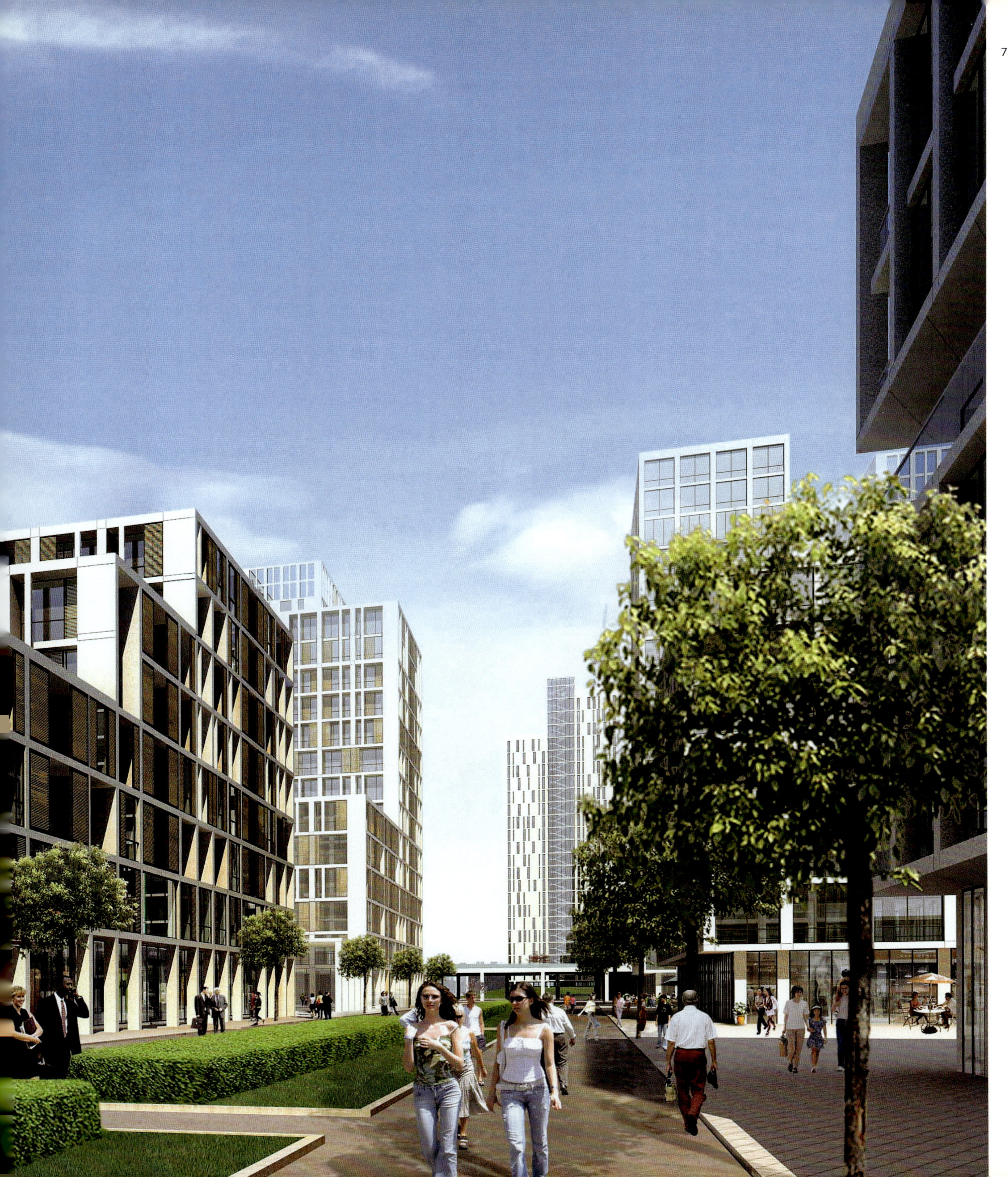

 The World Expo Village The World Expo Village is being built for the world's fair in Shanghai on a planning area of forty-four hectares in the northeast part of the Pudong district. The master plan, which was awarded the first prize in an international competition, will be implemented in 2010 as one of the significant building projects of the EXPO.

The new district on the bank of the Huangpu is an exceptional example of one of the great tasks faced by modern urban planning: the sustainable conversion of preexisting inner-city industrial waste land into lively, urbane city district. With this fact underlying the project, hotels and apartment buildings, as well as retail, cultural, and recreation facilities, will be realized in a multi-layered use structure. The modular concepts employed facilitate the construction of apartment units ranging from 30 to 250 square meters.

The official theme of the world's fair, "Better City, Better Life," is both the leitmotif and the requirement of the architectural design. Sustainable planning is already evident in the balanced division of open and built spaces, especially given the highly dense urban context. In addition to the 700,000 square meters of gross floor area, the World Expo Village also has approximately sixteen hectares of parking space, part of a network that includes the surrounding landscape space, the bank of the Huangpu, the urban surroundings, and the planned building structure. In order to keep the buildings' heat input to an absolute minimum through their positioning, the individual building structures are oriented in a north-south direction. This orientation, in connection with the offset, linear alignment of the buildings, also allows for optimal views of the river and the city.

The occasion for the master plan is the world's fair, so an employee and visitor district is part of the design. However, the requirement that the project be sustainable has necessitated that the design concept retain its validity after the period of the World Expo. The master plan thus makes possible the continued use of the district after the world's fair as a new, dynamic quarter that harmonizes with the preexisting urban structure of Shanghai. The planning of the individual buildings allows for maximum flexibility with a view to future marketing, because the building structure is set up in such a way that with few exceptions it can be converted and inserted into the private real estate sector. This will occur above all thanks to a conveniently organized construction grid and structures whose use is easily adapted. Modular planning, a high degree of prefabrication of the façades, and the deployment of energy-saving technical systems characterize the qualitative requirements of the individual buildings.

The architectural image of the World Expo Village has a European character. The guiding concept is based on the structures and three-dimensionality of the greatest European cities. While Shanghai's surroundings are heterogeneous and marked by isolated developments, the idea of the coherent structure and the unifying stone façades of historical European city districts was one of the foremost influences on the design.

In the overall cityscape of Shanghai, the perforated stone façades of the World Expo Village transmit stability and calm while also contributing something sustainable and energetic to the city. Because of the large scale of the construction, cooling and air-conditioning can be reduced to only what is needed. Thus, the material character of the World Expo Village not only mirrors the image of a European city, but also reflects above all a concern for the appropriate management of resources.

→ Site plan
↞ Perforated façade typical of the district

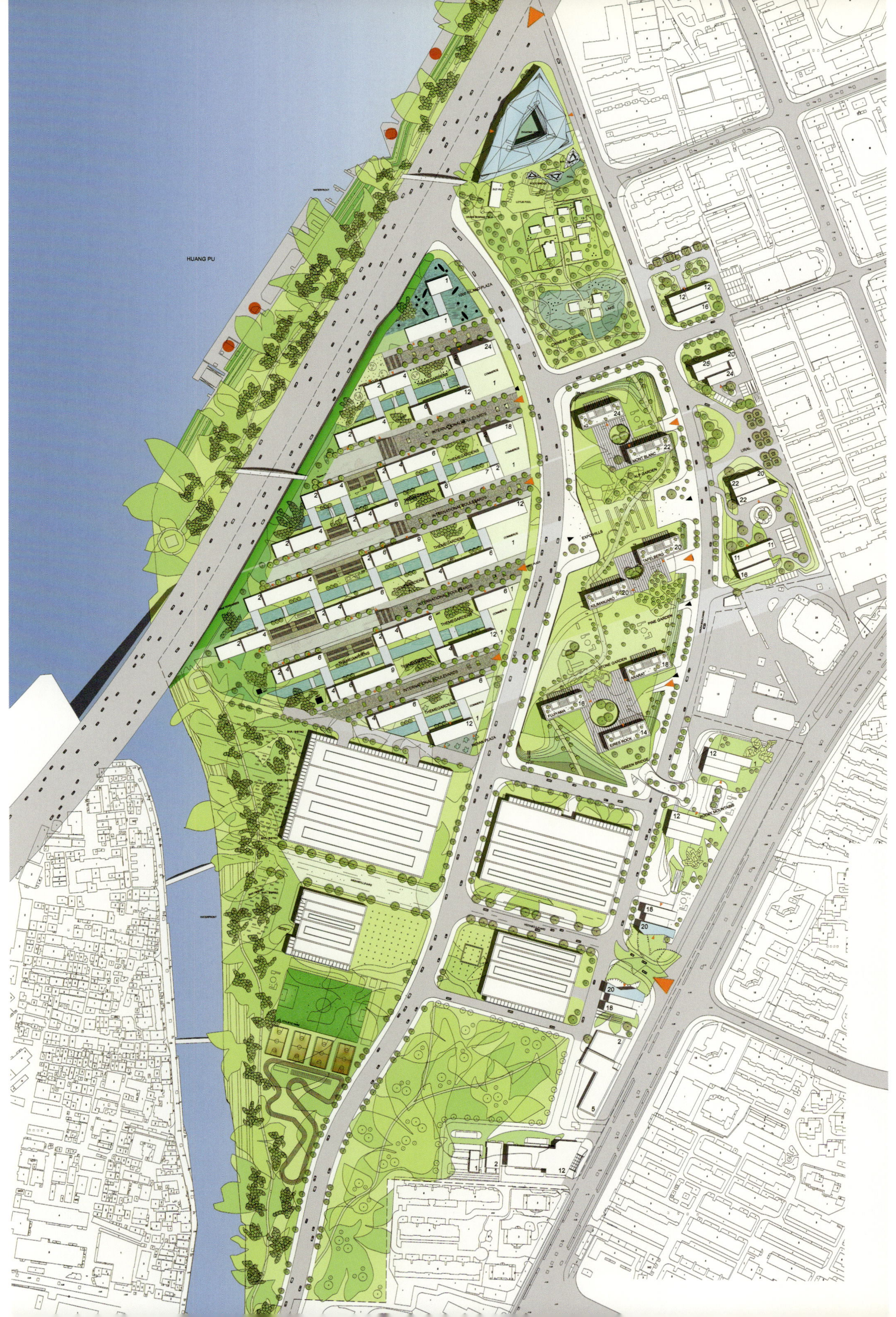
HUANG PU
MONT BLANC
PINE GARDEN
FUJIYAMA
AYERS ROCK
GREEN BRIDGE

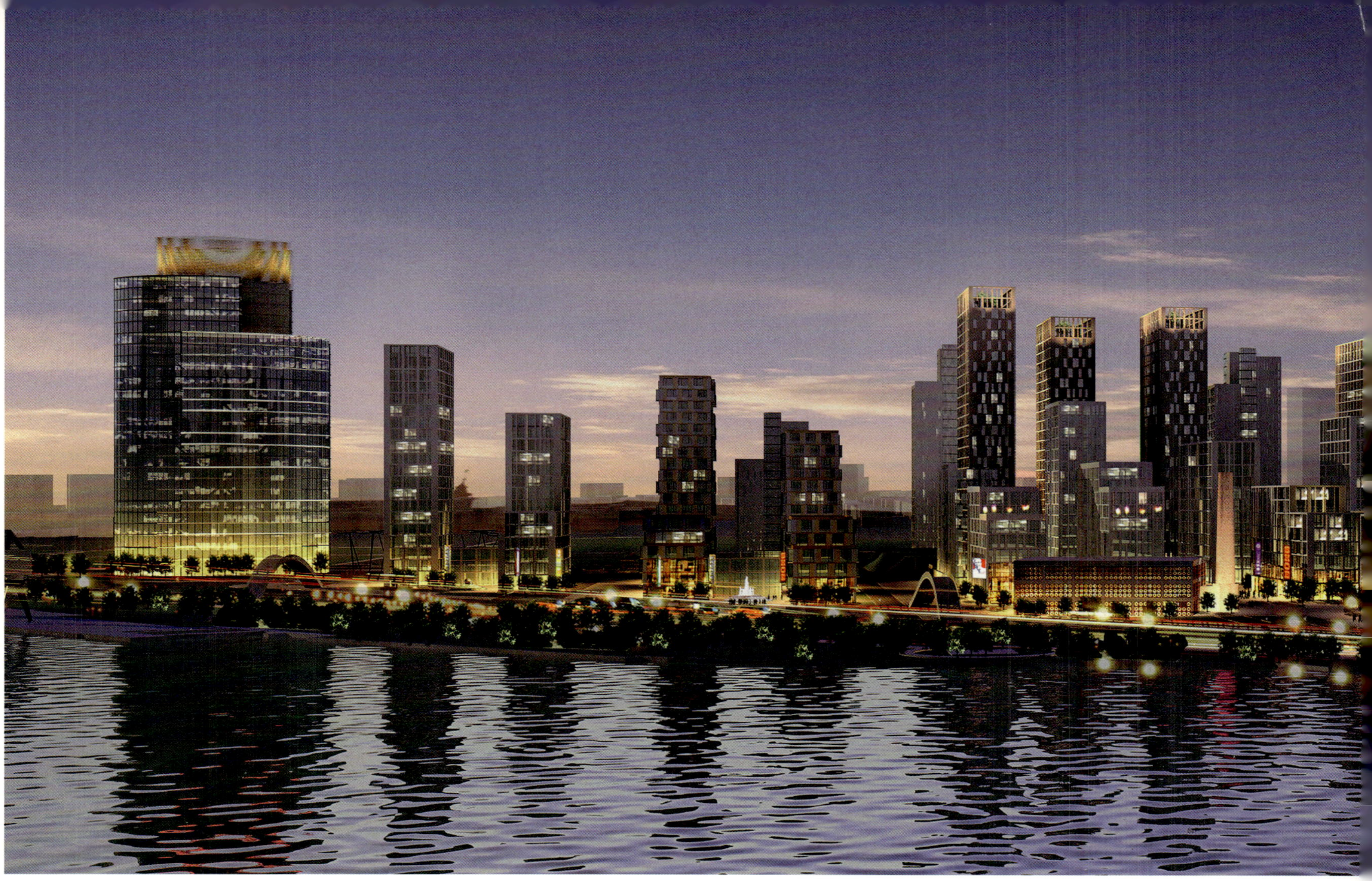

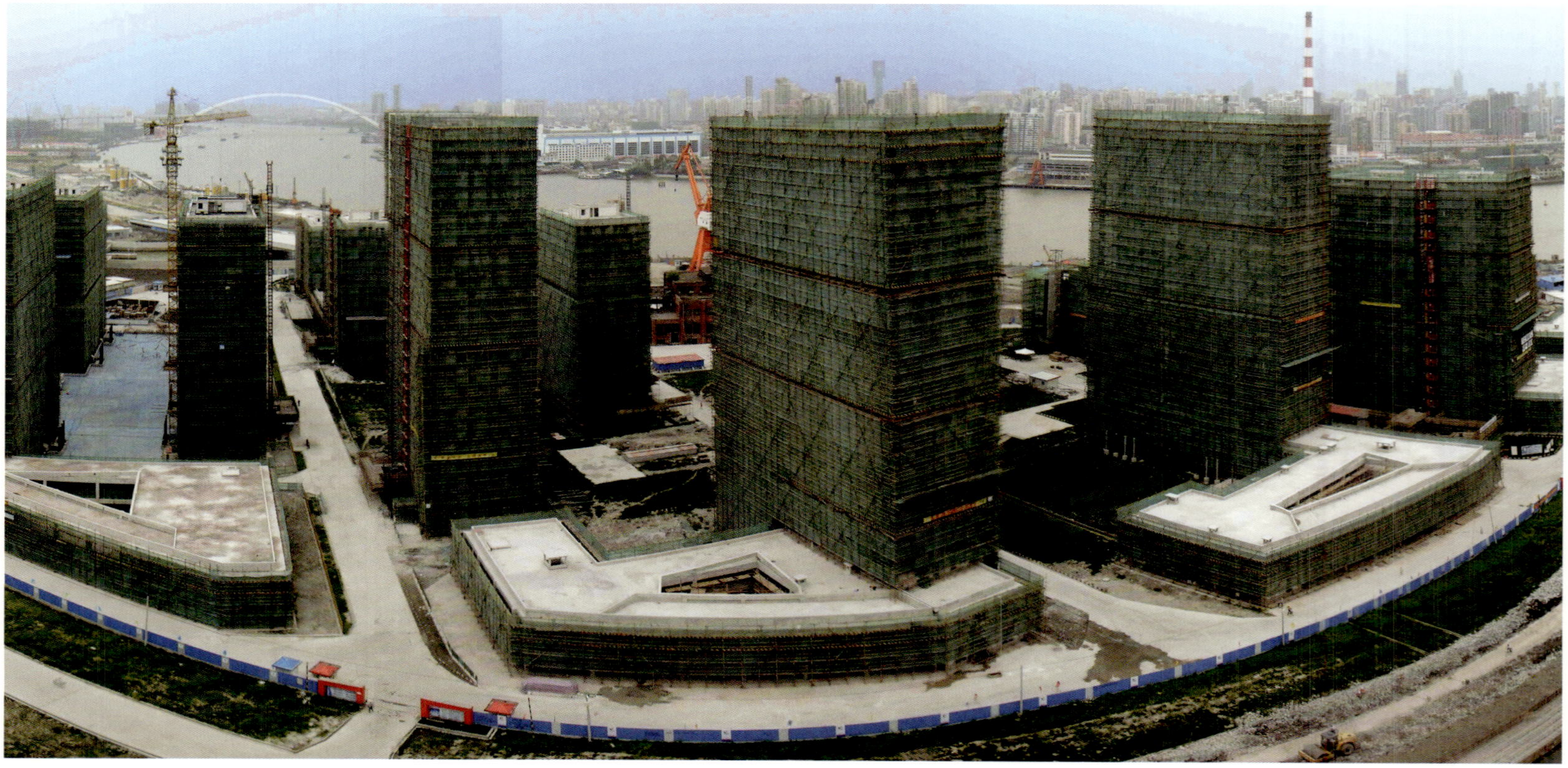

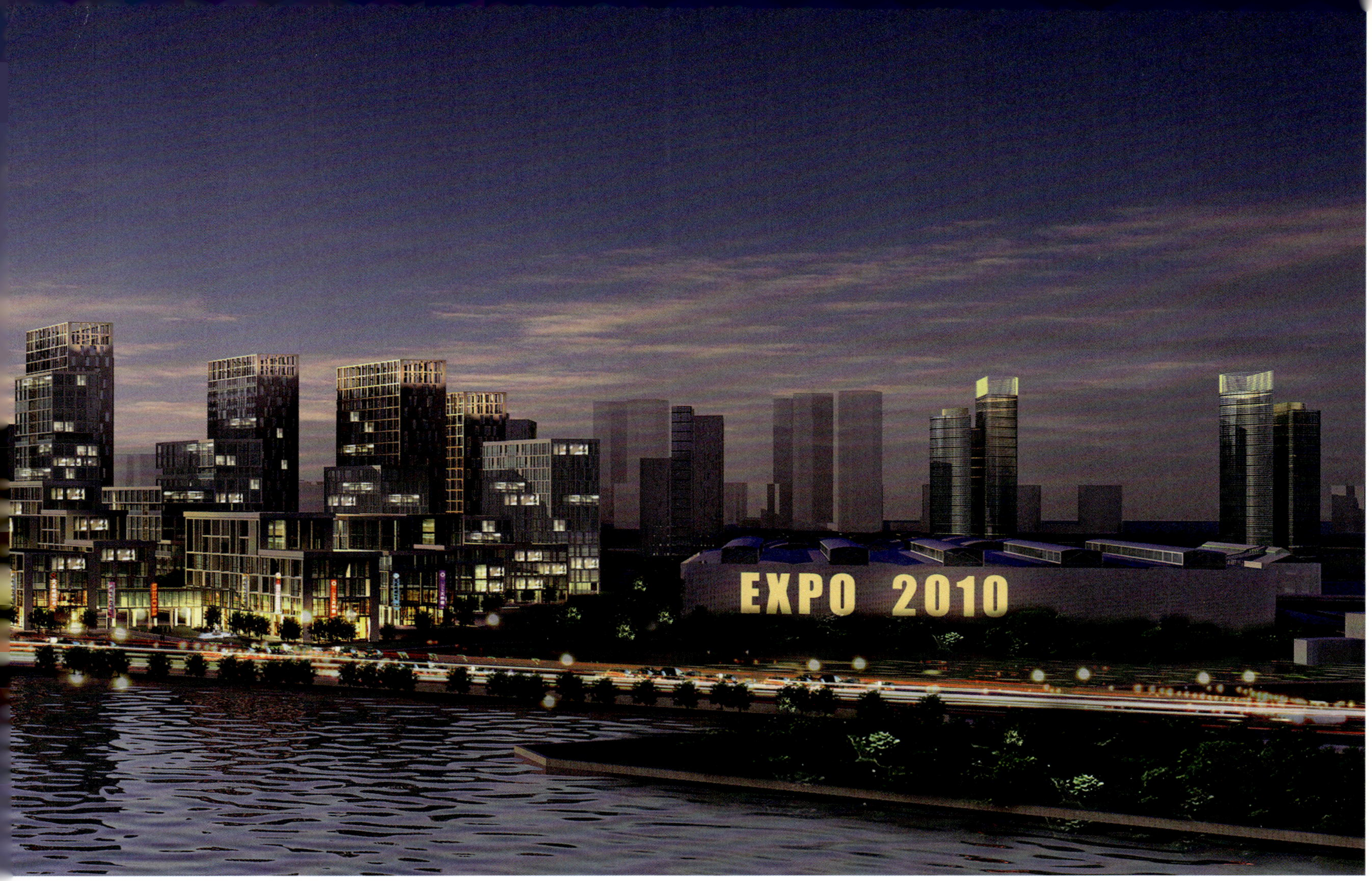

A new district along the Huangpu River

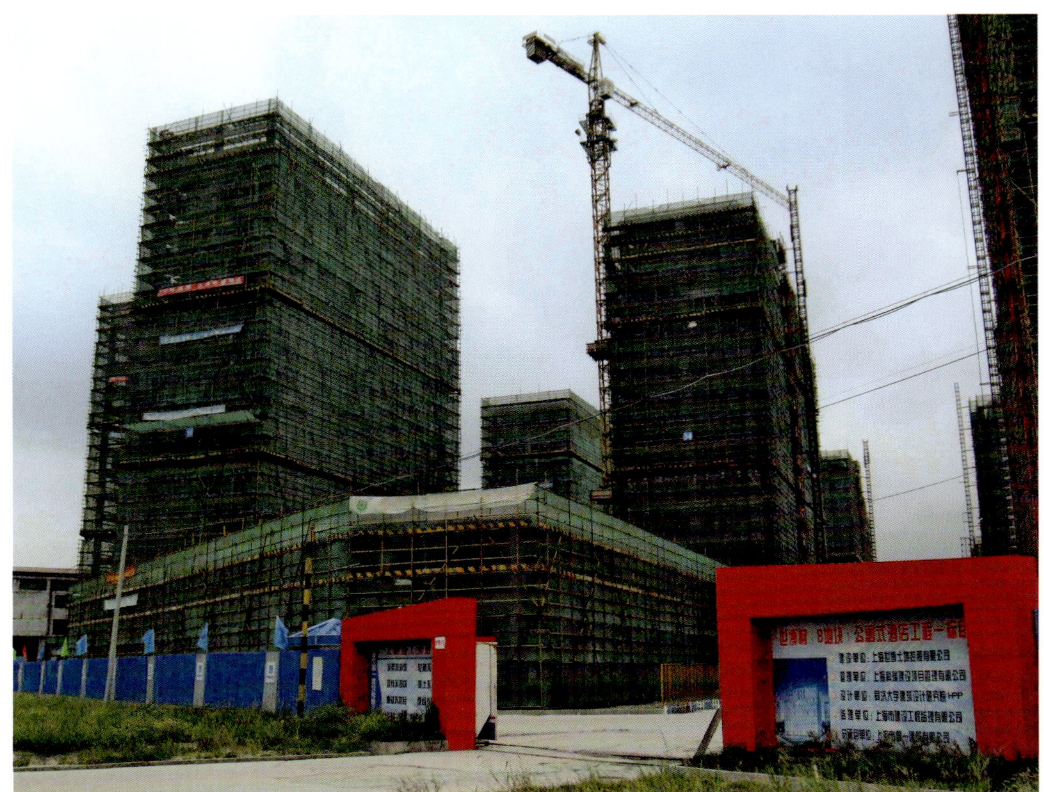

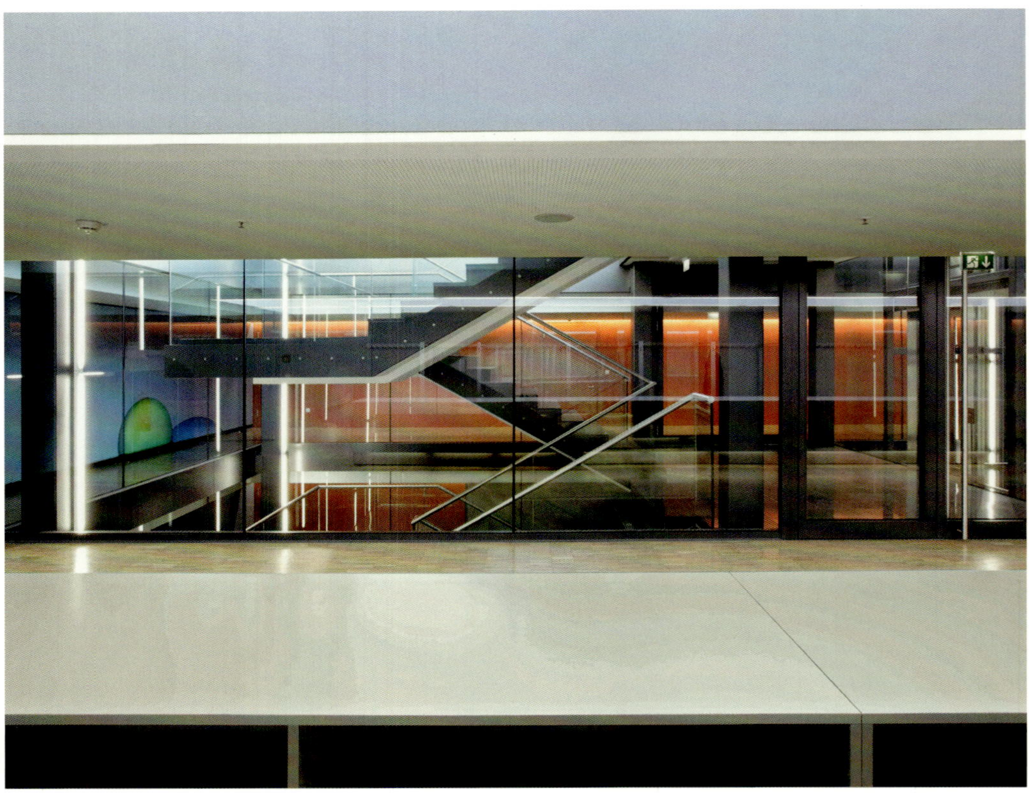

Dillmann Auditorium

This new building was inserted at a depth of six meters between the foundations of Dillmann High School, a protected historic structure. Due to this unusual location, the use of daylight became a central concern of the project's design. Horizontal rows of windows provide the multifunctional meeting room with natural light. The dematerialized glass pavilion ushers the visitor in and emphasizes the stairway, which seems like a sculpture set dramatically in front of a red wall.

Client: Dillmann Stiftung
Location: Stuttgart
GFA: 1,720 m²
Completion date: 2007

Materiality

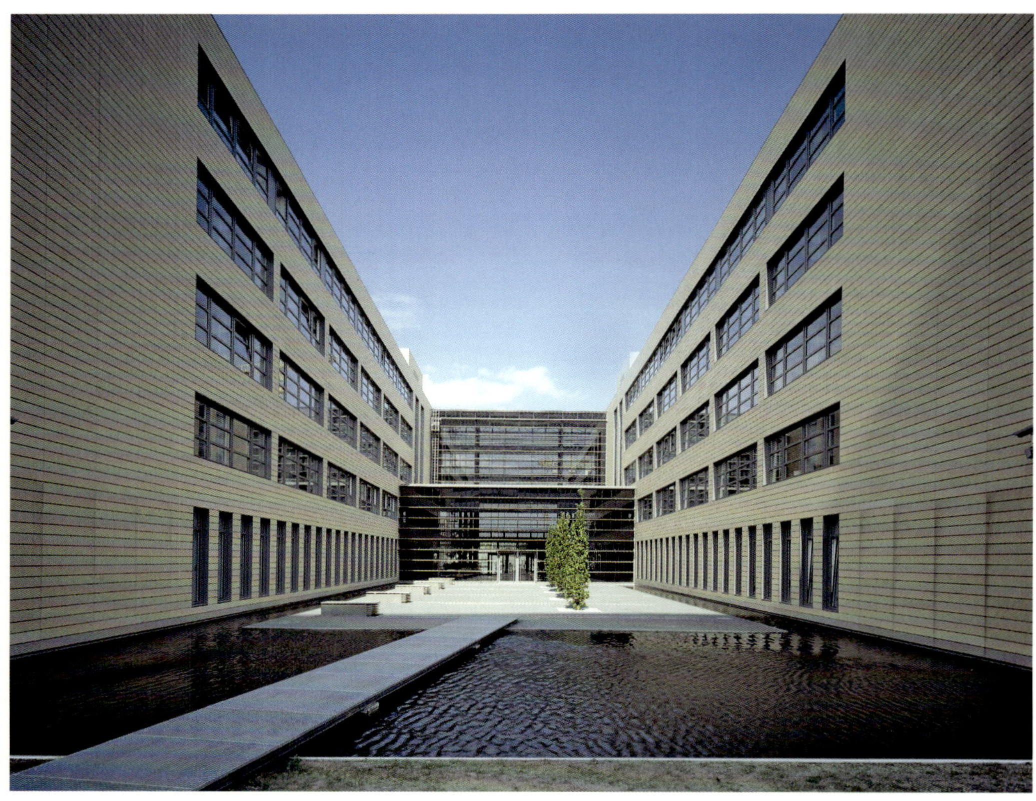

Hermes Insurance Building

The shell of this H-shaped, five-story building corresponds to the industrial architecture of the gasworks across the way in terms of materials, form, organization, and window division. The decision in favor of a rear-ventilated brick curtain wall façade reflects the desire to present a more contemporary interpretation of the traditional brick façade.

Client: Hermes Kreditversicherungs AG
Location: Hamburg
GFA: 14,871 m²
Work stations: 400
Completion date: 2001
Competition: 1st Prize, 1992

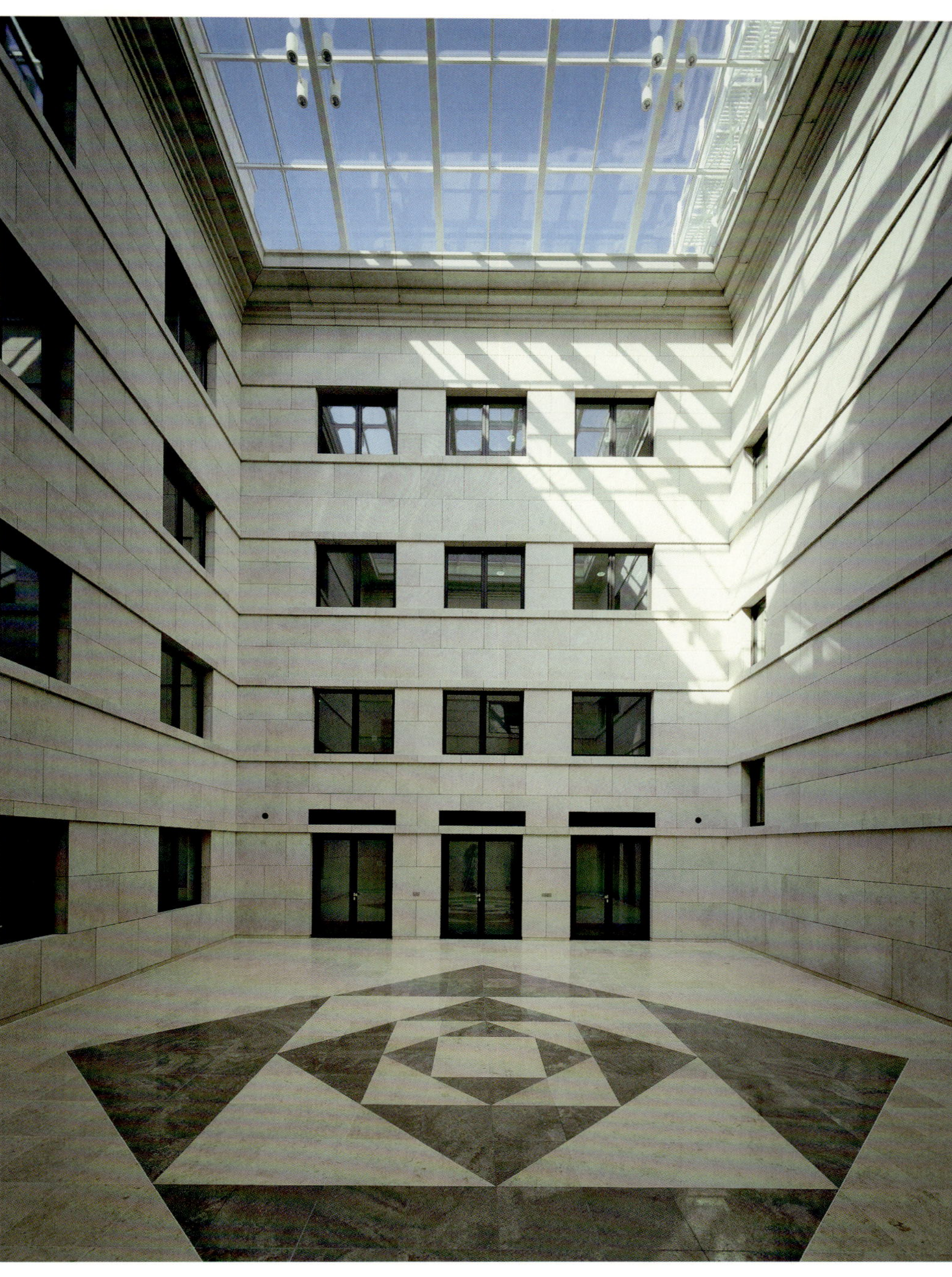

Japanese Embassy

After the decision to relocate the German capital to Berlin, the Japanese government decided to return to its former embassy building there, which had been used as a Japanese-German Center. However new use requirements dictated an expansion of the chancellery. As the result of a restricted architectural competition, the decision was made in favor of an expansion that allowed for the emergence of an homogenous overall building structure. The material and color concepts, as well as the design vocabulary, are all in keeping with the existing building.

Client: Japanese Foreign Ministry
Location: Berlin
GFA: 18,300 m²
Completion date: 2001
Architecture: HPP in collaboration with Ryohei Amemiya

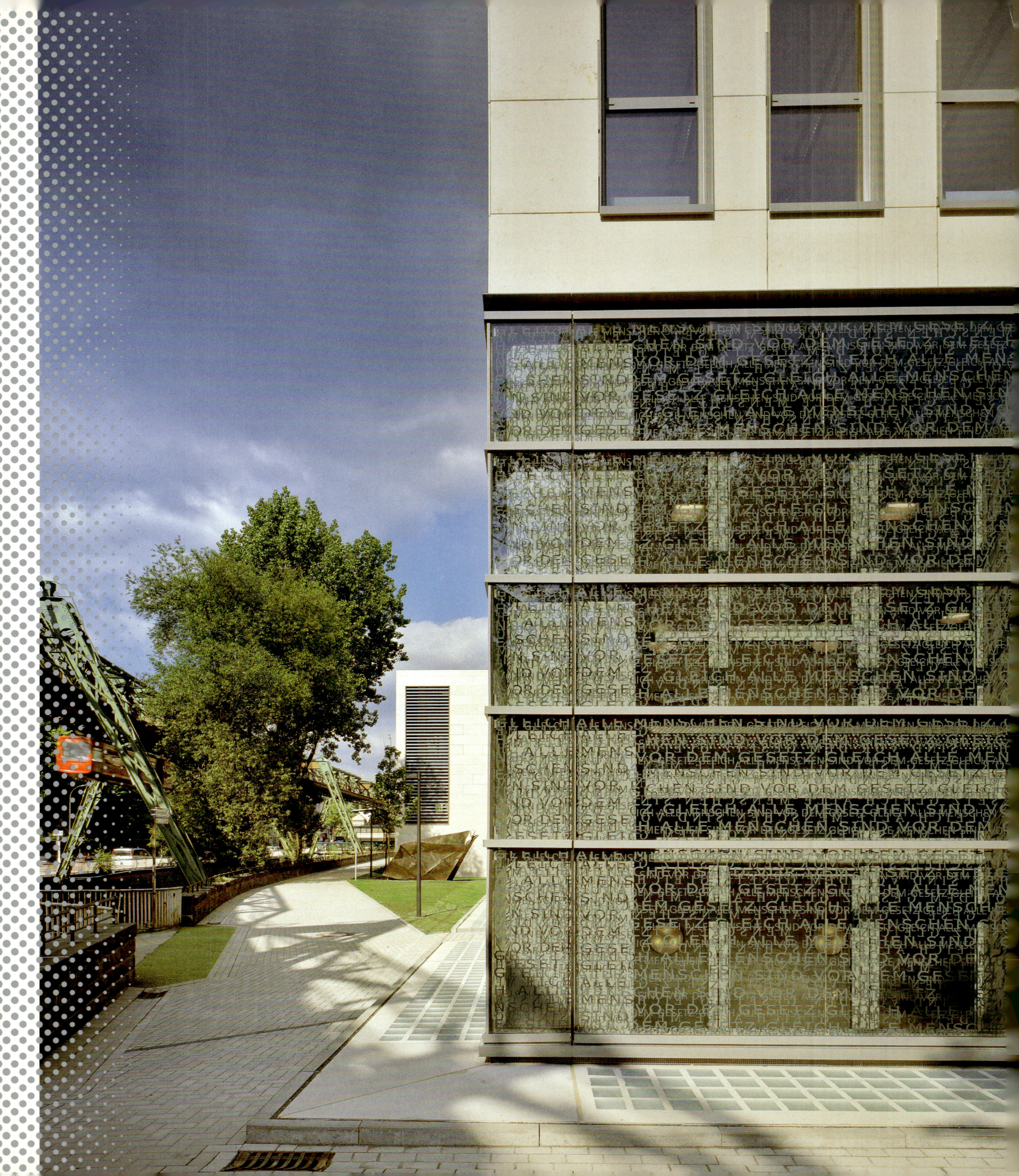
ALLE MENSCHEN SIND VOR DEM
VOR DEM GESETZ GLEICH

What constitutes the difference between the good and the extraordinary? What is it that fascinates us about a good shoe, the Cologne cathedral, or the Airbus A 380? Their distinction lies in their details and craftsmanship, in the understanding of the materials used to create them, and in the engineer-like handling of their construction and design characteristics, as well as in the scaled and proportional use of all of these elements after considering the objects themselves and their reflection within their environment.

The technology of extraordinary things is what generates our fascination. The sewn perimeter of the inner sole makes a shoe resilient and sets it apart from the short-lived, mass-produced shoe with a rubber sole. The Cologne cathedral acquired its importance in architectural history less for its size than for the unique craftsmanship of its masonry and the enormous engineering effort required to build it, both of which give the building its singular appearance. The breathtaking groined arches, the extremely slender piers, and the supporting structure of struts hold the cathedral within its "corset" and allow its double towers to extend upward and vanish into the sky. And with what magic power do our birds of steel fly high above our cities? They accomplish these feats faster and faster, becoming ever larger and longer, but not without fulfilling the most rigorous safety requirements. The recently inaugurated A 380 double-decker airbus is the latest sensation in the aerospace sector. A product of the highest engineering, it was made possible by committed planning, the greatest understanding of the task, and attention to countless details.

In architecture, tradition and engineering are to be found in equal measure. Both of these are expressed in the details, as demonstrated by the Justice Center in Wuppertal, a new structure erected in the historical context of the preexisting court buildings on a small island in the Wupper River. Here, the heavy reposes on the light: natural stone rests on a transparent plinth. Large, natural stone slabs of the Jurassic period set off by sand-covered joints acquire a monolithic appearance. They rest quietly on the double-shelled, formed-glass plinth, within whose interstice elevators travel, connecting the meeting halls with the cell block.

The handling and use of traditional materials on the one hand and the innovative function and individually designed form of the plinth on the other both underscore the uniqueness, the newness, and the quality of the Justice Center. And on the outer pane of the circumferential glass plinth, a message indicates in unmistakable clarity the essence of our basic social order: "All human beings are equal before the law." This silk-screened detail of the Justice Center appears in Rotis, Tahoma, and Times typefaces and its color is RAL 7000.

Detail Wuppertal Justice Center

Client: **BLB NRW** | Location: **Wuppertal** | GFA: **25,625 m²**
Completion date: **2005** | Competition: **1st Prize, 2001**
Award: **BDA Wuppertal 2007, for the recognition of good buildings**

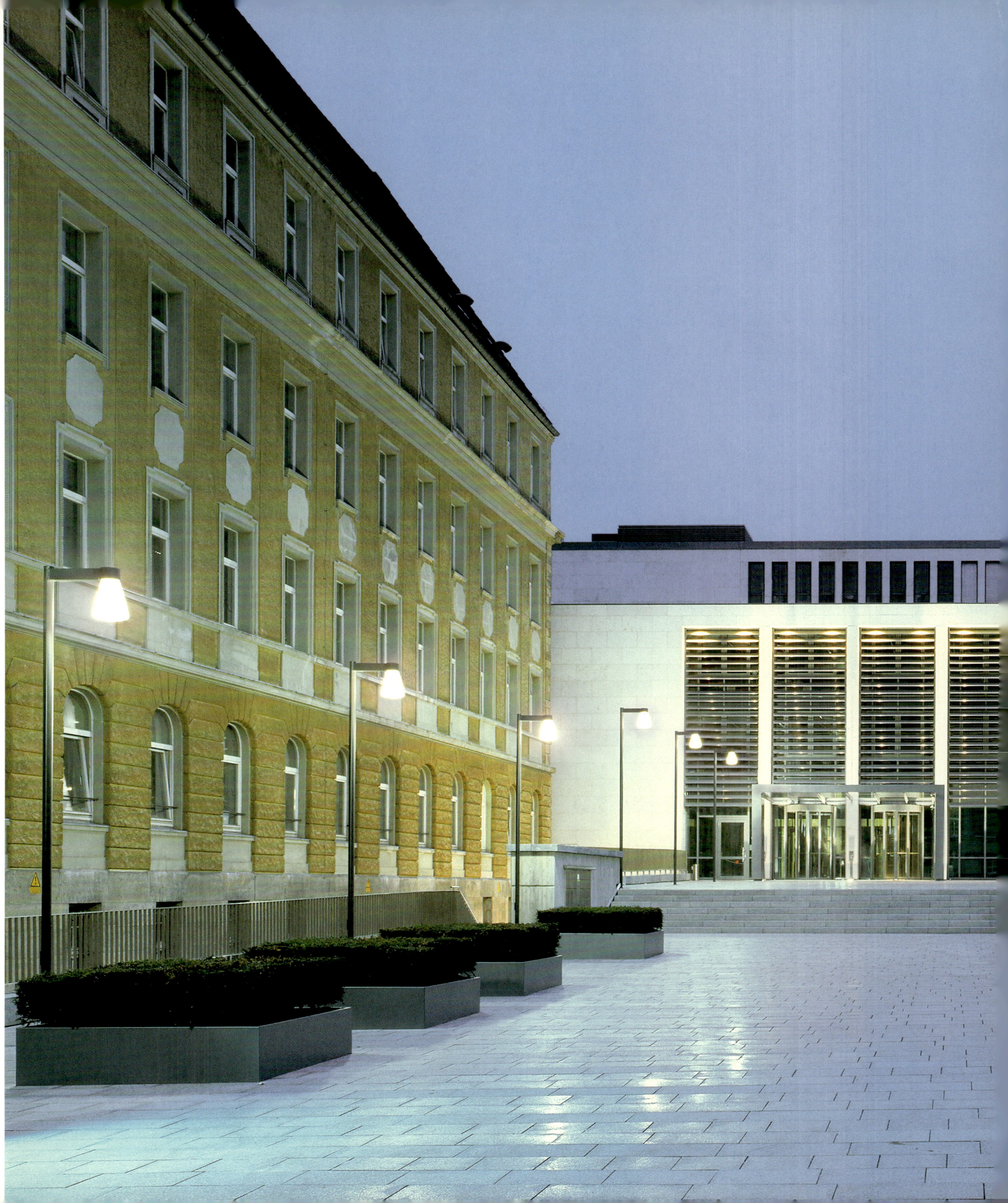

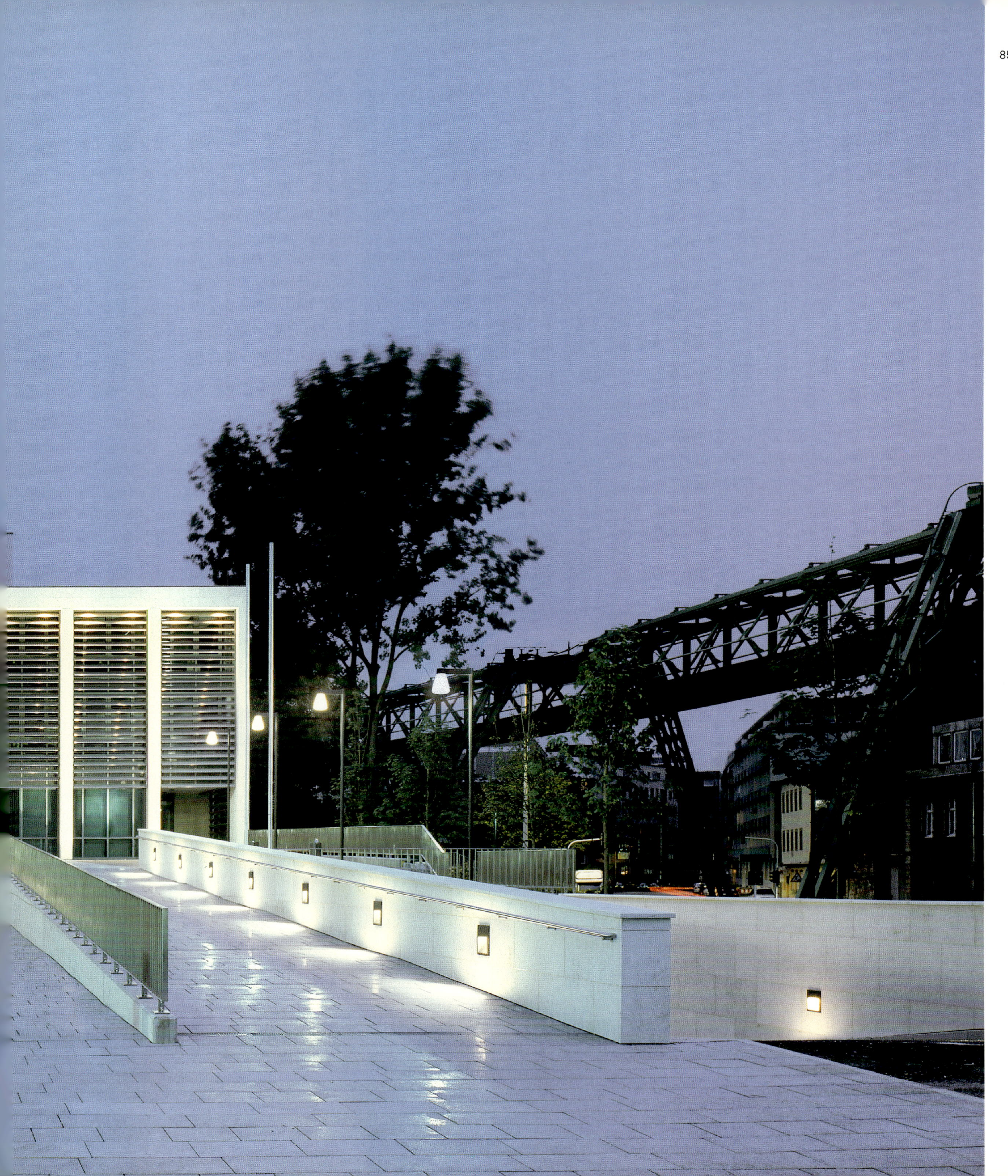

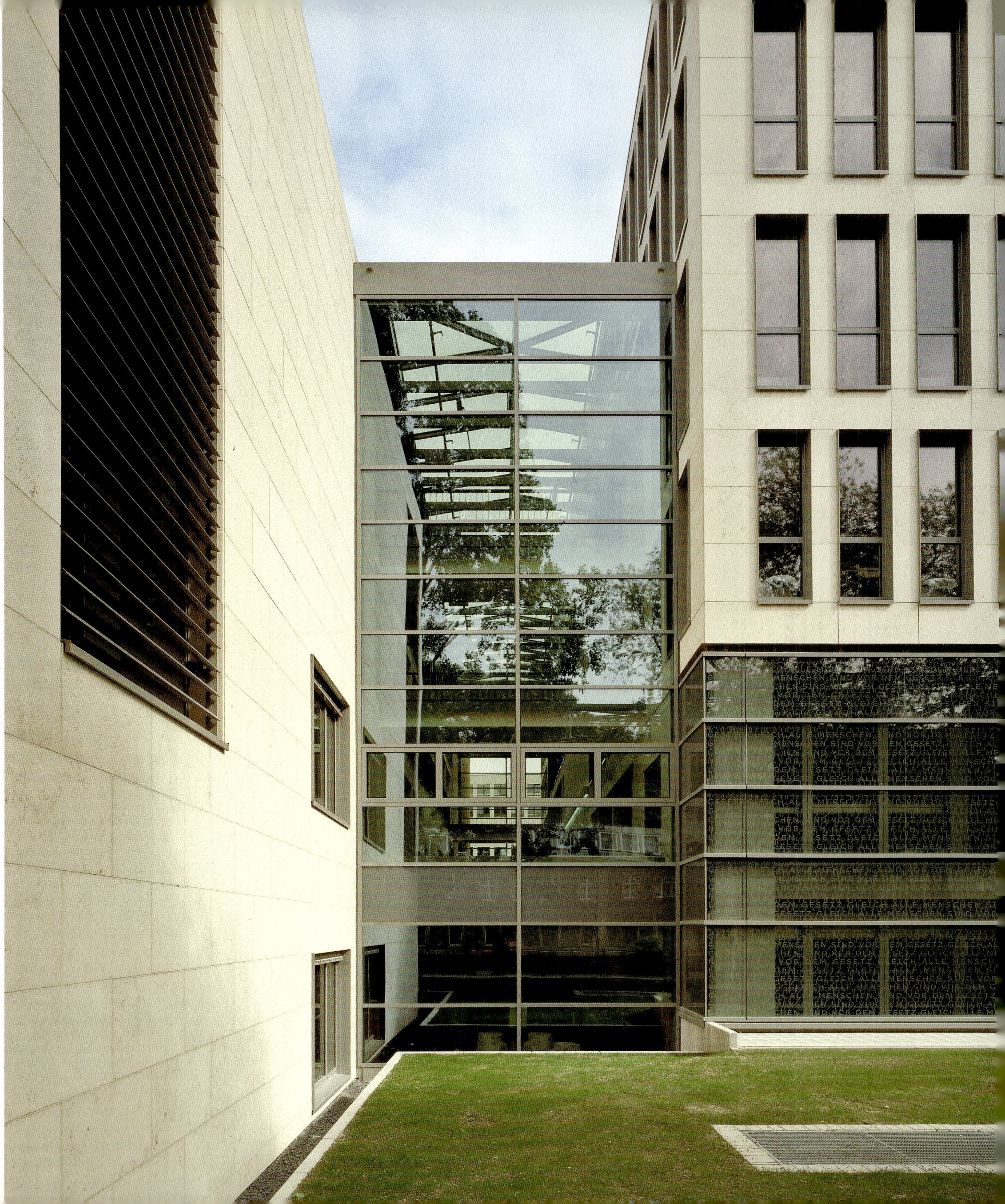
ALLE MENSCHEN SIND VOR DEM GESETZ

← Transition from access building to new building
↞ Courtyard of the Justice Center with a view of the new access building

Waiting area in the transition hall

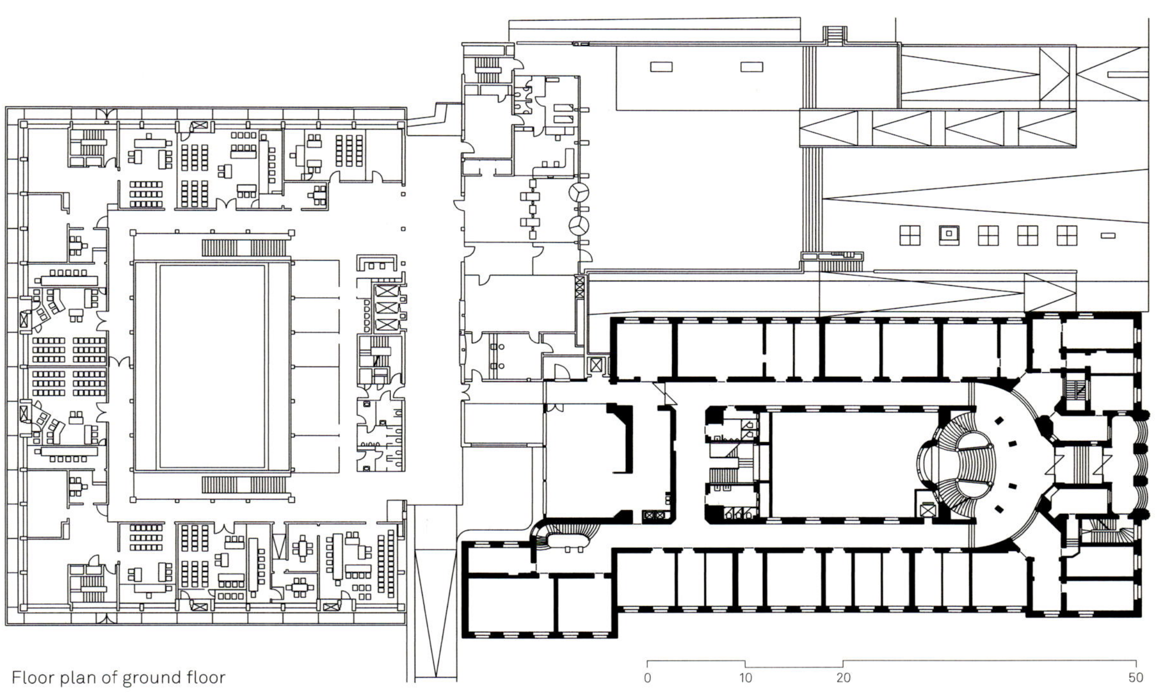

Floor plan of ground floor

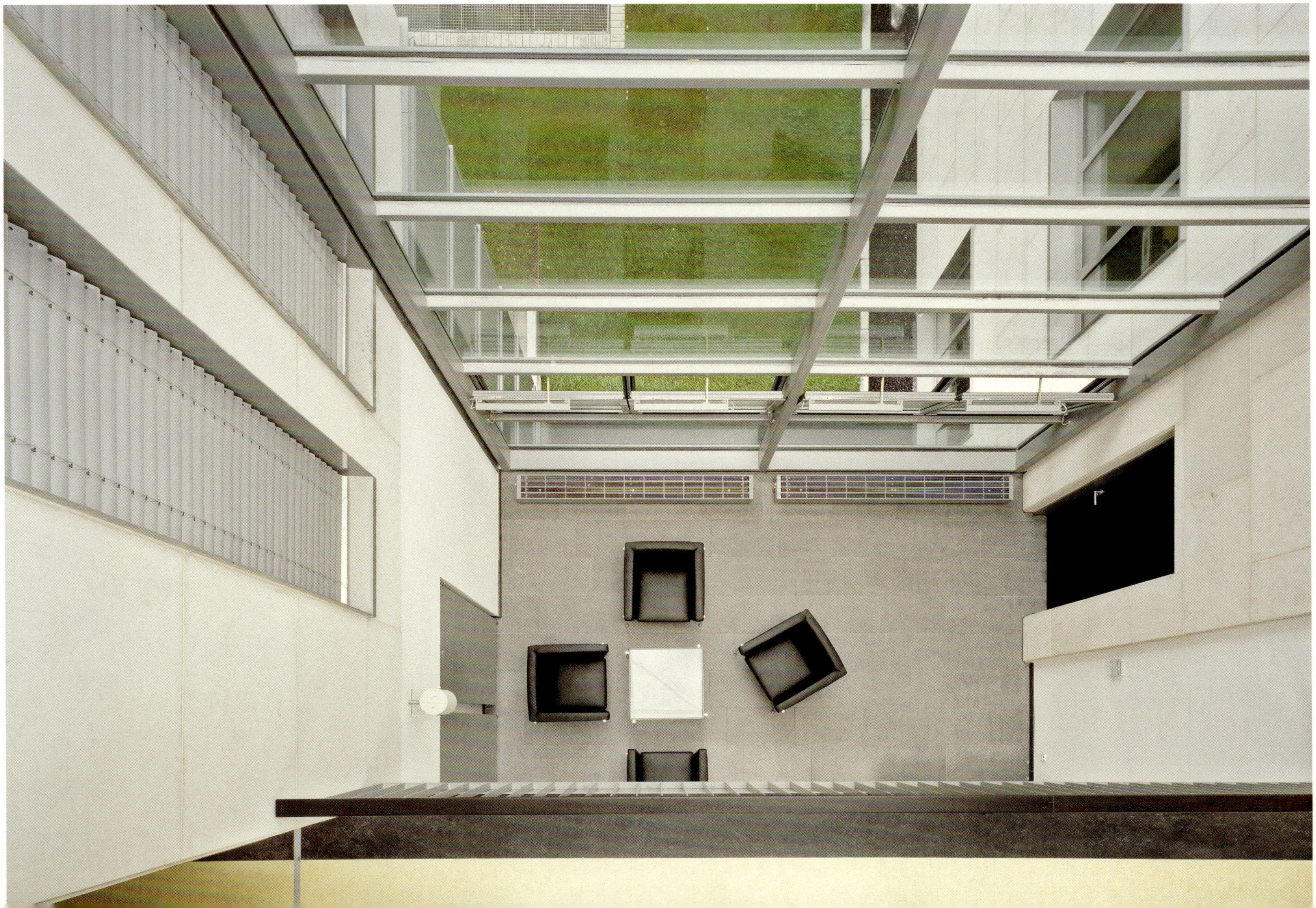

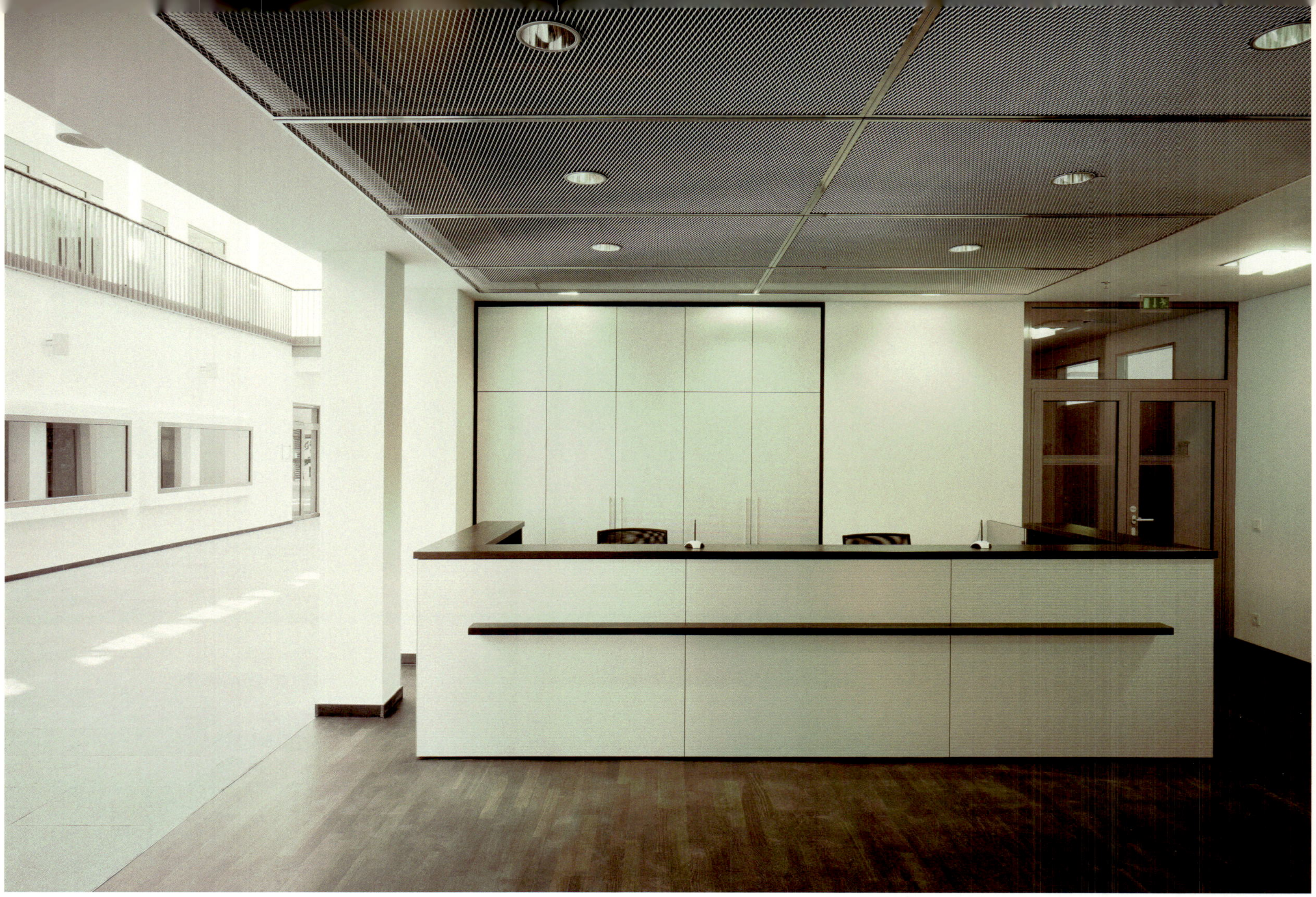

Central service point

→ Transition hall

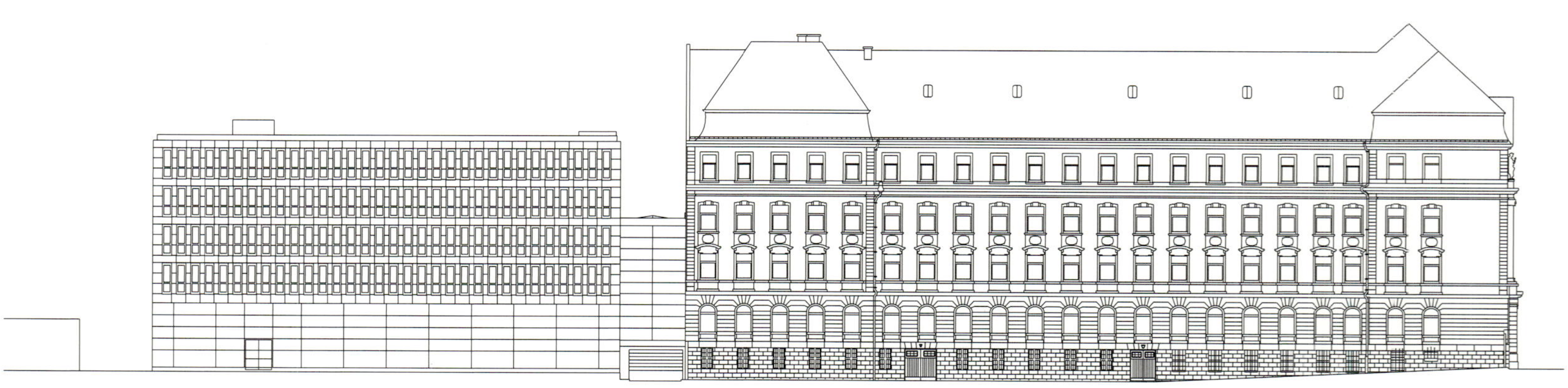

South view

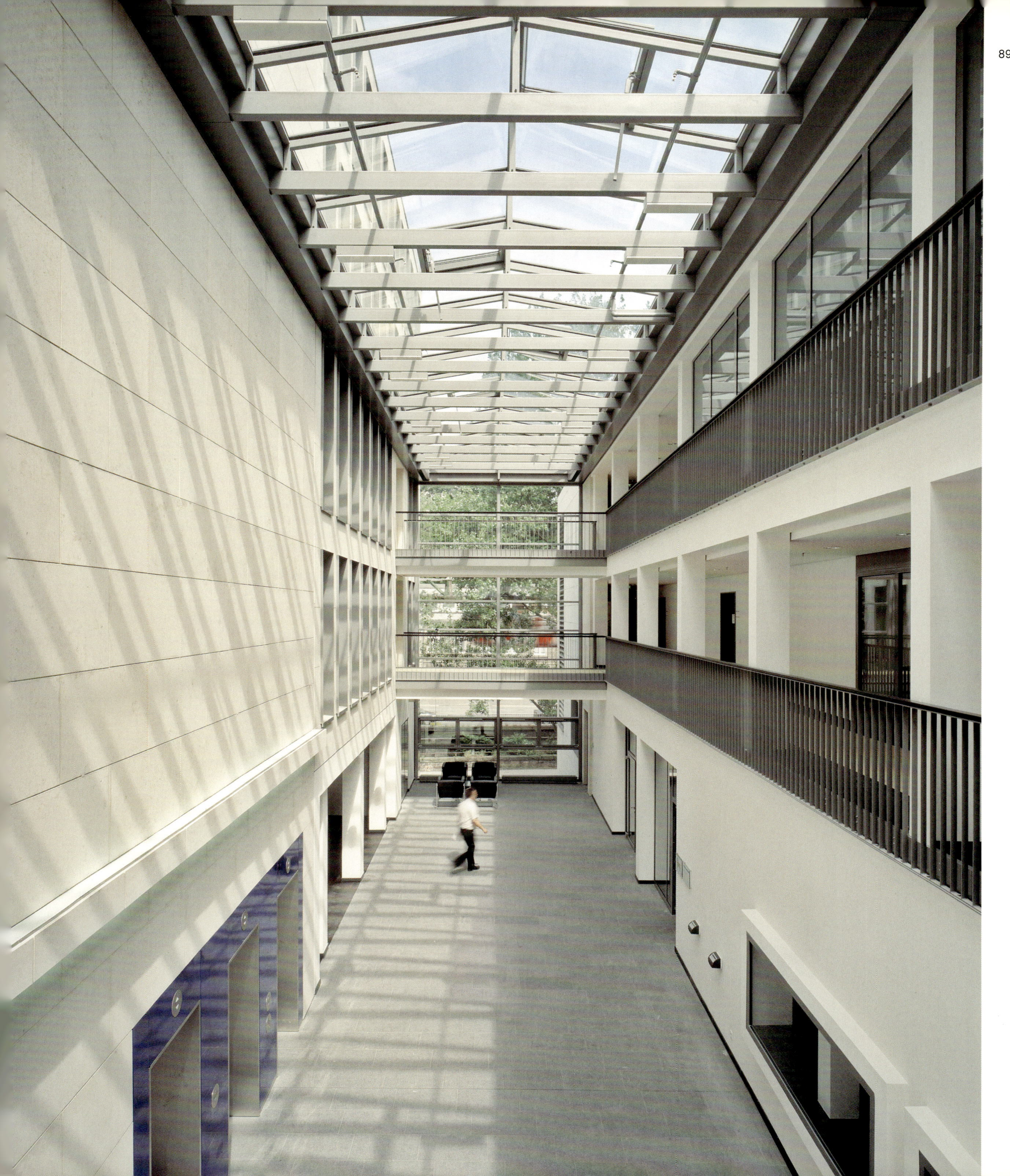

The Wuppertal Justice Center The new Justice Center erected in the context of two historic, landmark-protected court buildings on an island in the Wupper River known as the "Island of Justice" is a work of architecture caught between history and the zeitgeist of today. The new building's design measures up to the extraordinary urbanistic importance of its location and, in the process, the halls of justice become a transparent, citizen-oriented institution.

The demolition of the preexisting building on the site—an aluminum high-rise from the nineteen-sixties—made possible a new definition of the architectural complex on the island. Because of the special location, and in analogy to the existing Wuppertal urban structures, the new Justice Center was moved to a square that already had an identity. It is surrounded on three sides by the historical regional court, the district court, and the new building. The fourth side is defined by the Hartmannufer, the river, and the elevated rail line.

The Justice Center is divided into three areas: the new six-story building with its central access structure and the two preexisting buildings. The new structure continues the style of the traditional court building as a massive structure with a perforated façade, and with its proportionality and materiality, it provides the culmination of the building complex on the "Island of Justice." At the same time it opens up to the surrounding urban space thanks to its two-story, glassed-in lower level.

Entry to all parts of the Justice Center is gained via a three-story access building made of natural stone. The central service point for the incoming public is located on the ground floor and incorporates the constable's area with a security gate, the court cashier, and the newly designed cafeteria, which is found in the transition area that leads to the old building. The old and new buildings are thus equally accessible from the entryway. The training center, which has a view of the courtyard, is located in the two upper stories of the access building. A glassed-in distribution hall provides the spatial link to the new court building.

The new six-story building is presented as a single, monolithic structure. Large-scale natural stone slabs are placed above a glassed-in lower level. In this area of the court building, the detention and courtroom areas, which are clearly defined and easy to locate, are arranged around the atrium. The clear organization of the access and use structure facilitates optimal visitor orientation. Two flights of stairs along the inner courtyard façades connect the two hall levels. The detention area and the adjoining rooms are located in the basement. To facilitate the escort of prisoners between the cell block and the courtroom, there are innovative elevators between the layers of the double-shell glass façade. The other divisions of the county and state courts are located in the four upper stories of the new administrative building. The classically structured work rooms of the judges and the administrative officials are arranged along well-lit corridors within the building.

On the one hand, the glassed-in lower level of the new court building demonstrates the development of the justice system into an open, accessible institution: trials become transparent. On the other hand, it is also the structural foundation upon which the building's unmistakable message is found: the motto of Article 3 of Germany's constitution, "All human beings are equal before the law," is silk-screened on the outer glass surface of the building's lower level.

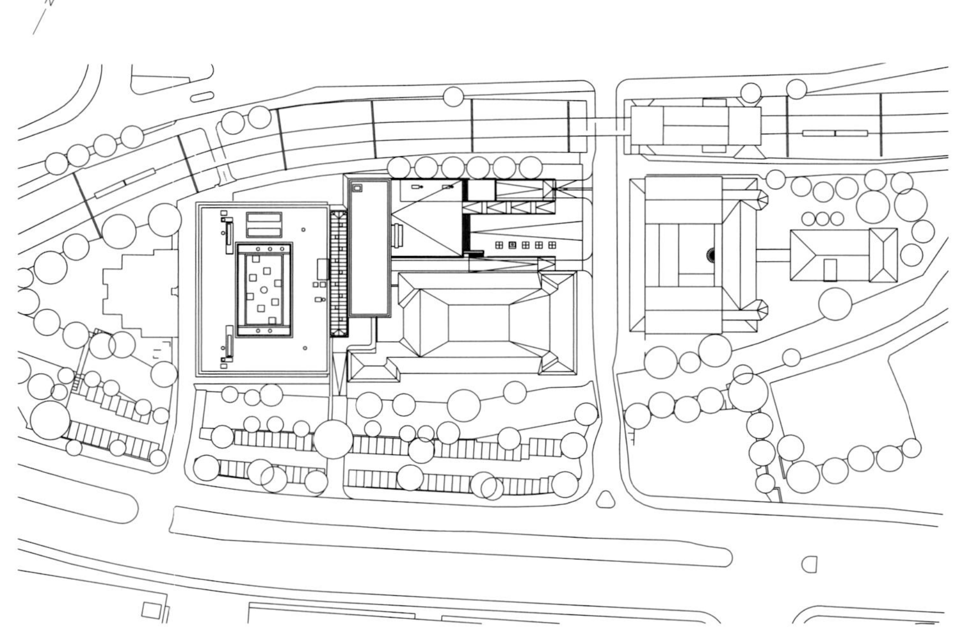

Site plan

→ Access building and county courthouse
→→ "Island of Justice" in the Wupper River

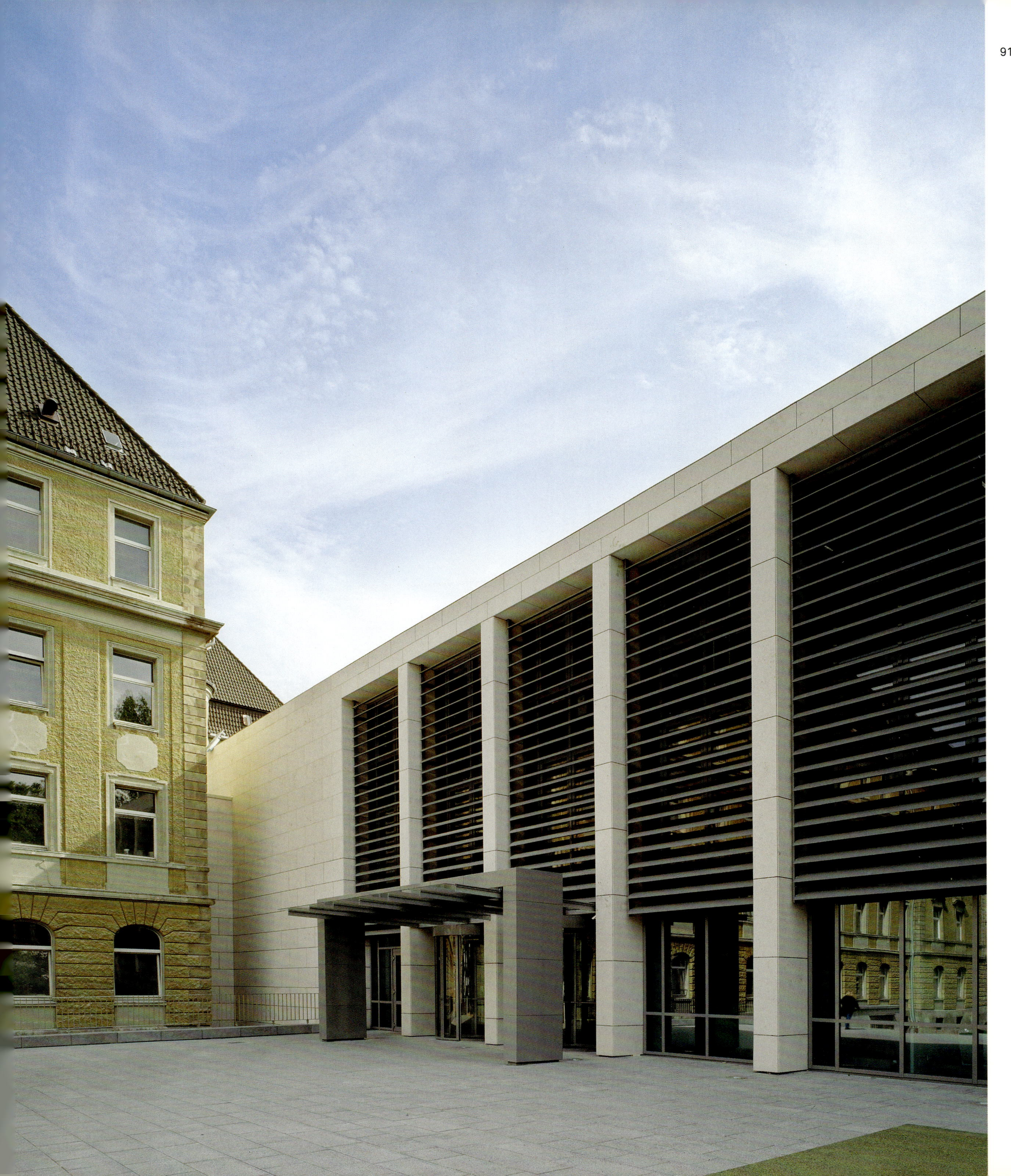

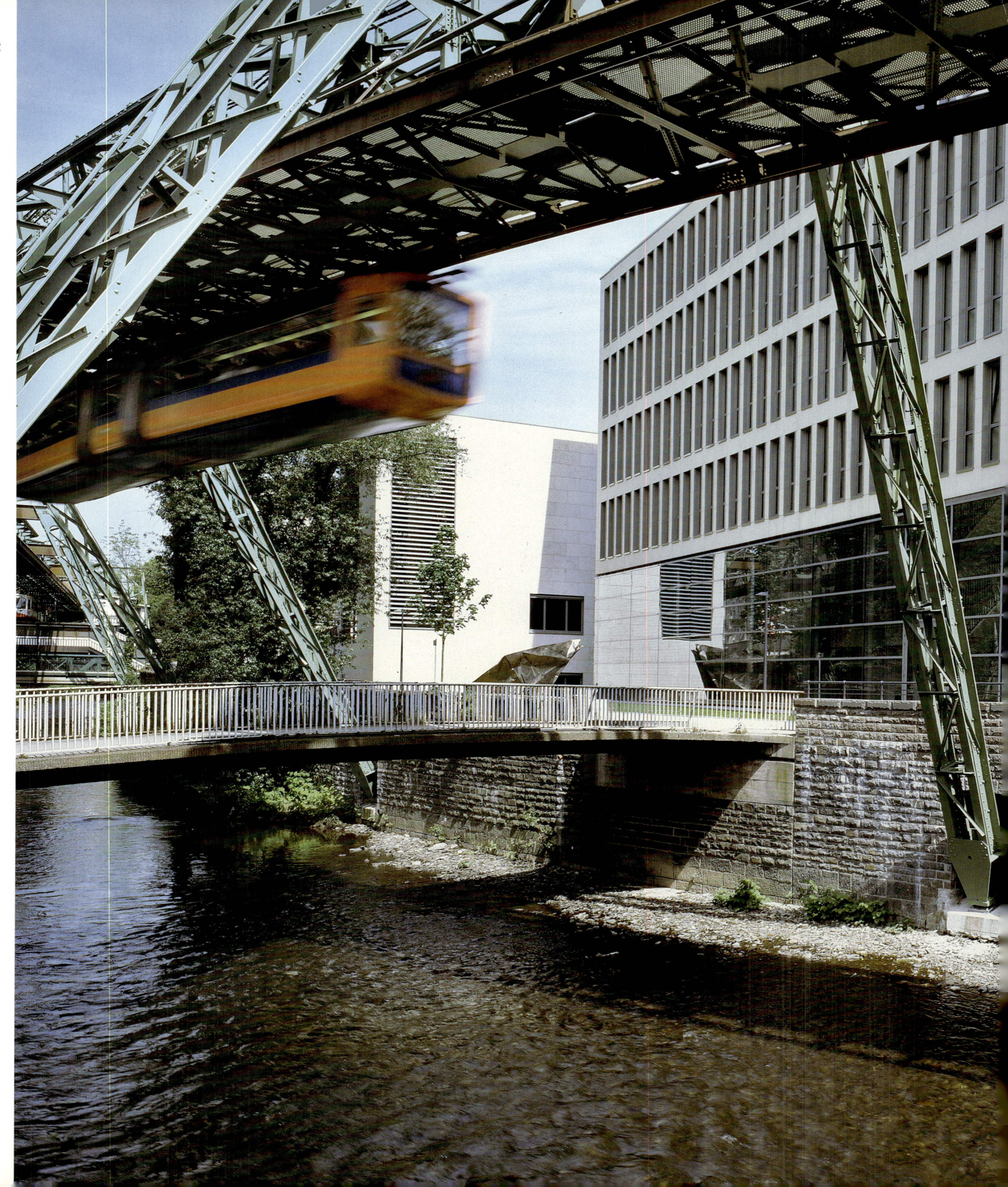

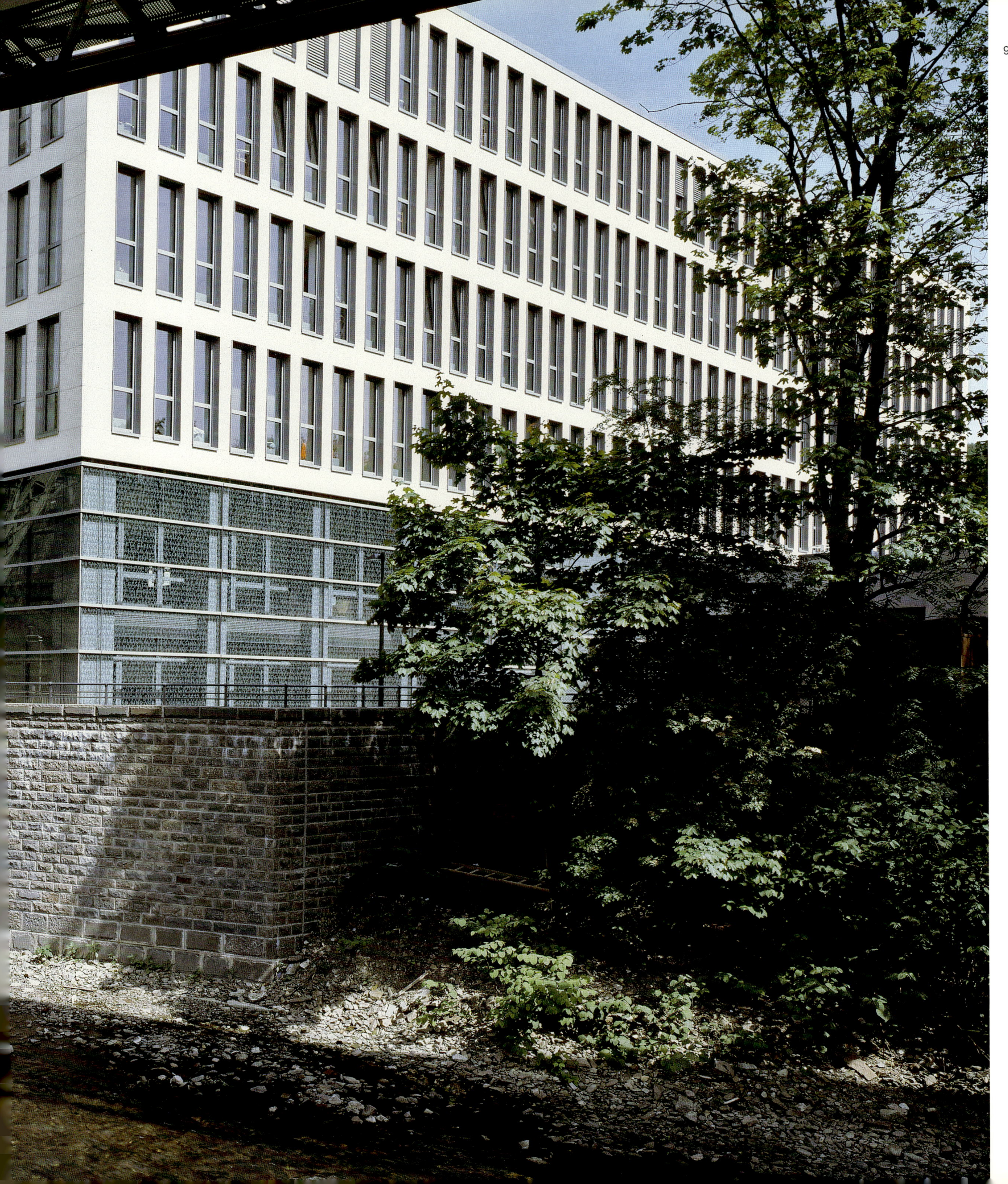

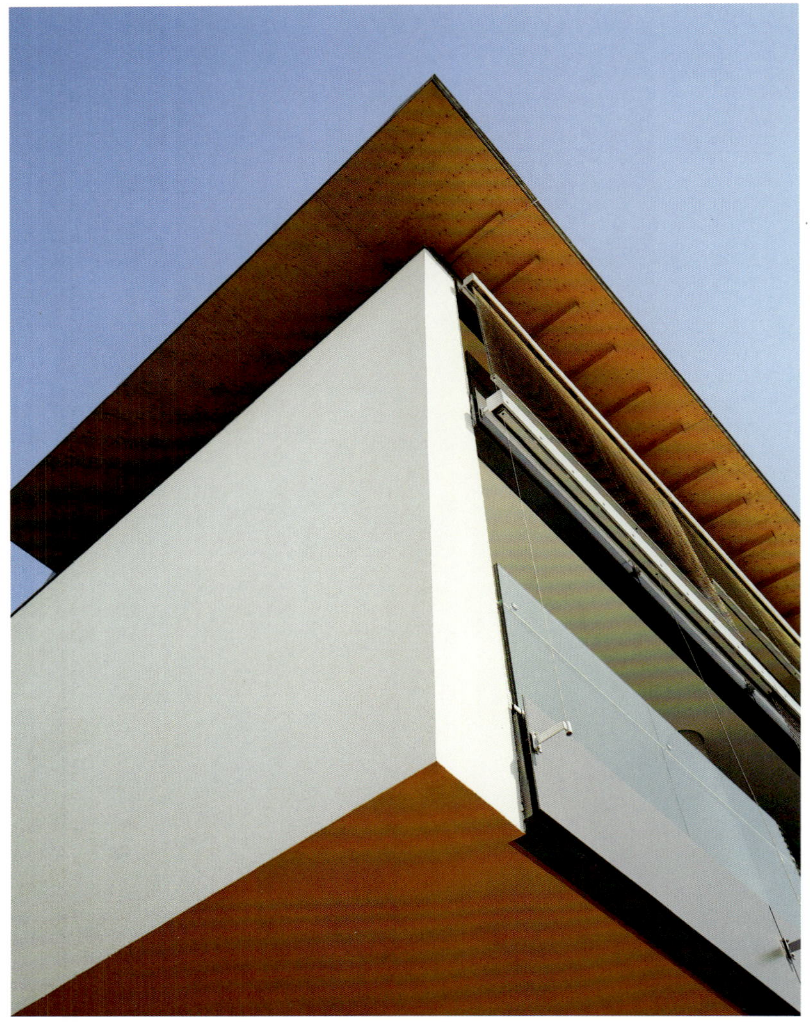

Detail

Robert Koch Clinic

A three-story expansion building based on existing structures was able to provide a design answer with a free form beyond the predefined grids and building sites. Starting from the necessary connection with the preexisting structure, two building wings playfully develop into an enclosed park. The molding of the lean-to roofs was fully exploited, thereby drawing a precise yet gentle boundary of the outer spaces. Depending on the situation, the façades are open and extroverted or closed and introverted. The imposing number of trees in the Robert Koch Park serves as a starting point for several considerations regarding the project's color concept: autumnal hues, ranging from pale yellow to the deepest of reds, are transferred to the building with verve in lines and surfaces of different intensities on the façades and within the structure's interior.

Client: Städtisches Klinikum St. Georg
Location: Leipzig
GFA: 9,737 m²
Beds: 144
Completion date: 2004
Competition: 1st Prize, 2001

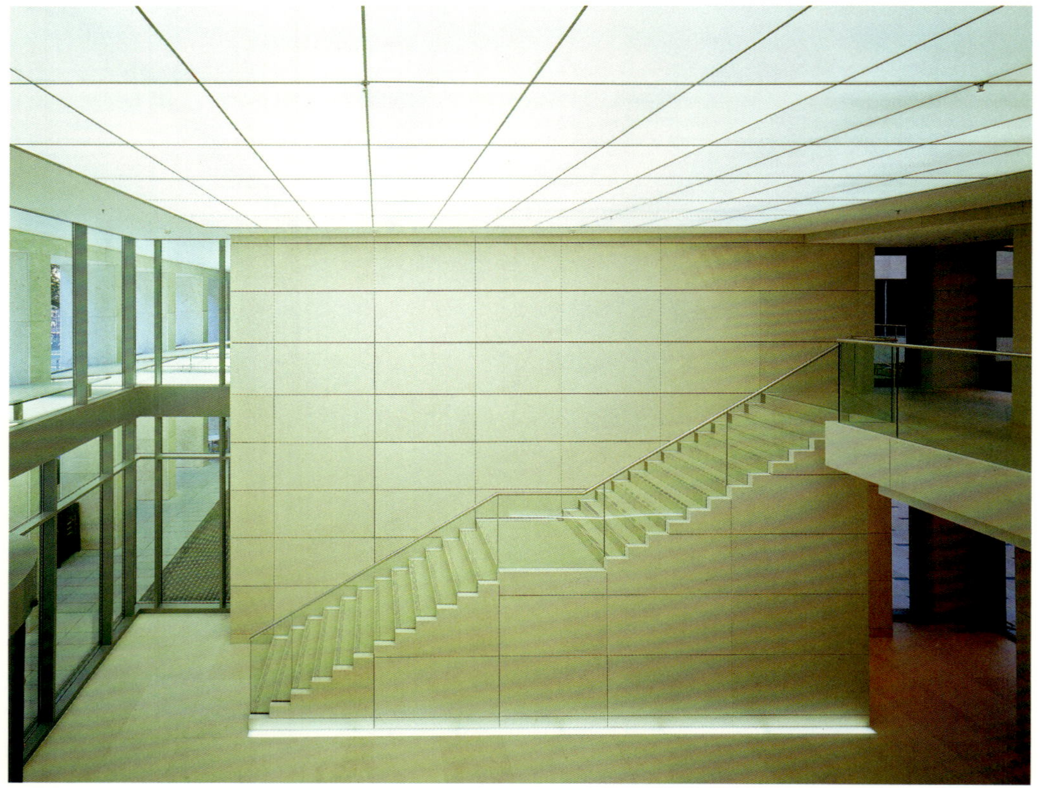

Clifford Chance

This urban building block located between Königsallee and Breite Strasse wins the viewer over with its compactness. The functions of office, hotel, school, restaurant, and wellness center are all combined in an exciting but—because of the disciplined detail and material language—nonetheless homogenous building complex. The office spaces are accessed by their own entrance on the Königsallee. The two-story space sets the stage for the extremely reductionist stair unit with its illuminated ceiling and the light-colored slabs of natural stone on the walls and the floor. The avoidance of anything superfluous directs the gaze to what is essential and creates a balance of lightness and weight.

Client: DKÖ-Objektgesellschaft
Königsallee Dr. Herbert Ebertz KG
Location: Düsseldorf
GFA: 9,500 m²
Completion date: 2005

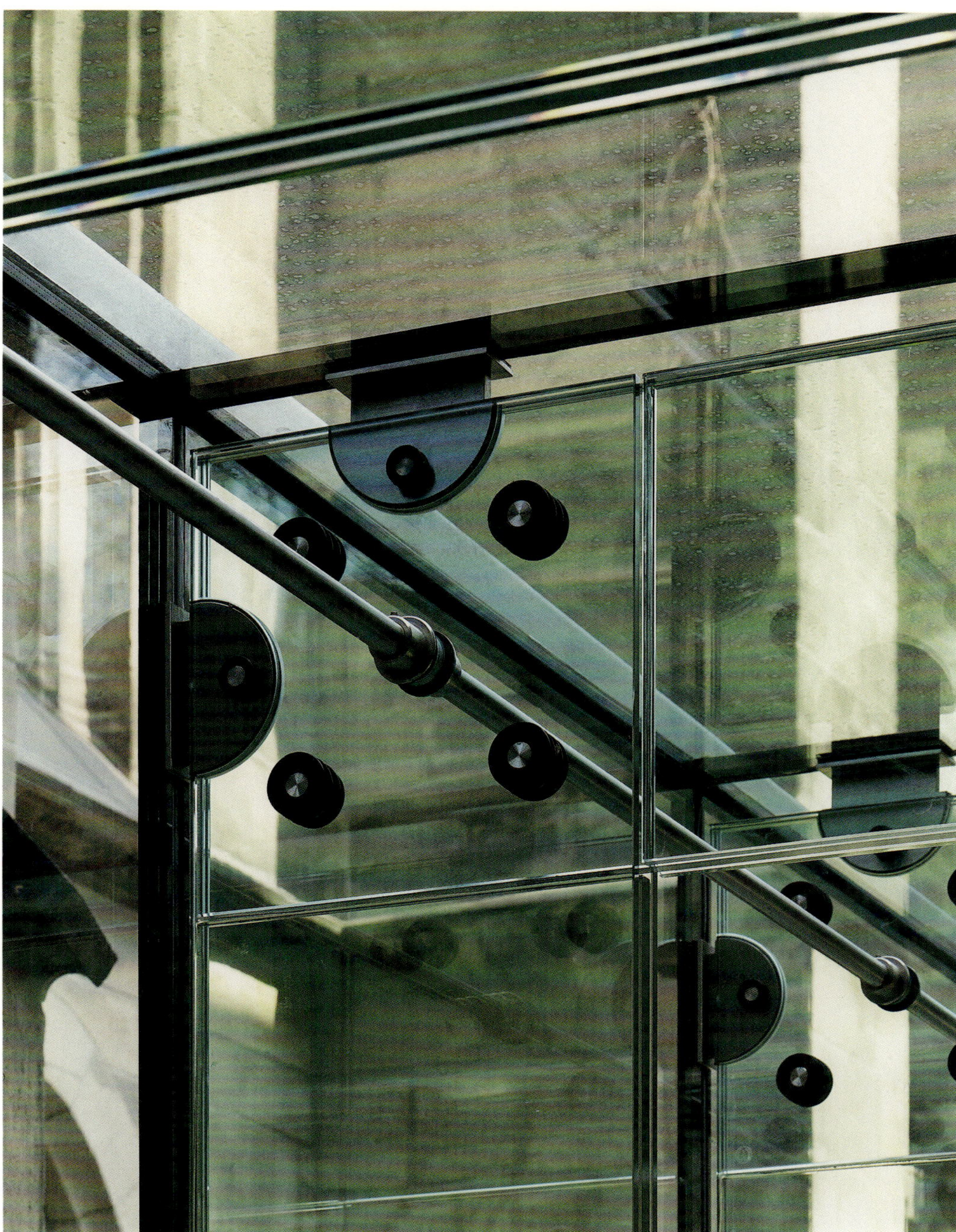

The Thomasshop in the Square of the Church of St. Thomas

For many years an unsightly souvenir store prevented an unencumbered view of Leipzig's world-renowned Thomaskirche (Church of St. Thomas) in Leipzig. But what could be done with this otherwise necessary facility? After several unsuccessful attempts were made, a suggestion was put forward that proved acceptable to all parties concerned. The project that resulted from this is an almost dematerialized glass cube, which in spite of the limited spatial context does not have a cramped feeling. It is a building structure reduced to a single material and a few details.

Client: **Ev.-Luth. Kirchengemeinde St. Thomas**
Location: **Leipzig**
GFA: **54 m^2**
Completion date: **2003**

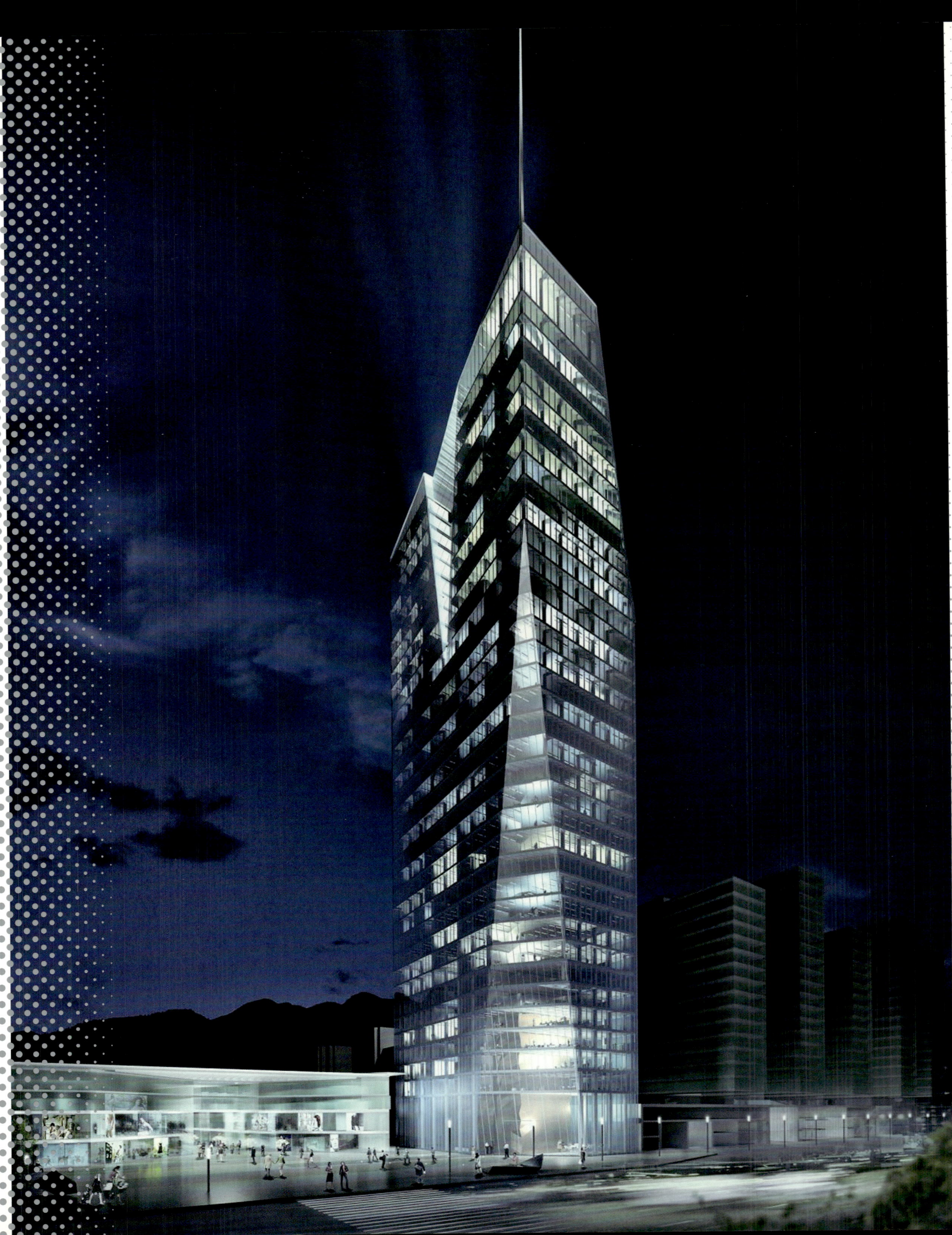

Significance Europe Tower

Client: **ECE-Gruppe and Advance Properties** | Location: **Sofia** | GFA: **69,000 m²**
Height: **209.5 m** | Completion date: **2011** | International competition: **1st Prize, 2007**

A summer stroll through glowing, straw-yellow wheat fields . . . Every single plant fascinates when seen from close up: borne by a stalk pushing up from the pale green leaves, lush ears crown the sheaves. It is an enchanting work of art wrought by nature. The path is fringed by soft, red poppy flowers. Cropping up every now and again in little groups at the edge of the field, they are no less fascinating to look at in the utter beauty of their otherness. From a distance, the wheat field gives the impression of a light-green carpet. The many sheaves melt into a multitude as one's distance from them increases. Only the corn poppies can be distinguished as individual points of red in the yellow sea of wheat.

Although both corn and poppy are comparable in size when seen from up close, the otherness of the poppy becomes more apparent in a glance from the distance. This is above all due to its signature red color, by which the poppy sets itself apart from the wheat at a sufficient remove.

Significance can be expressed in different forms, especially in the medium of architecture through factors such as height, breadth, materials, light, transparency, massiveness, and color. Significance is always expressed by external appearance. Volume, surfaces, and the materials employed all combine to create the unmistakable character of each building. Meaning lays bare and communicates. By the degree of its significance architecture occupies space.

Independence is a formulation of significance, and this identity allows conclusions to be drawn about a building's users and location or the company that commissioned the structure. Every building has a chance to become significant in the planning phase and at the same time by this uniqueness to develop an added value. For the city it is a "beacon project," an indicator of development. For the clients, on the other hand, it is a marketing tool, which works out as an additional sort of yield per square meter. And for a company, an appropriately custom-made piece of architecture communicates its corporate identity and attitude. Finally, in architecture, significance underscores the pride in the creation of something else: a clear, beautiful aesthetic.

Just like the poppy at the edge of the path, the Europe Tower in Sofia will also be seen from a great distance. Because of its physical characteristics, its height of more than 200 meters and its formal expression give it an imposing significance. The Europe Tower will broadcast power and dominance. However, at a second glance we will become aware of its other attributes, which go beyond the pure projection of power. The design of the building structure and the crystalline form of the surface are an homage to the omnipresent Vitosha Mountains, which almost completely surround Sofia and are visible from every point in the city. The mountains are part of the city's identity. The Europe Tower bears the expression of this crystalline, craggy, angular identity into the city. And the mountain chain is reflected from the surface of the façade, thereby completing the Europe Tower's main design ideas of significance, independence, and identity.

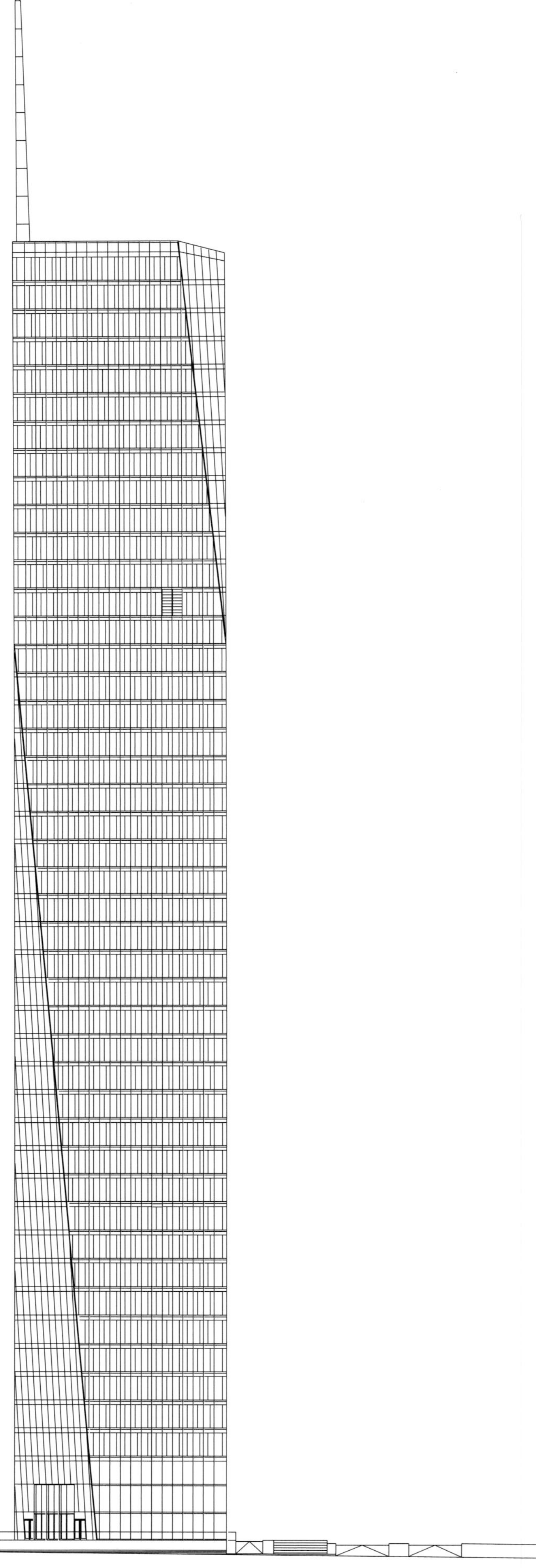

Southeast view

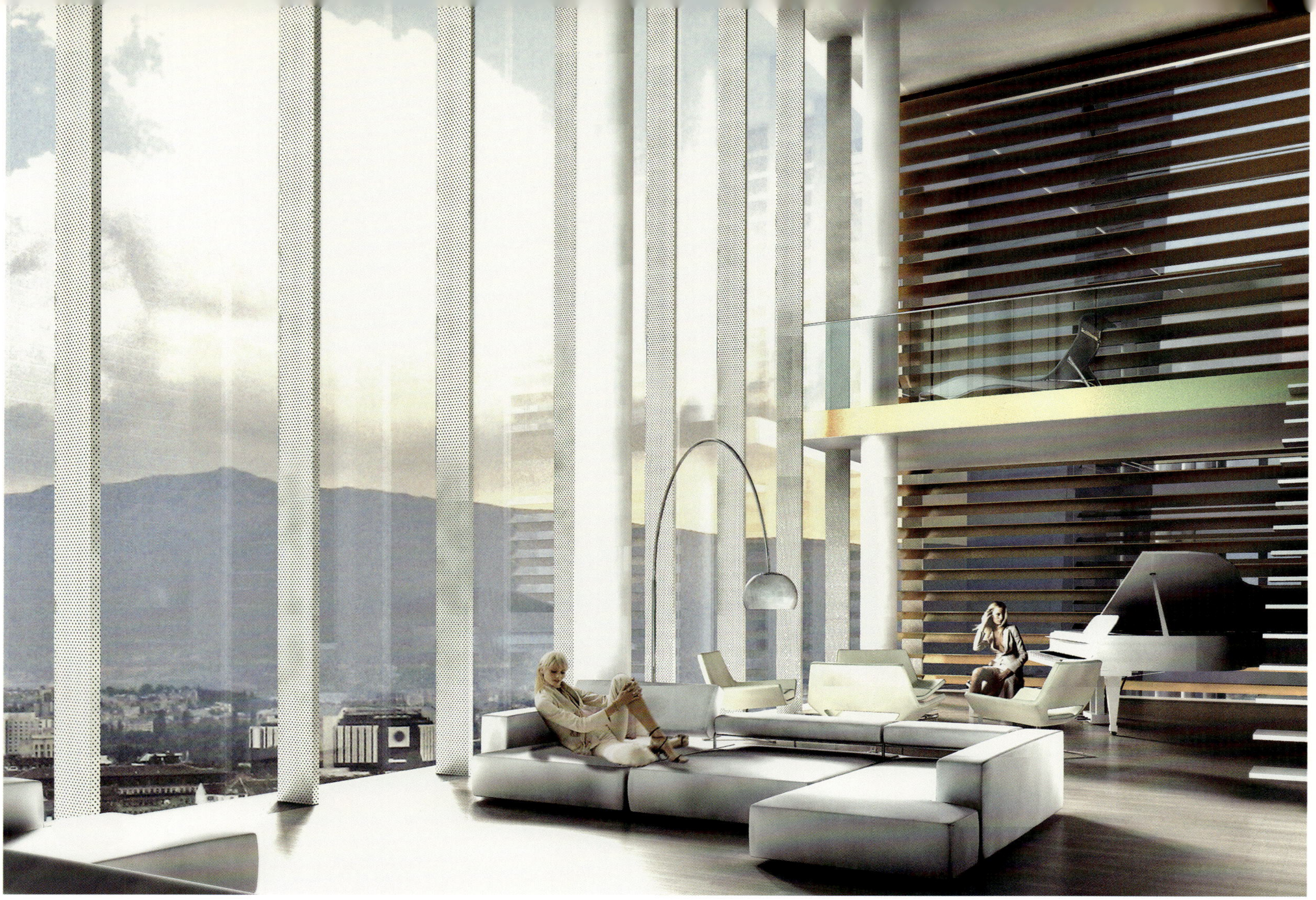

Apartment level 38

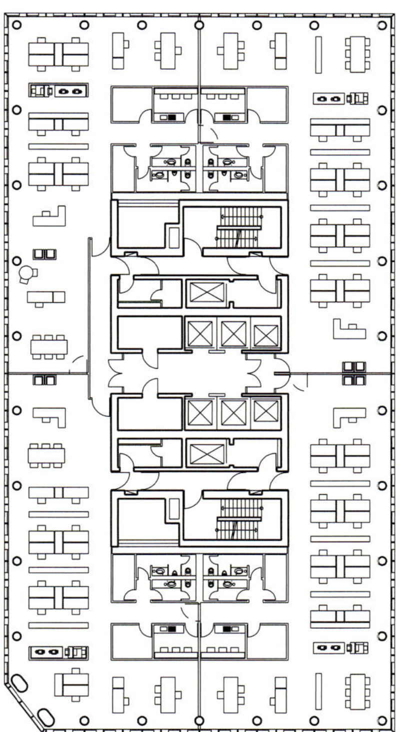

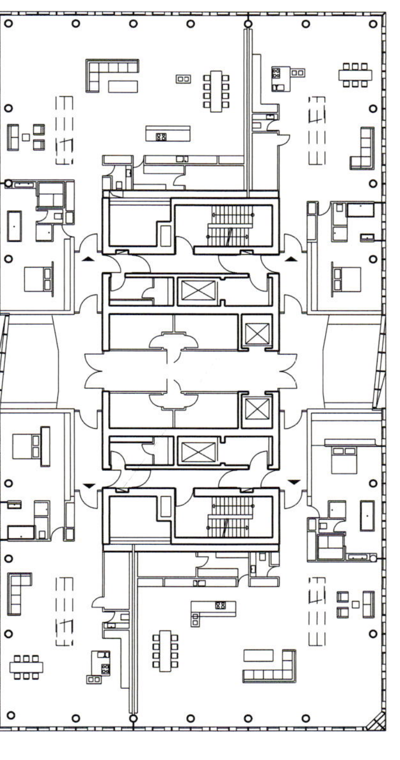

General floor plan and floor plan of apartment level

The Europe Tower The design for the highest building in Sofia originated with an international competition in 2007. Beginning in 2011, the Europe Tower will provide the initiating spark for urban development in a new district in the middle of the city on an industrial waste area. At the same time, with a height of 210 meters, it will become a significant new visual trademark of the rising Bulgarian metropolis.

The building's design idea is derived from a reflection of nature in architecture. Sofia's omnipresent massif led to the idea of sculpturally playing with a simple geometric form in such a way that the office tower forms an oversized V—an homage to the Vitosha Mountains. The composite steel skeleton structure of the building thereby receives its characteristic cubature from wedges cut out on the structure's southwest and southeast sides as well as the V-shaped sky atrium in the upper third of the building. The Europe Tower occupies a 53-by-28-meter area on one corner of the Europe Plaza, which will also host a shopping center on another corner. In addition, due to its height and formal qualities, the Tower references the historical city center of Sofia located three kilometers away. The building also relates to the surroundings thanks to its outer envelope: depending on one's point of view and the lighting conditions, kaleidoscopic fragments of the city are reflected in the smooth, double-layered façade made of glass and aluminum.

The Europe Tower was conceived as an office tower with luxury residences and a sky lounge, and it will have forty-six stories offering a total of 69,000 square meters of gross floor area. The office spaces are located from the second floor up to the twenty-ninth floor, and with an expansion grid of 1,375 meters as well as flexible layouts, the building will meet the requirements of the organizational forms of contemporary offices. The residences, which range in size from 120 to 400 square meters, are located from the thirty-third floor up to the fortieth. The V-shaped incision seen from the outside thereby creates the generous, open entryway area leading to the apartments inside the building. The sky lounge, with a restaurant and an observation platform, is located on the thirtieth and thirty-first floors.

Access to the building is provided via two central entrances on the south and northeast sides. Passing through the main entrance on the south side, one arrives in the Grand Lobby, and from here the office areas can be reached. The entrance on the northeast side of the building, in contrast, is intended for the use of the residents and their visitors. One elevator group will provide normal service to all floors and another will offer express access to upper floors.

An innovative building engineering concept is being realized for the construction of the Europe Tower. The creation of the double-layered façade with high-efficiency heat insulation glass as well as exterior sun protection will minimize the energy expended in heating and cooling, which will lead to a clear reduction of the building's operating costs. Air-conditioning the offices with climate convectors and openable windows in the residences help reduce the building's CO_2 emissions.

The Europe Tower will be the highest building in Bulgaria and has therefore been designed as a striking, freestanding structure, one that will soon be a trademark of the city of Sofia. As a model example of the new generation of high-efficiency, innovative high-rises, it will be the calling card of a new city center and make a significant economic and ecological contribution to the future of sustainable urban development. The construction of the Europe Tower is scheduled to start in April 2009 and should be completed by May 2011.

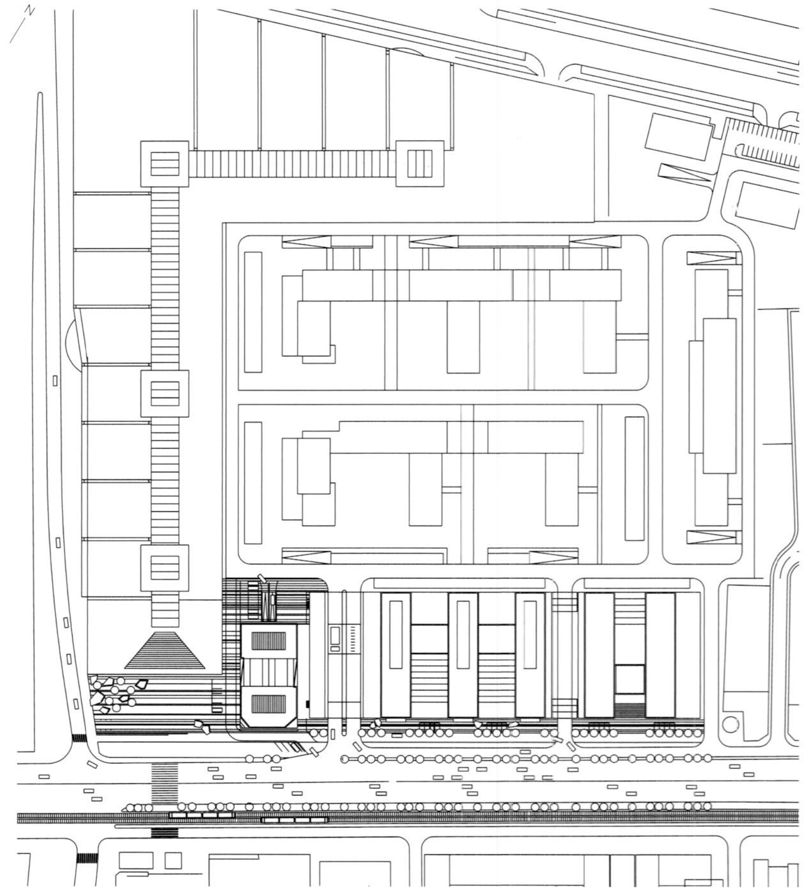

Site plan

→ New address in Europe Plaza

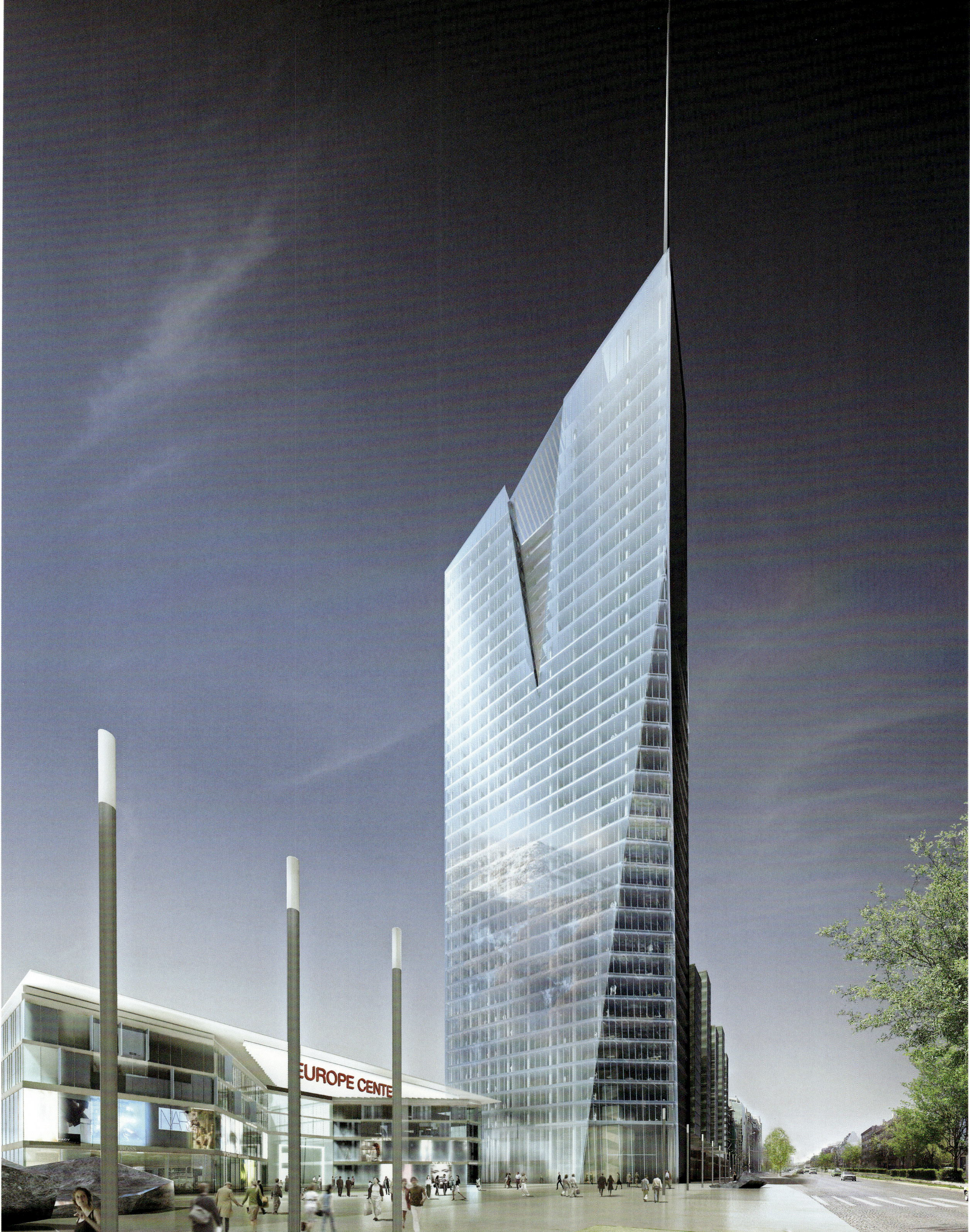
EUROPE CENTE

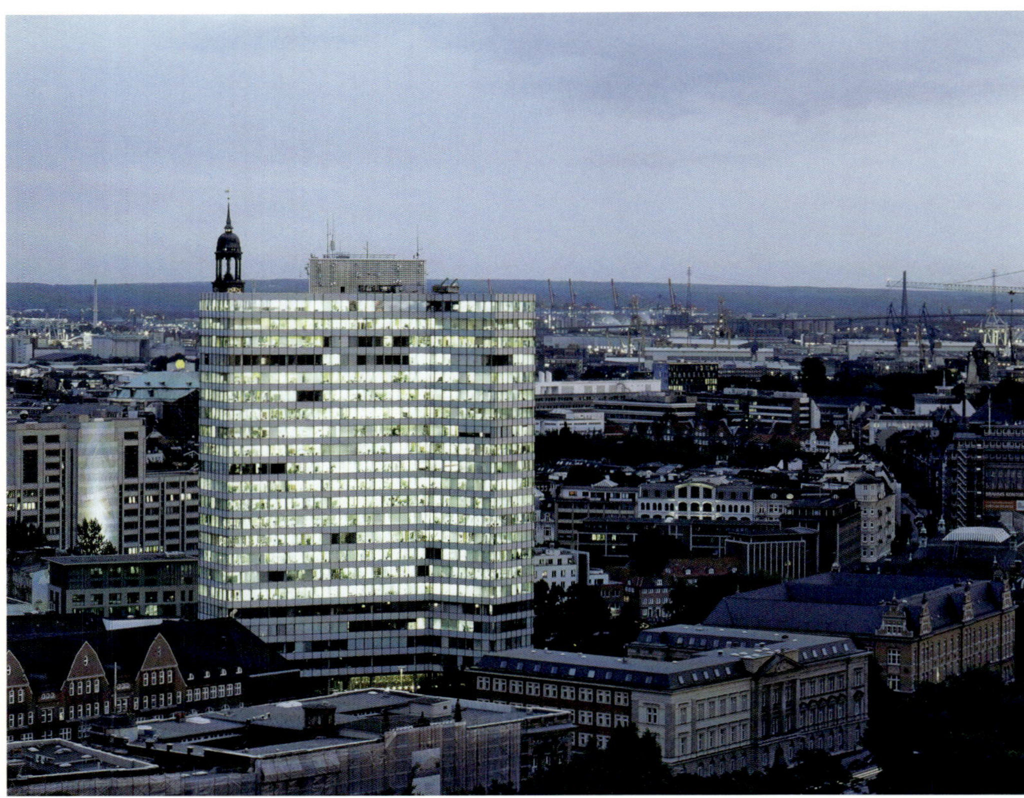

Unilever High-Rise

Forty years after it was built, the landmark-protected Unilever High-Rise has become a fixture of Hamburg's cityscape. The building's floor plan typology is an exemplary expression of flexibility and reversibility. This is another reason the building still stands today in gravitational defiance, almost unchanged. With the planned gutting of the structure, the building will retain its indelible contemporary character and simultaneously be prepared for a new life in terms of its energy use, construction, organization, and technology.

Client: Union Investment Real Estate AG
Location: Hamburg
GFA: 55,000 m²
Year of completion: 1964
Revitalization: 2009/2010

Significance

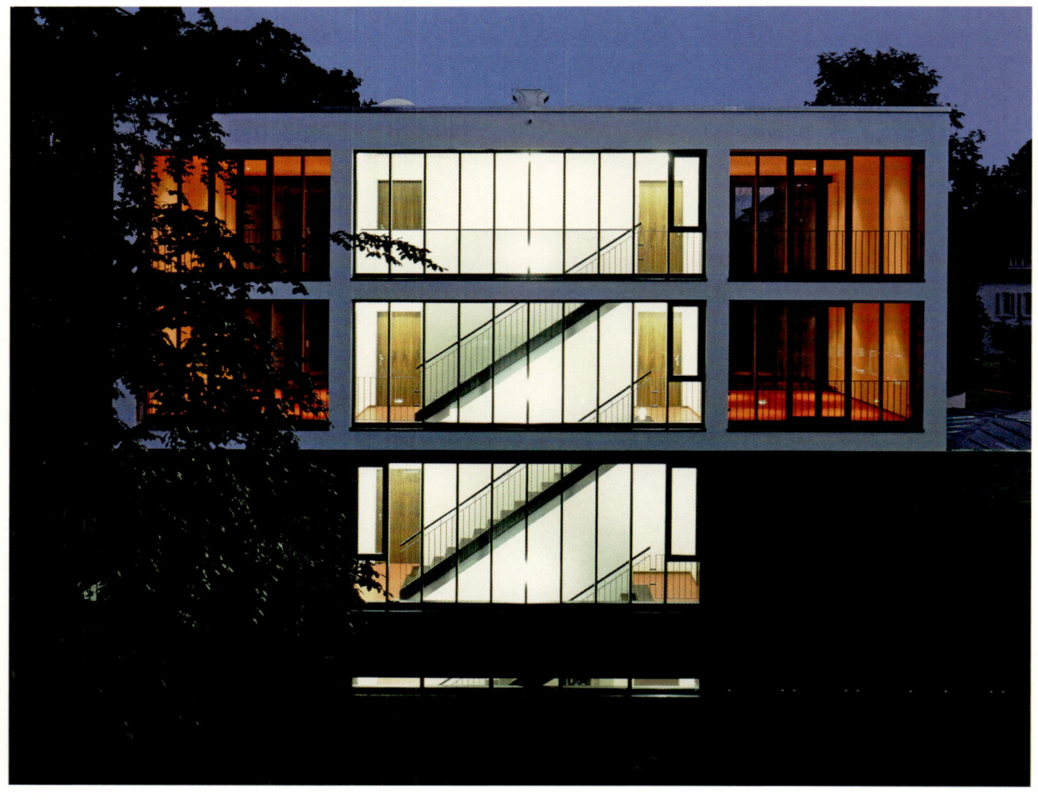

Villa Ida Media Campus

Shifts from open to closed surfaces and from light to shadow accomplished via jetties and setbacks are what lend this building ensemble its unmistakable personality. The project's physical context is characterized by the open construction of free-standing mansions and parklike open areas boasting a number of landmark-protected buildings. These elements are interpreted in a particularly contemporary way. The exposed flight of stairs leading to the garden also acts as an effective lead-in to the overall whole.

Client: Medienstiftung der Sparkasse Leipzig
Location: Leipzig
GFA: 3,250 m²
Completion date: 2006
Competition: 1st Prize, 2002
Award: BDA Prize of Saxony, recognition, 2007

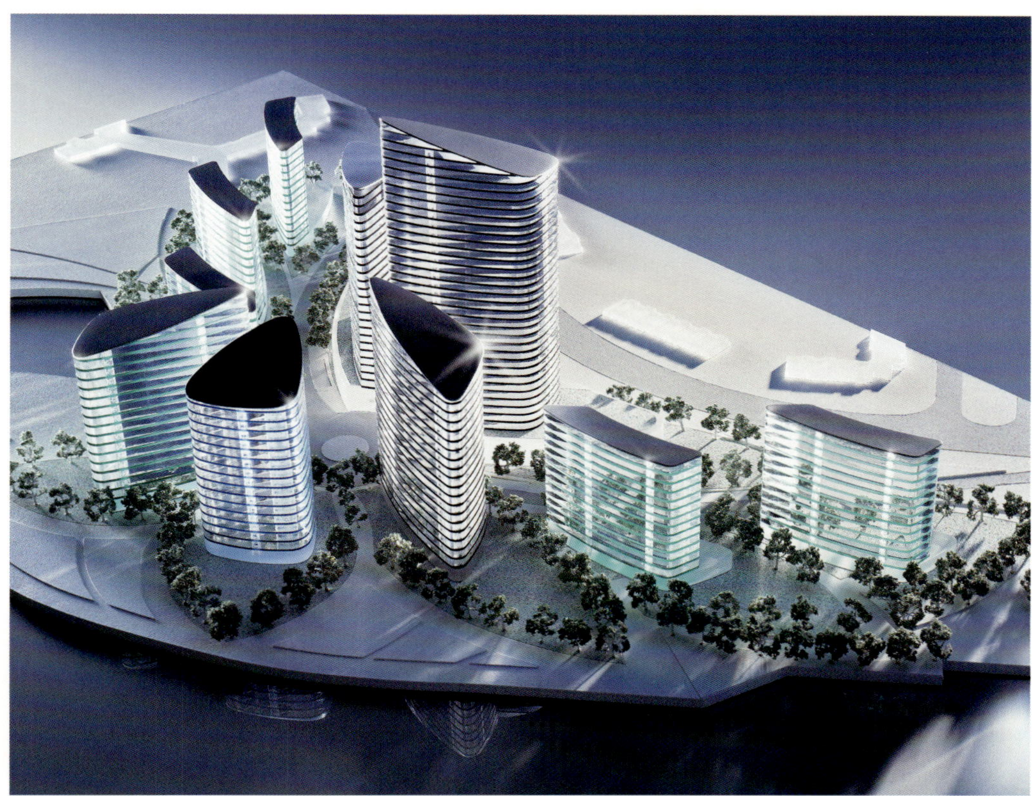

Multifunctional Complex, Krasnogorie-City

This project in the Moscow region will be executed on an exposed lot along the Moskva River. The design task consisted of the creation of a crystallization point—a new address within surroundings dominated by massive, prefab concrete buildings. Therefore, the project's concept contains an attractive mixture of uses, including hotel, residential, and office buildings, as well as recreation and restaurant facilities and a yacht harbor.

Client: **SU-155 Group of Companies**
Lead consulting: **Prosperity Project Management**
Location: **Pavshinskaya Poima, Moscow Region**
GFA: **326,500 m²**

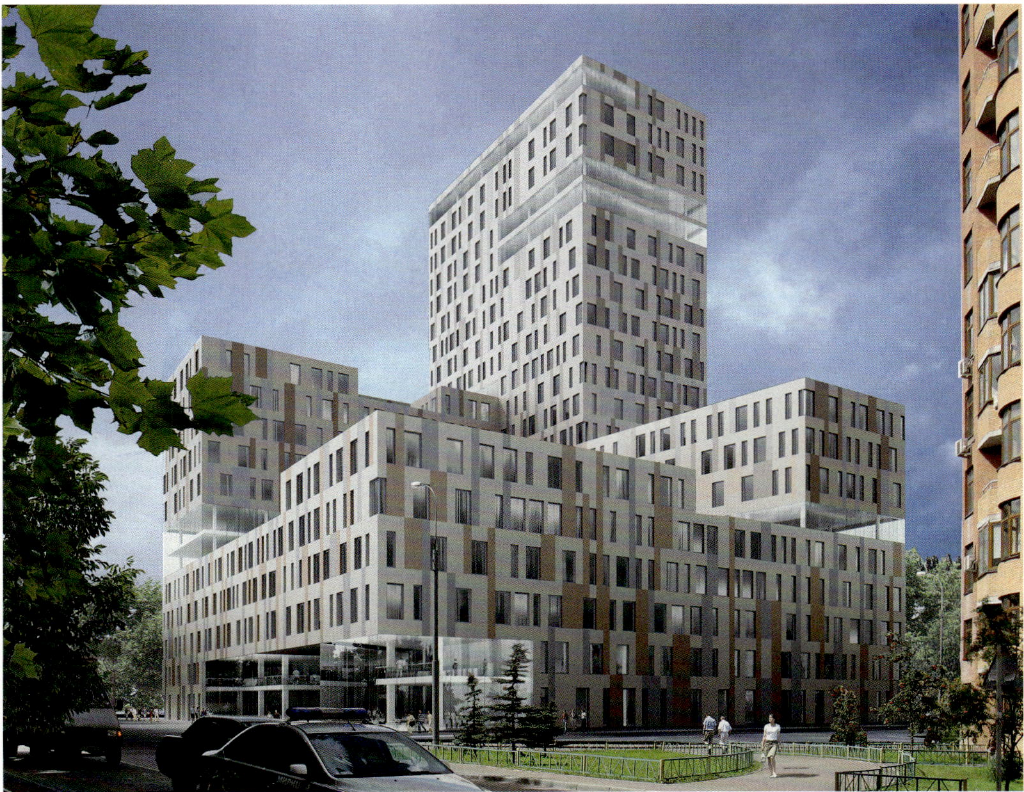

Office Complex, Moscow, Khromova Street

The design for this administration complex utilizes a rectangular base with an inward-leaning atrium on which the structure of the building ascends in stages to different heights. The structure's noticeable cubature communicates with the heterogeneous constructions of the surroundings and at the same time creates a new point of orientation within the district by means of its eighty-meter-high office tower.

Client: **Asata Construction Ltd.**
Location: **Moscow**
GFA: **60,000 m²**
Work stations: **approx. 2,500**
Completion date: **2012**
International competition: **1st Prize, 2008**

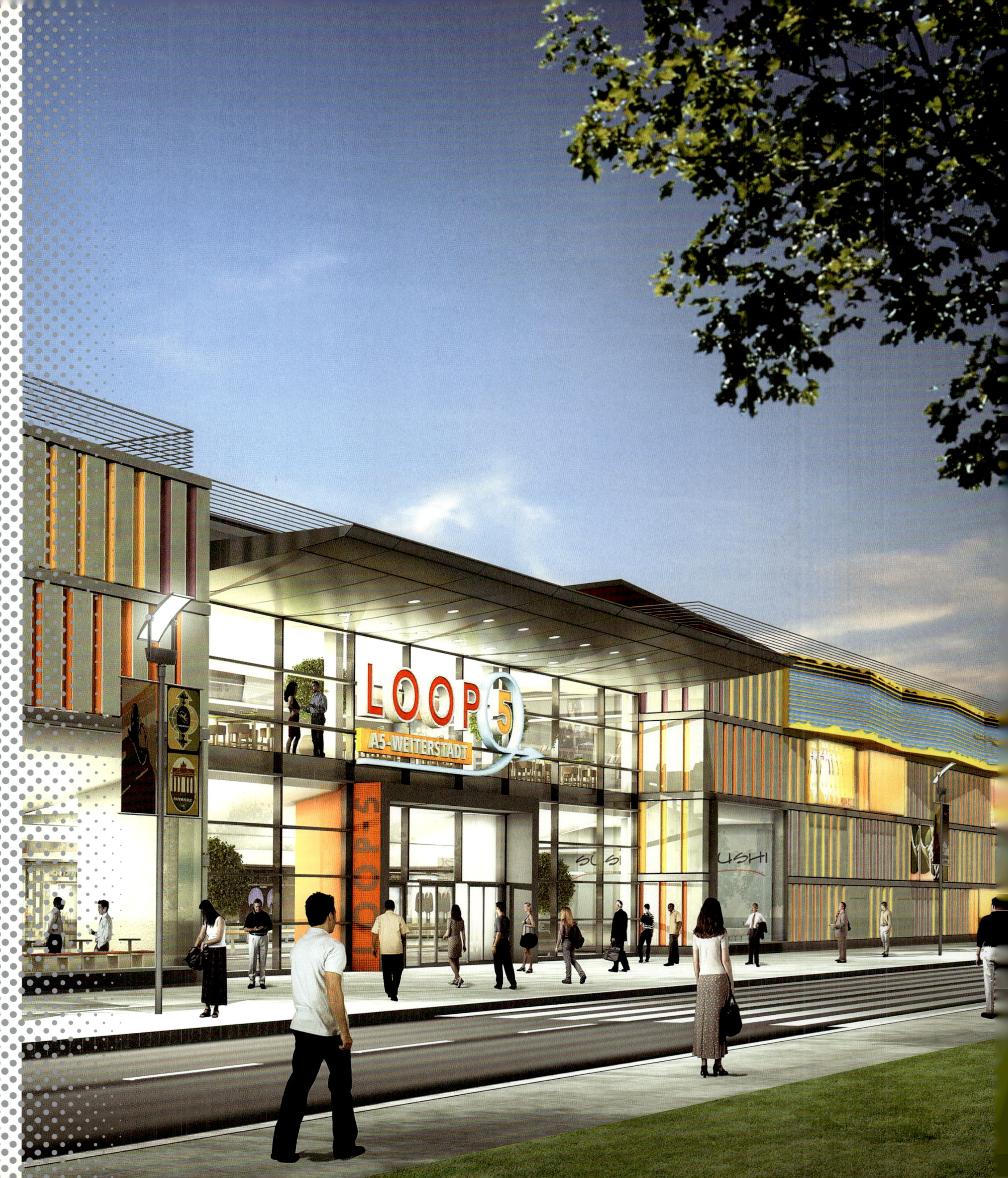

LOOP 5
A5-WEITERSTADT
LOOP 5
SUSHI

The term "destination" can be interpreted in a variety of ways: it can mean decision, the purpose for which something is destined, or the goal of a journey, as well as a location worthy of visiting. The term "destination" always communicates the idea of the endpoint of a negotiation, a process, or a voyage. When entering an airport, another meaning of the word becomes especially apparent: here, destination refers to the discovery of the foreign, as well as relaxation and pleasure.

The first buildings that were not erected for the purely functional purpose of meeting basic existential needs but had a higher purpose were temples and sacred buildings. In addition to the sacred, with the individualization of society, "destinations" of pleasure and commerce emerged in the form of fairs and exhibitions. With the onset of technological progress and the development of the railroad, cathedrals of travel were established as destinations of departure and arrival. Destinations that have been built leave a mark. They describe locations and physically embody the concept of movement.

Additional destinations were established in the wake of increasing urbanization, the growth of cities, and the concomitant changes in patterns of consumption, those of retail trade. Even if most of the goods offered were too expensive for the majority of the population, concourses and department stores became meeting points for all strata of society. No one at the time would have called this "destination shopping," but in a figurative sense the designation can also be applied to the venerable department stores of Europe.

Today the purchase of goods itself has become a social event with entertainment value. In addition to retail activity, the large shopping centers also feature cafés, bars, restaurants, and cinemas. Commercial destinations have come to outshine spiritual and cultural ones. Consumption has acquired an ever-increasing importance in our lives. The temple of commerce is what we seek, a place where shopping is provided with the appropriate framework in which to celebrate consumption.

For traveling consumers, the next destination of this kind will be Weiterstadt, where the Loop 5 shopping center offers a true temple of commerce, a veritable adventure world of shopping. The theme of "aviation" characterizes the malls, plazas, and skylights with different interpretations and designs. Loop 5 is becoming a port of call for travelers using the A5 autobahn near the Frankfurt Airport and the headquarters of the European Space Operation Center (ESOC) in Darmstadt. The appearance of the shopping center and its adjoining parking garage has been developed from the concepts of velocity and a jewel box. The first refers to the mall's location next to the autobahn, while the latter makes reference to the building's use.

Loop 5's exposed position on the autobahn and immense size—100,000 square meters of gross floor area with 3,000 parking places—are the vision of a true shopping pilgrimage. In addition, because of this new "destination," the city of Weiterstadt will gain popularity, and this will mean that the new shopping center will have achieved a significant part of its purpose.

Destination Loop 5 Shopping Center

Client: **Sonae Sierra** | Location: **Weiterstadt** | GFA: **100,000 m²**
Retail surface: **58,300 m²** | Rental units: **152** | Completion date: **2009**

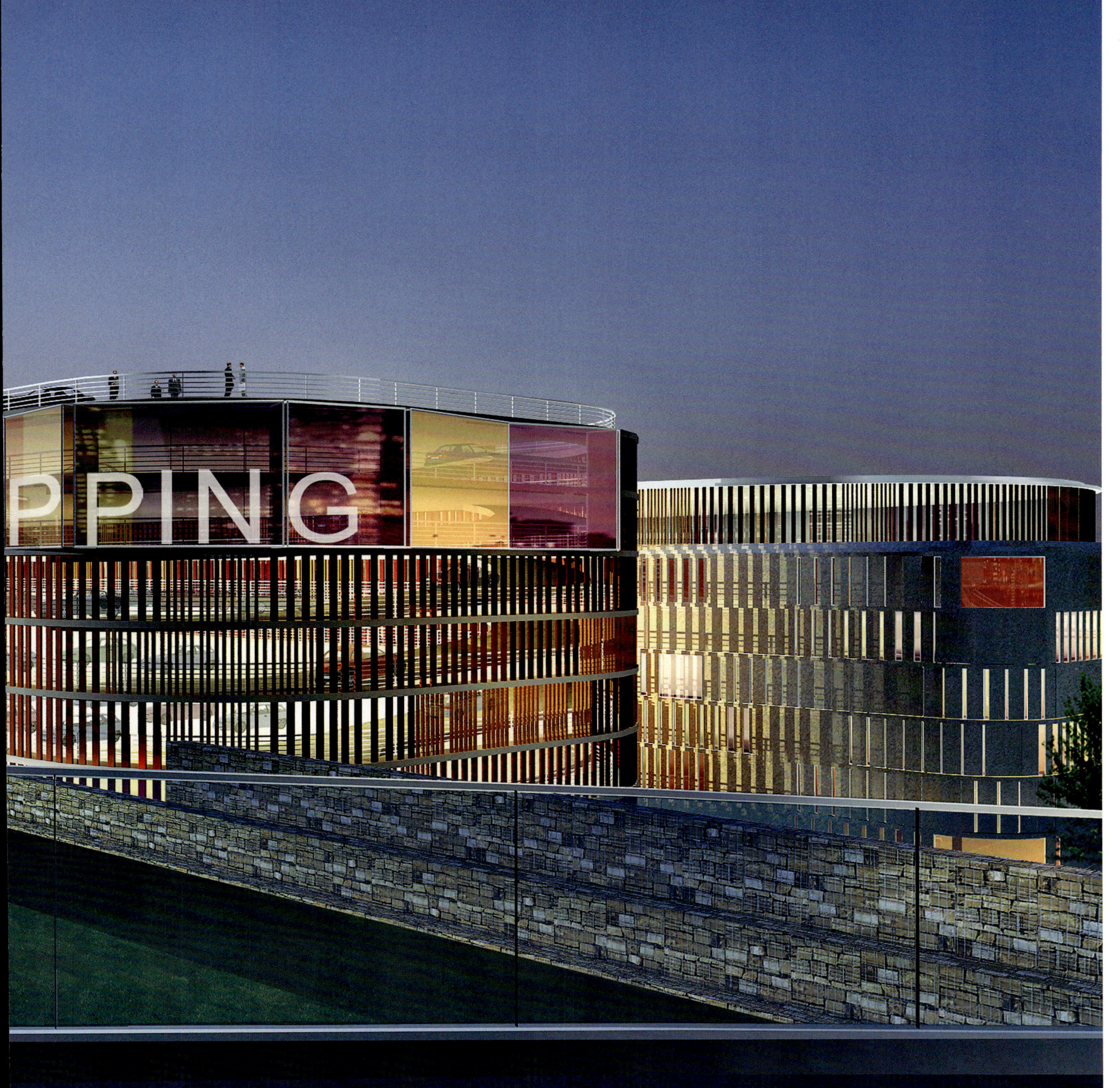
PPING

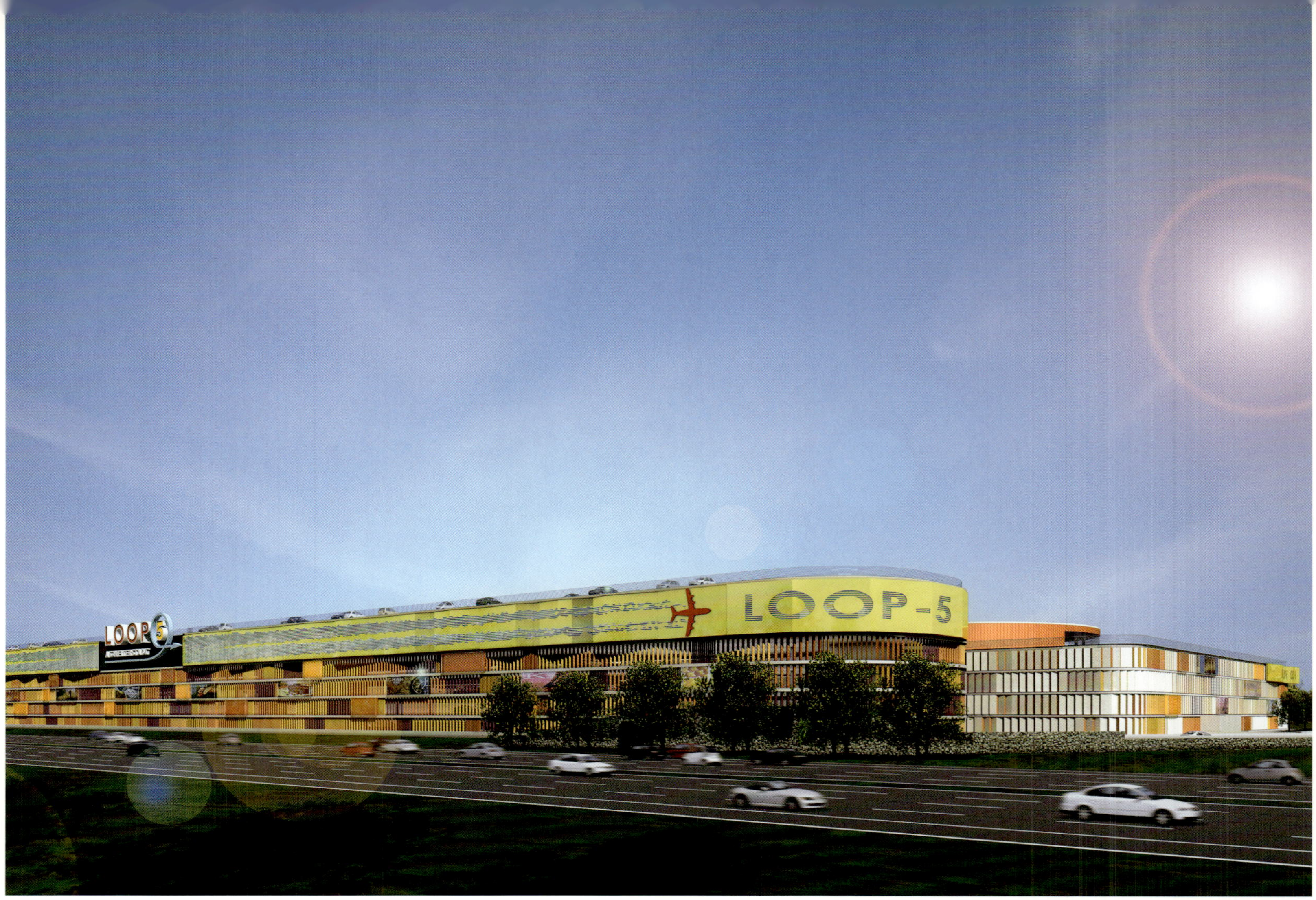

View of parking garage from A5 autobahn

→ Design idea of "aviation" in side mall
↞ View of parking garage from A5 autobahn

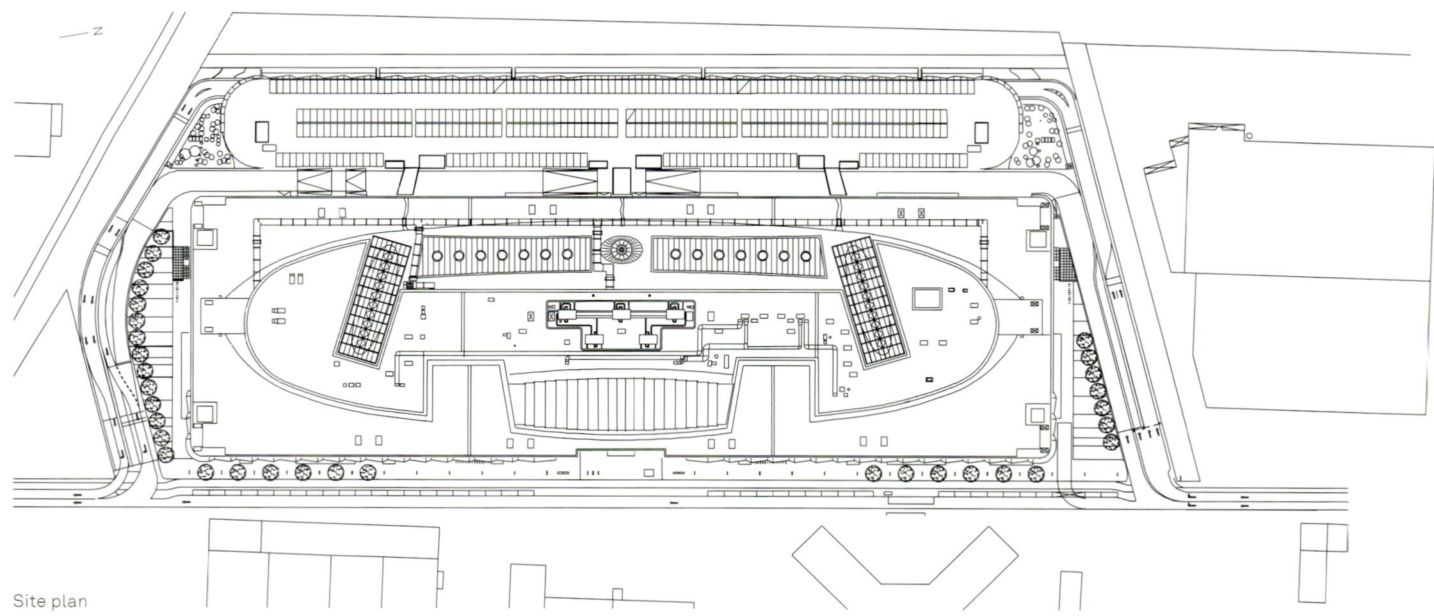

Site plan

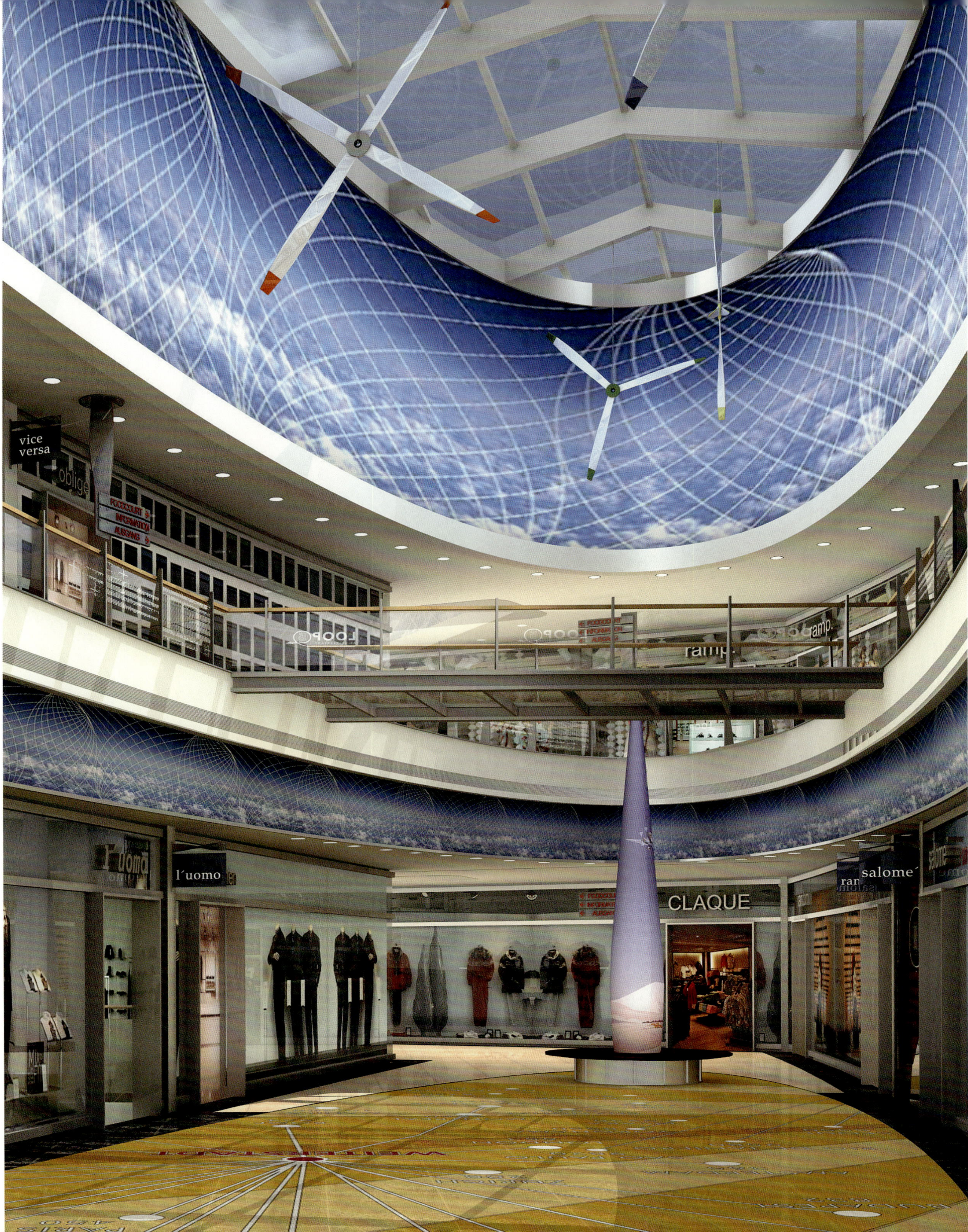
vice versa
oblige
l´uomo
CLAQUE
ramp.
salome´

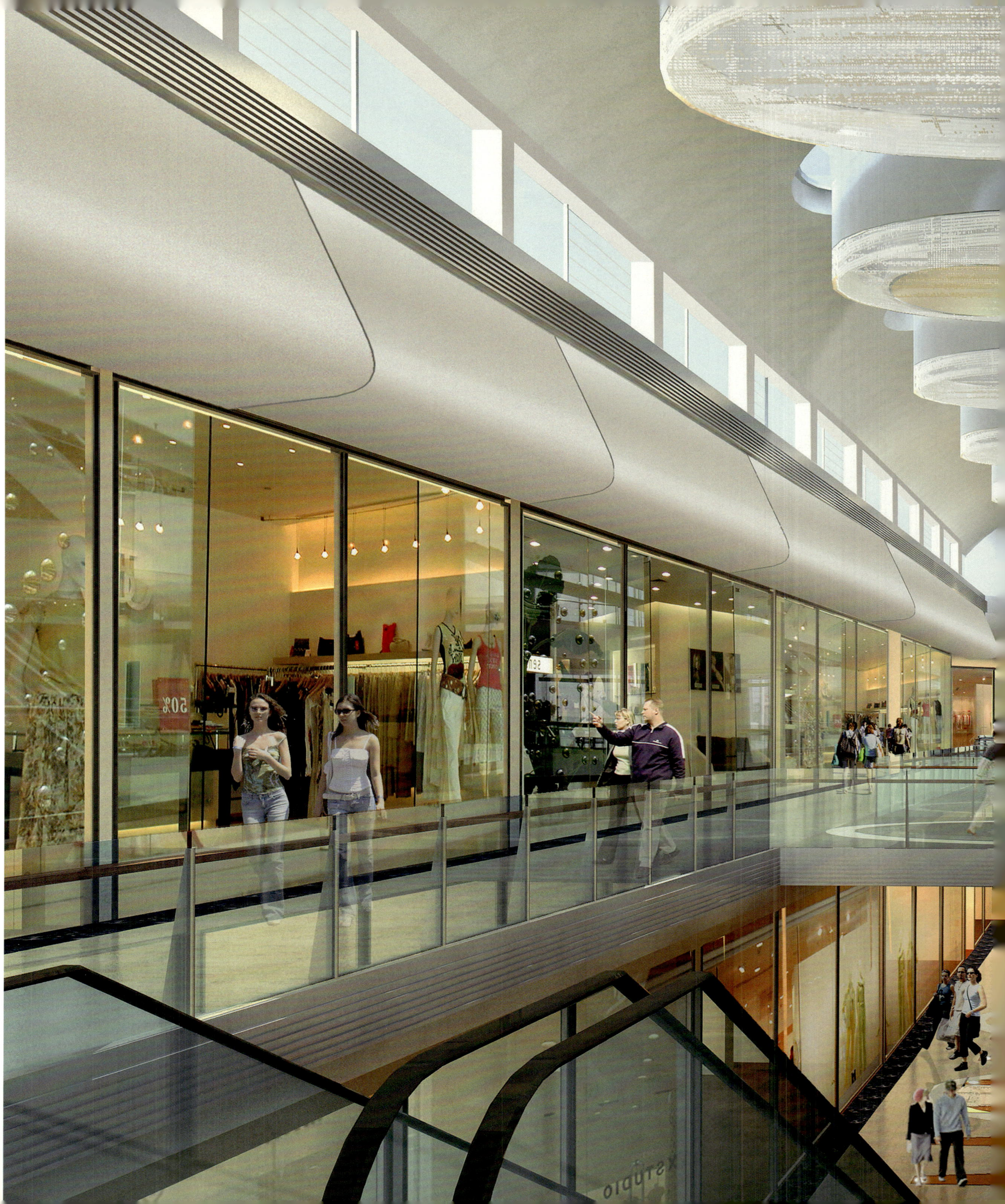

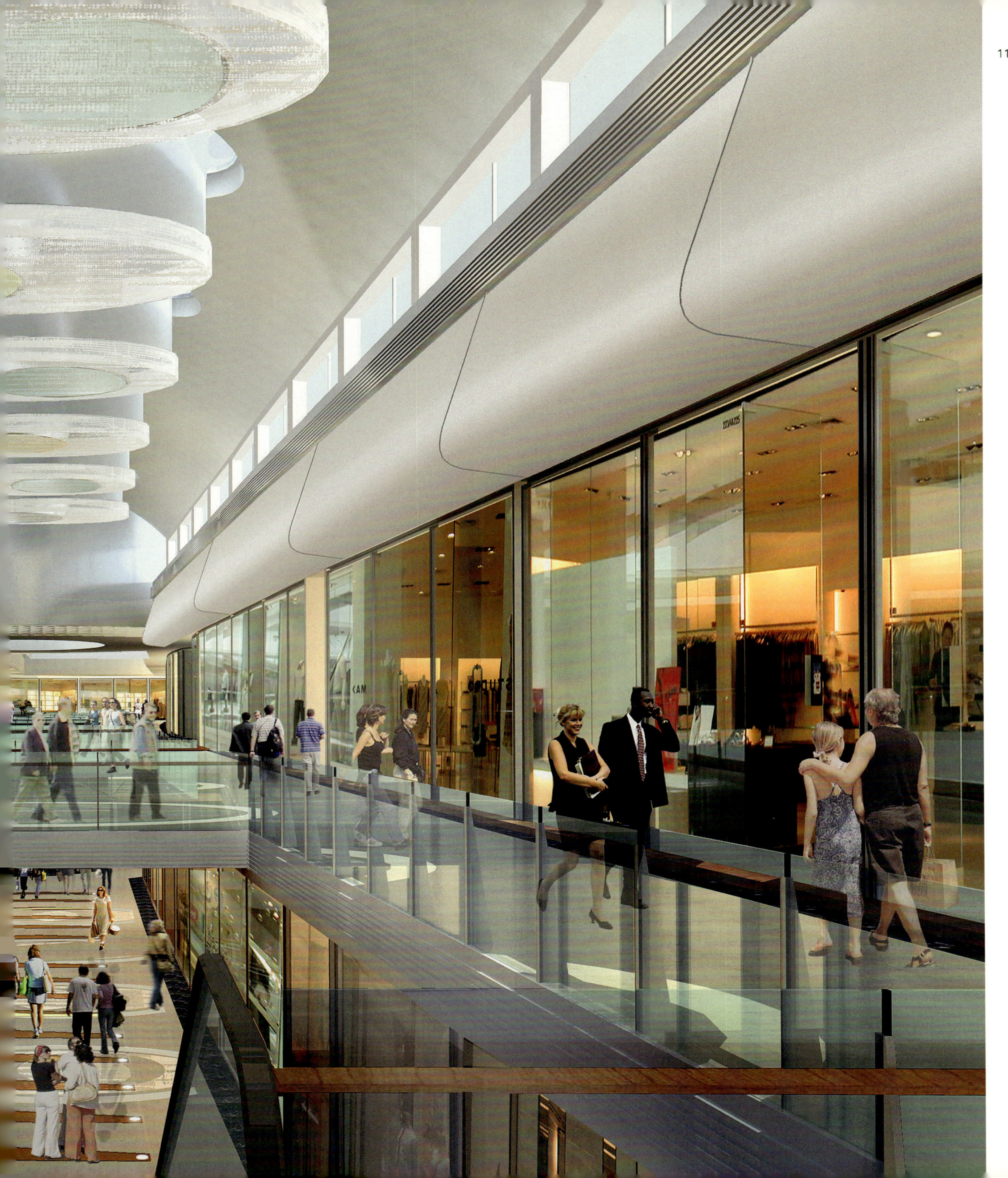

The Loop 5 Shopping Center Distinctive, accessible, and unmistakable—these were the key concepts to be incorporated in the design of the new shopping center in Weiterstadt called Loop 5. With 100,000 square meters of gross floor area, it is one of the largest shopping centers in Germany, and it is currently under construction on the A5 autobahn between Frankfurt and Darmstadt at the Weiterstadt exit. The shopping center and its adjoining parking garage will feature more than 58,300 square meters of leasable space, which is comparable with that of the downtown consumer and recreation area, as well as a unique amusement park inspired by the theme of "aviation." Beginning in 2009 it will become a destination for the 700,000 residents of the surrounding communities.

With its dimensions of 320 by 150 meters, the building complex consists of a shopping center comprised of two full floors, a basement, and an upper floor set back eight meters, as well as a nine-story parking garage that accommodates 3,000 cars. Both construction elements are connected by a supply street on the lower floor and bridges above, and are unified in a coherent architectural form by the rounding off of the building corners and the continuous running façade. In terms of their construction method, both buildings are characterized by a high degree of prefabrication—the shopping center in its use of finished concrete parts, and the parking garage in its steel structure.

The shopping center's external appearance is derived from the concepts of "velocity" and a "jewel box." The rhythmically raised, sand-colored slabs of the façade expose to view the permanently changing, recessed, colored levels of the building envelope. With the vertically arranged façade slabs being of different widths, the dynamic course of the outer façade surface suggests the notion of velocity, while the colored joints provide a sensual reference to precious stones nestled within a jewel box. The design culminates in a crownlike top of perforated metal that is animated day and night by a twinkling play of light and shadow.

Most visitors reach the shopping center by car via the A5 autobahn or by way of Robert-Koch-Strasse or Friedrich-Schaefer-Strasse. The access point is in the northern part of the grounds. Customers and employees enter parking level 02 of the nine-story parking garage via a two-lane entrance at street level. While three of the nine parking levels are connected directly to the main building by the supply street and bridges, the visitors who park on the other levels enter the shopping center by using one of six elevator groups. Pedestrians access Loop 5 via a grand main entrance overarched by a broad canopy.

The fully air-conditioned shopping center is typologically formed as a circular mall—with the exception of the basement, which is T-shaped. The basement houses sales areas featuring food, electronics, and domestic appliances, as well as the shopping center's central supply and waste disposal units. Three escalator units connect the lower floor with the streets below and the stores above, and because of their closed form, they allow visitors to make a complete round trip. With this arrangement, the shopping center offers space for 150 retail stores ranging in size from 25 to 3,420 square meters, 1,430 square meters for sixteen restaurants, and 1,200 square meters for an unusual recreation opportunity: the food court, as a central theme space, is located on the second floor above the entryway atrium. From there, the visitor reaches the recessed, staggered floor via the escalators. All levels are also connected by passenger elevators oriented toward the inner core area.

Because of Loop 5's proximity to the Frankfurt Airport, the aviation theme was the leitmotif for the elaborate interior design. The impression made by the structure's interior design is marked by it, with references being made to everything from the dawn of manned flight to the golden age and the era of the jet. The visitor notices the formal analogies in the incorporation of the forms of propellers, wings, rudders, and rotors, as well as in the graphic design of the banisters, floor surfaces, and ceilings, whose layout is based on a runway guidance system. Even the skylights over the main mall and the boulevard offer a visual connection to airplanes. Lighting units that look like oversized plane engines provide the interior with generous amounts of light, and the artificial light directs the gaze of the visitor skywards.

Loop 5 is scheduled to be completed in September 2009, and when it opens, Weiterstadt will become a new attraction, a place to visit. Loop 5 will initiate a new impulse for theme-related shopping-center architecture in Germany.

⇐ Boulevard
→ Illuminated parking garage

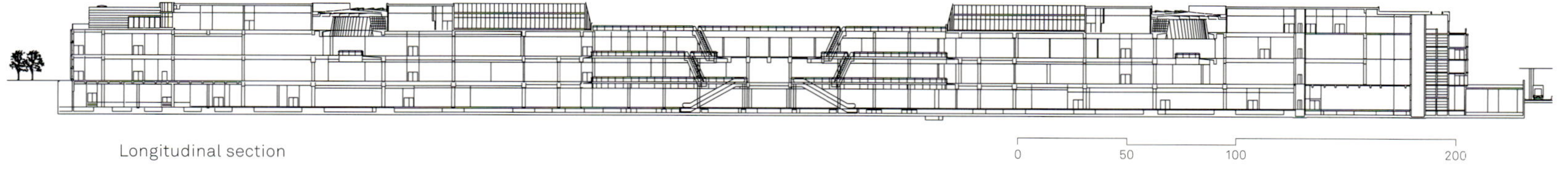

Longitudinal section

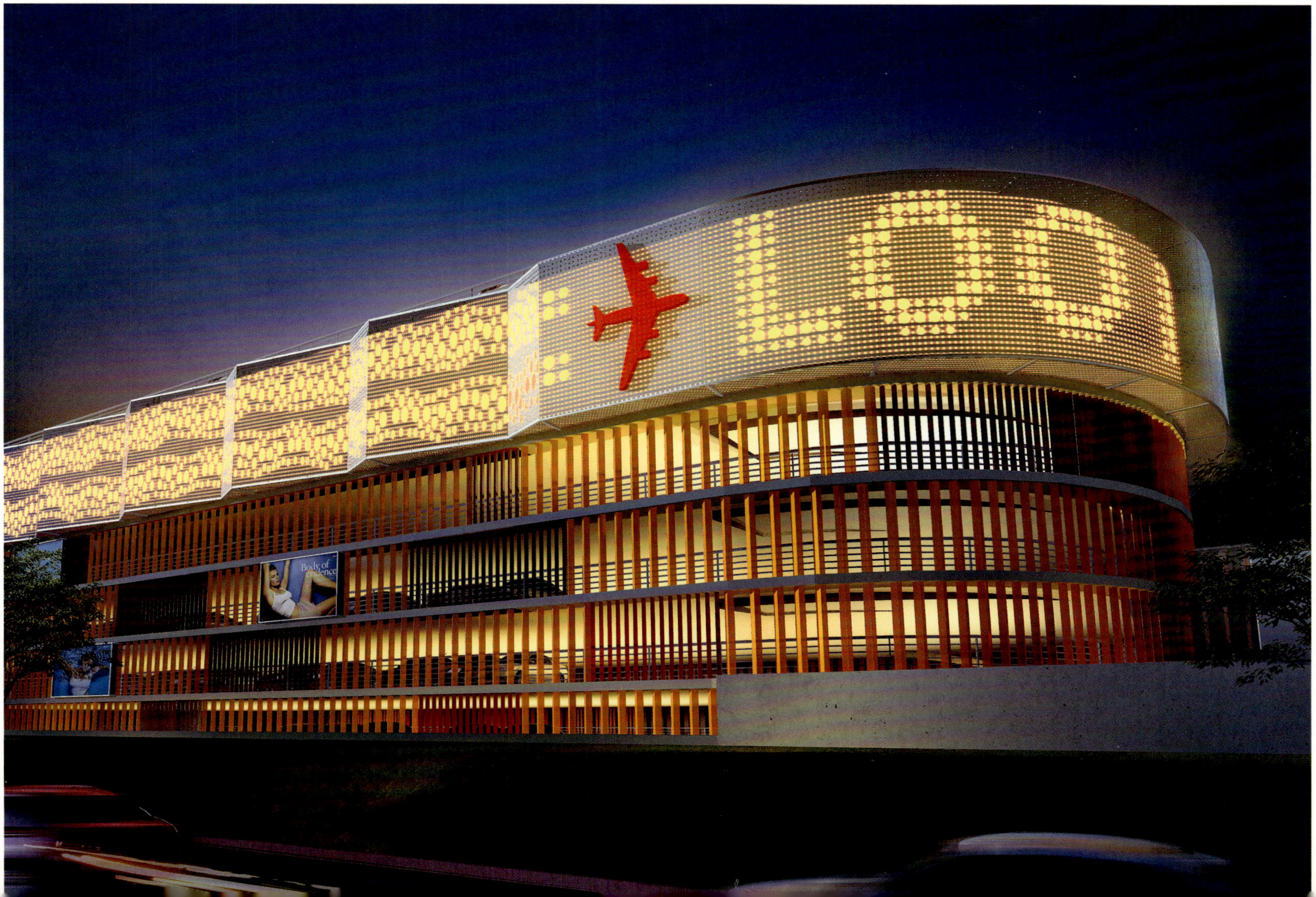

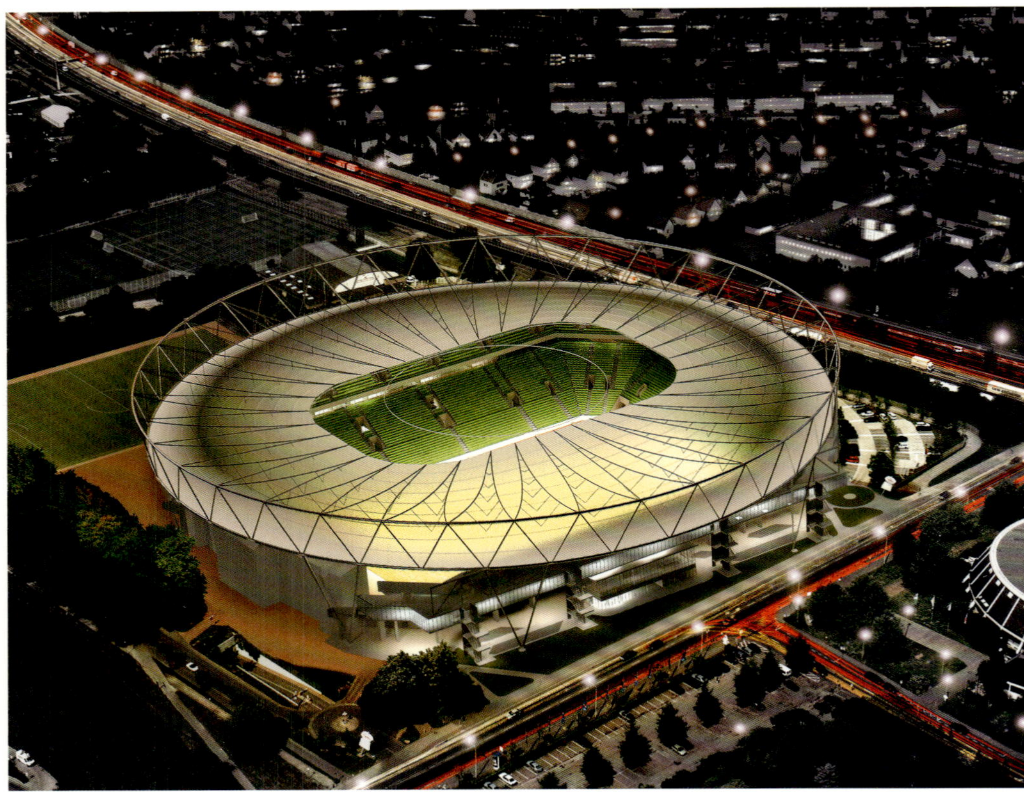

BayArena

In the course of its modernization, this "pilgrimage site" will be prepared to host more than 30,000 soccer fans. This is being made possible by the augmentation of the bleachers through the addition of another upper tier. Along with a stadium roof that is designed to be perceived, a new four-story west building is being erected. In the basement of this west building a new team area is being constructed with state-of-the-art infrastructure. There will also be more VIP, restaurant, and press areas on the other levels, as well as additional event spaces.

Client: Bayer 04 Leverkusen
Location: Leverkusen
GFA: 17,560 m²
Seats: 30,000
Completion date: 2009

Destination

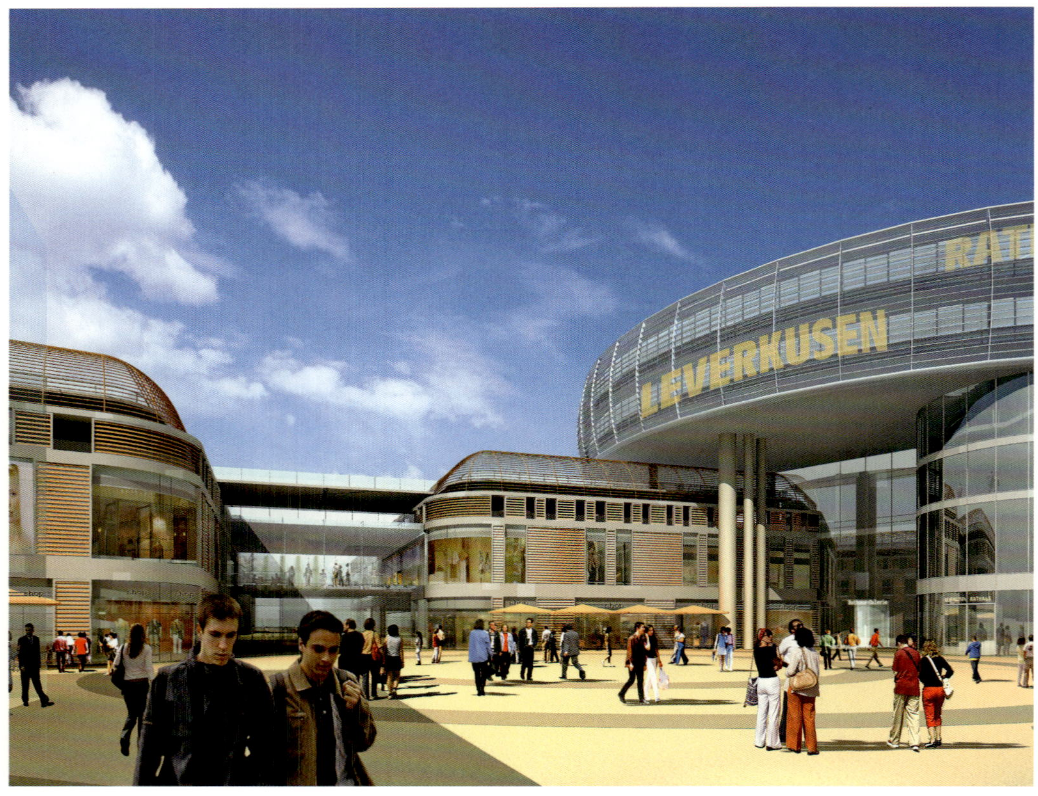

Town Hall Gallery, Leverkusen

Leverkusen's Town Hall Gallery is part of the city's newly revived downtown and emerges as a discernible, people-friendly city center. Combining elements of an urban square, retail stores, a town hall, and restaurant and entertainment facilities, the gallery becomes a new point of attraction within the existing urban structures.

Client: ECE Projektmanagement
Location: Leverkusen
Retail surface: 22,600 m²
Completion date: 2009/2010
Competition: 1st Prize, 2005

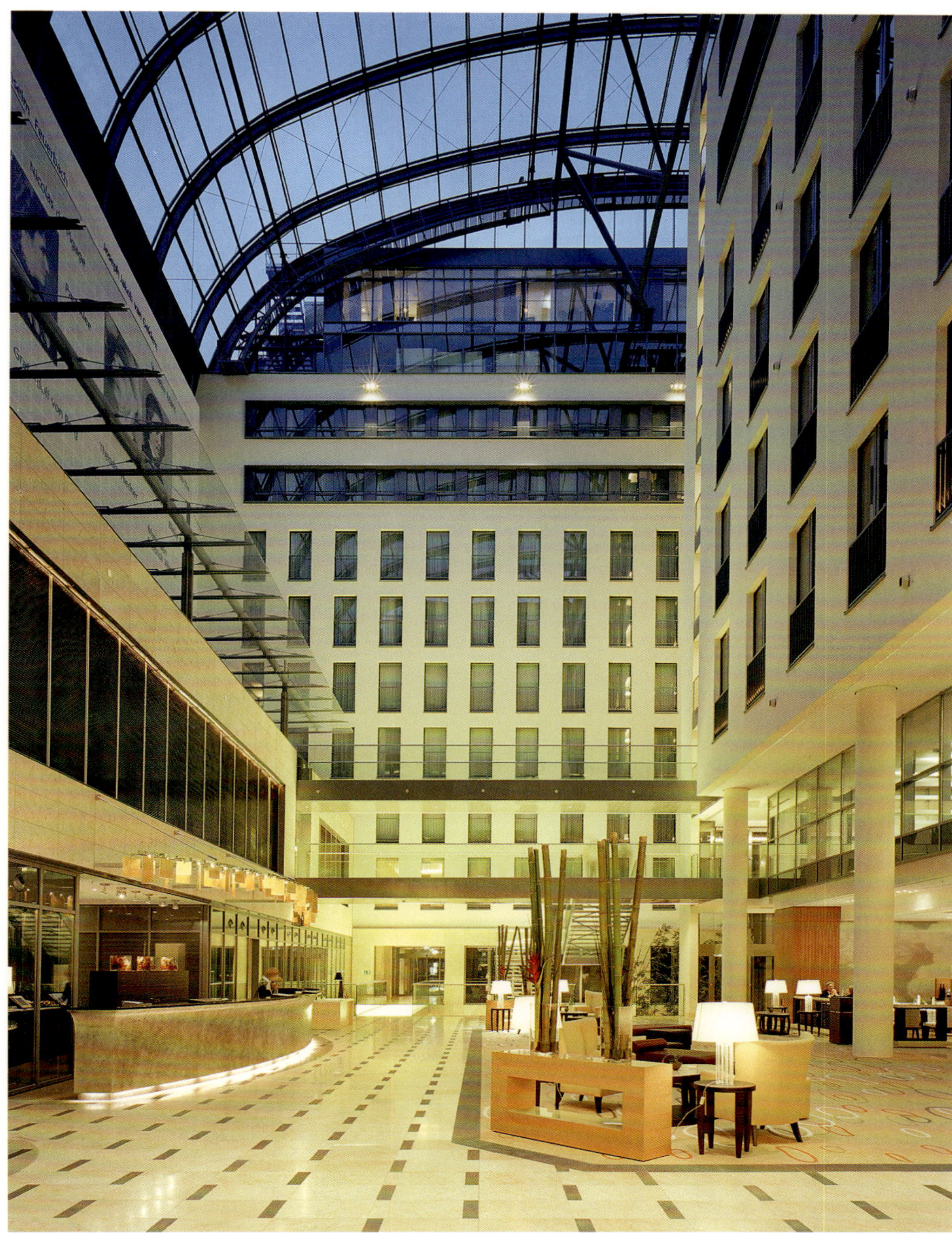

Grand Hotel Intercontinental

This five-star hotel at the south end of Düsseldorf's Königsallee receives its guests in a large, glass-covered atrium in which all public functional areas are clearly arranged. This typologically conditioned space becomes the middle of the overall ensemble and fulfills all significant expectations of travelers: a positive experience of both arrival and departure, a pleasant place to linger and meet, and an indulgence in the pastime of observing and being observed.

Client: DKÖ-Objektgesellschaft Königsallee Dr. Herbert Ebertz KG
Location: Düsseldorf
GFA: 50,000 m²
Hotel rooms: 287 guest rooms and suites
Completion date: 2005

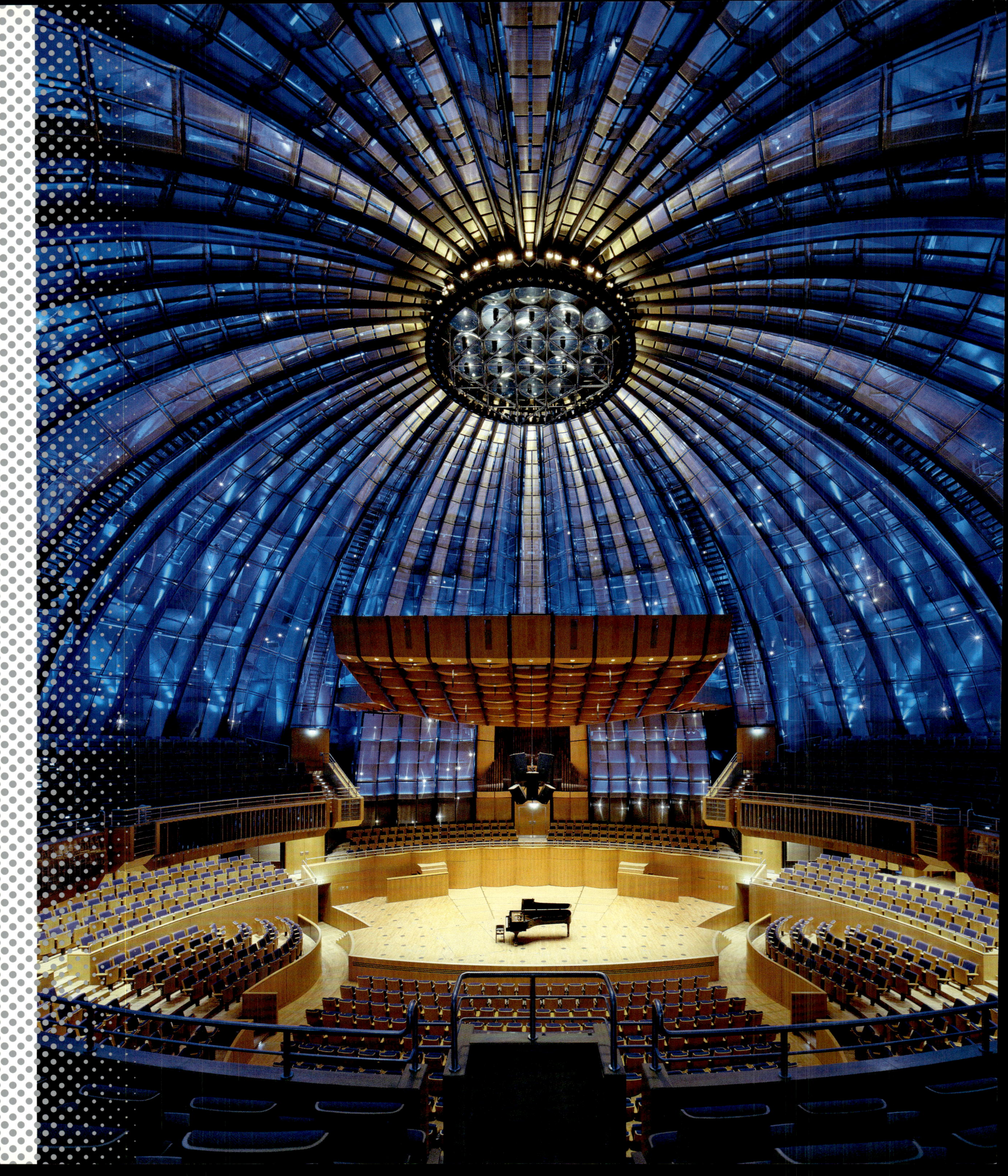

Continuity Düsseldorf Concert Hall

Client: **Landeshauptstadt Düsseldorf** | Location: **Düsseldorf** | GFA: **9,682 m²**
Seats: **1,854** | Year of completion: **1926** | Conversion: **1978** | Revitalization: **2005 and 2008**
Award: **Europa-Nostra-Prize 1979, exemplary building in North Rhine-Westphalia**

Philosophers of all eras, beginning with those of ancient Greece, have been interested in the term "continuity." But what does continuity mean? Some synonyms include steadiness and invariance. Procedures and processes that are always running in one direction possess continuity. Continuity also means that some sense of order and calm is maintained, and as a consequence it affords the opportunity to concentrate on what is essential.

The term "continuity" is multifaceted and can be applied in a variety of contexts. For instance, human relations require continuity, and the path of the sun from east to west is also "continuous." If the world appeared differently every day, it would not allow human beings and animals to orient themselves, and they would thus have to expend a great deal of energy to learn about and understand their constantly changing circumstances.

Continuity in the spatial sense, and hence in the architectural sense, refers for the most part to two factors. Firstly, it refers to architectural structures, which help us orient ourselves within our surroundings. Exceptional buildings and urban design are the cornerstones of the kinds of structures we identify as architectural landmarks. Secondly, typological design aspects also exert an influence on the continuity we sense or experience in our surroundings. In short, "continuity" in relation to architecture is primarily concerned with the shaping of our physical environment and our perception of this.

Since 1926 Düsseldorf has felt the continuous presence and influence of a notable building on the bank of the Rhine, the Rheinhalle, which today functions as the city's Tonhalle, or Concert Hall. The building was originally a planetarium constructed for the Gesolei (Grosse Ausstellung für Gesundheitspflege, soziale Fürsorge und Leibesübungen), or Great Exhibition for Health Care, Social Welfare, and Physical Exercise. The Rheinhalle was severely damaged during a bombing in 1942, after which it was provisionally repaired and put to use as a multipurpose hall. Thanks to the efforts of Helmut Hentrich, however, the old planetarium was converted into Düsseldorf's Concert Hall in the nineteen-seventies.

The Concert Hall underwent a much needed refurbishment in 2005. Structural modifications were made and the acoustics of the space were improved. The wooden paneling of the interior has been replaced by a stretched metal mesh, thereby retaining the formal appearance of the former planetarium: although the architecture of the interior is contemporary in character, modern lighting installed behind the metal fabric creates the effect of constellations of light recalling the heavenly bodies and stars in the night sky, an homage to the building's original function.

As a consequence of these changes, Düsseldorf has been able to keep the Rheinhalle. For almost ninety years now it has enjoyed its place in the social life—and the skyline—of the city.

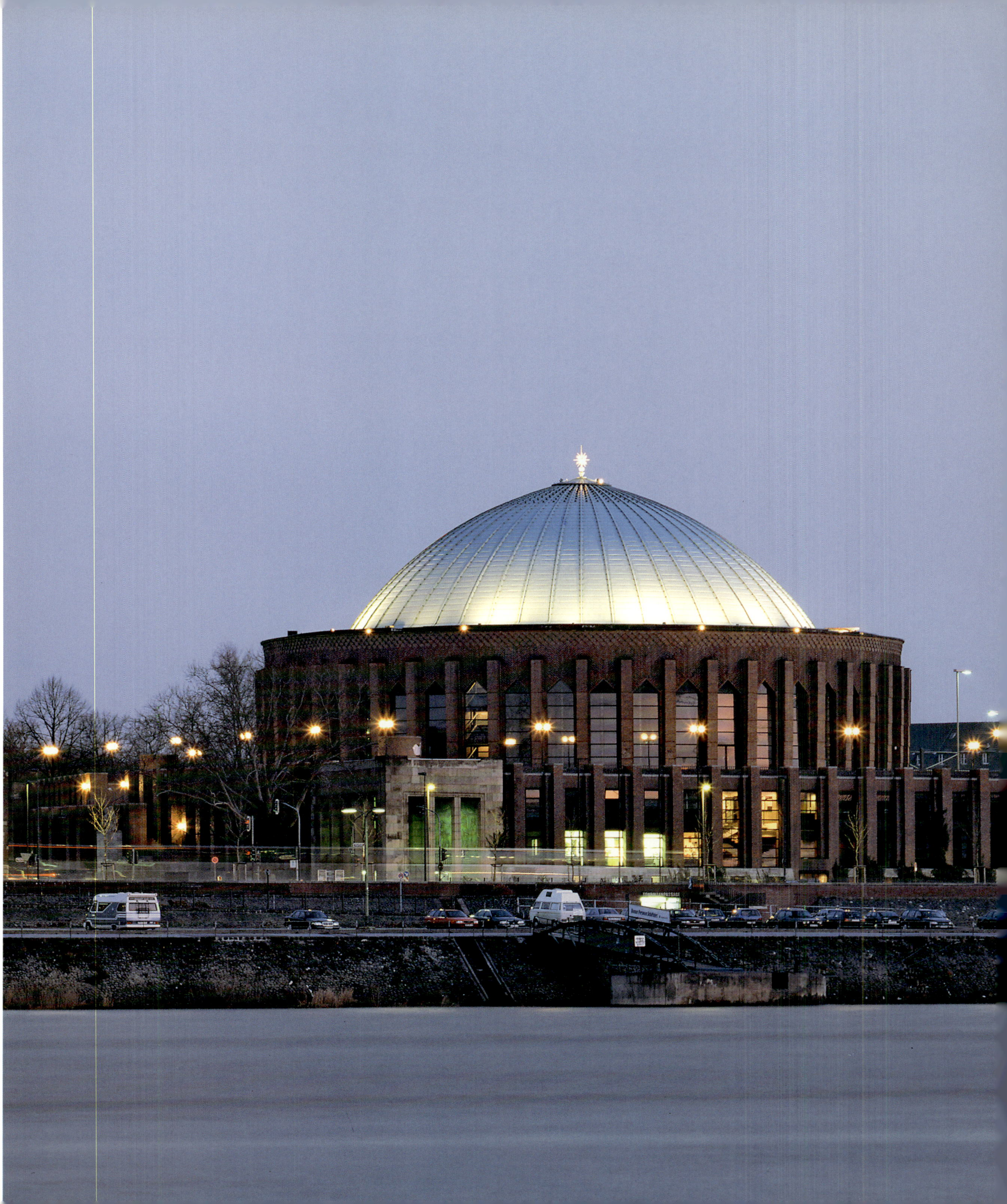

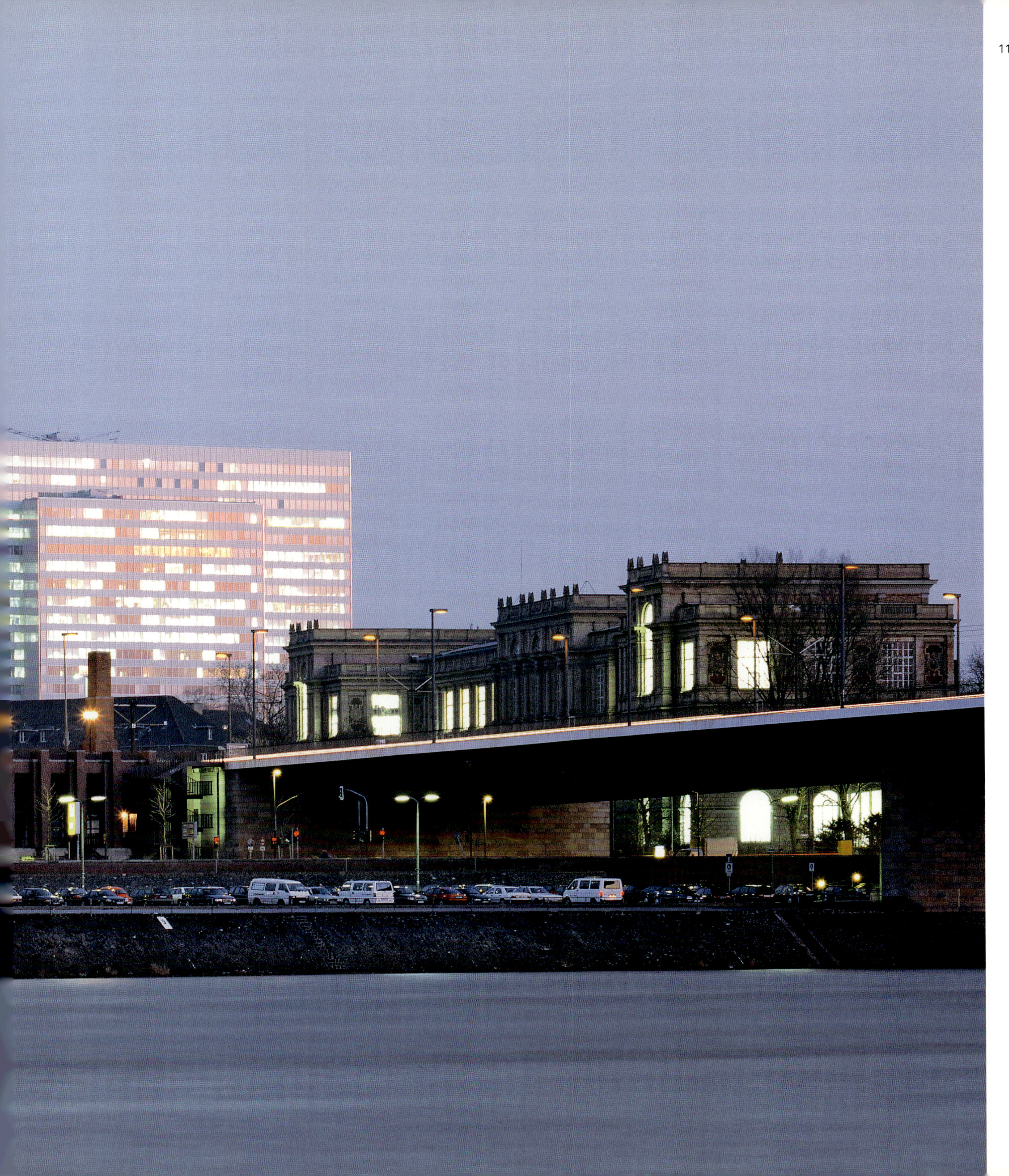

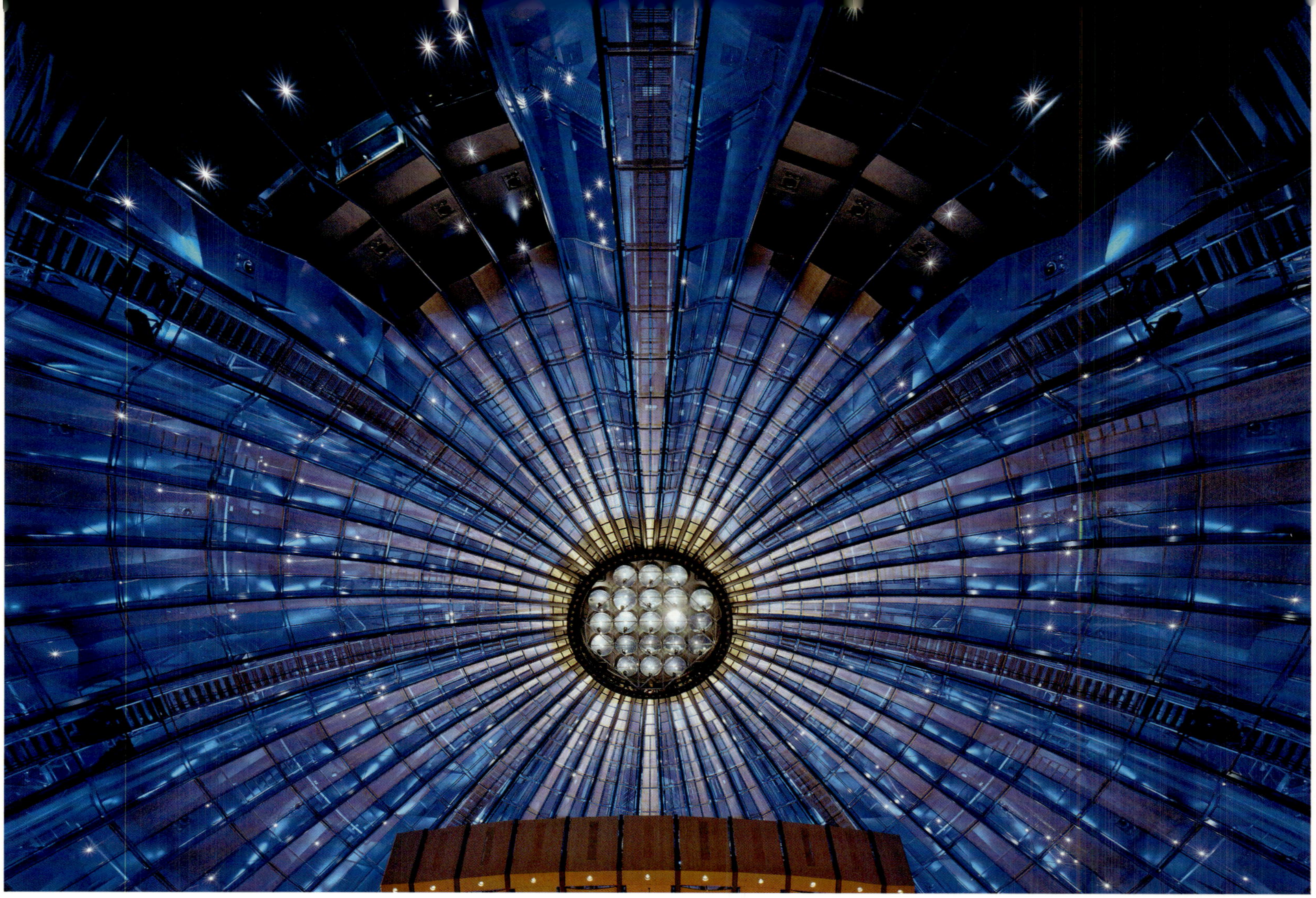

View of dematerialized dome construction

→ View of Ehrenhof
↞ Rhine side of Concert Hall

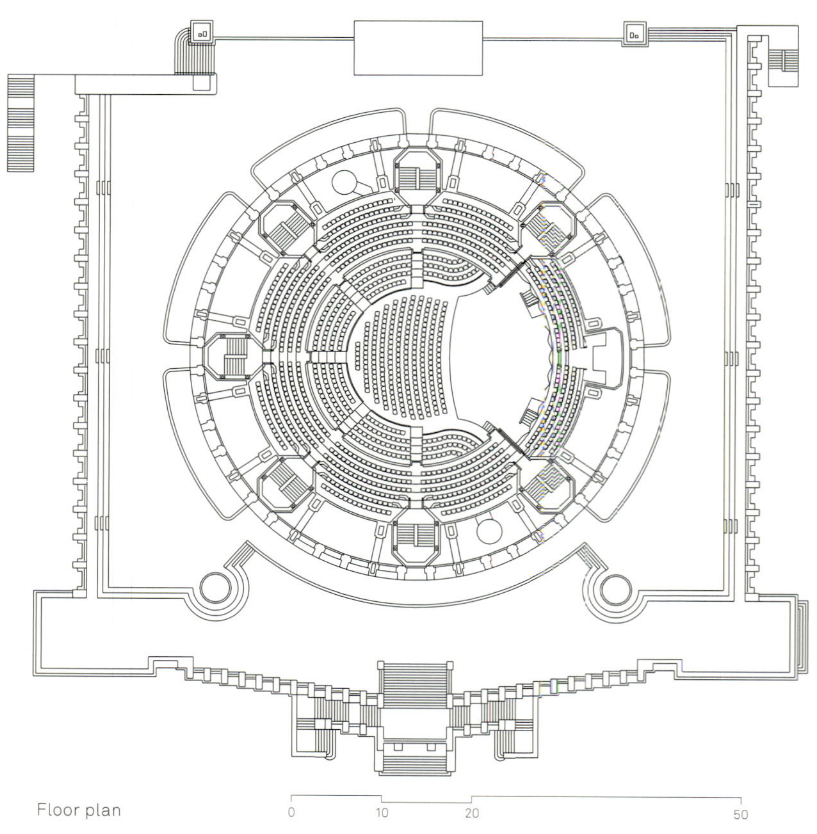

Floor plan

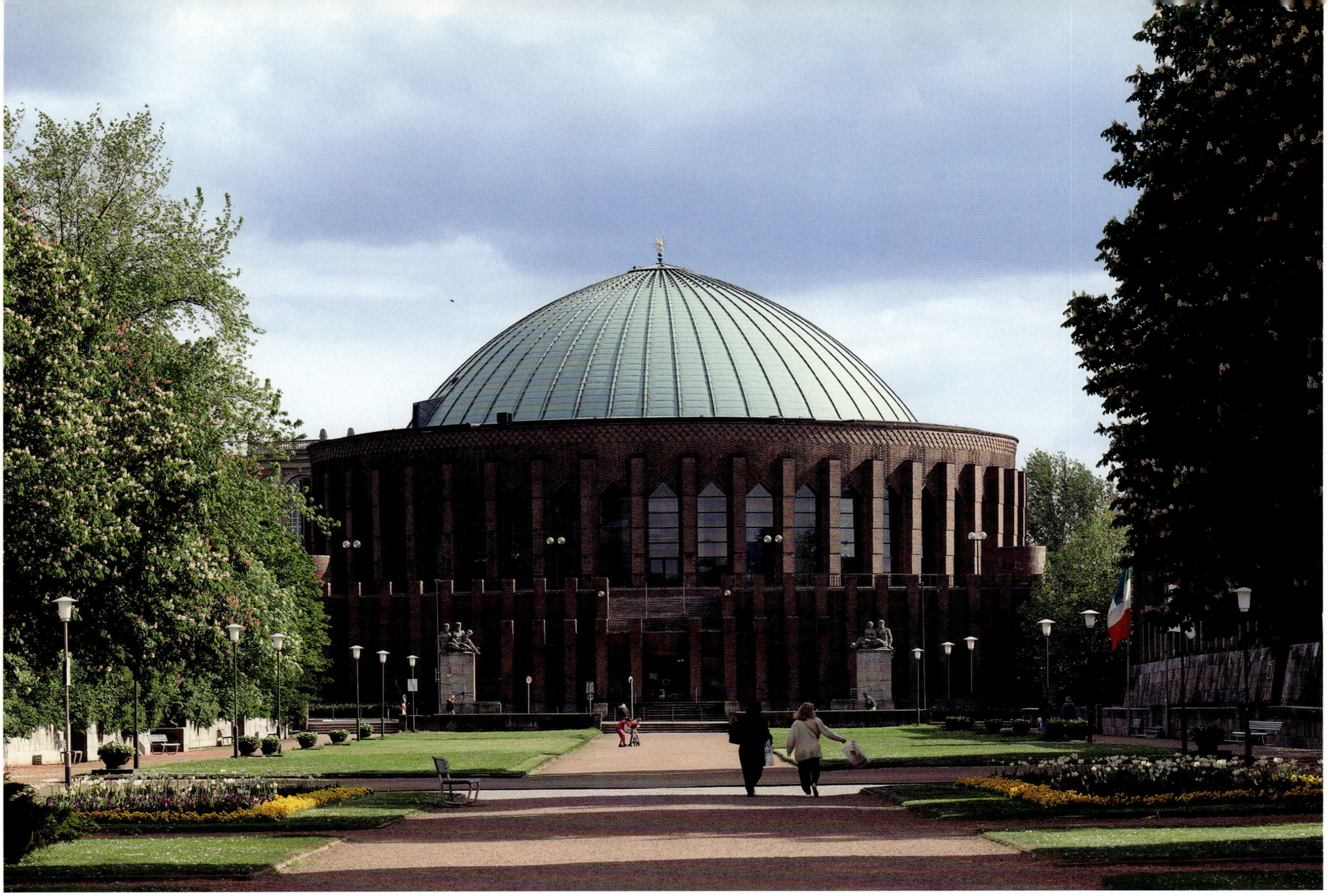

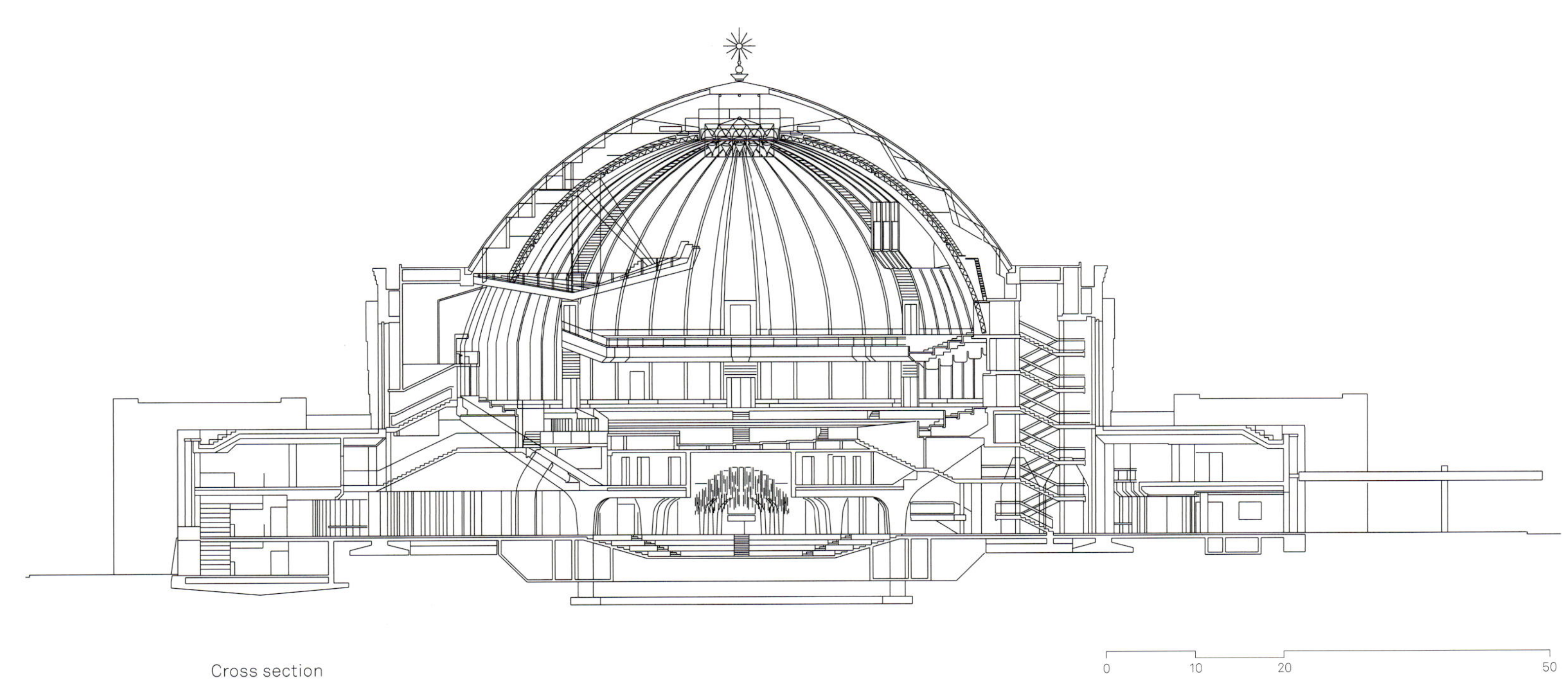

Cross section

 The Düsseldorf Concert Hall The Düsseldorf Concert Hall on the Rhine, originally called the Rheinhalle, was built in 1926 by Wilhelm Kreis as a planetarium. Together with the Ehrenhof-Komplex and the Rheinterrasse, it belonged to the so-called *Dauerbauten* (structures designed to last) of the Gesolei, or Great Exhibition for Health Care, Social Welfare, and Physical Exercise, that was held in Düsseldorf in 1926. In its materiality, proportions, and quality of detail, the Expressionistic brick architecture of the round dome structure is of timeless beauty. Severely damaged in World War II, the building was subsequently converted into a concert hall at the suggestion of Helmut Hentrich. By retaining the exterior façade, the dome, and the *Grüne Gewölbe* (Green Vault) north of the domed hall, the structure was successfully transformed into a completely new work of architecture characterized by a very special and intense atmosphere.

After almost thirty years of operation the need for revitalization became evident. The technical facilities were refurbished during the season break in 2005 and the building's protection against fire was improved to satisfy current standards. Particular attention was devoted to a drastic improvement of the problematic acoustics of the dome structure, including the elimination of what had become known as the *Klopfgeist,* or "knocking ghost," the disturbing echo produced by the dome. Together with the acoustic engineers, the dome vault was completely redesigned. The elimination of the echo effect and the maintenance of appropriate volume levels were accomplished with the aid of a complex system of polygonally arranged deflectors placed behind an acoustically transparent inner dome made of bronze fabric. The result is that the sound is reflected several times by the deflectors and thereby uniformly distributed. Since its refurbishment, the concert hall has been able to meet the highest international demands. By means of a special lighting design, the changes made to the hall through the acoustic intervention allow the space to be gradually transformed from a classic vaulted dome into a celestial canopy that generates a metaphysical effect—an echo of the hall's original use as a planetarium.

Another part of the concert hall is currently being renovated: the *Grüne Gewölbe,* one of the most beautiful examples of Expressionist architecture, is being restored. In addition, parts of the chamber music hall are being redesigned. Following the model of the large concert hall, it, too, will receive a new acoustic ceiling. The box office will be also enlarged in order to make more space for a separate ticket window for subscribers. These measures make a contribution to the ongoing, almost ninety-year history of the building, thanks to which people will still be able to experience the fascination of the Düsseldorf Concert Hall in the future.

→ Lighting of Concert Hall's dome

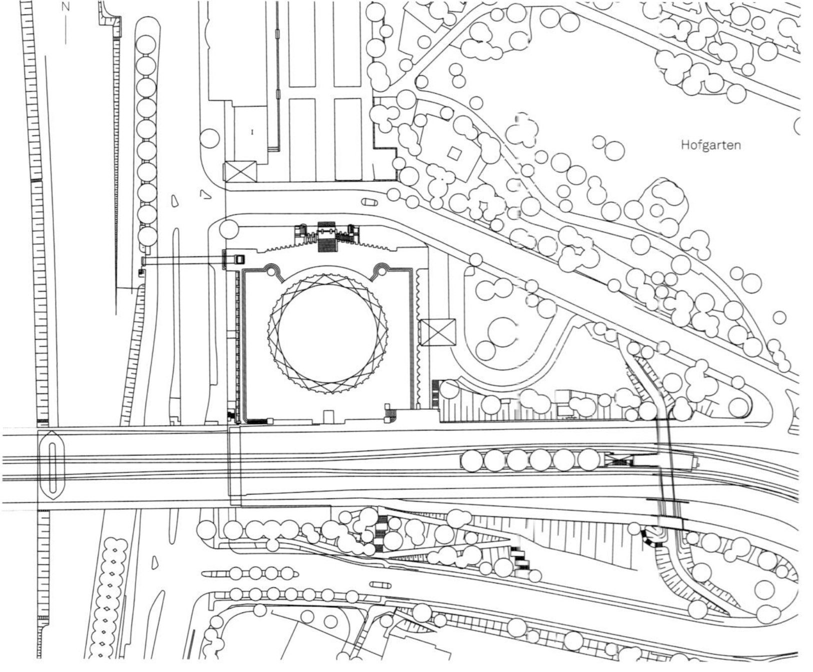

Site plan

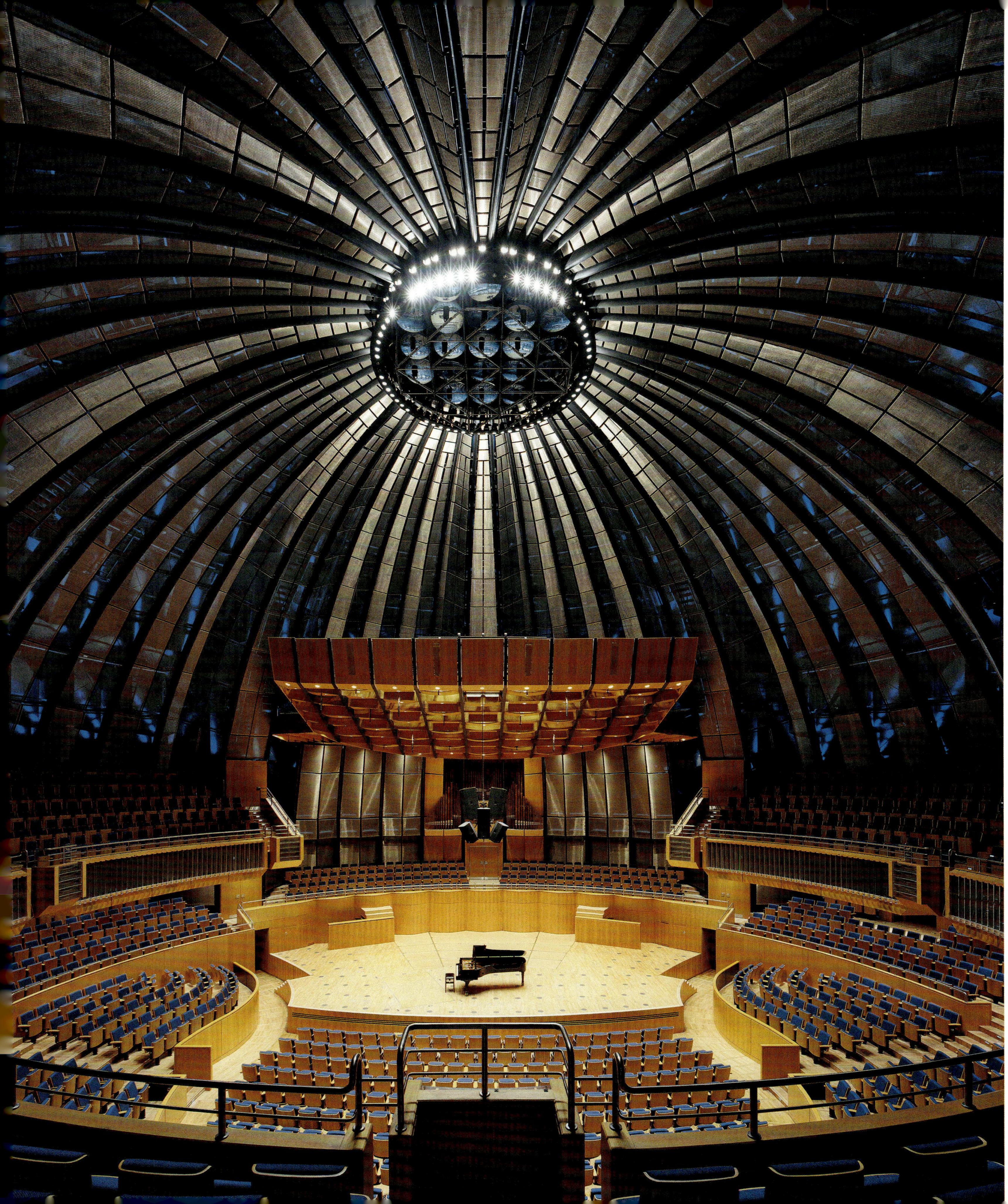

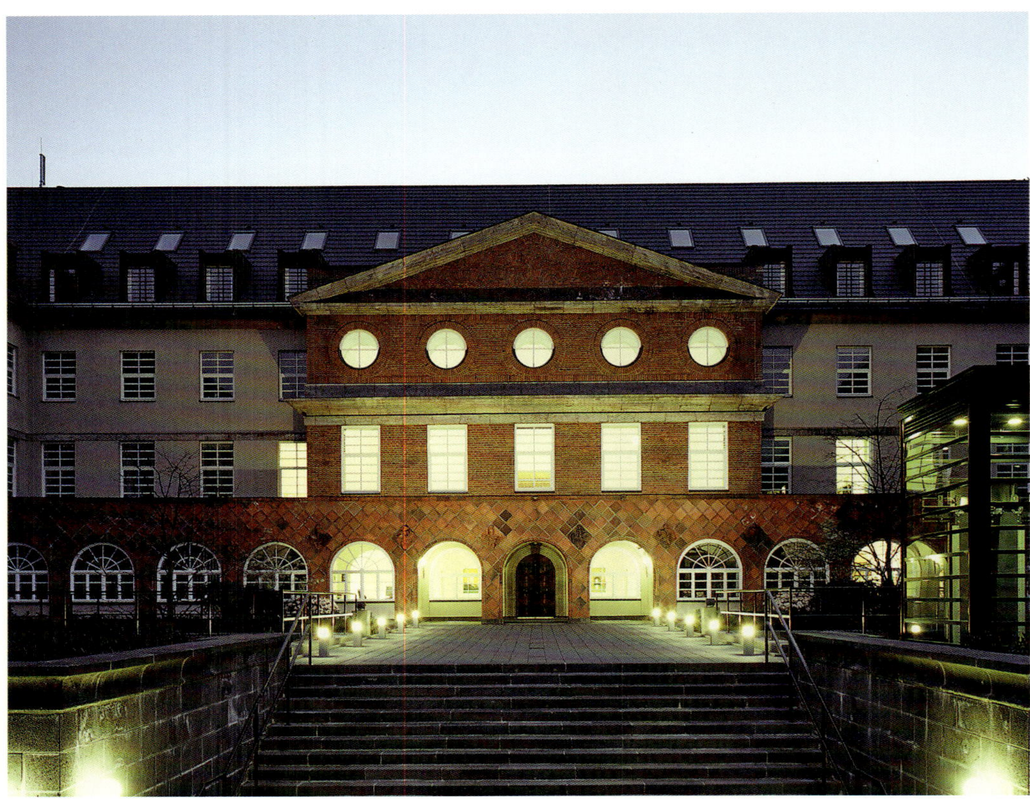

Phoenix Building

The original company headquarters of Phoenix AG and later headquarters of the labor bureau was converted and refurbished for the Düsseldorf district attorney and sections of the Düsseldorf county court. In order to expand the floor space, the top floor was completely removed and reconstructed. By retaining the landmark protected exterior façade, the entrance hall, and the stairwell as well as two imposing meeting rooms with stucco ceilings, the original character of the house was restored.

Client: LEG NRW GmbH
User: Amtsgericht und Staatsanwaltschaft Düsseldorf
Location: Düsseldorf
GFA: 17,063 m²
Year of completion: 1926
Restoration according to landmark protection criteria: 2002

Continuity

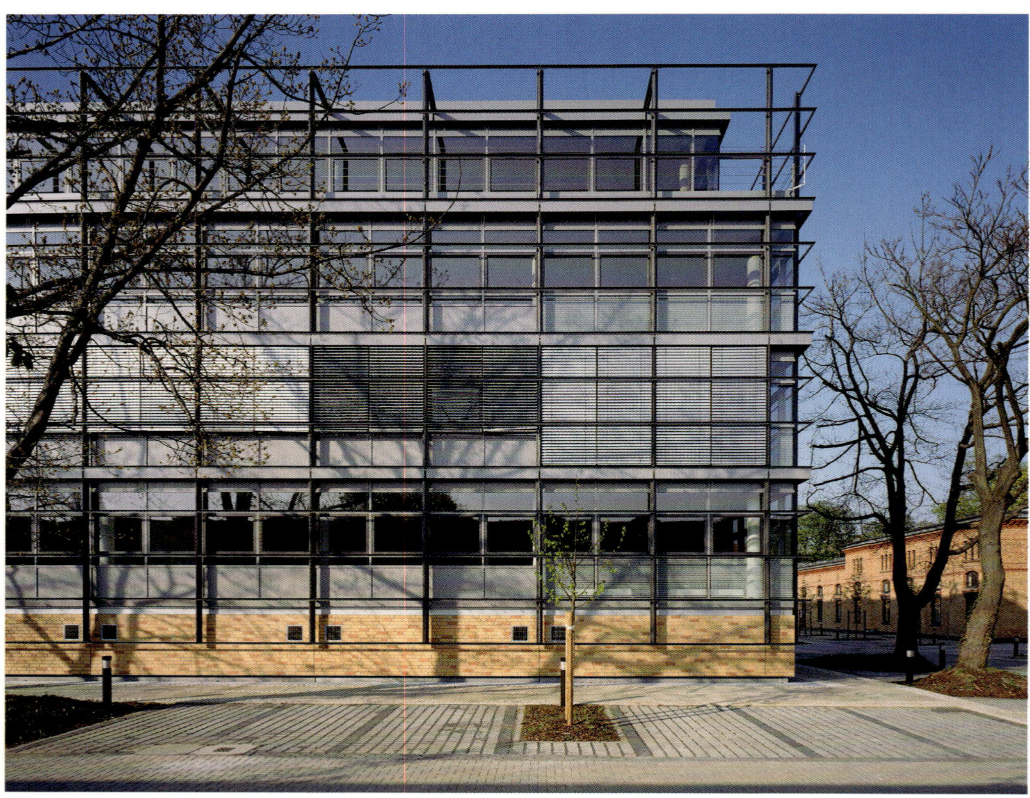

Telekom Potsdam

The building of the former barracks of the royal bodyguards was reconstructed according to the historical model and converted for office use. The new buildings complement the historical tone and create a sense of overall unity. In reference to the historical building, the main material used is brick, which has been paired with glass and metal.

Client: DeTeBau Deutsche Telekom Potsdam
Location: Potsdam
GFA: 32,000 m²
Year of completion: 1893
Conversion and revitalization according to landmark protection criteria: 1995

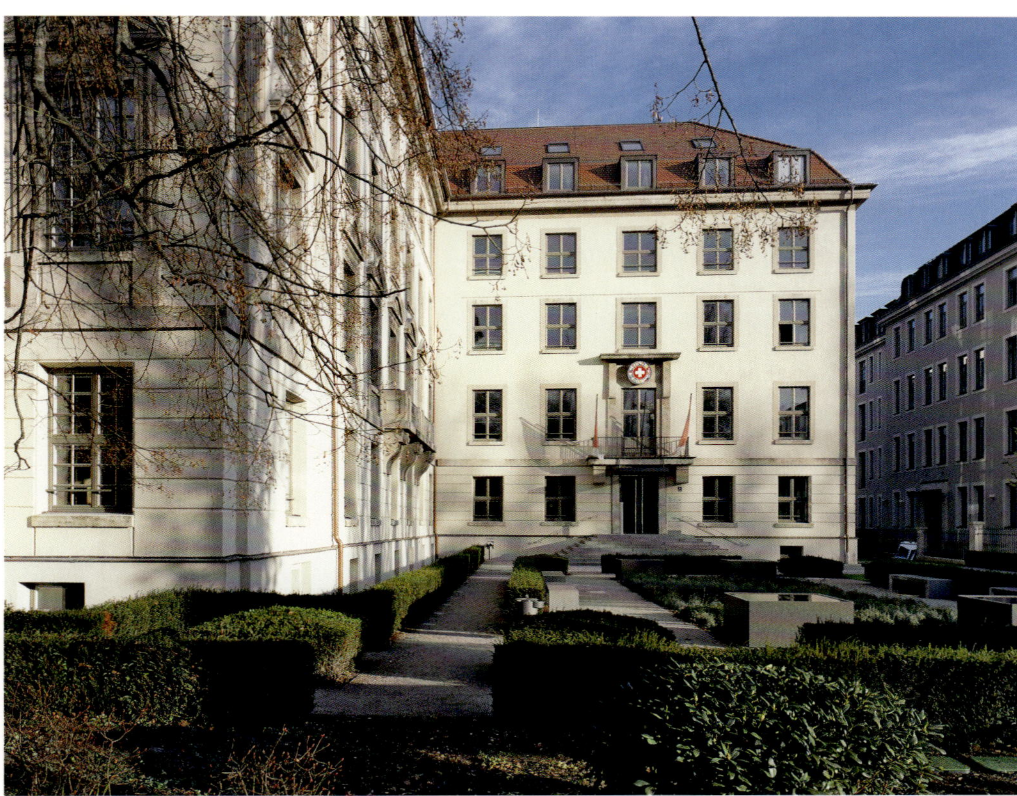

Palais Leopold

After Swiss Life moved out, the building complex was completely gutted, converted, and expanded. The landmark-protected sections 1 and 2, whose structure defines the surrounding urban space, were upgraded, and section 3 was replaced with a delicate, economical new building. The concept consisted of the development of a new, central, prestigious access setting leading directly from Leopoldstrasse. The building project realized in the course of the conversion planning facilitated a multifaceted, flexible use pattern.

Client: Swiss Life
Location: Munich
GFA: 13,568 m^2
Work stations: 500
Completion date: 2005
Award: Façade Prize of the Capital City of Munich, honorable mention, 2005

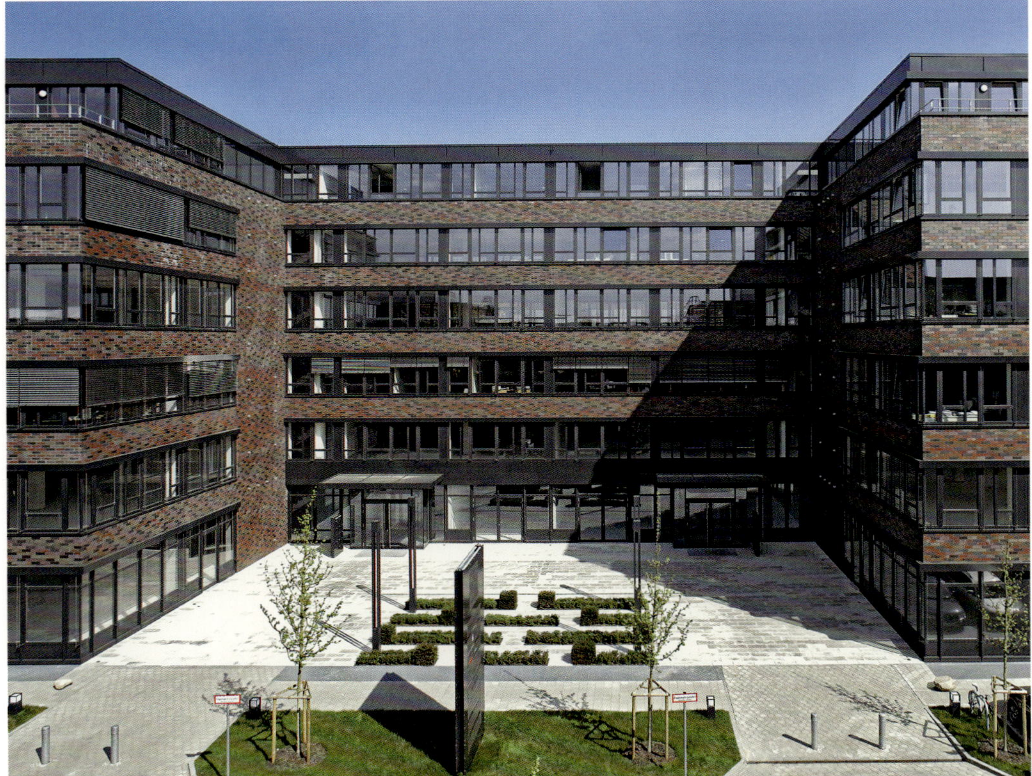

Quartier am Zeughaus (Armory District)

The Quartier am Zeughaus (Armory District) was realized on property formerly belonging to the telecommunications warehouse on Osterfeldstrasse in Hamburg. The starting point was the historic armory, with its characteristic brick details from the 1930s. With a minimum of intervention in its historical fabric, this structure was transformed into an attractive office building. Thanks to two further construction phases, a highly flexible office complex emerged whose familiar outlines and materials make reference to the historic armory. The result is the creation of a lively, mixed-use district featuring offices, residences, services, restaurants, and recreation opportunities.

Client: Calliston Gesellschaft für Projektentwicklung mbH
Location: Hamburg
GFA: 33,000 m^2
Completion date: 2008

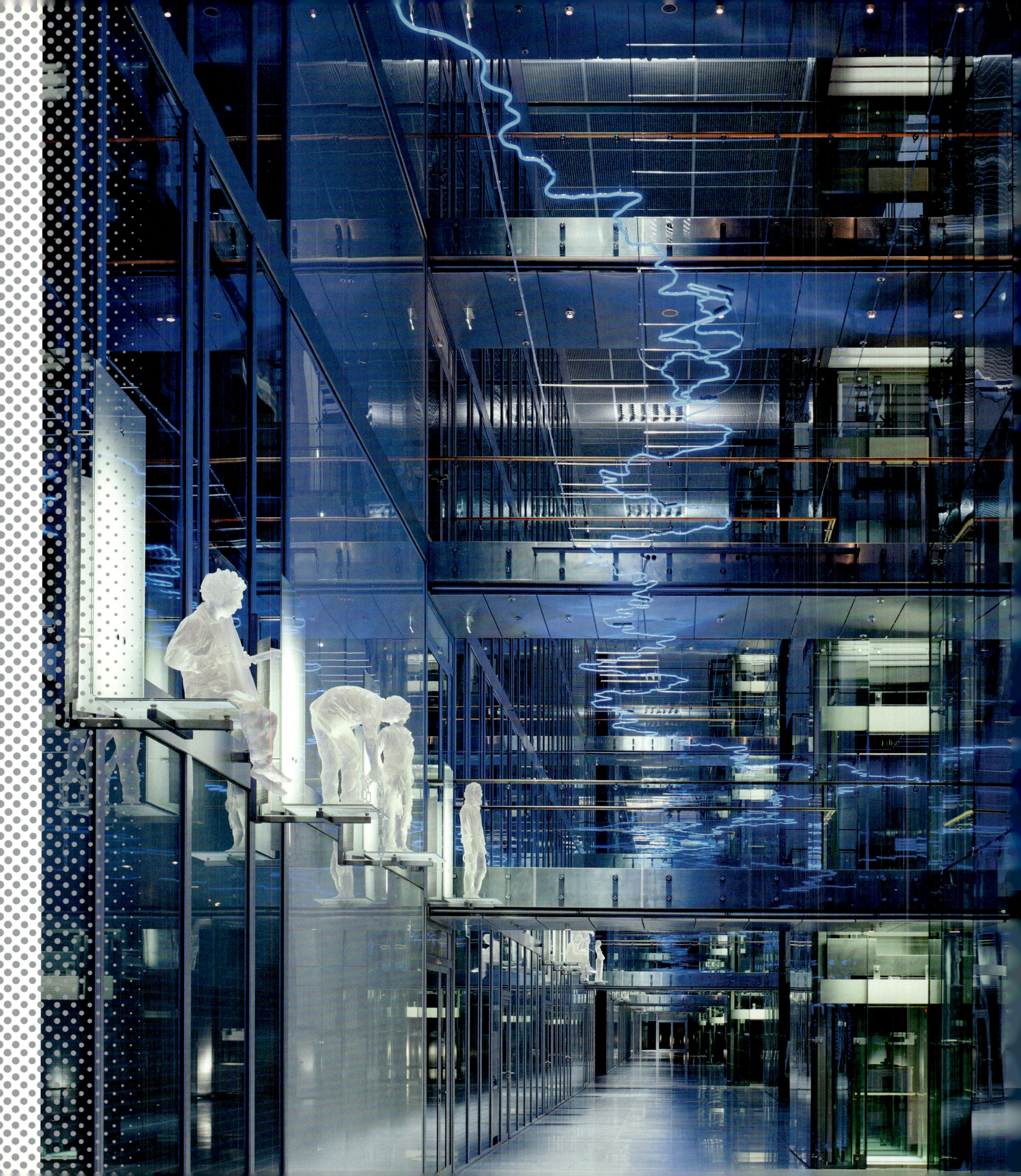

Poetry involves a kind of condensation. A poem consists most of the time of an image that moves us and that we can only describe with difficulty. The process of designing a building is comparable to the composition of a poem. Architectural poetry is created from an image, a thought, an idea; it is an interweaving of proportions, relationships, and measure.

Human beings often create likenesses of nature, putting these "borrowed" images in a new, artificial context. The appearance and the design are the mirror image of a condition that strongly compels the author or designer. Poetry moves us to the depths of our souls, operating at the very roots of our perception and understanding.

The poetry of architecture is three-dimensional. The task of the architect is to fit together images and metaphors in a graspable, constructive design. While the poetry of words plays with the inner imagination, the poetry of architecture, in contrast, appeals to the use of our senses. It is plastic, and therefore can be sensuously experienced at any time. According to Friedrich Wilhelm Joseph Schelling, the fine arts, and therefore also architecture, are a kind of "mute poetry" that is "expressed not with language, but, like the silence of nature, with design and form."

The image that distinguishes the architectural poetry of the Allianz Kai on the Frankfurt bank of the Main is the river itself. The flowing of the water and the force behind that flowing are symbolized in the building. Human beings apparently instinctively seek proximity to water; our physical and psychic well-being depend directly upon it. On the other hand, the riverbank as a concept often stands for desire in works of poetry. It evokes a romantic image that speaks to the innermost desires of the soul, whose fulfillment seems to be waiting unattainably on the other side of the ocean, lake, or river.

The Allianz Kai is in a location involving both water and riverbank, and this feeling should be palpable in the entire building. Like a hand, the fingers of the administration building open up to the Main and draw the image of the current flowing by towards the building itself. The open spaces between the individual building "fingers" are arranged with reference to the Main. The design's elongated riverbank zone succeeds in keeping the architecture at a distance, thereby creating a contrast to the water. The river is led all the way up the building through the inclusion of roof gardens. The Main is present everywhere and enriches the work's atmosphere.

The Main, along with all its patron saints, is even to be found inside the building. Where the individual building structures facing the Main are connected by the 160-meter-long main thoroughfare, the flowing current is signaled by a luminous work of art by Stephan Huber that hangs in space, proportionally shortened to the length of the "path" running through the building. Twenty-one river saints frozen in their poses accompany the bright-blue neon current, watching over the events as they transpire in an enchanting allegory. After everything has been said and the last sound has died away, the space remains and manifests itself in its three-dimensional state, providing further proof that, as Schelling said, architecture is mute poetry.

Poetry Allianz Kai

Client: **Allianz Lebensversicherung AG** | Location: **Frankfurt am Main** | GFA: **100,000 m²**
Work stations: **2,450** | Completion date: **2002** | Competition: **1st Prize, 1997**

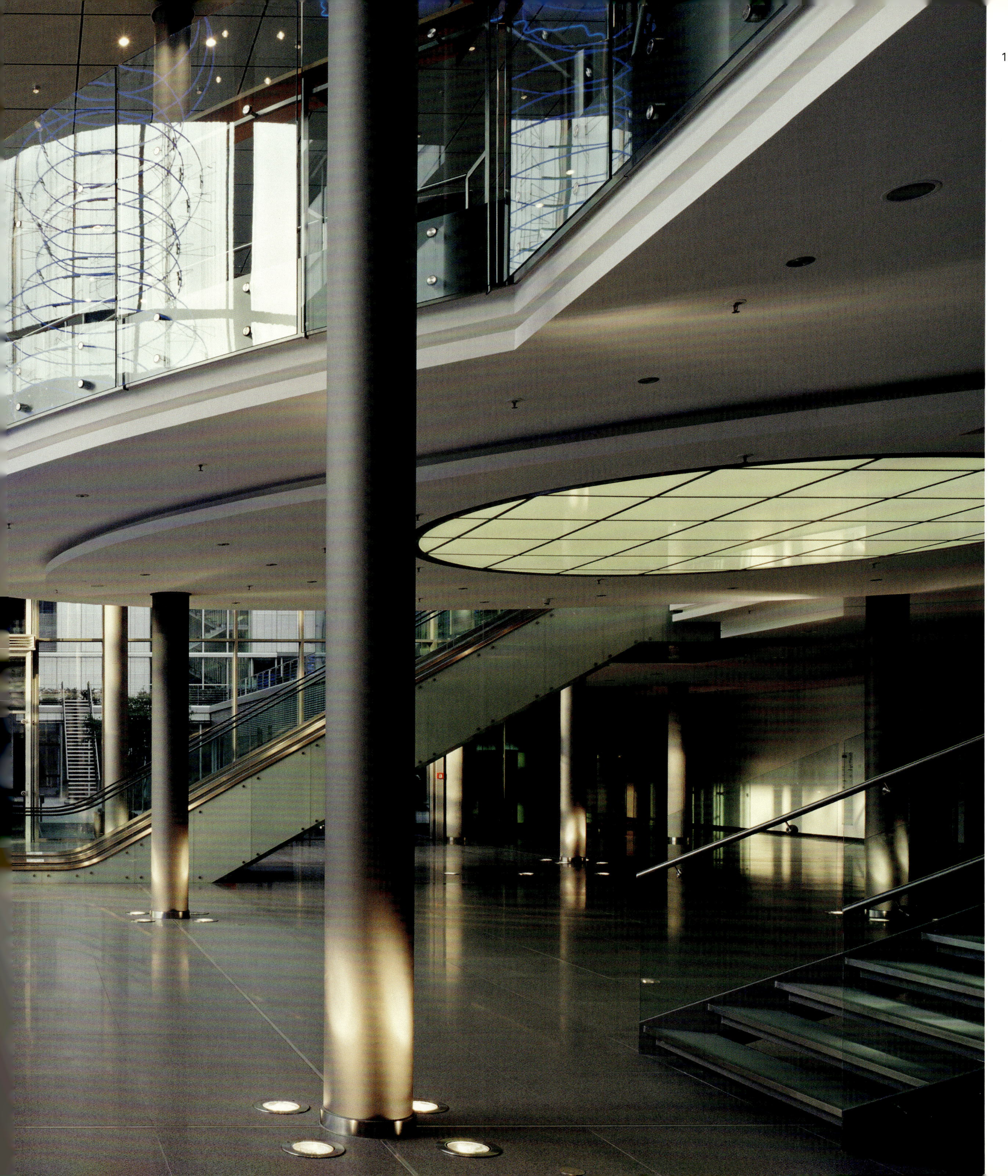

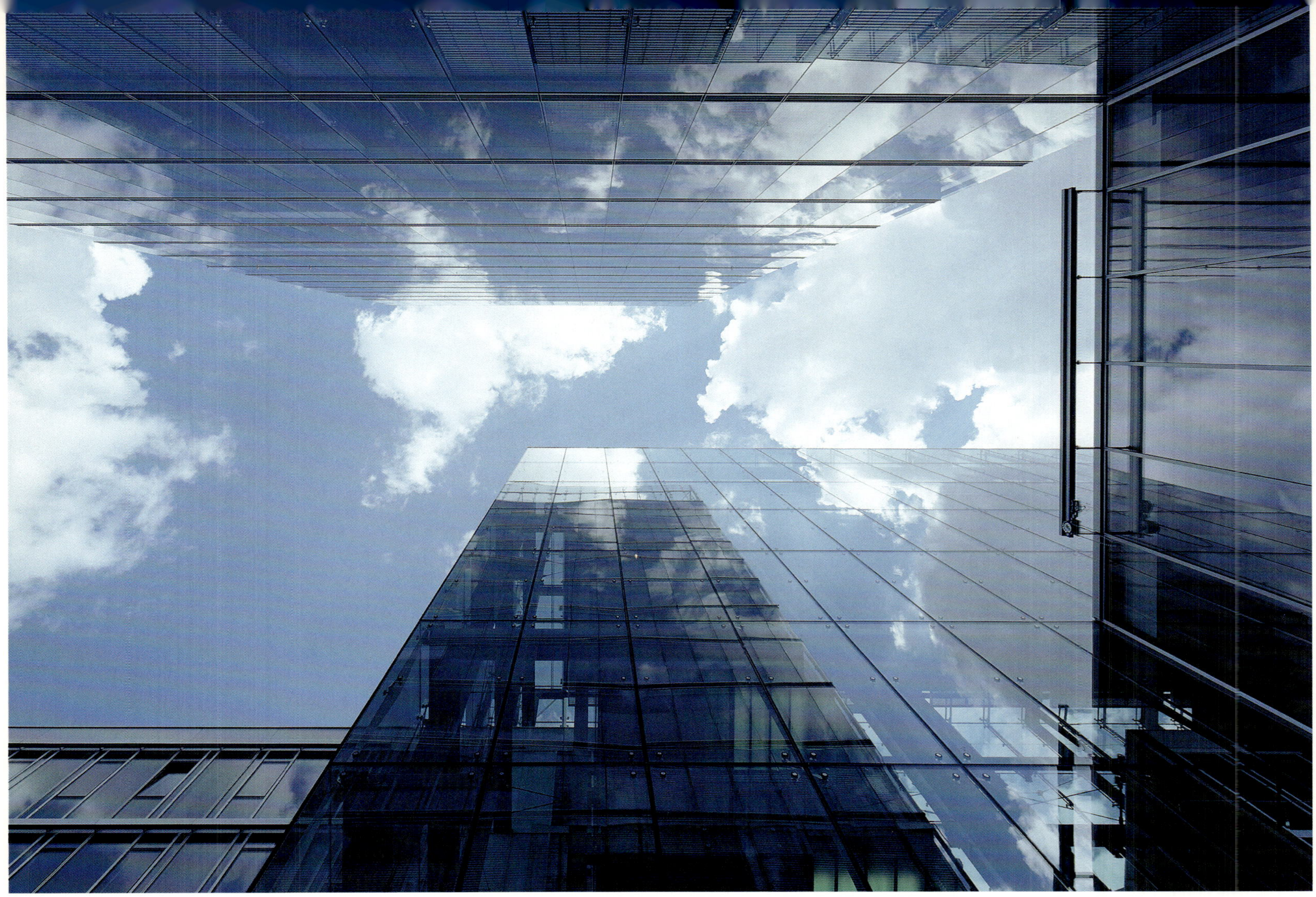

Atrium between high-rise and comb-shaped buildings

↞ Entrance foyer with the artwork *Im Fluss*
→ Atrium between high-rise and comb-shaped buildings

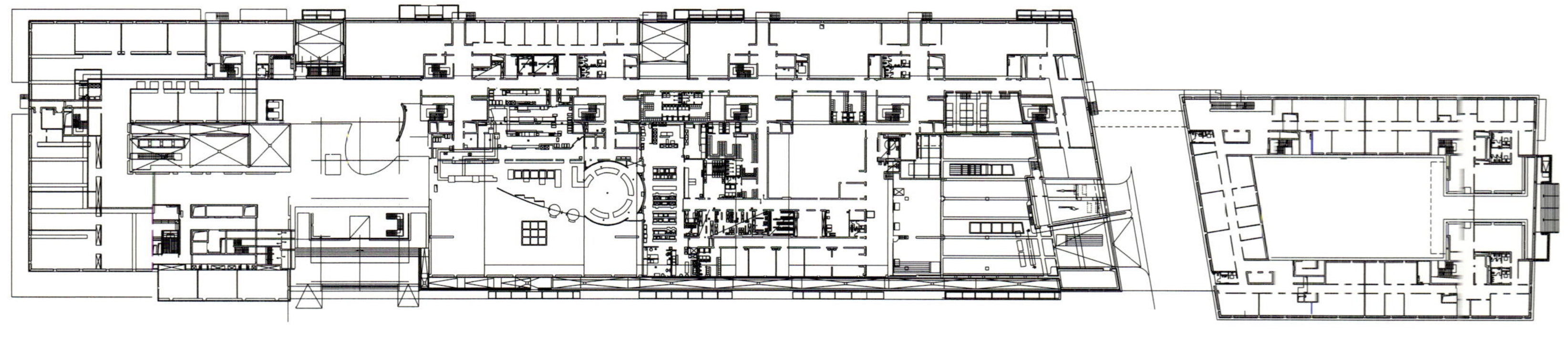

Floor plan of ground floor

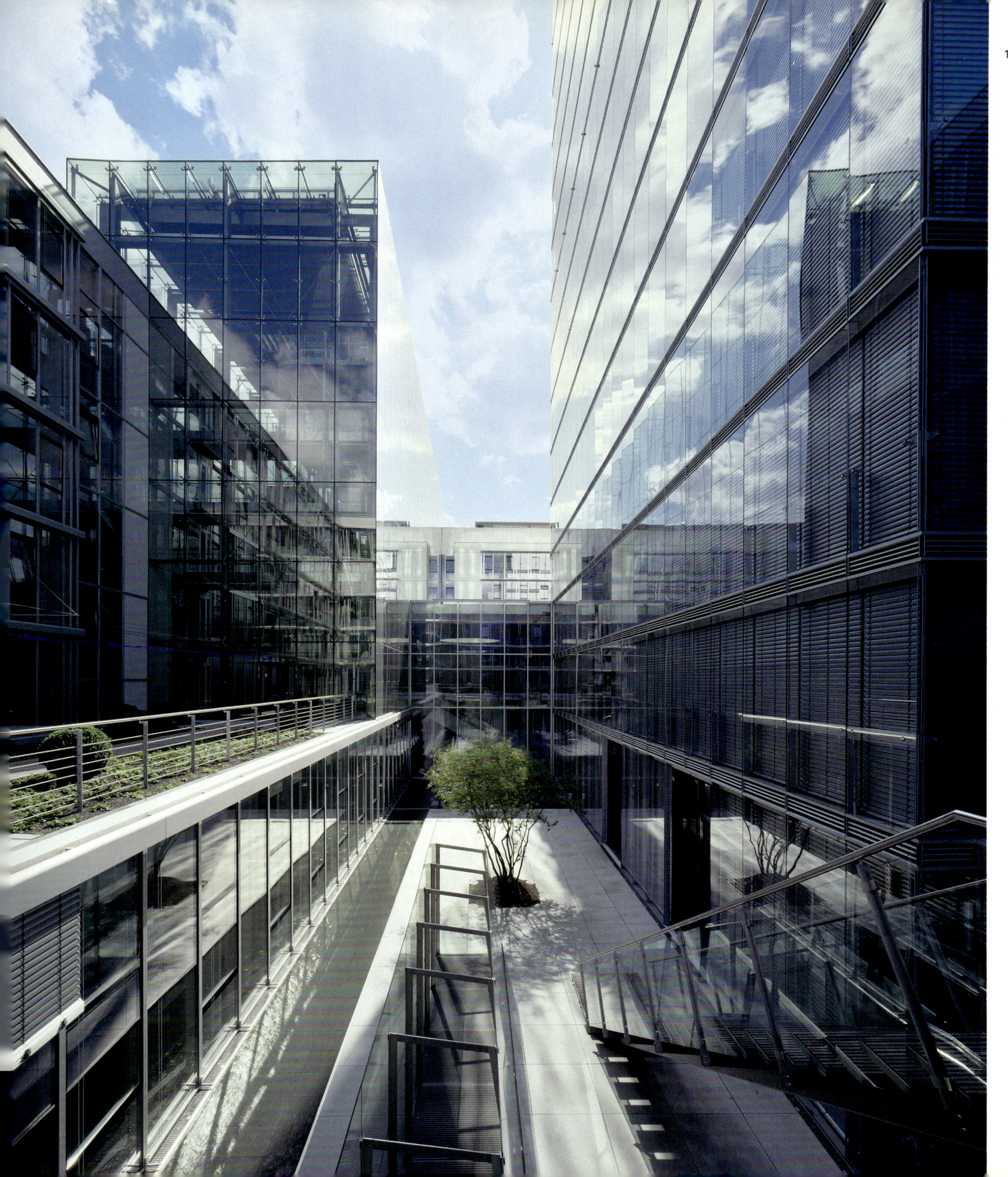

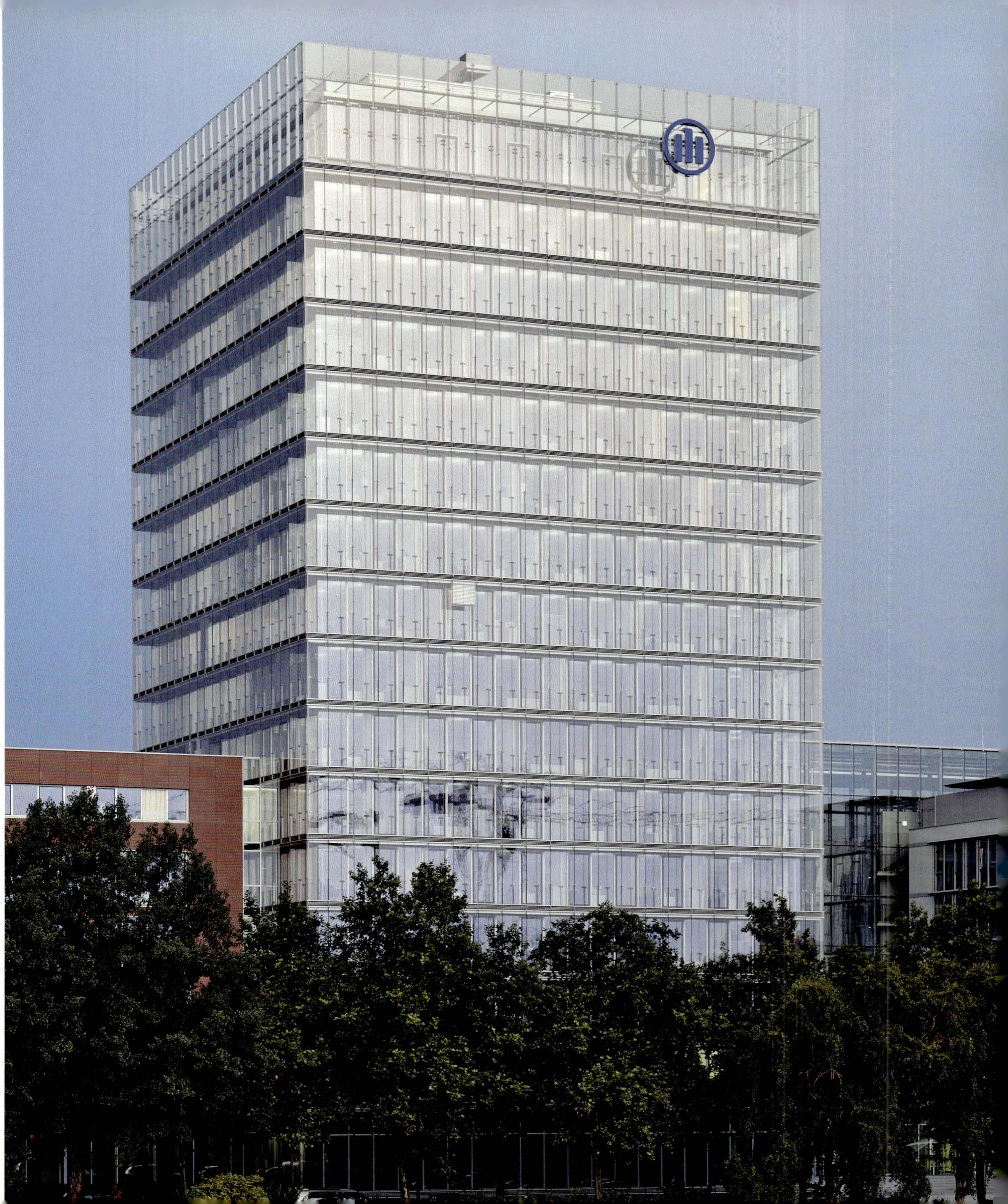

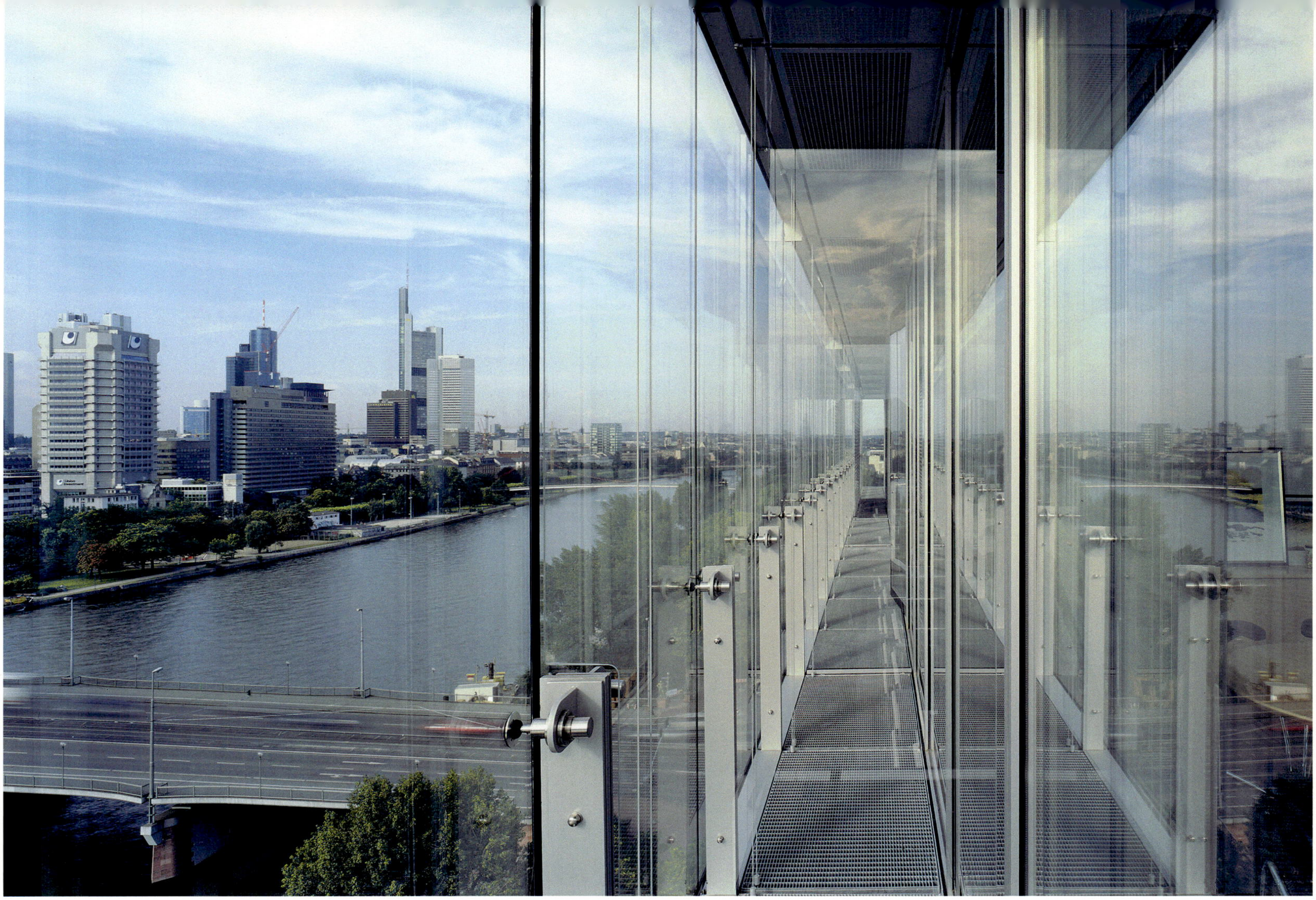

Merging of exterior and interior space

← Allianz High-Rise

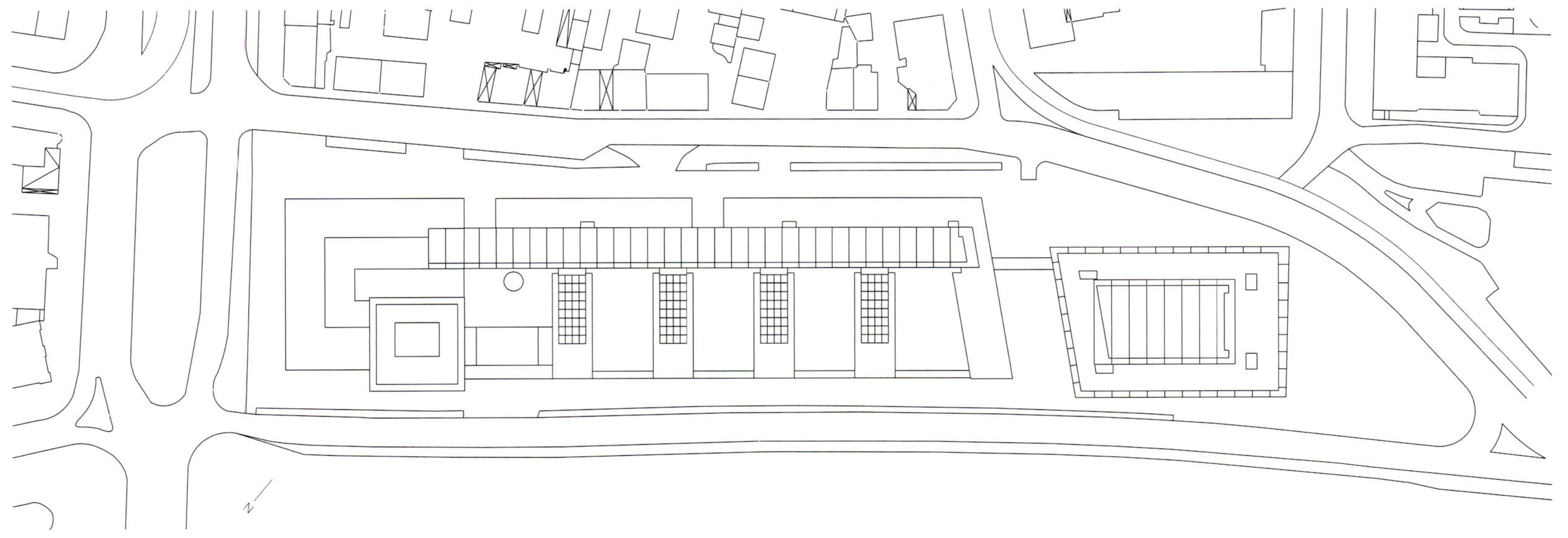

Site plan

The Allianz Kai The design for the new building complex was the entry that won first prize in a competition held in 1997. From 2000 to 2002 the new office and service center, which consolidated nine Allianz insurance firms and about 2,500 employees at this location, was erected on the former AEG grounds at Theodor-Stern-Kai, with a view of the Frankfurt skyline.

The new building is located directly on the Main River in the Sachsenhausen district. In order to do justice to the special situation as well as the necessary urban development order, the preexisting construction was torn down. However, with its urban developmental and typological disposition the design for the Allianz Kai refers to the earlier AEG buildings and is presented on a lot of 23,000 square meters as a differentiated comb and transom building complex of 100,000 square meters of gross floor area. A six-story perimeter development clad in natural stone and running along Stresemannallee provides the prelude for the 300-meter-long, eighty-meter-wide, and up to sixty-meter-high new building. At this location the building accommodates the scale of the adjacent housing structure and at the same time closes the road space. The main entrance on Theodor-Stern-Kai is addressed by the sixteen-story high-rise, which in addition marks the transition between the closed construction and the transparent comb structure along the Main. There the glass-skinned building opens and connects with the river and its bank. The glass façades of the five office wings generate a varied merging of interior and outdoor space and allow pedestrians and residents a glimpse inside. This openness is continued in the interior of the building. A 160-meter-long, seven-story-tall inner access street ties the separate buildings together. Glassed-in connecting bridges, elevators, and stairwells break up the space of the main thoroughfare and expose its function to view. In all office spaces the work stations are well-lit, naturally ventilated, and placed close to windows, a concept that was also rigorously applied in the high-rise by the extension of a double façade.

As a poetic gesture and a tribute to the location, the Main River was diverted into the interior of the building. In imitation of the Main, the work of art entitled *Im Fluss* by the Munich sculptor Stephan Huber presents a blue neon line in a scale of about 1:1,500 that winds through the entry hall and the main thoroughfare. Accompanied by twenty-one disembodied, radiantly glowing patron saints, this neon "river" creates an effective tension with the rational clarity of the architectural structure that houses it.

The Allianz Kai offers its employees a symbiosis of an atmosphere that is equal parts functional and sensual: it is a house that receives its guests with a generous spatial welcome, opening its arms to neighbors and pedestrians. Nestling into the bank of the Main, it almost melts into the river in the reflection of the water in the façade.

→ Main entrance
→› Main River side of the Allianz Kai

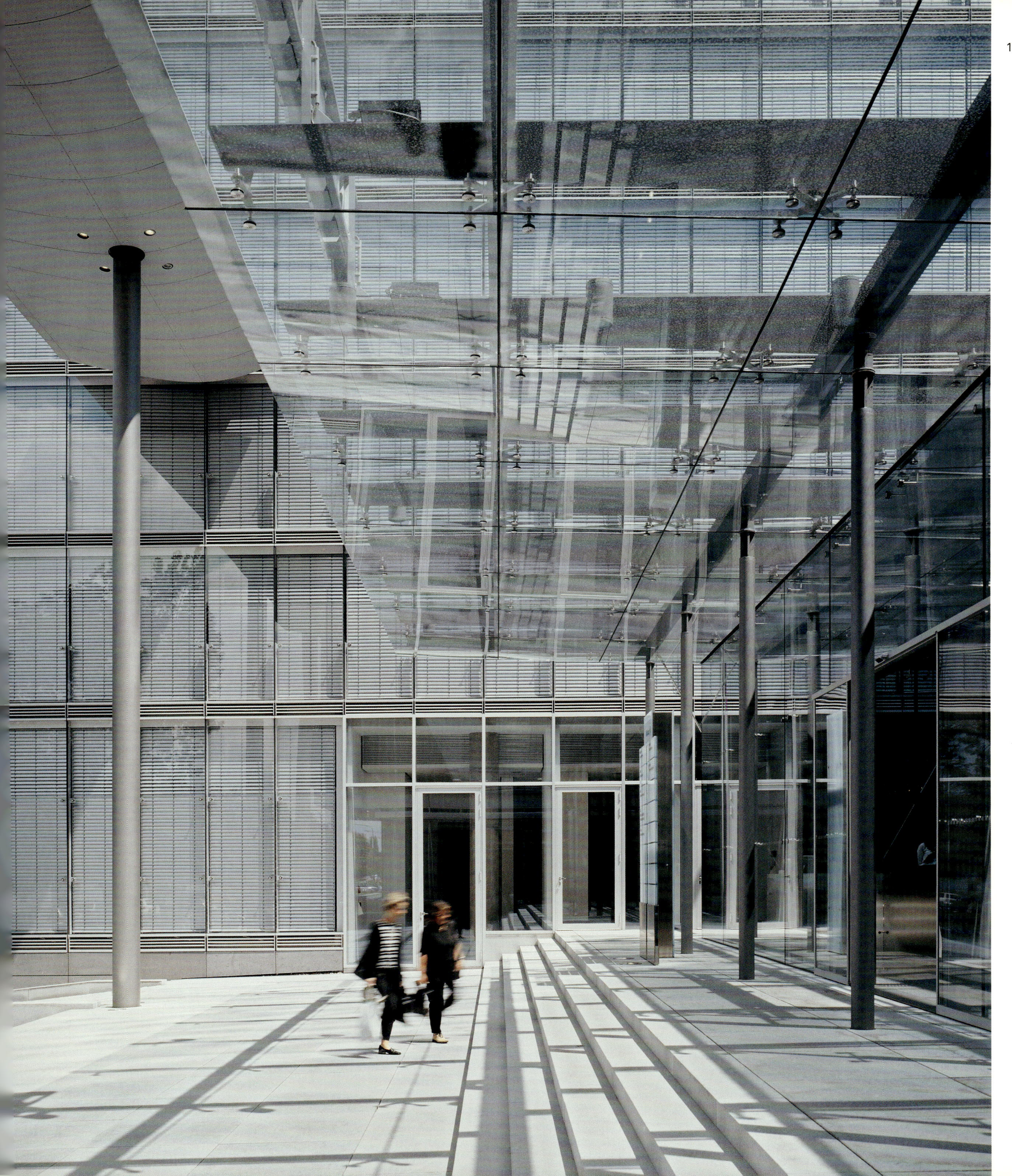

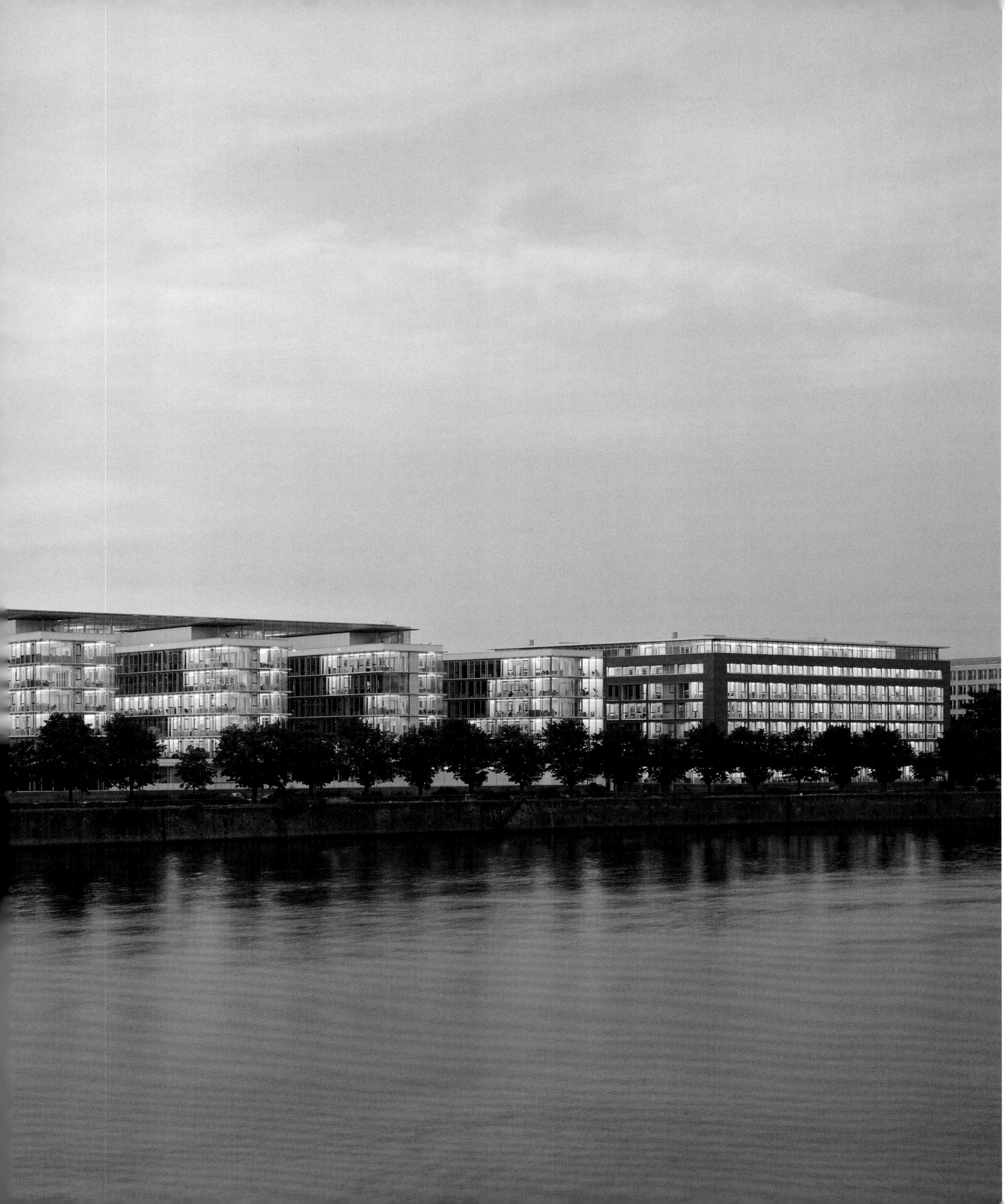

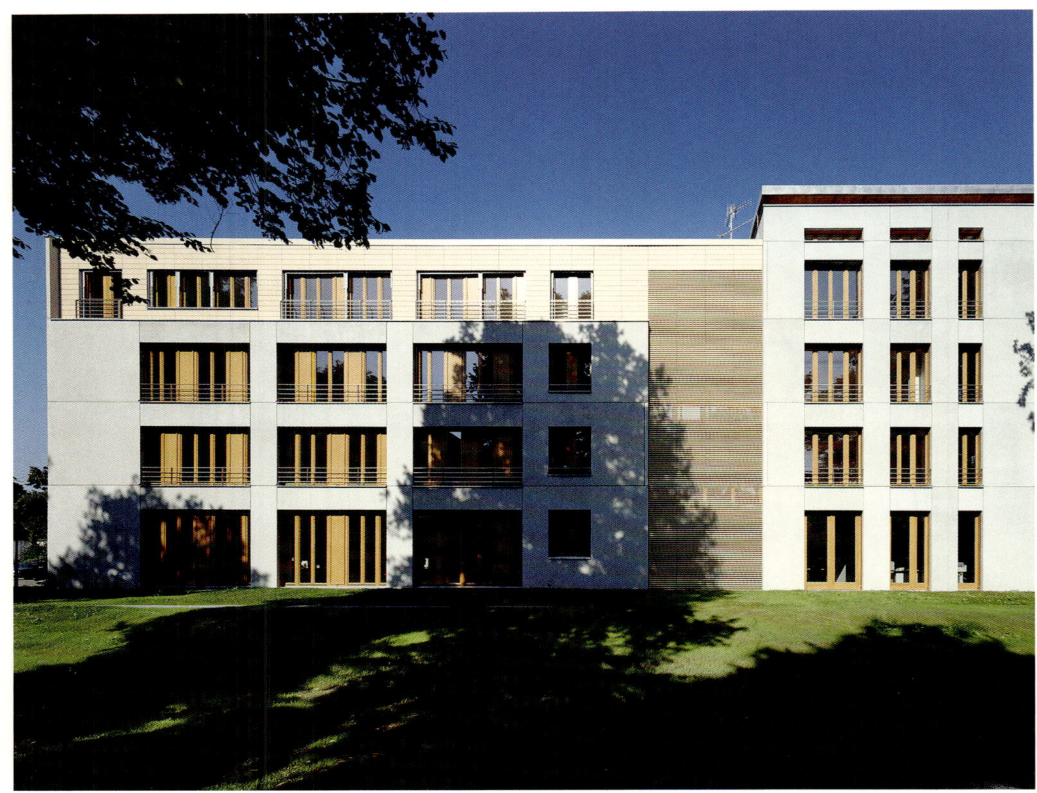

Headquarters of the Order of St. John

Located in an old park, the Order of St. John's new headquarters nestle gently into their surroundings. The use of green concrete blocks, oak, and ochre-colored clay slabs creates a perceptible relationship to the natural surroundings. The playfully arranged window formats are effectively juxtaposed with the clear, stone grid of the façade. The appearance of the building's exterior appropriately communicates the guiding principle of the Order's discipline and uprightness.

Client: Der Johanniterorden Balley Brandenburg des Ritterlichen Ordens St. Johannis vom Spital zu Jerusalem
Location: Berlin
GFA: 1,944 m²
Completion date: 2001
Competition: 1st Prize, 1998

Poetry

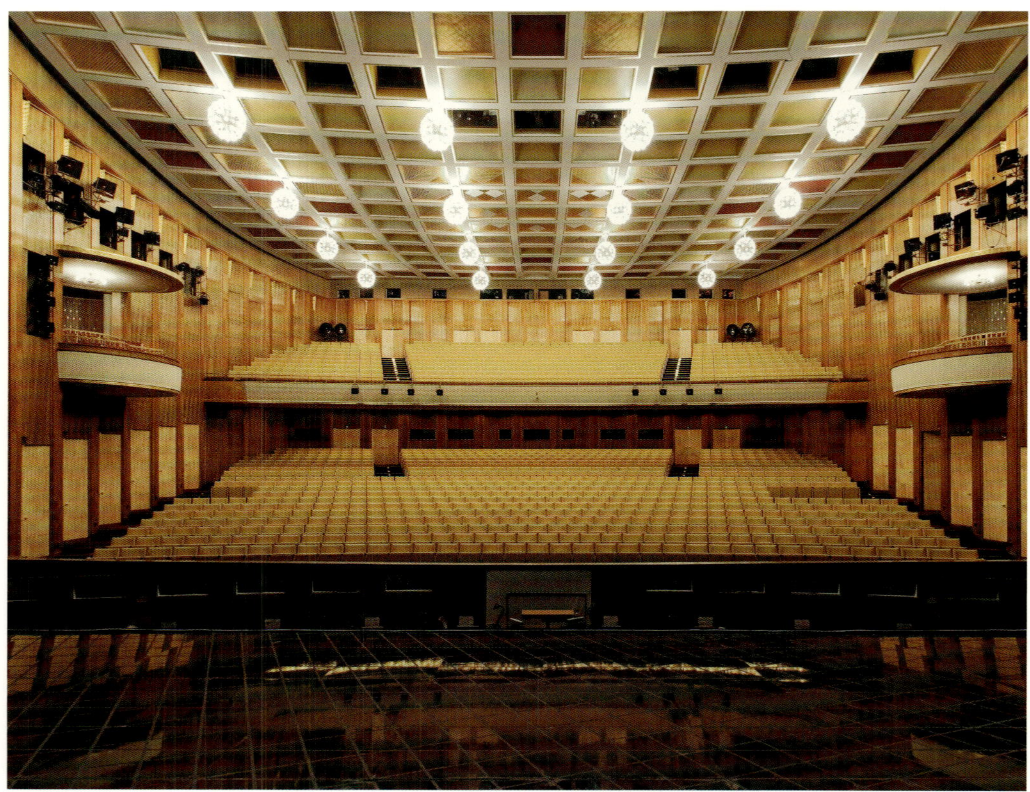

Leipzig Opera House

In the reconstruction of this building according to the original landmark-protected interior, the foyer and auditorium have taken on a new radiance. Fire protection upgrades, the improvement of the acoustics, and the raking of the auditorium were additional measures taken in the renovation of the tradition-laden opera house.

Client: City of Leipzig
Location: Leipzig
GFA: 21,100 m²
Seats: 1,250
Year of completion: 1959
Conversion and restoration according to landmark protection criteria: 2007

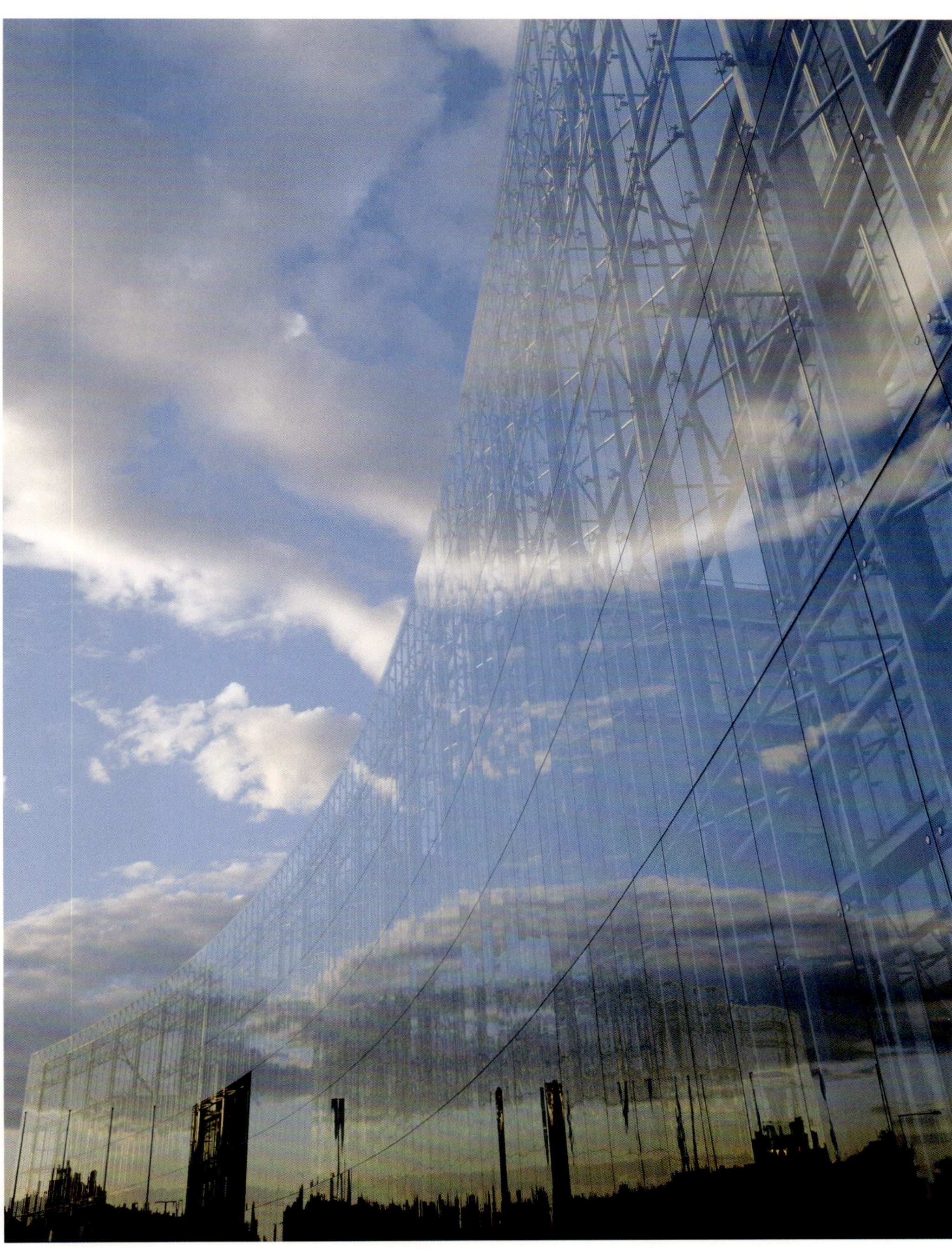

Neven DuMont Building

To a great extent, this project's appearance is determined by a freestanding, concave glass façade. This building shell is, on the one hand, an analogy to the idea of an open, transparent, people-oriented publishing house, while on the other it performs the useful function of sound-proofing the office spaces, which are equipped with windows that can be opened.

Client: Sagittarius Verwaltungs- und Beteiligungs-Gesellschaft mbH & Co. KG
Location: Cologne
GFA: 47,500 m^2
Work stations: 1,200
Completion date: 1998

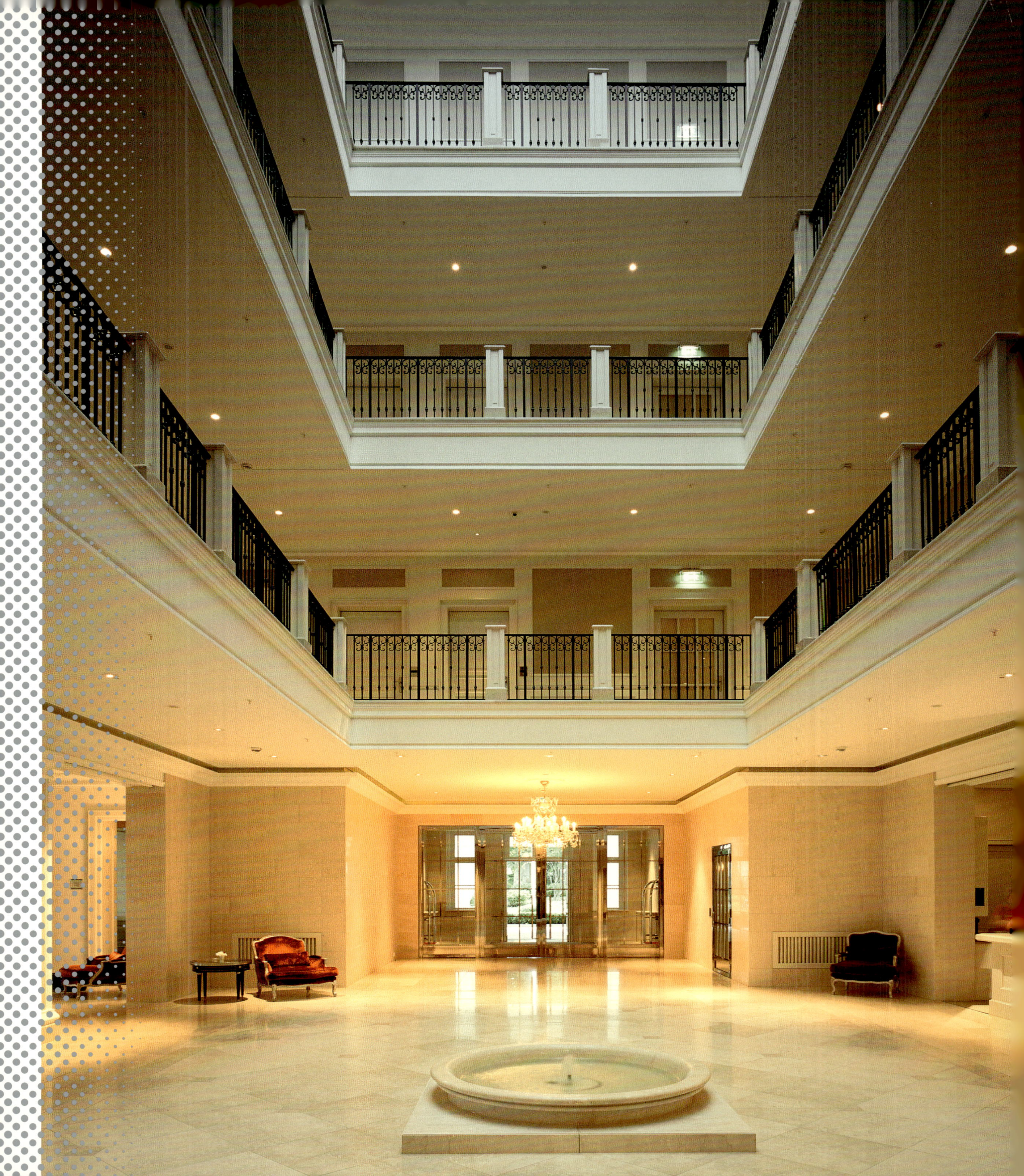

Identity Kempinski Grand Hotel Heiligendamm

Client: **ECH Entwicklungs-Compagnie Heiligendamm GmbH & Co. KG** | Location: **Bad Doberan–Heiligendamm**
GFA: **34,467 m²** | Hotel rooms: **107 suites and 118 hotel rooms** | Year of completion: **1793** | Restoration and revitalization according to landmark protection criteria: **2003** | Award: **MIPIM Award for "Hotel & Tourism Resorts," 2004**

Identity is based essentially on people, things, forms, and locations. A multitude of characteristics and qualities make up the human character. Fortunately, a perfected, idealized "identity" in the case of human beings—for instance, in the sense of a scientifically engineered clone— is only theoretically conceivable. The core of "personality" and its development of human identity is influenced to a significant extent by the interaction of the factors of "inclusion" and "demarcation." Something similar is at work with regard to the identity of a location. Just like a person, it is marked by its own unmistakable characteristics. Identity is often conditioned by evolution, and the "definition" that results from climate parameters, specific surroundings, or human interventions can result from natural as well as social motives. "Inclusion" is a necessary aspect of the identity of locations, for they always belong to a region, a country, a continent, and, in the final analysis, to the Earth as a whole.

One of the more unique places is the Bay of Mecklenburg. It extends from east to west from Fehmarn to the Darss peninsula. At the westernmost point of the bay, the coast is bordered by luxurious forests of beech. The fine sand extends almost to the roots of the trees, and from the bay one can see the chalk cliffs of the Fischland-Darss region and Hiddensee. In the midst of these idyllic surroundings is Heiligendamm, a location built up from the moraine debris left behind by a glacier in the Ice Age. The bay's natural characteristics have marked it for millions of years and contribute to its distinctiveness, its identity.

The location became known as a spa in 1793, when Dr. Samuel Gottlieb von Vogel sent his patient, Duke Friedrich Franz I of Mecklenburg-Schwerin, to the "hallowed" place. The personal physician to the duke had recognized the healing effect of the sea water, and the exceptional climatic conditions of the location acted as a remedy for a number of illnesses. The noble guest attracted other prominent visitors. In order to provide appropriate accommodation for them, bathing and lodging facilities were built from 1793 to 1870. Master builders Johann Christoph Heinrich von Seydwitz, Carl Theodor Severin, and Gustav Adolph Demmler created a unique and total work of art. The interaction of the human interventions and the surrounding landscape left its mark on the location and has lent it its uniqueness.

After its establishment, Heiligendamm became the most elegant spa in Germany and remained such until the nineteen-thirties. By the end of World War II, however, it had almost lost this "identity." The main building had come to lead un unhappy existence as a converted professional college and vacation camp for children, and it was just waiting for the run-down spa to be restored to its original glory. The five white buildings, which are now home to the Kempinski Grand Hotel complex, were augmented by the addition of a new building, the Severin Palais. Today, the five-star hotel continues the tradition of the historic Heiligendamm spa, but in a contemporary fashion. There is yet work to be done to the complex in order for it to be on a par with its original state. The cottages in the west, for example, have yet to be restored. The core of the facility, however, has been effectively revitalized and is more splendid than ever.

Once the uniqueness—the striking identity— of a location or an individual has been properly revealed, it behooves us to maintain this image, and this is precisely what has been done in Heiligendamm.

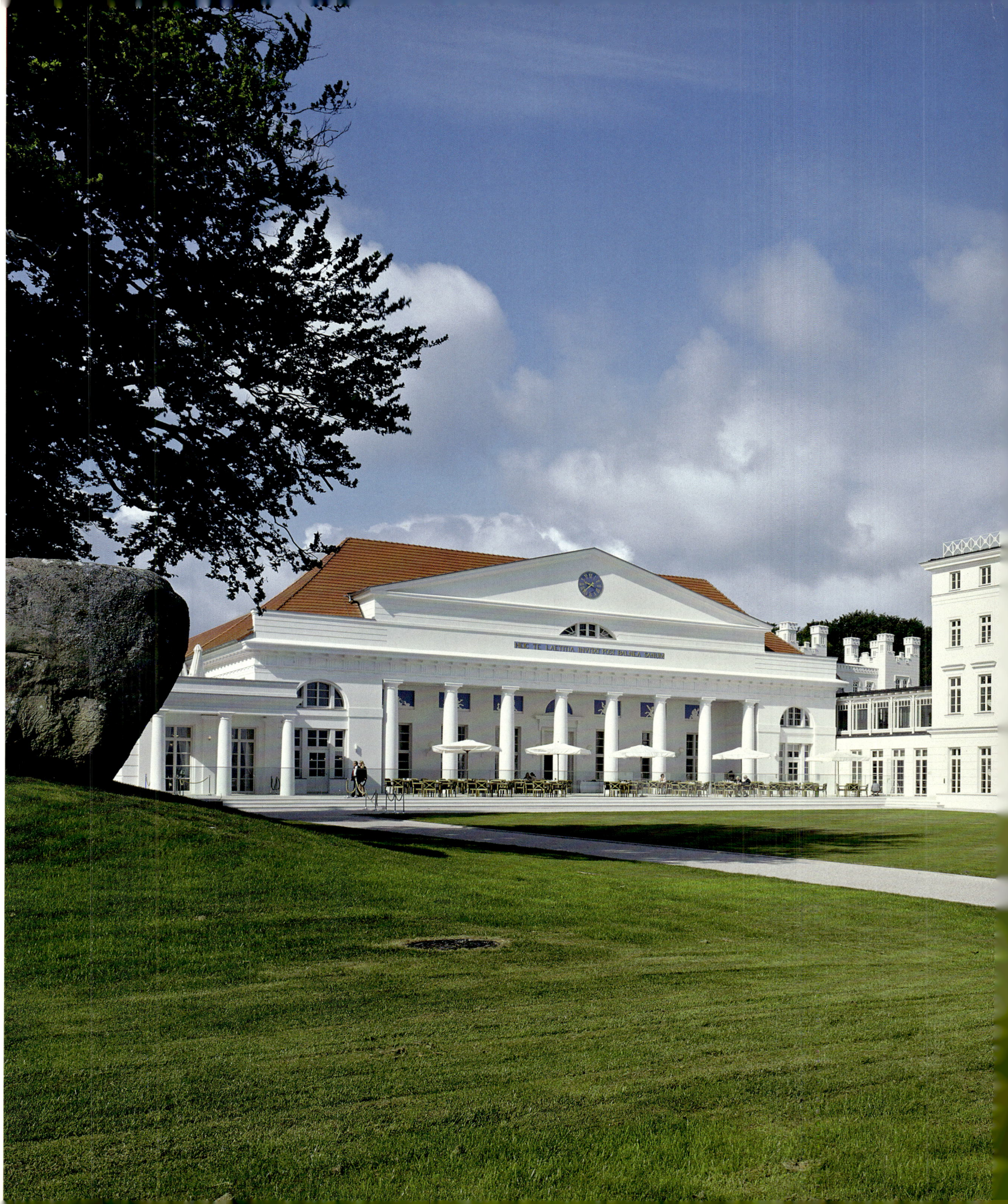

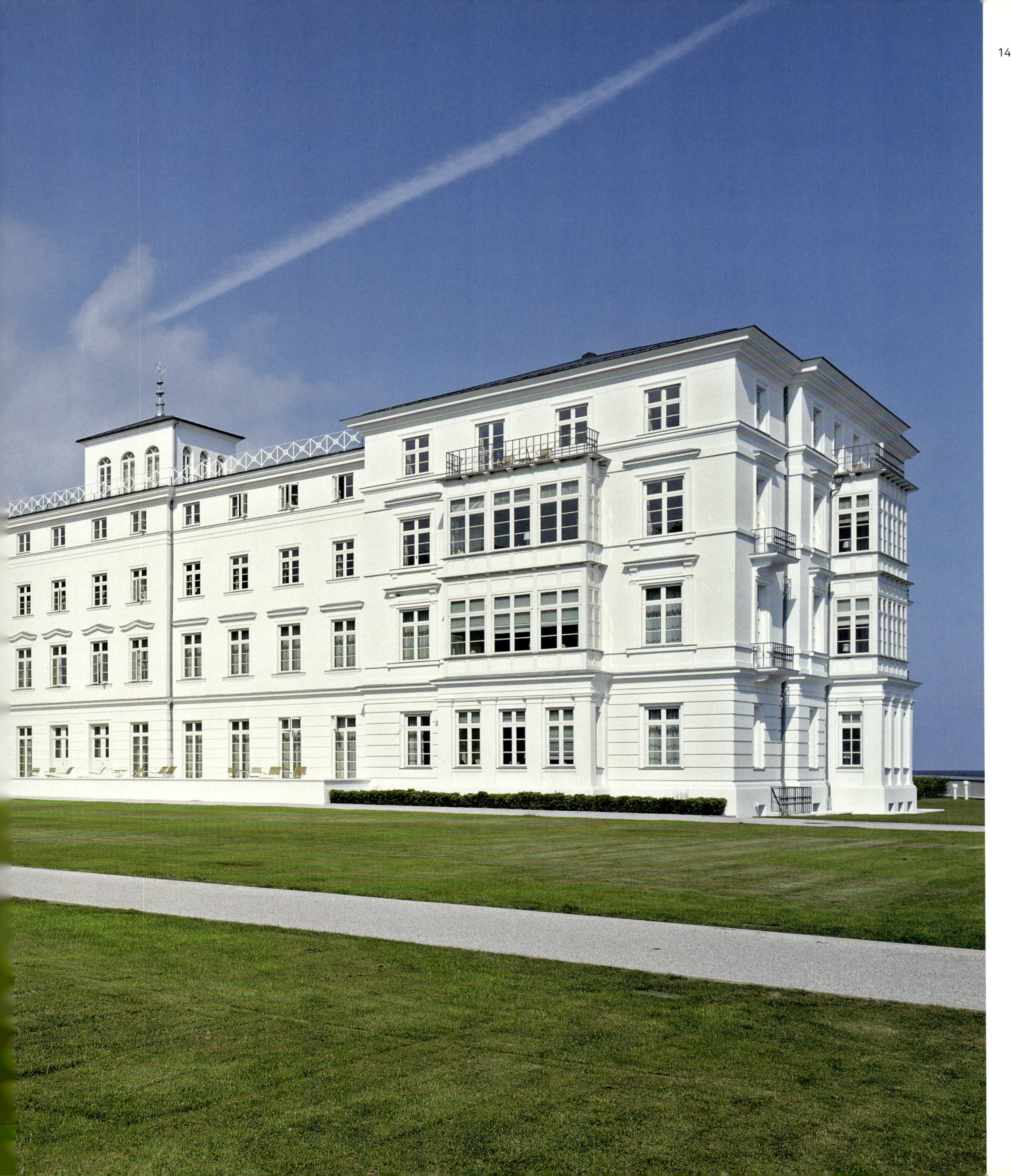

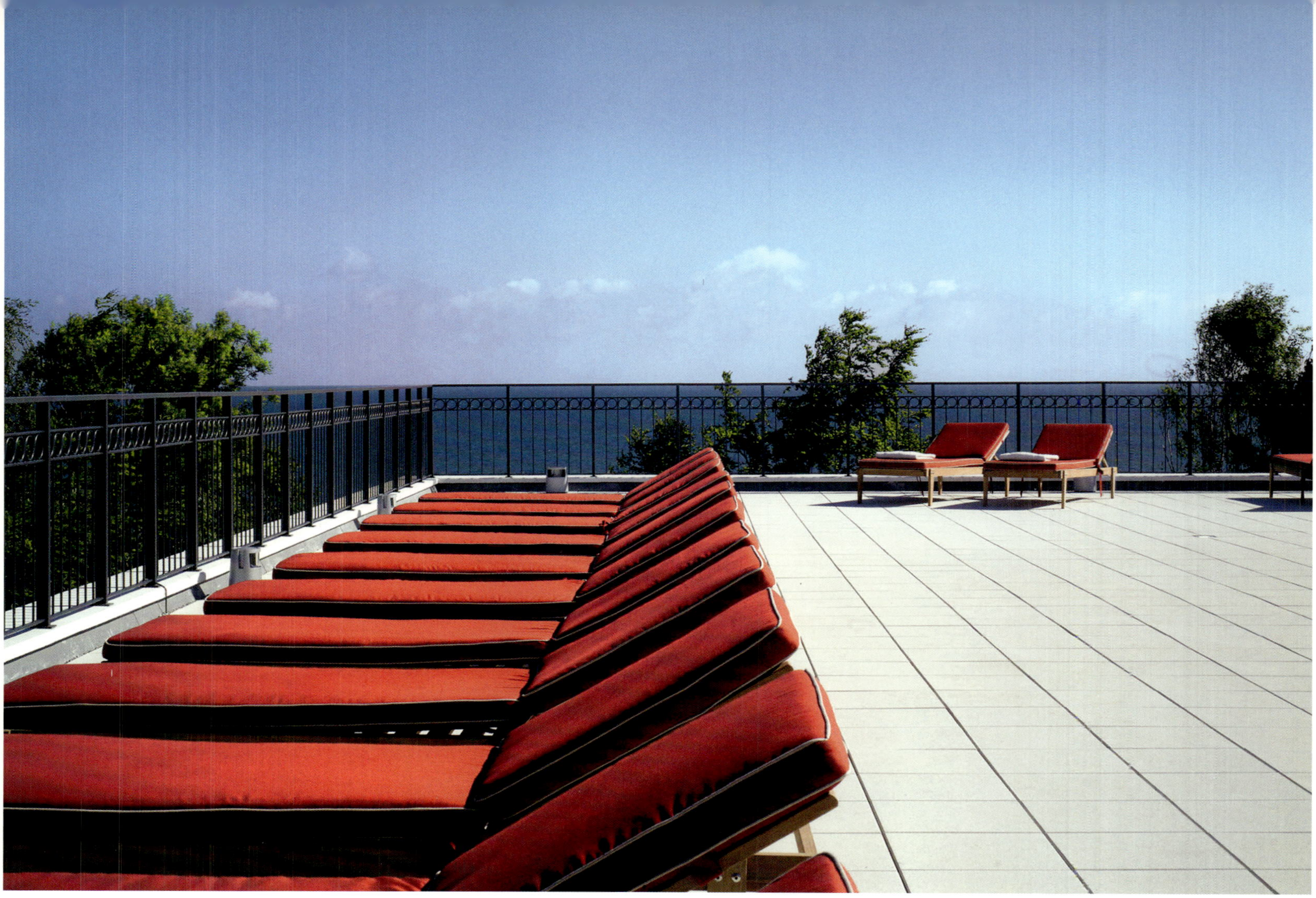

Roof terrace of Severin Palais

↞ Kurhaus with Mecklenburg House
→ Severin Palais
→ Kurhaus

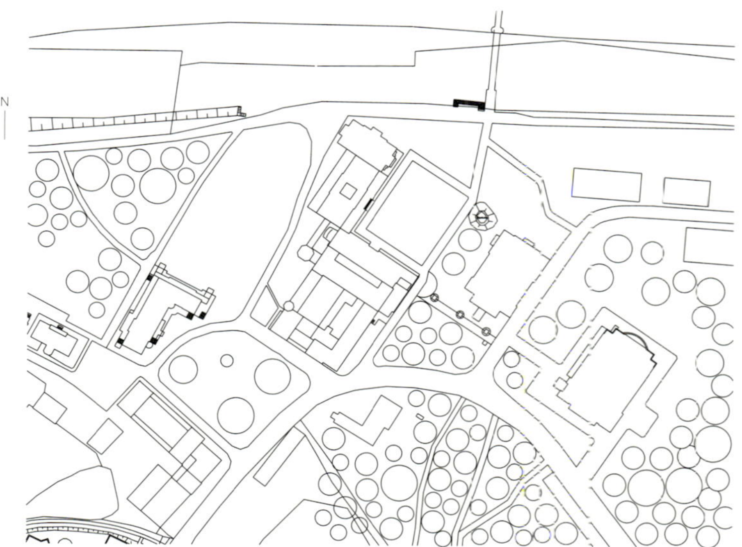

Site plan

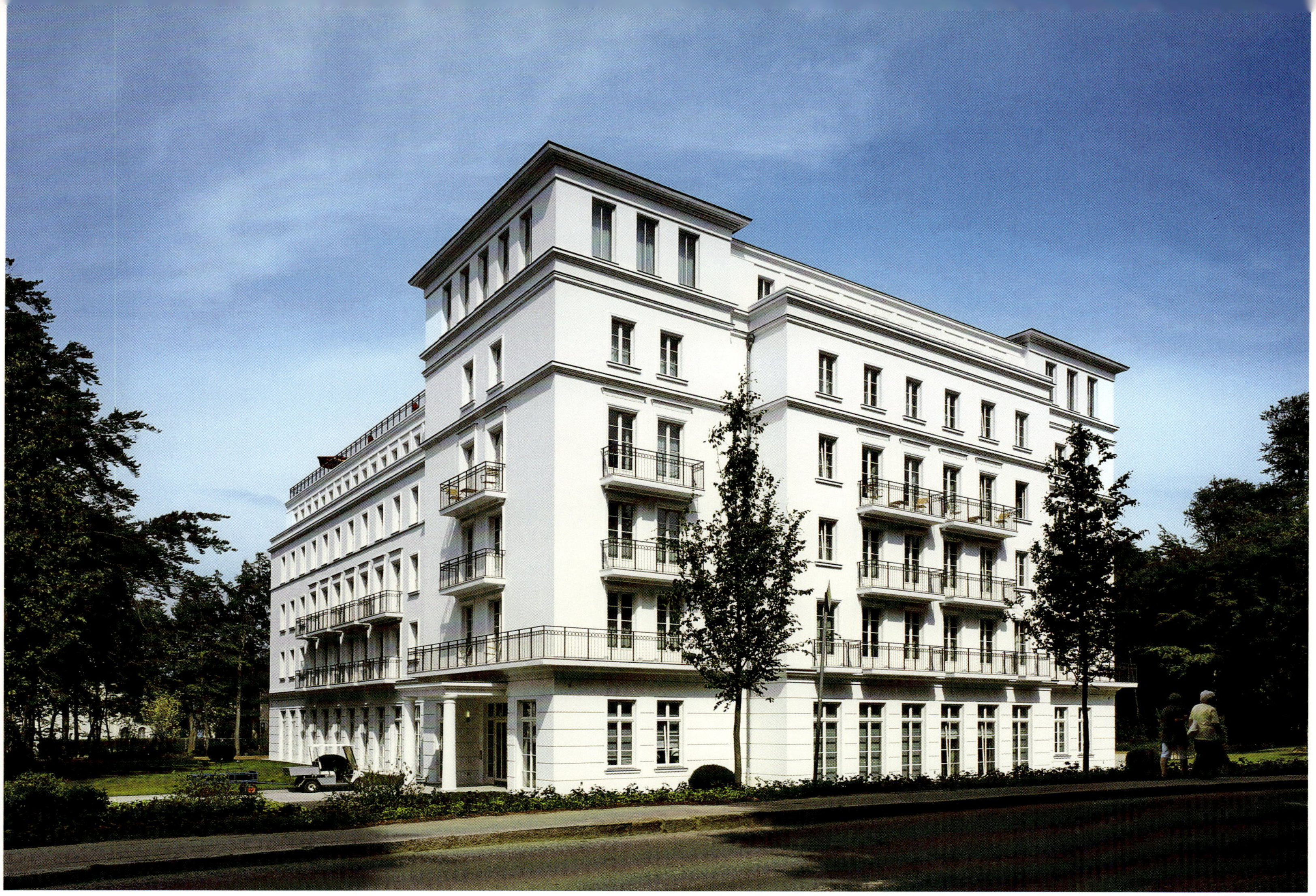

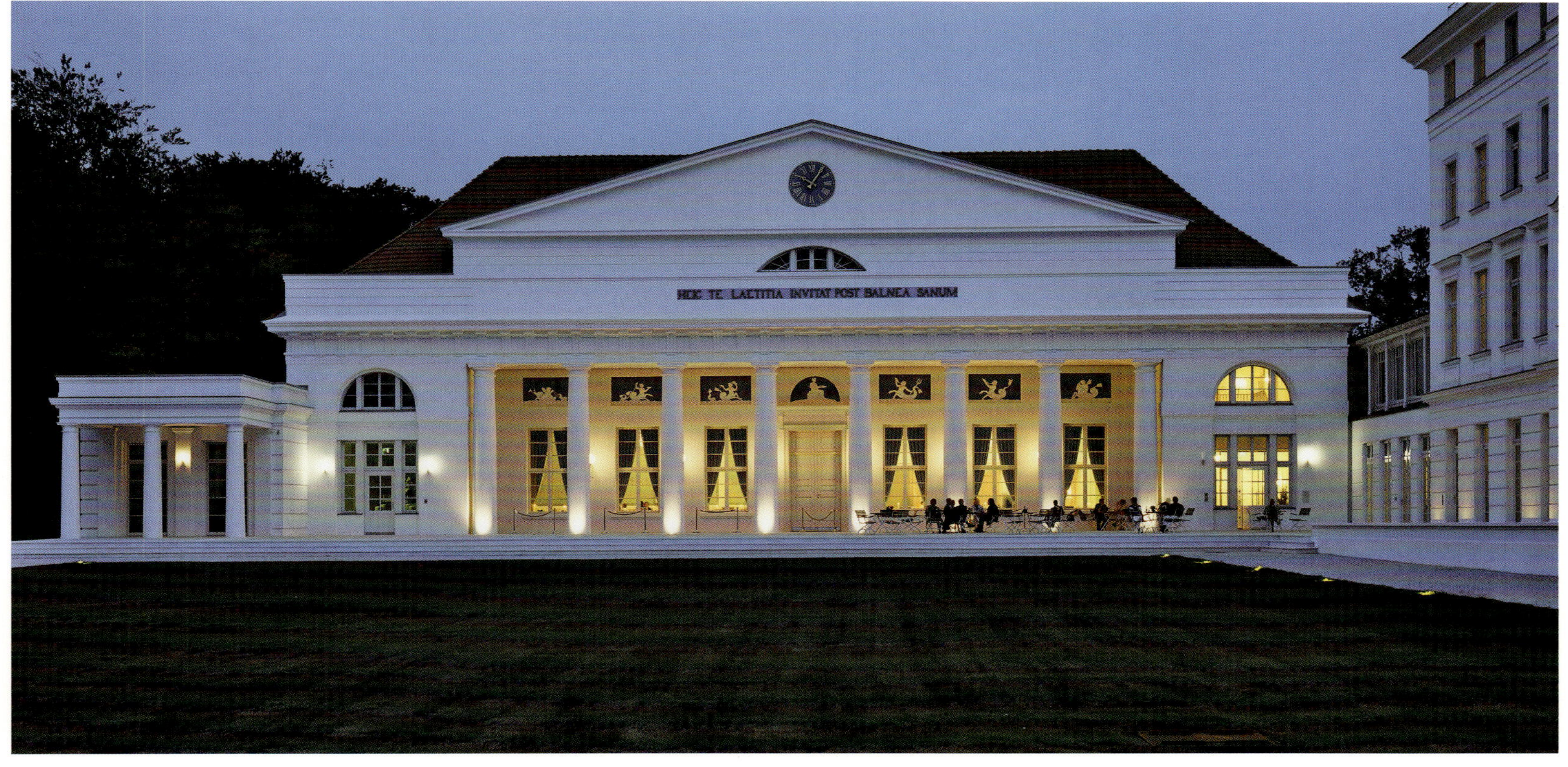
HIC TE LAETITIA INVITAT POST BALNEA SANUM

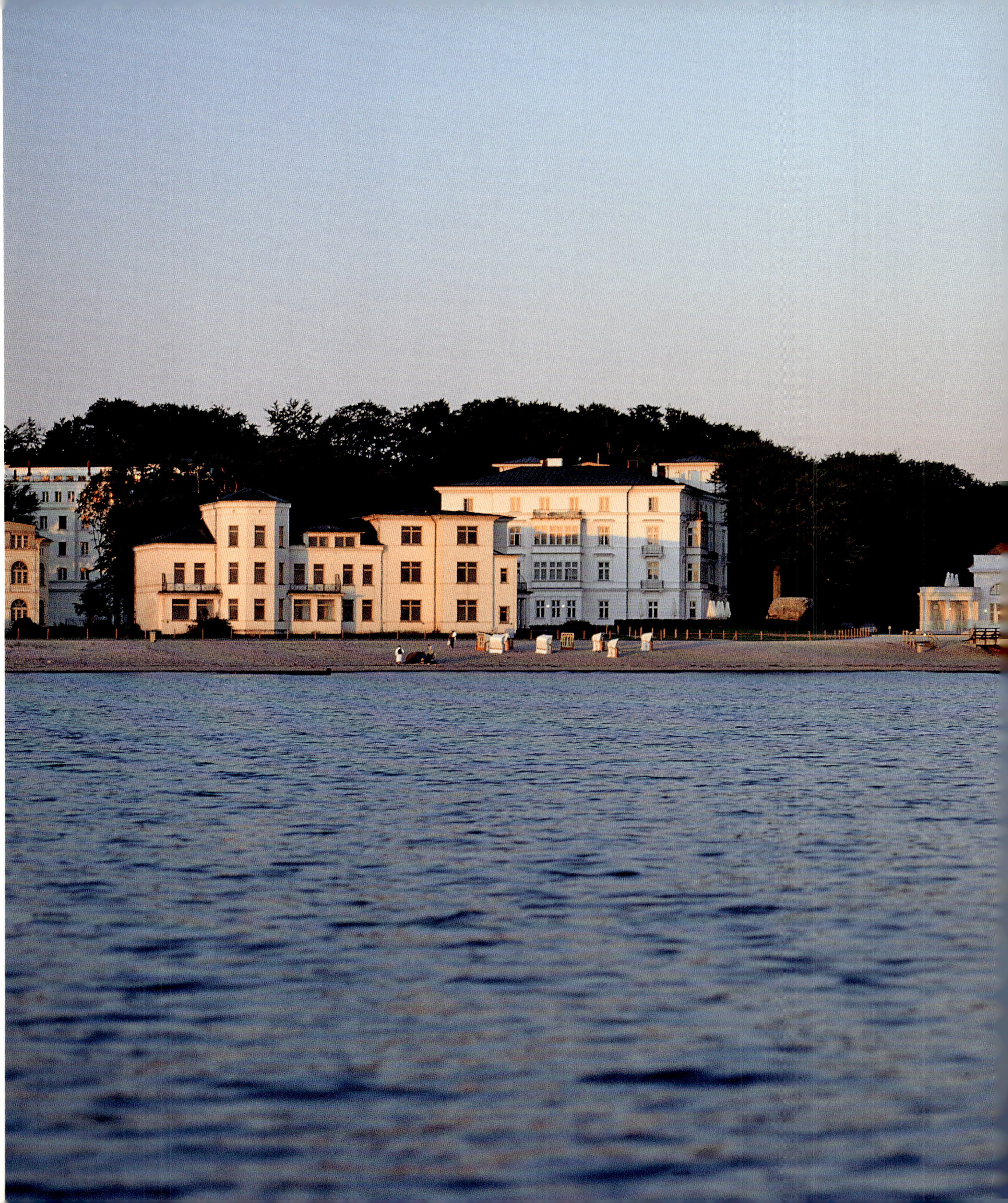

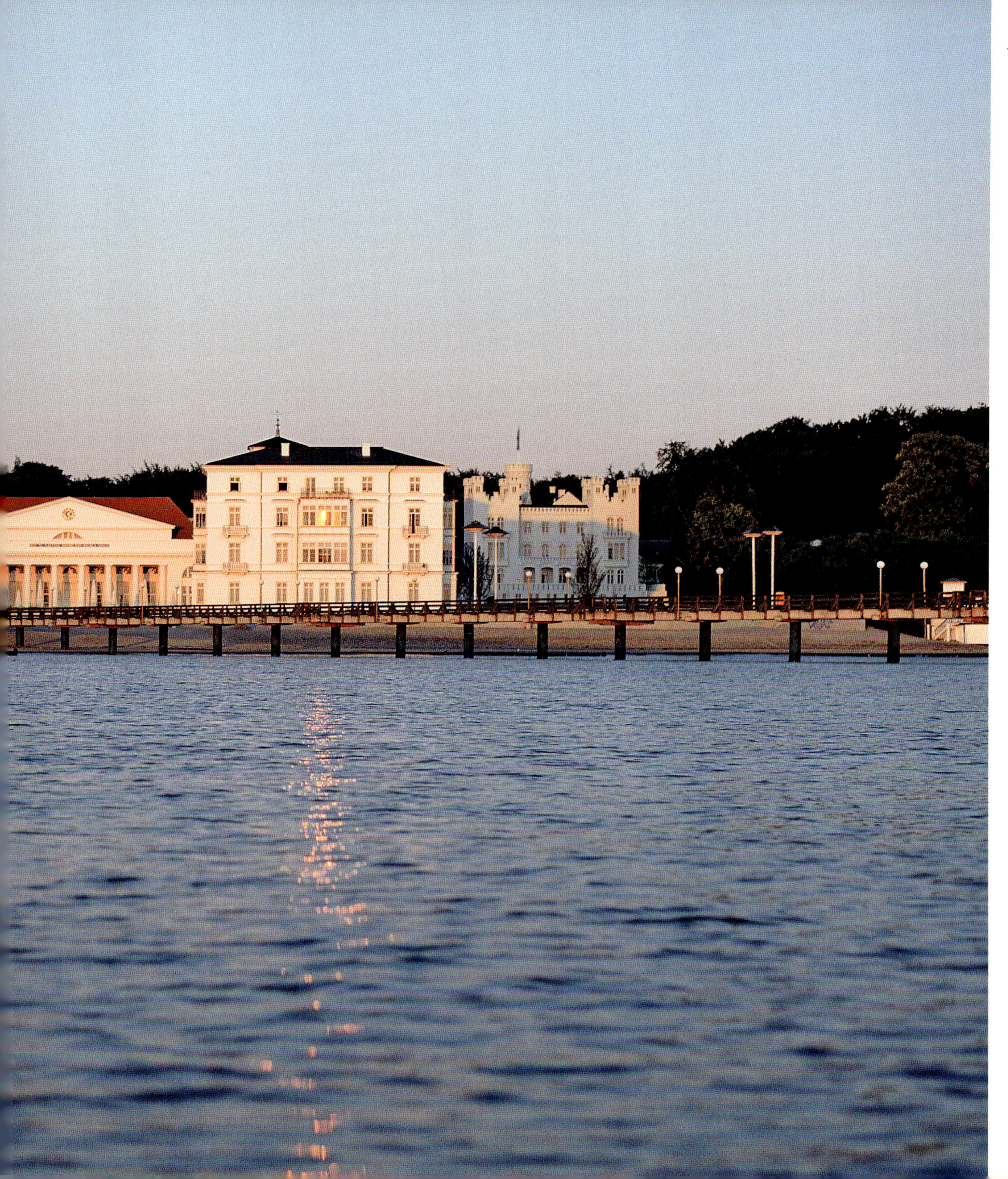

The Kempinski Grand Hotel Heiligendamm Duke Friedrich Franz I of Mecklenburg visited the shores of Doberan for the first time in 1793 on medical advice, thereby beginning the history of the Baltic Sea spa of Heiligendamm. In the years that followed, the spa town became increasingly popular, and in 1796 a bathhouse on the location of what would later become Mecklenburg House was built. The spa, cottages, Hohenzollern Castle, and Grand Hotel that followed comprised the final historic building complex that still characterizes the appearance of what has come to be known as the "White City on the Sea."

After a decades-long process of decay, the landmark-protected structures were renovated in 2000 in order to restore what had been one of the most distinguished spa locations in Europe. On the basis of a few drawings and photographs the five historical buildings—the Orangerie, Hohenzollern Castle, Mecklenburg House, the Kurhaus (medical center), and the Grand Hotel—were reconstructed and modernized to create a five-star "Plus Hotel" with integrated spa, wellness, and conference center facilities according to modern standards. In close collaboration with local landmark officials the buildings were completely gutted, leaving only the façades intact.

On its 29,500-square-meter lot, the hotel facility is today comprised of six classicizing and Romantic buildings offering 107 suites and 118 hotel rooms. The newly erected sixth building, the stylistically appropriate Severin Palais, fills out the architectural complex to the northeast and, in addition to fifty hotel rooms and eighteen suites, is outfitted with an elaborately equipped wellness and spa area.

The image of Heiligendamm is marked to a significant extent by the imposing Kurhaus. It was built in 1816 by Karl Theodor Severin and is located at a right angle to Mecklenburg House, directly facing the sea. Its severe, symmetrical façade recalls a Greek temple, with its portico creating a connection between interior and exterior, thereby including the environs in the overall urban plan. The Latin inscription *Heic Laetitia invitat post balnea sanum*—"Joy greets you here, leave the baths healed"—crowns the portico. This guiding principle is just as valid today, as is demonstrated by the large ballroom and restaurant found in these halls. Several side rooms can be used for conferences and banquets. Mecklenburg House is exclusively used for accommodation for the Grand Hotel. Most of its thirty-five hotel rooms and seventeen suites offer a unique view of the sea. The former Grand Hotel has also reclaimed its former generous feeling of space. Distributed over four levels, there are thirty-four hotel rooms and sixteen suites with individual room plans and designs, some including terraces. After the reconstruction, the Orangerie, the former telegraph office, also now houses suites. By recreating the distinctive historical decorative elements, Hohenzollern Castle has been restored to its original state, too. The flat, battlement-decorated roof was destroyed in a fire in 1950 and in the reconstruction was replaced by a simple hip roof.

The Mecklenburg master builders Carl Theodor Severin and Gustav Adolph Demmler defined the architectural and urbanistic image of Heiligendamm, an image that was shaped by two great intellectual currents, those of classicism and Romanticism. With the aid of a few historic photographs, the original character of the five landmark-protected buildings was restored: every building has its own personality but is nonetheless a part of the larger whole. Finally, a new building adapted to the historical imprint of the whole was added so that its identity would not disturb the equilibrium of the historical complex. With its modern comfort, Severin Palais has been effectively incorporated into the "White City."

⇠ The "White City on the Sea"
→ Façade of Grand Hotel

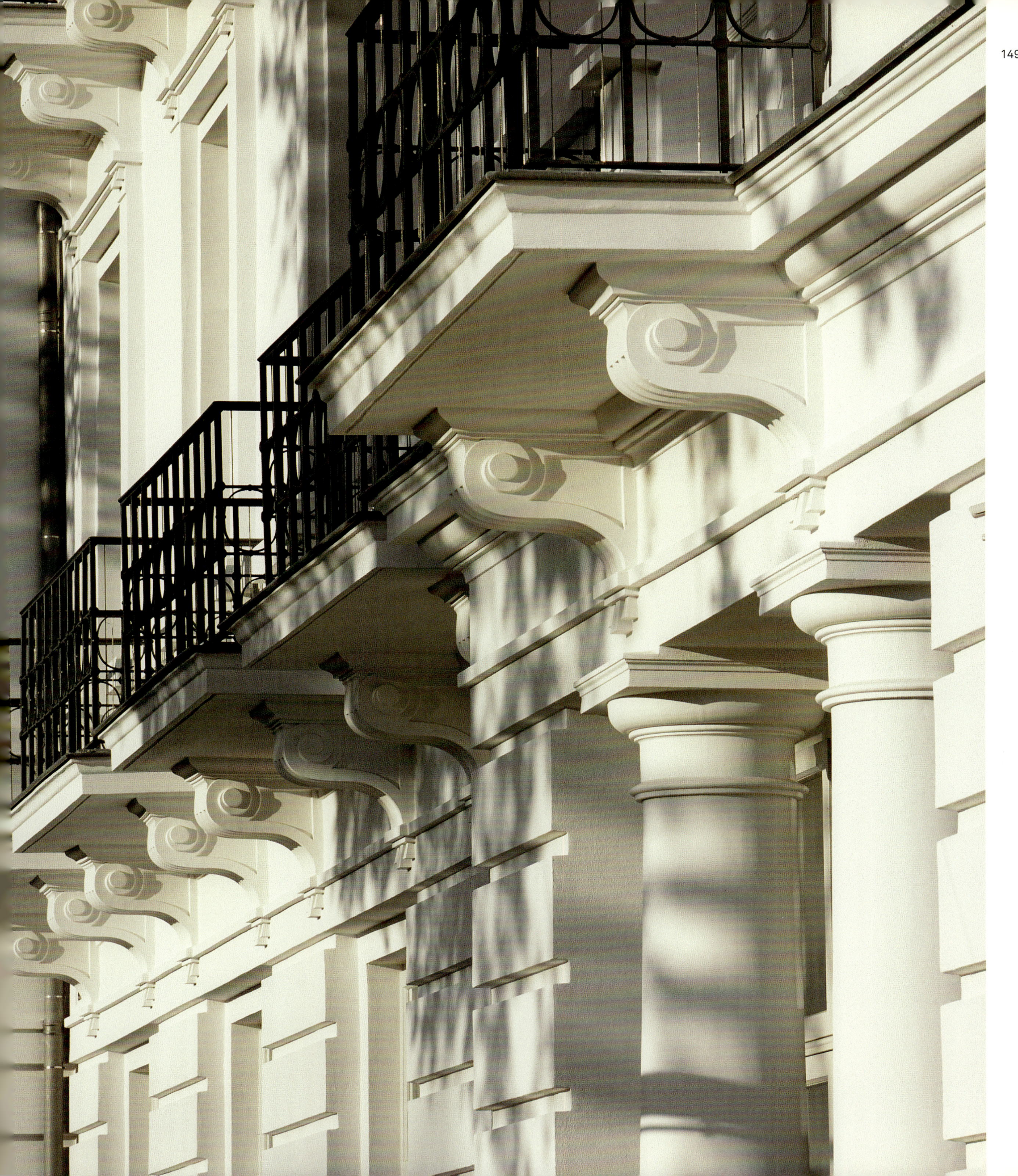

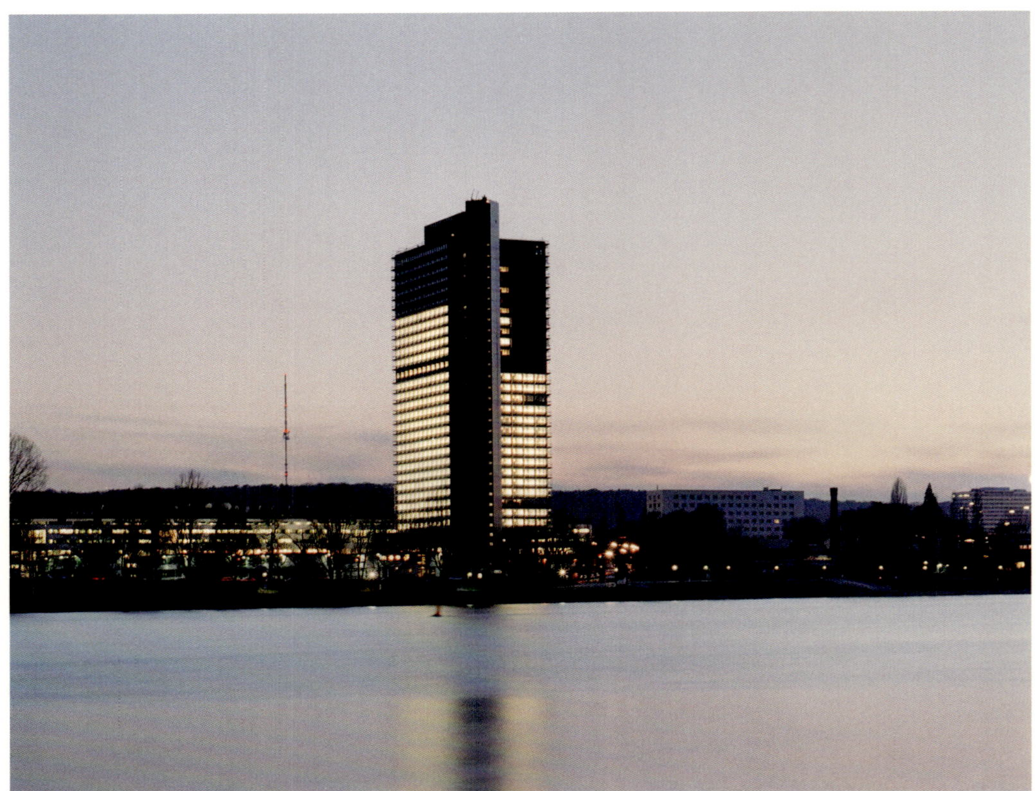

"Langer Eugen"

This architectural trademark of Bonn was built by Egon Eiermann in 1969. After the German parliament moved to Berlin, the landmark-protected building was equipped with a new fire protection system and was brought up to modern standards in terms of aspects of its physical construction, technology, and energy use. All necessary changes were executed according to landmark protection requirements, and after its revitalization, the high-rise was in complete accord with Eiermann's original ideas.

Client: BLB NRW
Location: Bonn
GFA: 55,650 m²
Year of completion: 1969
Restoration according to landmark protection criteria: 2006
Design architect: Egon Eiermann

Identity

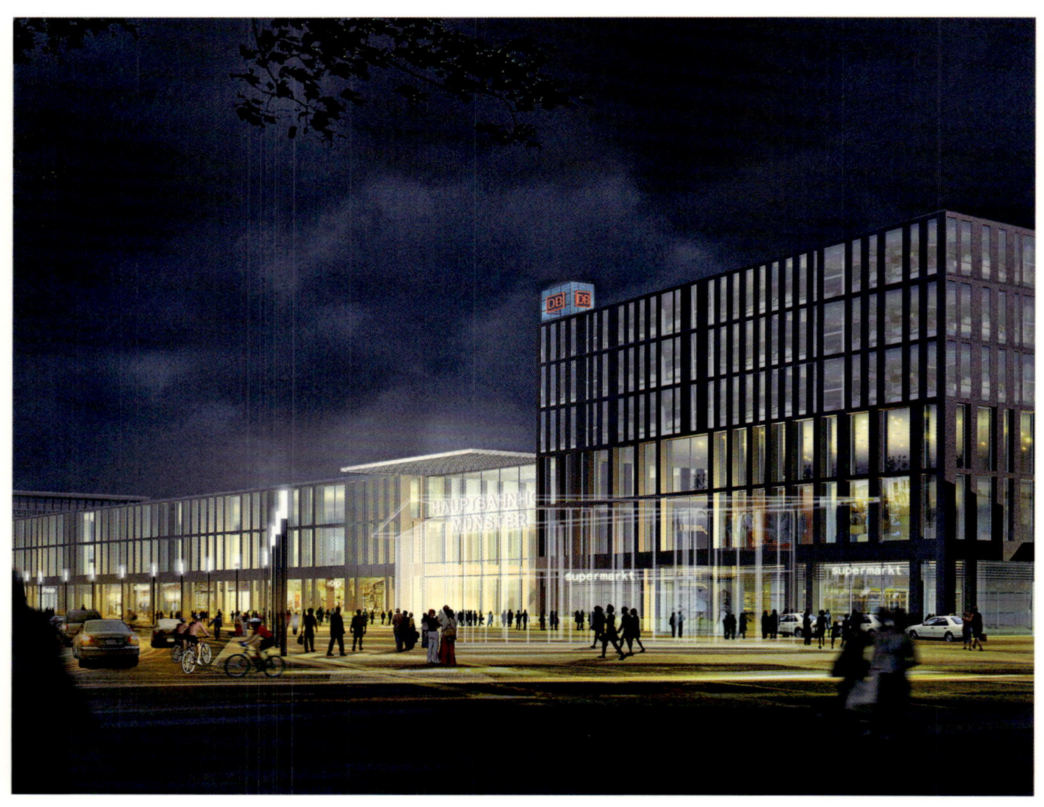

Münster Central Train Station

The design is based on the construction of two new reception buildings that are intended to connect the downtown district and the harbor district more closely. In addition to their original train station function, the new structures will also have retail and office space as well as restaurants. The two prestigious buildings create an increased urban density in the area.

Client: Bahnhof Münster Entwicklungsgesellschaft mbH & Co. KG
Location: Münster
GFA: 42,700 m²
Completion date: 2012
Investors competition: 1st Prize, 2008

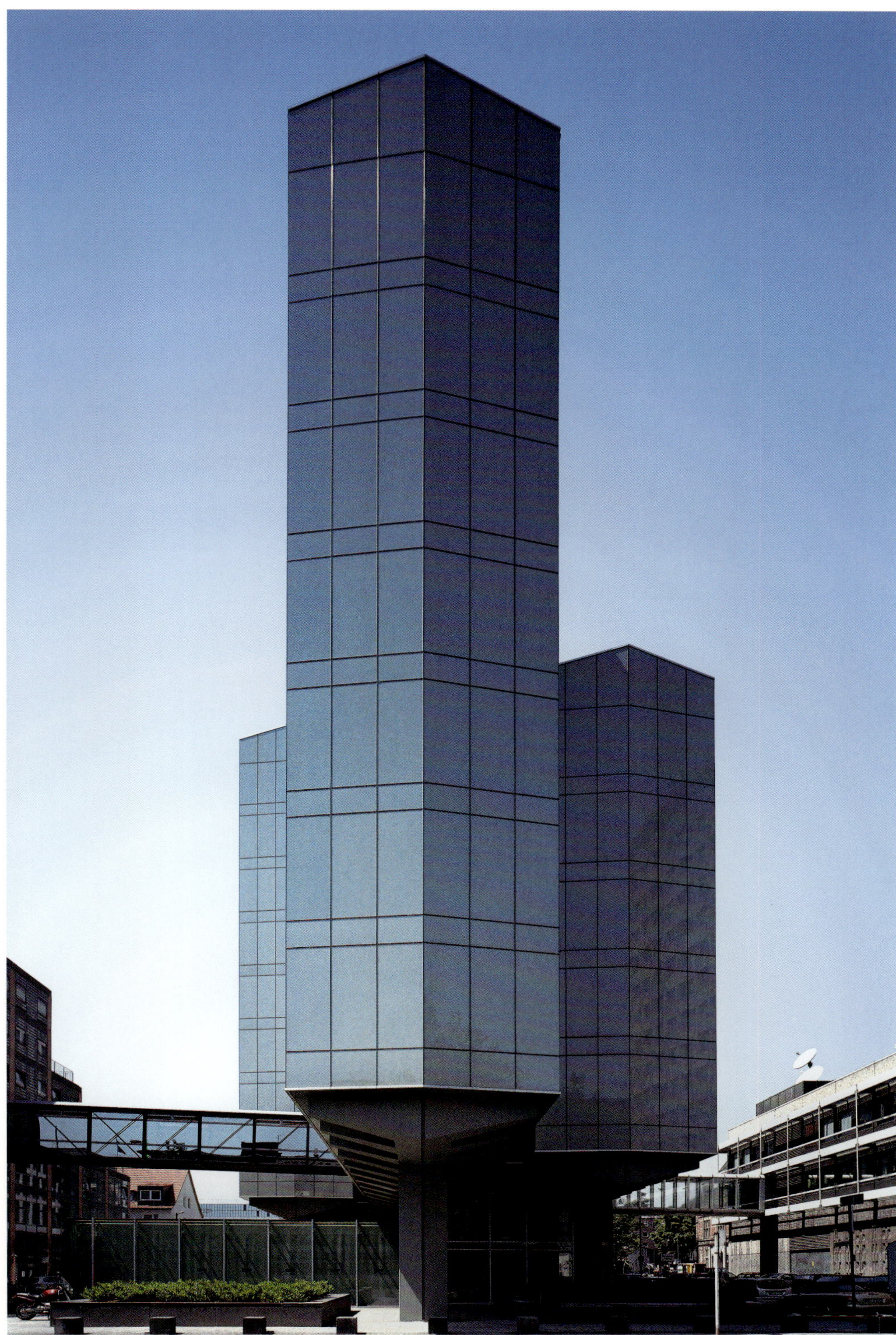

WDR Vierscheibenhaus ("The Four-Slice Building")

For almost forty years the administration building of the Westdeutscher Rundfunk (WDR) has represented an urban developmental point of orientation in Cologne. Its striking appearance, the exposed location, and the project's proximity to the adjacent facilities of the WDR encouraged a sweeping renovation in 2002. A new façade with improved soundproofing and insulation, the optimizing of the use of space, and the design of brighter, friendlier office areas made a substantial contribution to the upgrading of the building to modern standards.

Client: **Westdeutscher Rundfunk Köln**
Location: **Cologne**
NFA aboveground: **18,230 m²**
NFA underground: **23,860 m²**
Work stations: **approx. 800**
Year of completion: **1970**
Conversion and restoration: **2002**

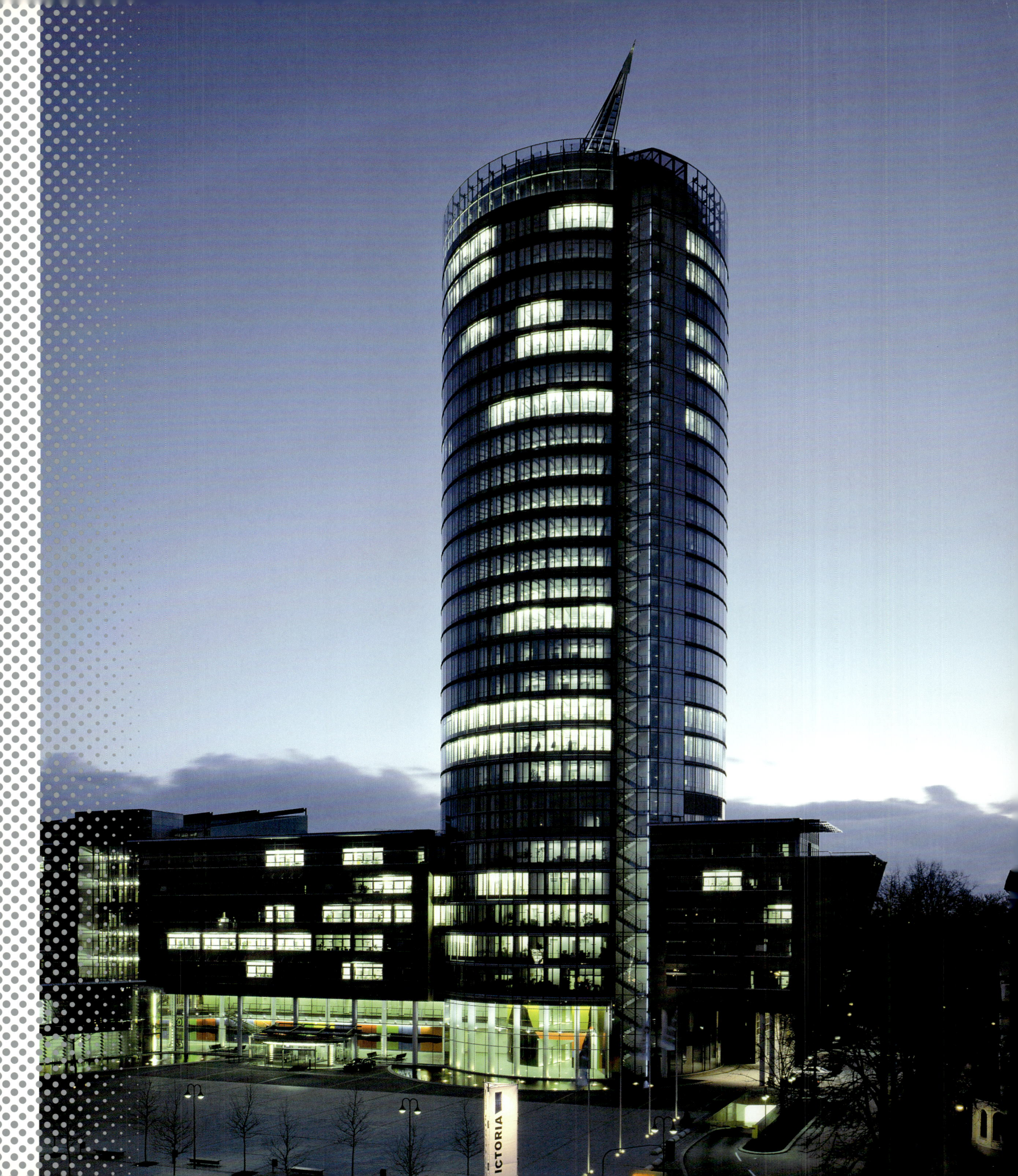
ICTORIA

Over a century and a half ago, Ernst Haeckel defined "ecology" as the study of the relations of living creatures to their environment. Today's general understanding of this term, however, only made its way into common parlance in the last few decades. In the early 1960s the term was placed in a new context. Biologists and environmental activists began warning about the dangers chemicals posed for human beings and nature. From this point on, ecology was understood as the effect of human actions on nature and was rapidly assimilated and accepted as such by all levels of society.

Ecology was increasingly included in an environmentally politicized context, and as this happened it underwent a change in meaning. "Ecological" became equated in part with "environmentally compatible," "clean," "considerate," or simply "good," and in this way the principle of environmental consciousness made its way into everyday life.

In architectural design, ecology has become an ever more frequently considered factor in connection with the issues of energy efficiency and CO_2 reduction ever since it was recognized that greenhouse gases and the concomitant air pollution of our ecosystem represent an accumulative danger. In addition, with the increasing cost of energy, a new consciousness of the need for the frugal use of energy has also been emerging.

Various certifications have been developed for the "ecological evaluation of buildings." The Energy Saving Regulation prescribes standard technical building requirements for energy efficiency and is an important tool in helping to reduce energy use and the emission of CO_2 and other greenhouse gases. However, it considers only one aspect of ecologically relevant measures. Certifications such as LEED (Leadership in Energy and Environmental Design), which cover other aspects, provide a sort of seal of approval for ecological and sustainable building, which encompasses the whole gamut of factors that an ecological approach to architecture must consider.

In the context of architectural design, the incorporation of ecological measures may be a less obvious component, but it has the important effect of creating sustainability. It contributes to a greater sense of responsibility in the use of energy and natural resources in planning and building. There is still a lot more to do in this area of architectural development.

In the planning of its headquarters in Düsseldorf, Victoria Grundstücksverwaltungs-Gesellschaft GbR placed especially great emphasis on goals for ecological building. As a result, the building was awarded the Intec Facility Management Prize in 1999 and Victoria received the EMAS Award from the European Commission for Verified Environmental Management in 2002. These awards reflect the project's energy efficiency as well as its qualitative aspects.

Victoria's ecological demands of the building are reflected in the multitude of plants distributed throughout the complex. However, the project's numerous high-quality green zones were not only planned as a measure of optical upgrading; they are also intended to make the work environment more attractive to employees.

If one considers the development of ecological measures in building planning in relation to the development of the term "ecology"—which is only 150 years old and has been used in its contemporary sense for less than fifty years—one can be assured that it will yield significant innovations over the next decades. After all, building has been going on for thousands of years.

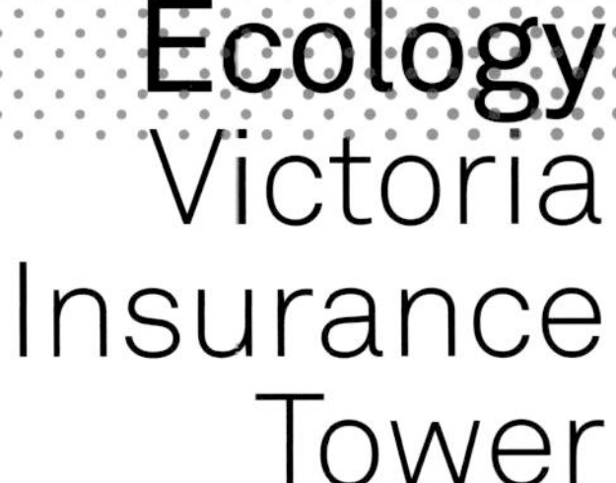

Ecology
Victoria Insurance Tower

Client: **Victoria Grundstücksverwaltungs-Gesellschaft GbR** | Location: **Düsseldorf** | GFA: **135,445 m²** | Height: **108.8 m**
Work stations: **1,915** | Completion date: **1998** | Award: **Intec-FM-Prize, 1999; EU-EMAS Award for Best Practice in Environmental Management, 2002**

Expansion of Victoria Headquarters, third construction phase | Client: **Victoria Grundstücksverwaltungs-Gesellschaft GbR**
GFA: **28,845 m²** | Work stations: **656** | Completion date: **2001**

Expansion of Victoria Headquarters, fourth construction phase | Client: **Victoria 4. Bauabschnitt GmbH & Co. KG**
GFA: **40,972 m²** | Work stations: **900** | Completion date: **2010**

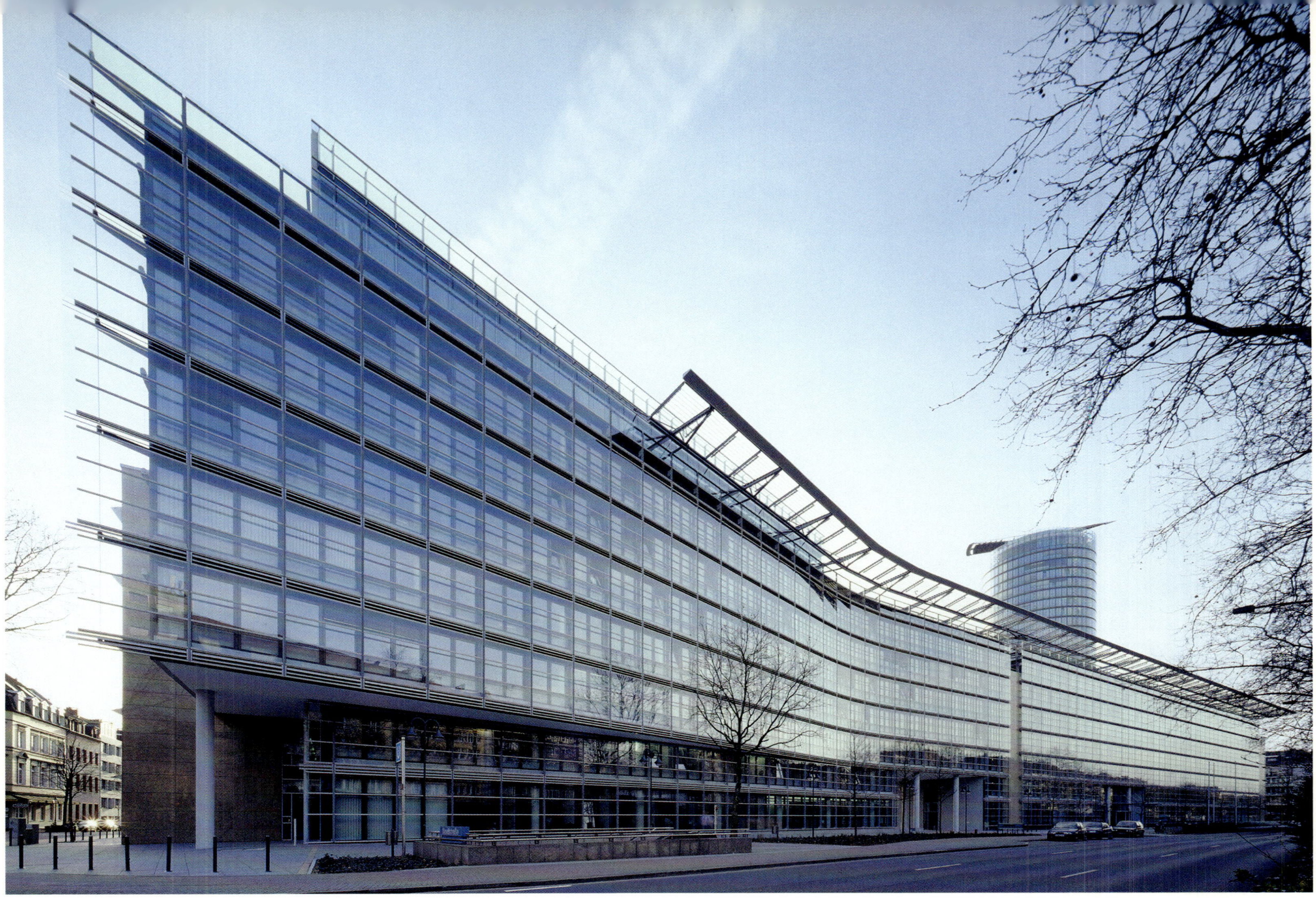

View of Fischerstrasse
→ Green inner courtyard

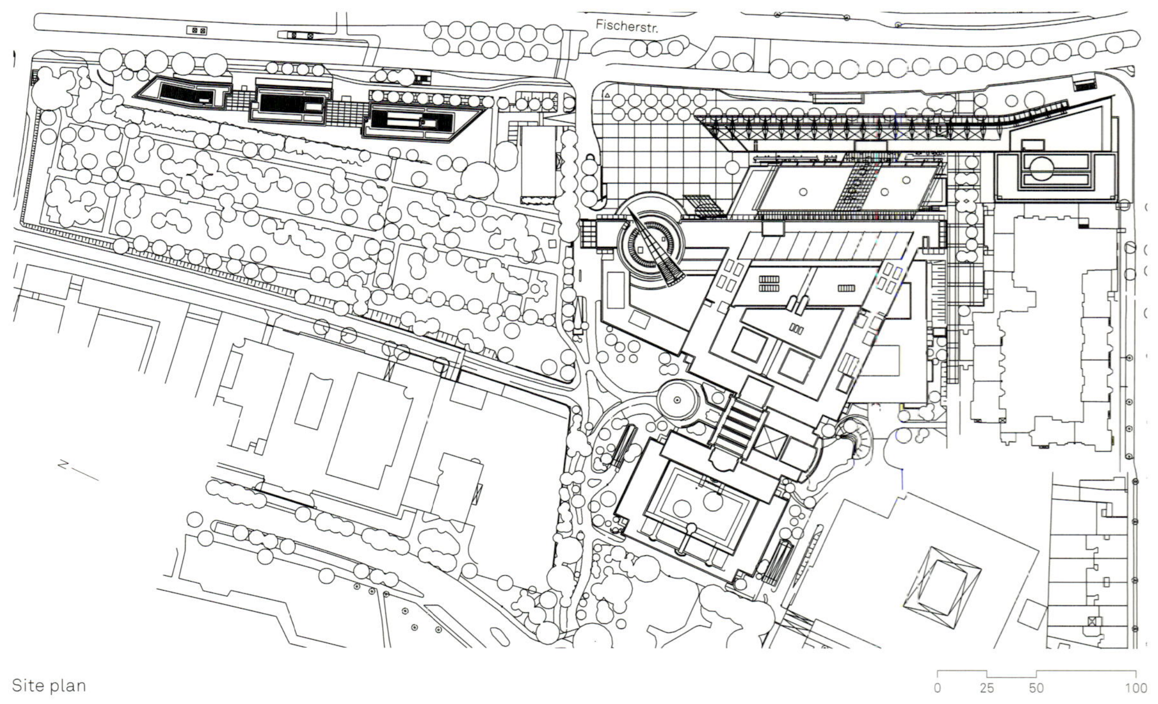

Site plan

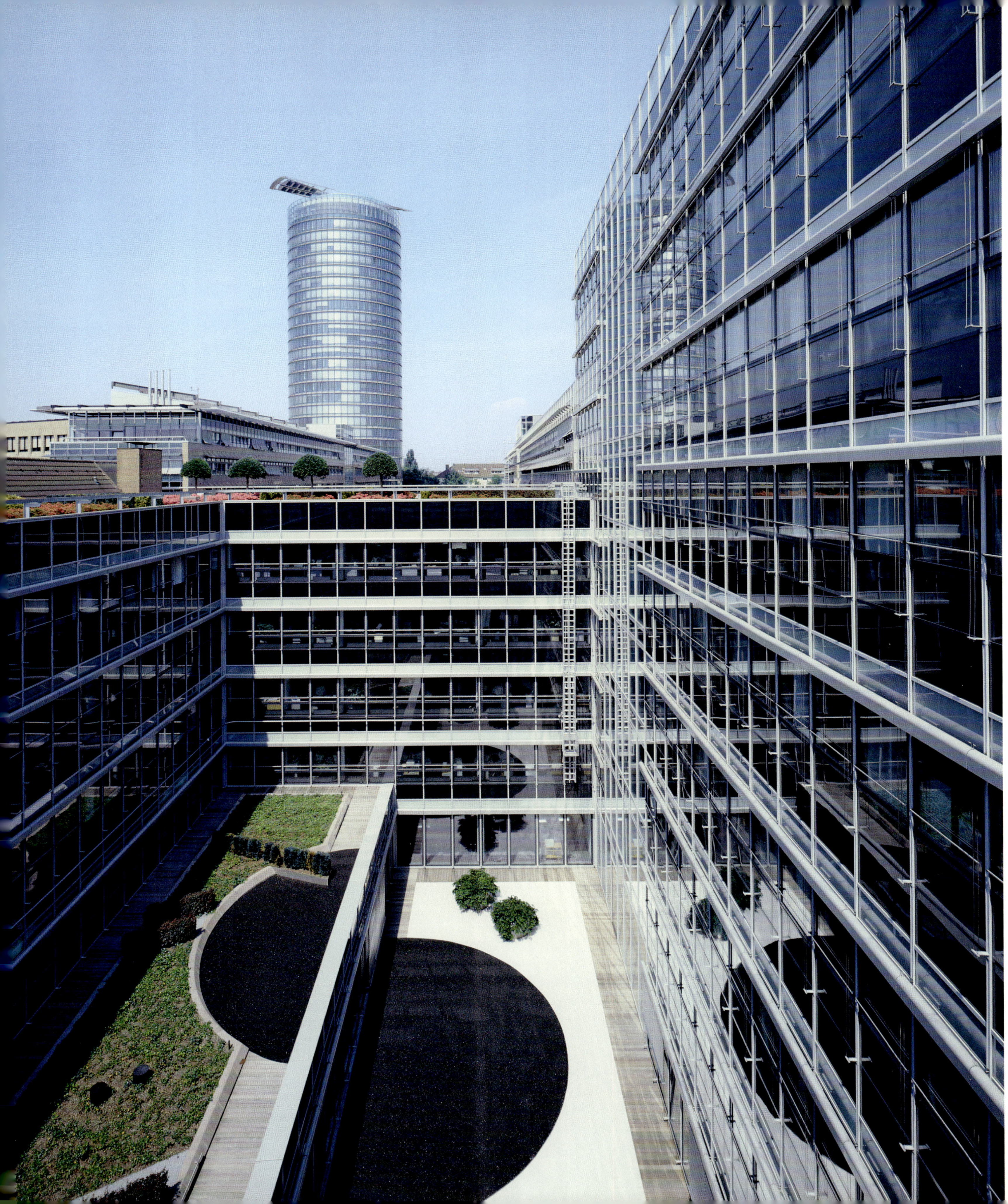

The Victoria Insurance Tower As the result of moving Düsseldorf's exhibition grounds, the insurance company Victoria was able to acquire the former fairgrounds at the Hofgarten between the district seat of government and the Ehrenhof in the 1970s. The corporate headquarters of the company has thus been located here since 1986 and is currently being expanded in a fourth stage of construction. A twenty-nine-story office tower was at the center of the first phase of expansion, carried out between 1993 and 1998. The cylindrical building structure, situated between the open space of the former Golzheimer cemetery and the downtown on Fischerstrasse, constitutes the architectural focus of the urbanistic design. In the third construction phase from 1998 to 2001 a hundred-meter-long building structure was added to the complex along Fischerstrasse within the context of the preexisting urban fabric. The necessity for these expansions was dictated by the need for additional capacities as well as the merging of different corporate areas in the Düsseldorf location. The current and fourth construction phase complements the main administration building of the insurance firm by an aboveground building complex with 158,000 square meters of gross floor area offering a total of 4,600 work stations. Between the landmark-protected artist studio and the Victoriaplatz to the south and Klever Strasse to the north, the new 169-meter-long building will be comprised of three elements connected by two glassed-in halls. The transparent and openly designed structure should be completed by 2010.

However, the grounds of the insurance company will always be characterized by the 108.8-meter-high Victoria Tower. As a commanding element visible from a great distance, it has become a visual trademark of the capital city of North Rhine-Westphalia and features an extraordinary panoramic view from the meeting rooms at the top. The tower is crowned by a flying roof construction made of steel that incorporates photovoltaics. However, the office tower provides more than just a significant urban planning accent—it also protects the environment with its exceptionally low primary energy consumption. The tower is one of the first high-rises in Germany with natural ventilation. This was made possible by the use of a double façade, which was a completely new concept designed especially for the tower and for the construction project along Fischerstrasse. The double façade consists of an inner layer made of hinged, bottom-hung windows and an approximately forty-centimeter-thick pre-positioned glass membrane. This construction makes it possible to open the inner windows in order to provide a natural ventilation of the offices, including those on the upper floors of the high-rise. A specially designed computer system automatically shuts off the heating as soon as the windows are opened. The sun protection units and the interior illumination of the offices are also continuously adapted to the daylight conditions thanks to EDP controls. The necessary energy input for the building is provided by an in-house cogeneration unit. This has made it possible to reduce the building's CO_2 emissions by about 16,000 tons per year. The tower's optimal energy management also allows for a drastic reduction of energy consumption, even in the preexisting main administration building. As a result of these ecological measures, Victoria was the first insurance company in Europe to receive certification from the EU-issued environmental audit.

→ Corner detail of double façade

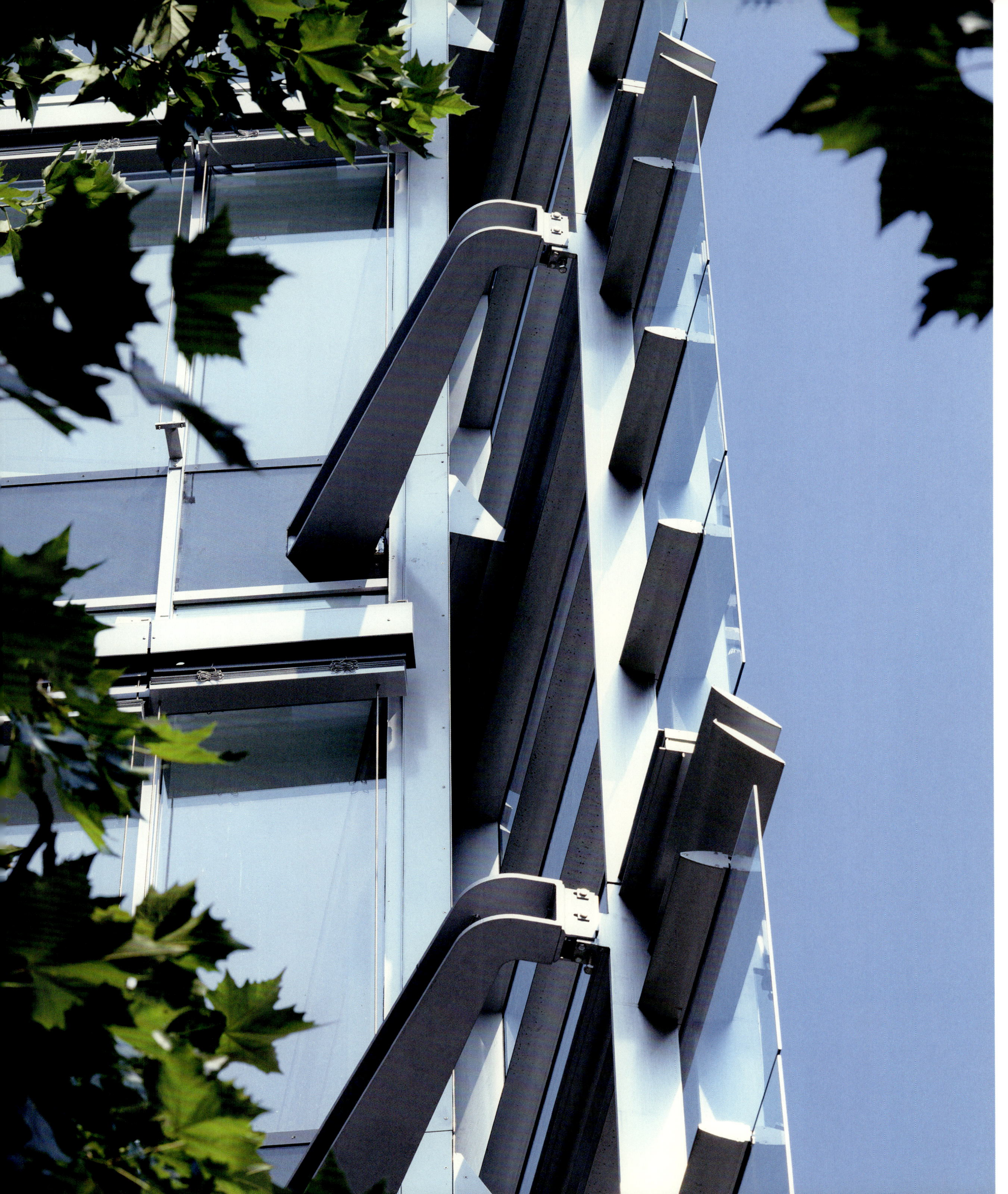

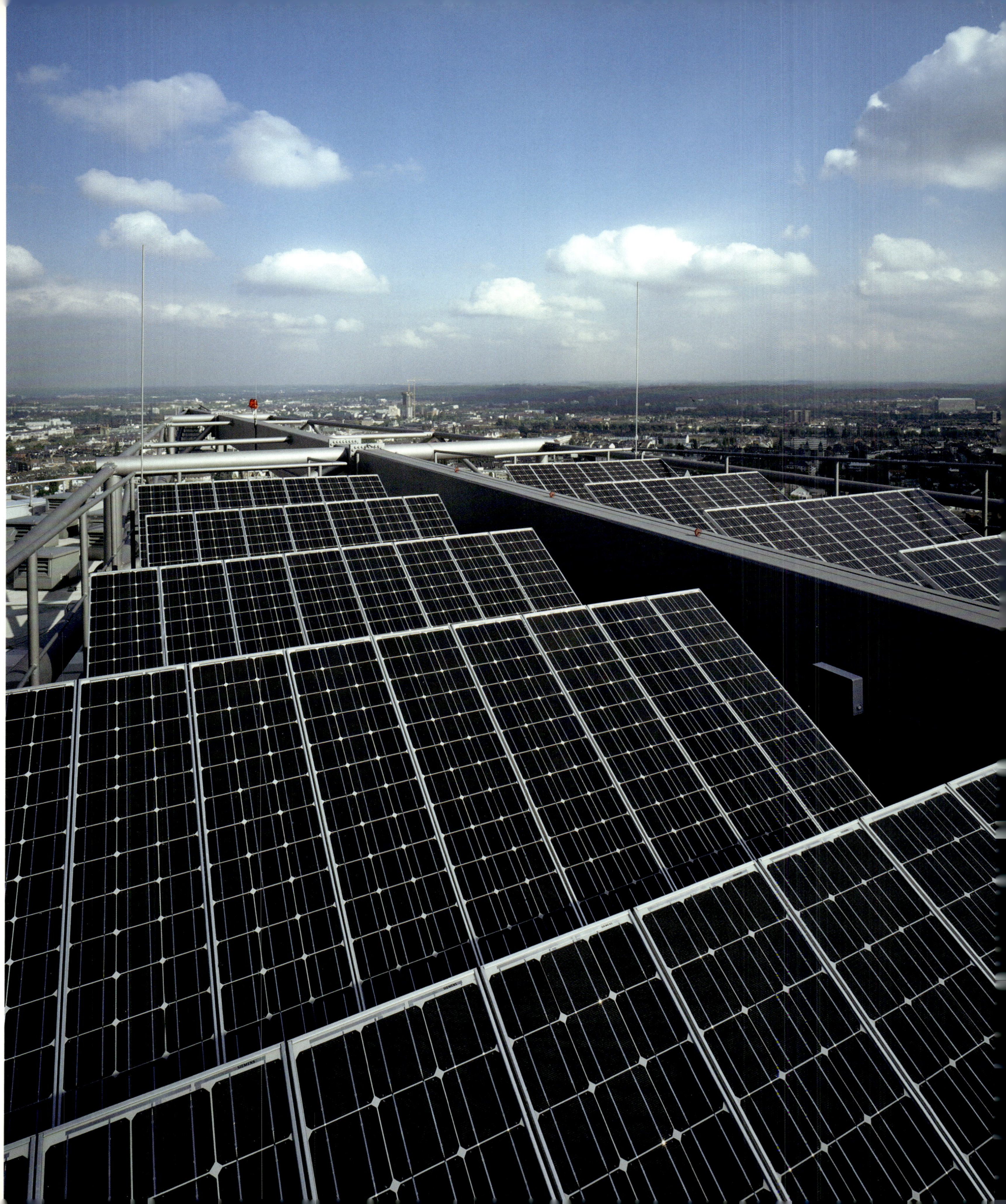

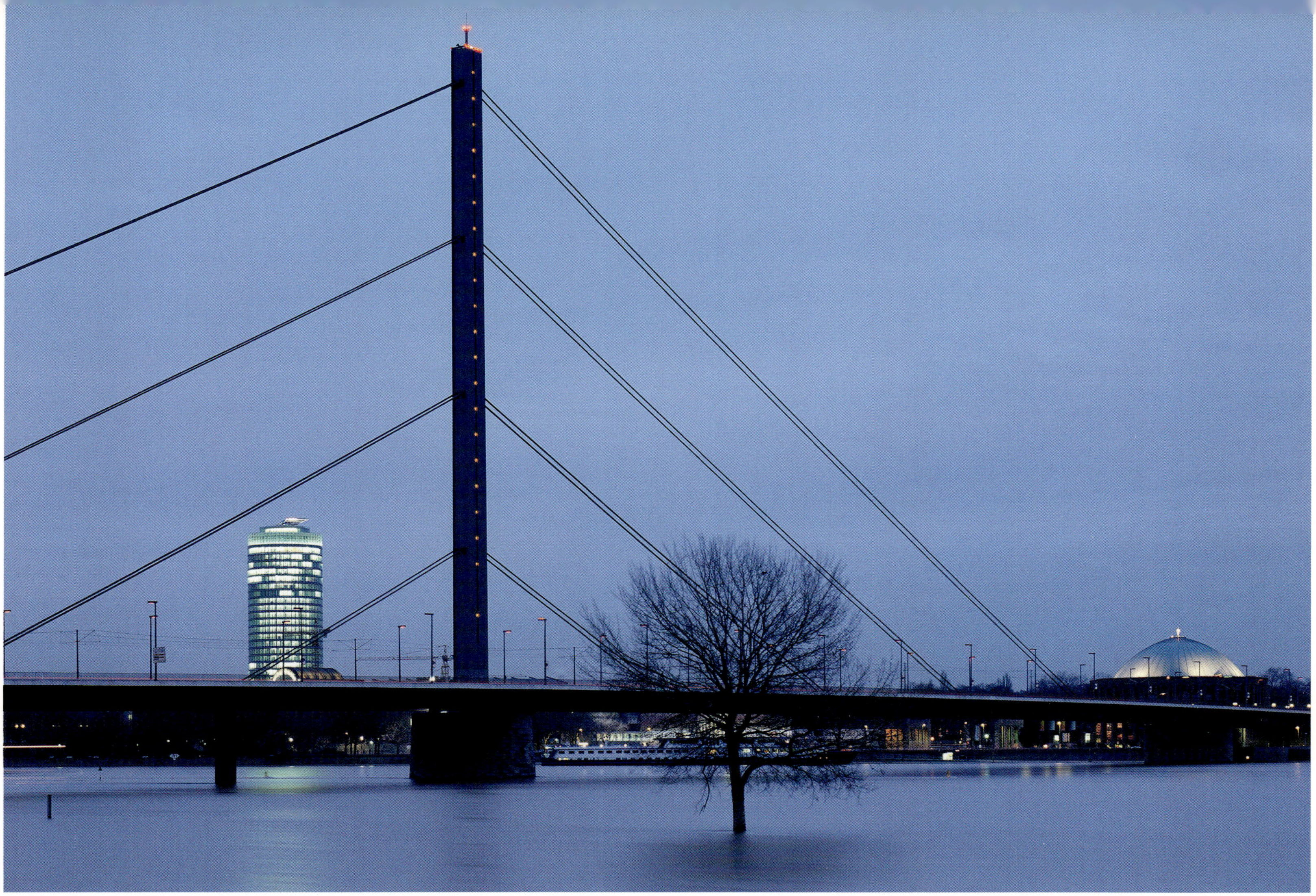

Panorama of the Rhine with the Victoria Tower and the Concert Hall

← Photovoltaic unit on the Victoria Tower

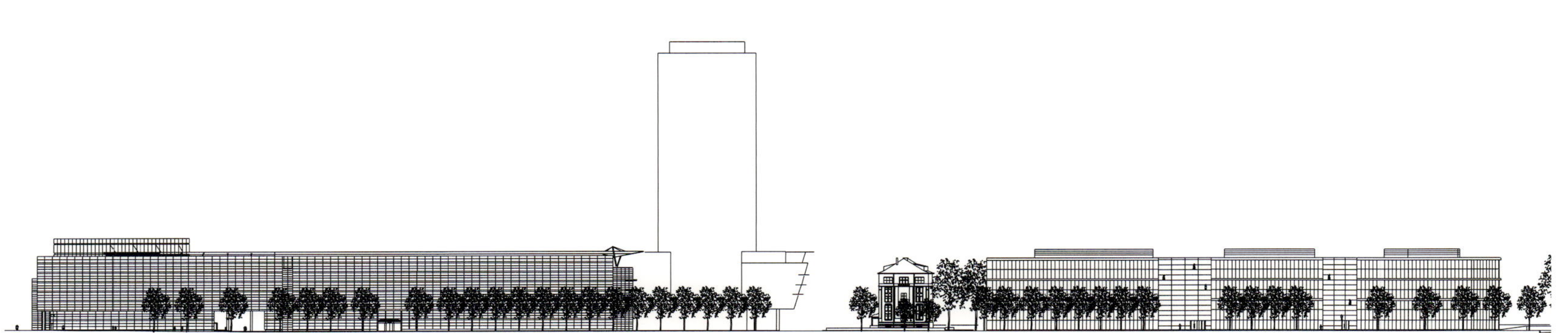

View of Fischerstrasse with fourth construction phase

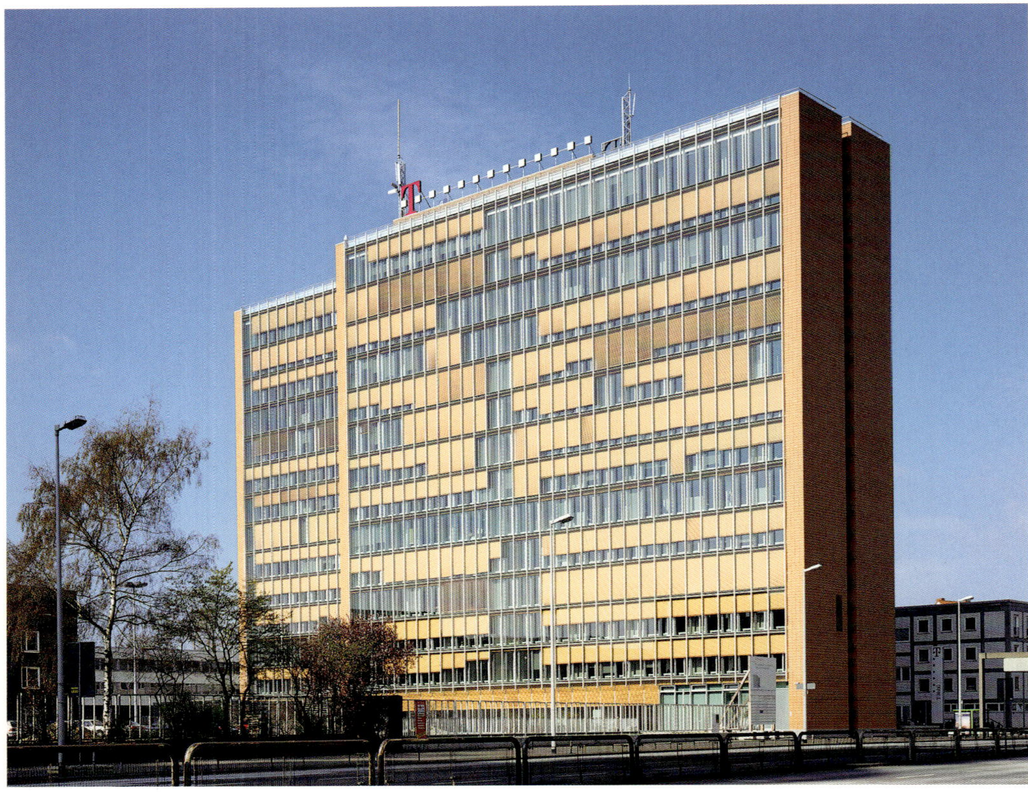

Telekom High-Rise, Hannover

In the course of its renovation, this standout high-rise in the vicinity of Hannover's central train station received a multilayered skin: on the long sides of the building, the skin is a glass-enclosed, modular façade, while on the building's gable sides it takes the form of a heat-insulated, rear-ventilated, modular brick façade. In addition, an external sun shield and openable windows contribute to the structure's energy efficiency.

Client: DeTeImmobilien
Location: Hannover
GFA: 16,590 m²
Work stations: 1,040
Year of completion: 1971
Conversion and modernization: 1999

Ecology

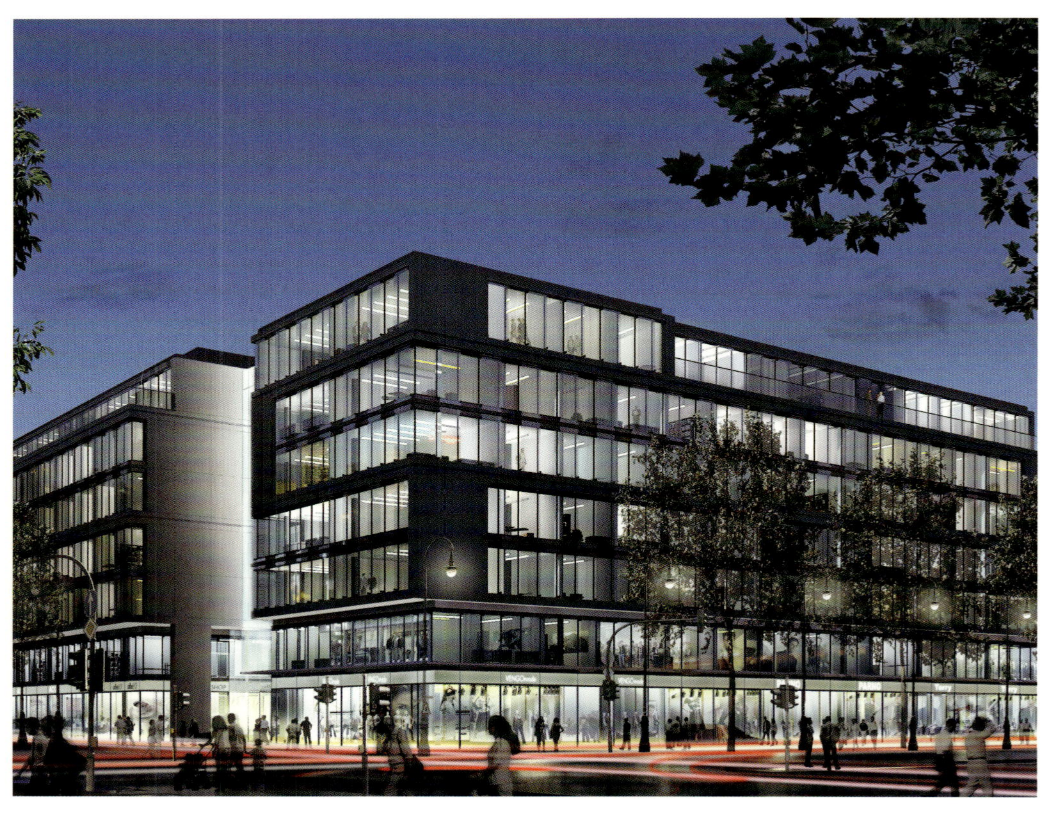

Office and Commercial Building, Habsburgerring

This new, clearly articulated, seven-story office and commercial building is located at one of the most important interfaces of downtown Cologne. A hybrid façade provides natural ventilation as well as soundproofing. A special feature of the project's ecological concept is that the energy for heating and cooling is derived chiefly from groundwater.

Client: MEAG MUNICH ERGO Asset Management GmbH
Location: Cologne
GFA: 31,661 m²
Work stations: 880
Completion date: 2010
Competition: 1st Prize, 2005

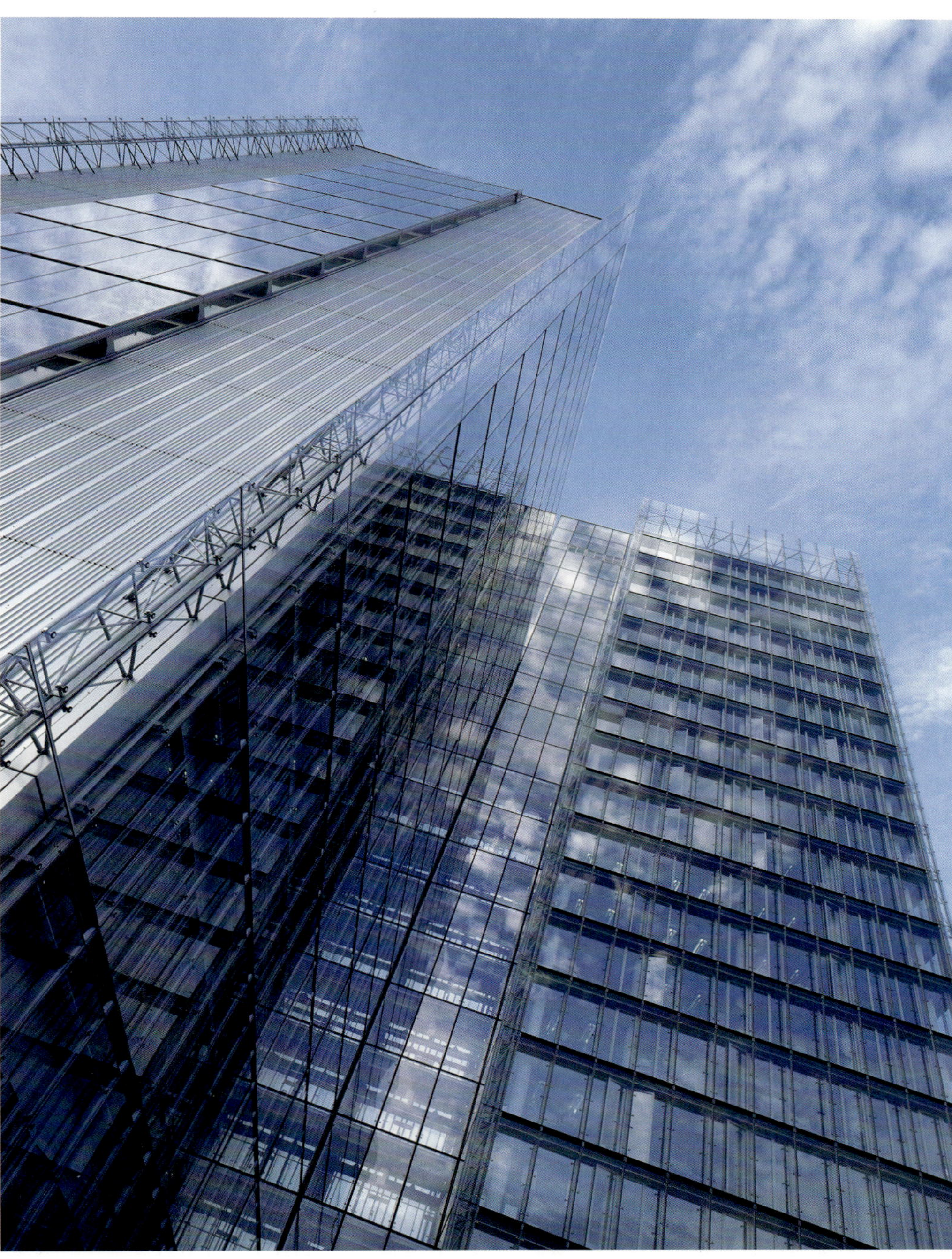

LVM High-Rise

The narrow high-rise dating back to 1967 was extensively renovated, augmented, and expanded with a more cubic, centrally planned building.
In addition to the repetition of five stories, the building was furnished with a double façade to facilitate natural ventilation as well as windproof sun protection on the exterior. By using intelligent control systems, the building can be operated for many weeks in the year without heating or cooling.

Client: **LVM Landwirtschaftlicher Versicherungsverein Münster a.G.**
Location: **Münster**
GFA: **26,768 m²**
Height: **70.0 m**
Work stations: **658**
Year of completion: **1967**
Restoration and expansion: **1998**

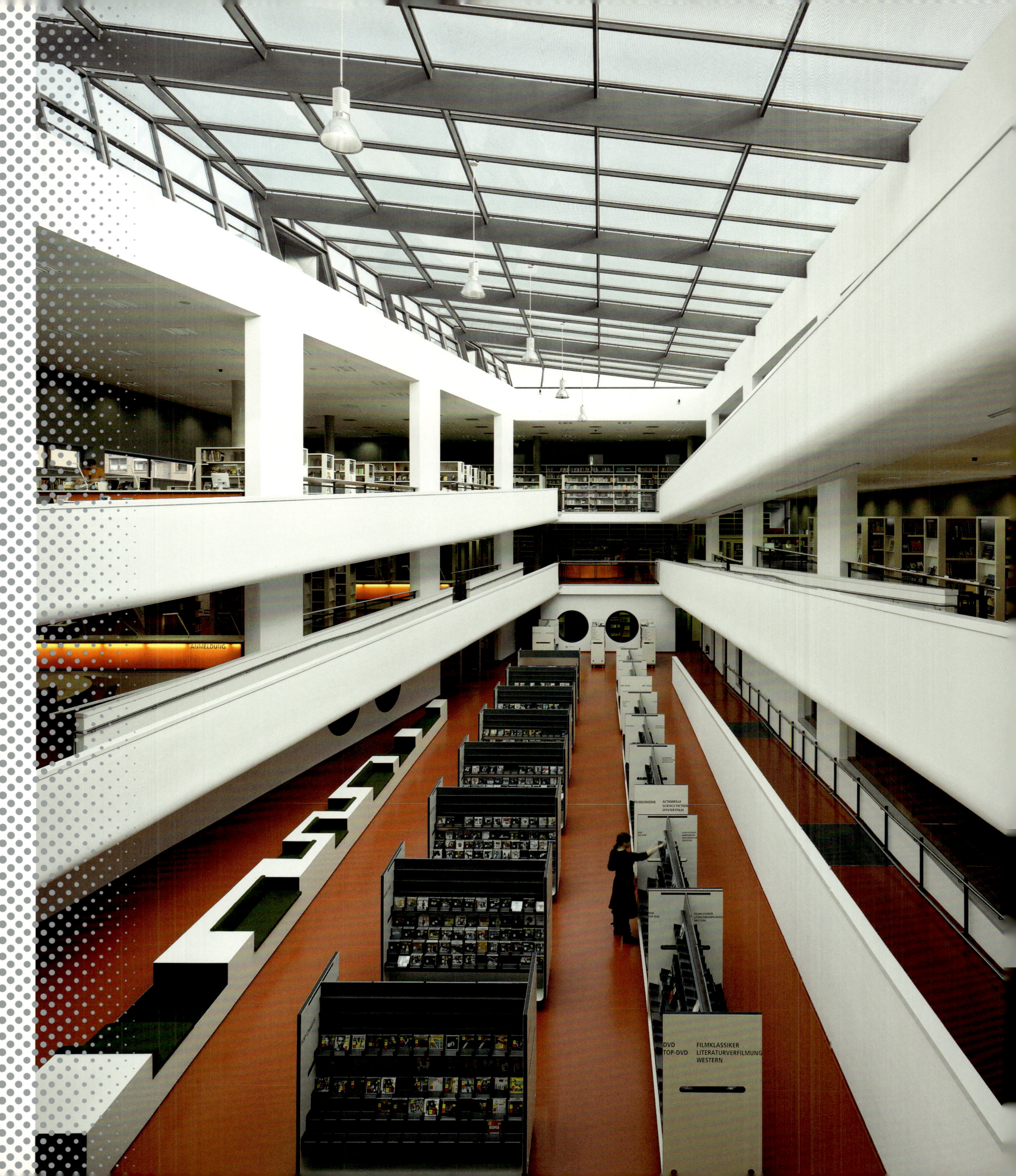
ANMELDUNG
DVD
TOP-DVD
FILMKLASSIKER
LITERATURVERFILMUNG
WESTERN

Economy Krefeld Media Library

Client: **City of Krefeld** | Location: **Krefeld** | GFA: **7,500 m²**
Completion date: **2008** | Competition: **1st Prize, 2002**
Architecture: **HPP in collaboration with Dieter Berten**

The conditions for construction were clearly defined from the start: a budget of 100,000 pounds, a lot in Hyde Park, and an unusual design task. On the occasion of the first world's fair in 1851, a building that could later be disassembled was to be erected in London on a lot of 6.4 hectares. The structure to be built was to be subdividable, so that spaces of different sizes could be placed at the disposal of the various exhibitors.

The first stage of the design competition drew 233 entries, but all of the proposals greatly exceeded the project's planned financial parameters. After this unsuccessful round of competition, and after the jury had proposed a design employing a more permanent construction system, Joseph Paxton entered the picture. Paxton, a landscape architect who had particular experience with the construction of greenhouses, submitted a design that utilized nothing but glass and cast iron. His design was accepted, and the building was erected from prefabricated iron railings and panes of glass in just seventeen weeks. The Crystal Palace, as the greenhouse-like building was quickly christened by the satirical magazine *Punch,* could be expanded as necessary.

The building quickly generated an enthusiastic response and earned respect for both its architectural qualities and its economical construction. As a result, the Crystal Palace was left intact after the world's fair had ended. It was subsequently used in Sydenham as a museum and exhibition building until it burned to the ground on November 30, 1936. With his design, Paxton did much more than just respect the project's restrictive budget. He also gave the people of London something unique. This uniqueness and the eighty additional years of use were the Crystal Palace's added value, or its dividends, as it were.

Innovation, trust, and foresight are the factors that determine the value and success of any achievement. Cost-effectiveness, however, is always paramount, and in architecture, cost-effectiveness is by no means limited to just controlling expenses and working with a low budget; it also means the rational and responsible handling of resources. Today, because of the dwindling of raw materials and climate change, architects are increasingly expected to build in a cost-effective manner.

The Media Library project in Krefeld was under just this kind of budget pressure. In order to keep within the project's restrictive budget, a low-tech design was conceived. This is underscored by the building's high energy efficiency and use of natural ventilation. It has already become evident that the library's low operating costs will not overburden the city of Krefeld's budget.

As a design, the Media Library opens up onto the Theaterplatz in front of it. The transparent central inner area also creates a spatially impressive effect. The building has registered a record number of visitors since it was opened in the spring of 2008. In that short time, the Media Library has gained the reputation of being one of the most modern and communicative facilities of its kind, and not only because of its spatial and color concepts. In spite of the project's low budget, an atmospherically inviting building has been created, one whose added value has contributed directly to an increased appetite for information on the part of the citizens of Krefeld.

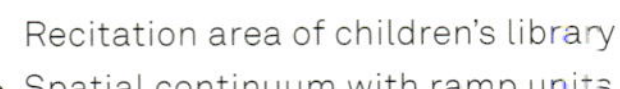

Recitation area of children's library
→ Spatial continuum with ramp units

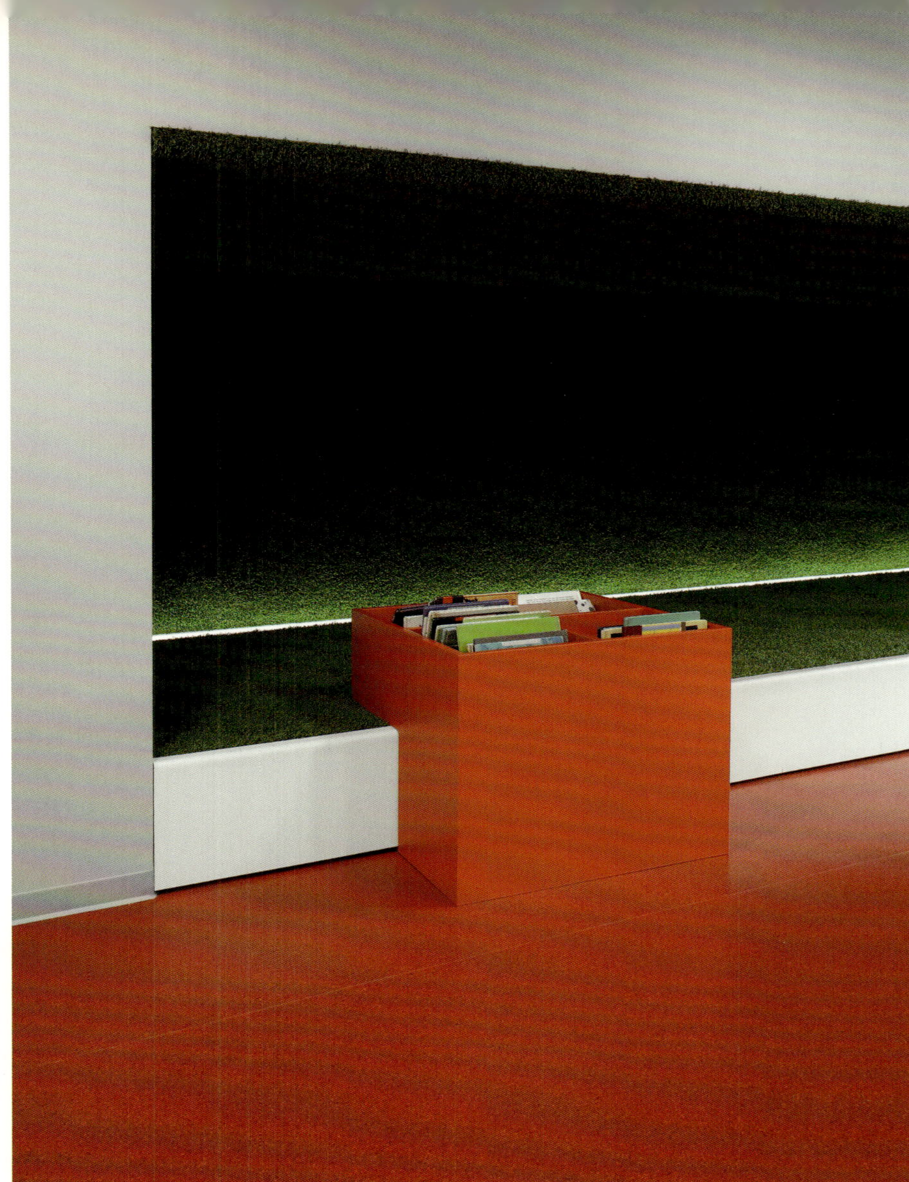

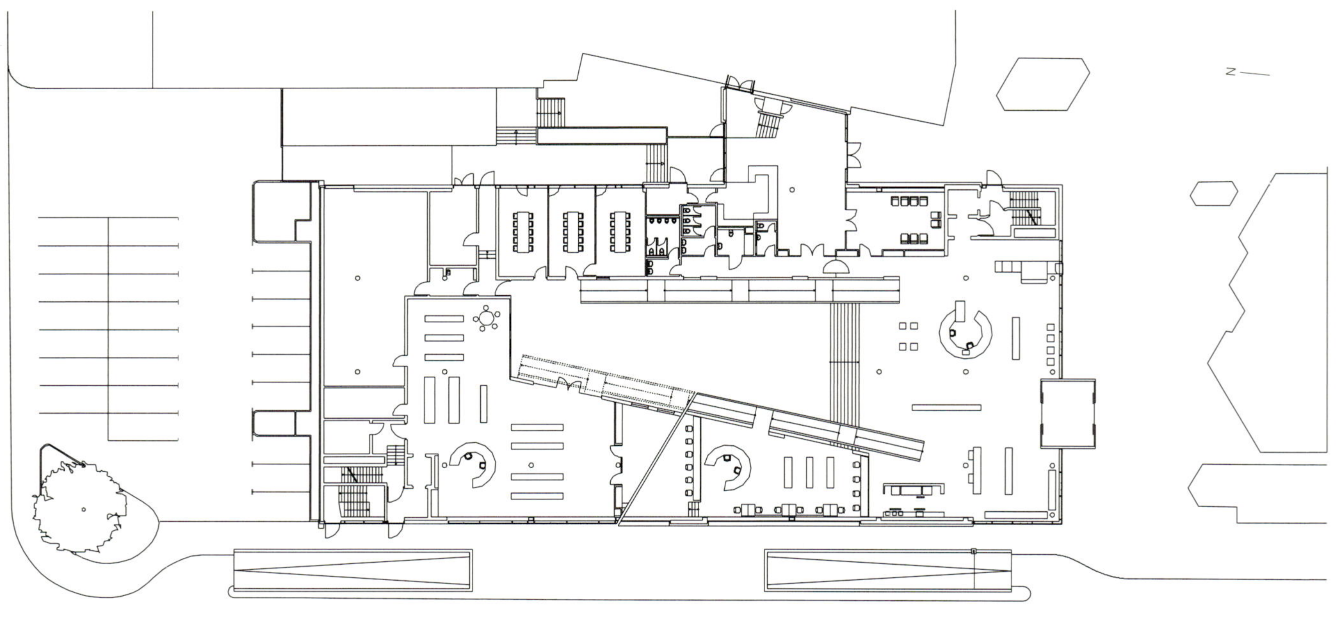

0 10 20 50

Floor plan of ground floor

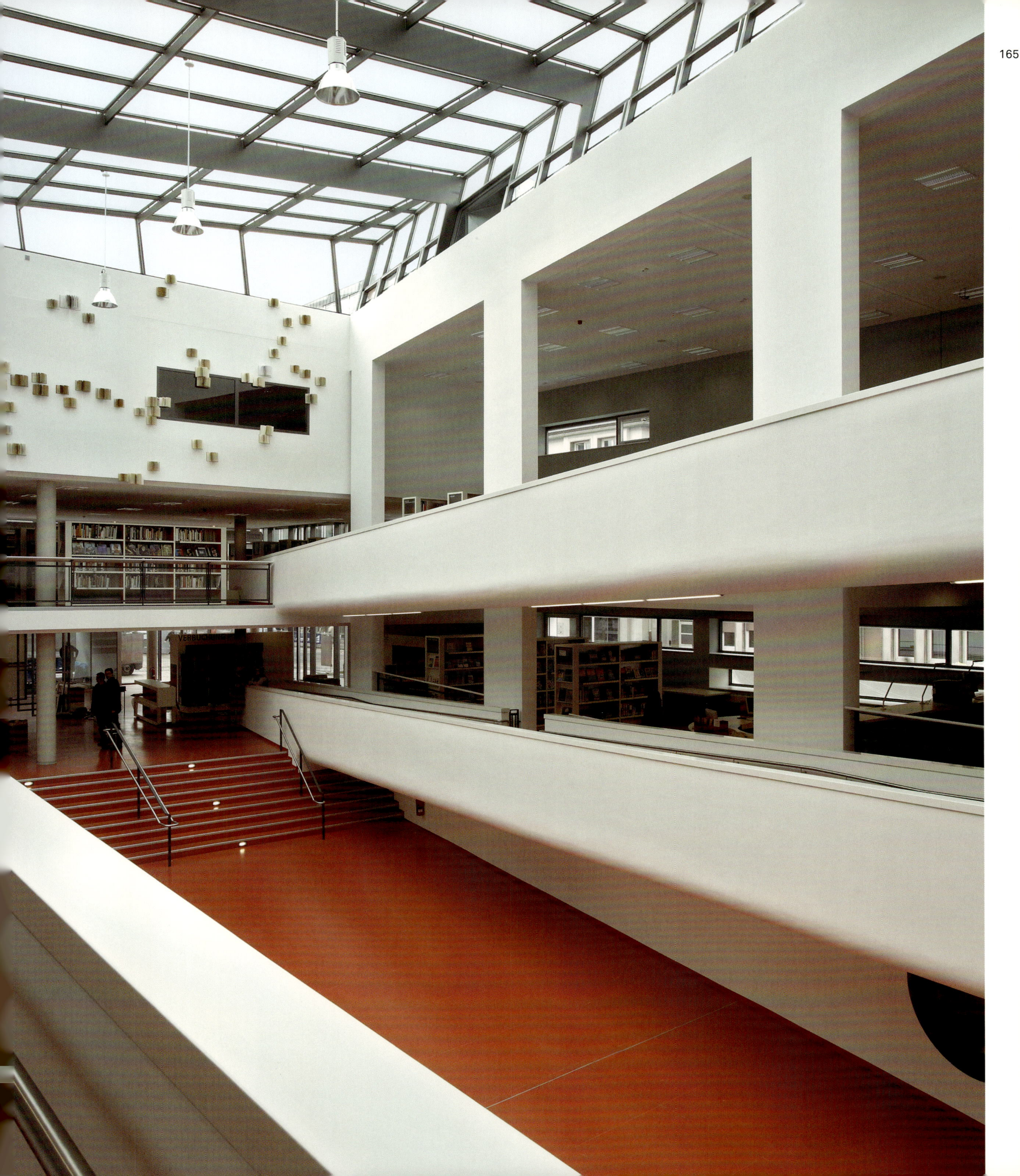

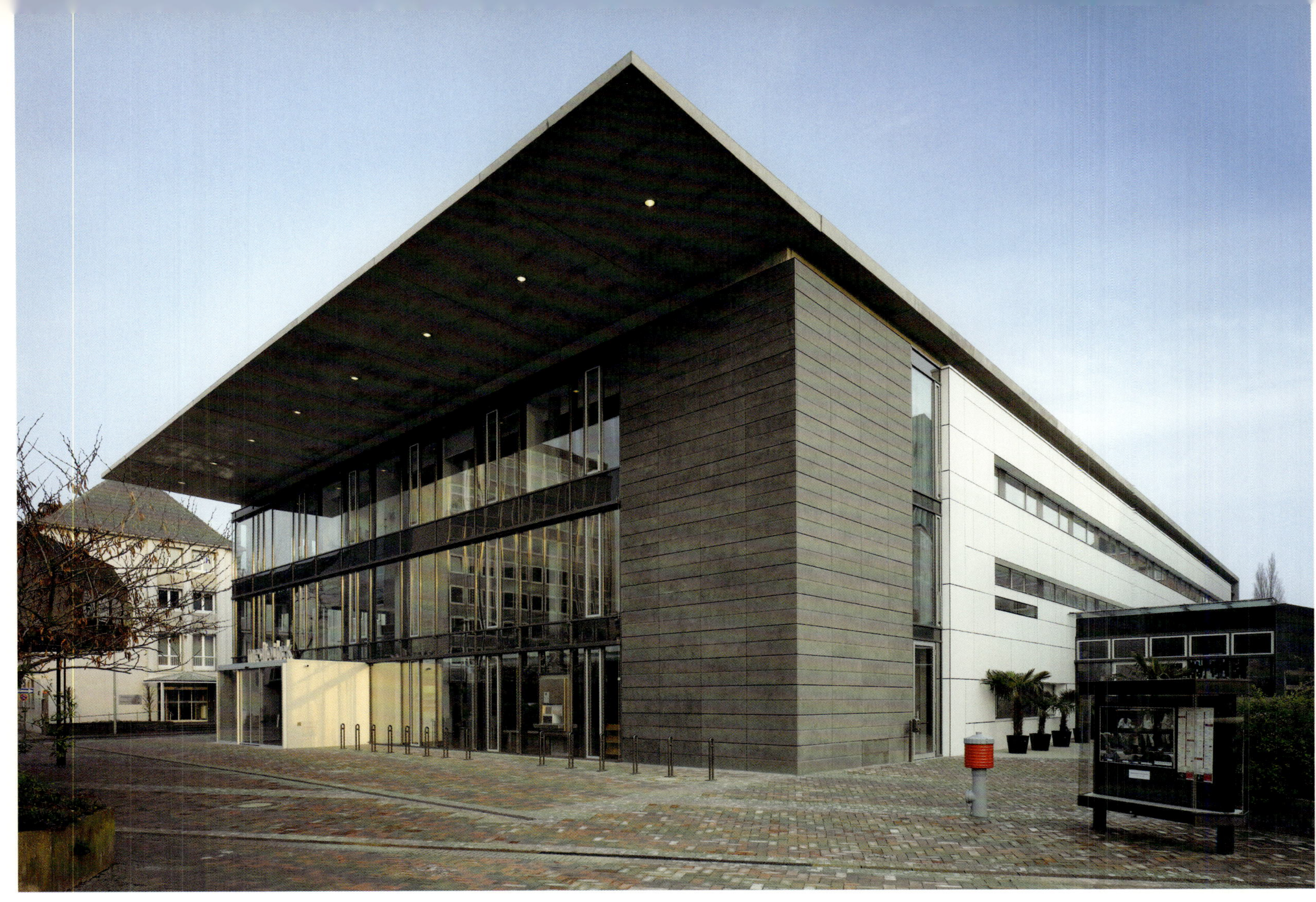

Entrance façade giving onto the Theaterplatz

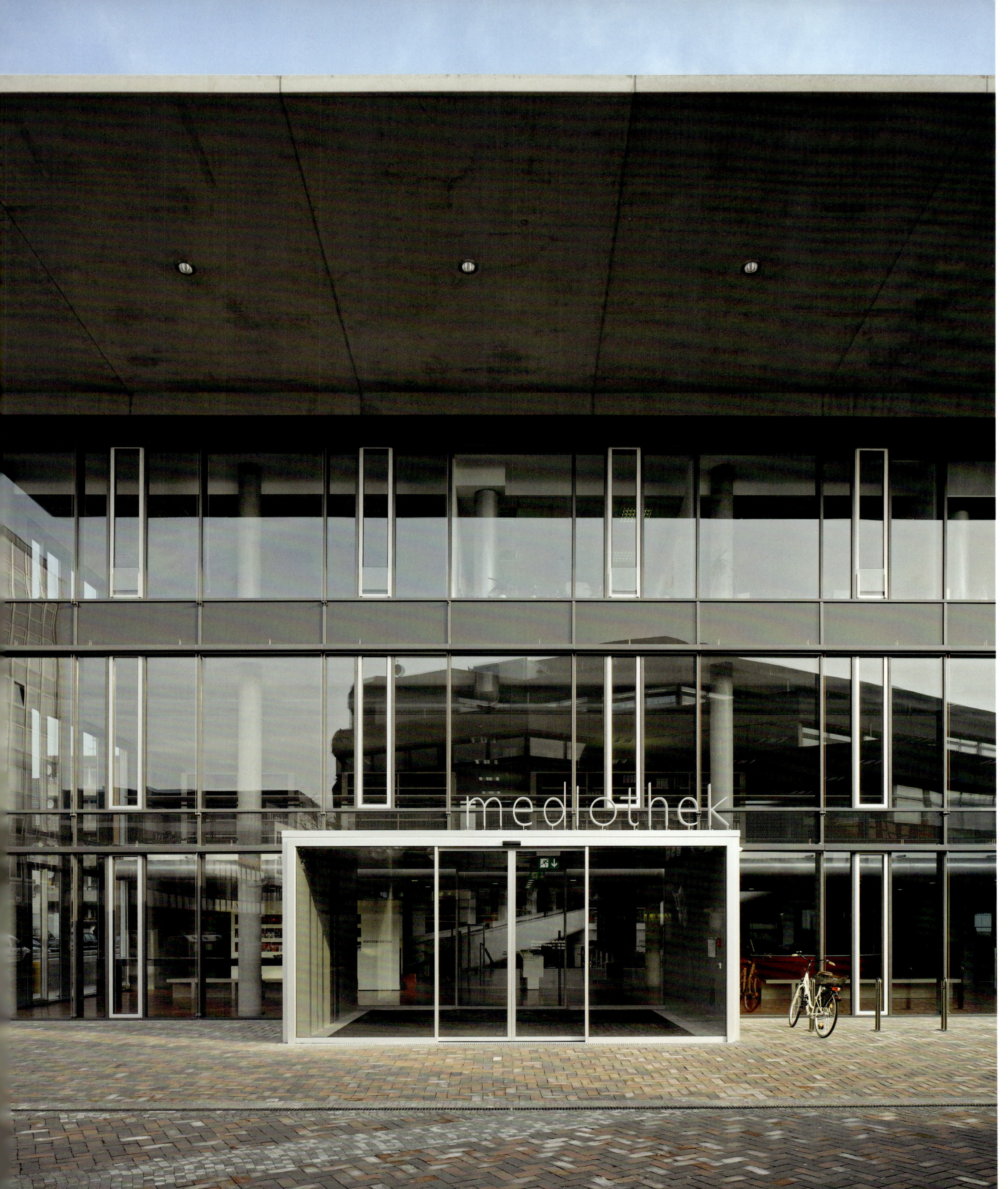
mediothek

 The Media Library in Krefeld A lack of inclination to spend time in the city of Krefeld's Theaterplatz was what led the city to hold a competition for a new urban development plan for the district between Ostwall, St. Anton-Strasse, and Königstrasse. The new Media Library is the first stage of the planned development of this public space, where the Seidenweberhaus, a historic building which houses the municipal theater, and the state theater are also located. From an urbanistic standpoint, the new building, like the old municipal library that preceded it, is situated parallel to the landmark-protected Seidenweberhaus on the west side of the Theaterplatz.

A clearly delineated, three-story building was created on a rectangular ground plan with a glass entry façade that gives onto the Theaterplatz. The inviting windows are framed on the sides by dark grey natural stone. Large, white slabs on the façade shape the building exterior on the structure's longer sides. Strip windows that have offset heights and can be opened establish the spatial arrangement of the building's interior when the structure is viewed from the outside. A protruding, exposed concrete slab binds the different façade elements together while at the same time serving as a canopy that introduces the building.

The Media Library is accessed via the extended main entrance on the Theaterplatz. From the foyer, where the information, exhibition areas, and booking counters are located, the visitor enters the glass-roofed atrium. The unusual interior design, which is based on the concept of a "continuous space," can be seen here in its full dimensions: ramps that take off upwards around the foyer and the central exhibition and lecture area connect the terraced, ascending book dispensing levels in a flowing, and wheelchair-accessible, fashion. The visitors stroll through the Media Library as if they were on a boardwalk and, depending on their location and level as they do this, they continually experience new spatial impressions.

The ramps, which are suspended in open space, have a steel construction covered with white, rounded-off plasterboard elements. In addition, the dynamic space continuum is given definition by the orangey-red floor surface of synthetic rubber and is accented by the red-and-white furniture and the grey-green walls.

All windows can be opened, in order to provide natural ventilation for the building, and are equipped with exterior sun protection. Supplementary mechanical ventilation ensures the requisite circulation of air through the building, thereby preventing the need for additional cooling or air-conditioning.

By means of the basic idea of a continuous space, the architecture of Krefeld's new Media Library playfully reflects the ubiquity of the media. The unconventional character and generous disposition of the library space are underscored by the building's economical manufacture and energy-efficient operation. This building offers further proof that unconventional ideas can also be cost-effective.

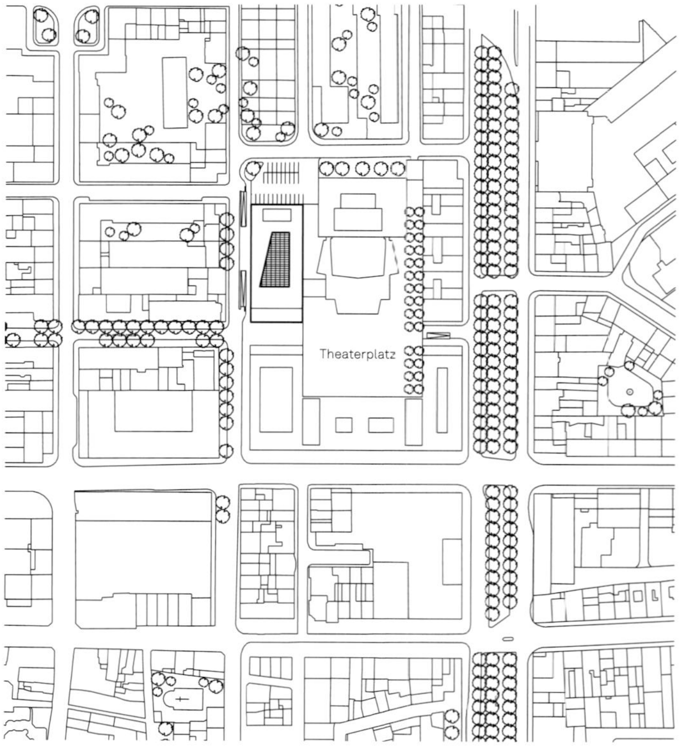

Site plan

→ Longitudinal façade
→→ Media Library in the Theaterplatz

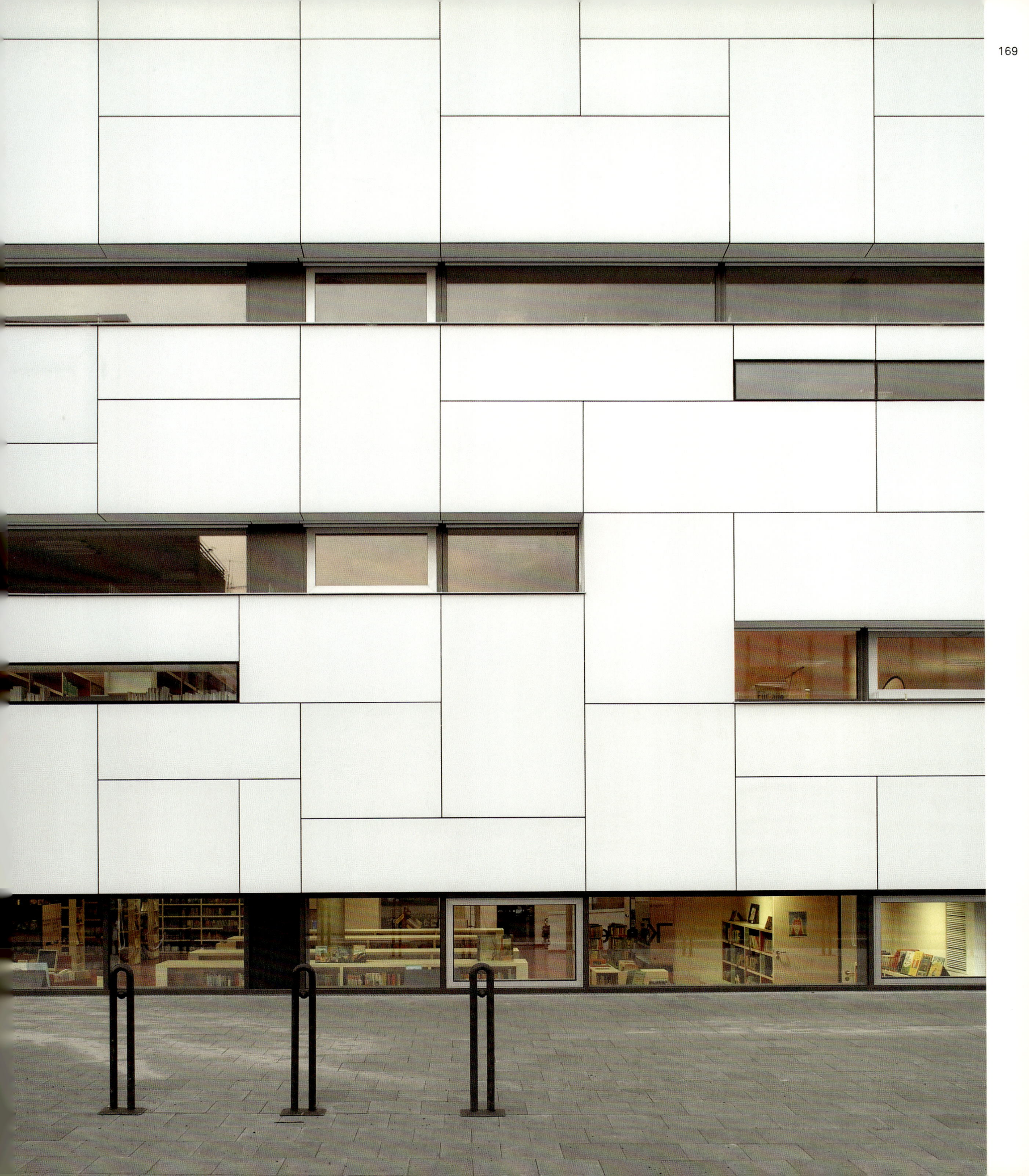

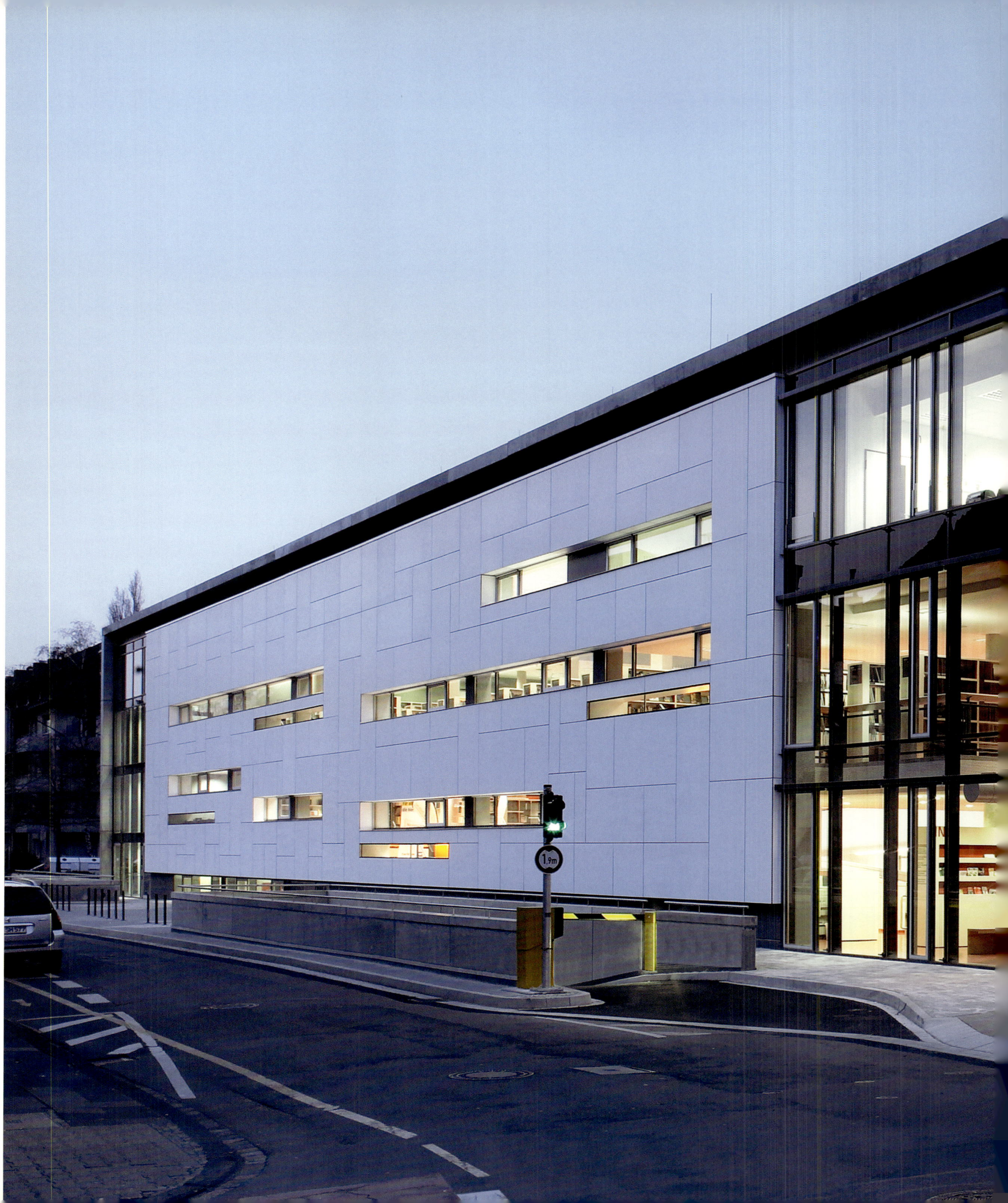

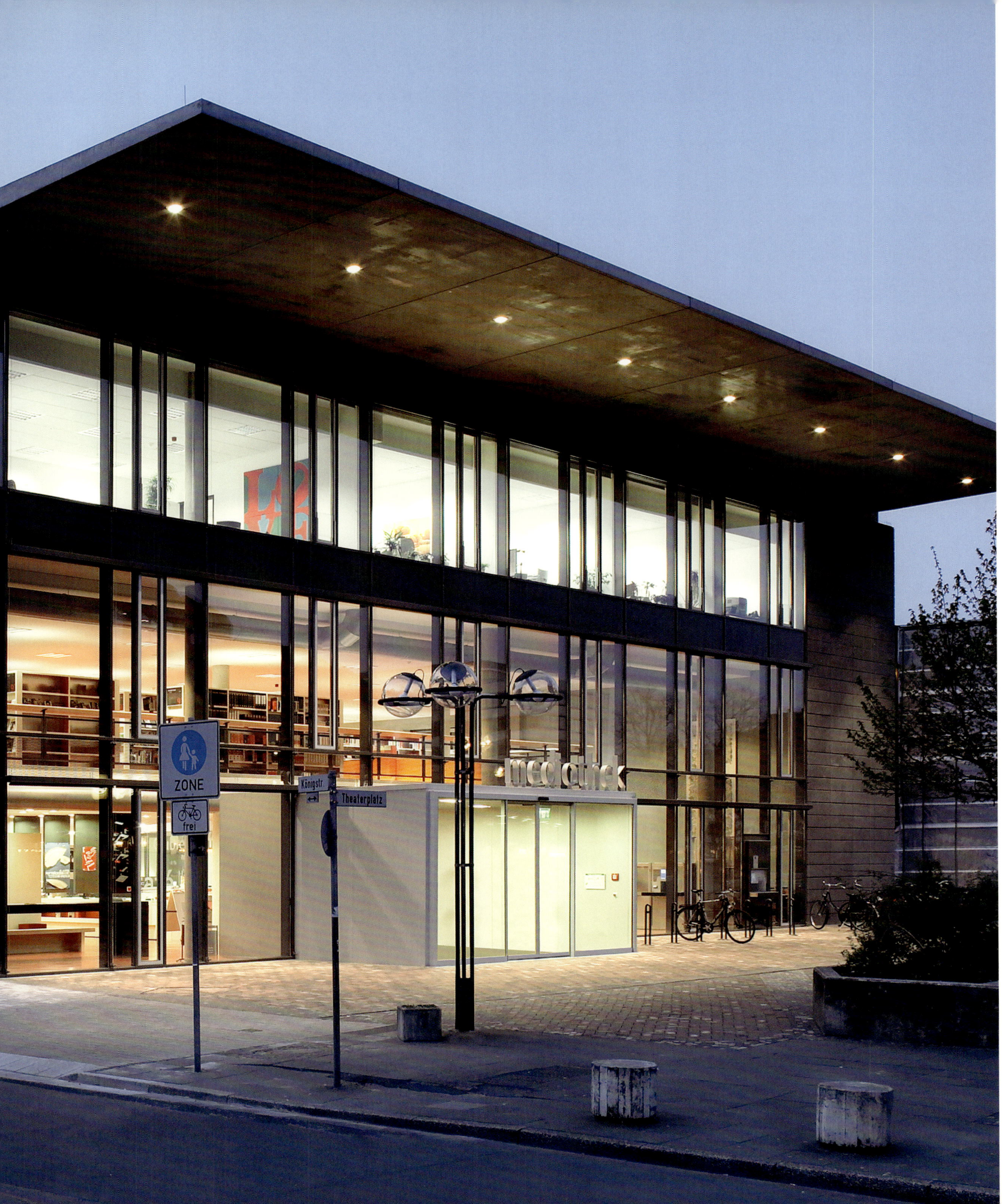
ZONE
frei
Königstr
Theaterplatz

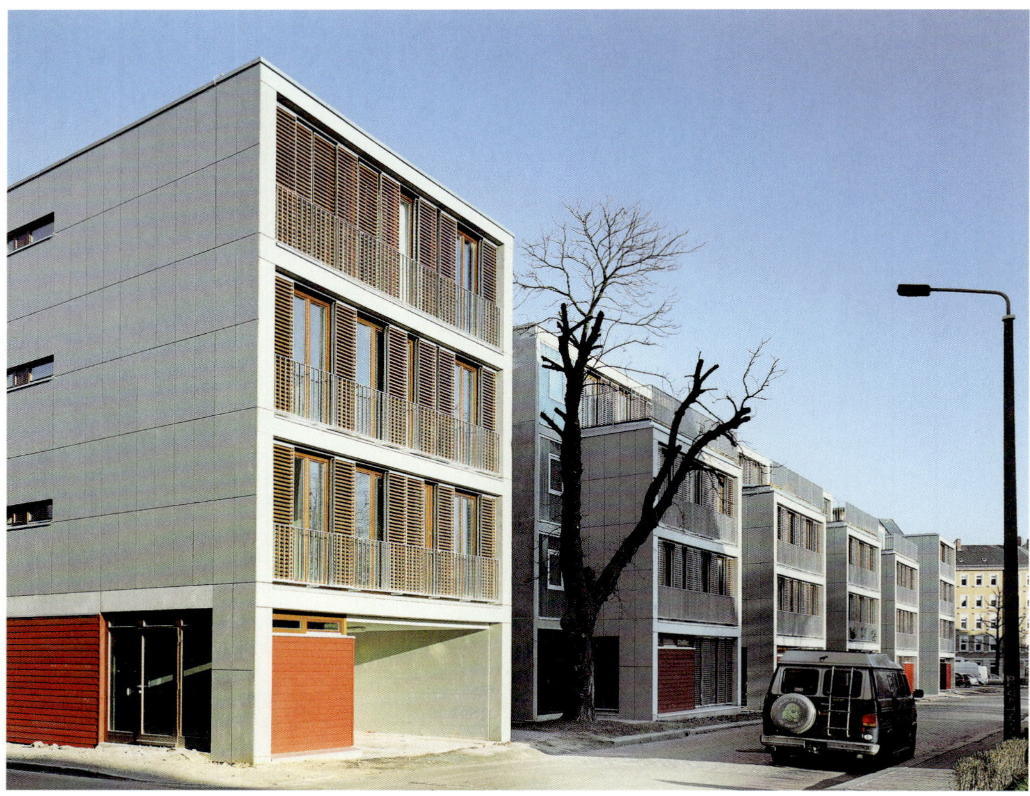

Housing for Young People

This project exemplifies the symbiosis of maximum economy, high design standards, and the highest functional adaptability. Excepting only the core sanitary infrastructure, the apartments created allow for a completely flexible division of space. In addition, due to the project's especially economical construction, it was possible to glaze the street side of each apartment.

Client: Wohnungsbaugenossenschaft Kontakt e.V.
Location: Leipzig
GFA: 2,951 m²
Residential units: 26
Completion date: 2000
Competition: 1st Prize, 1998
Award: Architecture Prize of the City of Leipzig, honorable mention, 2001

Economy

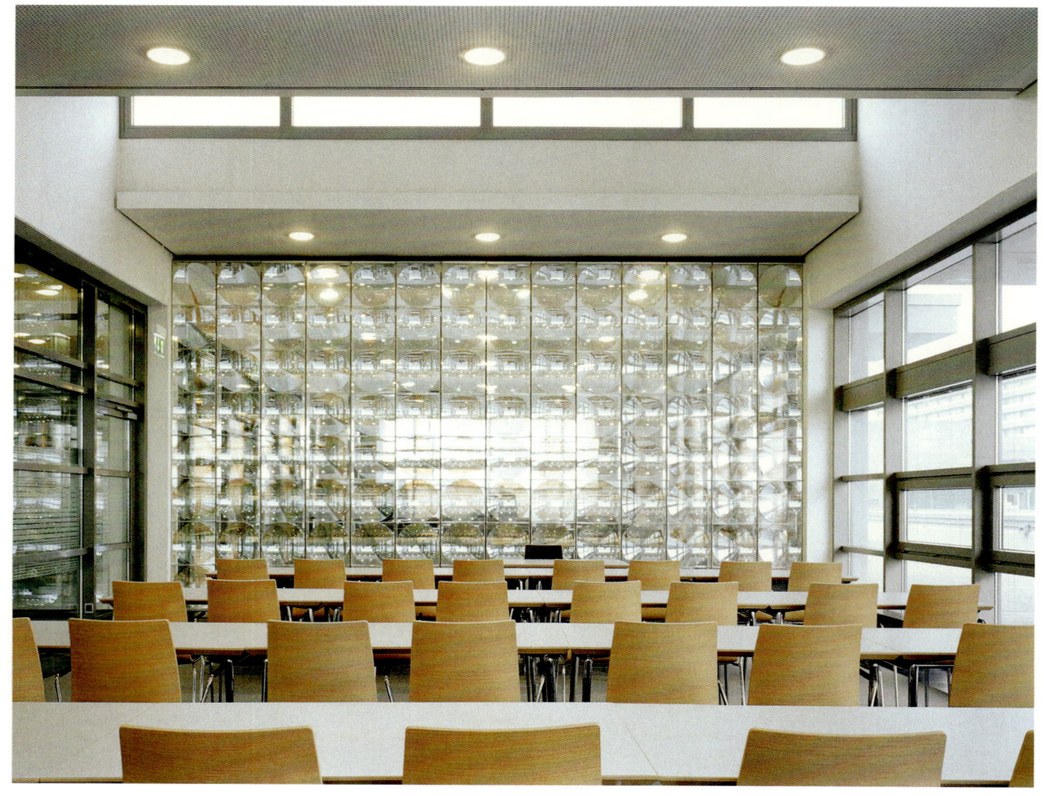

Cafeteria of the Ruhr University in Bochum

While retaining its exterior contour, the cafeteria of the Ruhr University in Bochum was extensively renovated after almost thirty years of operation. The main areas of the interior were redesigned to create more openness and transparency. Formal clarity and contemporary design elements in combination with the latest kitchen technology as well as an innovative hygiene concept allow for energy efficiency and environmental compatibility.

Client: BLB Dortmund
Location: Bochum
GFA: 19,000 m²
Year of completion: 1970
Restoration and revitalization: 2006

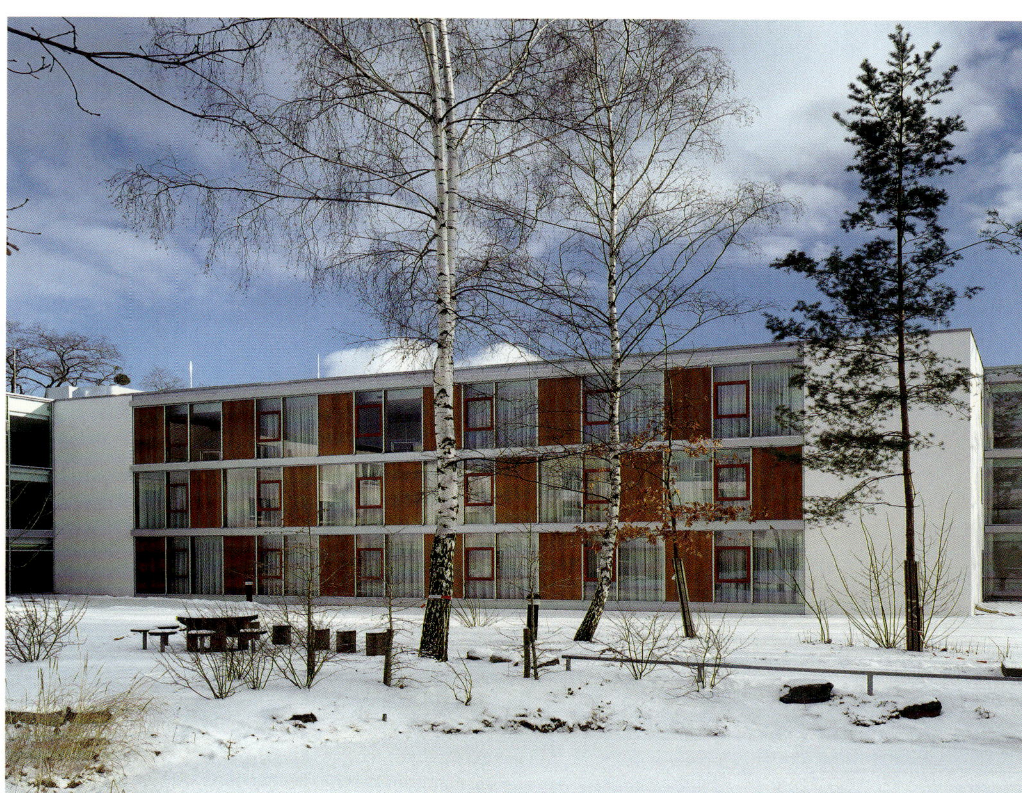

Saxony Vocational Training Center

The vocational training center in Saxony offers young physically disabled or chronically ill people manifold training opportunities and comprehensive medical care. Through the use of modular construction, a simple geometry, and a reduced approach to materials, a very economical building resulted. In spite of its austerity, the building exudes a playful cheerfulness thanks to the story to story reflection of the sanitary units and their colorful design.

Client: Berufsbildungswerk Sachsen GmbH
Location: Dresden
GFA: 1,974 m^2
Beds: 36
Completion date: 2004

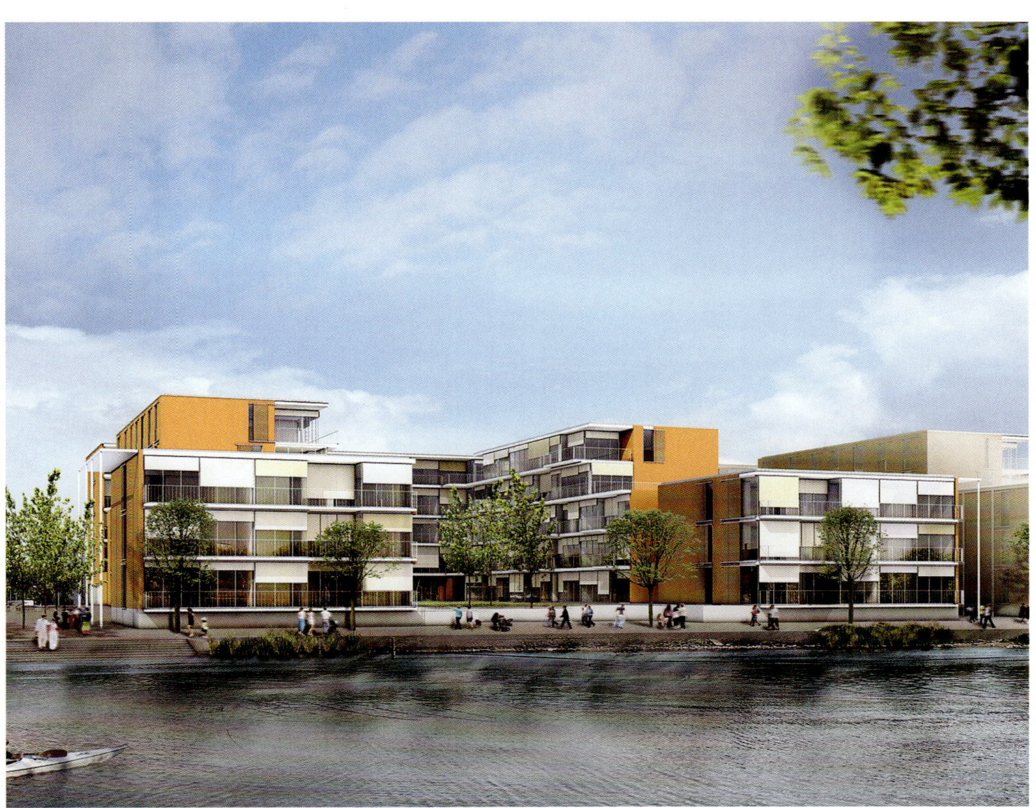

Housing on the Seerhein River

This building complex is located on the north bank of the Seerhein River in Constance and optimally oriented to the sun and the water on its open south side. The building structure is set up to make possible a maximum flexibility in the design of the apartments' ground plans. This allows the residential units to be adapted to new needs at any time, a characteristic which also helps prolong the life of the building.

Client: Euroland Wohnen am Seerhein GmbH & Co. KG
Location: Constance
GFA: 12,687 m^2
Residential units: 54
Completion date: 2009

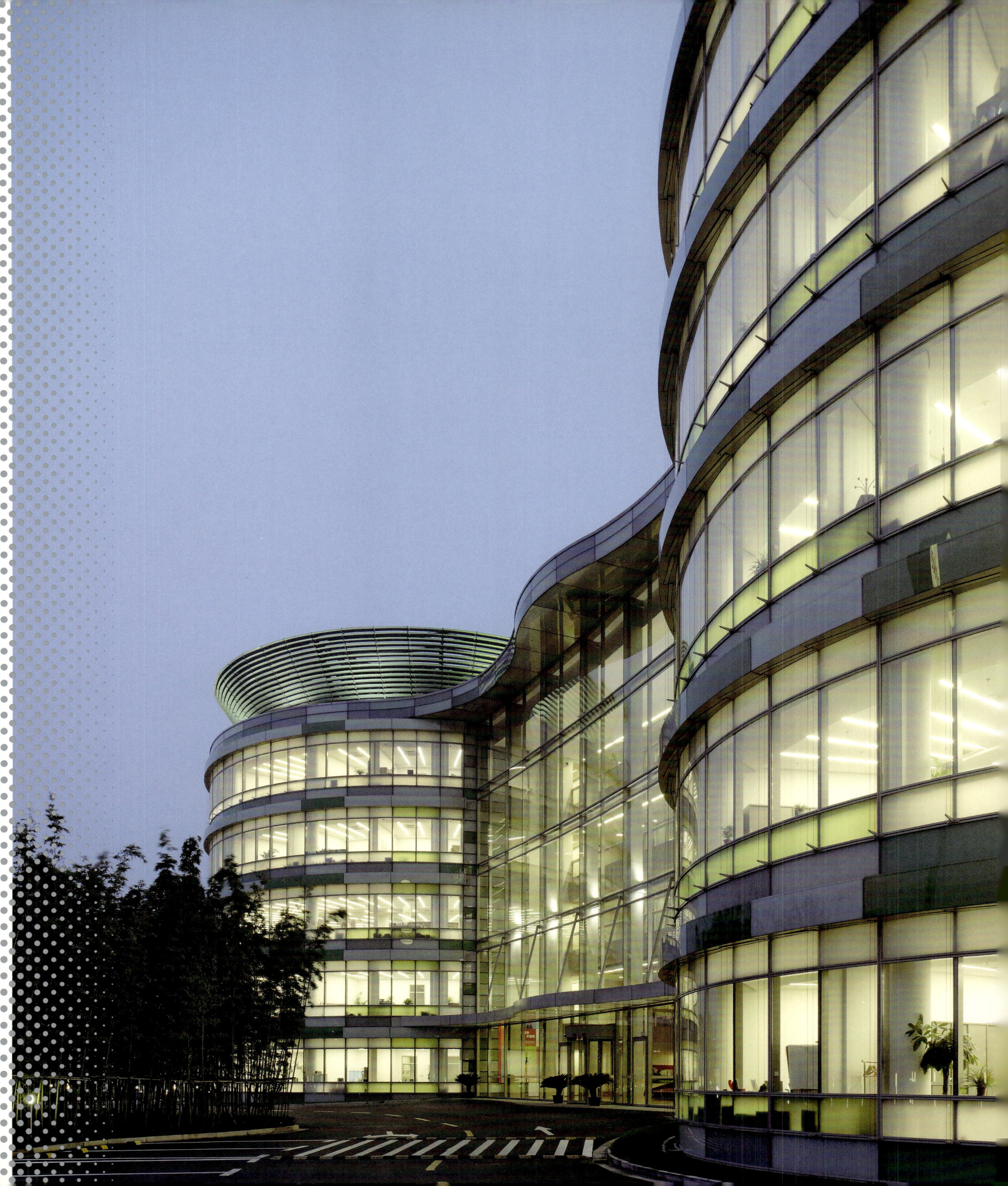

The term "sustainability" is being heard more and more often in the context of sociopolitical debate about climate change and increasing energy prices. The meaning of the word is clear: ongoing, long lasting, abiding. This also helps to explain the meaning of "sustainable development." These terms indicate tendencies which correspond to the needs of the current generation but do not endanger the opportunities of future generations.

Agenda 21, which was adopted at the United Nations Conference on Environment and Development (UNCED) in Rio de Janeiro in 1992, and the extension of its decisions at the World Summit for Sustainable Development in Johannesburg in 2002 form the basis for sustainable development projects throughout the world. The goal is to adapt the economic, energy, agricultural, and trade policies of industrialized nations in order to reduce the consumption of natural resources. In threshold and developing nations the Agenda focuses on the issues of poverty, population growth, education, health, drinking water and sanitation, wastewater and garbage disposal, and rural development.

It was at this point that the term "sustainability" was also acknowledged in architectural circles. At HPP, a comprehension of sustainability is a significant part of the basis of our planning activities. The goal of sustainable building is to build in an economically and environmentally compatible way that spares natural resources. In addition, sustainable buildings should be comfortable and healthy for their users and fit well into their surroundings.

Sustainability has a limited significance, however, in growth markets and threshold nations. To clients and investors in these contexts, the resources that are available for building appear inexhaustible, and everything seems doable if one can afford to pay for it. Money, financial power, and a desire to project a certain image still take priority over the idea of sustainability; a sense of responsibility to society and the environment have made only tentative inroads in these countries.

It is all the more important, therefore, to work to create extraordinary "beacon projects" of sustainability in threshold nations, and HPP recently designed just such a project for the Henkel Asia-Pacific and China Headquarters in Shanghai. The interplay between the building's engineering and the design of its façade has led to an energy use reduction of about forty percent in comparison with other buildings in the area. The structure's exterior sun protection may seem to be only a small design detail, but it actually significantly reduces the building's energy consumption. Although this kind of approach to architectural design is taken for granted in central Europe, it is seldom seen in Asia.

Drawing on the form and color of the magnolia bloom, the façade's design communicates the desire to incorporate national and area-specific themes and materials in the project. For instance, bamboo, a locally available wood, was used in the building's interior. This also helps the building to achieve a positive energy balance and reflects today's demand for a more responsible handling of resources. The building itself elucidates the principle of sustainability, a concept which is usually difficult to convey or explain to visitors through architectural planning and design. All in all, the result is highly satisfying, and every visitor takes the building's message away with them.

Sustainability
Henkel Asia-Pacific and China Headquarters

Client: **Henkel KGaA** | Location: **Shanghai** | GFA: **23,000 m²** | Work stations: **500**
Completion date: **2007** | Interior design: **HPP in collaboration with Fingerle & Woeste**

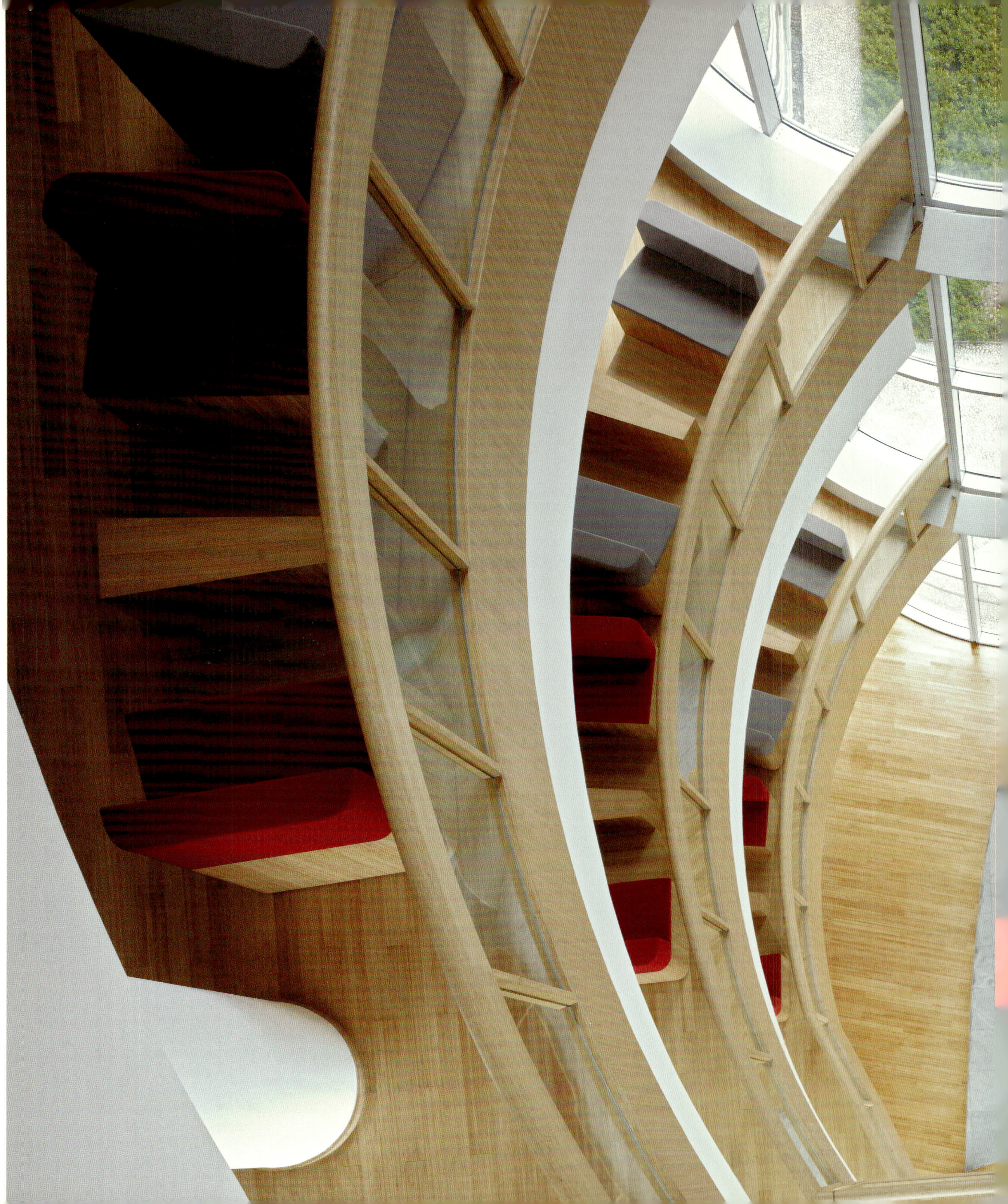

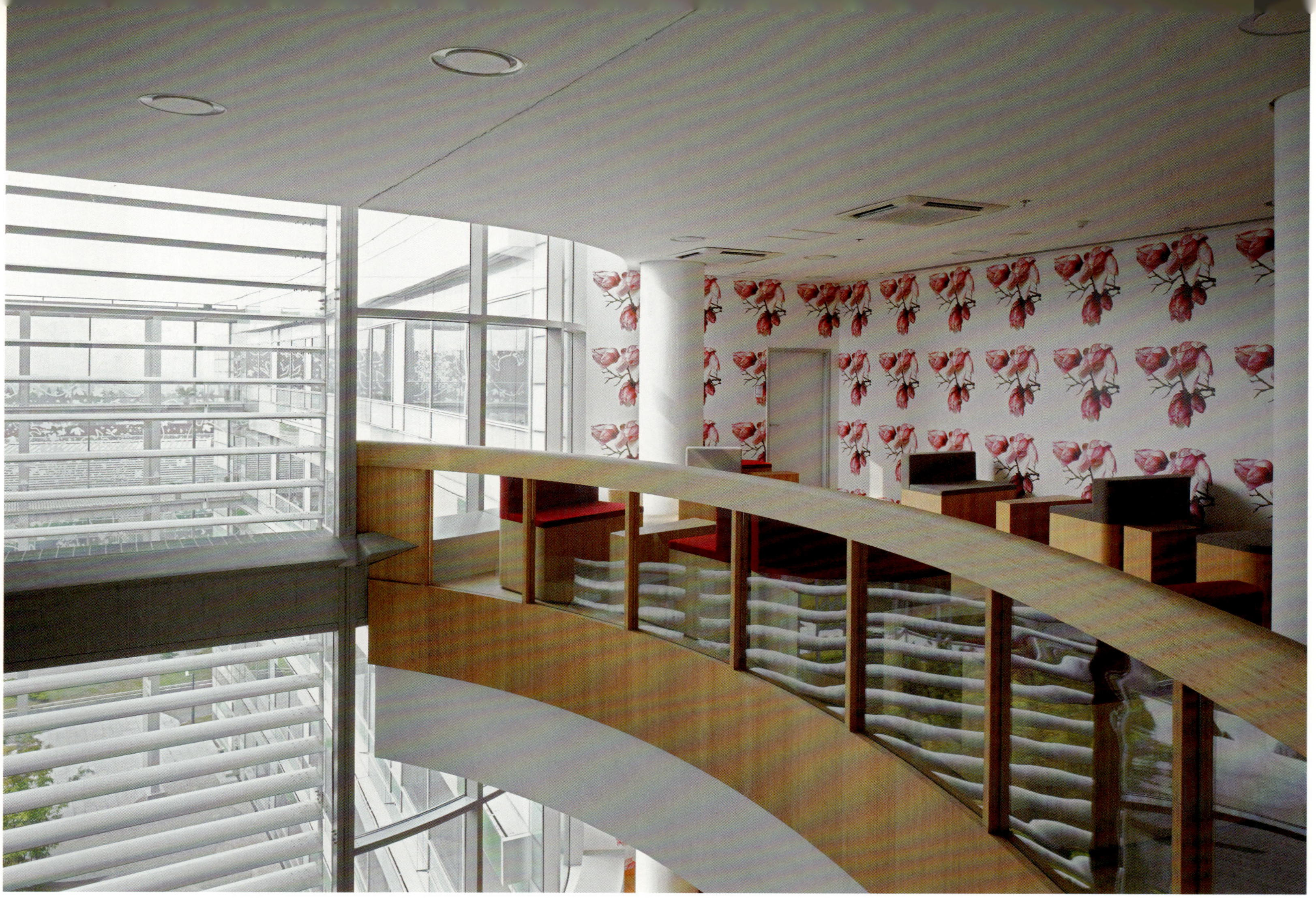

Communication zones

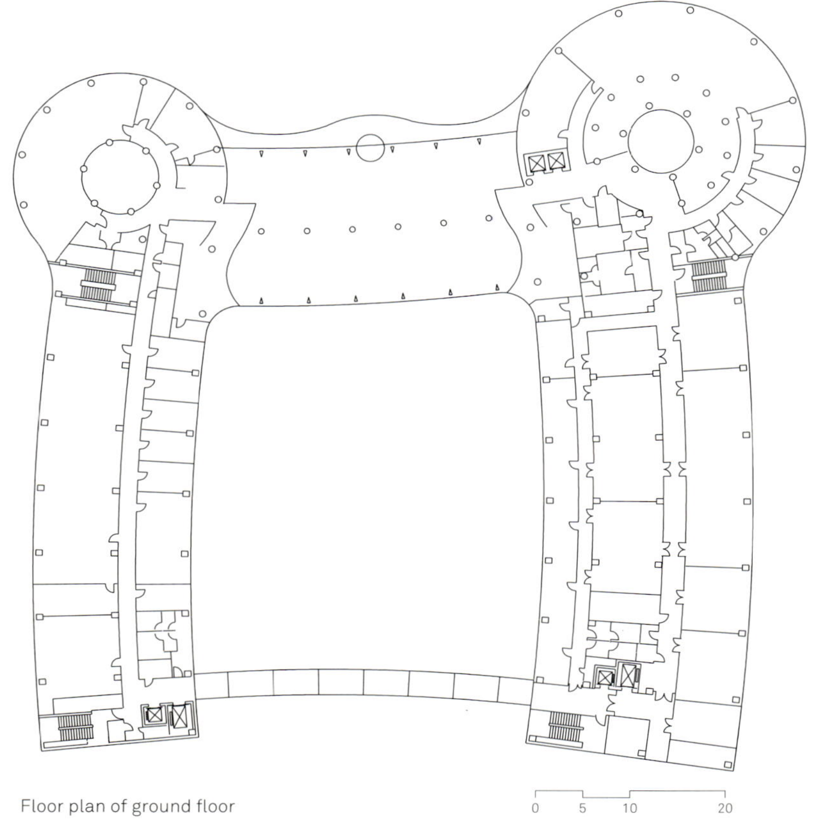

Floor plan of ground floor

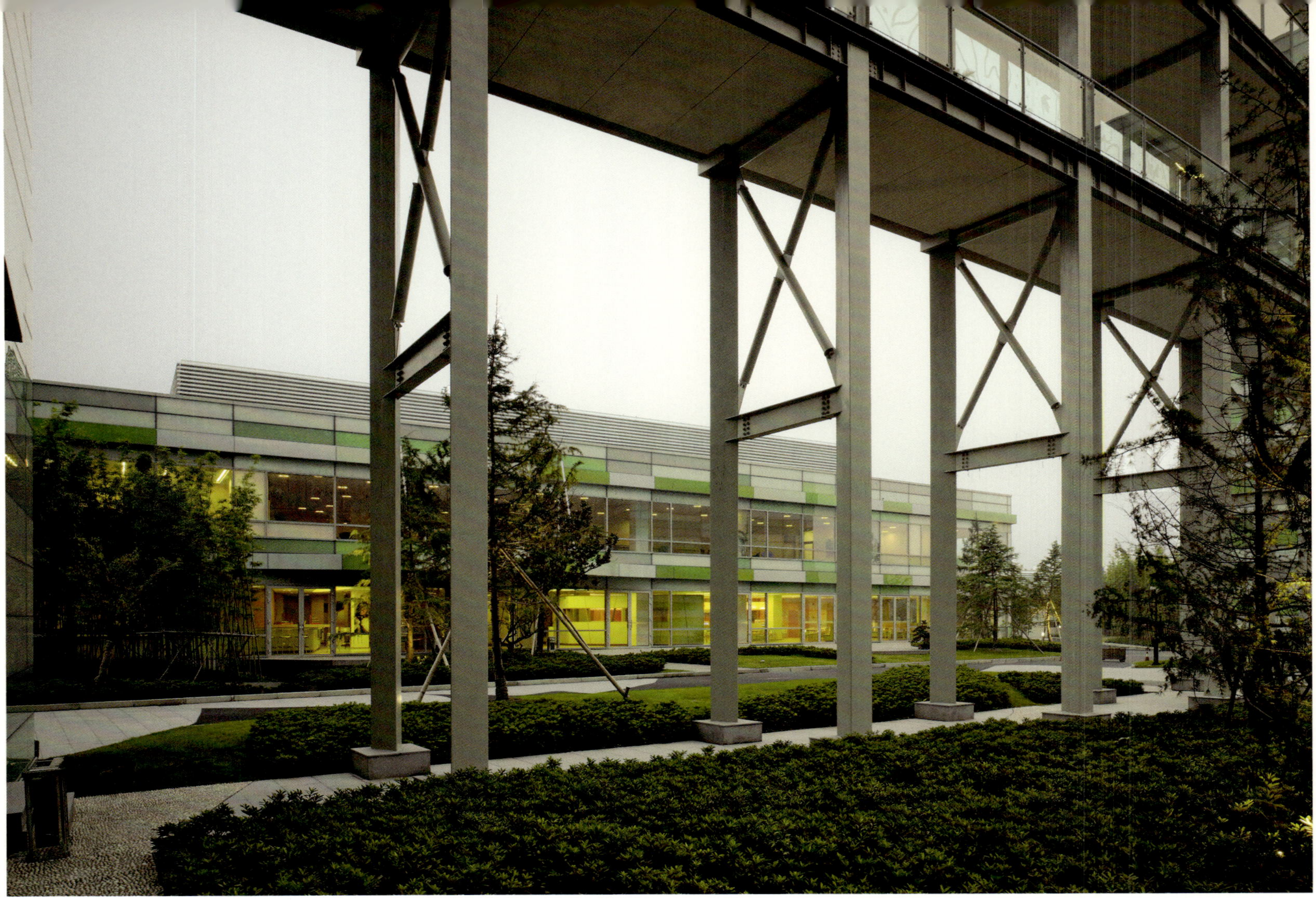

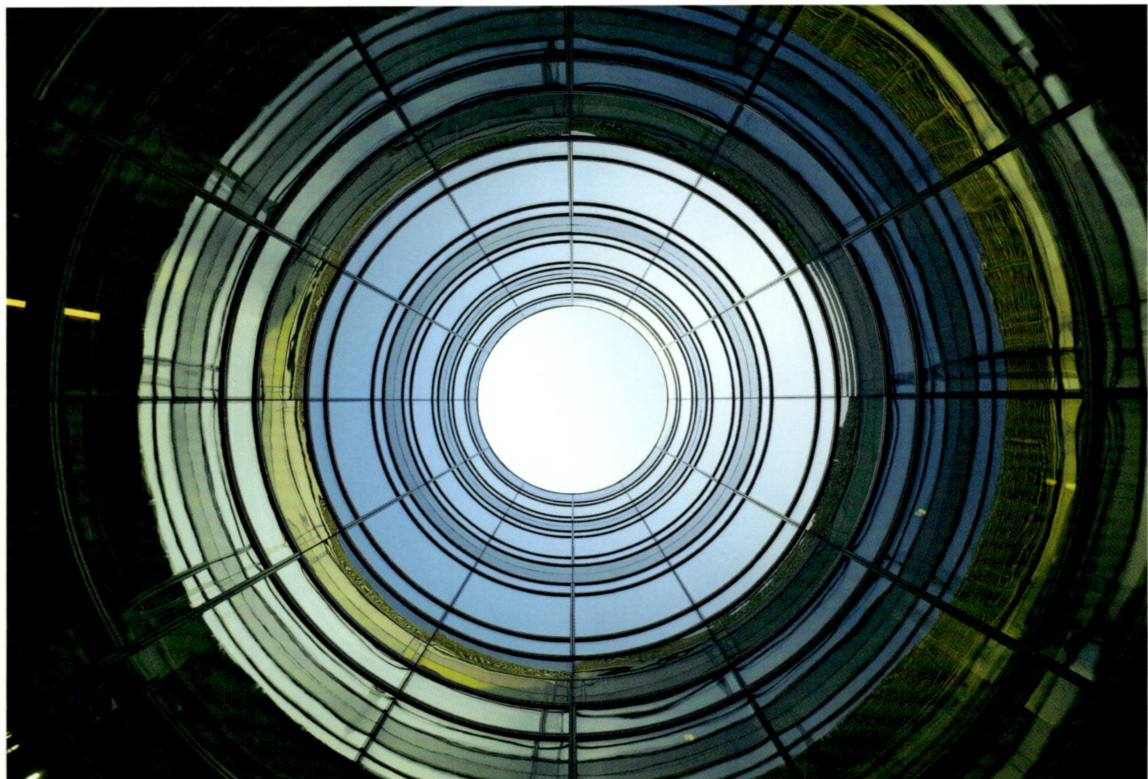

View of auditorium
Rotunda

→ Inner courtyard with magnolia blossom motif

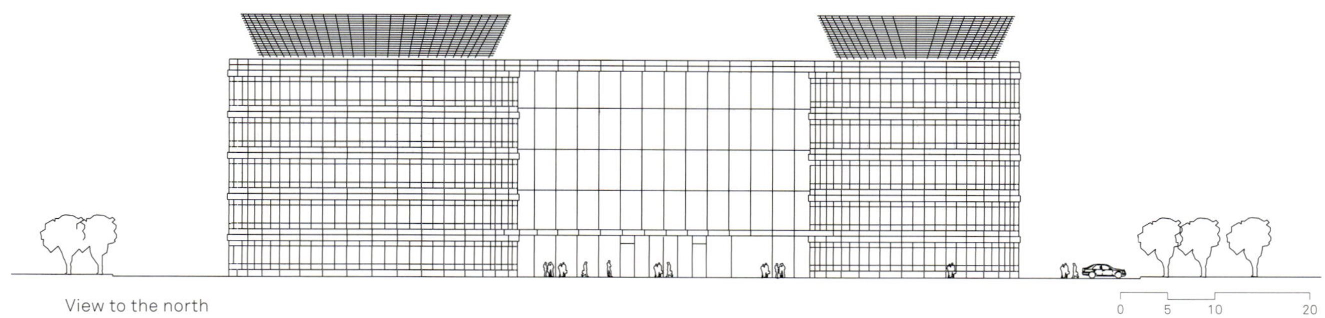

View to the north

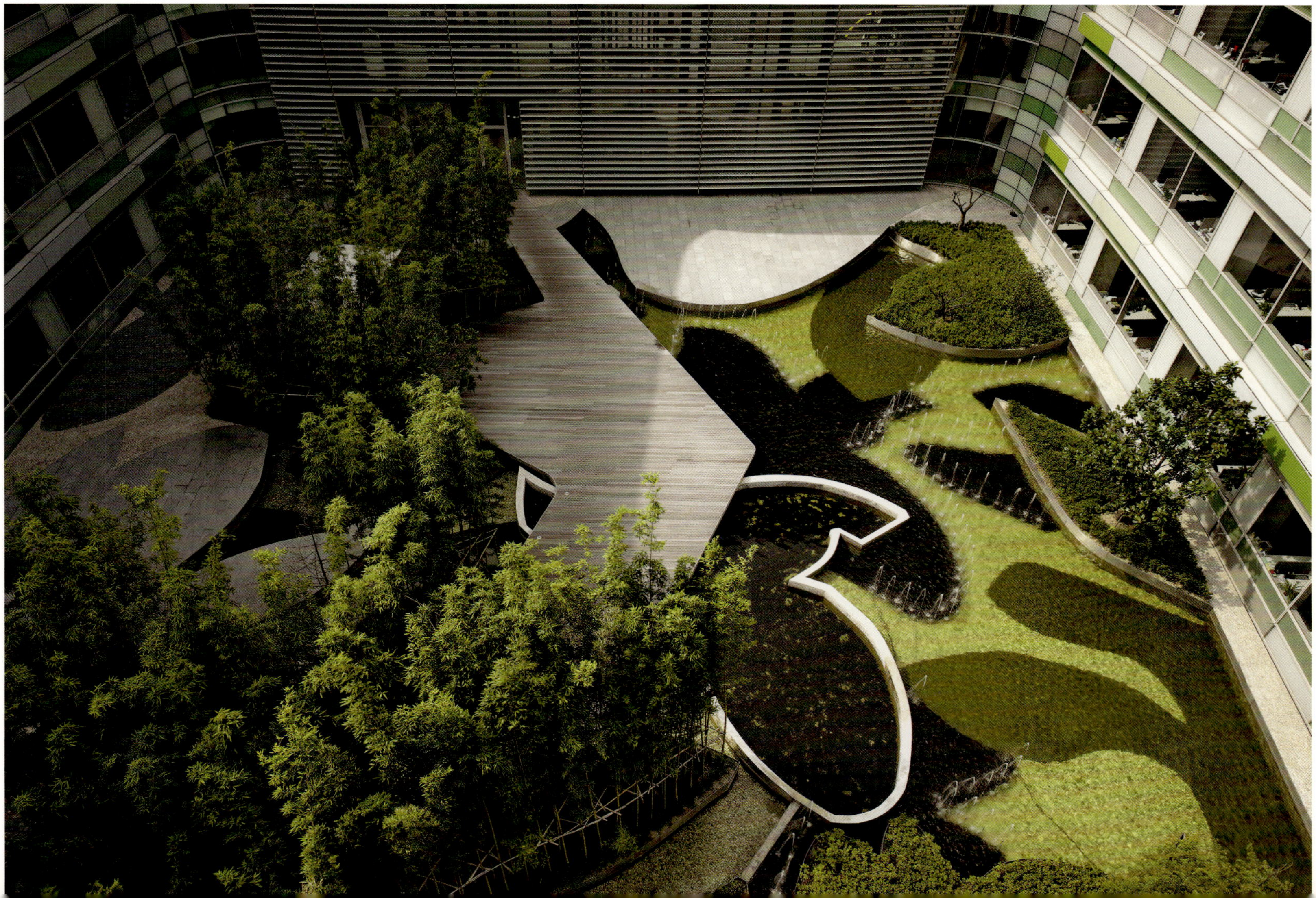

Henkel Asia-Pacific and China Headquarters In the summer of 2007 the headquarters in China of Henkel KGaA was completed in Pudong, Shanghai's booming economic center on the east bank of the Huangpu River. The new administration and research center stands in a green field and in its basic form represents an asymmetrically curving U.

The design for the new building is based on the concepts of "skin" and "mantle," as well as the reflection of nature within architecture. As the official city flower of Shanghai, the magnolia was the inspiration for various design ideas. From a functional standpoint, the new headquarters mirror Henkel's identity as a leading high-tech company. The designers' guiding principles were environmental compatibility as well as the most modern building standards with respect to sustainable building. In addition, the values of Chinese culture were to be integrated into the design. A feng shui consultant was specially hired for this project to analyze the design from the perspective of the application of traditional Chinese building orientations and configurations.

The building is an earthquake-proof construction with a concrete and steel framework. The most conspicuous sign of the influence of feng shui is that there are no right angles in the entire building. With five stories and a basement, the new building has a gross surface area of 23,000 square meters and approximately 500 work stations. A continuous construction grid of 5.5 meters and a façade grid of 2.75 meters ensure the greatest flexibility as well as variable office and laboratory layouts.

The main point of access is via the five-story entryway atrium located on the north side of the building, which also connects the two side rotundas. At the level of the third and fifth floors the atrium takes over the function of conference and meeting rooms in the form of glass cubes inserted within the space. Access to the two wings of the building occurs from the cylinders. While the circular construction and wings on the northeast side house ultramodern laboratory areas and an imposing showroom on the ground floor, the office spaces—designed as a mixture of open areas, cubicles, and team offices—are located in the rotunda and in the wings on the northwest side. One of the two elevator groups is centrally located in each of the transition zones of the entry hall in the rotundas as a means of vertical access and are joined here by the supply units and coffee areas. Fire escape stairways are placed on the outside of the façades. Bridges also connect the upper three stories at the rear of the building in order to facilitate communication between the laboratory and office wings. These wood-covered catwalks are protected from the weather by a canopy and a glass membrane printed with magnolia blossoms. On the south side, a two-story structure completes the building ensemble in front. It contains more training and seminar rooms as well as an additional lecture hall, which in cooperation with the Fraunhofer Institut is being used as an "Adhesive University."

The façade was realized as a continuous, all-glass curtain wall in an elemental construction system in order to fulfill the planning requirement of building an energy-efficient building according to Western standards. By using heat-insulating glass and thermally decoupled window frames, a transmission value of 1.86 W/m-K was achievable. These choices, together with the exterior sun protection, which is also unusual in China, lowered the energy consumption of the building by a total of forty percent in comparison with the regional average.

In the choice of the façade's color, the design once again turned to the inspiration of magnolia blossoms: the upper and lower lights of the convex and concave double glazing is coated with colored film in shades of light green and white, thereby integrating the building with its surroundings in a lively and harmonious way. That the integration of Chinese culture also plays an important role in the design of the building's interior and outdoor landscape can be seen in the public areas. The form and color scheme of the magnolia blossom was also used in the organically shaped pond and garden facilities of the inner courtyard, in the floor covering in the entryway atrium, and in the company restaurant. The design is also characterized by the use of traditional building materials, such as bamboo and granite or gravel embedded in mortar.

The combination of Western building standards with Asian feng shui led to an unusual model administration building—and not just because of its positive energy balance.

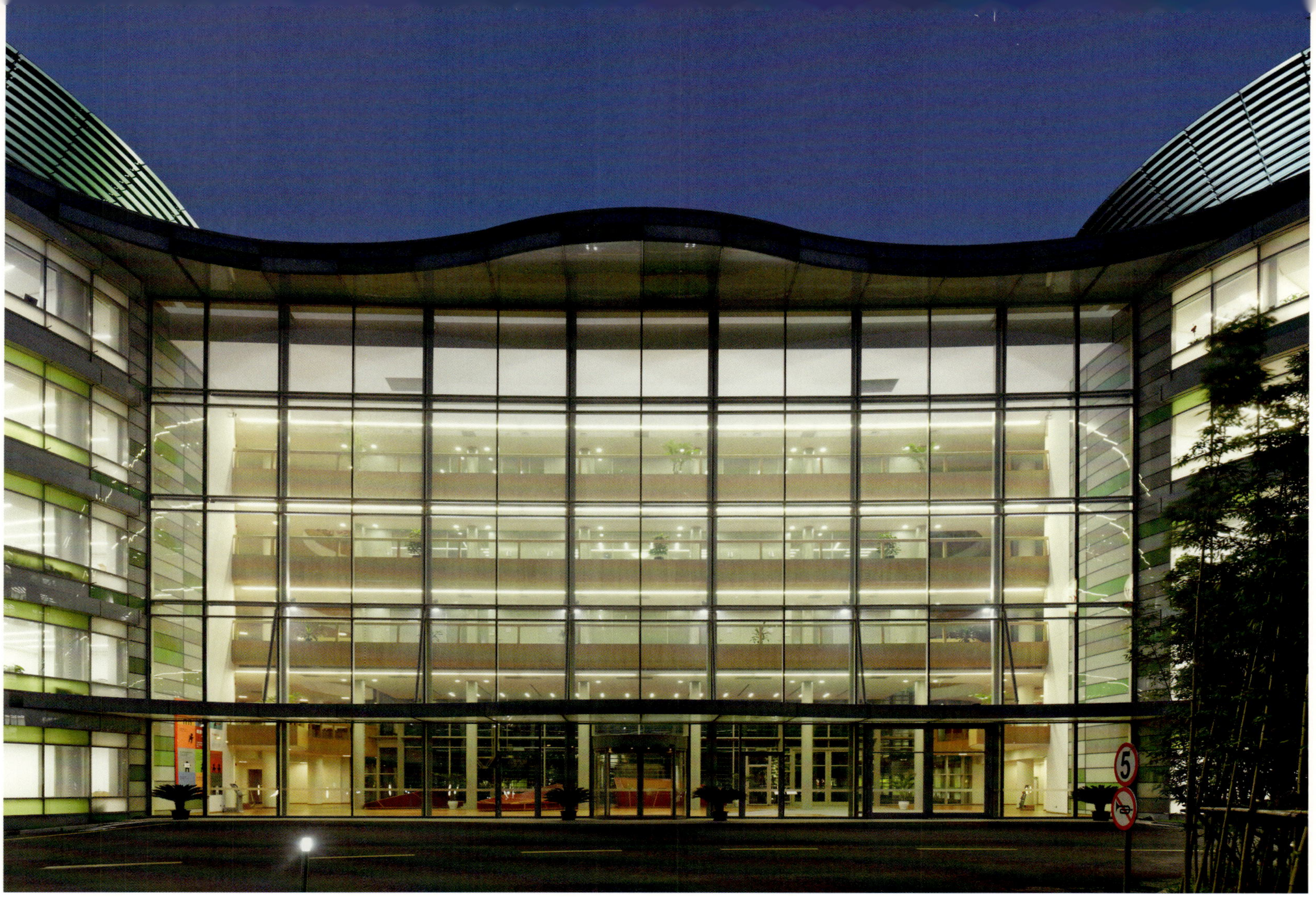

Main entrance
→ Main entrance with rotundas

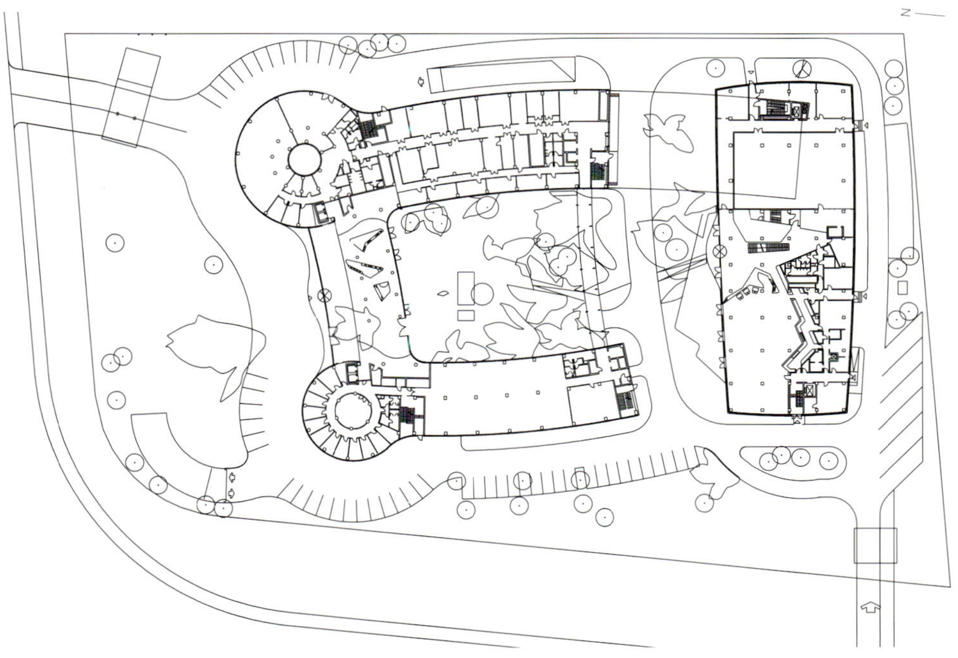

Site plan

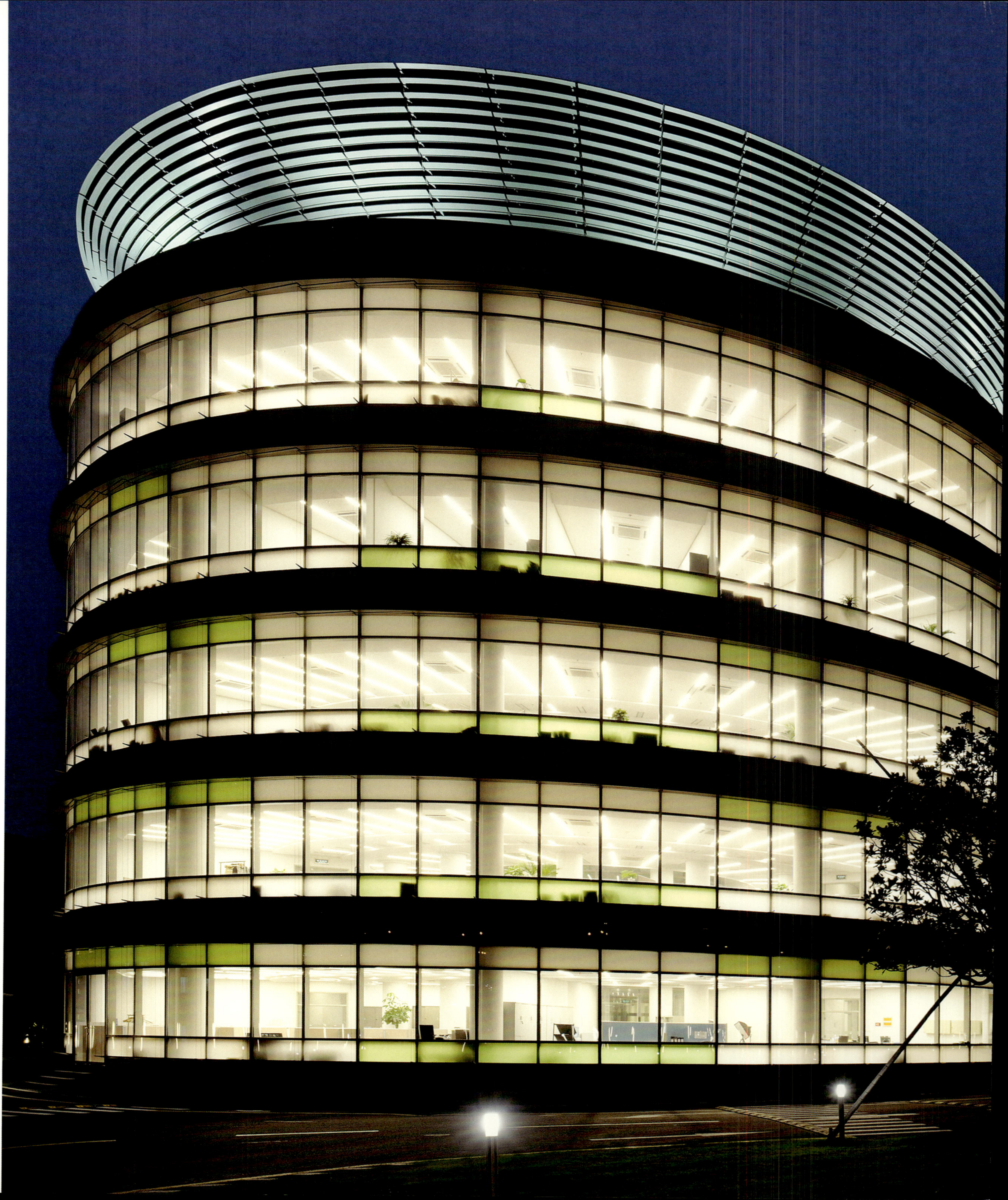

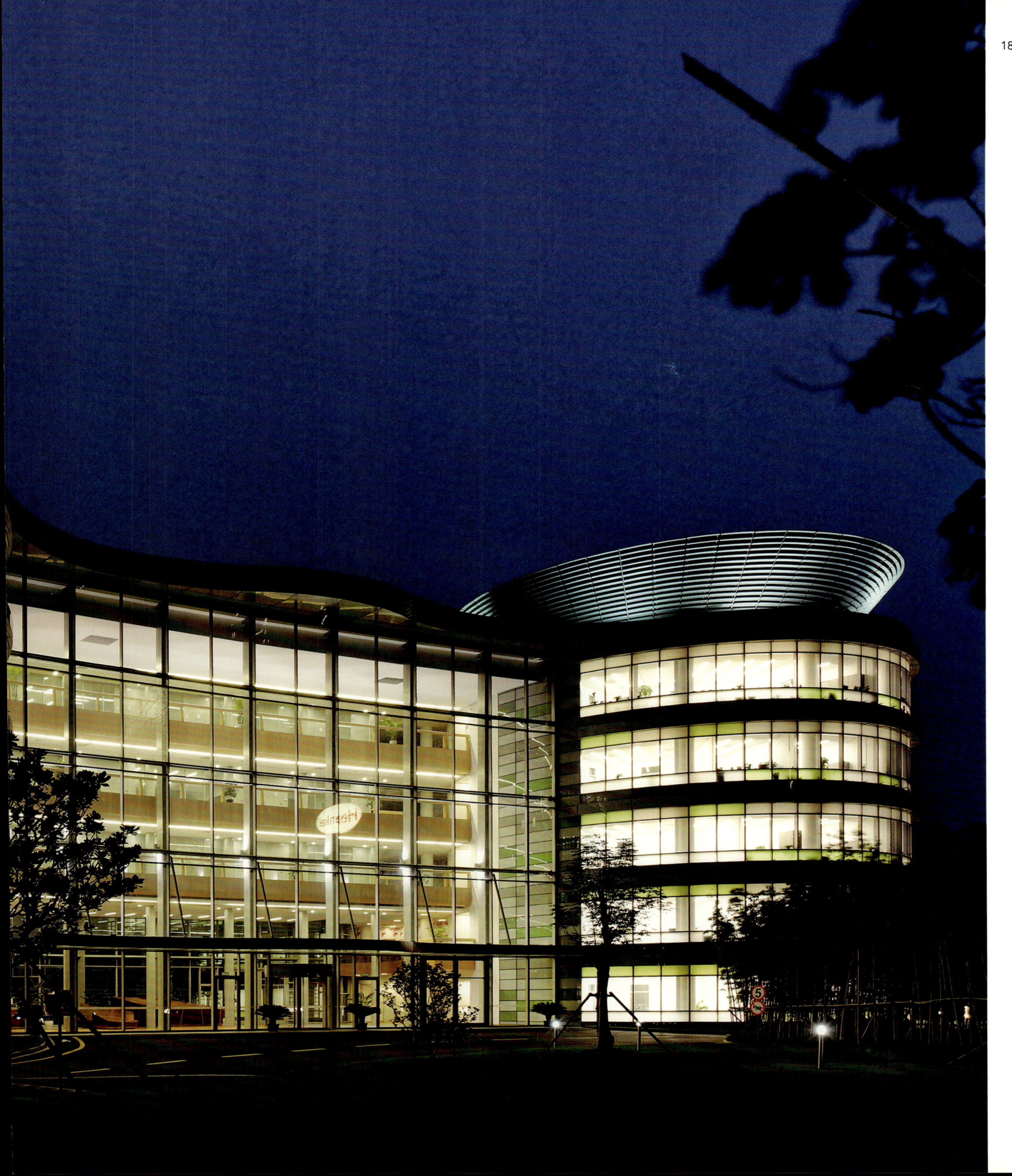

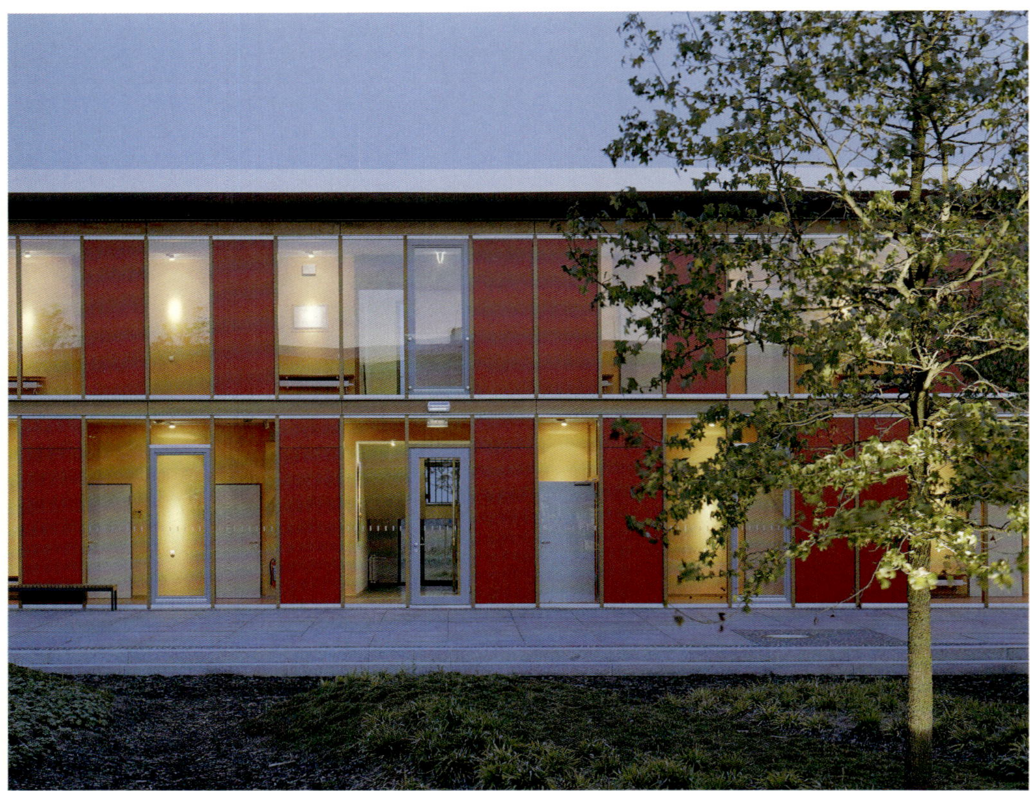

Xanten Youth Hostel

The new building, whose design won first prize in the project's competition, is located on the bank of Xanten's South Lake. The typology of the house with a courtyard used for this building establishes connections between the new structure and Xanten's Roman history and archaeological excavation sites. The two-story building is equipped with a wooden façade with story-high window elements. Another sustainable feature of the design is the environmentally compatible wood pellet heating unit.

Client: Deutsches Jugendherbergswerk Landesverband Rheinland e.V.
Location: Xanten
GFA: 4,572 m²
Beds: 180
Completion date: 2004
Competition: 1st Prize, 2000

Sustainability

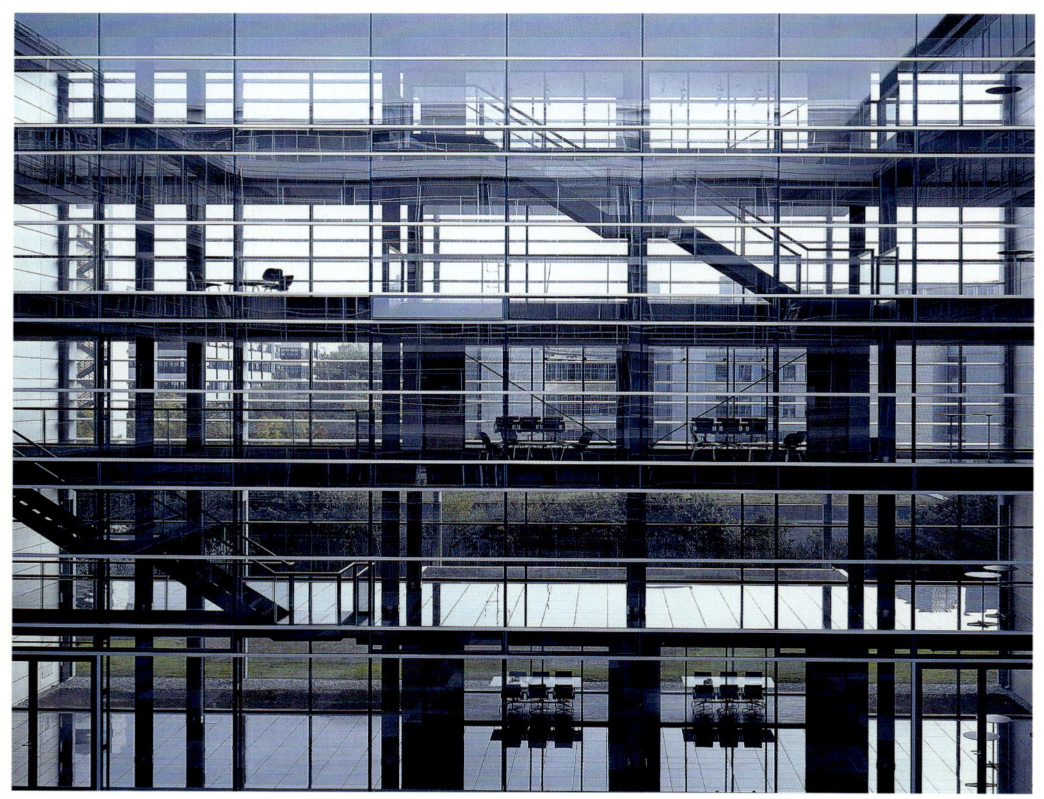

Generali Headquarters

The new building complements the two preexisting structures at the Munich-Neuperlach location, resulting in an office complex for 2,200 employees. The backbone of the entire facility, which has been continuously expanded over the last thirty years, is an east-west running thoroughfare that connects the three buildings in a functional unity. A transparent glass façade with shading elements structures the access axis, providing the opportunity for solar energy generation with photovoltaic units.

Client: Generali Versicherung AG
Location: Munich
GFA: 54,900 m²
Work stations: 1,150
Completion date: 2005

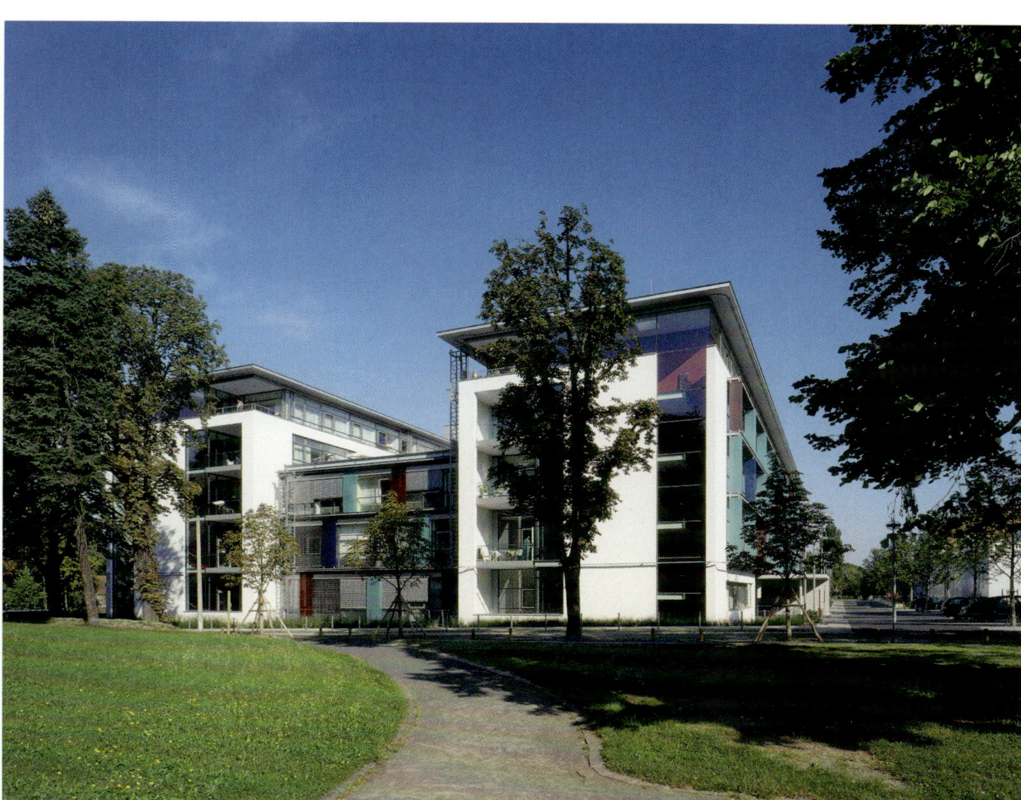

City Clinic, St. Georg

This new central building logically fits into the typical pavilion system of the clinic's 1908 master plan. Two parallel longitudinal sections are connected by two intermediate buildings. The construction of the new buildings with their delicate glass façades is consciously set apart from the older landmark-protected buildings from the turn of the century. The design of the patient ward represents a welcome break from the typical hospital clichés. The individual patient rooms are carefully designed down to the last detail and exude a discreet charm thanks to their color and material concepts. That a hospital facility conceived over one hundred years ago can still be expanded today in a logical way testifies to the concept's longevity.

Client: Städtisches Klinikum St. Georg
Location: Leipzig
GFA: 23,500 m^2
Beds: 246
Completion date: 2002
Competition: 1st Prize, 1998

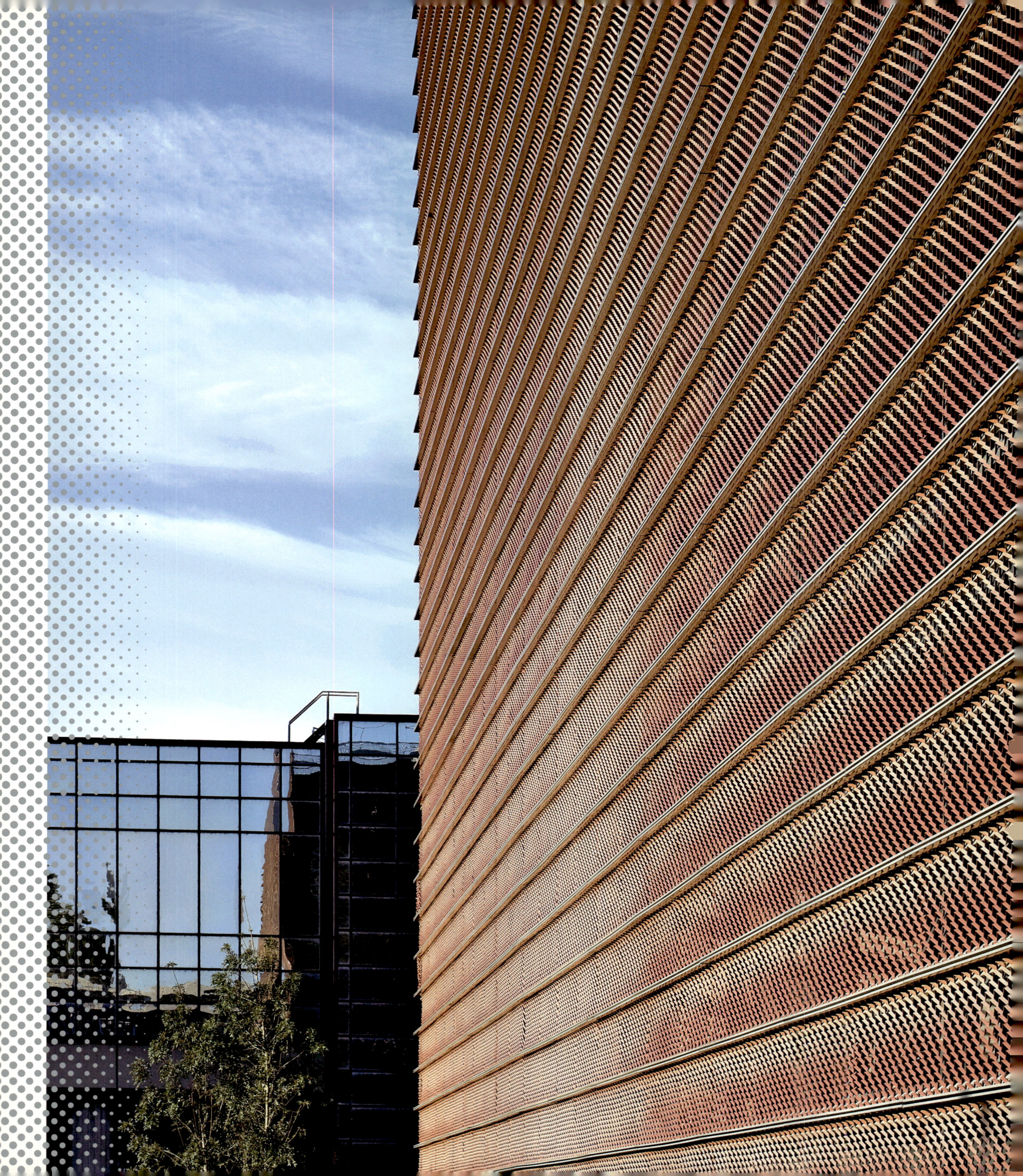

How fast time passes depends on an individual's perception of a given situation. Waiting for a person who is dear to us can become an interminable moment, while an involuntary departure can be over before we know it. But regardless of the pace of time as we perceive it individually, we all experience it as something that marches on, that accompanies the progress of events and organizes them in an unfolding order; this is how terms such as "the past," "the present," and "the future" structure our understanding of time. In turn, this is all closely related to the idea of causality, the notion that cause and effect occur unavoidably one after the other.

Time also accompanies processes such as architectural design and stands for a change in circumstances. Although the historic incidents that are part of a building cannot be changed, the progress of that history can naturally be influenced by changes made to the building.

The Cologne Rheinhallen's past is a very turbulent one. The halls were built on the meadows of the Rhine across from the cathedral in the nineteen-twenties. The purpose of the facility was to host the Cologne Fair. It was intended to give a new face to the city and to bolster its hegemony on the Rhine. The complex's festive inauguration occurred in 1924, and four years later the halls received a unified façade designed by Adolf Abel, along with another trademark of the grounds, the tower. In the years to come, the tower outlived the highs and lows of the fairgrounds and even became a media star in the nineties when Erich Böhme and Sandra Maischberger's weekly talk show, *Talk im Turm,* was broadcast from it.

But between the erection of the tower and the media event significant events which are a part of the Cologne fairgrounds had occurred. For instance, less than twenty years after the completion of the tower, the main hall and the south, east, and west halls were destroyed. After the chaos of the war, they were replaced with a continuous, overlapping hall construction extending throughout the entire inner fairground area. What remained intact from the early years of the Rheinhallen was the brick façade. The halls, therefore, have for the most part maintained their appearance down to today. But from the standpoint of functionality and building structure, the complex was not ready to meet the demands of a contemporary exhibition facility. The brick corset of the old halls was thus gutted, and the Cologne Fair was moved to a new location.

A new tenant soon moved into the historic Rheinhallen. The private television station RTL has transferred its headquarters there, and the grand opening is not far off: their goal is to open the facility in the spring of 2009. The surrounding brick façade, the tower, and the vestibule of the old structure remain, while in behind them a contemporary office structure is emerging. As a result, the city of Cologne has retained an urban trademark, one which will also have a place in the city's future.

At its old location, the fair is a part of the past; the future of the old fairgrounds now belongs to RTL. Beginning next year, it will be from here that the program which transmits the pulse of the world into Germany's living rooms will be broadcast every evening in discreet bits, one after the other.

Time Cologne Rheinhallen

Main users: **RTL Television, Talanx** | Location: **Cologne-Deutz**
GFA: **163,000 m²** | Work stations: **4,000** | Completion date: **2009**

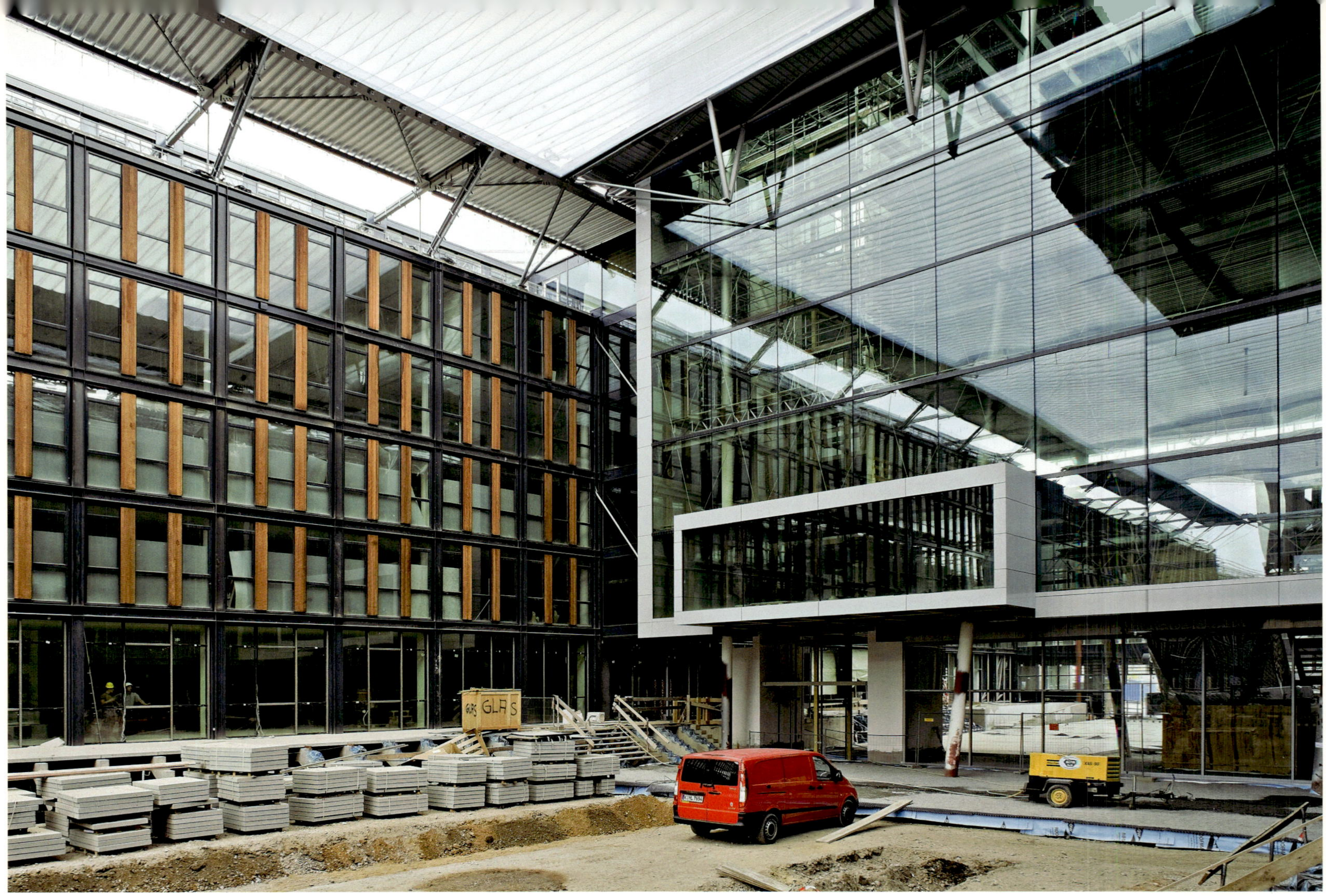

RTL connecting building

→ Parking garage
→ Fair tower
↞ RTL's main entrance

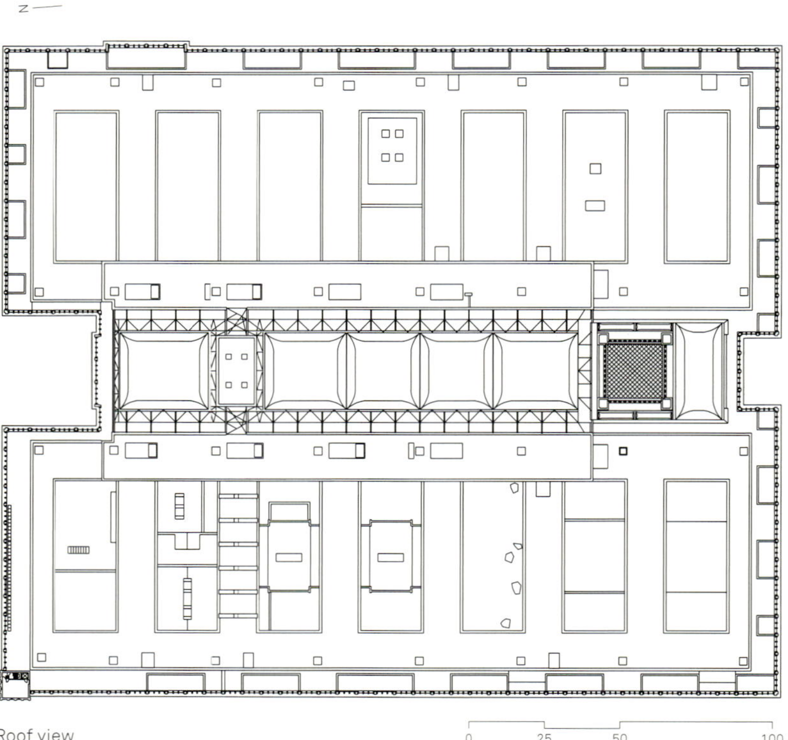

Roof view

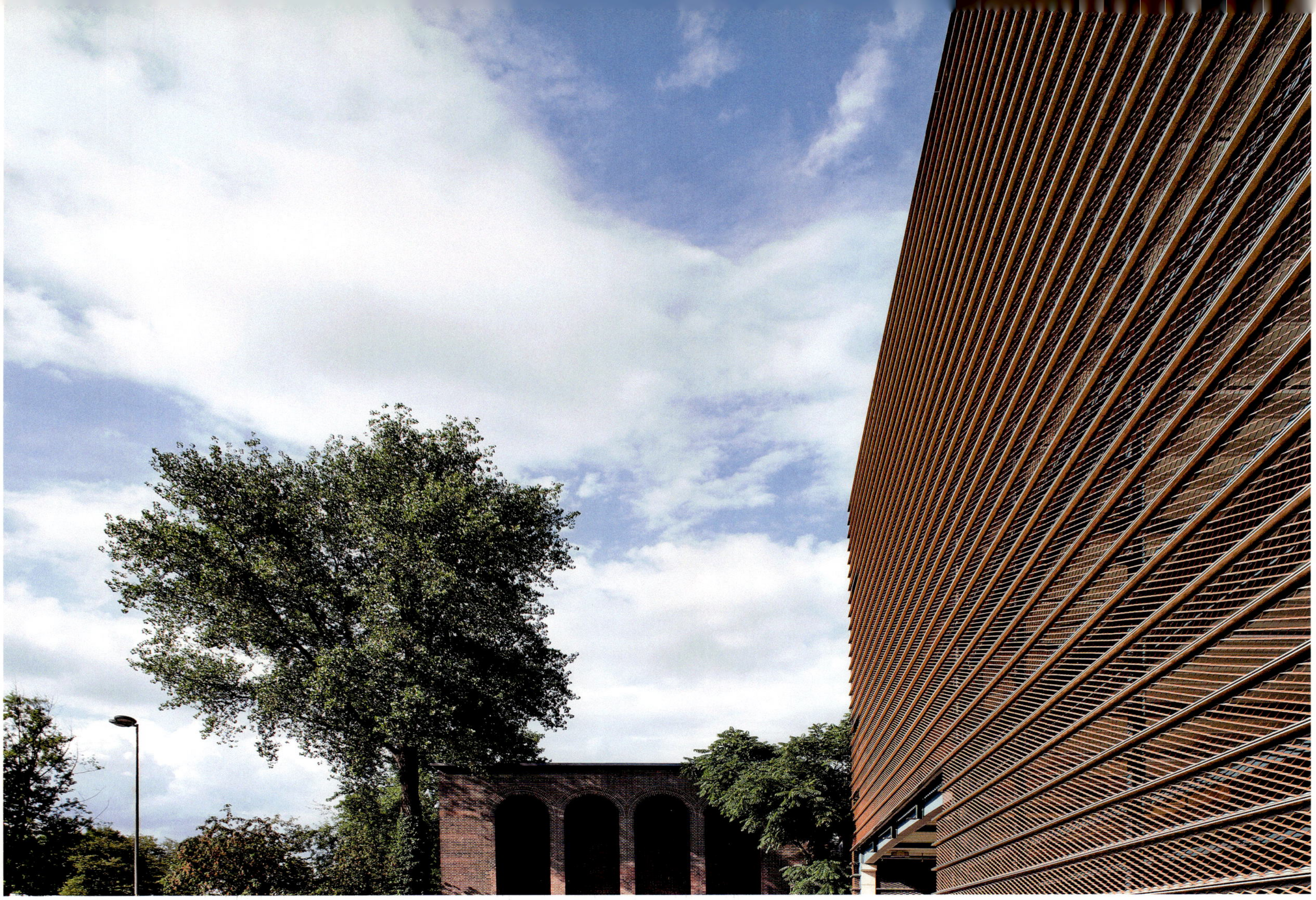

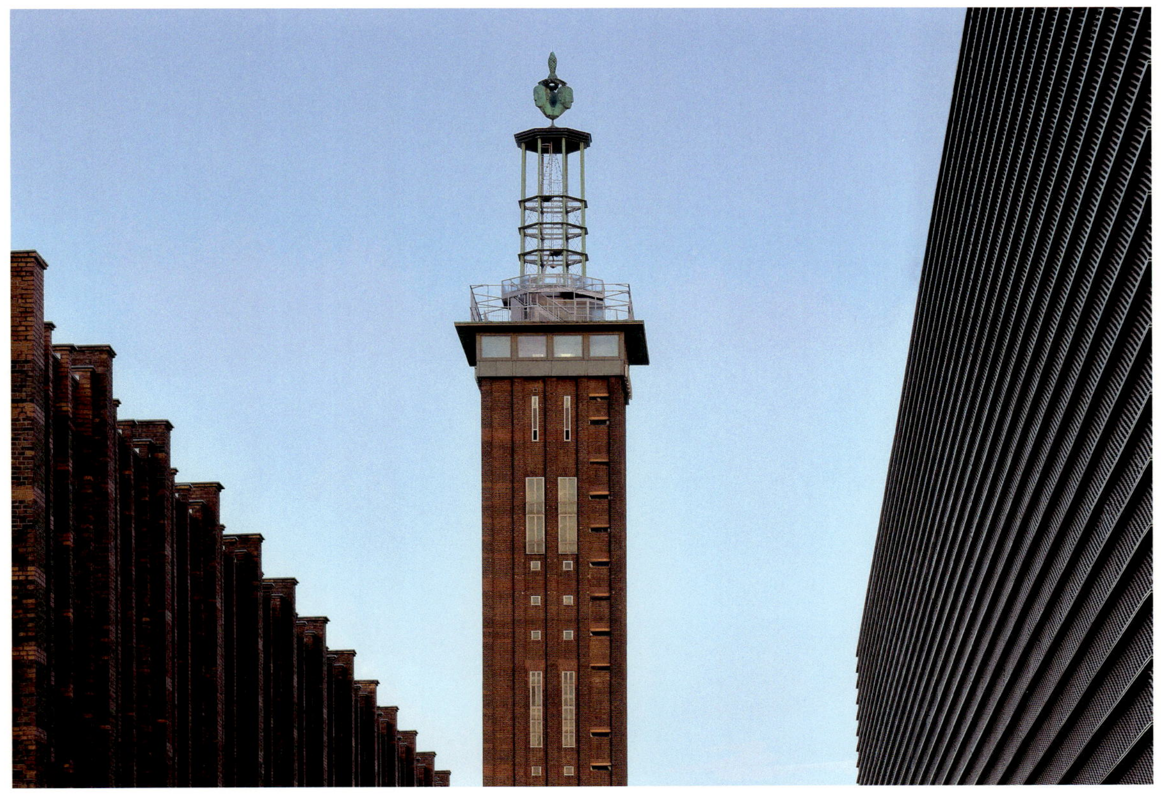

The Cologne Rheinhallen The Rheinhallen in Cologne were built in 1924 on the initiative of the mayor, Konrad Adenauer, on the right bank of the Rhine in Deutz with a direct view of the city cathedral. Several expansions carried out within a short period of time, however, led to a state of disorder. Therefore, on the occasion of the International Press Exhibition (Pressa) in 1928, the heterogeneous exhibition halls were consolidated into a single complex through the addition of a unifying brick perimeter façade. In 2005 the halls, which the Cologne Fair organization had long used as their fairgrounds thanks to a hereditary lease, were returned to the city of Cologne. When the most prominent future tenant, the private television station RTL, decided to move into the halls, the landmark-protected complex, which was comprised of the Expressionistic brick façade, the fair tower on the northwest side, and the Ehrenhof, was converted and completely refurbished.

To maintain the outward architectural and urban design appearance of the historic Rheinhallen, an ultramodern administration complex with an integrated broadcast center is being built behind the landmark-protected façade for the two main users, RTL and the insurance group Talanx AG. In order to do this, the original halls were torn down and replaced with two chamberlike, four-story structures that correspond to the height of the original façades. In the access hall located in the middle of the two structures, the building height rises to six stories. With a length of 200 meters, the hall constitutes a connection between the Ehrenhof and the Tanzbrunnen, and thanks to its innovative roof made of a plastic pillow construction, it can be also used as a flexible space for hosting special events. A central, glass-encased structure in the north of the new access hall functions as the main entrance to and connecting structure for the RTL area and as a contemporary counterpart to the historic Ehrenhof to the south. A “sky lobby” was integrated within it as a main entrance to Talanx’s spaces. The ensemble is being expanded on its northeast side by a new seven-story parking garage, which has space for about 2,000 cars and a bridge that connects it to the Rheinhallen. The SAT television antennae are positioned on the roof of the parking garage.

The historical brick façade is statically supported by a steel skeleton construction that has been cleaned and furnished with new zinc sheet facings. The façades of the new structures are conceived as story-high, glass-encased, light metal façade elements. Every other window axis has a wing-shaped opening, so that the offices can be naturally ventilated by opening the windows. The new hall façades are furnished with a hanging steel frame construction as an articulating element. The closed panels of these façades are also equipped with a perforated wooden facing that takes acoustics into account and their reddish hue makes reference to the original, unifying red brick façade, lending a warm atmosphere to the hall.

The upper stories of the two structures are occupied exclusively by office spaces. Thanks to the comb-and-transom shaped design of the building, there can be great flexibility in the offices’ organization of space, including traditional cellular plans, two- and three-unit combinations, or open plans. Special areas such as cafeterias and meeting rooms are located on the ground floor as well as on parts of the second and third floors, while the building engineering and warehouse spaces are located in the basement. Using approximately 80,000 square meters of gross floor area, RTL occupies the larger part of the halls. Broadcast operations and the editorial division are located on the west side, while broadcast development is located on the east side.

In accordance with the architecture of the existing buildings, the interior structure represents an effective symbiosis of the respectful handling of the landmark-protected areas and the contemporary architectural language of the new construction. The sheer mass of the exterior skin of the dark brick façade and the delicate transparency of the interior structure generate a coordinated overall effect that is rich in visual contrasts.

→ Events hall
→→ View of the entire complex

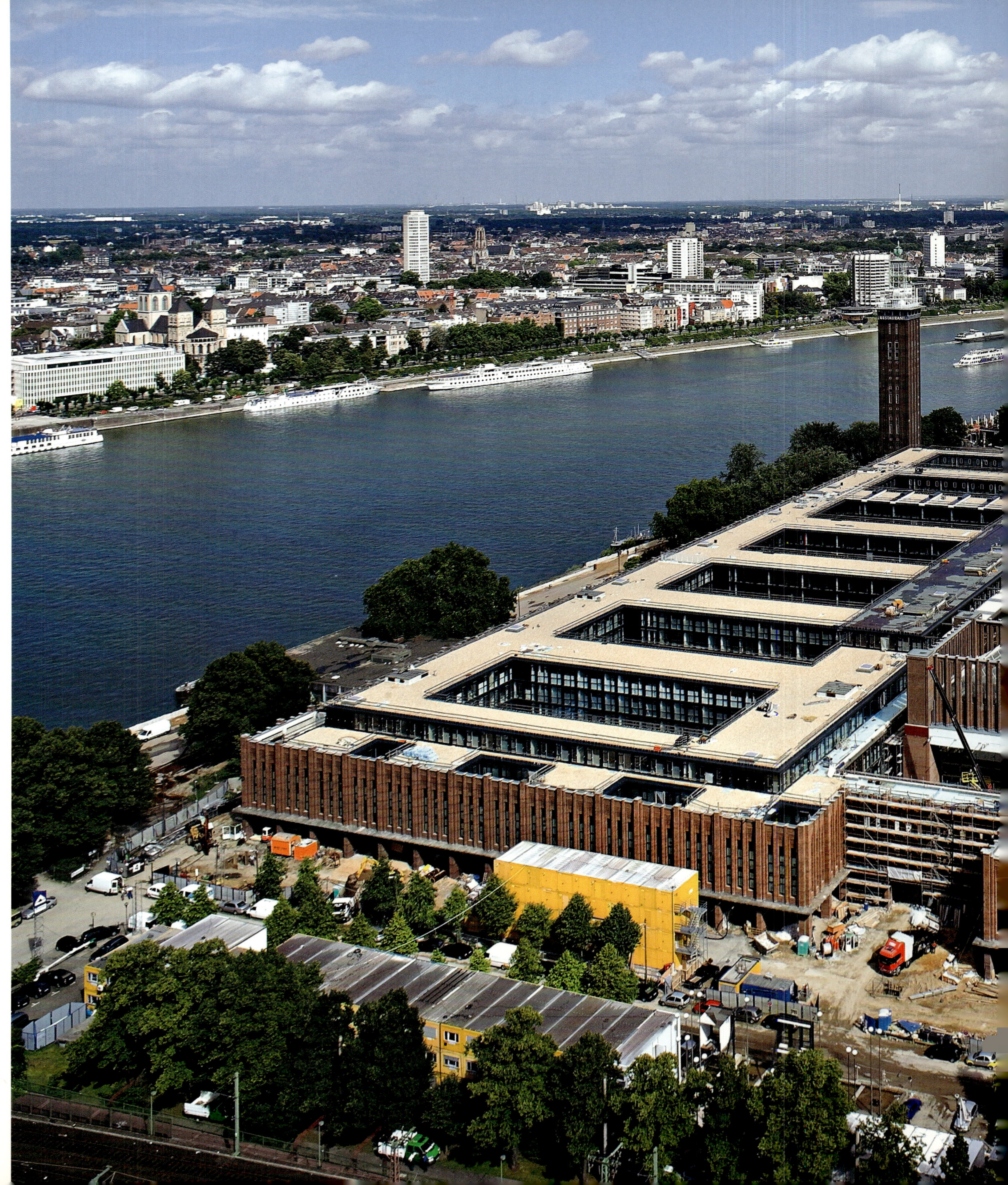

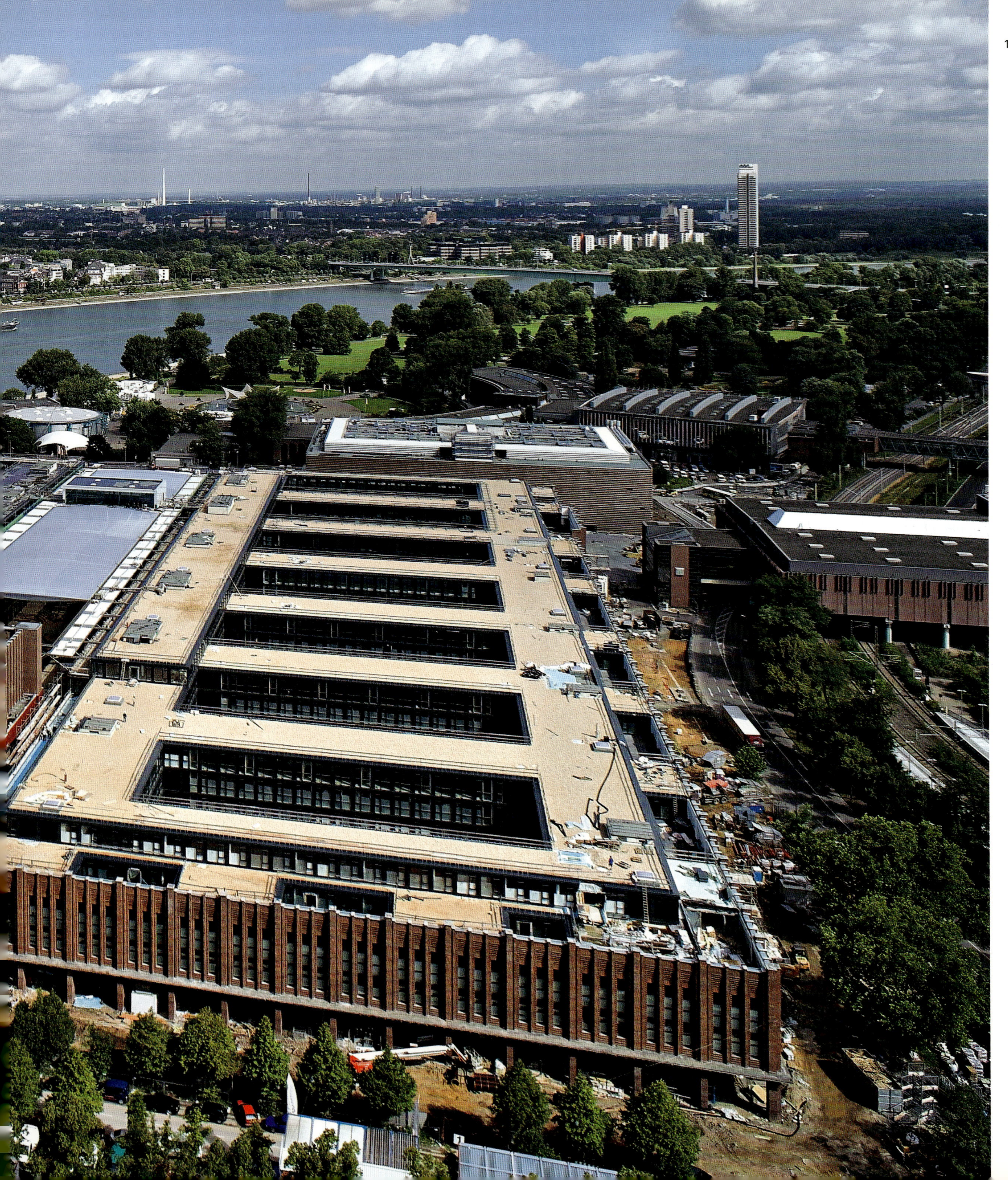

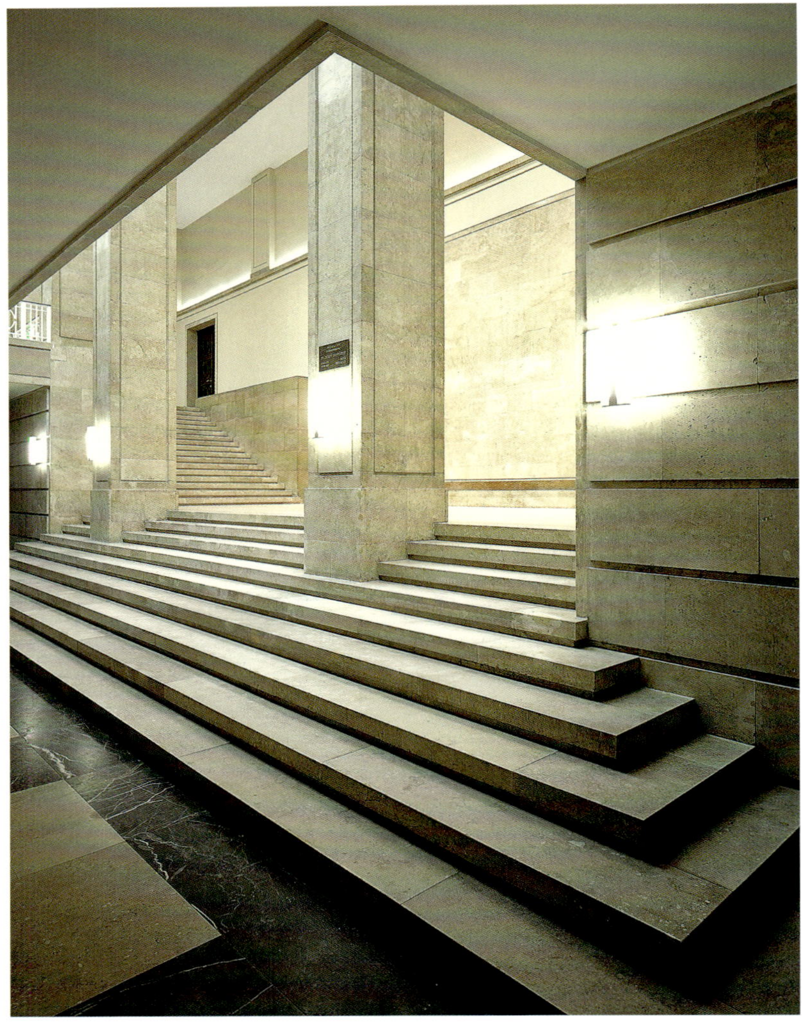

Federal Ministry of Finance

Since it was erected in 1936, this building has had a checkered and largely unpleasant history. However, instead of yielding to an assessment which encouraged the structure's demolition, the historic challenge that this building represented was taken up. The final solution respected the historic phases of the building and retained its structural geometry, and above all took care of repairs which had been put off for decades.

Client: Bundesbauamt Berlin III
Location: Berlin
GFA: 111,293 m²
Work stations: 2,500
Year of completion: 1936
Conversion and restoration according to landmark protection criteria: 2000
Award: Light Architecture Prize, 2001

Time

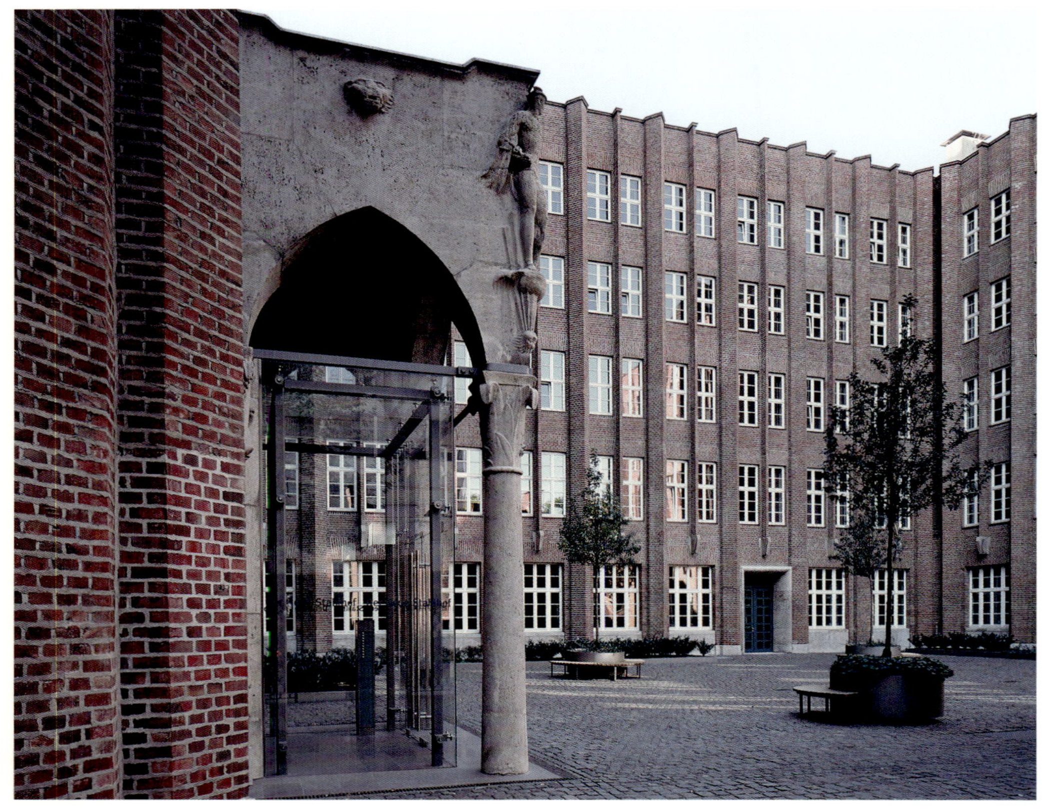

The Stahlhof

The Stahlhof, or "steel court," which was built by Paul Bonatz in the 1920s, underwent a series of structural changes until the late 1990s that were necessitated in part by damage caused by war. The renovation project especially pursued the goal of retaining the aesthetic and historical value of the building, which has historic landmark status. In this effort, the exterior and parts of the interior were recreated by rigorously following Bonatz's original plans while the floor space was simultaneously modernized.

Client: Tishman Speyer Properties Deutschland GmbH
Location: Düsseldorf
GFA: 16,250 m²
Year of completion: 1928
Restoration and revitalization according to landmark protection criteria: 2002

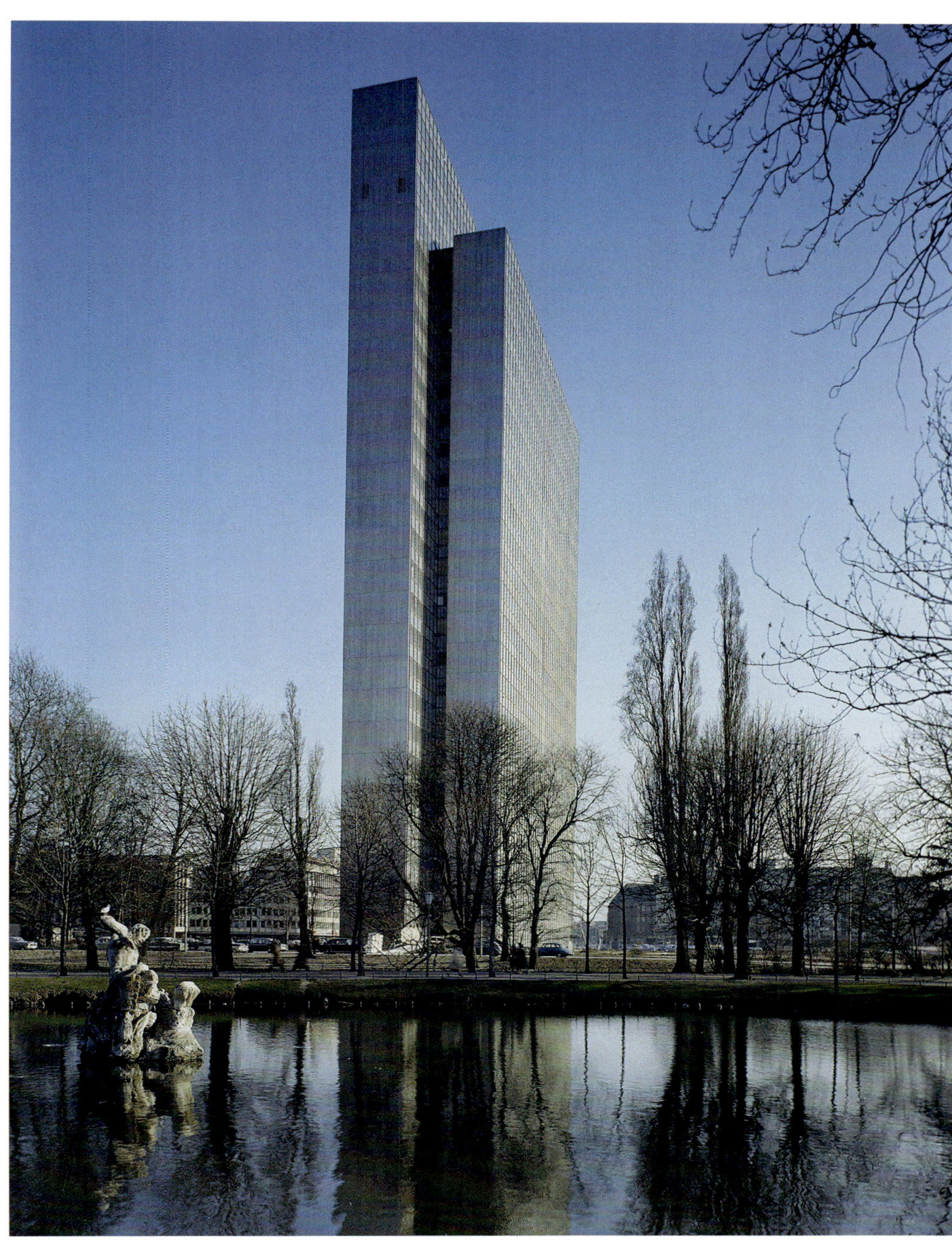

Dreischeibenhaus ("The Three-Slice Building")

This administration building for Phoenix-Rheinrohr AG (a Thyssen company as of 1964) is considered one of the high points of postwar German architecture. Today the Dreischeibenhaus continues to fulfill its communicative, urban planning function with symbolic character, while as a stand-alone structure situated between the Hofgarten and Schauspielhaus it is also simply a unique architectural achievement.

Client: Thyssen AG
Location: Düsseldorf
GFA: 33,700 m²
Year of completion: 1960
Revitalization: 1994
Competition: 1st Prize, 1955
Award: BDA Badge, 1969

Essays

Rudi Assauer
Gregor Bonin
Daniel von Borries
Willi Fährmann
Hans-Dietrich Genscher
Annette Görtz
Wolfram Goertz
Peter Hennicke
Peter Kern
Mischa Kuball
Bernd M. Michael
Alexander Otto
Fritz Pleitgen
Peter Cachola Schmal
Zheng Shiling
Raimund Stecker
Frank R. Werner
Hans-Werner Zawisla

Five New Stars in the "Little Cosmos" of Downtown Düsseldorf

Gregor Bonin on the Breidenbacher Hof

If one understands Düsseldorf as a kind of little cosmos, then the individual buildings in their configuration of closed blocks are like stars in a constellation. The constellation in the center of Düsseldorf—that is, the spatial structure of the buildings—is difficult to discern at first glance and is even more difficult to comprehend. There is hardly another city district that is so varied, multifaceted, exciting, and compact as the area around the Königsallee, the historic district, and Schadowstrasse. Here there are retail businesses in all possible permutations, a broad spectrum of art and culture, and restaurants for even the most diverse of culinary tastes. In this charged atmosphere, one would wish that the surrounding architecture would provide a kind of orientation that calms and unites on the one hand, and creates identity and generates an image on the other. In this context, buildings are bearers of economic, social, cultural, and even political significance.

With the new construction of the Breidenbacher Hof hotel, the constellation of the center of Düsseldorf has been augmented by the addition of five new stars. But what do these stars mean in the context of downtown Düsseldorf's "little cosmos"? They certainly stand for luxury, prestige, and elegance. For me, as the head of the city's planning department, the five stars of the new Breidenbacher Hof stand for five concepts:

Integration into the existing structures of the Kaufhof an der Kö and Carschhaus department stores as well as the completion of the downtown complex at the most central point in Düsseldorf: between Königsallee, Theodor-Körner-Strasse, and Heinrich-Heine-Allee. By integration I mean an effective arrangement of the new building within the preexisting urban fabric, not a copying of the old or a subordinating of the new. The historic character of this area is respected through the conscious selection of materials, building height, form, and the planning of details. The Breidenbacher Hof guarantees new and better possibilities for spatial orientation in the context of downtown Düsseldorf.

A multitude of uses, by connecting high-quality retail areas, upscale apartments, and offices along with the hotel itself. This creates a fluid transition between the two retail zones on Flinger Strasse and Königsallee on the one hand, and special living and work forms along the lines of concepts like "the big city as habitat" and "back to the city" on the other.

Quality of life, with the uppermost goal being to make the quality of the experience of the "new scenery" of the Breidenbacher Hof in the center of Düsseldorf perceivable. This augments the already manifold settings for the different lifestyle groups of a rainbow-colored urban society.

"Traditional modern" in the sense of a connection between the past and the future. The history of the location in downtown Düsseldorf is skillfully interwoven with the different demands of future developments. The new Breidenbacher Hof stands symbolically for this bridging of the maintenance of traditional elements and a simultaneous adaptation to modern requirements.

Unification in the total environment of downtown Düsseldorf. The newly erected Breidenbacher Hof, with its high-quality architecture in the urban context, in the functional terms of its mixed uses, with its social orientation to experience, and, at the same time, with its consciousness of the site's history, is the manifestation of the desire to uphold, strengthen, and distinguish the city and its attractions as a great urban center.

With a departing glance at the stars, I wish the "little cosmos" of downtown Düsseldorf continued creativity and ongoing enthusiasm and liveliness, so that the stars appearing in the near future, such as the Wehrhahnlinie (a new city railway line) and the Kö-Bogen (an office complex that creates a connection between Königsallee and the Hofgarten), will radiate just as much force and energy—because this is what one feels when one experiences our city.

Dr. Gregor Bonin is the head of Düsseldorf's urban planning department.

Great!
Let's Do It, Manager!

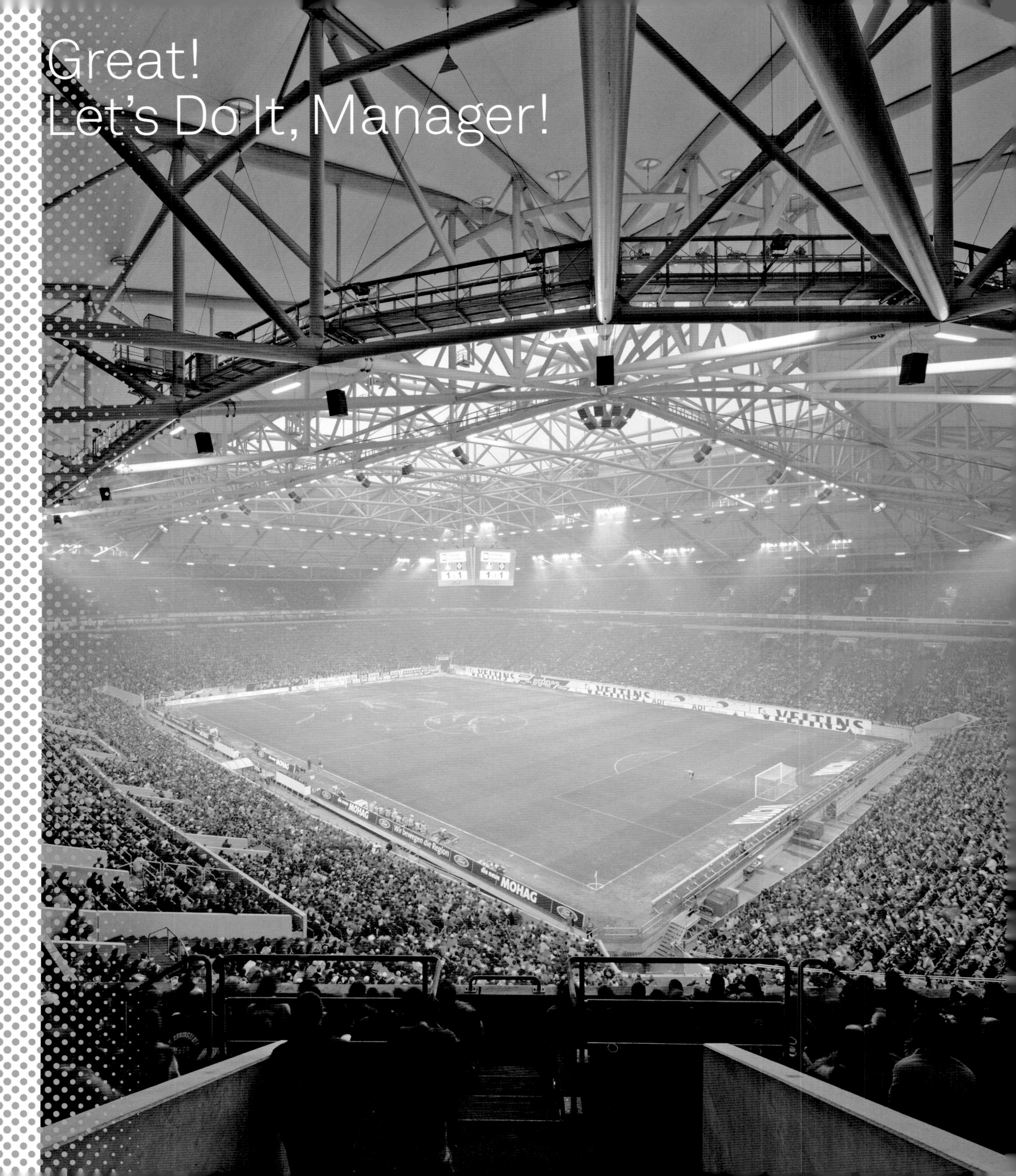

After a detour via Oldenburg, I came back to Gelsenkirchen in April 1993. At the time, the situation with FC Schalke 04, the soccer club, was not especially good, and my declared goal was to reach the top of the national league and to play internationally. At this point, there was already some discussion of renovating the team's stadium or building a new one. The issue was raised by problems with subsidence in the mining area in which the old Park Stadium had been built. As a consequence of the exploitation of the coal deposits in the region, there was a danger that from one day to the next the stadium's foundations would shift, thus causing parts of the bleachers to collapse overnight. When the concrete structure actually began to show signs of cracking, the risk was judged to be too great to ignore anymore and it was decided that something had to be done. Of course, I first informed myself about how a conversion of the existing stadium or the construction of new bleachers could be made to work during the playing season, how much time would be needed for the work, and especially how many spectators would be able to fit into the stadium during this transitional time. The old Park Stadium had a capacity of 70,000 spectators. New bleachers would take two years to build and would mean a maximum spectator capacity of 35,000 during the period of construction, something which was absolutely unacceptable to both the club and its fans. This led to the joint decision with the club's board to construct a new stadium.

Hans Sanders and I got the idea for the AufSchalke Arena on a walk one Sunday. At the time, Hans was working for HBM Stadien- und Sportstättenbau GmbH, which was then in the process of building the Gelderland stadium in Arnheim, the little brother of the AufSchalke Arena. We discussed, philosophized, and began to sketch the first drafts of the project. After that, we met every Sunday morning in my office and developed the project as a kind of two-man team. From the beginning, I wanted to build a multifunctional arena. The vision for the project consisted of the goal of visibly leading the soccer club into a new era by building an ultra-modern stadium which would be unequalled in Europe, thereby also giving a new stimulus to the surrounding region. The idea for a roll-out playing field was inspired by the Gelderland stadium. A similar concept had been used there for the first time not long before, but not without serious problems: the grass did not get enough sunlight or natural irrigation and thus had to be constantly replaced. I drove to Arnheim regularly at the time, in order to inspect the shunting principle in operation there and to look for ways to improve it.

But I made my personal decision to make the project happen after we went with 5,000 Schalke fans to Arnheim. After our UEFA cup victory against Inter Mailand in the winter of 1996–97, we invited our fans, the Royal Blues, to travel with us to the Gelderland stadium in a hundred buses for an exhibition game which was to take place there between Vitesse Arnheim and FC Schalke 04, and on this occasion we presented the stadium to them. After the match, I said: "Ok, fans, that's how I imagine our new stadium. Do you have any objections?" The Royal Blues' answer was: "Ok, great! Let's do it, manager!"

I remember well the resistance and the thousands of doubters that dogged the project from the beginning to the end. Not a few people considered me insane, especially due to the design's roll-out playing field. After the financing of the stadium's construction was secure —the building is, by the way, completely privately financed and was constructed without any public subsidy—the DFB president, Egidius Braun, did the groundbreaking on November 21, 1998. More than two and half years later, on August 13 and 14, 2001, the new AufSchalke Arena was officially opened with an exhibition match. All the soccer VIPs were on hand: Braun, Blatter, Beckenbauer, and company. I was granted the great honor of opening the arena and I still remember that I started crying just beforehand. My dream had become a reality. Such a project cannot be created alone—one needs the right people, the right team. I am still proud today, especially because no one had thought that the "Mickey Mouse" club of FC Schalke 04 would be the first in Europe to build such a stadium, or that the structure would host 60,000 spectators for national league matches as well as for other events—operas, pop concerts, and especially the biathlon with 54,000 seats. The arena is regularly filled to capacity. This brings in gigantic sums, from which the region also profits. Nothing better could have happened to this region than building the stadium at that point in time.

For me, the AufSchalke Arena is the greatest story of which I have ever been a part. Although I can tell many stories, what the stadium has meant is something extraordinary. AufSchalke Arena may not be a place for drinking champagne and eating caviar, but it is nonetheless the most modern stadium in Europe, and its multifunctionality is truly astounding.

Rudi Assauer, a former soccer player, national league trainer and manager, testimonial speaker, and moderator, was manager of FC Schalke 04 from 1981–86 and 1993–2006.

Rudi Assauer on the AufSchalke Arena

When an Envelope Becomes a Sensual Experience

Annette Görtz on the Parking Garage of the Leipzig Zoo

The perfect "envelope" faces the same challenges in fashion that it does in architecture—the need for visual impact, a haptic quality, and functionality. Bringing all three of these components together in harmonious accord is what makes for good design.

In many cases, what looks good does not necessarily feel good, or even serve a purpose. And by the same token, everything that works is by no means beautiful. For me, the most important criterion in design is individuality. I find it interesting when architecture and design leave the beaten path and experiment with new materials and forms. In fashion it is always exciting to use unusual materials, because they can lead to new possibilities for design but also show the limits of design. That is what makes fashion ultimately so exciting. Bamboo—a raw material that I have used as a fiber for making cloth—is a resistant natural material that is sensual and visually very pleasing.

Unusual materials often have more expressive power when employed in a simple manner. An example of this is the impressive parking garage of the Leipzig Zoo. Although it has a closed effect from the outside, the parking garage's bamboo façade nonetheless creates a very light, transparent effect on the inside. Daylight filters through the stalks everywhere and illuminates the interior. One can imagine what happens beyond the bamboo stalks, from inside as well as outside—they form a boundary and are at the same time an unusual exterior wall that simultaneously functions as both railing and window. Here bamboo demonstrates all of the important components of an effective envelope: an element of protection, a pleasant sense of "interior," and an attractive exterior.

The expression of personality and character should be important for every human being, and it should also be considered in the urban landscape. Unfortunately, it is neglected in many cities for financial or commercial reasons. By their nature "sins of design" are a more lasting impertinence when they are architectural than when they take the form of quickly abandoned trends in the world of fashion. Then again, when it comes to positive examples of design I envy architecture for its longer "shelf life." Sometimes I would prefer to concentrate on a work of art and not on the 200 new designs of this season. The common goal is to mirror the zeitgeist of the moment in one's work and, without having made oneself ridiculous years later, to remain unmistakable. Naturally, if one wishes to tease the "sensuality" out of inexpensive materials, it requires more creativity. In the fashion industry as in architecture there are many examples which show that good does not have to mean expensive.

If we were to reduce fashion and architecture to functionality, which is just one of their many important components, then our world would lose its individuality and multifacetedness. Fortunately, prefab buildings and Mao jackets have exceeded their half-lives.

Annette Görtz is a fashion designer who founded and manages Görtz-Welsch Modedesign. Her fashion label, annette görtz, stands for clarity, timelessness, and meticulousness, and it won her the Fashion Design Prize of North Rhine-Westphalia in 1995.

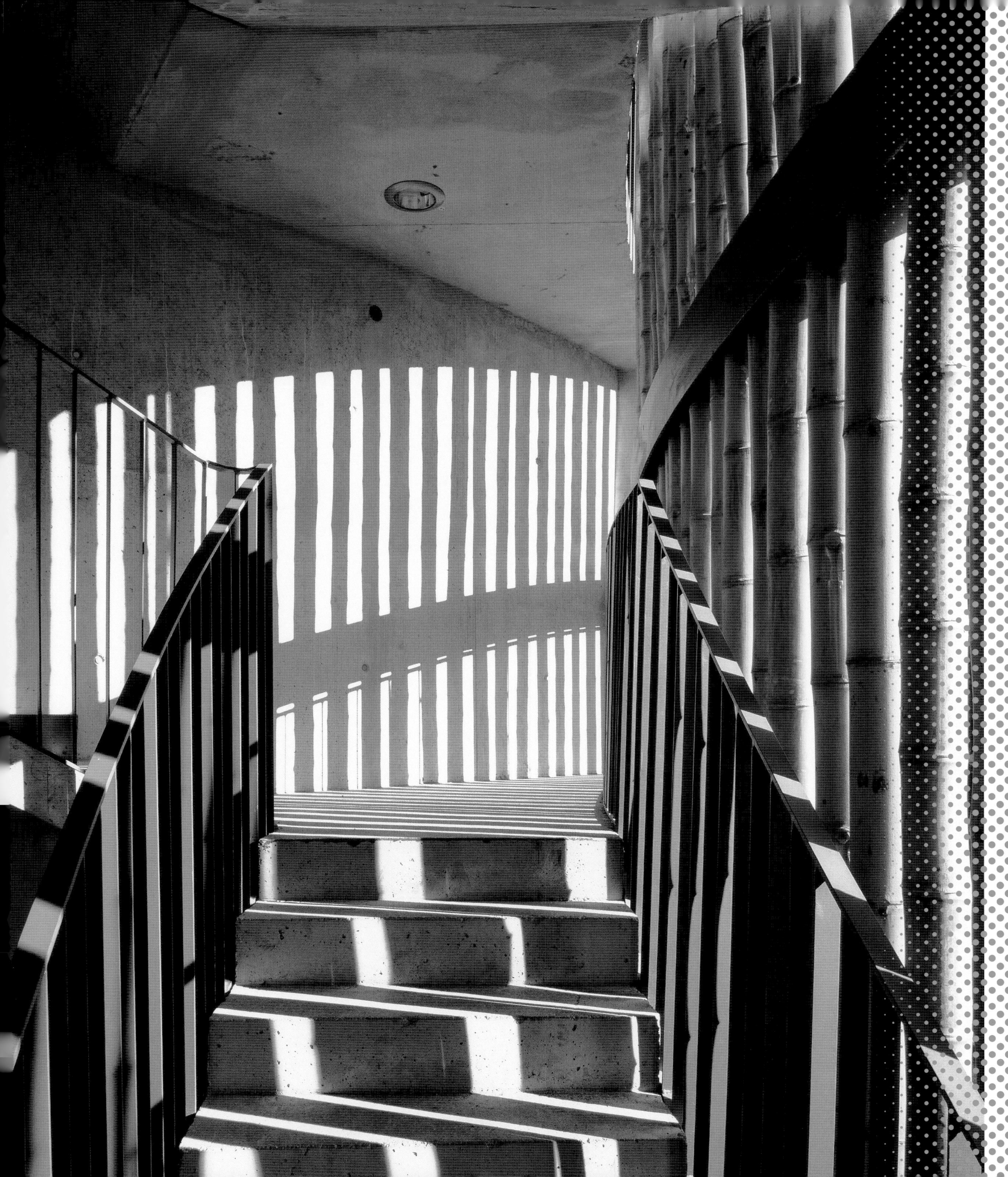

A Successful Vision of a Central Train Station for the Twenty-First Century

Alexander Otto on the Leipzig Central Train Station

With their unmistakable and impressive architecture, Germany's railway stations have left their mark on the identity of German cities in a multitude of ways. For new arrivals to a city, the railway station provides their first impression of the city, making it a kind of calling card. It is therefore all the more important that railroad stations be perceived as positive locations that are full of life. An attractive, clean, and transparent station interior reverberates throughout its urban surroundings.

In order to confront the problem of dwindling numbers of passengers after the German reunification, the German railroad company Deutsche Bahn AG began to revitalize highly trafficked centers by making their railroad terminals more attractive. In the process, the new design of the concourse of Leipzig's central railroad station by HPP and the master planning of the project by ECE Projektmanagement GmbH & Co. KG became a pilot project. While the project retained the station's historical architecture, it also introduced an incomparable new shopping center offering a variety of services within the terminal, the Promenaden Hauptbahnhof Leipzig.

The great change our society is undergoing offers significant opportunities for the revival and upgrading of the image of our railroad stations. We are considerably more mobile today, which has led to us subjecting ourselves to ever longer journeys to work and elsewhere. As a kind of optimization of their time management, many commuters and travelers use the layover time in the station to take care of their shopping. This is especially true in the case of goods that would be unavailable elsewhere on Sundays and holidays. Eating, too, is increasingly taking place while people are on the move, and large, highly trafficked railway terminals that experience as many as several hundred thousand visitors per day can benefit from this trend. Hosting more than 100 long-distance trains, 550 commuter trains, 230 urban trains, and about 150,000 travelers per day, the Leipzig central railway station is an important German transit hub. Its commercial promenades are also some of the most heavily frequented shopping centers in the nation. As impressive entryways, the promenades create a perfect connection to Leipzig's historical center and can be demonstrated to be an enticement to visit there. In this way, the development of shopping centers in the train station has provided an important spark for the revitalization of the entire Leipzig downtown area.

The upgrading of the central railroad stations in Cologne and Hannover followed after Leipzig's example by following ECE's master plan. They embody a successful vision of a central railroad station in the twenty-first century: a more attractive, safer hub for the travelers, a symbol with which a city can proudly identify itself, an image-bearer for Deutsche Bahn, and a source of guaranteed earnings for investors. The proof of this concept's success has been provided by an economic survey conducted by the Infas Institute which revealed that customer satisfaction in these three terminals is the highest in Germany.

More than ten years after the revitalization of the Leipzig railroad station, we still look back with pride on the project. The conversion was a great challenge, one that was met only because all of the participants—the city, Deutsche Bahn, investors, citizens, architects, and ECE—had jointly vouched for the realization of this project as partners. Since that time, ECE has had a special attachment to Leipzig. This is reflected by the fact that assuming the management of the city's new station is an honor for our managers.

Alexander Otto is chairman of the management of ECE Projektmanagement GmbH & Co. KG.

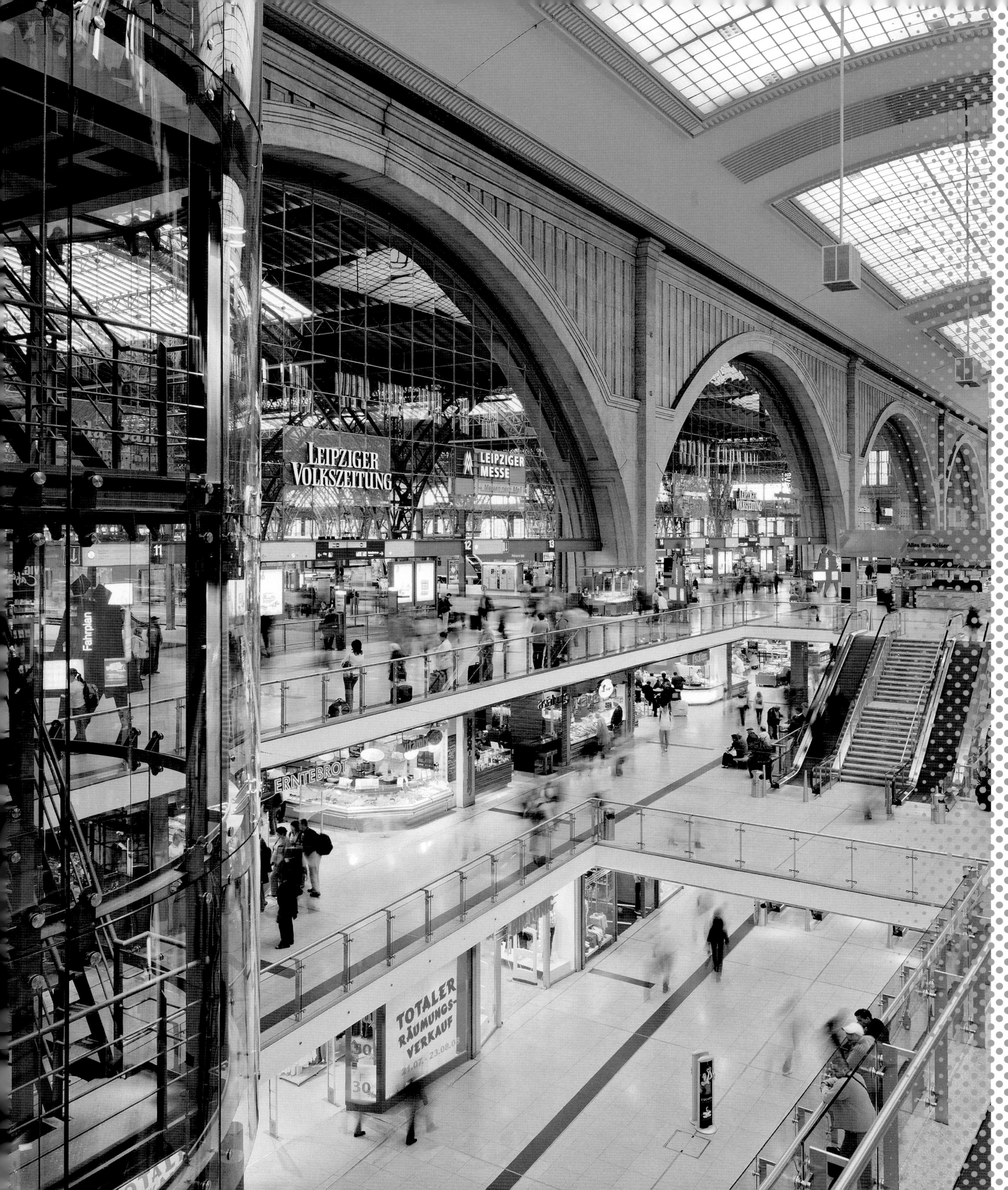
LEIPZIGER
VOLKSZEITUNG
LEIPZIGER
MESSE
Fahrplan
ERNTEBROT
TOTALER
RÄUMUNGS-
VERKAUF

The Santander "New Work" Project

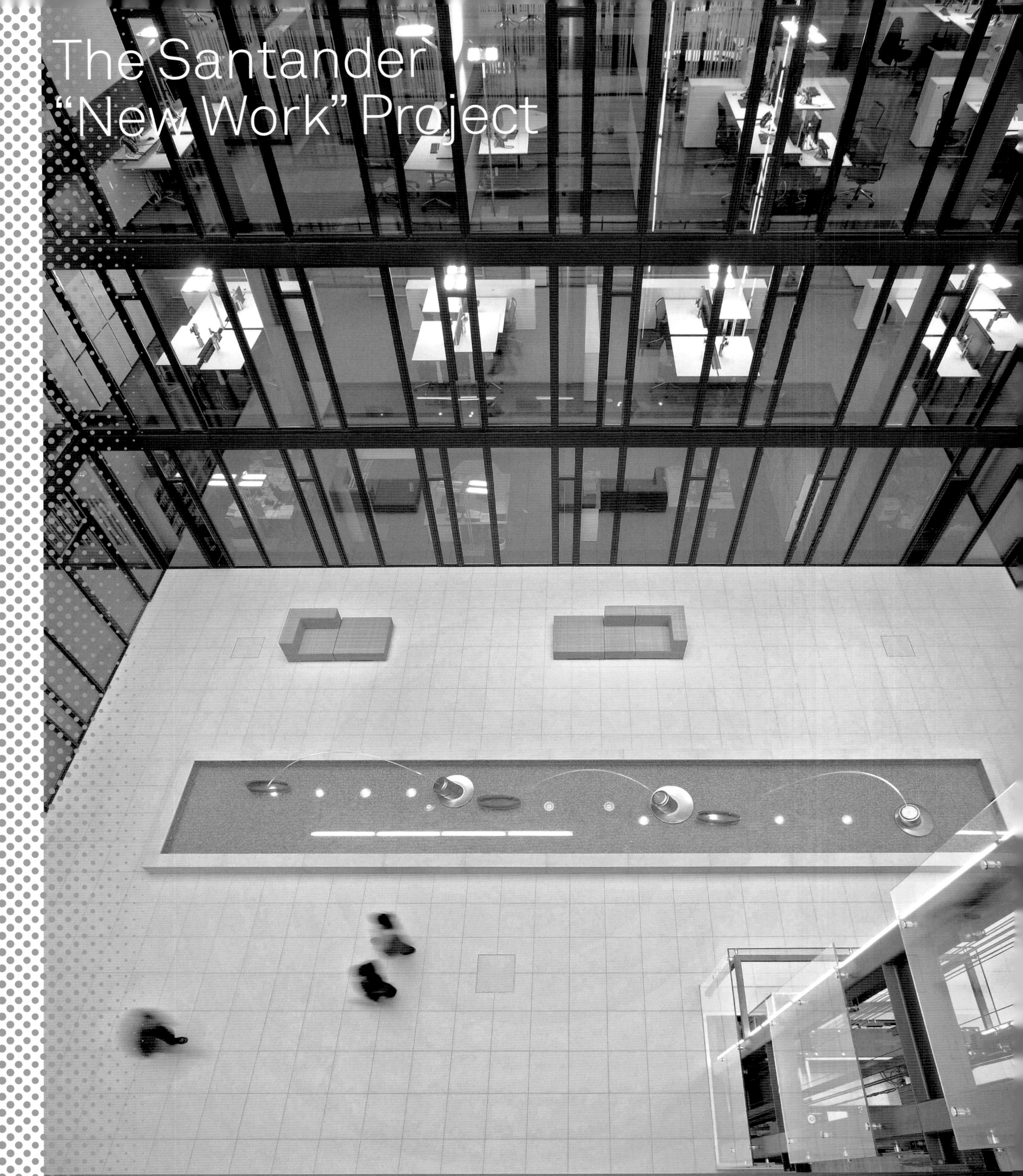

Peter Kern on the Santander Consumer Bank Building

Today great changes in the structures and processes of service performance make it necessary to rethink the design of office work spaces and the implementation of new concepts and solutions. Work is changing radically: structures, work areas, and also work times are becoming less and less stable. As a result, flexibility and adaptability are the most significant factors in today's working world.

We can observe this trend from several standpoints. On the one hand, work is growing beyond the confines of the office building: Work can now happen in the car, on the train, or in airplanes via W-LAN and UMTS. Work can now be done in the train station, in the airport, and in cafés thanks to Internet access points. Work can also happen in the offices of clients and suppliers or at home via VPN. Such practices are becoming taken for granted by many employees.

On the other hand, work in the office is becoming ever more flexible and mobile. Employees can work at the office in a variety of different locations: at their own desk, in meeting rooms, in project rooms, at meeting points, or in the cafeteria, all of which is facilitated by wireless LAN, portable computers, and mobile phones. In more and more workplaces, work is being done with a system of desk sharing, and as a result non-territorial working methods are increasingly emerging.

An office that perfectly responds to the needs of all tasks and activities does not exist. What we need today—and in the future—is offices that enable the most diverse work activities. I like to talk about the "multi-space office," or an office in which there are different rooms and zones with different work spaces. This means that every employee can find the space he or she needs on demand.

This is the road that the Santander Consumer Bank took with their new building project in Mönchengladbach. Recognizing the challenges of the future early on, the company debated the future in the framework of the group research project "Office 21" and implemented the group's insights through a strategic development process in a new work and office world. The guiding principles of the development are more support for teamwork, less spatial hierarchy, more spatial transparency and openness, more extensive digitization of work processes, higher flexibility with standardized work stations, and an agreeable spatial ambiance.

Due to its flexibility and transparent design, the building supports the free organization of work procedures and promotes a team-oriented and communicative work culture. More than fifty "think tanks" and more than one hundred informal communication zones—for instance, "chill-out zones," "lounges," or "touch-downs"—were integrated into the building to promote and support internal communication among the employees.

An especially powerful IT infrastructure supports—indeed, makes possible—today's more flexible working methods: laptops where needed, desktop computers with single logins, wireless LAN in the office and central areas, voice over IP, telephones in conjunction with DECT, and mobile work solutions with a 3G connection are the relevant components. Thoroughgoing digitization in conjunction with a reduction of the storage space for paper has also helped to change how work is done today.

An important key to success is the involvement of the employees as much as possible in the process of development and change. Using the motto "Making participants out of victims," goal-oriented change is important. Plans for office change that suggest things like "Next Monday we move into the new offices and everything will be completely different!" are doomed to failure. The targeted preparation of employees through the communication of information and employee participation is important. This is something we did on an extensive scale with the Santander "New Work" project. Together with a "Change Agent Team" made up of employees from all sectors of the company, we discussed the impending changes systematically and communicated with and prepared all employees.

The result of the project is respectable. The employees' approval of the design concept is extraordinarily high, the positive effects expected by management have been convincingly achieved, and previously uttered fears have been for the most part proven unfounded. Courage is rewarded if one sets out to reach a goal unfalteringly and in full awareness of the consequences. This approach was very successfully implemented in the Santander "New Work" project.

Dr. Peter Kern was the leader of the Santander "New Work" project. He is the former director of the Fraunhofer Institute for Labor Economy and Organization and continues to serve as a member of its board of directors.

The Material and Mental Character of Architecture

Zheng Shiling on the World Expo Village

Our world is a material one as well as a mental and cultural one, but the material world, the mental world, and the cultural world are all erected on a material basis. At the very beginning, we learn about the world from its material side, and this is the reason why we regard its materiality as its essential aspect. Throughout history different notions of substance have inspired different worldviews and religious beliefs, instigated numerous historical events, and even exercised their influence on historical progress.

Because of the peculiar material character of architecture, the entire history of architecture is constantly pervaded by investigations into the internal relationship between the material and mental aspects of architecture. Materiality relates to the perception and holistic comprehension of architecture; it is the essence of the existence of architecture and at the same time the central element of any individual experience of architecture. Materiality refers to space, time, structure, technology, form, sound, building material, color, perception of reality, outer skin, composition, and nodes. Through materiality, architecture expresses beauty, sublimity, and, at the same time, life itself. Through its materiality architecture shapes the human world in time and space, and also mankind itself. In this way, it also expresses its mental character.

Architectural space is the core of the unity of material and mental objects. The Italian architecture theorist Bruno Zevi believes that space is the main factor in architecture—that architectural history is predominantly a history of our notions of space, and that the assessment of architecture is to a great extent based on the assessment of the space within a given structure. In traditional Chinese culture, space and materiality form a unity. The eleventh chapter of Lao Tzu's *Tao Te Ching* contains the following passage:

> We put thirty spikes together and call it a wheel; but it is on the space where there is nothing that the usefulness of the vehicle depends. We turn clay to form a vessel; but it is on its emptiness that the usefulness of the vessel depends. We pierce walls with doors and windows to make a house; but it is on the empty spaces that the usefulness of the house depends. Therefore, just as we take advantage of what is, we should recognize the usefulness of what is not.

Architecture is like a vessel that is able to contain, separate, connect, enhance, elevate, and even distinguish human actions related to space. The materiality of architecture draws people into experiencing the changes of time, light, and shadow, and leads to an integration of time and space in the distance.

Materiality is marked by material, mental, technological, and cultural elements; the materiality of architecture exerts an influence over the system of human sensory perception and is the basis of metaphysics, as it stimulates imagination, generates associations, and inspires poetry. In one of his poems, the German poet Hoelderlin praised how "poetically man dwells on this earth," thus connecting man and mental matter; this is about the integration of materiality and mental objects. From its very beginning, Chinese philosophy has been arguing that man is connected with the divine, and in the world of traditional Chinese philosophy life itself is the essence of all living beings. The classic *Yi Zhuan* (Commentary on the *I Ching*, or Book of Changes) states: "The great virtue of heaven and earth arises anew each day." Heaven and earth foremost embody themselves in all living beings; the essential nature of heaven and earth is the continuously changing creation of new life. The creation of life is the most sublime and virtuous act of the universe. The life of man is different from that of other creatures, for he is able to approach heaven, to know his own fate and form a unity with heaven in order to fulfill the saying "heaven and man as one"; this is the link between rationality and human nature. In this way, the principle aspired to by Chinese architects—"heaven and man as one"—is just the linkage between materiality and mental objects.

In China, a discussion about "substance" (materiality) and "cultivation" (the mental) emerged as early as millennia ago. Confucius said: "Natural substance prevailing over cultivation begets roughness; cultivation prevailing over natural substance begets pedantry; natural substance and cultivation duly blended make a superior man." Materiality and mental matter are factors that are dependent on each other, regardless of whether they relate to objects or human beings; all of them are in need of the reciprocal enforcement and complementation of cultivation and material substance, as well as the integration of technology and culture, in order to enable the spirit of architecture to arise. To take environment, technology, and the logic of space all seriously, to deal with each project with a basic attitude of rationality—this is the aspiration of architects and, at the same time, also the inspiration imparted by the buildings of HPP.

Architects are always in search of a certain state of mind. This state of mind can be illustrated by three lines from poems of the Song Dynasty that describe it on three different levels. The first state of mind can be described as follows: "Yesterday night the west wind made the green trees wither. All alone I climbed the tall tower, and with my gaze I followed the paths across the sky to their end." This is nothing other than standing on higher ground to clearly recognize all those paths walked upon by our forefathers and to recapitulate and completely penetrate their artistic endeavors and scientific thinking. The second state of mind can be described like this: "Although my clothes are already hanging loose, I do not regret in the end; it seems as if I had become weak and feeble because of longing for my true love." Deeply immersed in thought and engrossed in work, unfailingly striving—it is like being amorous in a state of unrequited love, completely devoting oneself to the task at hand. The third state of mind is like this: "I have searched for him far away and in all directions, but as I turn my head, he all of a sudden appears and comes into the light." It is as if, after a long search in a sea of illuminated lanterns in a great crowd of people during a festival night, one suddenly encounters the beloved person that one has been longing for day and night. All of a sudden one feels enlightened, and the long and hazardous search has finally produced a result: a perfect state of mind is reached.

The first exhibit of the 2010 World Expo is the World Expo Village, an innovative experimental community that is a far cry from ordinary architectural design. As early as 2004, HPP had been selected from among more than thirty international architectural design firms to participate in the drawing of the master plan for the World Expo area. The office has submitted a highly sophisticated concept that clearly marks areas separated according to their functions while at the same time ensuring their overall integration. Each single group is marked by the excellent quality of its environment, and the individual country pavilions can be set up in a flexible way. The concept attaches great importance to social, economic, and ecological progress as well as to landscape and urban design, provides for an appropriate allocation of basic infrastructure, and, furthermore, emphasizes overall security and rationality. Among the ten concepts submitted at the time, the goals of this concept—namely, an outermost structuredness, an inner logic, and an integrated approach—were clearly discernable. Several of the design ideas of the HPP concept that displayed an excellent design quality and facilitated sustainable development have been incorporated into the final plan for the World Expo area.

During the competition for the design of the World Expo Village, the concept of HPP was awarded the highest rating by placing first in the competition. The concept has also been unanimously praised because of its precise logic and creativity. On the basis of a deduction from the 2010 Shanghai World Expo motto "Better City, Better Life," it advocates an international lifestyle as well as flexibility in the urban space and serves to create an outstanding, forward-looking urban community.

Due to the location of the 2010 Shanghai World Expo Village within a former industrial area of the city, its design possesses a singular character: on the one hand, it has to protect the historical and industrial buildings remaining on site, while on the other, it has to adapt to the complicated course of the urban terrain and take into account the present state of the area as well as make adequate use of the scenery and living conditions for families along the Binjiang riverside strip of land. On one hand, the use of the village during the World Expo has to be taken into account, and on the other, the requirements for the functioning of an urban community after the end of the World Expo have to be fulfilled. The World Expo Village realizes the ideal of sustainable development and materializes the first Green Architecture Urban Community of such a size in Shanghai with respect to its technology and architectural design. This international community is presently under construction and will become a future model community for Shanghai.

Dr. Zheng Shiling is the director of the Institute of Architecture and Urban Space at Tongji University and the senior consultant on theme concepts for Expo 2010's organizing committee.

Mischa Kuball on the Wuppertal Justice Center

What follows is a conversation with Mischa K., who was challenged by his counterpart, *, to actually visit the court at the Justice Center in Wuppertal in the guise of Josef K., the character from Franz Kafka's novel *The Trial*. Selected passages from Kafka's novel (as translated by David Wyllie on the Project Gutenberg Web site at http://www.gutenberg.org/etext/7849) have also been interspersed within Mischa K.'s commentary and these appear in italics.

Someone must have slandered Mischa K., because one morning he was arrested without having done anything bad. The most important thing was that K. had some previously acquired art-historical knowledge, and was a member of the Association for the Maintenance of Urban Art Landmarks for awhile. Mischa K. had this to say:

"Yes, not without opposition from certain investors, as an artist I had joined different groups which were resisting the pure commercialization of urban space—a resistance which also created friction with the executive jurisdictional authority. But this resistance also generated a demonstrable public sensitivity, as the first performative actions showed. It was no coincidence that Joseph Beuys was the 'resident godfather' in this parentless, house-to-house battle and he thereby initiated the first convincing and sustainable connections between society and artistic practice. Actually, beginning in the late 1970s and early 1980s, there was also a strong artistic attention to public space, to the urban significance of what we call 'urbanity.' So, I had actually not done anything bad, but . . ."

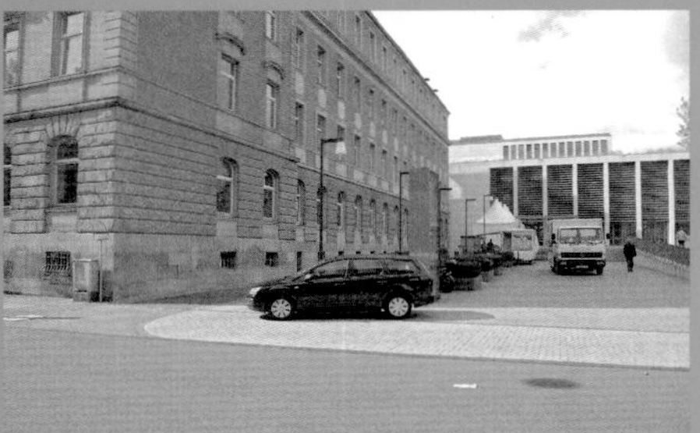

He had thought that he would recognize the building from a distance by some kind of sign, without knowing exactly what the sign would look like, or from some particular kind of activity outside the entrance. . . . K. went further into the street, slowly, as if he had plenty of time now, or as if the examining magistrate were looking at him from one of the windows and therefore knew that K. had found his way there. It was shortly after nine. The building was quite far down the street[;] it covered so much area it was almost extraordinary, and the gateway in particular was tall and long. . . . In contrast with his usual habits, he remained standing a while at the entrance to the yard, taking in all these external details.

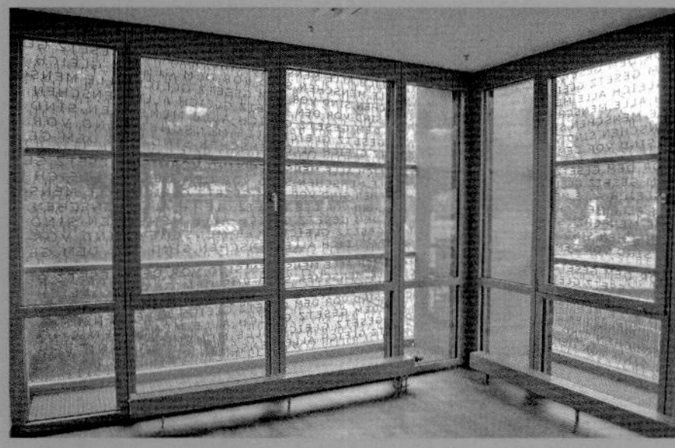

"I can still hear the murmuring of the Wupper River and the noises of innocent children playing in the neighborhood day care—and also the iron-on-iron banging of the overhead railway. I am already running up the ramp. The old pillared building with its watchful façade becomes a film sequence. The new revolving glass sluice separately admits visitors and attendants. The X-ray-like scan verifies my good intentions: I already seem to be inside. . . . The New is now shrouded in glass instead of stone. It gives me an unencumbered view—through the new building to its exterior!"

K. went over to the stairway to get to the room where the hearing was to take place, but then stood still again[,] as besides these steps he could see three other stairway entrances, and there also seemed to be a small passageway at the end of the yard leading into a second yard.

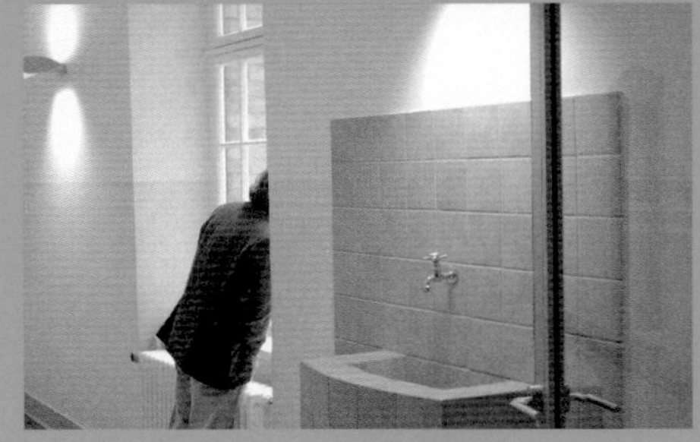

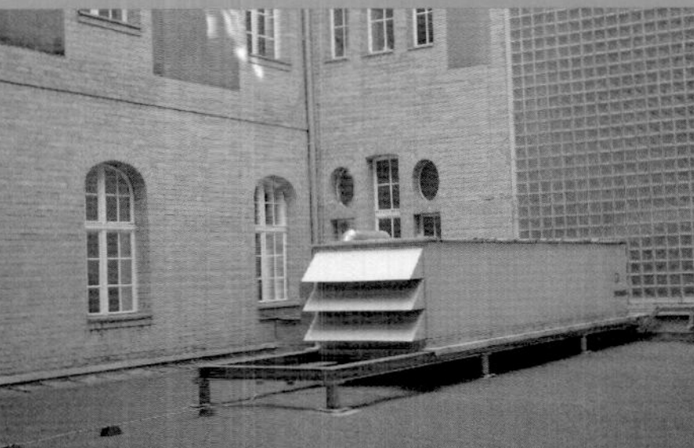

"I step into the lucid new hall—and pause. In all the magnitude of a little game of playing with the light of the sun, Günter Fruhtrunk extends a greeting from the upper balcony wall like a nature prostrate . . . 'art and nature on the building site.' And on the first floor, individual attendants have demonstrated their passion to collect with empty tankards presented in a showcase that seem to want to take on a human dimension. I duck into a hallway. . . ."

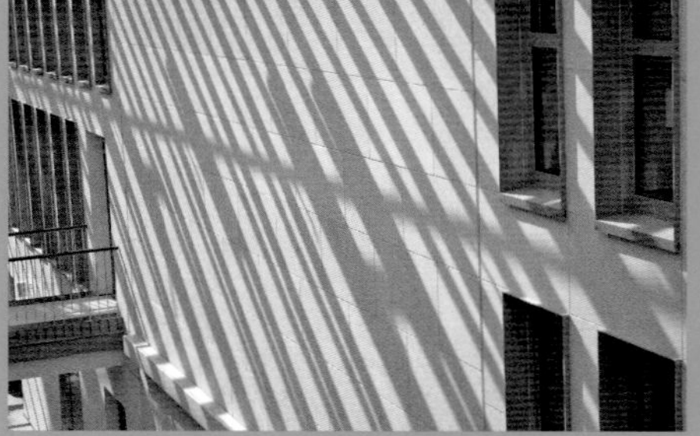

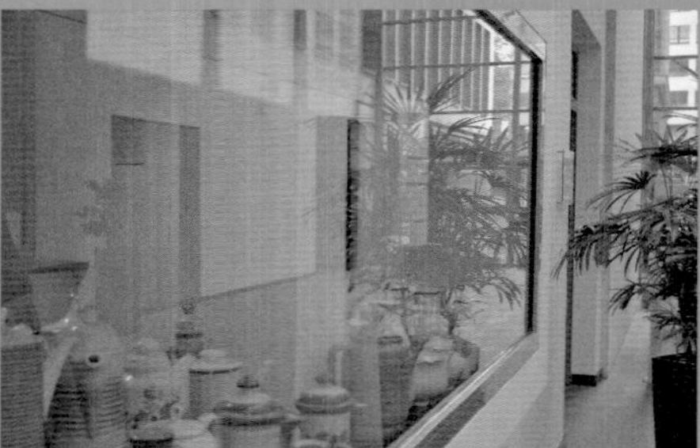

Most of them were small, one-windowed rooms. . . . At the entrance he nearly fell over, as behind the door there was another step. "They don't show much concern for the public," he said. "They don't show any concern at all," said the usher, "just look at the waiting room here." It consisted of a long corridor from which roughly made doors led out to the separate departments of the attic. There was no direct source of light, but it was not entirely dark. . . .

"I hesitantly and respectfully pass by those waiting (witnesses, plaintiffs, defendants?). Announcements on the blackboards of the trial rooms yield a brief insight into files pertaining to the cases of the human fates about to be negotiated. . . . In one of the courtyards I read a sign: 'No parking.' I read in shimmering letters on the panes: 'All human beings are equal before the law.' I ask *, my counterpart, 'Are all laws equal before human beings?' The question is drowned out by a consistent rumbling as the attendants push the file carts down the corridor. I look into a courtyard covered with gravel. . . .”

One evening, a few days later, K. was walking along one of the corridors that separated his office from the main stairway—he was nearly the last one to leave for home that evening, [as t]here remained only a couple of workers in the light of a single bulb in the dispatch department—when he heard a sigh from behind a door which he had himself never opened but which he had always thought just led into a junk room. . . . Now, K. remained at the window, he did not dare go back into the junk room, and he did not want to go home either. The yard he looked down into was small and rectangular, [and] all around it were offices. . . .

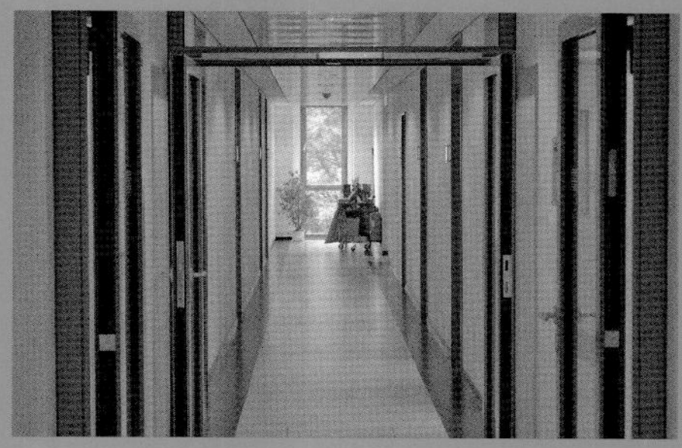

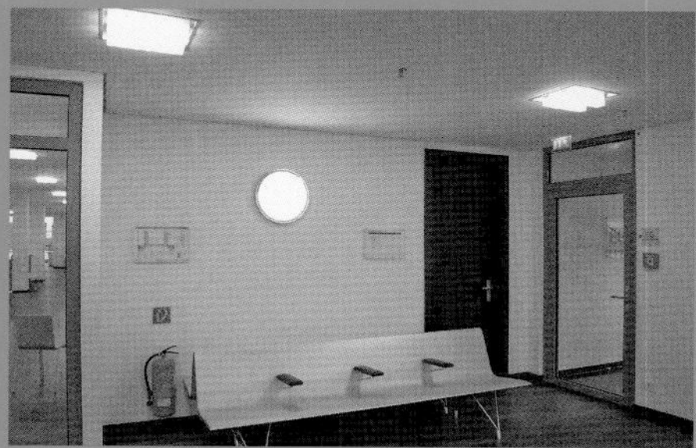

“The regular arrangement of the windows repeats the initial impression of the film experience. I turn faster. The windows melt into a ribbon: they reflect light. I stagger, catch a strange body in one of the courtyards, stagger on, and grasp for a bench . . . The call comes abruptly: ‘The witnesses in the criminal case of K., please come to trial room 1.04!’ My inner eye searches for the telltale sign of the ‘Men’s Room’ . . . Relief!”

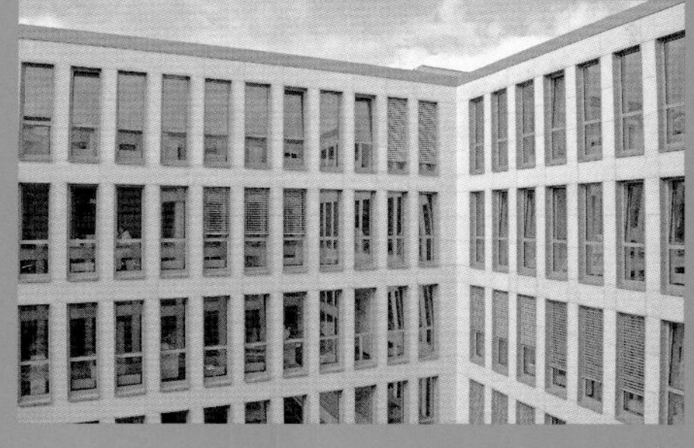

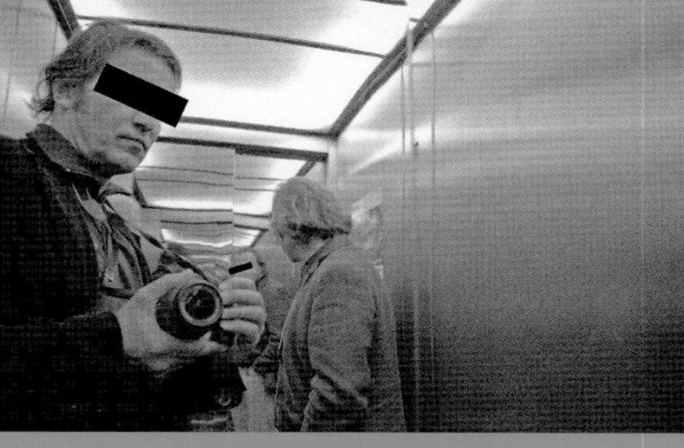

As he reached the fifth floor, he decided to give up the search . . .

“In the mirrored elevator I adjust my clothing when the door closes. I don’t want to suggest anything suspicious with my appearance. But I am always startled a little when the door opens and attendants step into the elevator and we—of necessity—continue the journey together with them. Enzensberger’s compartments! I look unavoidably—but actually against my will—at the hair on the ear of *, my counterpart. A small electric chime reminds us of the exit on the uppermost floor of the building. I read the number ‘4.’ We get out and we look awkwardly at the surrounding city . . .”

“Now that I’ve seen what it looks like here, I’d like to go.”

“You haven’t seen everything yet,” said the usher ingenuously.

“I don’t want to see everything,” said K., who was also feeling very tired. “I want to go, what is the way to the exit?”

“You haven’t got[ten] lost, have you?” asked the usher in amazement[. “Y]ou go down this way to the corner, then right down the corridor straight ahead as far as the door.”

“Come with me,” said K., “[and] show me the way. I’ll miss it; there are so many different ways here.”

“It’s the only way there is,” said the usher, who had now started to sound quite reproachful[.] “I can’t go back with you again[;] I’ve got to hand in my report, and I’ve already lost a lot of time because of you as it is.”

“The officials in the green robes give us a friendly nod at the exit. The red plastic number 019 in the pocket of my pants reminds me of the photographic capability of the mobile telephone I had to leave upon entering as a deposit for my future ‘exit.’ It reminds me that in this building, with all its doors and windows and courtyards, very significant and personal things are being negotiated!”

They were standing on the front steps of the bank; as the doorkeeper seemed to be listening to what they were saying, K. drew his uncle down further, where they were absorbed into the bustle of the street. . . . “[T]he court doesn’t want anything from you. It accepts you when you come and it lets you go when you leave.”

“Now I finally perceive that my heart is slowly resuming its day-to-day beating. I see how the more than one-hundred-year-old overhead railway drags by and with a derisive cawing I stare at the court building—and also at an unmarked, unruly steel sculpture. Now I look at the parking spot: yes, it is there, in the same place as I locked it . . .”

The painter observed the effect his explanation had had on K. and then, with a certain unease, said, “Does it not occur to you that the way I’m speaking is almost like a lawyer? It’s the incessant contact with the gentlemen of the court [that] has that influence on me. I gain a lot by it, of course, but I lose a lot, artistically speaking.”

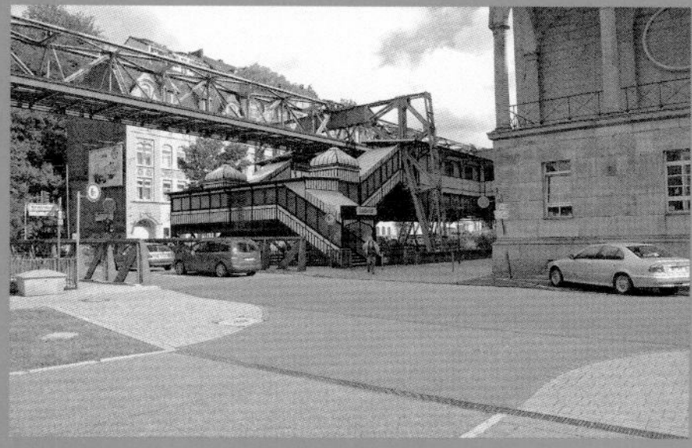

Mischa K., also known as Mischa Kuball, is a graphic artist living in Düsseldorf. He is especially well known for his conceptual light installations in public spaces and he holds a professorship in media art at the Kunsthochschule für Medien in Cologne. Kuball’s counterpart, *, is the historian and theoretician of art Raimund Stecker. He was the founding director of the Arp Museum Bahnhof Rolandseck and is now an honorary professor of the history of contemporary art at the Kunstakademie in Münster.

A Statement of Change

Fritz Pleitgen on the Europe Tower

When I was a foreign news correspondent, I had the privilege of being able to work in a series of world-class cities. Each time I arrived in one, I quickly gravitated to the cities' landmarks. These served as the backdrop for my "stand-ups," which is what we call on-site news broadcasts in television parlance. Seen in the background, the Arc de Triomphe, the Kremlin, the Brandenburger Tor and the Berlin Wall, the White House, and Times Square gave me an added authority in the eyes of my viewers when I reported on camera about the situation of the world at the time from the vantage point of a correspondent.

I use the expression "the world at the time" advisedly. The end of the confrontation between East and West with the fall of the Wall and the Iron Curtain had a liberating effect on the whole world—politically, spiritually, and intellectually. It loosed a tremendous dynamic. It banished the stagnation of a divided Europe. New "global players" stepped onto the stage and new ideas began to circulate, some of which assumed mythic proportions, especially in the realm of architecture. Buildings of unheard-of elegance and boldness were created, monuments of a time of boundless opportunity. At any rate, that is how it looked. They were statements of dramatic change. We discover fewer of them in the "New World" of America than in the homelands of the oldest cultures on the Arabian peninsula and in the Far East. Where just a few years ago there were only humble huts, gigantic apartment and office towers shoot up hundreds of meters into the sky. There are especially conspicuous examples in Dubai and Shanghai.

These buildings are viewed as challenges to the West. This does not bother me; intellectual competition cannot do us any harm. Do I like everything that has been built? Certainly not! Some buildings border on a defiance of nature. But the first skyscrapers were also seen this way, so I do not want to sound a timid note.

In order to comprehend the changes that have recently occurred, I do not need to take a long journey to the Orient. I can find something that is just as powerful as the "anything goes" towers being built in Asia—and a lot more sympathetic to me—in my own capital city. As a correspondent stationed in East Berlin, I only needed to look out my window to know what the situation in the world was. Across from me was the Wall. Today, that structure of the last century is gone. The ruin-studded Platz der Akademie, which once presented its dreary countenance when I looked out the rear windows of my apartment, is also gone. In its place, the Gendarmenmarkt has been resurrected with its old name as one of the most beautiful squares in all of Germany. Each time I go to Berlin I check in on it. Every "auf Wiedersehen" is an emotional experience for me.

It is the same for me in other Eastern and Central European cities. Whether I find myself in Tallinn, Riga, Vilnius, Warsaw, Prague, Bratislava, Budapest, Bucharest, or Sofia, I always have two superimposed images before me: the before and the after. I love it when the new architecture has the courage to look to the future. Let us take Bulgaria as an example. As a Socialist people's republic, it was the poorest in the early Soviet bloc and had the least freedom. I remember that when I took a flying tour of Sofia on a family vacation to the Black Sea, the Bulgarian metropolis made a cheerless impression. Today, however, Sofia is a totally different city: it is full of life despite problems that cannot be ignored. Located in the former Soviet Balkans, Sofia was close and stuffy just a short time ago, but now it is acquiring a European freshness and openness. One of the signs of the new city that will be visible at a great distance is the planned Europe Tower. The design is compelling. With its great height, the building's clear profile transmits a sense of increased self-confidence. A sustainable political impulse is being initiated here with the help of architecture: Bulgaria, the new EU member, has arrived in modern Europe.

I am certain that when television news correspondents report about the new Bulgaria in two or three years, they will choose the Europe Tower in Sofia as their backdrop. Then the building will be able to broadcast its effective political message around the world.

Fritz Pleitgen has left his mark in the public sector as a broadcast journalist, especially during his long tenure as director of the WDR (Westdeutscher Rundfunk). Since 2007, as chairman of Ruhr 2010 GmbH he has been involved in the planning of the city of Essen as the cultural capital of Europe.

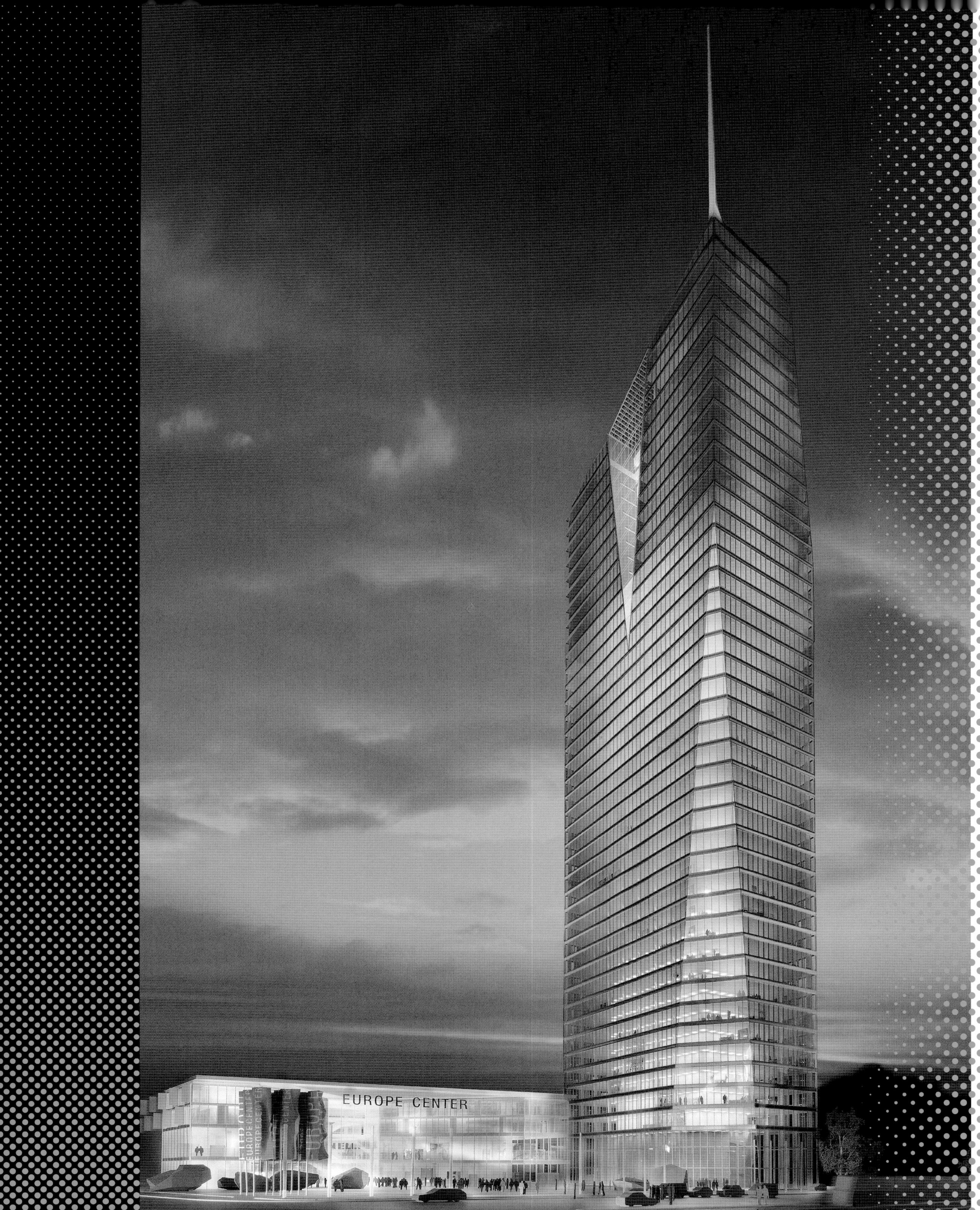
EUROPE CENTER

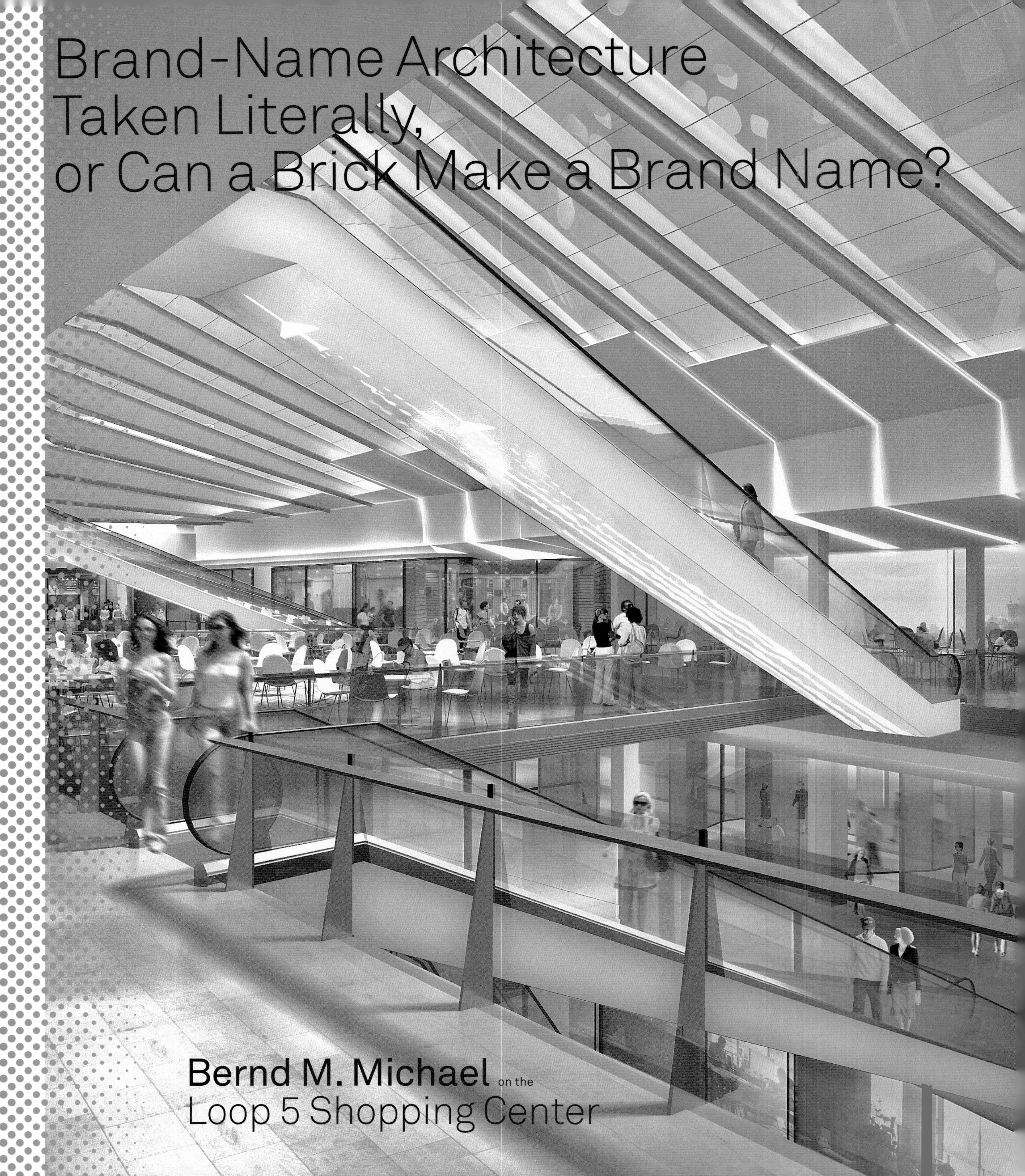

Brand-Name Architecture Taken Literally, or Can a Brick Make a Brand Name?

Bernd M. Michael on the Loop 5 Shopping Center

When architecture becomes a trademark it suddenly embodies a two-fold value: in addition to its function as a building, it accrues the representative value of a trademark. In the BMW main administration building in Munich, the four cylinders of the building symbolize an automobile manufacturer's competence in building motors unmistakably and handsomely: it is forward-looking. Frank O. Gehry's Guggenheim Museum in Bilbao signals the awakening of a formerly tasteless, gray industrial city to culture, style, and higher expectations. Coincidence turned a structurally tilted tower in Pisa into a trademark for a city—it was entirely unintentional. But in the cases of the Eiffel Tower or the Atomium in Brussels the intent was deliberate. Countless firms such as Nokia, Vitra, Oracle, Pan Am, Thyssen, and Citicorp have had their company philosophy translated into an architectural trademark. In the age of corporate brandings, the trademarklike gestalt of the company building has assumed a new inner as well as outer dimension. The goal is to encourage internally the identification and the pride of the employees—but also to transmit attractiveness and a certain sort of image to the outside world. Design and architecture have thus become building blocks of corporate culture and corporate identity. The number of interchangeable buildings set out uniformly and identically, and motivated only by the desire to fulfill their practical function, is dwindling. A new way of thinking has begun: the more a building makes a mark, the more re-"markable" the design of a space is, the better and faster it will be "remarked" upon and the more it will become a trademark!

But what is the advantage of a building "being a trademark"?

For manufacturers of products or for service providers, having a trademark offers a competitive edge. A trademark helps to influence business in two significant aspects: uniqueness and identification. Thanks to the oversupply of everything in our world, people have learned that exchangeability prevails because there are hardly any differences in quality and service between one company and another; the differences are too subtle and hard to discern and experience. From the standpoint of emotion the story is very different. The sympathy or the feeling, that is, the non-topical effect, that a trademark can radiate gives it a strategic added value which goes beyond the pure characteristics of a product or service. A trademark is the difference between reality and perception! It is from the combination of the "felt" and practical values of a trademark that a consumer's preference emerges, and this preference often becomes an enduring bond.

So, what does this have to do with architecture? What can "being a trademark" mean in the real estate business? Let us start with the large role that the emotional presence of houses or cities plays for human beings. Terms like "homeland" or "at home" are laden with emotion. We have already mentioned the gray, no-name place that the word Bilbao once conjured. However, because of the creative architecture of a single building, the city suddenly began to construct a new image, first to create pride among the citizens, and then to make the city attractive to visitors. Year after year in Bilbao the weight and presence of art and culture have grown and led to a balance between a liveable ambiance and industrial strength. We now call this process professional urban marketing. Real estate has become a market dealing in trademarks, because striking architecture creates added value that goes beyond the purely spatial aspects of the building.

Today corporations are thinking far beyond classic modes of communication, and the integrated leadership of their corporate trademark includes architecture, which facilitates the expression of the corporation's philosophy in the form of building. The traditional, functional stacking of bricks is not enough anymore. Whoever wants to purchase a building that offers more than just its use value must think about trademark strategy in order to find an adequate architectural solution.

In this regard, the example of Weiterstadt has set new standards. The basic concept is a trademark idea. An emotional, atmospheric effect is achieved via architectonic means, which then serves as a stage for the presentation of goods and services. This stage circles around the fascinating, desire-laden, dream-unfolding world of aeronautics: the sky, freedom, travel, flying, technology, luxury, desire, adventure—all of this is packed into this mystical stage, which is created by the architecture and its materials, design, and effects. In its entirety, it is a palpable atmosphere that lifts us above the day-to-day and lets us take a "sky-high" stroll. It provides stimulation and distance from the customary. The monotony of shopping centers and the mall phenomenon is renowned. And together with the uniformity of the perpetually recurring stores that are represented there, a new form of "upscale boredom" at world-class prices has been established. Whether it be in Shanghai, Milan, New York, Moscow, or Delhi, the homogeneous appearance of the putative shopping paradises of such cities will soon reach a peak. If one cannot tell where one is except by looking at the destination on one's airline ticket, then it becomes clear that this one-mall-fits-all experience is the same in all places and at all times. It would be something along the lines of "Let's go mall-hop in the next big city."

The trademark concept of Weiterstadt, however, evades the negative sense of this phenomenon. It stages its own unmistakable and emotionally stimulating world, which gives shopping a spirit of adventure steeped in the world of airports and airlines—a world that symbolizes the mobility of the twenty-first century. From the façade to the building materials, and from the design's light-flooded ambience that bathes the shopping street to the execution of light and form: everything about the architecture exudes the "sky-flair" of a destination where one can shop as if in mid-flight. The "Loop" trademark precisely broadcasts its message with the structure's architectural building blocks and thereby creates a uniqueness and attraction that can quickly become the talk of the town. The eager curiosity has an allure, and the "Loop" trademark building becomes a fresh, new stage for today's "high flyers"—or those who would aspire to become such.

That architects in this instance have built a fascinating architectural "trademark" is something new. It is a new and rigorous approach to architectural thinking. To conclude, one must say that this place has started to sell not just bricks, but trademark-worthy adventures. In a time when value creation is everything and the battle against uniformity and boredom must be fought, creative architecture has opened a new market strategy, assuming that one wants to learn what it means to think in terms of trademarks and trademark philosophies from the beginning.

Bernd M. Michael was founder and chairman of the Grey Global Group until 2006 and is one of the most acknowledged trademark experts in Europe.

The Eternity of the Stars

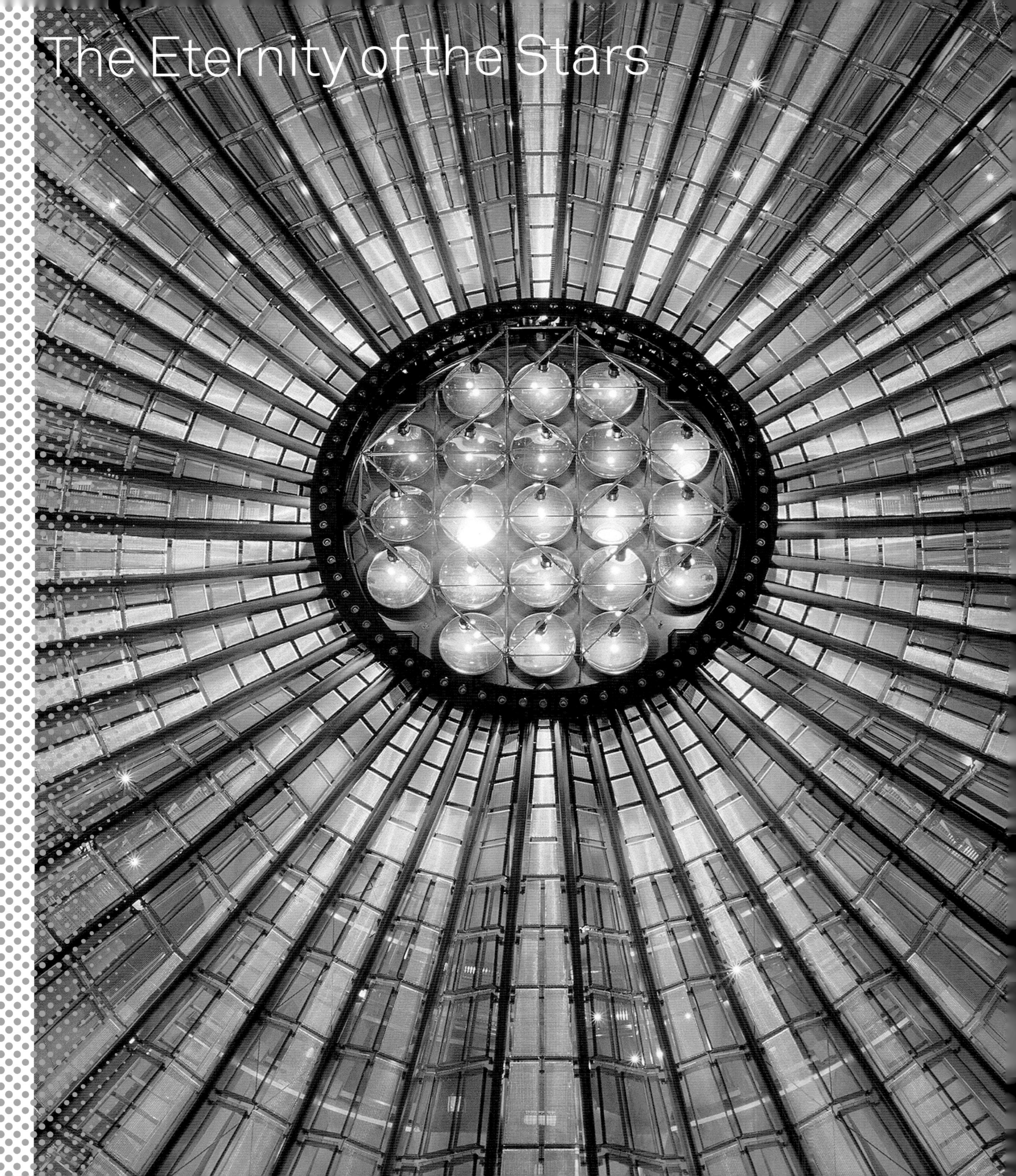

Wolfram Goertz
on the Düsseldorf Concert Hall

I always felt as if I were in a shipyard here, or inside the hull of a ship. The only things that were strange were the armchairs. Above me were hard, light wooden planks, and beneath was hard ground; there was always too little air around me, and there was a constant clacking noise that penetrated the ear. It did this with such a precise delay that, part in desperation and part lovingly, this phenomenon was commonly called the "knocking ghost." The shipyard was near to the water, and ultramodern, but it was still haunted.

That has been my experience of the Düsseldorf Concert Hall since it opened in 1978: an amphitheater-style structure that permitted the most beautiful contact with music yet at the same time triggered something foreign. It was not music itself, but rather the distorted product of a merciless exercise in physics that had resulted in the execution of a sorry piece of acoustical work within the much-too-small framework the hall had to offer. The music echoed brutally instead of gigantically, and it had little volume and even less reverberation. "How else should a dome construction sound?" sighed an acoustics professor from Cologne, who promptly received a bitter complaint from the city of Düsseldorf: "People from Cologne should keep out of this matter, if you please." The complainants had no reason to react so huffily; they knew the man was right and that the concert hall was, in fact, acoustically beyond rescue.

But the hall had good fortune and loyal domestic gods, its invisible but never forgotten star performers. Previously, the concert hall had been a planetarium in which grown-ups and children alike had stared into space—a place in which promise and poetry had made its way down to mortals. The idea of the new concert hall was to "reach for the stars" a second time and give the inside of the dome a new inner skin and introduce multiple right angles. The concert hall was converted following a model that had long served for the carrying out of acoustic experiments. The dome now arches up, salvaged and broadened, over a perforated metal meshwork which processes and spreads the sound. The planks had simply been ripped out, and the new right angles that had been introduced fractured the sound so that it lingered awhile under the ceiling before sinking downward. It was unbelievable—a trick, pure cleverness. But it was just physics. And fantasy.

When the hall was finished, thanks to the acoustics experts and architects, the grown-ups and the children began to marvel in the space once more, gazing transfixed at the dome with fascination, as if they were encountering a continuum of time and space. The stars were back again in a nocturnal, sky-blue mantle, twinkling contentedly as if nothing had happened and everything had stood still in order to give them the opportunity to make a triumphant return. All the world hummed in unison: "What a wonderful concert hall—pure light, pure magic!"

When the orchestras moved in, they almost fainted. How could it be that with a couple of prestigitations there was such an increase in majesty? Aside from our own irritation, we had always imagined what it must have been like for the musicians, sitting on the podium under badly adjusted sound reflectors and making music but never enjoying the experience of a hall that let the music ring, let alone allowed them to breathe. No one had ever heard what the others were playing; everyone had just played morosely for themselves. But now it is suddenly there, this collectively perceived brilliancy—the space offers the enlightenment of a commonwealth of sound and no longer harbors the estranged.

And that is how I experienced—and continue to experience—the concert hall every day anew: as a hard-earned gift that came after all of the drawn out discontent and griping. Now we can comfort ourselves with the uplifting feeling that the whole world envies us for our hall—including the residents of Cologne. We would welcome a visit from them. We hold no grudge, but think instead in greater spans of time and about the stars of the past that have now returned to the firmament. As we all know, there is no beginning or end up there, just a continuum that is as eternal as the music of the great masters, who have finally found a home in Düsseldorf on the Rhine. The hall has truly become hallowed.

Wolfram Goertz is the music editor of the *Rheinischen Post* in Düsseldorf.

The Allianz Kai on the River Main

What is it about that diaphanous figure, standing as it does at a lofty height on a plate of glass? He is a barefooted man holding an angular architectural model in his hands with his glance directed to the heavens and his hair wafting in the wind: it is Heinrich, the patron saint of the city of Bamberg and its churches. Here in Frankfurt, he has been given a place in the great *Im Fluss* art installation on the banks of the Main, which the Munich sculptor Stephan Huber has dedicated with a subtle humor to the work's clients. For the work, a total of twenty-one patron saints of the Main accompany a path of nervously quivering neon light that winds its way through the main hall on the second floor of the Allianz building and can be seen glowing mysteriously from outside at night. The gleaming blue trail is a true-to-scale image of the course of the Main and Rhine rivers from their sources to their outlets, and it culminates in a giant spiral in the building's main entrance on the bank of the Main.

In this location, the closed effect of the combination of the functional and design aspects not only opens up the riverbank, but it also becomes connected to it. A two-lane, waterside street in the courtyard leads away, down stairs and ramps from the upper bank of the Main onto a newly created river embankment (paid for by the client) with an impressive length of 800 meters, which completes the park on the riverbank. Further east, a transverse street running through the property was extended to the Main's banks, thereby dividing the complex in two. This lane serves as a delivery route and as a means to access the underground garage. Even more important is the pedestrian network within the quarter. Such interests show the striving on the part of the architects for an office building espousing a positive urban planning model characterized by a very high construction density (100,000 square meters of gross area on a 25,000-square-meter property) in contrast to the small-scale prewar constructions of the surrounding area. The resulting conflict between scale and use is typical and cannot be solved through design. However, it does make clear that the future of the city center is to be found in higher densities, something which the large-scale residential constructions immediately adjacent to the riverbank demonstrate. The office complex offers office space for 2,500 employees and parking for 550 cars on its lower levels.

The rear of the building facing south is bordered by a six-story closed-perimeter development that is almost completely enclosed in glass. To the north, the construction is connected in a honeycomb-like fashion. It turns to the river with five completely glassed-in, narrow boxes jutting out of a lower story. Wide block buildings enclosed with red sandstone complete the picture to the west and the east. Next to the entrance and in the vicinity of the Friedensbrücke, the fifteen-story glass high-rise sends a clear message regarding urban planning, and together with the cylinder-shaped Westhafen Tower across the way, it forms a gate to the city center near the Main. With the disembodied effect of its double-layered skin of non-reflective, translucent white glass, especially in the case of the roof parapet, the Allianz high-rise bears a slight resemblance to Jean Nouvel's unrealized project for the 425-meter-tall Tour Sans Fins of 1989, which was to be constructed in the high-rise district of La Défense in Paris.

The most striking design aspect of the Allianz building is its structural envelope and the material characteristics of its louvered exterior blinds made of aluminum. The choice of material is certainly primarily based on considerations of climate, but the deliberate application of the design on the north side, which receives very little direct sunlight, establishes a strong conceptual identity for the building from a functional standpoint with regard to the choice of material. Seen from the Friedensbrücke, the impression given by the building is always completely different, depending on the time of day, the day of the week, the season, and, naturally, the weather. Thanks to the structure's aluminum skin, this variability is even more striking than with other buildings. On the weekend, the building appears as a closed metal castle, because all of its louvered blinds are shut. During the week, however, the individual aluminum elements move, as they are either pulled up or positioned at different angles by the occupants of each of the various offices. The evening sky in the west is also reflected especially well, because of the convenient angles of incidence and reflection: the reflection displays the entire color spectrum. Seldom does one see a large building in an exposed location that offers non-users such an agreeable visual experience. It would seem that St. Barbara, the patron saint of architects and construction workers, is pleased with the building project: the artist Stephan Huber put a tower in her hands as her attribute.

Peter Cachola Schmal is the director of the German Architecture Museum.

Peter Cachola Schmal
on the Allianz Kai

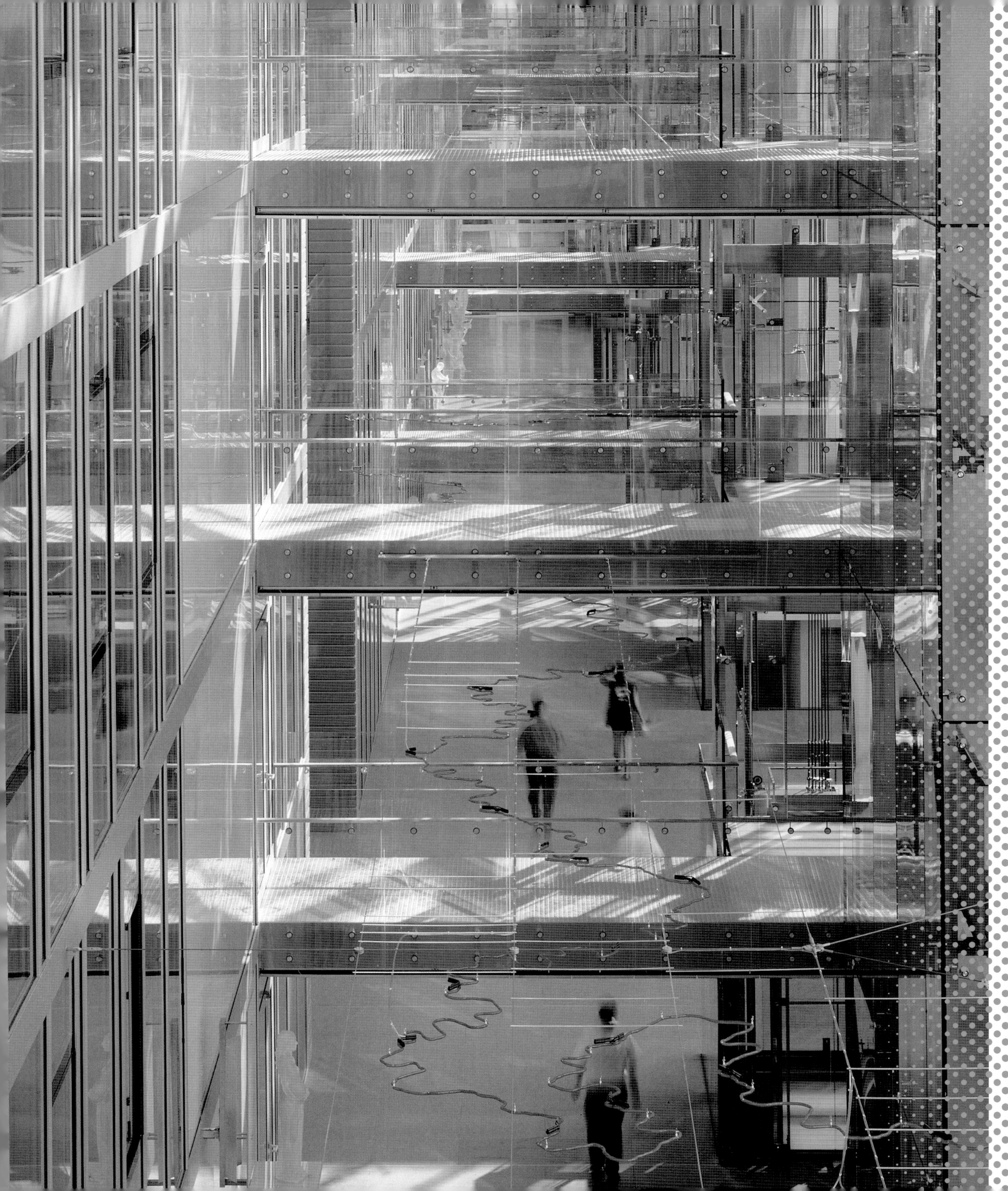

The Symbol of a Cultural Region

Hans-Dietrich Genscher on the Kempinski Grand Hotel Heiligendamm

Heiligendamm and its revitalized building complex became known throughout the world during the world economic summit held under German chairmanship in 2007. Was it a sort of Baltic Nizza, or a hearkening back to the spa culture of days gone by, that the world at large perceived with curiosity and surprise in Heiligendamm? And was this also the reaction of the German public?

One could almost say that Heiligendamm has been resurrected. With its impressive architecture it has become a symbol of the time when it was created, the expression of a historical era in which spiked helmets and the rattling of sabers by no means determined people's mental processes. From its inception, the building ensemble we connect today with Heiligendamm was a part of the image of Mecklenburg, an image of the cultural landscape of the southern shore of the Baltic Sea. Seen this way, the revitalization was not only a bold commercial initiative, but also a reaffirmation of an entire region of Germany. A unique architectural experience awaits the traveler here, a singular landscape on the Baltic coast characterized by magnificence and style. Magnificence and style have rarely been factors as successful at identifying a time and a landscape as they were here.

But can it really be said that this architectural complex is a symbol of an era? What distinguishes Heiligendamm is that it has become a timeless symbol. As it was on the verge of decay, the landscape became the poorer for it. It was a cultural region, an expression of a flavor for life of those who were seeking out the Baltic Sea and could appreciate the very special and unique atmosphere to be found there. At first glance, this may seem to be a contradiction, when one begins to trace back the history of Mecklenburg and the character of its people. But indeed one will arrive at the conclusion that, in a sense, the clarity of the architecture's classicizing rigor echoed the upright character of Mecklenburg's inhabitants. What became known as the "White City on the Sea" signaled impressively that one had arrived in a wonderful landscape inhabited by a strong, vibrant people; here one was under the spell of an architecture that did more than simply serve as human accommodation. One cannot describe the cultural region of the Baltic, northern Germany, and Mecklenburg without also having the "White City" before one's eyes. It is cosmopolitan, not "narrow" in any sense of the word, and it indeed facilitates an understanding of the Baltic as a sea that provides physical, and hence political, access. If one had ultimately allowed Heiligendamm to decay beyond rescue, the cultural region of the Baltic would have suffered a great loss; in a completely ideal sense, Heiligendamm had become not just a part but also a symbol of this region and thus also an expression of its identity.

Hans-Dietrich Genscher was a member of the German parliament for more than three decades. He was Foreign Minister and Vice Chancellor from 1974 to 1992.

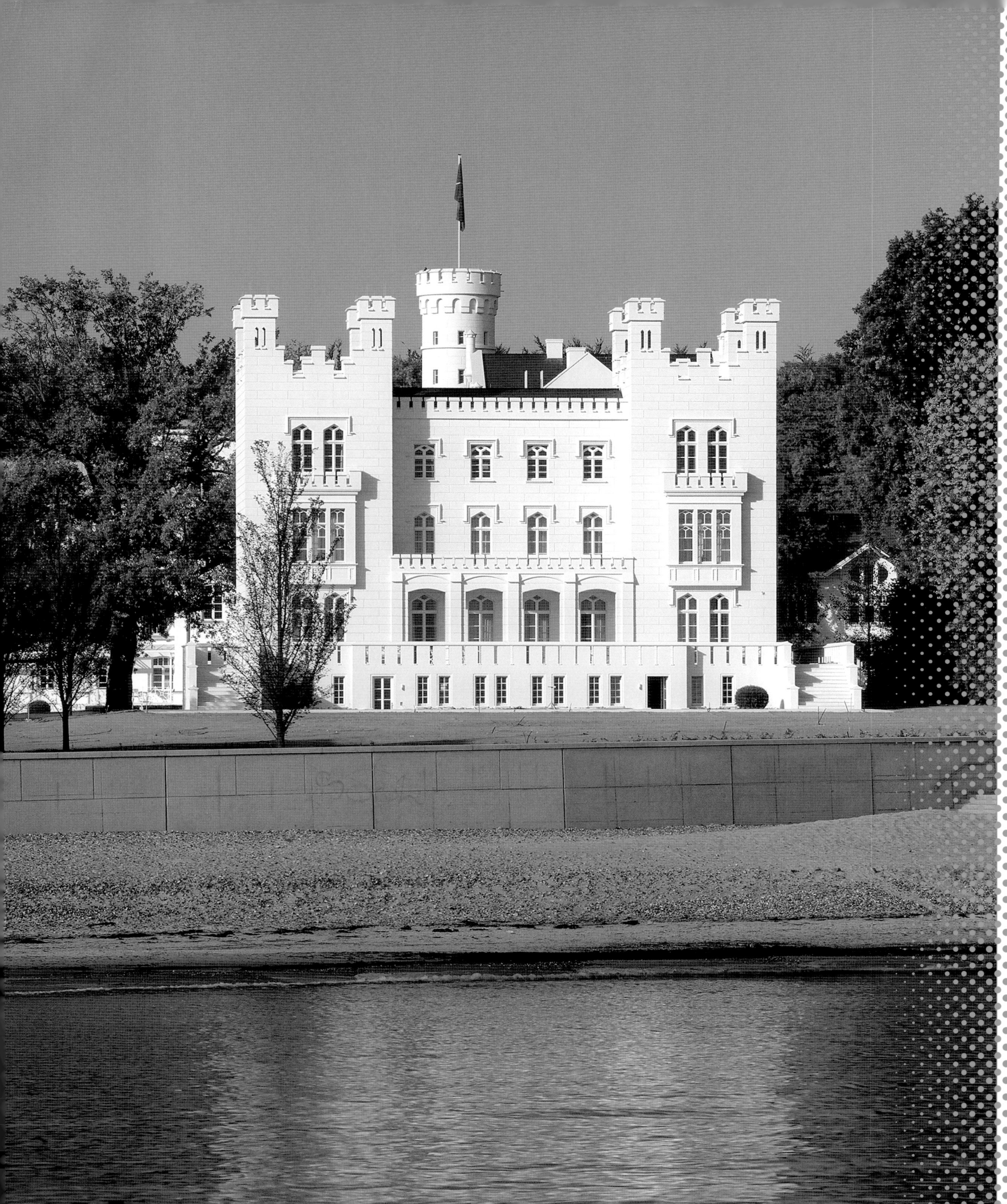

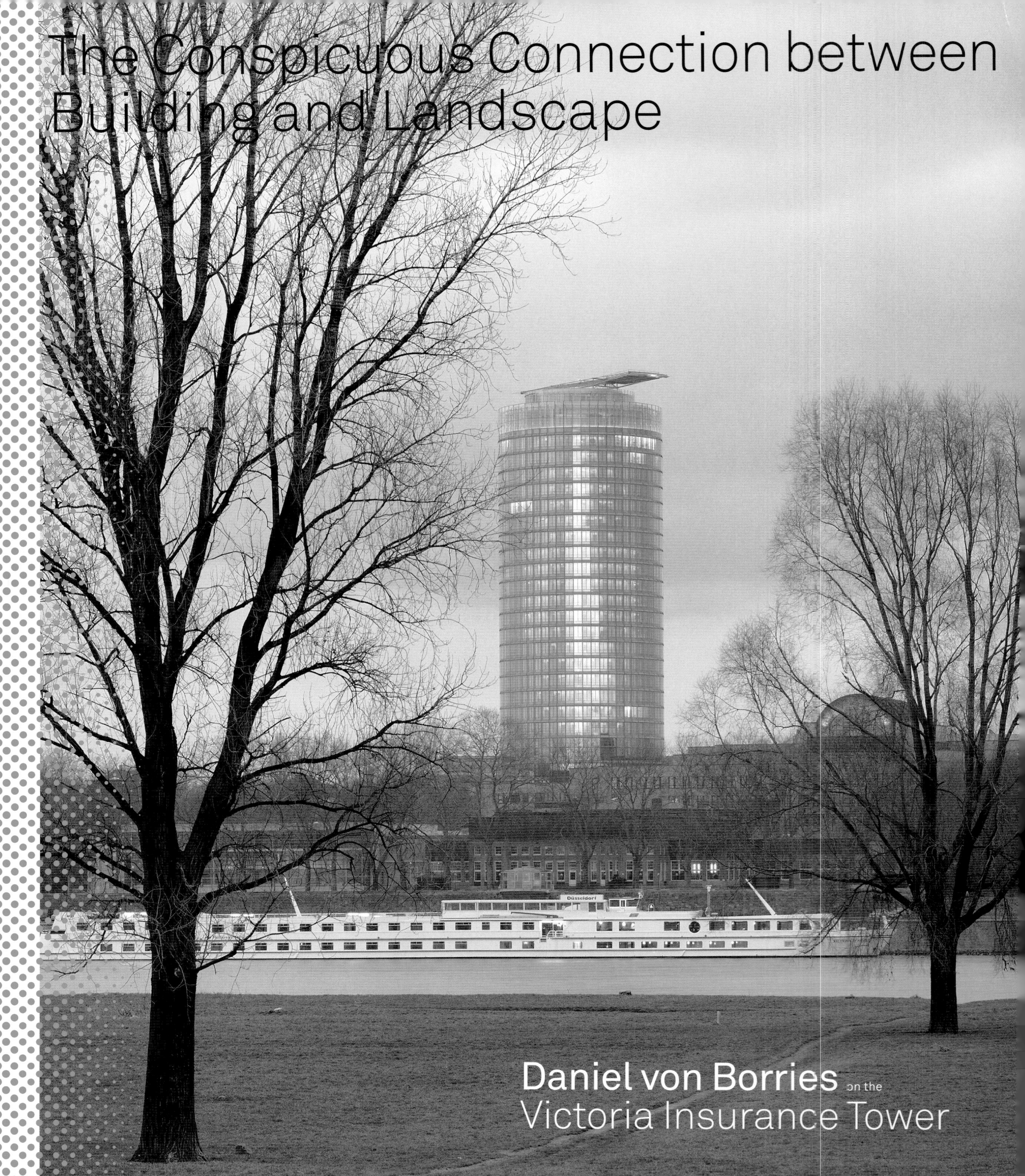
The Conspicuous Connection between Building and Landscape
Daniel von Borries on the
Victoria Insurance Tower
Düsseldorf

Architecture is the physiognomy of a city. Düsseldorf's architectural character has always been determined by a desire for modernity and awakening. The diverse building culture of the city bears witness to this—from the Ehrenhof to what has become known as the Media Harbor.

Not far from the Ehrenhof, Victoria Grundstücksverwaltungs-Gesellschaft GbR erected its administration building. The ERGO Insurance Group, Victoria's parent organization, has also established its headquarters here. The complex is located on one of the most beautiful pieces of land in Düsseldorf, an area along the Rhine River that also adjoins the Rhine Park, which is used by inhabitants and visitors alike as an open, green landscape for recreational activities. In such an environment, sustainable building is not only a task for an ecological urban development, but, for the company establishing roots there, it is an important prerequisite for architectural and landscape design. Together with the architectural firm of HPP, Victoria has erected its headquarters in Düsseldorf in several phases of construction, beginning in 1986. In an interview with the former chairman of Victoria's board, Edgar Jannott, Helmut Hentrich emphasized, "Whoever builds has a lot of responsibility. There is only one thing that is important for me: getting back to the basics. And the basics mean good proportions, beauty, sensible functionality, and good materials." In 1999, the buildings were selected as the three best buildings in the world at the international architectural competition in Cannes, where Victoria also won the coveted investor prize, the MIPIM Award.

In the case of Victoria's architectural project, characteristics such as the proper proportions and functionality are evident to a great degree in both the architectural and ecological aspects of the administrative building. Roof gardens, which reflect the luxurious vegetation of the surrounding parks, green inner courtyards, water surfaces, light-drenched atria—all of these aspects of the building's design establish a conspicuous connection between the structure and the landscape. A leitmotif of the former planner was: "Instead of art, put something green on the building." This thought is still alive at Victoria's administration building in Düsseldorf.

ERGO and Victoria recognized the meaning of environmental protection very early on. Already in 1985, during the construction phase of the first administrative building, Victoria applied to carry out a research and development project addressing the "experimental application of the EC Environmental Audit System in the Insurance Sector." This research project was initiated by Angela Merkel, former Federal Minister for the Environment and current Chancellor of Germany. The subject of the research was the transferability and applicability of industrial norms for environmental protection in the service sector. Within the framework of this research and development project, Victoria implemented an environmental management system and had it validated by the EC Eco-Management and Audit Scheme (EMAS). This made Victoria the first insurance company in Europe to do so.

ERGO and Victoria have also shown responsibility in dealing with resources through the use of energy in their administrative buildings. One will look in vain for air conditioners in the offices of their headquarters in Victoriaplatz. The newer buildings employ double façades with openable windows for indoor climate regulation. In the approximately 110-meter-tall high-rise, which already dominates the view of the building ensemble from a distance, cooling ceilings with circulating water are used to air-condition the complex.

More than sixty percent of the electricity and heating requirements are now covered by the company at the main administration headquarters in Düsseldorf with a combined heat and power plant (CHP), thanks to which the building's CO_2 emissions were reduced by about 26,700 tons of CO_2 per year in comparison with similar buildings without a CHP. This reduction corresponds to the average annual CO_2 emissions of roughly 2,700 single-family homes. Additional heating needs are covered by environmentally compatible space heating, while the rest of the electricity needs are met by the purchase of certified "eco-electricity."

The importance that this subject will have in the future is demonstrated by the current data of the international real estate surveyors, the Royal Institution of Chartered Surveyors (RICS). According to their calculations, forty percent of the world's anthropogenic carbon dioxide is emitted by buildings. This fact places the onus on large companies to engage in sustainable building practices.

The administrative headquarters of ERGO and Victoria is now to be augmented by another new building. The plans designed by HPP are characterized by an architectonic concept that is completely integrated into the urban developmental environment and neighborhood of the former Golzheimer cemetery. The design envisions a construction comprised of individual structural shells that are connected to each other with great transparency by large glass halls. The building concept features high-quality, as well as energy-efficient, office space and thereby connects practical user value, ecology, and aesthetics in a harmonious way. In addition, the new building, which is being built on a former parking lot, will make a valuable contribution to the geological cycle in the city after it is erected. If one compares the biotope type of the previous parking lot use with what is currently planned for the building, there will be a 5,200-point increase of the area's ecological value due to the removal of the parking lot's asphalt surface. This corresponds to a sixty-six percent rise in the biotope value.

For many years, Victoria has professed a gentle handling of the environment. The firm has embedded its basic principles of sustainable company policy in a binding environmental outline: "The Victoria organization is committed to environmentally sensitive, sustainable development. We promote measures that protect the environment, in order to maintain it for the generations to come. According to our tradition as a service organization, we strive to prevent and protect against damage, in order avoid a negative environmental impact." With this sense of responsibility in mind, we will also continue to develop the administrative headquarters in Düsseldorf, and in so doing, make a real contribution to sustainable urban development.

Dr. Daniel von Borries is a board member of the ERGO Insurance Group.

Paths through the Worlds of Reading

Willi Fährmann on the Krefeld Media Library

"Fritz Ott is an educated man," said my father, when the subject of our house barber was brought up. When I was a child, house barbers were men who presumed to be able to cut hair. Mr. Ott came to us once every two weeks on Friday evening. He charged only twenty-five pfennigs per cut. Other house barbers charged fifty pfennigs. Those who could afford to went to the barbershop where they had to put seventy-five pfennigs on the counter, which was, by the way, approximately the hourly wage of a craftsman at the time. Since Mr. Ott charged an unbeatable sum, five men from our apartment building regularly assembled for the haircutting evening in our kitchen.

There was, however, another reason that moved these men to miss the appointment seldom. My father worked as a machinist in the König brewery. It was a known fact that the brewery workers were not paid a full wage in marks and pfennigs, but that a part of their wage was paid in kind. As a consequence, my father regularly brought home six half-liter bottles of beer. On the aforementioned Fridays, the men who came over could enjoy one or two glasses of the delicious beverage "on the house," and with a choice of pils, alt, or export! Mr. Ott, for his part, received a bottle of beer for every freshly barbered head. I was glad that I was always the first object of his labors, because he always became more and more creative with each successive head of hair. Some of the men thus went home with rather adventuresome haircuts, which were not always appreciated by their wives, but no one wanted to miss out on the opportunity to save a considerable number of pfennigs twice a month.

One evening, Mr. Ott saw me browsing through the one book that I owned, which my Aunt Mimi had given me for my birthday. The picture book began with the following sentence: "I hate to say it, poor little pig, but you won't live long or dance a jig." The pig was turned into sausage on the last page. Was it perhaps an early work of nonfiction? Mr. Ott looked at the book and shook his head, saying nothing. But on the next haircut Friday he brought a book covered in black paper with a yellow number written on the spine. "Read this," he said, "but it is only borrowed. Be careful with it. If you like it, I'll have a surprise for you in two weeks."

I read it feverishly. The book was called *Kai in a Box*. I liked it so much! Mr. Ott was happy. "Where did you get that wonderful book?" I asked him.

"I am the director of the library across from the church on Flotten Street. I'm a volunteer! The library is open on Wednesdays and Sundays. If you want, you can borrow books there. It costs just 5 pfennigs."

I went to the library that very day. I was a little afraid. It was a long, rather dark room divided along its length by a narrow counter with a bookcase behind it that reached all the way to the ceiling. Books, books, and more books, all bound in black. It was my first visit to a library. I went there so often in the years that followed that the doe-eyed woman dressed in dark colors who was responsible for the children's books, Miss Bia Hüger, soon got to know me. She even called me by my first name, although she addressed all the other children, as well as the teachers from the school, by their family names. She sensed that I was developing a close relationship with books.

With all the other children, Miss Hüger put three books on the counter for them to choose from, but she always asked me what I wanted. Of course, she also said to me, "Willi, you have to read this." And I did. And even if I did not like the book she had recommended, I never dared to say so.

My parents observed my growing passion for reading with limited enthusiasm. In spite of this, however, my father read a few pages to me almost every day, sometimes even from his own reading material. The melodiousness of his voice allowed me to ignore the fact that I did not understand much of what I heard.

The high point in my world of letters always happened during Advent. That was when Mr. Ott would bring a large leather bag full of books that, for whatever reason, had been removed from the library inventory. He would later leave with a bag full of beer. He bartered literature for beer. My father made a little bookcase of light-colored wood and hung it in the kitchen next to the kitchen cabinet.

I especially remember one particular evening with Mr. Ott. The barber had come earlier than usual. This time he had brought *two* bags full of books. He gave them to my father with a conspiratorial remark: "Paul, don't tell anyone about these. They are great books, but their authors are ones that Hitler doesn't like, so they have been banned. They started to be burned, so now they can't be kept in the library. Paul, put them away where no one can find them, or else you can get into trouble."

My mother put them way in the back of the clothes closet, but she was still afraid that someone would discover them. Once, when she made the suggestion that it might be better to get rid of them, my father said gruffly, "Fritz Ott is an educated man, Franziska. He thinks these books are good, so they'll stay where they are." My mother drummed into me, "Don't tell anyone a word about them, Willi. Not at school, not to your friends . . . Not one word! Do you hear me?" I had heard indeed, but I had not understood.

I sometimes ask myself whether I would have become a lifelong reader without father's beer, Mr. Ott, and the Flotten Street library. And then I stand in a library in some town or city, where I have gone to do a reading from one of my books, and I am amazed. Everything is completely different in the libraries of today. They are sometimes captivating, beautiful, clear, well-lit structures, both inside and out. They can be wonders of architecture, as is true of the new Media Library in Krefeld. I was especially impressed by this structure's side façade. Lots of right angles. Big ones, little ones, square ones, portrait format, landscape format, like lots of pictures of books . . . Oh, yes, and the windows in this wall . . . Aren't they patches of light, like the ones in those books on the shelf that you slide out of the tightly packed row? The ones that yield those glimpses into the "magic land of literature"? Reading journeys that transport us to realms unknown, or islands of poetry in the ocean of day-to-day life? The entryway suffused with light emboldened me to draw near and enter, overcoming my initial fear.

When I stand in front of the Media Library in Krefeld, the library in Flotten Street seems like a dwarf. The rather dim reading room that I remember is the counterimage of the new building's clear, bright spaces. The books bound in black of long ago stand in stark contrast to the colorfully designed book jackets of today. The expanses of the building, with its enticing, gently inclined paths leading to its upper levels, contrast greatly with the cramped paradise of my childhood world of books.

But I also had the "educated man," Fritz Ott. Perhaps he might be an early example of the "hands-on" approach. He inspired a child in our kitchen with the desire to read. He personally opened the gates of the library to that child.

And then there was my father, who gave me a taste for texts by reading and reading out loud. My mother did, too. When she read her thirty-pfennig romance novels, which she borrowed in considerable quantities from our neighbor, she would often be so moved that tears would well up behind her thick glasses. And finally, so did my grandmother Mathilde, who was a spellbinding storyteller of tales "from long ago." Most of the time she would give in to me when I would say "Grammy, tell that one again!" Her stories often seemed to occur to her as if they were new. A few times she had to stop telling stories in order to laugh.

To be moved, to laugh and to cry, and to recognize the world, and oneself, better—all of this can happen between the covers of a book, but not without opening them. The new, wonderful library could be an important aid in making this happen, and the members of the Krefeld city council know this. They also assume that one can judge a city according to its involvement in cultural programs. I would conclude with a piece of commonplace wisdom: even the best Media Library cannot win over new readers by itself. Parents, kindergartens, schools, book dealers, neighbors, the media, and, as far as I am concerned, even one's barber, all have to do their part in encouraging people to read books.

Willi Fährmann is one of Germany's beloved, award-winning authors of children's and juvenile books.

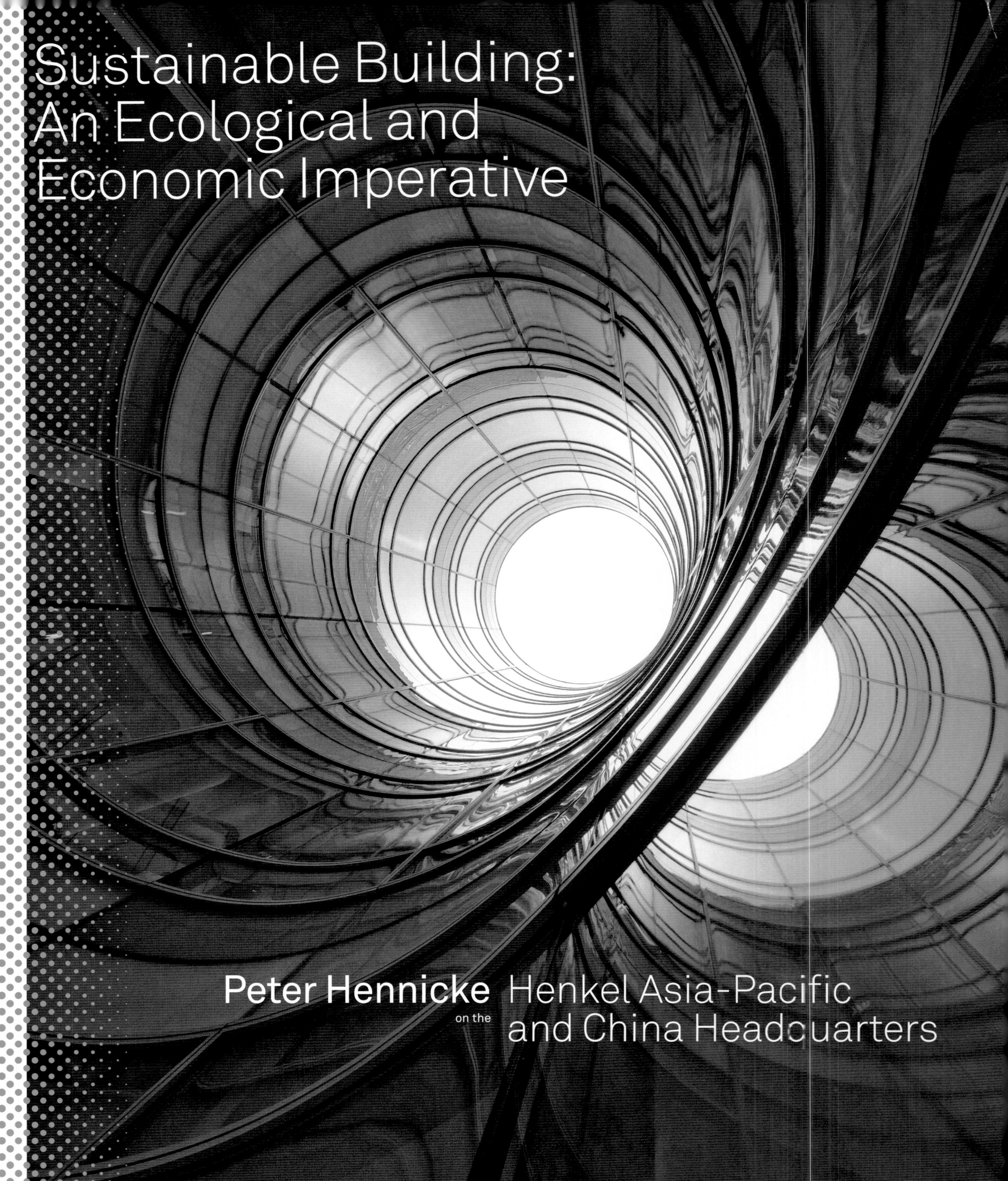

Sustainable Building: An Ecological and Economic Imperative

Peter Hennicke on the Henkel Asia-Pacific and China Headquarters

The scientific insights of the Intergovernmental Panel on Climate Change (IPCC), together with the growing empirical evidence, such as the increase in weather anomalies and resource conflicts, indicate that worldwide energy and climate politics are approaching an epochal moment of decision. With a continuation of the current trends and increasing risks of climate change, and given the increasing scarcity of resources and dependence on nuclear power, the world community could be heading for disaster. Pessimists believe that the self-destruction of humanity as a result of a "punctum saliens" in the climatic system—for instance, a seven-meter rise in sea level due to the melting of polar ice—can no longer be ruled out in the long term. As a counterreaction to this alarming perspective, a multitude of diplomatic initiatives for the protection of our climate and countless encouraging examples and activities on the part of companies, governments, and civilian organizations have been launched. These "good deeds," which still occur on an individual basis, must be "scaled up" by an intelligent political effort into an exemplary "green market" of energy efficiency and renewable energies as well as sustainable development, so that a change in outlook regarding energy and resources can be brought about.

Increasing the quality of life does not need to mean the unbridled use of natural resources if the productivity of the available resources is strategically increased by technical and social innovation. In this effort, time is the scarcest resource. If the worldwide emissions of climate-relevant gases—especially CO_2—are to be reduced by at least half in order to implement effective climate protection by the middle of this century, then the until now unchecked increase of CO_2 production must reach a high point in ten years at most and then be drastically reduced. Today, each investment that is made without reflecting on this problem when alternatives that would be less of a burden on our climate and more economical in the long term exist is therefore counterproductive and irresponsible.

This pertains to infrastructure with long investment cycles, such as power plants and the building sector, and it is especially true for populous countries such as China and India, whose enormous rates of growth lead to the construction of buildings that result in decades of excessive energy consumption and costs, including the CO_2 emissions that this kind of building generates. Every energy-inefficient new building in China or elsewhere is a missed opportunity to avoid future direct and external energy costs, which are then passed on to society.

A new scenario released by the German Federal Ministry of Economics (Germany 2008) has estimated a severe rise in oil prices from approximately 55 to 250 dollars per barrel by 2020. It is therefore a matter of interest for everyone that, through a partnership between German architectural firms and the Chinese construction business, the most modern, energy-efficient building technology be used in China. This would include the by-product of an economically dictated insurance against spikes in the cost of energy. Roland Berger estimates the current worldwide market potential for technology that protects the environment in the areas of energy efficiency, production, and storage, mobility and circular economy, water management, and efficient raw materials management at about 1,000 billion euros, and by 2020 this figure could already double. Some are talking about a "third industrial revolution" defined as the shift from the efficiency revolution to a solar energy economy. This is the first revolution in history that benefits all national economies and civil societies worldwide (except for the corporate boards of directors that profit from wasting energy), and it helps to protect the world's resources and climate with the slogan "No more oil!" In addition, it increases the security of supply, makes a contribution to crisis prevention, avoids unnecessary energy costs, creates a new quality of economic growth, and generates more areas of employment. An increase in energy efficiency is therefore indisputably the largest, cheapest, and fastest—though most often neglected—area of potential for the protection of the world's climate and resources. With a technological increase in efficiency and more intelligent management, a multiple use effect can be achieved for every kilowatt-hour of electricity and barrel of oil in the future.

Thirty to forty percent of world energy consumption occurs in buildings. With the refurbishing of energy-production facilities and efficient building technology, up to fifty percent of energy consumption can be avoided. An emerging trend suggests that by 2050 private buildings worldwide will be responsible for the release of 2.1 gigatons of carbon, with commercial buildings accounting for 1.7 gigatons of that total. On the other hand, by employing currently available energy-efficiency measures in the building sector, up to forty percent of these emissions could be avoided by 2050 (IPCC 1996).

In 2000, China used about 130 Mtce (Mega Tons of Coal Equivalent, or million tons of carbon units) for heating in its cities. This represents a tremendous burden, not only for the global climate, but also for China's citizens and environment. According to a scenario calculation (Suding 2004), with current Chinese methods of construction this value could grow by 2015 to 450 Mtce, a 3.5-fold increase. By simply deploying conventional energy-efficiency technologies rigorously, the rise could be limited to 2.5 times. The application of low-energy or passive housing standards in China would lead to even greater energy efficiencies: "If one takes into account the high solar heat gain in the winter in northern China, then passive solar energy houses (i.e., low- or even zero-energy houses) in China are even more promising than in northern or central Europe, where they are already in commercial use (Suding 2004)."

Because of demographic, social, and political pressure to build new houses as fast as possible and because of a multitude of limitations—for instance, a lack of capital or information, the unavailability of life-cycle cost analysis, minimal quality standards, or the unavailability of technologies—the energy-efficiency of new buildings in emerging and developing economies is very low. Very often the cheapest start-up investment is used as the basis for decisions, but due to rising energy prices, such decisions can become very expensive. About half of the stock of public buildings in China was erected between 1990 and 1998, as a rule with low energy efficiency. It is all the more important that the current, most modern building standards be exported to China in cooperation with European architectural firms. This pertains especially to the kinds of high-quality building technologies and optimized heating, cooling, and lighting systems that were used in the Henkel office and laboratory building in Shanghai. This project represents one of the "good deeds" that set the example.

Dr. Peter Hennicke is the former president of the Wuppertal Institute for Climate, Environment, and Energy.

The Rheinhallen: A Monument to Time

Hans-Werner Zawisla on the Cologne Rheinhallen

The Cologne Rheinhallen had already existed for an astounding eight decades when the decision was made a few years ago to discontinue their use for fairs and build new halls for this purpose at another location. The successful use of the older facility for large national and international fairs for eighty years was only made possible by its continuous adaptation to the needs of the exhibitors and their products. In this regard, the building decisions were made on the basis of technical requirements and exhibition strategy, thus making architectural ambitions play only a secondary role. If one considers the facility's interior design of 1922–24 to be successful, what was lost in design quality over the years was not due just to the destruction caused by the war. The halls' façades were less than convincing from the start, and although they were sculpturally touched up, they were still known as "Adenauer's stables," the "festively draped factory plant," and an "all-too-hasty product of inflation."

From an architectural and urban planning standpoint, the buildings measured up to the standard set by the community of the old trade city for the large utility buildings across from the city's downtown. This architecture had rapidly become out of date, and on the occasion of the international press exhibition in 1928, it was supposed to be replaced by a design appropriate to the overall significance of the city featuring the new objectivity that was a sign of the times.

The director of the municipal office of structural engineering, Adolph Abel, designed a new mantle for the entire complex: a seven-meter-high circumferential ring of arcades strung with vertical elements and a conspicuous, slender corner tower capped by a lantern. The tower, the approximately kilometer-long façade made of abutments with two-colored facing masonry around the steel supports, and the forecourt, standing out prominently from the flat roof and also redesigned by Abel, were the hallmarks of the Cologne exhibition halls' familiar image. It was considered important to maintain this appearance not only as a document of economic history and commercial architecture, but also as a reminder of the halls' wartime use for deportation and imprisonment.

The reconstruction of the buildings, almost ninety percent of which were destroyed during the war, had not ultimately threatened the elaborate façade. Much had changed on the fairgrounds since the end of the war. The façade, tower, and forecourt had survived. The architects from HPP undertook their task in the spirit of Abel's idea of a circumferential ring and executed it accordingly. Aside from the recessed one to two new stories, nothing had to be mantled. The outer mantle was already in place, and the inner structure was to be arranged and designed so that the idea of the mantle with its accents on the south and north sides also retained its functional meaning. Through the north-south alignment of the day-lit middle axis, the building wings' placement at right angles, and the connection of these to Abel's circumferential ring, a building of superior quality was created, one which followed the guidelines of the historical façade and at the same time offered attractive contemporary settings within the ring. Abel's mantle architecture had now been infused with a rigorously planned and ambitiously designed content, thereby creating an opportunity for the facility to distinguish the right side of the Rhine, hopefully for many decades to come. If investors and users should indeed develop an idea for how to put to use the tower—which seems doomed to a conspicuously wallflower-like existence—and not just view it as an advertising pylon, then the future of the landmark would be secured. The reactivation of the high lantern's beam of light in the Cologne night sky could be achieved with relatively little effort and could become the finishing touch of the successful feat of reconstituting Cologne's Rheinhallen while preserving a building that is very significant for the history of our city.

Dr. Hans-Werner Zawisla is the assistant curator of the landmark commission of Cologne.

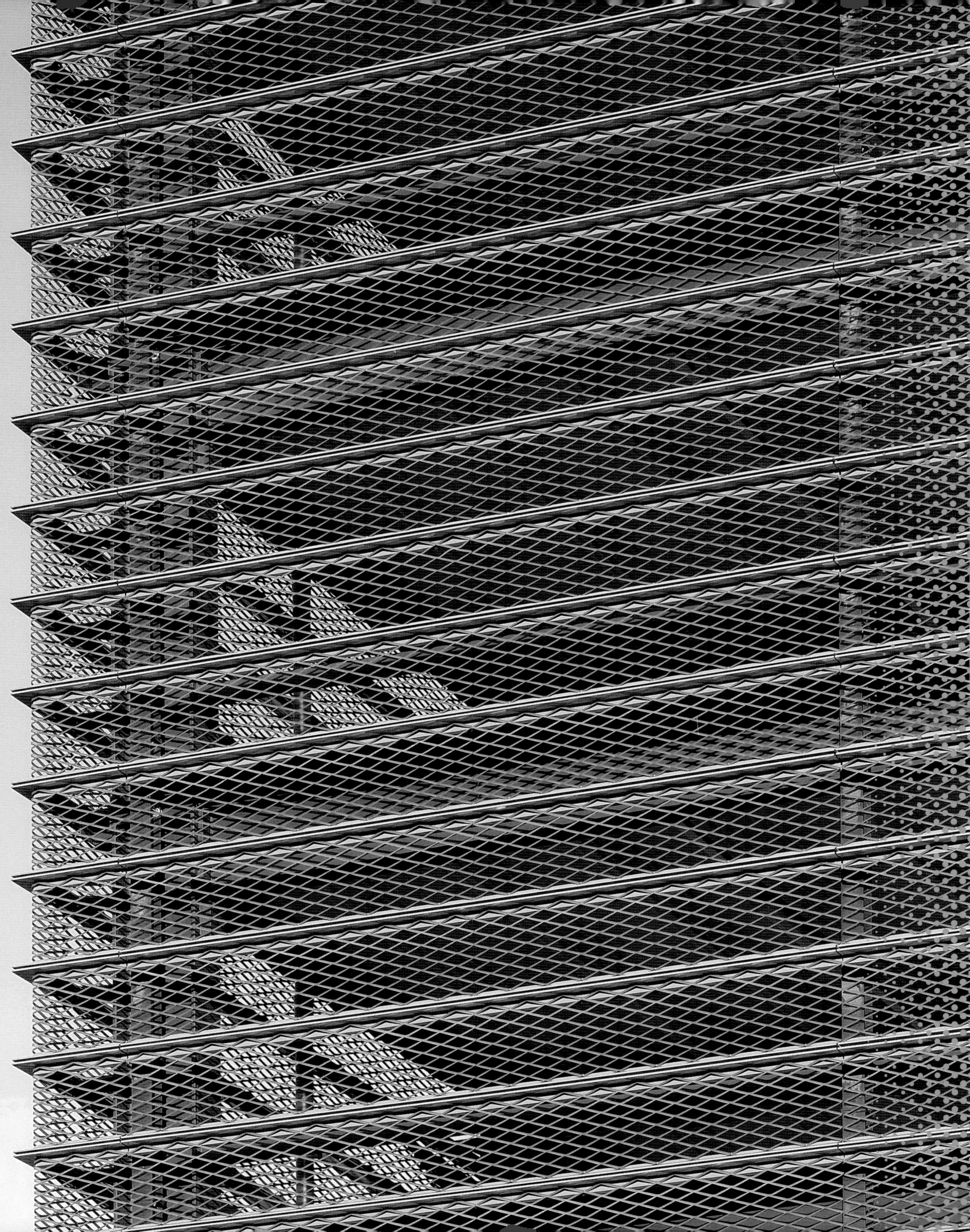

HPP is a seventy-five-year-old architectural partnership that is now led by the fourth generation of successors to its founder, Helmut Hentrich. The basis for the perpetuation of the firm beyond Hentrich's own lifetime was the transfer of power by Hentrich and his partner, Hubert Petschnigg, to the second generation in 1974. The cornerstones and the spirit of the contract concluded at that time are still valid in an almost unchanged form today. An organizational framework is the basis for a freedom of work based on the trust of each individual partner as well as of his or her team. From an organizational point of view, the collaboration and division of labor of the partners occurs within clear guidelines, whereby the continuous renewal of personnel at the leadership level has top priority. This means that although HPP is still a young architectural firm today, it has at its disposal immense knowledge and a uniquely rich treasure-house of experience. HPP is currently working with more than 250 employees in eight office locations in Germany and three offices in eastern Europe and Asia.

Over the course of the last decades, we have successfully dealt with the planning of a multitude of different building projects of all sizes. The current emphases of our work in Germany are in the areas of office and administration, retail, sports, health, hotel and recreation, and traffic management; on an international level, they are the urban development of entire districts and the design of multifunctional complexes. In addition to the planning of new buildings, working with preexisting structures is gaining in significance. As with new buildings, we are in a position to provide all architectural services, from the first sketch to the modern adaptation of a building that is already ready to be occupied. Lead consulting, or offering the full gamut of planning services under one roof, has been playing an ever greater role in recent years.

We see, however, that in a planning process that is becoming ever more complicated due to technological and social developments, the fields of architecture, design, and urban planning are increasingly merging with one another, and the professional self-consciousness and autonomy that had developed in the past are losing their validity. Therefore, solutions that are viable over time can only arise if all subjects have been addressed and combined in a dynamic system at the very beginning of the creative process. The requirements of maximum energy efficiency and the protection of resources have placed the highest priority on the development of holistic concepts of technology. Our goal over the middle term is to become a system provider by acquiring our own competencies.

While one can choose to put down a book or refuse to watch a film, we are constantly in the midst of buildings and cities whether we want to be or not. Our ever-expanding megacities are literally engulfing us, and this complicates the responsibilities of architects by obliging them to operate in a multitude of design and planning fields all at once. More than 2,000 years ago, Vitruvius had already determined that the architect must practice two professions at once, those of the artist and the engineer. Duality thus becomes a driving force of our creativity at HPP: rationality and emotion, ecology and economics, homogeneity and contrast, form and function, order and chaos, manageability and beauty. These are all apparent contradictions, but their rapprochement effectively stimulates ideas, without which good architecture—and, therefore, sustainable architecture—cannot be created.

The working out of ideas and the definition of content are some of our most important tasks. The right execution has never helped improve a concept that was wrong to begin with. The content is carried forward and introduced in dialogue. In the process, social, cultural, and legal aspects are placed on the table, as are the particular circumstances of the location, and the question and function of technology. Of equal importance are the subjects of management, cost, and deadlines, with excellence, of course, always remaining the top priority. Ultimately, the quality of this dialogue determines the nature of our products and, thereby, the quality of the spaces in which move about every day.

HPP's architectural language is determined by a nondogmatic handling of numerous issues of content, such as a building project's function, urban context, typology, history, etc. Fostering an easy recognition of our work is not our goal. It is much more important to us that each building becomes a unique specimen with its own design and personality. If the context demands the "healing" of a delicate urban development situation, as in the case of the Breidenbacher Hof, a "commerce-enhancing" project results. If a location must first be created, then a striking, typologically innovative, and materially autonomous building is created, as in the case of the Santander Consumer Bank Building. If, on the other hand, a location offers the opportunity to create something that cannot be repeated, then buildings such as the bamboo-covered parking garage at the Leipzig Zoo become possible. Despite their differences, all of them are HPP works. The element that unifies them is that their respective designs demonstrate a common striving for typological clarity and an integrity of detail and materials, thus ensuring their ability to age with dignity without sacrificing functionality and architectural quality.

Many HPP buildings have even achieved the status of brand-name products. While in the past such a status was defined by a project's typological clarity, architectural quality, productivity, longevity, and sustainability in terms of urban development, today and in the future our architectural works must also be functionally flexible, energy efficient, and frugal in their use of resources. Due to this approach, many HPP buildings have already become modern classics. Some have even been placed under landmark protection, not because they are timeless, but because they are permanently contemporary.

So how does architecture come into being at HPP? It all begins as an idea or concept. After this there is a multitude of analytic processes to be run through, questions to answer, and feelings to sort out. In order to define a common goal and then steer a project in the right direction we make use of the relevant task-specific concepts. These then condense into a model and, finally, into a story.

The present publication does not only document a selection of our recent projects. Instead, in its way, it is a likeness of our architectural approach to our work. This book takes up important subjects of our architecture exemplarily, especially the issues of architectural project models and the design concept of duality. At the end of the book, we have let guest authors say something about our buildings. These are all people who not only are public figures, but also have very personal connections to the buildings they discuss. It is true that we at HPP build not for ourselves, but for companies, organizations, and public entities—in fact, we do what we do for the benefit of communities and individuals. As a unifying element, the graphic concept of the book mimics or echoes the demands we make of our architectural works at HPP. It lends the book a little bit of sovereignty, and this, in turn, makes the book itself another HPP project.

The History of HPP

1935 Helmut Hentrich opens an architecture office.

1935 Helmut Hentrich and Hans Heuser found the architecture firm.

1953 With the early death of Hans Heuser, the consortium is continued under the leadership of Hubert Petschnigg.

1969 By taking on of new partners, the firm is now called HPP Hentrich-Petschnigg & Partner.

1971 HPP Bau- und Projektmanagement GmbH is founded.

1972 The partnership is transformed into a limited commercial partnership.

1974 The direction and liability of the firm is transferred to Hans Joachim Stutz and Rüdiger Thoma. Helmut Hentrich and Hubert Petschnigg continue their work at HPP as part of the firm's management.

1977 HPP International Planungsgesellschaft mbH, which is devoted to increasing the firm's foreign activities, is founded.

1985 Michael Zotter joins the firm's management.

1995 HPP Laage & Partner Planungsgesellschaft mbH, which specializes in the construction of hospitals, is founded.

1997 Helmut Hentrich and Hubert Petschnigg transfer their advisory capacities to Hans Joachim Stutz and Michael Zotter. Hubert Petschnigg dies at the age of 84.
Joachim H. Faust along with Hermann Henkel becomes a general partner of the firm's management.
HPP Service GmbH is founded.

2001 Dr. Helmut Hentrich dies at the age of 95.

2002 Gerhard G. Feldmeyer becomes a general partner and assumes direction of HPP KG together with Hermann Henkel and Joachim H. Faust.

2005 Hermann Henkel joins the advisory board of the company.

2007 The partnership becomes a GmbH + Co. KG (limited liability company and limited commercial partnership) with managing partners Joachim H. Faust and Gerhard G. Feldmeyer and partners Gerd Heise, Remigiusz Otrzonsek, Werner Sübai, and Volker Weuthen.
The firm's headquarters are moved to the Düsseldorf Media Harbor.

Range of Services

Urban Planning, Lead Consulting, Landscape Planning, Architecture, Interior Design, Construction Management, Reconstruction, Revitalization, Historic Preservation, Organizational Planning, Art Consulting, Model Building

Building Typologies

Office and Administration Buildings, Shopping Centers, Residential Buildings, Hotels, Hospitals, Stadiums and Arenas, Cultural Buildings, Teaching and Research Buildings, Transportation Buildings, Industrial Buildings, Banks, Computing Centers, Penitentiaries

Partners

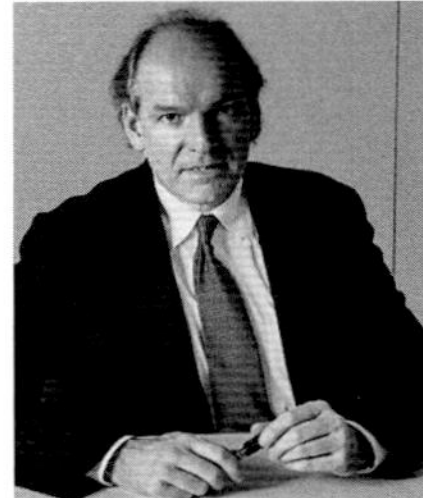

Joachim H. Faust
M.A. in Architectural Engineering
Managing partner of HPP Hentrich-Petschnigg & Partner GmbH + Co. KG
Director of HPP International Planungsgesellschaft mbH

Faust was born in 1954 in Mainz and studied architecture at the Technische Universität in Berlin and the Rheinisch-Westfälische Technische Hochschule in Aachen. In the 1980s he received a grant to study in the U.S., where he also received a Master's degree in architecture at Texas A&M University. After working in the offices of Skidmore, Owings & Merrill (Houston and New York) and Eggers / Kohn, Pedersen, Fox (New York) he came to HPP, where he began as director of the Frankfurt office and of which he became a limited partner in 1994. Faust has been a member of HPP's general management since 1997.
Faust has published in professional publications and speaks on subjects concerning architecture and interior design. In 2002 he was awarded the Distinguished Alumni Award by Texas A&M University.
He is a member of the Association of Architects in Hessen and the German Academy for City and Regional Planning.

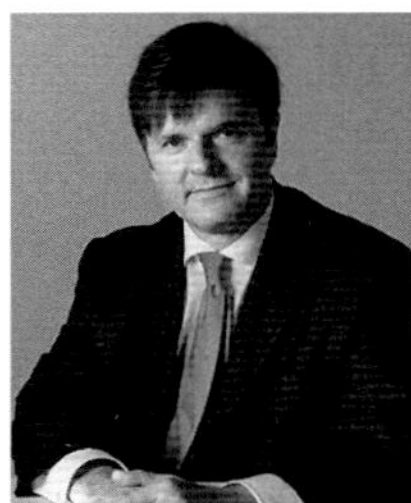

Gerhard G. Feldmeyer
Degree in Architectural Engineering
Managing partner of HPP Hentrich-Petschnigg & Partner GmbH + Co. KG
Director of HPP International Planungsgesellschaft mbH
Director of HPP Laage & Partner Planungsgesellschaft mbH

Feldmeyer was born in 1956 in Aalen. He studied architecture at the university in Stuttgart and the London South Bank University. In the 1980s he worked in the office of Kikutake Architect & Associates in Tokyo and in the office of Gerkan, Marg und Partner in Hamburg. He has been at HPP since 1989, where he began by heading the Hamburg and Berlin offices. Since 2002 Feldmeyer has been a member of HPP's general management.
Feldmeyer occupied a teaching position in the faculty of architecture at Nippon University in Tokyo, regularly gives guest lectures, and has published books and magazine articles. Among his publications are *The New German Architecture* and *HPP Hentrich-Petschnigg & Partner 1988 – 1998*. Feldmeyer is a member of the BDA and the Hamburg Association of Architects.

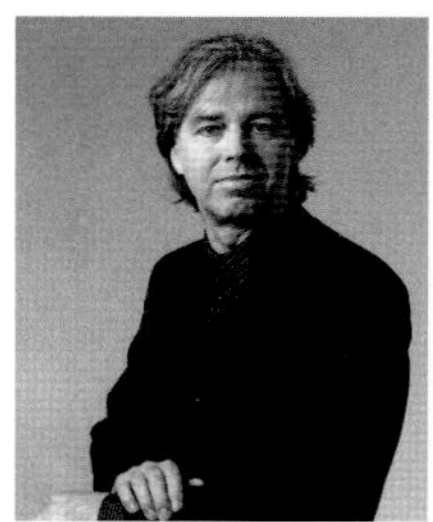

Gerd Heise
Degree in Architectural Engineering
Partner

Heise was born in 1953 in Oberhausen. After completing his architecture studies at the Polytechnic Institute in Cologne, he went to the Max Planck Institute of Art History and the Biblioteca Hertziana in the Palazzo Zuccari, both in Rome. He started work for HPP in 1980, first as a project director and then as the director of the HPP offices in Leipzig and Hamburg. In 1994 Heise became a limited partner of HPP. Today he directs the HPP office in Leipzig as a partner.
Heise is a member of the BDA and the Association of Architects in Saxony.

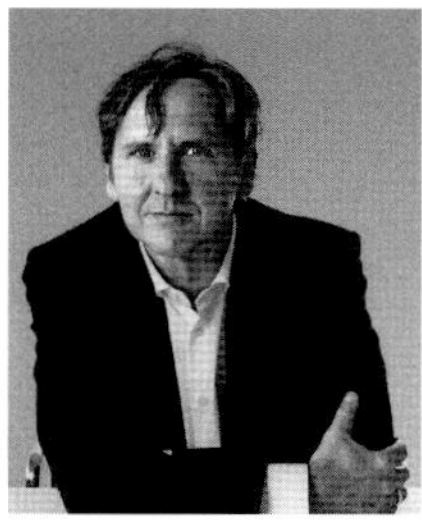

Remigiusz Otrzonsek
Degree in Architectural Engineering
Partner

Otrzonsek was born in 1962 in Breslau, Poland. He completed his architectural studies at the Technische Hochschule in Breslau and the Rheinisch-Westfälische Technische Hochschule in Aachen. At the beginning of the 1990s, he worked in the office of JSK. He came to HPP in 1992. Since 1999 he has directed the Cologne office and been a project partner, and he became a partner of HPP in 2007.
Otrzonsek is a member of the Association of Architects in North Rhine-Westphalia.

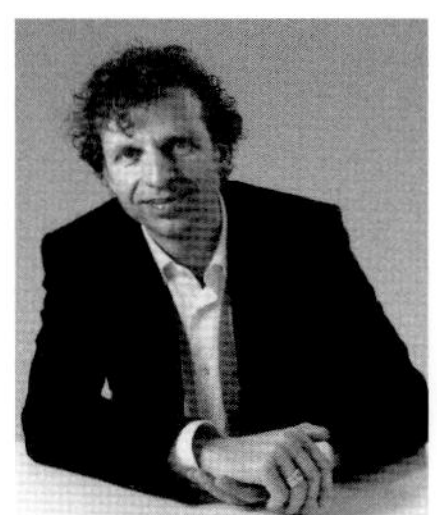

Werner Sübai
Degree in Architectural Engineering
Partner

Sübai was born in 1962 in Düsseldorf. He completed his architectural studies at the Bergische University in Wuppertal. After working in the office of Overdieck and Petzinka in the 1980s, he came to HPP in 1989, where he has worked as a project partner since 1999 and as an associate in the Düsseldorf office since 2008. Since the 1990s he has been chiefly responsible for monitoring the growth markets of China and eastern Europe.
Sübai is a member of the Association of Architects in North Rhine-Westphalia.

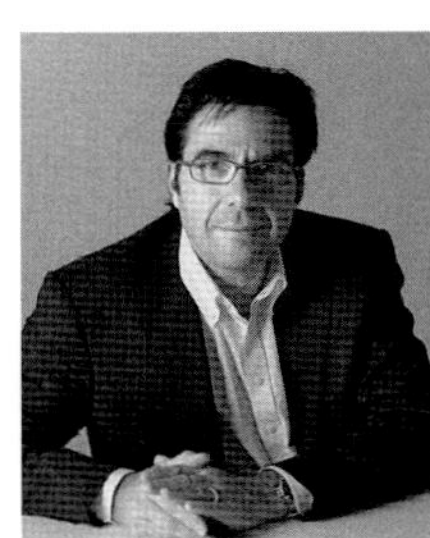

Volker Weuthen
Degree in Architectural Engineering
Partner

Weuthen was born in 1957 in Mönchengladbach and studied architecture and city planning at the Rheinisch-Westfälische Technische Hochschule in Aachen. His undergraduate thesis was awarded the Hochschule's Springorum Prize in 1985. He worked in the offices of HPP and JSK until 1992 and directed an architect's partnership in Hagen with Jürgen Bahl. In 1992 he went to HPP's Düsseldorf office, first as a project director and then as a project partner from 2000. Weuthen has been a partner of HPP since 2007.
Weuthen is a member of the Association of Architects in North Rhine-Westphalia.

Thomas Becker
Degree in Civil Engineering
Project Partner

Becker was born in 1958 in Arnsberg. He completed his civil engineering studies at the Westfälische Wilhelms-Universität in Münster. He has worked for HPP since 1987 in the area of site coordination.
He was in the Leipzig office from 1993 to 1999 and has been a project partner in the Hamburg office since 2001.

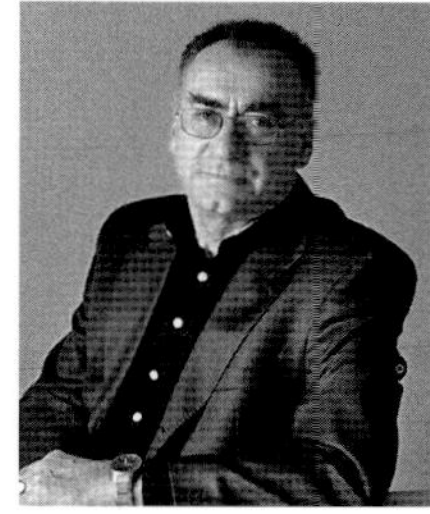

Günter Kus
Degree in Architectural Engineering
Project Partner

Kus was born in 1943 in Knittelfeld, Austria, and studied architecture at the Technische Universität in Graz. He has worked for HPP since 1971.
From 1989 he was a project partner in the Düsseldorf office, and beginning in the mid 1990s he became specialized in the area of stadium construction.
Kus is a member of the Association of Architects in North Rhine-Westphalia.

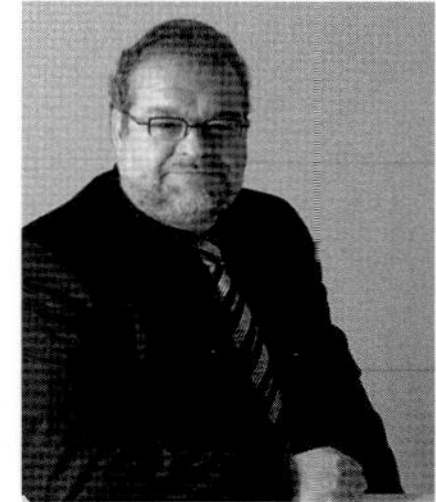

Gerhard F. Müller
Graduate Architect
Project Partner

Müller was born in Leverkusen in 1953 and studied architecture at the Technische Hochschule in Cologne. He has worked for HPP since 1987 and is responsible for site coordination. In 1989 he was promoted to project director and since 1999 has been a project partner in HPP's Düsseldorf office.
Müller is a member of the Association of Architects in North Rhine-Westphalia.

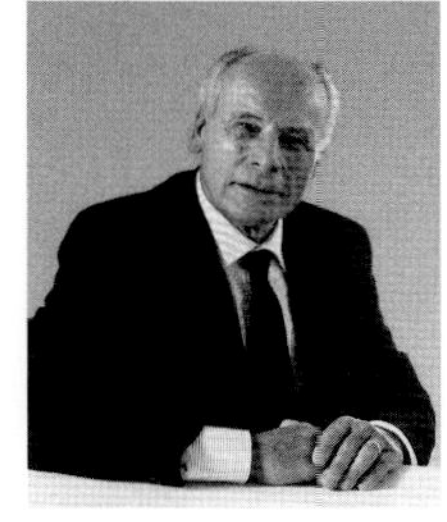

Hermann Henkel
Degree in Architectural Engineering
Advisor

Henkel was born in 1939 in Mühlhausen and studied architecture at the University of Kassel. After completing his studies he worked on the HPP planning team of the university in Bochum and then for two years for Suter + Suter in Basel. In 1969 Henkel came back to HPP as a project director. From 1974 he was a project partner and the director of the HPP offices in Duisburg and Cologne. In 1981 he was elected to the general management as an associate and directed HPP until 2005. He is now active on HPP's advisory council.
Henkel is a member of the BDA and the Association of Architects in North Rhine-Westphalia.

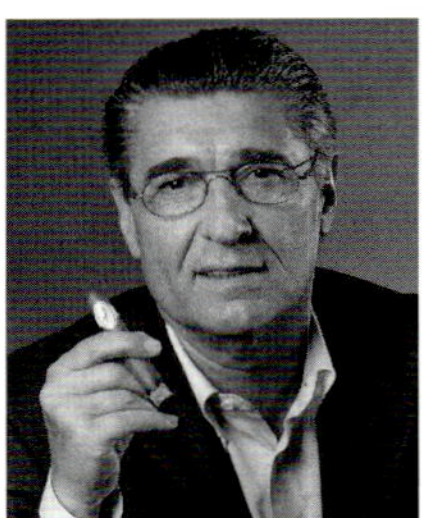

Rudi Assauer
* born in 1944 in Altenwald (Saar)
Former manager of the FC Schalke 04 soccer team
Career: Assauer signed his first contract as a soccer player in 1962 with the Spielvereinigung Herten and then went to Borussia Dortmund and SV Werder Bremen. In 1976 when he began playing for SV Werder Bremen he became the youngest National League manager in history. He went to FC Schalke 04 in 1981, managed VfB Oldenburg in 1990, and finally returned to FC Schalke 04 in 1993, where he remained until 2006.

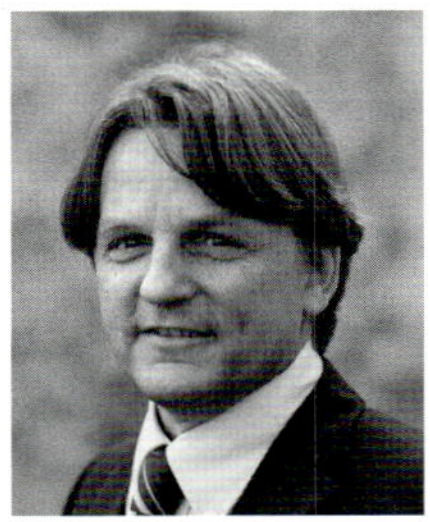

Gregor Bonin
* born in 1960 in Münster
Deputy of planning and construction for the city of Düsseldorf
Career: Bonin studied architecture in Aachen (1981–88), had a doctoral grant from the region of North Rhine-Westphalia (1988–90), and then carried out an internship (1990–92) until he completed his doctorate in 1992. From 1993 to 2004 he worked in the Düsseldorf planning office, where he became the assistant head. From 2004 to 2006 he was the head of planning, construction, transportation, and real estate management in the Düsseldorf mayor's office, and in 2006 he became deputy of planning and construction.

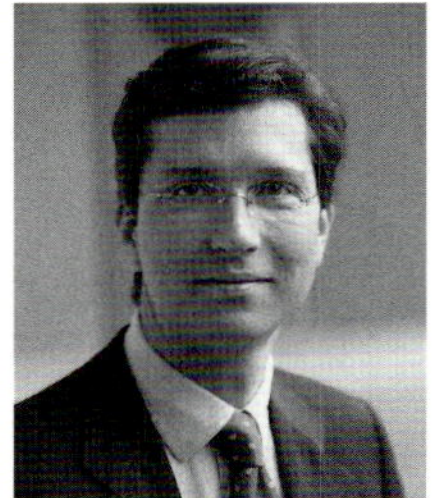

Daniel von Borries
* born in 1965 in Stuttgart
Member of the board of ERGO Versicherungsgruppe AG
Career: Borries studied banking from 1983 to 1985, and then studied economics at the University of Bonn from 1987 to 1992. From 1993 to 1998 he held different positions at Deutsche Bank AG. Since 1998 he has been with the Münchener-Rück-Gruppe, and in 2004 he joined the board of ERGO Versicherungsgruppe AG (in charge of finances and investment). Since 2007 he has also been in charge of life insurance.

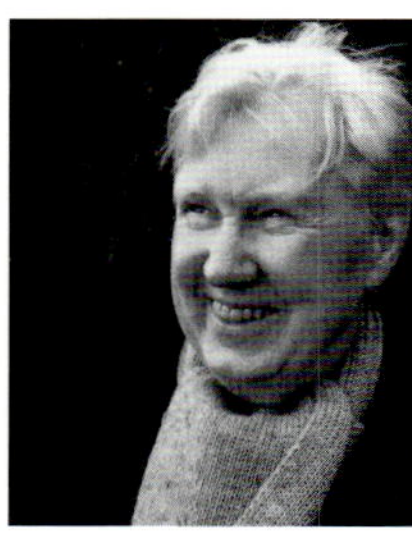

Willi Fährmann
* born in 1929 in Duisburg
Author of children's and juvenile books
Career: Fährmann learned stone masonry and studied in Oberhausen and Münster. In 1954 he became a teacher, and then later became a principal and school inspector. In 1956 he started publishing children's books, novels, and poetry.
Awards: Fährmann has received the Grand Prize from the German Academy for Children's and Juvenile Literature. In 1981 he received the German Juvenile Literature Prize, the Austrian State Prize for Juvenile Literature, and the Catholic Juvenile Book Prize. In 2000 he received the Media Prize of the History Teachers Association.

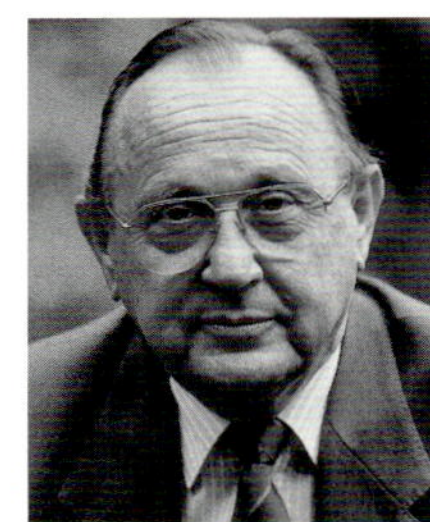

Hans-Dietrich Genscher
* born in 1927 in Reideburg, Saalkreis
Retired Federal Minister
Career: Genscher studied law and national economy in Halle and Leipzig (1946–49). He joined the FDP in 1952, and while he was a member of German Parliament from 1965 to 1998, he was the parliamentary leader of the FDP faction, the Assistant National Chairman of the FDP, Minister of the Interior, Chairman of the FDP, a member of the national executive board, and Foreign Minister of the Foreign Office and Vice Chancellor. He has been the honorary chair of the FDP since 1992 and a lawyer in Berlin since 1999. In 2000 he became the director of Hans-Dietrich Genscher Consult GmbH.
Awards: Genscher received the German Grand Cross of the Order of Merit (1980), the Grand Cross of the French Legion of Honor (1986), and the Polish and Hungarian Grand Award for Merit (1992). He also received the Order of Merit from North Rhine-Westphalia in 2007.

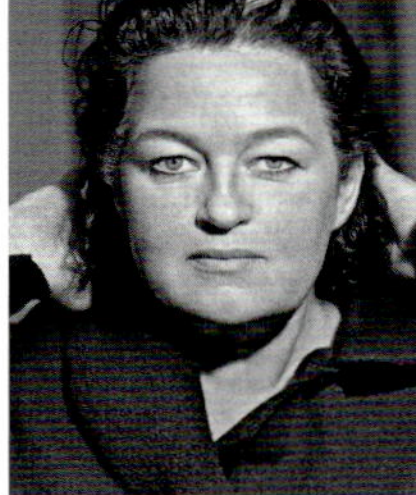

Annette Görtz
* born in 1959 in Marl
Fashion designer and founding director of Görtz-Welsch Modedesign GmbH
Career: Görtz studied fashion design at the Fachhochschule für Gestaltung & Design in Bielefeld from 1978 to 1983. In 1984 she presented her first collection under the name Görtz-Hoffmann and in 1991 founded Görtz-Welsch Modedesign with the annette görtz label. In 2001 she exhibited at the Prêt-à-Porter in Paris, and in 2006 she opened the designer boutique MILIAN.
Awards: Görtz received the Fashion Design Prize of North Rhine-Westphalia in 1995.

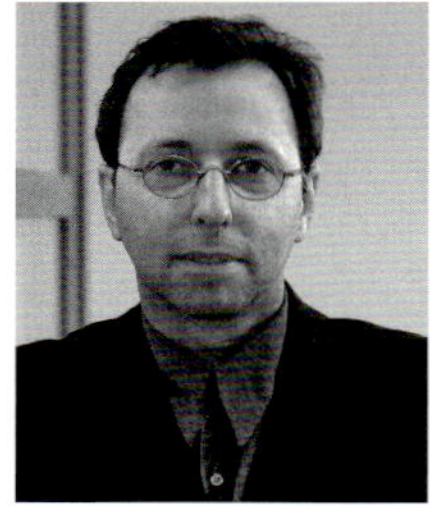

Wolfram Goertz
* born in 1961 in Mönchengladbach
Journalist, musician, and musicologist
Career: Goertz studied musicology and philosophy in Cologne and Bochum. Since 1978 he has written music and theater criticism for publications including the *Süddeutsche Zeitung* and *DIE ZEIT*. Since 1989 he has been the *Rheinische Post's* music editor and a lecturer on interpretation analysis at the Robert Schumann Hochschule, Düsseldorf. In 2005 he became a research assistant in music psychology in the St.-Franziskus Hospital in Mönchengladbach, and he will graduate from the faculty of medicine at the RWTH in Aachen in 2009.

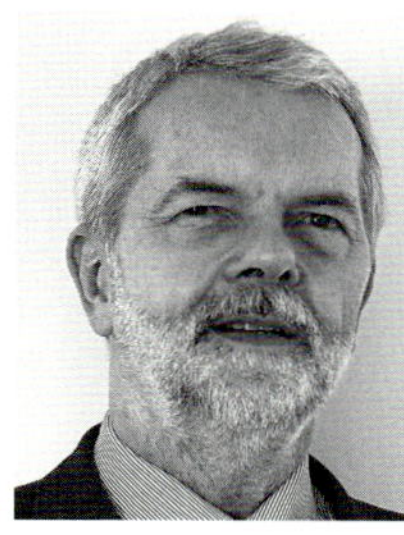

Peter Hennicke
* born in 1942 in Landsberg am Lech
Former president of the Wuppertal Institute for Climate, Environment, and Energy
Career: Hennicke studied chemistry and economics in Heidelberg (1962–70). He has since been an advisor on energy policy theory for the Hesse Ministry of Environment and Energy, a professor at the university in Wuppertal, director of the Energy Division of the Wuppertal Institute, a member of three German parliament commissions of inquiry concerned with climate and energy, and a member of the Scientific and Technical Committee (STAP) of the Global Environment Facility (GEF).

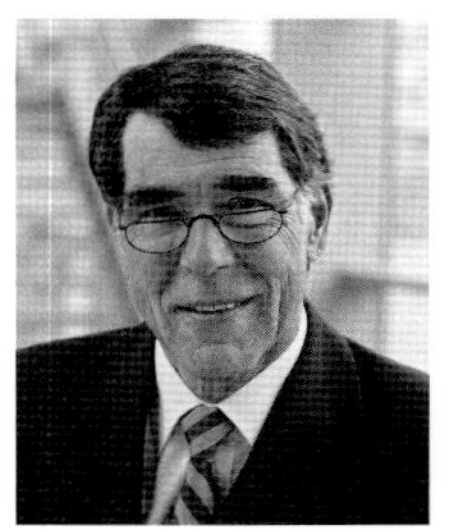

Peter Kern
* born in 1941 in Heilbronn
Member of the board of governors of the Fraunhofer Institute for Labor Economy and Organization (IAO)
Career: Kern studied machine construction, receiving his doctorate from the University of Stuttgart. He was an initiator of the "Office 21" network research project and is an honorary professor at the State Academy of Fine Arts in Stuttgart.

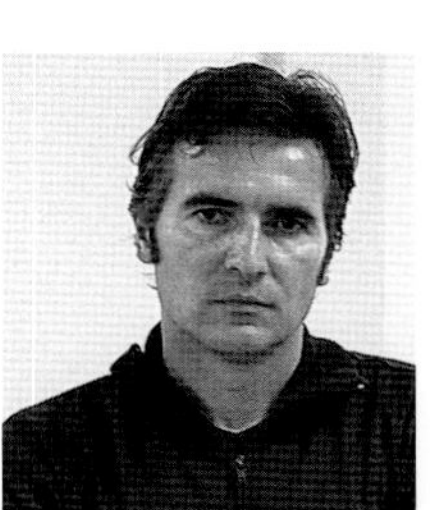

Mischa Kuball
* born in 1959 in Düsseldorf
Visual artist
Career: Kuball has been creating spatial projects since 1984. He has received artist's grants from the Alfried Krupp von Bohlen und Halbach Foundation (1991), the Kunstfonds Bonn (1996), and the Art and Culture Foundation of North Rhine-Westphalia (1997). From 2005 to 2008 he was a professor of media art at the College of Design in Karlsruhe. Since 2006 he has been a Visiting Artist Tutor at Goldsmiths College. Since 2007 he has held a chair in media art at the Art College for Media in Cologne.
Awards: Kuball has received an Ars Viva Advancement Award (1990) and an Advancement Award for Fine Art in the State of North Rhine-Westphalia (1993).

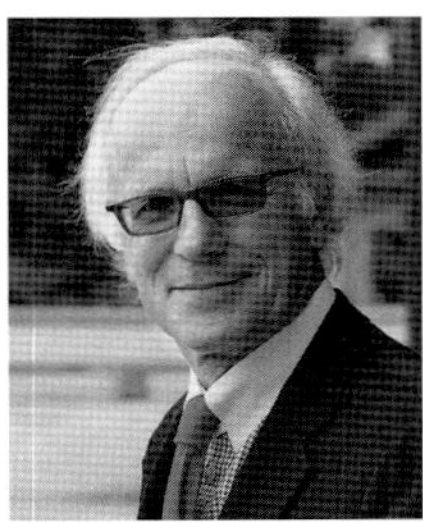

Bernd M. Michael
* born in 1942 in Dresden
Owner of the Büro für Markenarchitektur
Career: Until 2003, Michael was president of the European Association of Communications Agencies. From 2003 to 2006 he was chairman of the Grey Global Group Europe, an organization he himself founded, and he is president and longtime member of the board of GWA. Since 2008 he has also been president of the German Marketing Association.

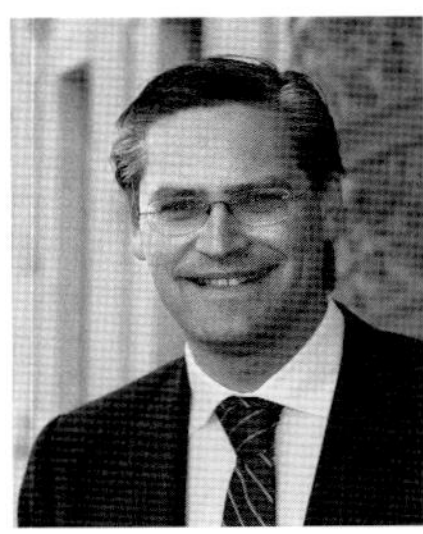

Alexander Otto
* born in 1967 in Hamburg
Chairman of management for ECE Projektmanagement GmbH & Co. KG
Career: Otto studied at Oxford, Harvard University, and Harvard Business School. Beginning in 1994 he held different positions at ECE, of which he has been chairman since 2000. He is also chairman of the Urban Land Institute Deutschland, a member of the board of the Zentraler Immobilienausschuss e.V., and an initiator of the Stiftung Lebendige Stadt.

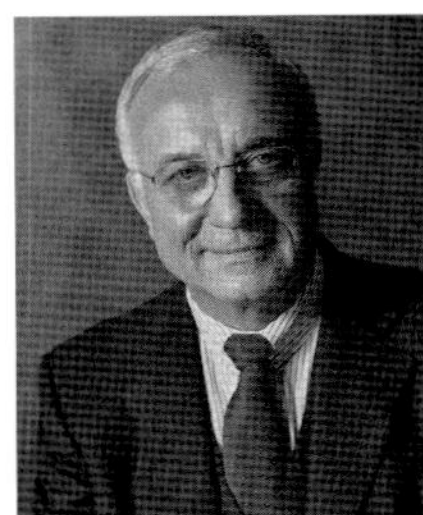

Fritz Pleitgen
* born in 1938 in Duisburg
Journalist and chairman of management of Ruhr.2010 GmbH
Career: Pleitgen has been the director of Germany's ARD studios and editor in chief at WDR Cologne. He was the director for radio and director of WDR Cologne from 1994 to 2007, chairman of ARD from 2001 to 2002, and then vice president (2002–05) and president (2006–08) of the European Broadcasting Union. Since 2007 he has been chairman of management of Ruhr.2010 GmbH.

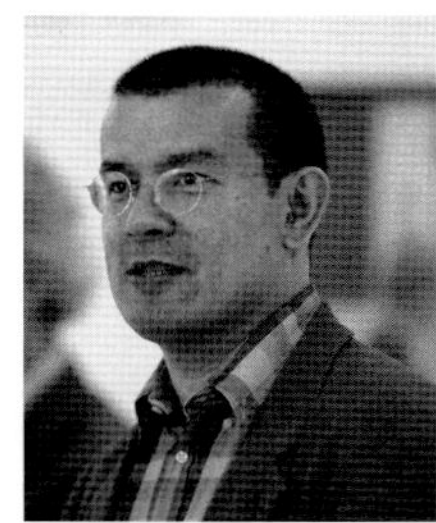

Peter Cachola Schmal
* born in 1960 in Altötting
Architect, architecture journalist, and director of the German Architecture Museum (DAM)
Career: Schmal studied architecture at the Technical University in Darmstadt and then worked at Albert Speer & Partner in Frankfurt, at Behnisch & Partner in Stuttgart, and at Eisenbach in Zeppelinheim from 1981 to 1989. From 1992 to 1997 he was a research assistant at the university in Darmstadt, and from 1997 to 2000 he lectured on design at the Fachhochschule Frankfurt. Beginning in 2000 he was the curator of DAM, of which he became director in 2006.

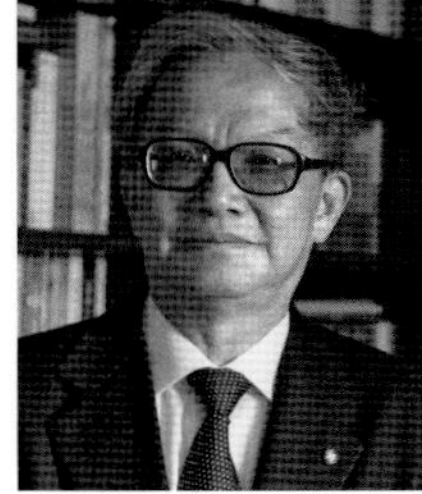

Zheng Shiling
* born in 1941 in Chengdu, Szechuan Province, China
Director of the Institute for Architecture and City Planning, Tongji University, Shanghai
Career: Zheng Shing is a member of the Chinese Academy of Sciences, has an honorary doctorate from the university in Rome, and is a member of the French Academy of Architecture and an honorary member of the American Institute of Architects. He is also an advisor to the organizational committee of EXPO 2010.

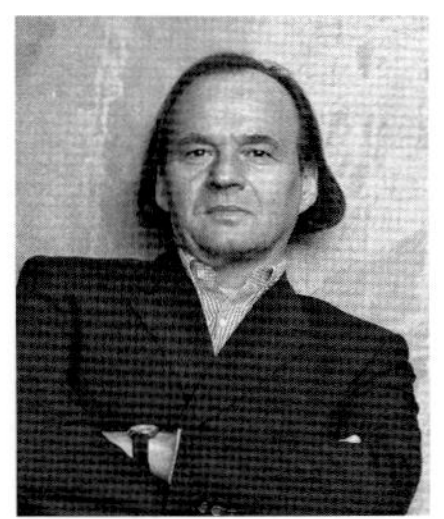

Raimund Stecker
* born in 1957 in Duisburg
Art historian and honorary professor of contemporary art at the Art Academy in Münster
Career: Stecker studied art history, philosophy, modern history, journalism, and communication in Bochum, Hamburg, and Florence. He has been a correspondent for the *Westdeutsche Allgemeine Zeitung* and the *Frankfurter Allgemeine Zeitung*, the director of the Rhineland and Westphalia Art Association. He is a founding member of the Arp Museum Bahnhof Rolandseck and publishes on twentieth-century art and architecture.

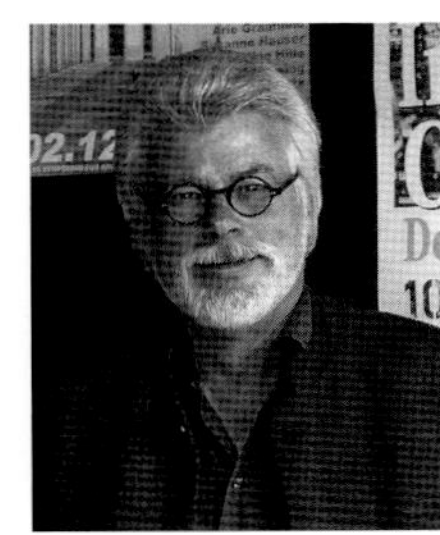

Frank R. Werner
* born in 1944 in Worms
Director of the Institute of Architectural History and Theory at the University of Wuppertal
Career: Werner graduated in architecture in 1972 from the university in Stuttgart, where he was also a scientific assistant until 1982. In 1982 he became a lecturer in architectural history at the Stuttgart Art Academy, where he became a professor of architecture and design history in 1990. In 1994 he became director of the Institute of Architectural History and Theory at the university in Wuppertal, where he later became dean of the faculty of architecture (1999–2003) and then dean of the faculties of architecture, design, and art (2005–07). He has held guest professorships in Los Angeles, Barcelona, Vienna, Mendrisio, and Milan.

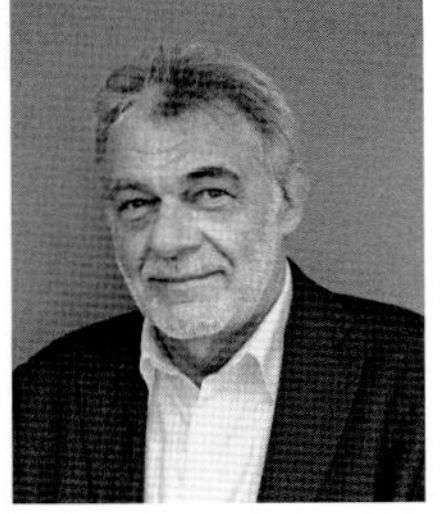

Hans-Werner Zawisla
* born in 1948 in Leverkusen
Assistant director of the office of the city conservator of Cologne
Career: Zawisla studied architecture at the RWTH in Aachen (1969–75), and then worked with Peter Neufert in Cologne, Georg von der Goltz in Bensberg, and Norbert Hilden in Cologne from 1975 to 1985. In 1982 he graduated in architectural history and since 1985 has been an employee in the office of the city conservator of Cologne.

Clients

A.T. Kearney
AachenMünchener
ABG Allgemeine Bauträger- und Gewerbeimmobiliengesellschaft
Adolf Würth
Aengevelt Immobilien
AIG Global Real Estate Investment Ltd.
ALDI
ALIDA Grundstücksgesellschaft
Allianz
Alte Leipziger
AMEC
ARCA East Investment
Archon Group Deutschland
AREAL GmbH
Arena Mannheim Besitzgesellschaft
ARGOMEX
Armani
Asata Construction Ltd.
Atisreal
Aurelis Real Estate
Außenministerium Japan
Auswärtiges Amt der Bundesrepublik Deutschland
B. Metzler seel. Sohn
Bahnhof Münster Entwicklungsgesellschaft
BAM Deutschland AG
Bankhaus Lampe
BASF
Bauwens
Bauwert
Bayer 04 Leverkusen
Bayer AG
Bayerische Immobilien AG
BBR Bundesamt für Bauwesen und Raumordnung
BEMA Unternehmensgruppe
Berufsbildungswerk Sachsen
BIG Bau-Unternehmensgruppe
Bird & Bird
BLB Dortmund
BLB NRW
Boehringer Ingelheim
Booz Allen Hamilton
Börsenverein des Deutschen Buchhandels
Bundesbaugesellschaft Berlin
Bundesbauamt Berlin
Bundesbaudirektion
Bundespräsidialamt
Calliston Gesellschaft für Projektentwicklung
Casacuberta Villamil S.L.
Central Krankenversicherung AG
Centrum Grundstücksgesellschaft
China Jiansu Repräsentanz für Investitionsberatung
Citibank
City of Dresden
City of Düsseldorf
City of Erkrath
City of Heidelberg
City of Krefeld
City of Langenfeld
City of Leipzig
City of Mannheim
City of Mönchengladbach
City of Nürnberg
City of Ratingen
City of Shanghai
City of Stuttgart
City Projektbau Leipzig
Clifford Chance
Commerzbank
Crédit Agricole
Credit Suisse
Daimler-Benz AG
DAL Deutsche Anlagen-Leasing
DB Real Estate Investment
DB Station & Service AG
DBV-Winterthur
DEFO Deutsche Fonds für Immobilienvermögen
DEGI Deutsche Gesellschaft für Immobilienfonds
Deka Immobilien Investment
DeTeBau
DeTelmmobilien
Deutsche Bahn AG
Deutsche Bank
Deutsche Bundesbank
Deutsche Rentenversicherung
Deutsche Vermögensberatung
Deutscher Herold AG
Deutscher Ring
DIBAG Industriebau AG
DIFA
Dillmann Stiftung
Diorit
DJH Rheinland e.V.
DKÖ-Objektgesellschaft Königsallee Dr. Herbert Ebertz KG
Dorint AG
Dr. Materna
Dresdner Bank AG
DUNA Mall S.R.L.
E.ON
EC Harris
ECE Projektmanagement
ECH Entwicklungs-Compagnie Heiligendamm
E-Plus
ERGO Versicherungsgruppe AG
Ernst & Young
Esch Unternehmensgruppe
Esprit
Euler Hermes Kreditversicherungs-AG
Euro-Invest KTS Ltd.
Euroland Projektierungen
Europahaus Gundstücksgesellschaft
Europäische Zentralbank
Ev.-Luth. Kirchengemeinde St. Thomas
EXPO Land Shanghai
F.A.Z.
fagus
FC Schalke 04
Flughafen Berlin Brandenburg
Flughafen Düsseldorf International
FOM Real Estate
Frankfurter Sozietätsdruckerei
Frankonia Eurobau
Freie und Hansestadt Hamburg
Freshfields Bruckhaus Deringer
FSN
Fundus Fonds-Verwaltungen
Gazprominvestarena
Generali Versicherungen
Gerling
Gewerbegrund
Goldman Sachs
Goodman
Grey Global
Gross & Partner Grundstücksentwicklungsgesellschaft
Gucci
Habarent Immobilien Marketing
Hafencity Hamburg
Handelsblatt
Hansainvest
HBM Stadien- und Sportstättenbau
Heidelberger Druckmaschinen AG
Heinrich-Heine-Universität
Hengeler Mueller
Henkel China Company Ltd.
Henkel KGaA
Henlly Enterprise Management Co. Ltd.
Hermes Kreditversicherungs-AG
HIH Hamburgische Immobilien Handlung
Hilton International
HLG Solingen
Hochbauamt Leipzig
Hochbauamt Stadt Düsseldorf
Hochtief
Hochtief Construction AG
Hochtief Projektentwicklung HTP
Hochtief Real Estate
HSBC Trinkaus & Burkhardt
HUK-COBURG
HypoVereinsbank
IDR Industrieterrains Düsseldorf-Reisholz AG
IKB Deutsche Industriebank AG
Industrie-Club e.V. Düsseldorf
infineon
Interboden
Interlace
International Property Asset Management
Intiativkreis Ruhrgebiet
IVG Development
JER Europe Fund III
Johanniterorden Balley Brandenburg
Jones Lang LaSalle
Justizministerium NRW
Karstadt
Keppel Seghers Belgium NV
Kienbaum
Klinikum der LMU München
Klöckner Werke AG
Land Nordrhein-Westfalen
Landeshauptstadt Düsseldorf
Landeshauptstadt Stuttgart
Landesregierung Düsseldorf
A. Lange & Söhne
Lanxess AG
LBB NRW
LBBW Immobilien
LEG NRW
LIXXUS Projektentwicklung
L'Oréal
Lovells Rechtsanwälte
LVM Versicherungen
Mader Capital Resources
Mannesmann
Marks & Spencer
Max-Planck-Institut
MEAG Munich Ergo
Medienstiftung der Sparkasse Leipzig
Mercedes Benz
Metro Group
Metzler Grundstücksverwaltung
mfi Management für Immobilien AG
Momeni Projektentwicklung
Multi Development Germany
N.I.C. + Partner
NPC Holding AG
Oaktree
OFB Projektentwicklung
Park-Hotel
Patrizia Projektentwicklung AG
Pearl of Kuwait Real Estate Co.
Porsche
Procter & Gamble
Prosperity Project Management
Provinzial
Quantum Immobilien AG
Redevco Service Deutschland
Rheinmetall Service
RIAG Shamrocking Immobilien
Rothenberg & Frank
Rothmann Immobilien
RTL Television
Ruhr-Universität Bochum
Sagittarius Verwaltungs- und Beteiligungsgesellschaft
Sal. Oppenheim jr. & Cie. KGaA
Santander Consumer Bank
Schauspielhaus Leipzig
Schnabel GmbH
Schweizerische Lebensversicherung und Rentenanstalt
Seeste Bau
Shanghai EVE Design
Shanghai Orient International Tendering Co. Ltd.
Siemens VDO
Signal Iduna
SITC Shanghai International Tendering Co. Ltd.
Sonae Sierra
Sparkasse
Sparkasse Essen
Sparkasse Krefeld
Stadtbauplan GmbH
Städtisches Klinikum St. Georg
Stadtsparkasse Düsseldorf
Stadtsparkasse Köln
Stadtwerke Düsseldorf
Stadtwerke Frankfurt am Main
Stadtwerke Leipzig
Stadtwerke Lüdenscheid
Stadtwerke Münster
STEAG
Stiller Immobilien
Julia Stoschek
SU 155
SWAN Property S.R.L.
Swiss Life
Techem AG
Tenkhoff Properties

The Boston Consulting Group
The Carlyle Group
Thyssen AG
ThyssenKrupp Real Estate
Thyssen Stahl
Timon Bauregie
Tishman Speyer Properties
TriGránit Development Corporation
TÜV Rheinland
Unilever Deutschland
Union Investment Real Estate AG
Universitätsklinikum Bonn
Universitätsklinikum Düsseldorf
Versicherungskammer Bayern
VfL Wolfsburg e.V.
Victoria Grundstücksverwaltungs-Gesellschaft GbR
Vivacon AG
Vivico Real Estate
Vodafone D2
Volkswagen Immobilien Service
VR Bauregie
VR-Leasing ONYX
Warburg-Henderson Kapitalgesellschaft für Immobilien
WDR
WestInvest Gesellschaft für Immobilienfonds
Westwind Capital
Witte Projektmanagement
Wohnungsbaugenossenschaft Kontakt e.V.
Wolfsburg AG
Wüstenrot
ZDF
Zechbau
Zoo Leipzig
Züblin AG

Team

Britta Albus
Fritz Altland
Sema Arda
Detlev Armeloh
Walter Auer
Philipp Aust
Matthias Bartsch
Ulrich Bast
Klaus Baudach
Martina Bauer
Meike Behmann
Melanie Behnke
Mirja Beinert
Olga Beisel
Hendrik Beller
Sandra von Berg
Claudia Berger-Koch
Eleonore Berndsen
Gabriela Bessert
Katja Bethmann
Anja Biechele
Volker Biermann
Katrin Bihler
Barbara Bitners
Sven Blau
Jasmin Bohnenkamp
Ole Bohnenkamp
Julia Bongers
Michael Braun
Götz Oliver Broichheuser
Frank Brühmann
Sandra Buff
Christa Burkhardt
Melanie Buschbell
Jan Cepek
Bing Chen
Yvonne Christensen
Claus Coumont
Alexander Deines
Birgit Dieckgreber-Kickel
Klaus Dietrich
Marion Dietrich
Vera Duell
Karin Dyck
Christoph Ebert
Nurgül Ece
Alexandra Eichenlaub
Uta Esselmann
Etel Fabriz
Philipp Forchheim
Cornelia Franke
Lothar Franzen
Richard Freitag
Andreas Friedrich
Martin Fuchs
Götz Gagelmann
Birte Gandert
Simon Gassner
Monika Gläske
Simon Glogowski
Alexander Graf
Sabine Greißinger
Martina Grobusch
Martin Gross
Elena Gutierrez
Sonja Hagl
Mahmoud Halvai
Myriam Hamdi
Stefan Haupt
Stephan Heimann
Sebastian Helm
Thomas Hengst
Eireen Herz
Martina Herzog
Sandra Heupel
Elke Heuser
Andrea Holler
Johannes Holthausen
Detlef von Homeyer
Carrie Huang
Steffen Huhn
Jens Jackowski
Karl Jacob
Stephan Jacoby
Catharina Jahn
Jürgen Jänicke
Wolfgang Janiszewski
Maria Josephine Jaspers
Edeltraud Jauster-Dorider
Jin Jing
Yuan Jing
Volker Johannsen
Marco Jungelen
Monika Jungen
Rainer Kaiser
Silke Kampen
Selma Karagöz
Faruk Karagöz
Robert Kellermann
Eva Kesting
Stefanie Kettler
Uta Kielstein
Daniela Koch
Oliver König
Axel Kostorz
Ramona Krenn
Michael Krieg
Uta Kühn
Jens-Michael Kump
Marianne Kunze
Gabriele Kurz
Jochen Lamerz
Sybille Lammann
Alexander Lebe
Christina Leder
Hann Lee
Lei Lei
Markus Leiting
Achim Leschinger
Wolfgang Liebergesell
Bingyi Liu
Zichuan Liu
Peter Loth
Hans Lotz
Petra Marx
Falko Matthäs
Dietmar Maurer
Johannes Meiners
Rainer Mende
Wolfgang Miazgowski
Brigita Mijatovic
Nadja Moche
Kun-San Moon
Karin Müller
Ines Müller
Oliver München
Petra Neuhaus
Kirsten Neumann-Kleinpaul
Uwe Neuschulz
Klaus-Dieter Noelte
Ralf Oelke
Christina Olteanu-Lissai
Ernst Pampus
Heike Pauckert-Noelte
Kathleen Perkuhn
Anke Piepenstock
Volker Poth
Zhengyu Qiu
Detlef Redeligx
Frank Reineke
Tobias Martin Reinhardt
Nathalie Rehm
Martin Reichel
Tobias Martin Reinhardt
Frank Reineke
Christoph Reischböck
Helmut Ritzki
Diana Rogasch
Claudia Roggenkämper
Anne Röttsches
Claudia-Bianca Ruoff
Ralf Rustemeyer
Hüseyin Sahin
Axel Samsel
Volker Scharfenberg
Walter Schelle
Dennis Scherer
Karen Schlömer
Doris Schmitz
Carolina Schöber
Reiner Schulz
Alfred Schwab
Katja Schweizer
Frank Schwensfeier
Joachim Schwitalla
Sebastian Seibold
Maike Seifert
Monika Senger-Wögebauer
Guerogui Siarov
Bugrahan Sirin
Marcus Sirl
Bettina Spix
Martin Stang
Claudia Stephan
Robianto Sugiri
Nina Sundermann
Barbara Taha
May Lin Tan
Astrid Temminghoff
Steffi Tennstedt
Peter Thon
Dorothee Vicario
Dietmar vom Bey
Michael Wahn
Bärbel Walger
Dominika Wallach
Qi Wang
Yu Wei
Stefan Winkelmeyr
Lars Wöhrmann
Karl Heinz Wolff
Davor Zagrajski
Alexander Zanke
Maris Zanke
Yanlai Zhou

Image Credits

Aldinger & Wolf 109
Assauer, Rudi 236 (Rudi Assauer)
avp group 193
Binsack, Gunter 55
Bolk, Florian 81
Bünten, Christoph 236 (Daniel von Borries)
Crystal Digital Technology 72, 74, 78, 104, 106, 108, 110, 113, 114 bottom, 150 bottom, 216
Dettmar, Uwe 237 (Peter Cachola Schmal)
DIGITALARCHITEKTUR 96, 99, 101
ECE 237 (Alexander Otto)
Esch, H.G. 46 top, 47, 70 top, 71 bottom, 80 bottom, 126, 128, 130, 131, 132, 133, 135, 136, 138 top, 139, 154, 155, 157, 161, 174, 176, 177, 178, 179, 181, 182, 196 top, 221, 228
Fährmann, Willi 236 (Willi Fährmann)
Fang Honghui 237 (Zheng Shiling)
Godehardt, Michael 24
Grundner, Thomas 140, 142, 145 top and bottom, 146, 149, 223
Hagemeyer, Tom 236 (Annette Görtz)
Hampel, Max 124 top
Hanisch, Manfred 22, 26, 27, 28, 29, 31, 34 top and bottom, 118, 121, 152, 159, 160 top, 196 bottom, 224
Hayden, Ken 144
Heiermann, Dorothea 237 (Hans-Werner Zawisla)
Helle, Jochen 32, 52, 202
Huthmacher, Werner 150 top
Kern, Peter 237 (Peter Kern)
Kiefer, Aloys 124 bottom
Kirchner, Jens 68, 69
Korczowski, Marek 21, 103 bottom, 160 bottom
Koslowski, Reinhard 103 top, 151
Krebs, Andreas 236 (Wolfram Goertz)
Kuball, Mischa 212, 213
Landeshauptstadt Düsseldorf 236 (Gregor Bonin)
Maus, Burkhard 237 (Raimund Stecker)
Meisen, Manos 12, 115, 172 bottom, 184 top
Michael, Bernd M. 237 (Bernd M. Michael)
moka studio 58 bottom, 173 bottom
Müller-Naumann, Stefan 46 bottom, 125 top
PUNCTUM Bertram Kober 20 bottom, 138 bottom
PUNCTUM H.Ch. Schink 20 top, 36, 38, 40, 41, 43, 44, 45, 95, 102 bottom, 172 top, 205
Rakete GmbH 59
Rehfeld, Rainer 94 bottom
Reisch, Michael 158
Riehle, Tomas 116, 120, 123, 219
Schmidt, Axel 14, 16, 17, 19, 48, 50, 53, 56, 82, 84, 86, 87, 88, 89, 91, 92, 201, 207, 215
Schulze, Helmut R. 236 (Hans-Dietrich Genscher)
Seggelke, Karen 234, 235
Strauß, Dietmar 184 bottom
Stüber, Jochen 58 top, 60, 62, 63, 64 top and bottom, 65, 67, 70 bottom, 80 top, 94 top, 125 bottom, 163, 164, 165, 166, 167, 169, 170, 173 top, 185, 208
Sumalowitsch, Bernd 35
Sumesgutner, Daniel 102 top
Universität Wuppertal 237 (Frank R. Werner)
Virtuell FORMAt 114 top
WDR 237 (Fritz Pleitgen)
Willebrand, Jens 186, 188, 189, 190, 191, 194, 231
Wrubel, Arno 197
Wuppertal Institut für Klima, Umwelt, Energie 236 (Peter Hennicke)
Yun Lee 237 (Mischa Kuball)

Edited by
HPP Hentrich-Petschnigg & Partner GmbH + Co. KG, Düsseldorf

Managing editor
Sandra Heupel

Texts
Gerhard G. Feldmeyer, Sandra Heupel, Werner Sübai

Essays
Rudi Assauer, Gregor Bonin, Daniel von Borries, Willi Fährmann, Hans-Dietrich Genscher, Annette Görtz, Wolfram Goertz, Peter Hennicke, Peter Kern, Mischa Kuball, Bernd M. Michael, Alexander Otto, Fritz Pleitgen, Peter Cachola Schmal, Zheng Shiling, Raimund Stecker, Frank R. Werner, Hans-Werner Zawisla

Assistants
Jasmin Bohnenkamp, Falko Matthäs, Anne Röttsches, Daniel Stollfuss

Copyediting
Krystina Stermole

Translations
Axel Kassing, Geoffrey Steinherz

Graphic design
Heimann und Schwantes, Berlin
Assistance: Haig Walta

Production
Christine Emter (Hatje Cantz)

Reproductions
LVD Gesellschaft für Datenverarbeitung mbH, Berlin

Typeface
Akkurat

Paper
Galaxi Supermat, 170 g/m²

Binding
Conzella Verlagsbuchbinderei, Urban Meister GmbH, Aschheim-Dornach

Printed by
Dr. Cantz'sche Druckerei, Ostfildern

Published by
Hatje Cantz Verlag
Zeppelinstrasse 32
73760 Ostfildern
Germany
Tel. +49 711 4405-200
Fax +49 711 4405-220
www.hatjecantz.com

Hatje Cantz books are available internationally at selected bookstores. For more information about our distribution partners, please visit our home page at www.hatjecantz.com.

ISBN 978-3-7757-2307-7 (English)
ISBN 978-3-7757-2172-1 (German)

Printed in Germany